Reinsurance

Reinsurance

R.L. Carter

Kluwer Publishing

in association with

The Mercantile and General Reinsurance Company Limited

ISBN   0 903393 38 7

First published in Great Britain 1979 by
Kluwer Publishing Limited, 1 Harlequin Avenue,
Brentford, Middlesex, TW8 9EW
Second impression 1979
Third impression 1979

Printed in Great Britain by
Redwood Burn Limited
Trowbridge & Esher

Contents

Foreword

There may be some readers of this book who are expecting a sort of Mrs Beeton of reinsurance, whose indications if carefully followed will ensure the satisfactory outcome of any reinsurance operation undertaken. They will, I fear, be disappointed for reinsurance is first and foremost a commercial enterprise, whose successful conduct depends upon so much that cannot be written in books or committed to paper. Above all else, it depends upon people and on the personalities of people as much as on their technical skills. Most reinsurers are born and only some are made, but none the less for either sort this book will be of inestimable benefit as a guide to the principles that lie behind the transaction of a business at once as complex and widespread as reinsurance is by its very nature.

One of the main characteristics of this highly specialized business is the infinite variety of situations to which the reinsurer is called upon to adapt his business methods making any standardization of practice possible only on a broad, as opposed to a detailed, basis. This renders any attempt to encompass in one book all the practical alternatives and differences in approach to technical reinsurance problems a virtual impossibility.

But the reader of that which follows will find a mine of essential basic information that ranges over the whole subject and will provide not only a very thorough introduction to the subject for students and serious practitioners but will also act as a sheet anchor to which the well established reinsurer will return when needing to refresh his memory on techniques, abstruse or straightforward.

This book is the outcome of a joint endeavour between practitioner and academic; the latter in the guise of Professor Carter who as conductor has orchestrated the score as well as conducting the performance. The practical experience of a team of specialists in the M.&G. under a dedicated leader has provided the instrumentalists of the orchestra who, by careful study, have adapted the score to everyday commercial practice. Together they have completed the recording. Whilst it is for the reader to judge the performance, there can be no doubt that what has been produced is a major contribution to the reinsurance profession and worthy of the immense amount of hard and dedicated work that has gone into its production.

JULIUS A.S. NEAVE, CBE, JP
Director and General Manager
The Mercantile and General Reinsurance Company Limited

Preface

The layman can be excused for regarding insurance as a mystery but many insurance practitioners themselves view reinsurance in a similar light. Yet without reinsurance many classes of insurance could not be conducted on their present-day scale, or at least any attempt to do so would seriously undermine the degree of security insurers can provide for policyholders. The mobilization of underwriting capacity on an international scale is necessary to provide the amount of insurance cover required for many of today's very large industrial and transport risks, and the world-wide spreading of catastrophe losses, especially those caused by natural disasters, contributes to international economic stability.

It is hoped that this book will provide readers with an understanding of the role of reinsurance, and the first three chapters are concerned with that task. Besides covering the basic function of reinsurance they also deal with reinsurance markets and practices.

The aim, however, has not been to write a textbook dealing only with the theoretical aspects of reinsurance. Mainly it is intended for use by insurance and reinsurance practitioners, and indeed I must acknowledge the example set by the late Dr Golding with his internationally known work, *The Law and Practice of Reinsurance*. Therefore the remainder of the book is concerned with the very practical aspects of reinsurance business.

Chapters 4 to 9 inclusive deal with matters of general application to all classes of insurance and reinsurance business—the law relating to reinsurance contracts, the advantages and disadvantages of the various forms of reinsurance, the placing of reinsurances facultatively and by treaty, the form and operation of such contracts, and the fixing of retentions.

Chapters 10 to 13 comprise the third part of the book. They deal with the features of the individual classes of reinsurance. The final two chapters then cover the financial and international aspects of reinsurance operations.

There are four points I should like to make about the contents of this work. First, although it is far longer than originally envisaged, it has not been possible to cover in detail every nuance of reinsurance practice, which in any case is not static. Therefore, although experts in individual classes of reinsurance may be able to point out many exceptions to the practices discussed, it is hoped that nevertheless readers will obtain a good insight into the general principles and practice of each class of business.

Secondly, although it is inevitable that the subject-matter of a book has to be presented sequentially, neither buyers nor sellers of reinsurance can afford to ignore all of the elements that enter into the financial results of a reinsurance contract. The arrangements regarding the preparation and settlement of accounts, the rate of interest payable on deposits, foreign exchange controls applying to remittances, and so forth, can be just as important as the technical aspects of a treaty. Therefore, anyone dealing with reinsurance must have at least some grasp of the legal and financial aspects of the business, and of the constraints imposed by governments.

Thirdly, like other forms of insurance business, in response to changing risk conditions reinsurance practice is becoming far more complex and sophisticated. There will always remain a lot of room for subjective judgment—the so-called 'underwriting flair'—but today's underwriter needs more mathematical and statistical skill than his predecessor. Of course he can always turn to an actuary or statistician for expert advice but at least he should be aware of what is required and of the techniques that are available. In a very simple way, an attempt has been made to frame some of the principles and problems in a mathematical form and to provide references for further reading.

Fourthly, although the basic principles of the subject are universal, practice in various markets throughout the world is conditioned by local market organization, supervisory regulations, and so forth. It would be impossible within the scope of one book to deal with those differences, and any list of, say, supervisory or exchange control regulations would rapidly become out of date. Therefore, the practices described are those to be found on the London market but some reference is made to differences which may be encountered elsewhere.

The idea of writing this book arose out of a discussion I had with the President of the Reinsurance Offices' Association, Mr Julius Neave of The Mercantile and General Reinsurance Company Limited. We both felt that the time was ripe for a new book on the subject but as an academic I knew that I did not possess a sufficient knowledge of reinsurance practice. Julius Neave generously offered to provide that expertise from among his own colleagues. The result was a team of M.&G. advisers; although they modestly wish to remain anonymous I must record the great debt that I owe to them. They have supplied information, explained tricky points, read and criticized drafts and when all else has failed have written parts themselves. Although I must reluctantly respect their wish to remain anonymous I feel compelled to name Philip Flint who has acted as coordinator, adviser, friend and at times father confessor.

The M.&G. have offered more than advice. Julius Neave also provided the financial support which has made the work possible.

To Julius Neave, Philip Flint and their many colleagues I am deeply grateful. If the work is not worthy of the help they have given, or if any errors remain, the fault is mine alone.

I should also like to record my gratitude to Miss Margaret Roys. She must be thoroughly tired of the subject by now, but without her secretarial help and typing I should have been lost. She has deciphered my notes, typed endless drafts and given her help uncomplainingly.

Finally, my wife and family who for two years have lived with 'the book'. Even the dog has suffered from having fewer and shorter walks than usual! I thank my wife Rita for her patience, encouragement and forbearance.

R.L. CARTER

1
The role and development of reinsurance

1
The role and development of reinsurance

Introduction

Reinsurance is a form of insurance. Consequently many of the principles and practices applying to the conduct of insurance business equally apply to reinsurance. Like most insurers, the reinsurer is concerned with uncertain future events which produce losses; his underwriting skill lies in accurately estimating the probability of future losses; and the special legal rules governing insurance contracts similarly apply to reinsurance. Yet in other respects the practice of reinsurance so differs from direct insurance that it is recognized by insurance practitioners, the courts and insurance supervisory authorities as being in a category of its own.

Under a contract of insurance one party, known as the insurer, promises that on the occurrence of an uncertain specified event he will either indemnify the other party, known as the insured or the policyholder, for any financial losses he may sustain, or pay to him a certain sum, and in return the insured agrees to pay the insurer an ascertainable amount known as a premium. Reinsurance contracts differ essentially from other classes of insurance contracts in three ways:

(1) An insurer contracts with a member of the public, e.g. an individual person, business enterprise, public authority, or charitable institution. A reinsurance contract is between two insurers, the one known as the reinsurer, the other as the reinsured, the direct or primary insurer, or the ceding office. A reinsurer in turn may reinsure reinsurances he has accepted, the contract then being known as retrocession, with the ceding company being the retrocedent and the reinsurer being the retrocessionaire.

(2) The subject-matter of an insurance is some property, person or benefit exposed to loss or damage, or some potential legal liability the insured may incur arising out of activities undertaken by himself, his servant or agents. Thus an insurer directly insures against events

which may give rise to economic loss, such as the destruction of property by fire or other perils, and accidents giving rise to legal liability for injury to, or for damage to the property of, third parties. A reinsurer on the other hand only becomes indirectly interested in such primary losses in so far as he has undertaken to compensate his reinsured for payments the latter has made. Therefore, it would appear logical in the case of reinsurance to regard the subject-matter insured as all or part of the contractual liabilities which the reinsured has accepted under the insurance policies he has written. British courts, however, have taken a contrary view, holding that the subject-matter of insurance under a reinsurance contract is the same as the subject-matter of the underlying direct insurance, and the Department of Trade have adopted that principle for accounting and other supervisory requirements.[1]

(3) Not all insurance contracts are subject to the principle of indemnity; it is well accepted law that insurances covering human life (i.e. life, personal accident and sickness policies) are excluded from the principle[2] and therefore are sometimes termed benefit policies. All reinsurance contracts, including life reinsurances, are contracts of indemnity, being limited to payments made by the reinsured under insurances he has written. In practice most reinsurances provide only partial compensation, the reinsured bearing part of any loss himself.

Reinsurance contracts, therefore, are concerned with providing for the insurance of liabilities which may be incurred under contracts of insurance or, in the case of retrocessions, under contracts of reinsurance. Always the parties to a reinsurance contract are the reinsurer and another insurer,[3] and though reinsurance contracts are often discussed in such terms as 'ceding'[4] or 'passing to another insurer part of a risk or liability accepted',[5] the original insured acquires no rights or liabilities thereunder. A reinsurance contract constitutes a separate contract of insurance between the reinsurer and the reinsured; it is not an assignment of all or any part of the rights and liabilities already existing under a contract of direct insurance. Therefore, reinsurance may be defined briefly as:

> the insurance of contractual liabilities incurred under contracts of direct insurance or reinsurance.

---

1 See page 118 *infra*, for a fuller discussion.
2 *Dalby* v *India and London Life* (1854), 15 C.B. 365.
3 An American court said in the case of *Iowa Mutual Tornado Insurance Association* v *Timmons*, 105 N.W. 2d 209: 'The true reinsurer is merely an insurance company or underwriter which deals only with other insurance companies as its policyholders.'
4 C.E. Golding, *The Law and Practice of Reinsurance*, p.5, Stone & Cox, 1965 edition amended 1968.
5 W.A. Dinsdale, *Specimen Insurance Forms and Glossaries*, 2nd ed., p.142, Stone & Cox, 1963.

Finally in distinguishing reinsurance from insurance business one could add that whereas almost all direct insurance business, other than marine and aviation, is essentially domestic, reinsurance operates on an international scale. Typically direct insurance contracts are between two parties resident in the same country. Although a lot of reinsurance business is domestic, particularly in large developed markets such as North America, substantial amounts of reinsurance business are placed across national frontiers, and international reinsurance markets recognize no ideological barriers: for example, state insurance corporations of politically left- and right-wing countries trade actively with free-enterprise companies.

A reinsurer should always know about the insurance market conditions in each country from which he accepts business, including underwriting practices, details of the various types of policies available and the legal rules regulating insurance contracts and the business of insurers in general. It would be impossible, however, to attempt to cover in this book the many variations between countries in the principles and practice of direct insurance, nor would it be appropriate to do so. There are ample bibliographies available covering the law and practice of all major insurance markets.[1] Therefore, this book will concentrate on the principles and practice of reinsurance business, and will only refer to direct insurance when it is necessary to provide an understanding of reinsurance practice.

The purpose of reinsurance

The conduct of insurance business

Insurance is a mechanism for spreading losses over larger numbers of persons exposed to loss. Unlike some social-security schemes, all private insurances work on a funding principle. The insurer pools the premiums he collects from policyholders to form a fund from which to pay the claims of the unfortunate few. With life insurance the cost of death claims is also spread over time. Through the system of level annual premiums, life policyholders pay during the early years of their policies larger premiums than are necessary to cover the mortality risk: thus a fund is built up to cover the excess cost of claims in later years.

Therefore in fixing its premiums, an insurance company must aim to

---

1 In the case of Britain see R.L. Carter (ed.) *The Handbook of Insurance*, (London: Kluwer, 1973 updated), R. Colinvaux, *The Law of Insurance*, 3rd ed. (London: Sweet & Maxwell, 1970), E.R. Hardy Ivamy, *General Principles of Insurance Law*, 3rd ed. (London: Butterworth, 1975), *MacGillivray & Parkington on Insurance Law*, 6th ed. (London: Sweet & Maxwell, 1975).

obtain enough income, including interest that can be earned on its funds, to cover expenses and to pay all claims as they fall due. And if the company ceases writing new business, the fund must be sufficiently large to meet the run-off of its liabilities. Moreover, a proprietary company must try to earn enough profit to provide its shareholders with an adequate return on their investment, and if it wishes to expand its business, to attract extra capital. Therefore when dealing with short-term business (typically annual policies) the insurer aims to collect from each policyholder at the commencement of the period of insurance a premium P basically calculated as follows:

$$P = (q \times \bar{c}) + E$$

$$\text{where } q = \text{the probability of a loss occurring}$$
$$\bar{c} = \text{the average size of loss which occurs}$$
$$E = \text{the loading for expenses and profit}$$

The expression $q \times \bar{c}$ represents each policyholder's loss expectancy, that is the average cost of the losses he can expect to experience in each period (i.e. usually 12 months). So if the premium is correctly calculated, and given an infinitely large number of policyholders, an insurer may expect premiums to cover claims costs each year.

Normally the premium is payable at the inception of the insurance, but losses are distributed throughout the period of insurance. Moreover when losses do occur, usually some time elapses before they are notified and the claims are settled. Therefore the above premium equation can be modified to allow for the interest which the insurer can earn on the funds he holds. In other words, an insurer needs to collect a premium which represents the net present value of his liabilities, as follows:

$$p = [(q \times \bar{c}) + ec] (1+r)^{-t} + ei$$

$$\text{where } r = \text{the rate of earnings on funds}$$
$$t = \text{the average time lag (by payments) in the settlement of claims}$$
$$ei = \text{expenses payable at inception of the insurance}$$
$$ec = \text{expenses of settling claims}$$

In practice life is not so simple for an insurer. Underlying the above description of premium rating are a number of fundamental assumptions:

— there exist a very large number of homogeneous exposure units available to the insurer;
— all units are independently exposed to loss;
— past experience can provide a guide to the future; and conditions do not change.

Rarely if ever do underwriting portfolios fulfil all of the above conditions which are necessary to ensure that from year to year the company's claims costs will be closely in line with its expected loss experience. Often portfolios contain relatively few exposure units which in turn may vary considerably in size; possibly the occurrence of one loss event may affect several units; and over time risk conditions do change, sometimes both rapidly and dramatically. Consequently an insurance company's actual loss experience during any one underwriting year may fluctuate considerably from its expected experience averaged over a longer period. Part of the job of an underwriter is to anticipate changing risk factors in order to adjust premium rates to reflect expected future experience, and some provision may be made for claims fluctuations by carrying reserve funds and by adding a contingency loading to premium rates. However, competition and other factors impose a constraint on the size of reserves and of the premium loadings that a company can afford to carry. Consequently some additional form of protection is required against losses which at worst may imperil a company's solvency, or at least cause financial embarrassment. That protection can be provided by reinsurance.

The role of reinsurance

There are many reasons why insurance companies fail. Some are common to other industries, such as inefficiency, inadequate pricing, etc. The commonest single case of failure amongst insurance companies, however, is an unprovided increase in their largest cost item, claims. Such a situation may arise in several ways, notably:
(1) a general rise in claims costs due to an increase in either the underlying frequency and/or severity of losses;
(2) the random occurrence of one or more very large individual losses, or an accumulation of losses arising from one event, relative to premium income and reserves;
(3) the fluctuation of the annual aggregate claims experience around the mean.
The basic role of reinsurance is to offer protection against (2) and (3); the first cause is essentially a problem of premium rating, though in practice a reinsurer may find that at least part of the consequences of a ceding company charging inadequate premiums falls upon him too.

As will be shown, reinsurance evolved from first offering protection to ceding companies against very large individual losses which may strain their underwriting capacity, to dealing as well with fluctuations in aggregate portfolio loss experience. Essentially in the same way as an individual pays a premium to insure against any financially crippling losses he may suffer, so too an insurance company may pay part of its premium income to a reinsurer to obtain protection against part of the potential losses which may arise on the insurances it has written. Thus the technical role of reinsurance is to protect insurers against insolvency or financial strain by reducing the degree of variability in their retained claims costs. Expressed another way, an efficient reinsurance programme should produce a greater stability in the underwriting results of a direct insurer. This stabilizing effect has been described by Dr F.L. Tuma[1] as follows:

> The purpose of reinsurance is purely technical. It is a means which an insurance company uses to reduce, from the point of view of possible material losses, the perils which it has accepted. When a carriage fitted with a shock absorber passes over a rough street, the road becomes no smoother, but the passenger will feel the jerks less as these are absorbed by the contrivance carried as a special addition to the vehicle. So it is with reinsurance; it does not reduce losses but it makes it easier for insurance to carry the material consequences.

The availability of reinsurance provides other benefits too. It produces a further spreading of losses. Some countries, including the less developed ones, are particularly exposed to the risk of natural disasters such as earthquakes, floods and hurricanes which can place a grave strain on a national economy: reinsurance enables domestic insurers to spread such losses internationally.[2]

Reinsurance also provides an insurer with additional underwriting capacity in that he can both accept larger risks than otherwise would be possible and sometimes accommodate existing policyholders by writing types of business which normally he would prefer to avoid. Domestic insurance markets in most western countries are highly competitive, and the extra capacity and flexibility which reinsurance facilities provide can

1 'The economics theory of reinsurance', *Journal of the Insurance Institute of London*, 1933.
2 An analysis by one major professional reinsurance company of its own experience of two major catastrophes illustrates this risk-spreading effect of reinsurance.

	Darwin hurricane	*Flixborough explosion*
(1) Number of ceding companies from which reinsurance accepted	78	30
(2) Number of treaties involved	154	51
(3) Number of countries of domicile of ceding companies	8	5
(4) Number of retrocessionaires to which risks retroceded	262	160
(5) Number of countries of domicile of retrocessionaires	51	46

J.A.S. Neave, 'International reinsurance: changing patterns in economic relationship', *Policy*, May 1976.

particularly assist smaller insurance companies in competing for business.

The financial aspects of reinsurance

The preceding paragraphs cover what may be termed the technical role of reinsurance. Increasingly it has assumed a financing role too, partly in response to the way in which insurance supervisory regulations are framed and operate.

The availability of reinsurance may enable a direct insurance company to expand the volume of business it writes at a faster rate than otherwise would be possible without a corresponding increase in its capital base. In the American or other markets where unearned premium reserves for non-life insurance have to be maintained as a proportion of net premiums written (i.e. gross premiums written less premiums for reinsurances ceded) without any deduction for prepaid expenses, financing 'basically means unearned-premium reserve relief'.[1] Reinsurance premiums paid for reinsurances ceded reduce the net written premiums on which unearned premium reserves are calculated and thus reduce the strain on surplus.

Similarly where non-life insurance companies are required to maintain a minimum solvency margin (i.e. a surplus of assets over liabilities) expressed as a proportion of net written premium income, the ceding of business to a reinsurer, with the consequent reduction in net premium income, will enable a company to write a larger gross account than otherwise would be possible.[2] There are plenty of examples of companies that have encountered difficulties in meeting a prescribed solvency margin and have substantially increased the volume of business ceded to reinsurers in order to reduce their net premium income to an acceptable level. Similarly the imposition or raising of solvency margins usually leads to an increase in reinsurance purchases.

The use of reinsurance for such purposes can be taken too far. Therefore some supervisory authorities limit the amount of credit that can be taken for reinsurances ceded when calculating premium reserves and/or solvency margins, especially reinsurances ceded to foreign reinsurers over whom the supervisory authority can exercise no control.

The ceding of business to reinsurers with the object of obtaining large overriding commissions, particularly when the ceding company retains practically no business for its own account, may be sound financial practice in that the company obtains virtually a risk-free profit, but it is

1 G.F. Michelbacher and N.R. Roos, *Multiple-line insurers:. Their nature and operation*, 2nd ed. (New York: McGraw-Hill, 1970), p.83.
2 See page 65 for a fuller explanation of these two effects.

bad insurance practice. Under such conditions the ceding company is acting as a broker under another guise.

Provision of management and technical services

A further and wholly beneficial aspect of reinsurance operations is the range of services which ceding companies can obtain from large reinsurance companies and some reinsurance brokers which have a worldwide experience of many classes of insurance business. Besides the provision of advice on the planning of reinsurance programmes, such services range from advice on the handling of very large claims to setting up the underwriting, claims and accounting procedures and the training of staff required by a new direct insurance company.

Summary

The functions of reinsurance may be summarized as follows:
— The primary functions are:
    (1) to protect insurers from underwriting losses which may imperil their solvency;
    (2) to stabilize underwriting results;
    (3) to increase the flexibility of an insurer in the size and types of risk and the volume of business he can underwrite; and
    (4) further spread the risk of loss.
— Reinsurance may assist in the financing of insurance operations.
— Arising out of the growth of reinsurance business, major reinsurance companies and brokers can offer a range of secondary insurance underwriting, claims handling, administrative and technical services.

Development of reinsurance

Origins of the insurance industry

The origins of insurance, and so of reinsurance, remain a mystery despite the efforts of considerable historical scholarship. Devices for the spreading of risks have been discovered dating back to the earliest days of commercial enterprise. Chinese merchants, for example, would distribute their goods between several vessels for journeys along the hazardous rivers of China.[1] About 3000 BC the Babylonians evolved

1 David L. Bickelhaupt, *General Insurance*, 9th ed. (Homewood, Ill: Richard D. Irwin Inc., 1974), p.62.

methods of marine (or sea) loans which relieved the borrower of the duty to repay either the loan or the interest thereon in the event of certain accidents happening to the ship or goods. Such loans were developed by the Greeks to become bottomry and respondentia bonds.[1] In the ninth century BC the laws of Rhodes laid the foundations of the maritime practice of general average whereby if in time of peril any party makes sacrifices or suffers extraordinary expenditure for the common safety, all interests thereby saved contribute to his loss. None of these examples fulfils the basic elements of a contract of insurance, but it has been argued that the Romans developed such contracts and they certainly practised mutual life insurance.[2]

The development of the present-day form of insurance is generally credited to the merchants of the city states of northern Italy. Soon their activities spread to the Low Countries and England and it has been claimed that in 1310 the Duke of Flanders granted a charter for the establishment of a Chamber of Assurance at Bruges to carry on the underwriting of marine risks.[3]

The practice of marine insurance so flourished in London that eventually Parliament felt compelled to regulate the business, passing in 1601 an 'Act touching policies of assurance used among merchants'.[4]

In 1601, although the system of broker intermediaries was already in existence, insurance was virtually restricted to merchants and shippers seeking protection against the loss of their goods and ships at sea from a limited number of individual merchant underwriters operation in the Royal Exchange and the coffee-houses of London. Life assurance was in a very crude and early stage of development, while another 79 and 239 years respectively were to pass before the first fire and accident policies were issued in London.[5]

Until the end of the eighteenth century the supply of insurance remained in the hands of individual underwriters, the forerunners of the present-day Lloyd's. The Great Fire of London in 1666 stimulated interest in fire insurance and several companies were soon formed, the longest surviving being the Hand-in-Hand Fire Office established in 1696 and acquired by the Commercial Union in 1905.[6] In 1710 the Sun Fire

---

1 G. Clayton, *British Insurance* (London: Elek Books, 1971), ch.1.
2 Ibid.
3 Ibid., p.27.
4 H.E. Raynes, *A History of British Insurance*, 2nd ed. (London: Pitman, 1964), p.53. The Act contains the classic explanation of the purpose of insurance in the words:
   '...by means of which policies of assurance it cometh to pass on the perishing of any ship, there followeth not the undoing of any man, but the loss lighteth rather easily upon many than heavily upon few.'
5 Ibid.
6 P.G.M. Dickson, *The Sun Insurance Office 1710-1960* (London: Oxford University Press, 1960), ch.1.

Office was founded, followed by the Royal Exchange and the London in 1720. Elsewhere in Europe and North America insurance companies were formed in increasing numbers; in 1752, for example, Benjamin Franklin organized the first American fire insurance company, the Philadelphia Contributionship.[1]

Although the foundations of today's insurance industry were laid in the 18th century it was the industrial growth of the 19th century that established its importance in the economy. Alongside that growth came an increasing demand for reinsurance.

Reinsurance

Exactly when underwriters first sought reinsurance for the risks they had themselves accepted is a matter of speculation. It may be assumed that early underwriters limited their acceptances to amounts they could afford to bear themselves, so avoiding any need for reinsurance.[2] The practice of coinsurance in both marine and fire insurance business, whereby a number of underwriters would each take a direct share of any risk which was too large for any one underwriter to carry himself,[3] supports that hypothesis. On the other hand, Golding goes on to argue:[4]

> It is easy to surmise that those shrewd races inhabiting the shores of the Mediterranean, amongst whom marine insurance began, would neglect no opportunity of conducting the business on a prudent basis. If this were so, reinsurance would have been an early need and it would be doing less than justice to the business acumen of those early pioneers to assume that they knew nothing about reinsurance, nor had ever devised a means of laying off a liability too great to be comfortably held. But of actual record there is none.

Marine reinsurance

The first account of a marine reinsurance is given by Gustav Cruciger relating to the issue in 1370 of a policy for a voyage from Genoa to Sluys,

---

1 Bickelhaupt, *General Insurance*, p.63.
2 C.E. Golding, *A History of Reinsurance* (Sterling Offices Ltd, 1927), p.7.
3 See Raynes, *History of British Insurance* and D.E.W. Gibb, *Lloyd's of London* (London: Macmillan & Co., 1957). The first fire insurance companies placed limits on the sums they were prepared to insure. Dickson (*Sun Insurance Office*, p.38) records that when the Sun Insurance Office first began writing fire insurance in 1710 it limited the maximum coverage allowed to £1000, £500 on a house and £500 on goods. The Royal Exchange Assurance commenced business in 1721 with a much higher limit of £5000 but this was soon raised, see B. Supple, *The Royal Exchange Assurance* (London: Cambridge University Press, 1970), p.85.
4 Golding, *History of Reinsurance*, p.21.

the original insurer then reinsuring the most hazardous part of the risk from Cadiz to Sluys.[1] Clearly that was not a case of an original underwriter reinsuring a risk which he could not afford to carry himself, as evidenced by his retention of the full risk for the safer part of the voyage through the Mediterranean. Rather, he used reinsurance to avoid a hazardous risk which he preferred not to carry but which he had been obliged to accept in order to obtain the more desirable business, or perhaps to accommodate a valuable client. Thus it may be concluded that insurers soon learned how to put reinsurance to use to increase their underwriting flexibility.

Early records are somewhat confused by the use of the word 'reinsurance' to cover both transactions between two insurers, and cases where for some reason an insured effected a second insurance on the same property, possibly because the original insurer had died or gone bankrupt. The latter were really fresh, direct insurances, in some cases being double insurance. Dr Golding comments that:[2]

> Much confusion of thought existed on this point, especially in the early days of marine insurance, so much so that when marine reinsurance was made illegal (in England) by an Act of 1746, an exception was made if the original insurer became insolvent or bankrupt or should die. But of course that exception could only enable a fresh insurance to be taken out by the insured, since the first insurance had become valueless.

Despite such confusion in terminology it is clear from the records that reinsurance in its true sense had become generally practised amongst marine underwriters by the end of the 17th century. James Allan Park in a treatise on *A System of the Law of Marine Insurance* published in London in 1800 refers to an *ordonnance* of Louis XIV of France dated 1681 which delcared that 'it should be lawful to the insurers to make reassurance with other men of those effects which they had themselves previously insured'.[3] Park added that:

> It is not in France alone that this law prevails, for by the positive and express regulations and ordinances of Königsberg and Hamburgh and Bilboa, reassurances are allowed to be effected and consequently are lawful contracts.

---

1 Golding, *History of Reinsurance*, p.20.
2 Golding, *Law and Practice of Reinsurance*, p.2.
3 Quoted by Golding in *History of Reinsurance*, p.27.

During the 18th century marine reinsurance continued to develop on the Continent but in England it came to a temporary halt by the intervention of Parliament. Concerned about the growth of certain (unspecified) abuses the legislators inserted into an Act of 1746 'to regulate insurance on ships belonging to the subjects of Great Britain and on merchandises or effects laden thereon', a section which provided:

> And be it further enacted by the Authority aforesaid. That it shall not be lawful to make reassurance, unless the Assurer shall be insolvent, become a bankrupt or die; in either of which cases each Assurer, his Executors, Administrators or Assigners may make Reassurance to the amount of the sum before by him assured provided it shall be expressed in the policy to be a Reassurance.

Marine reinsurance in its true sense thus became illegal until the Act was repealed in 1864, though Golding says that some cases were recorded during the intervening period[1] If the purpose of the Act had been to stamp out the use of reinsurance as 'a mode of speculating in the rise and fall of premiums'[2] it is far from certain that it succeeded. Supple records that during the late 1880s the marine underwriter of the Royal Exchange, whose terms of appointment included a generous profit bonus, was paying away up to 50 per cent of his gross premiums in reinsurances.[3]

All of the early reinsurances were arranged facultatively; that is, each individual risk was offered to another insurer who was free to accept or reject the offer. It was not until the middle of the 19th century that the first marine reinsurance treaties were arranged which imposed obligations upon the direct insurer to cede part of his buisness and upon the reinsurer to accept what was offered.

Fire insurance

The development of fire insurance during the 18th century appears to have taken place without the assistance of reinsurance. P.G.M. Dickson, for example, in discussing the early fire underwriting problems of the Sun Insurance Office founded in London in 1710 commented that there were 'no facilities for reinsurance until the second quarter of the nineteenth century'.[4] Risks too large for a single company to carry were

---

1 Golding, *Law & Practice of Reisurance*, p.3
2 Sir J. Arnould, *A treatise on the law of Marine Insurance and Average*, 2nd ed. (London: Stevens & Sons, 1857), p.339.
3 Supple, *Royal Exchange Assurance*, p.259.
4 Dickson, *Sun Insurance Office*, p.83.

placed directly with a number of companies, that is, on a coinsurance basis. An obvious drawback was the introduction of a company's clients to its competitors. Reinsurance provided the means whereby a company could increase its own acceptances and reduce the need for coinsurance.

The first record of a fire reinsurance was an agreement by the Eagle Fire Insurance Company of New York in August 1813 to assume all of the outstanding risks of the Union Insurance Company (formerly the Jersey Bank).[1] Seven years later in 1820 a German company is reputed to have entered into a reinsurance treaty but the first case for which full details are available was a treaty between La Compagnie Nationale d'Assurances of Paris (then known as the Compagnie Royale) and the Compagnie des Propriétaires Réunis of Brussels.[2] In 1824 La Nationale concluded a treaty with an English company, the Imperial Fire.[3]

Although reinsurance was looked upon with some disfavour, it provided a further means of acquiring new business and other British companies soon began to accept reinsurances from other offices; including their competitors. The directors of the Royal Exchange Assurance declined their first offers of fire reinsurance, a facultative proposal from the Guardian in 1828 and a treaty for the exchange of surplus lines with the Union of Paris in 1829,[4] but the Sun Insurance Office started to accept reinsurances from the Newcastle Fire Office as early as the 1820s.[5] The Sun concluded its first overseas treaty with the Aächener and Münchener in 1838 and over the next 40 years accepted business from all over the Continent, India and North and South America.[6]

In Britain fire reinsurance was known as guarantee business, and in November 1863 the newly formed Fire Offices' Committee circularized its members as follows:[7]

> That guarantees be not given to or taken from any office which does not adhere to the tariff system as to any class of risks in London or elsewhere in the United Kingdom, whether tariff or non-tariff, and whether at tariff or non-tariff rates.

An amended version of the rule was included in the general rules of the Fire Offices' Committee issued in 1868, and finally in the 'Rules for the regulation of guarantee transactions in fire insurance business' issued in 1871.

---

1 Golding, *History of Reinsurance*, p.31.
2 Ibid., p.44 and app.
3 Ibid., p.46.
4 Ibid., p.33 and 48.
5 Dickson, *Sun Insurance Office*, p.160.
6 Ibid., pp.167 – 224.
7 Golding, *History of Reinsurance*, p.38.

The early treaties were arranged on a surplus basis, and Golding records in detail in *The History of Reinsurance* the evolution of those features now common to modern treaties, e.g. obligations regarding the ceding and acceptance of risks, retention limits, commission rates, exclusion clauses, the rendering of accounts, arbitration clauses, etc. Some time between 1880 and 1890 Mr Cuthbert Heath, a Lloyd's underwriter noted as an innovator in many classes of insurance business, introduced excess of loss reinsurance whereby the ceding company retains for its own account any fire loss up to a given figure, and reinsures any excess up to a fixed amount.[1]

It is notable that from the beginning the treaties provided for the reciprocal exchange of business between the parties, so that the contentious practice of reciprocity has a history that predates its bitterest opponents, the companies specializing in reinsurance business. The practice of retrocession also dates back to a treaty concluded in 1854 between Riunione Adriatica and Le Globe Compagnie d'Assurances contre l'Incendie which provided for the retrocession of reinsurances Le Globe had itself accepted.

Life reinsurance

The origins of life reinsurance in Britain lie in the growth of demand for life insurance and the associated formation of new life insurance companies which occurred during the first half of the 19th century. The early days, however, were beset by various difficulties and disputes attributable to a number of causes. On occasions behaviour left much to be desired; for example, original insurers did not always disclose retentions or even retain any part of the risk for their own account, and reinsurances were not always cancelled following the discontinuance of the original policy. In addition problems arose because rates of premium and policy conditions varied between companies.

Such problems led 17 Scottish life offices in 1849 to sign an agreement regulating reinsurance business in an endeavour to establish some acceptable standards of practice for the market. At that time life reinsurances were only placed on a facultative basis and the agreement covered such matters as premium rates, retentions and surrenders. A supplementary agreement was drawn up in 1873 covering retentions, extra premiums and commission rates, followed by a revised and extended agreement in 1887 dealing in more detail with surrenders.

In 1900 an agreement on similar lines to the Scottish agreements was

---

1 Golding, *History of Reisurance*, p.39

signed by 46 British life offices. This agreement, known as the Reassurance Agreement 1900, is still in force, regulating the practice of life reinsurances placed on a facultative basis.

It was not until 1918 that a specialist reinsurance company, the Mercantile and General, transacted life reinsurance business in Britain. Life reinsurance treaties likewise did not appear until after the First World War, the main impetus coming from the introduction by the Mercantile and General of risk premium rates for United Kingdom business in 1927.[1]

The development of life reinsurance markets took place somewhat earlier on the Continent. Some treaties were accepted by specialist reinsurance companies from the 1850s onwards, though from 1865 to 1880 only the Swiss Reinsurance Company transacted such business.[2]

Accident reinsurance

Accident reinsurance business has developed alongside the rapid growth of accident and motor insurance since the middle of the 19th century. The earliest record of accident reinsurance dates from 1872 when the Railway Passengers Assurance Company accepted from a life assurance company liability for accidental death claims in excess of £2000 in the aggregate in one vessel in respect of emigrants going to New Zealand.

The bulk of the early business was arranged on a facultative basis except for motor and liability business where excess of loss treaties soon found favour.

Specialist reinsurance companies

Reinsurances were first exchanged between direct insurers, sometimes competing in the same markets. Although reinsurance was an improvement on coinsurance, the reinsurer could still obtain valuable information about the ceding office's business whether the reinsurance was placed facultatively or by treaty, and possibly could use it to compete unfairly for direct insurances. The one main constraint on an unscrupulous insurer was the knowledge that in so far as his reinsurance business was conducted on a reciprocal basis his ceding offices had the same information about his own direct business. Nevertheless in those days of fuller disclosure between reinsurer and ceding office there must have been some merit in the idea of being able to place reinsurances with

1 The author is grateful to Mr J. Dougharty of the Mercantile and General Reinsurance Company for permission to use historical material regarding the British market contained in his unpublished paper, 'The history of life reinsurance in Great Britain'.
2 Golding, *History of Reinsurance,* p.41.

companies which could not conceivably offer any actual or potential competition in direct markets.

No one knows whether such thoughts entered the minds of the men who introduced to the world's insurance markets a new type of company specializing in reinsurance business only. However, Golding records that the first reinsurance company was established in 1842 by a German direct insurance company for the sole purpose of handling surplus lines from its parent company, so bypassing competitors.[1] Several other such subsidiaries were formed before the world's first independent reinsurance company, the Kölnische Rückversicherungs Gesellschaft, was promoted and commenced business in 1852.

The early development of what have come to be known as professional reinsurance companies took place on the Continent of Europe. Not until 1867 was an attempt made to found such a company in Britain and it lasted only four years, being wound up in 1871. The first successful British company was the Mercantile and General Reinsurance Company Ltd, founded in 1907. Likewise in America professional reinsurance companies were slow to evolve. The first record is of a company, the Reassurance Company of America, which was wound up about 1890.[2] Another 19 years passed before the next company was formed in 1909.

Table 1.1 summarizes the succesful promotion of reinsurance companies in Europe and America up to 1925, recording with relatively few omissions the numbers of reinsurance companies still in existence at that date.

State insurance and reinsurance corporations

The political and economic upheavals of the 20th century have markedly changed many domestic insurance and reinsurance markets. Throughout the Communist bloc and in many other Socialist states insurance has been nationalized, the business now being handled by state organizations, often part of the Ministry of Finance. Sometimes separate state reinsurance corporations have been established to transact business on international reinsurance markets, usually on a reciprocal basis with the corporation accepting foreign reinsurances in exchange for its own cessions.

The desire to build strong indigenous insurance industries capable of retaining most if not all of the domestic insurance business predates the 20th century. One of the objectives of the promoters of the Cologne Reinsurance Company in 1852 was the desire 'to preserve for a German

---

1 Golding, *History of Reinsurance,* p.75.
2 Ibid., p.90.

Table 1.1 Numbers of professional reinsurance companies formed in various countries and still in existence in 1926.

	1850 to 1859	1860 to 1869	1870 to 1879	1880 to 1889	1890 to 1899	1900 to 1909	1910 to 1919	1920 to 1925	Total
Germany	3	2	4	3	2	2	6	12	34
Switzerland	—	2	1	—	—	—	3	1	7
Austria	—	3	—	2	—	1	1	—	7
France	—	—	—	1	2	3	6	4	16
Sweden	—	—	1	1	2	2	5	—	11
Denmark	—	—	—	1	2	—	17	—	20
Norway	—	—	—	—	—	—	9	—	20
Holland	—	—	—	1	2	—	—	3	6
Belgium	1	—	—	1	—	1	2	1	6
Italy	—	—	—	—	—	—	3	5	8
United Kingdom	—	—	—	—	—	5	10	1	16
United States of America	—	—	—	—	—	1	10	5	16
Total	4	7	6	10	10	15	72	32	156

Source: Golding, *History of Reinsurance*, p.91.

company the surpluses which direct German offices had previously placed with German and Belgian companies'.[1] In 1927 the government of Chile seized on the same idea, prohibited the formation of new agencies for foreign companies and established a state reinsurance corporation, the Caja Reaseguradora de Chile. Foreign insurers were compelled to cede to the Caja a part of all of the risks they wrote in the country and it was given a monopoly of all reinsurance placed abroad. The Chilean example was followed in due course by Brazil and Argentina. Over the last decade developing countries have been encouraged by UNCTAD (the United Nations Conference on Trade and Development) to reduce their dependence on foreign insurers[2] and an evergrowing number (e.g. Kenya, Nigeria and Pakistan) have adopted the South American system of state insurance or reinsurance corporations and compulsory cessions to the state corporation.

Although a state reinsurance corporation may be able to harness the full capacity of its domestic market, for various reasons it still will be necessary to purchase some reinsurance from abroad. To minimize the foreign exchange costs of such external reinsurance a state corporation may seek the reciprocal exchange of business from its reinsurers, but over the last few years another device has been adopted. Developing countries in various parts of the world, sometimes as part of more

---

1 Golding, *History of Reinsurance*, p.75.
2 J. Ripoll, 'UNCTAD and insurance', *Journal of World Trade Law*, vol.8, No.1, (January—February 1974).

general economic groupings, have organized regional underwriting pools for the exchange of surplus lines.

Underwriting pools

The term 'underwriting pools' covers a variety of organizational arrangements.[1] Some are purely national in character being concerned with mobilizing sufficient capacity to handle the direct insurance of very large risks; the atomic insurance pools established in Britain and several other countries fall into this category. Other pools, though of a domestic character, operate as reinsurance organizations with individual members ceding to the pool direct insurances they have written, which are then shared out in agreed proportions between all members on a retrocession basis. An example of such an arrangement is the Philippines motor pool.

More recently regional reinsurance pools have been formed in various parts of the world. Examples of this type of pool are the four Arab Federation Pools covering engineering (formed in 1969), aviation (1970), fire (1974) and marine (1975) insurances, and the three Regional Cooperation for Development Pools operated jointly by Turkey, Iran and Pakistan. In each case the pool is managed by one participating company with shares of treaties being accepted from members and in turn shares of the risks accepted by the pool are retroceded to members.

Whatever the merits of such arrangements may be, the result is to reduce the flow of international reinsurance business, though some catastrophe protection may be placed with outside reinsurers.

Reinsurance brokers

The role of intermediaries in insurance markets is as old as that of insurers. For example, brokers have been an integral part of the Lloyd's market from its inception.[2] In the early days of reinsurance there was unlikely to be sufficient business to keep a broker fully employed, but undoubtedly some reinsurance business was placed by brokers. In 1829, for example, a Mr Cazenove arranged a fire treaty between the Union of Paris and the Royal Exchange Assurance.[3]

According to Golding, the first broker to specialize in reinsurance was a Mr Martin Heckscher who in 1865 started his own business under the name of Heckscher and Gottlieb in St Petersburg in 1865. Twelve years later, after having opened branches in Berlin and Vienna, he commenced

---

1 For a fuller discussion see *Reinsurance problems in developing countries*, UNCTAD document TD/B/C.3/106/Rev.1 (United Nations, 1975), ch.4.
2 Gibb, *Lloyd's of London*.
3 Golding, *Hi tory of Reinsurance*, p.95.

business in London, where his firm continued to trade until amalgamated with Sterling Offices Ltd in 1918.

Over the last 100 years many other specialist reinsurance broking firms have been established, some as independent organizations, others as subsidiaries of insurance broking firms. Today the major reinsurance brokers operate on a worldwide basis, often maintaining offices in all of the major insurance centres of the western world. Out of the many British firms that have been formed only a few now operate as independent firms, the remainder are all part of larger broking and underwriting groups.

REINSURANCE

2
Reinsurance markets

2
Reinsurance markets

Types of markets

Whenever the buyers of any commodity are in contact with its sellers a market can be said to exist. Although physical contact between the two parties at some recognized place may be normal, it is not a necessary condition for the existence of a market. The essential requirement is that there exists some method of communication between potential buyers and sellers either directly, e.g. by telephone or letter, or indirectly through an intermediary.

The development of reinsurance companies throughout the world has led to active and sometimes highly competitive markets operating in many cities where local direct insurers can place their reinsurances. In addition there are a few places recognized as international reinsurance centres where much of the business transacted originates from abroad. Contact between insurers and reinsurers in some markets is direct whereas in other countries much of the business is dealt with through the agency of reinsurance brokers who play a particularly important role in the placing of reinsurances internationally, especially on the London market. A feature of reinsurance markets is that because of the ways in which insurers and reinsurers operate, a company may be trading simultaneously as both a buyer and seller of reinsurance.

So the organization of reinsurance markets ranges from a group of local insurers placing all of their reinsurances with a monopoly corporation to something as complex as the London reinsurance market which is illustrated in Figure 2.1. Indeed the multiplicity of organizations operating in the London market and their different ways of doing business led one observer to suggest that 'London would be more accurately described as consisting of a number of overlapping markets loosely linked by practice and tradition'.[1]

Given such diversity, an attempt will now be made to analyse the characteristics of national and international reinsurance markets and of the parties involved therein.

---

1 R.A. Handover, 'The London non-marine reinsurance market', *Journal of the Chartered Insurance Institute*, vol.64 (1967), p.121.

Figure 2.1

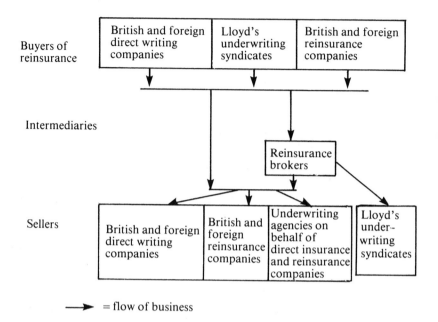

= flow of business

International markets

Why have some reinsurance markets developed from serving local direct insurers into international centres? There is no single answer. In the case of London the development of overseas underwriting agencies and later of branches and subsidiaries by the major direct insurance companies gave their London head-office officials a unique knowledge of insurance practice and conditions throughout the world. As local markets developed, the same companies through their old connections were able to attract reinsurance business to London in place of the insurances they previously wrote direct. London too was able to offer a variety of different types of insurers and reinsurers—major tariff and independent companies, the so-called fringe companies consisting of smaller companies writing overseas business through underwriting agencies, branches and subsidiaries of major foreign insurance and reinsurance companies, and most notably the individual underwriters forming the Lloyd's market with its highly developed broker system. At the time of its early development London possessed the additional advantages of a strong international currency, exchange-control regulations favourable to international reinsurance transactions, and the backing of banking and other financial institutions experienced in the conduct of overseas business. Finally there was considerable freedom from government interference in the conduct of insurance business, so encouraging flexibility in rating and wordings and the establishment in London of foreign companies. Thus London possessed all of the attributes which J.A.S. Neave has listed as the prerequisites of an international insurance centre, i.e.:[2]

> A sound financial background and a thorough technical expertise ... a currency freely negotiable and exchange-control regulations favourable to the free transaction of reinsurance business internationally ... flexibility, implying a certain size and variety of technical opinion, and with it a willingness to consider all types of cover so that competitive quotations can be obtained.

The strength of London rests principally on Lloyd's, the direct writing companies and its extensive broker connections. Largely it has failed to breed specialist reinsurance companies, and even today only one British company figures amongst the big league of reinsurance companies (see Table 2.2). In contrast, the growth of the New York, Tokyo, Zurich and other Continental reinsurance markets has stemmed mainly from the enterprise and growth of companies specialising in reinsurance business.

It is perhaps unfortunate that the specialist reinsurers have come to be known as professional reinsurance companies: the implication that companies whose main business is direct insurance are amateurs when it comes to dealing with inwards reinsurance business is often far from the truth. What the major professional reinsurance companies can offer (and here must be included reinsurers that deal either mainly direct or through brokers, and the reinsurance subsidiaries of large direct companies) are the services of specialist underwriters. Thus they can handle all of the main classes of business and they possess a thorough knowledge of conditions throughout the world gained from years of experience and extensive travel. The development of some specialist reinsurers has been based principally on the size and growth of their domestic markets, e.g. the American companies, but the Swiss reinsurance companies have demonstrated that an international business can be built on a small domestic base.

National markets

By definition, national reinsurance markets are narrower in the scope

---

2 J.A.S. Neave, 'Reinsurance today: a general survey', *Journal of the Chartered Insurance Institute*, vol.63 (1966), p.47.

of business transacted than their international counterparts. Usually the same is true of their structures too, though they display widely differing patterns. Throughout the Communist world all insurance business has been nationalized and state insurance organizations seek international reinsurance protection only to protect foreign-currency commitments. Several African and Arab countries, and the states of the Indian subcontinent, have followed the Communist example, but because of the more limited size of their domestic markets they tend to have greater recourse to international reinsurance. In other countries where private direct insurance companies are still permitted to operate, state owned reinsurance corporations have been formed to which all companies are required to cede part of their business. Some state reinsurance corporations, notably in South America, have a monopoly of domestic reinsurance, and alone are permitted to place business abroad. Elsewhere, the state reinsurer is entitled to only limited compulsory cessions, leaving direct insurers free to place any balance with other reinsurers (e.g. Turkey), and in France the state company competes with other private reinsurance companies. Lastly there are competitive reinsurance markets catering principally for domestic direct companies, though, as in Scandinavia, they may contain a professional reinsurance company very active in world markets.

The uniqueness of London is that it encompasses within the market as buyers and sellers of reinsurance all of the types of insurance and reinsurance enterprise that can be found throughout the world. The remainder of this chapter, therefore, will be concerned mainly, though not exclusively, with an explanation of the roles of the various bodies shown in Figure 2.1.

Buyers of reinsurance

Direct insurers

The main buyers of reinsurance are the direct writing companies. How much reinsurance the direct insurers operating in any country need depends partly on the structure of the insurance market.

When retentions are considered in Chapter 9 it will be shown that the size of any one loss or an accumulation of losses arising from one event which an insurance company can retain for its own account tends to increase directly with (*a*) the volume and spread of the business it transacts and (*b*) the size of its reserves relative to its premium income. Therefore, the more fragmented is a country's insurance business amongst large numbers of small and new companies, the greater will tend to be the total market demand for reinsurance.

It follows that changes in market structures, such as the mergers that have taken place between insurance companies in many countries over the last 25 years, may significantly affect the demand for reinsurance. In Britain, for example, between 1956 and December 1968, 22 of the leading non-life insurance companies merged to form seven groups. The effect of those mergers on the market shares of the largest companies is shown in Table 2.1. After allowing for inflation and the devaluation of sterling, the three largest companies on average have more than trebled the scale of their operations, and naturally their group reinsurance arrangements have been reviewed accordingly.

Table 2.1 Leading companies' share of the worldwide net fire and accident premium incomes of British insurers, including Lloyd's

	Leading companies' premium incomes (£ million)				Share of total premium income			
	1956	1963	1968	1976	1956 %	1963 %	1968 %	1976 %
Three largest companies	220.2	412.3	811.0	2715.7	27.2	32.9	40.4	41.5
Six largest companies	313.4	600.2	1134.1	3882.9	38.8	47.9	57.1	59.3

Source: R.L. Carter, *Economics and Insurance* (London: P.H. Press, 1972) tables 1.2 and 1.5, and *Policy Holder Insurance Journal*, 16 December 1977.

Following a merger a group underwriting pool may be formed with retention limits fixed in relation to the group's combined financial resources in place of the individual retentions of the formerly independent companies. Thus the group may aim to retain for its own account a larger share of its gross premium income and thereby improve its profits in two ways. First, as the change in retentions should not affect its business-acquisition costs and may marginally reduce administration expenses, its ratio of expenses to retained premium income should fall. Secondly, it will keep for itself any profit earned on the previously reinsured part of its business. Against those gains, however, must be offset the appropriate share of the reinsurance commission and any profit commission the companies previously received.

The fixing of retentions is far from a precise science and much depends on the degree of risk a management is willing to tolerate. Also when dealing with portfolios that are subject to some interdependence between exposure units, it is possible that the combining of two portfolios could result in high concentrations of units, so creating a severe risk of accumulations of losses from one event. Therefore, it is possible (and in practice it sometimes does happen) that following a merger a group may set its retentions at higher levels than the individual limits of its previously separate members but less than their aggregate retentions. Theoretically, however, a merged group is more likely to reinsure a smaller proportion of its total business because generally the combining of two separate portfolios should produce a more stable claims experience relative to total premium income.[3] This relationship between the volume of business transacted and retentions will be explored more fully in Chapter 9, but in the meantime the following example will illustrate this point. For the sake of simplicity all exposure units are taken as being of the same size and the possibility of catastrophe losses is excluded too.

Example. Two engineering insurance companies A and B insure a class of machines against breakdown. All machines are independently exposed to loss and the probability of a failure occurring in any one year is 0.05. The cost of repairing a machine is £100. Company A insures 50,000 machines and company B insures 25,000.

    Expected losses each year as separate companies and as a merged group are:

	Expected number of losses		Claim per machine		Total expected claims
Company A	$50,000 \times 0.05 = 2,500$	×	£100	=	£250,000
B	$25,000 \times 0.05 = 1,250$	×	£100	=	£125,000
Group	$75,000 \times 0.05 = 3,750$	×	£100	=	£375,000

The expected variability in the numbers of losses each year can be measured by the standard deviation σ as follows:[4]

$$\sigma = \sqrt{pqn}$$

where p = probability of no loss ($=0.95$)

               q = probability of loss ($=0.05$)

               n = number of machines

---

3 This reasoning lies behind the encouragement given to developing countries to concentrate their insurance markets on fewer companies. See *Reinsurance Problems in Developing Countries.*
4 The standard deviation is a particularly useful measure for describing how far individual items in a distribution deviate from the mean. When used in conjunction with a frequency distribution as here, in the case of normal distributions it indicates the percentage of outcomes that can be expected to fall within specified ranges.

Company A $\sigma = \sqrt{(0.95 \times 0.05 \times 50,000)} = 48.7$

B $\sigma = \sqrt{(0.95 \times 0.05 \times 25,000)} = 34.5$

Group $\sigma = \sqrt{(0.95 \times 0.05 \times 75,000)} = 59.7$

The above information can then be used to estimate the size of premium loading, free reserves, or amount of reinsurance (or some combination of all three) which the companies would require to reduce their probabilities of ruin to an acceptable figure. As the probability distributions of the two companies and so the group are identical, it is reasonable to make further use of the standard deviation, one of its properties being that for normal distributions over 99% of all possible outcomes lie within three standard deviations of the mean. Thus it may be accepted that there will be less than a 1% probability that the companies' losses will be more or less than:

	Numbers of losses	Total claims	Relative variation from total expected claims
Company A	$2,500 \pm 146 = 2,354$ or $2,646$	£235,400 to £264,600	5.84%
Company B	$1,250 \pm 103 = 1,147$ or $1,353$	£114,700 to £135,300	8.24%
Group	$3,750 \pm 179 = 3,571$ or $3,929$	£357,100 to £392,900	4.77%

As can be seen, the merging of the two companies reduces the relative expected variability in the claims costs, which therefore could be covered by either building a smaller contingency loading into the premiums or by buying less reinsurance than before.

Once a group underwriting scheme has been instituted only business surplus to the group retentions will be passed to outside reinsurers. Subsidiaries writing separate accounts will first pass business to the parent company which will arrange any necessary reinsurances on behalf of the whole group. Such arrangements are analogous to the central purchasing departments of manufacturing groups. Central control ensures that premium income is not unnecessarily paid away in purchasing reinsurance, and that full advantage is taken of the combined bargaining power of the group in negotiating terms for reinsurance contracts.

It has been argued that reinsurers are doubly hit by the mergers of direct companies, in that not only do large groups increase their retentions but they also tend to switch from proportional to non-proportional reinsurances, which results in a further cut in premiums available for reinsurers. Thus 'every time two large companies merge reinsurers lose large slices of their income and their bargaining power gets weaker.'[5]

There have been other forces at work, however, which have operated against group underwriting and in favour of some reinsurers, such as the formation of state reinsurance corporations to which all companies operating in the country, including branches and subsidiaries of foreign companies, must cede a part of their business. Also the spread of floating foreign-exchange rates has made the holding of central funds to cover the liabilities of overseas branches and subsidiaries more risky. Finally, inflation, combined with social pressures, has caused potential liabilities to increase far more rapidly than premium incomes, while the rise in premium incomes has strained solvency margins so limiting the amount of business companies can retain for their own account.

The term *group underwriting* is also used to describe arrangements between a consortium of independent companies for a centralized system of placing business between themselves and for arranging any necessary reinsurances. Such arrangements are akin to underwriting pools and will be discussed later in this chapter.

Captive insurance companies

Another major development of the postwar period has been the formation by major industrial and commercial companies of so-called *captive insurance companies* to handle the insurance business of their parent company and fellow subsidiaries. It is the final stage in a self-insurance programme.

There are several sound reasons why a large group may decide to form its own insurance company.[6] Some of the earliest captives established in the 1920s and 1930s were prompted by difficulties encountered in trying to place very hazardous risks on conventional direct insurance markets. More recently as large manufacturing and commercial companies have become more interested in controlling the costs of handling their risks they have demanded more extensive forms of partial insurance (notably very large deductibles and sometimes large first loss covers) and more flexible premium rating schemes tied to the loss experience of the group. Both demands have met with resistance from insurers concerned with preserving their premium incomes. Excess of loss covers with premiums

---

5 J. Butcher, 'Insurance mergers—their effect on professional reinsurers', *Reinsurance*, September 1971.

6 J.A. Dixon groups the reasons under five headings: (1) the pooling of risks within the group; (2) to meet compulsory insurance requirements; (3) to reduce insurance costs; (4) to overcome a lack of availability of the type of insurance required; and (5) so that the group retains control over the funds generated. 'Captive insurance companies', in *The Handbook of Risk Management*, ed. R.L. Carter and N.A. Doherty (Brentford: Kluwer, 1974).

based on burning costs (i.e. on the reinsured's loss experience) are, however, common practice in reinsurance markets so that large groups developing their self-insurance programmes have found a more sympathetic response from reinsurers.[7] Also, because reinsurers do not incur the same costs as direct insurers in servicing their business, premium savings can be achieved by forming a captive, bypassing the direct insurance market, and placing business with reinsurers, though services previously provided by insurers and brokers will have to be paid for separately if required. In looking at American practices one writer suggested that the *raison d'être* of a captive 'seems to be its use as a reinsurance conduit.'[8] Whatever the reasons may have been, American companies in particular have formed a substantial number of captive insurance companies during the last ten years: in 1972 Arthur Mayes put the total number at 145 – 150.[9]

During the 1960s multinational corporations also discovered the advantages of establishing captive insurance companies in tax havens such as Bermuda, the Bahamas, and the Seychelles. Mayes estimated that in 1972 there were 15 – 30 captives with American parent companies registered in Bermuda:[10] since then the numbers have increased substantially,[11] and may now exceed 700.

How many captives can be said to operate in Britain depends partly on definitions. The Department of Trade records show that the number of insurance companies which are wholly or mainly owned by an industrial or commercial company for the purposes principally of handling the parent company's insurance business has increased from eight in 1963 to 15 in 1975. Like the Americans, British multinational groups have in recent years tended to set up new captives in tax havens, including Guernsey, though definite information about numbers involved is hard to find.

The net losers from the growth of captives have been the direct-insurance companies, with the reinsurance market probably having gained in so far as captive companies tend to be smaller and so fix lower retention limits than conventional insurers underwriting large industrial and commercial risks. However, among the six British captive companies that submit full returns to the Department of Trade, practice does vary.

7 The Chairman of the Reinsurance Offices' Association in discussing captive insurers said that if their establishment was part of a programme of cutting losses through improved prevention, then reinsurers will be sympathetic and support their formation. J.A.S. Neave, 'Current problems of the reinsurance market', *Policy Holder Insurance Journal*, vol. 89, (5 February 1971).

8 R.C. Goshay, 'Captive Insurance Companies', in *Risk Management*, ed. H.W. Snider, (Homewood, Ill: R.D. Irwin Inc., 1964), p.120.

9 A. Mayes, 'Captive companies updated', *Policy Holder Insurance Journal*, vol. 90 (22 September 1972).

10 Ibid.

11 T.R. Goulder, 'Self-insurance—the prospects', *Insurance*, February 1974.

In 1974, three (including the second and third largest in terms of gross written premium income) ceded over half of their United Kingdom premium income to reinsurers; the other three retained 90% or more of their gross premiums for their own account. Even if the formation of captives has produced an increase in reinsurance business it is questionable how much of it has passed to established reinsurance markets because some captive companies have participated in underwriting pools exchanging business between themselves.

Reinsurers

Although reinsurers are principally suppliers of reinsurance they also operate as buyers whenever they retrocede part of any business they have underwritten.

Technically a reinsurer will retrocede business for the same reasons as a direct insurer buys reinsurance, i.e. mainly because it does not wish to retain wholly for its own account some business it has accepted.

In many markets, including London, reinsurers accept larger potential liabilities, or business which they normally prefer to avoid, in order to accommodate valuable clients or brokers. They may then seek to offload some of the risk by way of retrocessions.

More important, however, is the risk of the accumulation of liabilities on one or more exposure units. Since the practice of providing detailed bordereaux under reinsurance treaties was generally abandoned, reinsurers have been unable to index acceptances to prevent over-exposure to losses at any one situation or area, or arising from any one event. For example, a reinsurer may become heavily interested in a particular mercantile risk through cessions received under a number of treaties. Similarly the company's property account may be over-exposed to catastrophe losses from natural perils such as windstorm or earthquake because of reinsurances accepted on properties concentrated in a relatively small area. Inevitably, therefore, a reinsurer must buy protection, usually in the form of non-proportional reinsurance, against the risk of (often unknown) accumulations.

Besides such cases where reinsurers seek to protect their own financial position through the use of retrocessions, often for competitive reasons they reluctantly retrocede business they would prefer to retain for their own account. Ceding insurers, including state insurance and reinsurance corporations, often regard an exchange of reinsurance business as a means of developing, and at the same time possibly improving the profitability and stability of, their own accounts. Consequently reciprocity is well-established practice in reinsurance markets: its merits and dangers will be considered in Chapter 3.

State insurance and reinsurance corporations

Brief reference was made in Chapter 1 to the formation of state insurance and reinsurance corporations. Their roles in relation to reinsurance vary considerably, depending largely on the extent to which they are given monopoly rights to domestic business.

State-owned insurance corporations are becoming an increasingly common feature of insurance markets throughout the world. In the Communist bloc and some developing countries they are the result of the wholesale nationalization of the insurance industry, and possess 100% monopolies of their domestic markets. Elsewhere they have been established to transact the insurance of certain types of risk, often subject to compulsory insurance provisions, that are normally handled by private insurance. Examples are the Länder and cantonal fire insurance companies in West Germany and Switzerland respectively, and the motor insurance corporation established in Canada by the dominion government of British Columbia. Other countries have state-owned insurance companies that compete in the market for business (e.g. France), though in some cases they are entitled to take compulsory cessions of all domestic business transacted by other companies (e.g. Nigeria). Although the main impact of such organizations is on direct insurance business, their effect is also felt on reinsurance markets in two ways:

(1) they *may* reduce the volume of reinsurance business that otherwise would have been placed internationally either because they take compulsory cessions from other insurers, or in the case of monopoly state insurance corporations they possess a greater underwriting capacity than the aggregate capacity of the former companies; and

(2) a state corporation may be its country's sole buyer of reinsurance from the international reinsurance markets, and be able to exercise more skill and bargaining power than that possessed by individual companies.

State reinsurance corporations are essentially sellers of reinsurance, but, in so far as they retrocede part of the risks they underwrite, like other reinsurers they also operate as buyers too.

The organization and practices of state reinsurance corporations display marked differences. Some possess a 100% monopoly of all domestic reinsurances (such as the Reinsurance Institute of Brazil), or are entitled to compulsory cessions from domestic and/or foreign companies operating in the country (e.g. the Bimeh Markazi of Iran). Many only encounter competition from foreign reinsurers when they enter international markets as sellers of reinsurance, as many do, though others have to meet it at home too.

No one knows to what extent international reinsurance markets are deprived of business by the existence of state insurance and reinsurance corporations because a substantial part of the risks underwritten by the corporations otherwise would probably have been absorbed by local direct and reinsurance companies, and the corporations themselves reinsure (or retrocede) some domestic risks to foreign reinsurers. It does seem inevitable, however, that there has been some reduction in the flow of business insured and reinsured internationally. Although some state corporations, particularly in developing countries with limited underwriting capacity and spread of risk, follow reinsurance and retrocession practices similar to those of private companies, others limit the amount of reinsurance they purchase abroad. For example, the very large state corporations like the Russian Ingosstrakh only tend to reinsure internationally risks involving potential foreign-exchange losses though, together with the other Eastern European state insurance corporations, they spread their reinsurance widely throughout the world, both through the medium of reinsurance brokers and directly with professional reinsurance companies. Much of the business is placed on a reciprocal basis so they play a role internationally as sellers of reinsurance.[12] Other state insurance and reinsurance corporations, particularly in the developing countries where domestic capacity and spread of risk are more limited, follow reinsurance and retrocession practices similar to those of private companies.

While recognizing that the formation of a state corporation may deprive foreign insurers of some business, it has been claimed that there can be offsetting benefits. In particular a better balanced portfolio of business may be expected from a national institution than from a collection of separate companies, and a state reinsurance corporation may impose a greater degree of discipline on the national market.[13]

Underwriting pools

Underwriting pools have been formed to handle both direct and reinsurance business. As their objective is to reduce the demand for reinsurance supplied by conventional reinsurance markets by mobilizing local capacity either to handle business directly or through the exchange

---

12 The Russian Ingosstrakh operates subsidiary companies in London, Hamburg and Vienna. The London company, the Black Sea and Baltic Insurance Company writes British and foreign direct and reinsurance business: in 1974 over one-quarter of its gross written premium income related to treaty reinsurances accepted.
13 *Reinsurance Problems in Developing Countries*, p.35.

of reinsurances, a description of their activities will be deferred until the next section on sellers of reinsurance. However, underwriting pools may seek external reinsurance protection and so must also be listed under potential buyers of reinsurance.

Sellers of reinsurance

Professional reinsurance companies

Since the foundation in 1852 of the first insurance company specializing in the transaction of reinsurance, professional reinsurance companies have been established in most countries. In 1965 it was estimated that there were almost 200 operating throughout the world with an aggregate annual premium income approaching £700 million.[14] Over the next ten years both the numbers of companies and premium incomes increased: in 1975 the net premium income of the 11 leading professional reinsurers alone amounted to over £2,500 million (see Table 2.2).

Germany, the home of the first company, still retains its pre-eminence as a base for professional reinsurance companies, with four among the 11 leading companies listed in Table 2.2. Before the First World War continental companies dominated international reinsurance markets, and despite their loss of business during the war and the ensuing economic upheaval, the German reinsurers were able to re-establish their position between the wars. The 1939 – 45 War was still more disruptive and the recovery of German companies, like their economy, has been an even more amazing feat of enterprise and energy.

Switzerland is the other main European base of reinsurance companies which have enjoyed the benefits of a more favourable political climate and more highly developed financial centres than their German counterparts. The largest company, the Swiss Reinsurance Company founded in 1863, vies with the Munich Reinsurance Company for the position of the world's largest international reinsurance company.

14 Neave, 'Reinsurance today', p.55.

Table 2.2 Net premium income of the world's professional reinsurance companies (conversions into US $ are at end-of-year rates of exchange)

	Domestic currency (millions)				US $ millions Total		Average annual growth rates 1971 – 75 total business	
	Non-life		Life				in domestic currency	in US $
	1971	1975	1971	1975	1971	1975	%	%
Munich Reinsurance Co. (D.M.)	2350.3	3616.7	310.5	474.8	814.2	1561.6	11.4	17.7
Swiss Reinsurance Co. (S.Fr.)	2307.1	2800.1	454.9	619.4	705.5	1305.2	5.5	16.7
General Reinsurance Co. ($)	252.6	428.8	—	—	252.6	428.8	14.1	14.1
American Reinsurance Co. ($)	184.6	263.7	—	—	184.6	263.7	9.3	9.3
Cologne Reinsurance Co. (D.M.)	361.4	483.6	115.4	168.2	145.9	248.8	8.1	14.3
Société Commerciale de Réassurance (F.Fr.)	530.8	1022.7	50.7	89.5	111.3	247.7	17.6	22.1
Mercantile & General Reinsurance Co. (£)	36.8	84.9	20.5	33.1	146.2	238.9	19.8	13.1
Gerling Global Reinsurance Co. (D.M.)	526.1	511.7	36.3	66.3	172.2	220.6	0.7	6.4
INA Reinsurance Co. ($)	116.8	205.3	—	—	116.8	205.3	15.1	15.1
Employers Reinsurance Co. ($)	153.0	198.3	—	—	153.0	198.3	6.7	6.7
Frankona Reinsurance Co. (D.M.)	278.8	381.4	76.8	102.4	108.8	184.7	8.0	14.1
Total					2911.1	5103.6		15.1

Source: *International Insurance Monitor.*

Rates of Exchange:		1971	1975
1$ =	D.M.	3.268	2.62
	S.Fr.	3.915	2.62
	F.Fr.	5.224	4.49
	£	0.392	0.494

The position of the American reinsurance companies is unique in that they operate in the world's largest domestic market where the direct insurance business accounts for a half of all of the non-Communist world's premium income. Given the size of the American direct insurance market, three aspects of its reinsurance market are hardly surprising. The business of American reinsurers is mainly domestic, though in recent years the major companies have entered the international market as sellers on a substantial scale. The sheer volume of business available has attracted Lloyd's and foreign reinsurers from all over the world, so making the United States a major importer of reinsurance. Most of the world's leading reinsurance companies have established branches or subsidiary companies in the country, and many write a substantial amount of business there. Finally, like specialist reinsurance companies in many other countries, American reinsurers are small compared with the major American direct insurance companies; for example, the worldwide general net premium incomes of the four largest American reinsurance companies amounted to only $1,096.1 million in 1975 compared to the $66,152 million net non-life premiums written by direct and reinsurance companies in the USA, i.e. only 1.7% of the total. Nevertheless four American reinsurers figure amongst the world's top 11 reinsurance companies listed in Table 2.2.

Undoubtedly the specialist reinsurance companies, whether operating mainly direct or through the broking system, play an important competitive role in the North American insurance industry. Moreover their technical skill and practices have attracted the admiration of their European counterparts.[15]

In contrast to other European countries, few professional reinsurance companies have been formed in Britain. The first company, the Reinsurance Company Limited, was established in 1867 but survived for only three years. Several other companies were founded but they too were short-lived until the establishment of the Mercantile and General Reinsurance Company in 1907. For several years it was a subsidiary of the Swiss Reinsurance Company but it is now owned by the Prudential Assurance Company. Its largest domestic competitor, the Victory Insurance Company, was registered in 1919 and remained independent until its acquisition by the Legal and General Assurance Society in 1974.

Many reinsurance companies have formal links with direct-writing companies. Some have been established by direct writers to handle their reinsurance accounts, e.g. INA Reinsurance Company which is a subsidiary of the Insurance Company of North America. Others have been acquired by direct-writing companies, and in a few cases the big

---

15 See, for example, Neave, 'Reinsurance today', p.57.

reinsurance companies have shareholdings in direct-writing companies with whom they are closely associated, e.g. the Munich Reinsurance Company and the largest German direct insurance company, the Allianz, have cross-shareholdings, and the Swiss Reinsurance Company has shareholdings in many companies throughout the world.

Market developments

One of the newer market developments has been the formation of new reinsurance companies as an international cooperative venture by insurance companies established in different parts of the world. One of the first major examples of such joint ventures was the formation in 1976 of the Norwich Winterthur Reinsurance Company by the Norwich Union Group of Britain, the Winterthur Insurance Company of Switzerland and the Chiyoda Insurance Company of Japan.

Lloyd's

The unique feature of the London market is the presence of Lloyd's, an organization of individual underwriters who can trace their history back to the merchant underwriters of the 16th and 17th centuries.[16] The organization owes its name to a Mr Edward Lloyd, a 17th-century proprietor of a London coffee house where many of the merchants writing marine insurance gathered to transact their business.

Since 1771 the membership of Lloyd's has been divided between underwriters and brokers, controlled by an elected committee which elects new members and supervises their financial standing through an annual audit and management of a Premium Trust Fund. Membership was limited to citizens of Britain and the Commonwealth until 1968 when the first foreign members were admitted, a year before the first women members. The Corporation of Lloyd's is purely an administrative body which provides the accommodation, information and other services (e.g. policy signing, claims bureau, appointment of Lloyd's agents) required by the members. The Corporation writes no insurance business itself and has no legal responsibility for any member's underwriting debts, though all members annually subscribe to a Guarantee Fund from which any such debts are paid on an *ex gratia* basis.

16 Gibb, *Lloyd's of London.*

Today the qualifications for admittance as an underwriting member are principally wealth and integrity; no knowledge of insurance is required. Consequently the members are organized into around 300 syndicates, mostly managed by underwriting agencies. Each member, however, remains severally liable without limit for his proportion of all risks written by the syndicate, though members have no liability for the debts of other members even of the same syndicate.

Business can be placed at Lloyd's only by approved Lloyd's brokers. Any other broker who wishes to deal with Lloyd's can only do so by channelling the business through a Lloyd's broker.

The underwriting syndicates handle both direct and reinsurance business, but no details are available of the composition of the business of either individual syndicates or the Lloyd's market as a whole. The only published breakdown of premium income is by class of business (see Table 2.3): the figures represent the total premium income received in the respective calendar years.[17]

Table 2.3 Lloyd's worldwide premium income in calendar years

Class of Business	1973 £m	1974 £m	1975 £m	1976 £m
UK motor	71	85	101	118
Marine and transit	380	442	580	734
Aviation	87	104	137	180
General	453	511	713	931
Short-term life	1	1	1	1
Total	992	1143	1532	1964

Only about one-quarter of Lloyd's premium income is derived from UK insurances. The largest source of business is the United States, which accounts for a half of total premium income, Lloyd's being particularly active in the market for surplus-line business, both direct and reinsurance. In order to meet the requirements of the state regulatory authorities, Lloyd's maintains a special guarantee fund in the United States.

Apart from the smallest risks, business placed at Lloyd's is shared between several syndicates, and in many cases the broker may interest one or more companies too. The skill of the broker lies in obtaining a

---

17 Under the Lloyd's system of three-year accounting, premiums are shown net of commissions and include premiums for self-reinsurance of outstanding liabilities from closed years. Thus Lloyd's premium income figures are somewhat higher than would be recorded by a company writing the same amount of business.

good lead from an underwriter recognized by the market as an expert in the particular type of business concerned: if companies are also to be interested a separate lead is needed from the company market too. The leading underwriter(s) are responsible for fixing terms for the cover required, and in order to establish a good lead must be prepared to write a significant share of the risk.

Basically the same procedures are followed for both direct and reinsurance business placed at Lloyd's. The monopoly Lloyd's brokers possess for placing business means that a direct office wishing to reinsure at Lloyd's must deal through brokers who both place the business and deal with all of the arrangements regarding premium and claims payments, the issue of documents, etc.

Direct insurance companies

Reinsurance business commenced with the ceding of reinsurances between direct insurers, and although no accurate global statistics are available, it is commonly believed that, in the aggregate, direct companies still handle a far larger volume of inwards reinsurance business than the professional reinsurance companies. The British market is not wholly typical of other countries but in 1969 the inwards non-life reinsurance premiums received by British-registered direct-writing companies under home and overseas treaties amounted to around £260 million compared with £80 million received by British-registered professional reinsurance companies, including the British subsidiaries of foreign professional reinsurers.

Major direct-writing companies typically establish a separate reinsurance department to handle both inwards and outwards reinsurance business, and in many cases have also either established or acquired a separate subsidiary company to specialize in the transaction of reinsurance. In view of the special knowledge and skill required to run an inwards reinsurance account successfully, small to medium-sized direct companies that wish to participate in such business tend to subcontract the work to underwriting agencies. Even large companies sometimes employ agencies to handle specialized classes of reinsurance business.

Thus the participation and organization of direct insurance companies as sellers of reinsurance follows no uniform pattern. In some groups reinsurance is conducted as an autonomous class of business by a separate subsidiary with little direct interference from the parent management. At the other extreme, inwards reinsurance may be little more than an appendage of the direct-writing operation, the inwards reinsurance activities being limited to the acceptance of facultative reinsurances. It is reasonable to conclude, therefore, that the attitudes and policies of direct-writing companies to reinsurance business likewise display wide differences and any generalizations about their behaviour must be treated with caution. Perhaps some are more concerned than their professional reinsurance counterparts with short-term profitability than with establishing long-term relationships with their ceding companies. On the other hand, any company that wishes to write a successful treaty account must gear its organization and objectives to dealing with that type of business.

Likewise, although direct insurance companies normally tend to acquire all or most of their reinsurance business through brokers, companies that wish to develop their reinsurance accounts must create the right conditions to do so. They need to build up professional staffs with specialist reinsurance knowledge and expertise, and must work hard to establish strong relationships with the brokers who act as their sales force.

Underwriting agencies

The transaction of reinsurance business internationally has the obvious advantage of enabling even direct insurance companies whose business is confined to their home market to obtain a geographically distributed portfolio of business. The transaction of international business is, however, highly concentrated on a few recognized centres so that a company wishing to participate on any scale in such business needs to be represented locally.

Absence of a local office with powers to accept business does not exclude a company from participating in international business, but it acts as a severe constraint on the ability to compete effectively. The company must rely on the willingness of brokers and other companies with whom it seeks to maintain friendly relations to incur the expense and delay of contact through telex and correspondence to provide it with a flow of business. Even if a company appoints a local representative or agent (usually a reinsurance broker) to provide it with a permanent presence in the market, the need to refer all offers of business to head office for acceptance will remain, together with the expense, the inevitable delay in obtaining decisions and the lack of personal contact between underwriters and the company's sources of business. On the other hand to establish a local office with full underwriting powers can be both very expensive, unless a company can be sure of writing a substantial volume of business, and may prove disastrous unless it can appoint a skilled underwriter with an intimate knowledge of local business practice and the types of business which will be offered.

The London market offers a compromise solution in the form of the underwriting agent. An insurance company which obtains authorization from the Department of Trade to transact insurance business in Britain can appoint an agent to underwrite reinsurance on its behalf. The terms of the agency agreement will specify the classes of business the agent is authorized to underwrite and his acceptance limits. Variations exist in the manner in which agencies operate but generally all matters affecting underwriting and claims settlement are left to the agent to handle within the terms of the agency agreement. Thus the agent is responsible for the local administration of the business, including the collection of premiums and other balances from ceding offices, maintaining the funds to cover technical reserves, and paying claims. Periodically the agent will report to his principal on the progress of the business, at the same time accounting for any profit or requesting settlement of any deficit on the account.

Remuneration of underwriting agents takes two basic forms, though it may involve a combination of both. One method is the payment of an overriding commission on premiums written. The other is by way of a share of any profits on the account.

No precise details are available regarding either numbers of underwriting agencies operating on the London market or premiums handled, but, ranked in order of importance, agencies are operated by reinsurance brokers, insurance and reinsurance companies, and by individual underwriters. Most, if not all, reinsurance brokers operate one or more underwriting agencies, generally on behalf of overseas clients, and will cover all classes of business if desired. Individual underwriters on the other hand tend to specialize in handling particular classes of business in which the underwriter is acknowledged by the rest of the market to be an expert. Therefore a company may appoint an individual underwriter to act as its underwriting agent for a highly specialized class of business while handling other reinsurance business itself.

The appointment of an underwriting agent may mark the decision of a company to be more closely identified with an international reinsurance centre, and it offers considerable advantages as a preliminary step to full-scale entry. It avoids the costs of opening a local office which in the early stages must either be spread over a small volume of business or be subsidized by the head office. At the same time the company should obtain the benefits of the skill and local knowledge possessed by the underwriting agent while building up its own experience of the types of business available on the market. Moreover the use of an underwriting agent need not necessarily be short term. Many London agencies are long established and have acted for some companies for many years, which is proof of the useful role they can perform.

On the other hand considerable care needs to be taken in the selection of the agent and the terms of his appointment. As some companies have discovered, a bad choice can prove an expensive mistake. First the underwriting record of the agent, particularly if he is an individual relatively new to the role of agent, will need to be scrutinized. Also the terms of the agreement, and each party's understanding of those terms must be such that the company does not find itself committed to liabilities it had no intention to accept.

State insurance and reinsurance corporations

As noted already, the positions of state insurance and reinsurance corporations in their domestic reinsurance markets vary considerably.[18] Even when the corporation is not given a monopoly of all the reinsurances ceded by direct companies operating in the country, there is usually some system of compulsory cessions. Sometimes the direct companies are allowed to exchange surplus reinsurances between themselves, but any balance must be ceded to the state corporation which alone can reinsure abroad. An alternative and more common system is for the state corporation to be entitled either to a quota share of all insurances transacted within the country, or to a fixed share of all surplus reinsurances ceded by the direct companies.

The result of these arrangements is that international reinsurers are either totally excluded from participating in the reinsurances of a country, other than through retrocessions from the state corporation, or their scope for participation is reduced.

Whichever system is employed, it is essential that great care be exercised by state corporations to avoid the risk of accumulations, especially in those classes of insurance business exposed to catastrophe risks. An overloading of the market's underwriting capacity could have disastrous consequences for the national economy in the event of a major loss occurring. Likewise, although one of the objectives of developing countries in forming state corporations is to ensure that the funds generated by insurance activities are invested locally to aid the development of the economy, great care is necessary to avoid undue concentration of those investments.[19]

---

18 See page 35 above.
19 The same point applies to reinsurance pools, see page 77.

Insurance and reinsurance pools

Under a pooling arrangement a group of insurers form a joint organization to handle the insurances of particular risks. As explained in Chapter 1,[20] pools may be arranged to handle business on either a direct or reinsurance basis.

The national (e.g. atomic energy) and multinational (e.g. oil) pools formed to underwrite particular classes of large risks on a direct basis ensure that the necessary market capacity is mobilized, and that the terms can be fixed in a single negotiation instead of the agreement of leading underwriter(s), coinsurers and reinsurers having to be obtained in turn. Although professional reinsurance companies and Lloyd's syndicates may participate, they do so as coinsurers and not as reinsurers of liabilities accepted by the pool, so that in the conventional sense such pools neither buy nor sell reinsurance. In fact rules of membership frequently restrict members from reinsuring liabilities accepted, the concept of the pooling arrangement being that each member's share is fixed in relation to what it can afford to retain for its own account.

Reinsurance pools have been formed on both local and regional bases. The organization may take the form of either a pool, perhaps managed by one of the member companies, or a separate reinsurance company with member companies participating as shareholders.

The formation of regional pools has been encouraged by the United Nations Conference on Trade and Development (UNCTAD) as a means of building up domestic insurance markets in developing countries and reducing the foreign-exchange costs of acquiring external reinsurance.[21] In addition to the Arab Federation and Regional Cooperation for Development pools cited in Chapter 1, regional pools have been formed in Asia, Latin America and the Caribbean. The Asian Reinsurance Corporation has participants, including international insurers, from Afghanistan, Bangladesh, India, Sri Lanka, Iran, Philippines, and Thailand.

If there were a substantial expansion of such regional groupings the international reinsurance market would be fragmented into a number of regional markets and the days of the truly international reinsurance company would be numbered. Although developing countries may see regional pools, with what are in effect formalized reciprocal reinsurance arrangements, as a means of strengthening their domestic insurers and minimizing balance-of-payments effects, it must be recognized that there

---

20 See page 20 and *Reinsurance problems in developing countries*, p.32, for the types of risks handled by direct insurance pools.

21 See para. 2 of resolution 42 (III) of the 1972 United Nations Conference on Trade and Development; and *Reinsurance problems in developing countries*, ch. 6.

is a price attached. That price is a more limited geographical spread of business, the forfeiting of the experience obtained from worldwide operations, and the elimination of choice in placing reinsurance. As in the general case of the reciprocal exchange of business, there is little satisfaction in exchanging profitable business with other companies whose results are consistently bad.

Reinsurance brokers

A discussion of reinsurance brokers is hampered by two difficulties: first there is no universally accepted definition of a reinsurance broker,[22] and secondly whatever definition one adopts there is no information available about the numbers of firms involved or the amount of business they handle. Partly these problems arise from the fact that even in countries where insurance business is closely supervised and where agents and brokers operating in the direct insurance markets must be licensed, intermediaries handling only reinsurance business are generally free from regulation.[23]

If the title reinsurance broker is used to describe all of the firms and individuals who act as intermediaries in the arranging of reinsurance contracts, whether acting principally as agent of the ceding company or the reinsurer, then it embraces a wide diversity of firms operating in a variety of ways. Moreover, as noted above, some brokers do not merely engage in arranging reinsurances but undertake, in their capacity as underwriting agents, the acceptance and underwriting of reinsurances for their reinsurer principals. Most brokers also become involved on behalf of one or other party to the reinsurance contract in the many administrative activities of reinsurance such as the preparation of contract documents and the preparation of statements of account in markets where this is not handled centrally by a recognized bureau.

The types of organizations acting as reinsurance brokers throughout the world vary considerably in size, location and types of business handled. They range from purely domestic to multinational enterprises with offices scattered around the world; from small partnerships to companies employing perhaps hundreds of staff; and from specialists in particular classes of business (e.g. oil or aviation risks) to organizations handling all classes of reinsurance.

---

22 See, for example, Stanford Miller, 'The intermediary in international reinsurance' in *Papers Presented at the International Reinsurance Seminar* (Reinsurance Offices' Association, 1973).

23 Until the state of New York introduced the licensing of reinsurance brokers in 1977, only brokers handling direct business had to be licensed in the United States. In Britain the compulsory registration of both insurance and reinsurance brokers was introduced by the Insurance Brokers (Registration) Act 1977.

The majority of reinsurance brokers now operating in London are subsidiaries of larger broking groups, but generally they operate independently of their direct-broking parent and associated companies. Whereas direct-broking business may be organized territorially, with separate organizations to handle home and overseas business, reinsurance broking is essentially international in character. The major firms maintain branch offices and are in contact with corresponding brokers in centres abroad, and their personnel, like those of the professional reinsurance companies, spend a substantial part of their time travelling overseas to visit clients. The presence of Lloyd's inevitably places brokers in a unique position in the London market.

Generally the large British direct insurance companies employ brokers to place some part of their domestic and foreign reinsurance covers, notably excess of loss treaties and proportional reinsurances where they are seeking reciprocity. Some small companies deal exclusively through brokers, others leave their reinsurance programmes in the hands of professional reinsurance companies.

In Western Europe the position of reinsurance brokers varies considerably between countries. For example, in Holland brokers handle a large proportion of the business whereas in Germany, the home of many large professional reinsurance companies, ceding offices tend to deal direct with their reinsurers. Elsewhere in the world the degree of market penetration achieved by reinsurance brokers varies considerably. In countries where the market is monopolized by a state reinsurance corporation obviously there is no role for brokers (though international brokers may be retained to place abroad the corporation's retrocessions). At the other end of the scale are countries such as Australia and Japan. In the former country, domestic and international brokers actively compete with the representatives of professional reinsurance companies for the reinsurances of the direct-writing companies. Japanese insurance companies tend to employ London brokers not only to place their reinsurances but also to act as underwriting agents to acquire inwards reinsurances.

The reinsurance market of the United States is complicated by the existence of separate insurance supervisory authorities for each state, and the distinction between 'domestic' (i.e. locally licensed), 'foreign' (i.e. licensed in another state) and 'alien' (not licensed in any state) companies. Most of the conventional reinsurance business is written by 'domestic' and 'foreign' reinsurers, and reinsurance brokers play an important role in placing that business. The market is broadly divided between a number of specialist American companies that deal direct with their ceding companies and compete for the complete reinsurance programmes of all but the largest direct-writing companies, and a brokerage market which is split between many specialist American and overseas reinsurers. Although there is intense competition between the two groups, a good deal of business is also shared between them.

Additionally a substantial amount of insurance and reinsurance for very large, substandard, and special risks for which cover cannot be obtained locally, is placed with non-admitted insurers, i.e. American companies not licensed to transact insurance in the state where the risk is located, or alien insurers. It has been estimated that premiums for such surplus-lines business (that is both direct insurance and reinsurance) 'topped the $ billion mark' in 1973, [24] of which Lloyd's wrote a substantial proportion. All of the surplus-lines direct insurances and reinsurances are arranged through specially licensed surplus-lines brokers, over 170 being licensed in New York. [25]

The reinsurance broker's role

The role of a reinsurance broker has been described as: [26]

> ... to professionally advise their client concerning the best type of reinsurance programme, proper retentions and adequate capacity based upon their experience and knowledge of market availability and then place the resultant programme for the client with secure markets at competitive price or terms.

Thus he is more than just an introductory agent. He holds himself out as being an expert who can be expected to bring to his duties a detailed knowledge of insurance law, supervisory regulations, market practice and conditions applying in all of the countries with which he deals. Furthermore, unlike the direct broker who will normally be advising the layman in relation to insurance, the reinsurance broker acts as an intermediary between expert professionals.

Provision of information

At the same time as the broker acts as an adviser to his client, the ceding office, he must also learn enough about its business, including the conditions under which it operates, to provide reinsurers with all of the facts they require to underwrite the risks he offers to them. In other words he must know his markets from the standpoint of both ceding

---

24 Sol Kroll, 'The past, present and future of non-admitted insurance in the United States', *Bests Insurance Digest*, November 1975.
25 Ibid.
26 Lothar Sudekum, 'The intermediary in international reinsurance', in *Papers Presented at the International Reinsurance Seminar* (Reinsurance Offices' Association, 1973).

insurer and reinsurer. To fulfil his role to the long-term satisfaction of his clients he must be capable of advising both parties so that they enter into the reinsurance contract with a reasonable equality of knowledge of all of the pertinent facts.

Thus an important part of the broker's role is to bridge the information gap between ceding office and reinsurer. Given sufficient time and effort no doubt the two parties could discover for themselves what they need to know, but often a broker can fulfil that need more efficiently. For example, whereas a broker in the normal course of his business can be fairly certain of learning about any new developments concerning types of reinsurance cover, rating methods, administrative procedures and so forth, a ceding insurer, lacking the same continuous contact with reinsurance markets throughout the world, would have to expend considerable special effort to be as well informed. The broker also has the added advantage of being able to spread the costs of gathering information over the many cases he handles.

A reinsurer for his part may feel that the limited share of the business he could hope to obtain from a country about which he knows little would not justify the necessary expenditure on research into prevailing market conditions and practices. A broker instructed to handle the whole account of a major insurer operating there can afford to invest time and money in becoming fully acquainted with all of the relevant facts. The rate of change in economic, social and political conditions throughout the world means moreover that information rapidly becomes outdated. In particular, governments throughout the world periodically enact new laws and decrees regulating the conduct of insurance and reinsurance business, including such matters as the deposit of assets and restrictions on the transfer abroad of funds, which have a vital bearing on the potential profitability of reinsurance business. Relatively few reinsurers can afford to match the market research activities of the major professional reinsurance companies, and therefore a company desirous of obtaining reinsurance from abroad may seek the assistance of brokers active in dealing with countries with which it would like to do business. At the same time the reinsurer will avoid the expense of sending out to the country its own representatives to canvass business.

The dual relationship of the broker to both ceding company and reinsurer in the provision of information and advice rests on more than strict legal obligations. If his business is to prosper he must seek to establish long-term relationships with both parties. This means that he must try to arrange contracts which will prove satisfactory to ceding companies and reinsurers over a long term. If the broker is to obtain continuity in the business he places, then both parties need to be fully aware of the benefits and obligations they accept. To provide ceding offices with unsuitable reinsurance cover can only result in the loss of their business. Likewise to induce reinsurers to enter into contracts which invariably produce losses because insufficient facts have been provided to enable adequate premiums and terms to be agreed will eventually leave the broker without a market.

Yet despite what has been said, reinsurers can be heard to complain that sometimes brokers fail to supply them with all of the information they would like. If that does happen, and clearly it is contrary to the broker's own long-term interests, then the fault may not always lie entirely with the broker. His information-gathering and dissemination task is not easy. Sometimes the problem may simply be one of communication between the broker, the leading reinsurer and other interested parties. Moreover a broker can know no more about his client's business than the client knows himself. Not infrequently, therefore, the broker must be prepared to advise clients on methods of improving their management information and control systems to ensure that reinsurers are not led blindly into contracts that may prove disastrous.

The demand for reciprocity in reinsurance business provides brokers with additional problems to solve and new responsibilities towards the parties with whom they deal. Clients seek introductions not merely to reinsurers prepared to supply reinsurance protection on acceptable terms, but also capable and willing to offer an exchange of treaties to their mutual satisfaction. So the exploratory and investigatory work of the broker is doubled and his relationship and responsibilities to the parties become more obscure.

Under such circumstances, however, one of the side benefits an insurer may obtain by employing a broker as intermediary, rather than approaching potential reinsurers direct, is that the preliminary investigations may be carried out anonymously. Thus it is possible to avoid embarrassment and possible loss of goodwill for the future if it is discovered that the terms obtainable or the business which could be offered in exchange are unlikely to prove acceptable.

Negotiation and administration of reinsurances

Although the main work of brokers lies in arranging and rearranging reinsurance treaties, they are also called upon to place reinsurances facultatively. For example, when an insurer is more or less obliged to accept a share of a very large risk which exceeds his own retention and treaty reinsurance facilities, the balance must be reinsured. Then a broker's extensive contacts can be invaluable in getting the business placed quickly.

Where a broker is employed to negotiate a new treaty, it will often be market practice for him to undertake all of the detailed work of drafting the treaty document, submitting it to the parties for their approval and preparing the final document in duplicate for their signature. A similar service may be provided when the parties to the treaty are small companies which lack the extensive experience of major insurers and reinsurers. In other cases the broker may be called upon to explain the terms of a proposed contract or of the underlying local customs and usages, and to help in reconciling any differences of opinion between the parties.

Upon completion of a reinsurance contract the broker will then concern himself in its administration, deal with its renewal, and when necessary renegotiate terms or arrange for the replacement of a reinsurer who gives notice that he wishes to terminate his interest in a treaty.

When a treaty is shared amongst a number of reinsurers the ceding office benefits from having to prepare only one account, drawing one cheque in settlement of balances due, and collecting one payment for any claim, leaving the broker to deal with individual reinsurers.

Regrettably delays in the settlement of accounts are a common source of friction between insurers and brokers and the reinsurance market is no exception. Sometimes it is difficult to speed up the process. Often following an agreement being reached that cover shall commence, the final completion of the contract may be delayed while negotiations take place about points of detail. The crux of the problem is the delay which frequently occurs between the dates when cases are closed, or at other times when payments are due, and the premiums being passed to the reinsurer(s). Again, however, the delay sometimes occurs because the broker has been unable to obtain payment from his client, perhaps due to the inability of the ceding company's accounting department to produce data on time in accordance with the agreed procedure.

The impression is that the problem is less acute in the United States than elsewhere. Possibly the accounting rules laid down by American supervisory authorities regarding the treatment of premium balances outstanding for more than 90 days may have made American reinsurers over the last decade more vigorous than their European counterparts in pressing brokers and ceding companies for settlement of accounts, though there is still scope for improvement. Recently steps have been taken in London to simplify and speed up the settlement of accounts between brokers and insurance companies, including reinsurers. Lloyd's operates its own accounting system, and at the end of 1975 the Institute of London Underwriters (ILU) modified its central accounting system so that each month a broker draws or receives one cheque in settlement of his accounts with ILU member companies for marine and aviation insurances and reinsurances, leaving the Institute then to settle individual balances with member companies. In March 1976 it was announced that a new Policy Signing and Accounting Centre was to be established in London for non-marine insurances and reinsurances, excluding life, aviation and motor business. The Centre commenced policy-signing operations in January 1977, and before long it will set up a central accounting system along the same lines as the ILU.

Losses

The broker may also assist in the settlement of losses. Where rapid settlement of a large loss is required it is not unusual for a broker to arrange for a banker's draft to be sent to the ceding office before he has received payment from all of the reinsurers. In other cases a broker may be able to help resolve disputes regarding, for example, the interpretation of a clause instead of the matter having to be referred to arbitration.

Brokerage

So reinsurance brokers render valuable services to many sectors of the market. In return they are remunerated by payment of an intermediary commission, usually payable by the reinsurer(s), on the amount of the premium. Occasionally the commission may take the form of a share of the profit under a treaty, and in rare cases where the business proves very difficult to place, the commission may be paid by the ceding office, or shared by the reinsurer(s) and ceding office.

Rates of commission based on premium are lower on quota share and surplus treaties than on excess of loss reinsurance treaties because of the much smaller premium volume generated by the latter. In London and other European markets rates currently range from $1\frac{1}{2}\%$ to $2\frac{1}{2}\%$ for the former and from 5% to 15% for excess of loss; in the American market commission rates are, in general, somewhat lower. The highest rate for excess of loss business applies only to treaties producing very small premiums. For excess of loss treaties rated on an adjustable basis, the brokerage is normally applied to a fixed rate of premium at a point somewhere midway between the minimum and maximum rates.

Services available from the market

The primary service provided by the reinsurance market is risk transfer for direct insurers, but as briefly mentioned in Chapter 1 it does in addition provide a variety of management and technical services for ceding companies.

Reference was made above to reinsurance brokers helping their clients to improve their management information and control systems. A reinsurer's operating results, particularly on proportional reinsurance business, will depend to a large degree on how ceding offices conduct their business. If, for example, selection and/or premium rating procedures are poor, or insufficient control is exercised over claims handling, then the chances of large losses being incurred on the direct account, and thus being passed on to the reinsurer, are greatly enhanced. Likewise poor claims records and estimating procedures may result in substantial losses being concealed for a number of years, during which time reinsurers reliant on available information on claims experience may be misled into charging inadequate premiums for excess of loss or other non-proportional reinsurances. Clearly reinsurers have an interest in the quality of management exercised by their ceding offices. Consequently companies writing substantial reinsurance accounts (notably the leading professional reinsurance companies) provide considerable assistance to small companies in the management of their business.

Such assistance takes various forms. It is common practice for large companies (and brokers) to provide training facilities at their head offices for staff of ceding companies, both at junior and middle management levels. Not infrequently a member of the reinsurer's or broker's own staff will spend some time at the office of a ceding company to help in setting up management systems, devising schemes for transacting new classes of insurance, arranging suitable reinsurance programmes, and generally guiding a new company in the conduct of its business. In other cases a large reinsurer may be able to draw on its own experience and knowledge of a particular class of insurance to comment on rating schedules or policy conditions proposed by a ceding company, though the extent to which a reinsurer will intervene in the affairs of its clients varies considerably between America and Britain.

Delays in the preparation of reinsurance accounts, and so in the settlement of balances due to the reinsurer, mean loss of investment income. Therefore reinsurers are naturally anxious to advise ceding offices on remedying any deficiencies in their internal accounting systems. Besides help with accounting a reinsurer may be able to advise a new company on investment policy.

Finally, technical assistance may be offered on the handling of claims, especially on large claims. For example, a reinsurer writing a substantial volume of excess of loss-liability business will gain far more experience in handling very large claims than the typical direct insurer which may suffer only a handful of such losses in a year. Thus the reinsurer may be able to offer invaluable advice at a critical stage of the claim negotiations or may be able to suggest ways to minimize the injured third party's loss. One major reinsurance company maintains extensive research laboratories, and its staff of engineers, physicists and other scientists are available to advise in both underwriting and loss handling for engineering and civil engineering risks.

The broking system compared with direct reinsurance

The continuing coexistence of brokers and of professional reinsurance companies that mainly deal direct with their clients can be interpreted as evidence that both systems possess advantages for ceding companies and reinsurers. If one excludes from the discussion the unique circumstances of the Lloyd's market where the underwriting syndicates could not operate in their present form without the support of brokers, it is clear that each system has its merits, and in large measure they complement each other.

Brokers provide a degree of flexibility in reinsurance markets which otherwise it would be difficult to achieve. Their extensive, often worldwide, market contacts can be particularly beneficial when a substantial amount of facultative reinsurance is required quickly, or cover is wanted either for abnormal risks, such as new or substandard risks, or for very large risks necessitating the mobilizing of market capacity on an international scale. The benefits of their knowledge and expertise also extend to the handling of the more mundane risks. In the United States, for example, the size and diversity of the brokerage market is such that a broker can turn to many reinsurers to obtain a good lead for almost any class of business, and thus brokers stimulate the quality of service, innovation and competition throughout the whole reinsurance market. The same remarks can also be applied in large measure on a worldwide scale.

A direct insurance company seeking the best reinsurance protection for its needs can obtain from a broker expert guidance on appropriate forms of reinsurance. It can also be sure that its business will be geographically well distributed and that especially for non-proportional reinsurances where premiums do not follow the original premium rates, the reinsurers selected will provide cover on fair terms. In turn a broker can provide a reinsurance company with both informed access to new markets without the necessity of engaging in expensive sales promotion, and with assistance in obtaining the market capacity required for placing its own retrocessions.

On the other hand there are advantages in the direct dealing between ceding office and reinsurer, as is typically practised by the large professional reinsurance companies. One reinsurer has listed those advantages as follows:[27]

1) The simplicity and clarity of a close direct relationship between two parties whereby there is no loss of some of the subtleties of information otherwise passed through a third party.
(2) More prompt fund transmittals between the parties (the 'float' many brokers maintain by holding funds in the transaction due to one or the other of the parties is eliminated thus benefiting the parties).
(3) The absence of a fragmenting of treaty participations (which otherwise makes underwriting study of a proposition uneconomical to the reinsurer).
(4) A type of underwriting, claims and actuarial service which a knowledgeable and technically staffed reinsurer can provide to some degree almost automatically as a part of direct contact and supervision of the reinsured's business.
(5) The absence of some accounting complexities resulting from fragmentation of shares of treaties and from frequent additions and subtractions from the participants in a given reinsurance programme.
(6) Simplicity of handling treaty bouquets for clients, in having available a reinsurer able to do across-the-board acceptances.

Which of the two systems may be judged the better must depend upon individual circumstances. Brokers and reinsurance companies vary considerably in the services they can offer, but as a broad generalization, the strength of brokers lies in dealing with reinsurances that either:
(1) require the mobilization of a large part of worldwide reinsurance capacity; as with catastrophe covers, especially for natural perils, or where a local direct insurer has been obliged to accept the whole of a very large insurance, such as for a local airline, which normally would have been partially spread through the use of coinsurance; or
(2) fall into the category of specialist covers, notably of a non-proportional type, where terms have to be negotiated with reinsurers. In property and marine business brokers tend to handle a far higher proportion of excess of loss covers than proportional reinsurances.

Therefore, given freedom to choose, the extent to which both direct and reinsurance companies either deal direct or employ brokers depends in part on individual needs and the type of reinsurance being handled, and partly on local practice.

It must be recognized too that circumstances change. Advances in computer systems may in the future lead to improvements in the amount of information available bearing on reinsurance needs and facilities which could be exchanged between companies. If such developments do occur then they could lead to radical changes in reinsurance markets to which both brokers and reinsurers will need to respond.

---

27 Miller, 'The intermediary in international reinsurance'.

3
Principles and practice of reinsurance

REINSURANCE

3
Principles and practice of reinsurance

Introduction

Three subjects will be covered in this chapter. First the needs of direct insurers for reinsurance, which were considered briefly in Chapter 1, will be examined in some detail, though the question of fixing retentions will be deferred to Chapter 9. Secondly, the different forms of reinsurance that have been developed to cater for the diverse risk characteristics of different classes of insurance business, and the methods of placing those reinsurances, will be outlined. Finally, some aspects of reinsurance practice and current problems will be considered.

The reinsurance needs of direct insurers

The need for protection

The primary reason why direct insurers purchase reinsurance is to protect themselves against the risk of incurring losses which may cause severe financial embarrassment and possibly insolvency. Here an insurer's motive for seeking reinsurance parallels that of its own policyholders, the main difference being that whereas an individual person usually owns or accepts responsibility for only one unit exposed to loss (i.e. his house, car or own life), an insurance company holds a portfolio of many exposure units for which it has accepted financial responsibility. Each year some of the units insured will suffer loss, so resulting in claims, but provided the insurer has calculated and been able to charge the correct level of premium rates, over the long run premiums, plus the investment earnings obtained on the funds it holds, should pay for all claims incurred, cover the costs of administering the business, and, it is hoped, yield a profit.

The insurance process in practice (ignoring investment earnings, fluctuations in asset values, and business-acquisition and administration expenses) can be illustrated as in Figure 3.1.[1] An insurer may commence a year's underwriting operations with reserves of R_0. Premiums received will add to those reserves and claims will deplete them. If the insurer has calculated premiums correctly then he may expect his business to expand and reserves to grow to R_1 at the end of the year, as shown by line R_0R_n. Actual outcomes, however, will be stochastic: neither the timing, frequency nor severity of claims can be predicted with absolute accuracy, though some types of insurance portfolio produce more stable results than others.

Therefore, provided the company can write the planned volume of business, deviations of outcomes from line R_0R_n will depend upon:
(1) The accuracy of premium calculations (and the ability to charge adequate premiums). An insurer's estimate of the loss expectancy may differ from the true loss expectancy either because of (*a*) sampling error, or (*b*) failure to identify and allow for changing risk conditions.

Figure 3.1

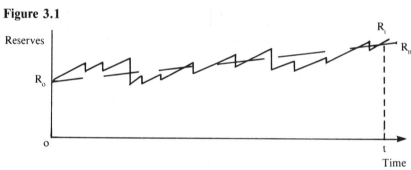

Figure 3.2

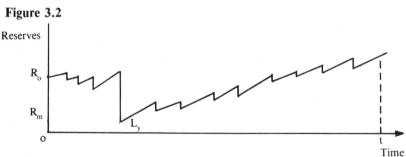

1 R.E. Beard, T. Pentikäinen and E. Pesonen, *Risk theory: The stochastic basis of insurance*, 2nd ed. (London: Chapman & Hall, 1977), p.3.

(2) The fluctuation of actual outcomes around the mean. The random occurrence of large individual losses or of accumulations of losses arising from one or more events may cause the sort of situation illustrated in Figure 3.2.

(3) The occurrence of fluctuations in the basic probabilities. For example, losses on an accident and sickness insurance account may be far higher in a year with prolonged periods of severe weather, or two or three widespread epidemics, than during a normal year.

Consequently the outcomes from year to year on an unchanging portfolio of insurance business may take the form shown in Figure 3.3. If it is assumed that after allowing for commissions, administrative costs and expected investment earnings on technical reserves, our insurer's overall operating result would just break even with a 65% claims to premium ratio, the range and probability of the overall outcomes may be represented as in Figure 3.4.

Figure 3.3 Annual incurred claims costs

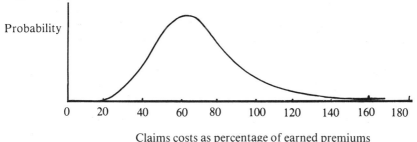

Claims costs as percentage of earned premiums

Figure 3.4 Annual operating results

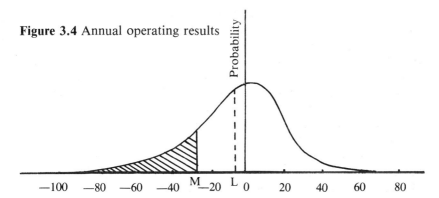

Operating results as percentage of earned premiums

Operating results = (earned premiums + investment earnings on technical reserves) — (incurred claims + commissions + expenses)

61

No insurer is likely to complain if outcomes are better than expected, but outcomes worse than the expected may at best cause minor inconvenience or additional cost (such as the forced realization of assets), and at worst may bankrupt the company. The notion of tolerable versus intolerable losses has been summarized in the concept of downside risk.[2] For example, perhaps an operating loss of 25% of earned premiums would take the insurer's reserves below the statutory minimum, so that the shaded area to the left of M would give its probability of ruin. On the other hand, the management may decide that the largest annual operating loss it could tolerate without serious disturbance would be, say, 5%, so that the probability of losses greater than L could be thought of as its downside risk. Depending upon the size of a company's reserves, the statutory solvency regulations, the rate of growth of premium income, and anticipated future capital requirements, the worst tolerable outcome may be pitched a few points either side of the breakeven point O. An insurer with relatively large free reserves and a fairly slowly growing premium income may be prepared to accept the risk of incurring a net operating loss in any one year of up to, say, 10 or 15% of earned premiums, whereas a rapidly growing company with fairly small reserves may find itself in difficulty if it failed to earn a profit.

Figure 3.2 illustrates the same sort of points. The lower the company's initial reserves R_0, the less capable it would be of surviving a loss of the size L_y. Moreover, the nature of the solvency regulations enforced by its supervisory authority would be of some importance. If the company was required to maintain minimum reserves of R_m, then if the supervisory authority continuously monitored solvency, the loss L_y would leave the company technically insolvent, but if the company was required to pass a solvency test only at the end of each year it would survive the shock.

Returning now to the reasons why an insurer's results may deviate from the expected, both sampling error and the fluctuations of outcomes around the mean are functions of sample size: an insurer with a relatively small portfolio of business is likely to be caught under both headings. If he bases his premiums solely on his own experience, there is a greater risk of premiums proving inadequate than if he had a larger statistical base for his calculations. Also, with a small sample of risks in his portfolio, claims costs will tend to display a larger relative variability than on a larger portfolio covering the same types of exposure units. Provided the insured units are homogeneous and statistically independent, both sampling error and variability will be inversely related to the square root

---

2 For a fuller discussion of downside risk, see G.M. Dickinson, 'Concepts of probability and risk', in *Handbook of Risk Management*, ch. 2.4.

of the number of units. Therefore, the larger the portfolio, the smaller the variability of outcomes from the expected.

The degree of variability in an insurer's claims costs, however, is also directly related to two other factors:

(1) The variations in the size of the individual units exposed to loss—the inclusion of a few large risks will expose a portfolio to the risk of large losses.

(2) The degree of interdependence between loss exposures, such as the geographical concentration of a property portfolio covering natural perils, or the exposure of a credit insurance account to the effects of a trade recession.

Therefore, if one function of reinsurance is seen to be that of reducing an insurer's probability of ruin, the amount of protection it will require to contain losses within tolerable limits (i.e. eliminating the possibility of losses such as L_y in Figure 3.2) will vary according to the type of business underwritten. Very stable results can be expected from, say, a geographically well distributed property portfolio covering only small household and trade risks against the perils of fire and explosion only. On the other hand, an account with a very similar premium income covering, say, properties concentrated within a relatively small area against earthquake or hurricane, or growing crops against hail damage, or composed of a relatively few very large risks (e.g. an aviation hull account insuring only airline risks), will be exposed to far greater fluctuations in its annual loss experience. Also although the risk of fluctuations in basic probabilities affects all classes of insurance, some may be more exposed than others.

Therefore, in examining a company's need for reinsurance protection the facts to be considered are:

(1) Whether its premiums are based on adequate data—it is not the function of reinsurance to protect an insurer against the consequences of inadequate pricing.

(2) The characteristics of the class of business insured in general, and the composition of the portfolio in particular, to determine its risk profile (i.e. its distribution by amounts at risk) and the likely probability distribution of claims results.

The probability of total claims in any one year exceeding some predetermined tolerable amount is, however, only a part of the problem. Figure 3.5 illustrates the probabilities and range of outcomes of two underwriting portfolios. Both have the same expected outcome, x, but the results of portfolio A are clustered much closer around the mean than portfolio B. Though there is the same probability under both portfolios of suffering results worse than a zero outcome (measured by the shaded areas under the curves lying to the left of 0), the degree of variability in

Figure 3.5 Annual operating results

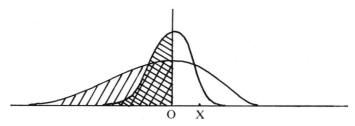

Operating result as percentage of earned premiums

possible outcomes under portfolio B warrants further consideration, and in particular the probability of incurring more severe losses than under the relatively more stable portfolio A. For example, the greater variability may be attributable to the presence of a few very large risks when greater stability of results could be achieved by limiting retentions, or by arranging excess of loss cover for any one loss any one risk. If on the other hand stop-loss reinsurance was being considered, a higher upper limit to the reinsurer's liability would be required for protection of portfolio B than for portfolio A.

Finally it must be emphasized that the process illustrated in Figure 3.1 ignores investment performance and management expenses. The failure of a company to control its business-acquisition and administrative costs, or to pursue a sound investment policy, also may impair its solvency, but these are matters outside the realm of reinsurance protection.

Underwriting flexibility and capacity

Possibly without any recourse to reinsurance, an underwriter could write an account that would produce fairly stable results and so have a low probability of ruin, but his potential market would be very limited. Great care would be needed to eliminate any possibility of interdependence between the exposure units insured, which would preclude the transaction of certain classes of insurance, such as insurance against windstorm and earthquake, and acceptances generally would have to be limited to risks with relatively low sums insured or limits of indemnity. Thus it would be difficult to accommodate the needs of all policyholders. The smaller the insurer, the greater the constraints on the types and sizes of risks he could safely accept. Every insurer would face the dilemma of whether to write business that could have a serious destabilizing effect on its claims costs, or refuse it and risk also losing other business to competitors.

Reinsurance offers a solution to such problems. It can provide protection against both large individual losses and accumulations of losses. Thus an insurer can accept individual risks and types of business that would be beyond his own underwriting capacity. Underwriting flexibility is also extended in another direction. Frequently insurers are asked by important clients to cover types of risks they normally prefer to avoid; for example, a life office may be asked to insure a substandard life, or an accident insurer may be offered the theft insurance for a jeweller's shop or other high-risk premises. Again a reinsurer may be able to assist by relieving the insurer of all or part of the risk, and in some cases advising on appropriate terms.

Professional reinsurance companies in particular play an important role in two areas of activity bearing on the flexibility of direct markets. In the absence of reinsurance, the paid-up capital required by a new company to transact safely most classes of insurance business would be prohibitively large. Also, lacking past experience of its own, a new company lacks the information required to rate risks correctly and to offer competitive policies. Professional reinsurance companies can help with both. In addition to supplying additional underwriting capacity, they can draw on their own market knowledge and experience to supply essential underwriting information. Likewise for certain classes of insurance, reinsurers provide special facilities for dealing with unusual risks, such as the special treaties and reinsurance pools arranged for the insurance of substandard lives.

The amount of reinsurance support an insurance company may require depends primarily upon (*a*) its own retention limits, and (*b*) the types and sizes of risk it may be called upon to accept. Generally reinsurers expect ceding companies to retain for their accounts a reasonable proportion of any insurances accepted so that a company is financially involved in the consequences of any shortcomings in its underwriting policies and standards. Thus even with reinsurance a small company may still be very limited in the size of risks it can accept compared with major insurance corporations. If it operates on a competitive market that may not be a severe constraint: although it may not be able to take the lead on, say, a large industrial fire insurance, it could still participate as a coinsurer and so build up its portfolio over time. State insurance corporations and similar institutions in developing countries may be in a very different position. They may be forced to accept the whole of a very large risk and then reinsure a high proportion, retaining perhaps less than 1% for their own accounts. Even then the aim would be to help the company over the years to increase its own underwriting capacity and thus reduce its dependence upon reinsurance.

Stabilizing claims costs

In discussing insurers' needs for protection, the emphasis was placed on the avoidance of insolvency, though reference was made to the possible desire of a management to contain fluctuations in claims costs within an even narrower band.

Even in relation to insolvency the distinction must be drawn between insolvency in the normal sense, that is the inability of a company to discharge its liabilities in full, and technical insolvency. Although an insurance company may have more than sufficient assets to meet all of its liabilities to policyholders and other creditors, it may fail to meet the margin of solvency laid down by an official supervisory authority, and so be judged technically insolvent. The consequences are the same; a company that is technically insolvent will be wound up. Therefore, it is critical that it should remain able to meet any minimum solvency requirements applying in any country in which it operates. The maximum size of loss it can withstand will thus be determined by the value of its free reserves in excess of the minimum solvency requirement: in practice probably no management would willingly accept the risk of a loss of such magnitude.

The degree of variability in claims experience that a management may consider acceptable depends upon (a) its corporate objectives, (b) its attitude to risk, and (c) the price of reinsurance.

Although exactly what objectives firms pursue is a matter of unresolved argument amongst economists and other observers of business behaviour, the matter is not one of purely theoretical interest. Economic theory demonstrates that the policies firms pursue are significantly influenced by corporate objectives, and in the field of risk management they play an important part in determining the optimal levels of insurance a firm will buy. Likewise corporate objectives and attitudes to risk must have a bearing on how much reinsurance an insurer will seek. For example, an insurance management that seeks to maximize profits in the short term will be prepared to pay less for protection, even though it may mean accepting the risk of greater variability in outcomes, than a management that ranks long-term survival high amongst its objectives.[3] The reason for such behaviour is simply explained: by reinsuring, a company can normally expect to pay each year more by way of reinsurance premiums than the losses which on average it can expect to recover from its reinsurer(s) because of the premium loading. For example, assume a company underwrites an individual risk where the probabilities of losses of increasing size are as shown in Table 3.1.

3 For a rigorous analysis, using utility theory, see K. Borch, *The Mathematical Theory of Insurance* (Lexington, Mass: Lexington Books, 1974).

Table 3.1

Probability (p)	Size of loss (c) £	Average loss ($\bar{c}$) £	$p \times \bar{c}$	
0.8	0	0	0	
0.075	0 – 10	5	0.3750	
0.05	11 – 50	30.5	1.5250	
0.025	51 – 100	75.5	1.8875	
0.019	101 – 250	175.5	3.3345	34.8865
0.014	251 – 500	375.5	5.2570	
0.010	501 – 1000	750.5	7.5050	
0.005	1001 – 5000	3000.5	15.0025	
0.0015	5001 – 10000	7500.5	11.2508	20.0010
0.0005	10001 – 25000	17500.5	8.7502	
	Total loss expectancy =		£54.8875	

The overall loss expectancy is £54.89. If the company reinsured all losses in excess of £5000, it would reduce its loss expectancy to £44.89. The actuarially fair premium for the reinsured part of the risk would be £10.00 but the reinsurer would want to make some allowance for a profit and to cover his expenses, so that the gross reinsurance premium would be greater than the expected value of the losses transferred to the reinsurer. Thus the premium would absorb part of the loading built into the premium charged by the direct insurer, thereby reducing his expected profit.

There are four important qualifications to that general conclusion. First, the example ignores interest which could be earned on premium and claims reserves, and any delay in paying the reinsurance premium would enable the ceding office to earn interest which would offset part of the premium cost. Secondly, because not all expenses are likely to vary directly with the size of the risk underwritten, if premium loadings are set proportionate to sums insured or the risk premium there could be some profit advantage to a direct insurer from underwriting larger risks, even at the cost of needing to purchase more reinsurance. Thirdly, a management may not have complete freedom in choosing the amount of reinsurance it purchases: supervisory regulations may directly or indirectly place a limit on the proportion of its business which a company can cede to reinsurers.[4] And finally because the amount of overriding commission which a ceding company can sometimes obtain from reinsurers on profitable business is sufficiently high to enable it to

---

4 See Michelbacher and Roos, *Multiple-line Insurers*, p.81. The 50% limit placed on credit for reinsurance recoveries, etc., by the EEC solvency margin indirectly constrains European companies in the amount of insurance they can afford to cede overall.

acquire a risk-free profit, it may choose to cede a high proportion of its business and write as much insurance as possible within the limits set by its capital reserves.

Modern behavioural theories have abandoned the idea that firms seek to maximize any one particular objective. Instead the theories emphasize the organizational aspects of firms and the limited amount of information available to decision-makers.[5] Consequently firms are seen as pursuing a number of goals but setting certain constraints, such as target profits or rates of return, which they seek to 'satisfice' rather than maximize. Despite the advances that have been made in risk theory over recent years and the rapid analysis of data made possible by the use of computers, the typical underwriter still lacks the precise information required to make the sort of decisions about reinsurance that will enable him to maximize any given objective. Decisions have to be taken under conditions of considerable uncertainty due to the vagaries of competition in direct and reinsurance markets, uncertainties about present and future investment conditions, and so forth. Therefore, underwriters tend to follow certain rules based on experience which, it is hoped, will keep outcomes within an acceptable band.

Financing

Reference was made in Chapter 1 to the growing use made of reinsurance for financing business expansion.

Supervisory regulations that require unearned premium reserves for 'non-life' insurances to be calculated as a proportion of retained premiums without any deduction for prepaid expenses place an additional financing strain on insurers. For example, take the case of two companies both having an annual gross premium income of £1 million from annual policies with commencement dates evenly distributed throughout the year, so that at the end of the year the unexpired periods of insurance on average would account for 50% of the written premiums. Both companies have paid out commissions and other business-acquisition costs equivalent to 20% of the premiums received, i.e. £200,000, but whereas company X is allowed to take credit for its paid expenses, company Y is required to base its unearned premium reserves on gross premiums. Thus their reserves at the end of the year would need to be:

5 H.A. Simon, 'A behavioural model of rational choice', *Quarterly Journal of Economics*, February 1955; R.M. Cyert and J.G. March, *A Behavioural Theory of the Firm* (Englewood Cliffs, NJ: Prentice-Hall, 1963) and H.A. Simon, 'Theories of decision making in economics and behavioural science', *American Economic Review*, June 1959.

	Company X	*Company Y*
Reserve 50% of:	£1,000,000 – £200,000	£1,000,000
	= £400,000	= £500,000

The only way in which company Y from its own resources could cover the additional liability of £100,000 would be by increasing its capital base accordingly. If, however, company Y reinsured part of its portfolio, ceding say, 60% of the written premiums, provided the regulations allowed unearned premium reserves to be calculated on premiums net of reinsurances ceded, it would need to reserve only £200,000 (i.e 50% of £400,000) as against a reserve of £160,000 which company X would need to carry if it too effected the same amount of reinsurance. Thus by reinsuring, company Y transfers part of the gross reserve liability to its reinsurers.

The other aspect of using reinsurance for financing purposes is the application of solvency margins to net (of reinsurances ceded) premiums. Again a simple example will illustrate the point. If supervisory regulations require a non-life insurer to maintain an excess of assets over liabilities equal to 10% of net premiums, then a company with capital and free reserves of £500,000 theoretically could support a net premium income of £5,000,000 but that could consist of either a gross premium income of £5,000,000 wholly retained by the company for its own account, or a premium income of, say, £20 million, 75% of which it reinsures to reduce its net premium income to £5 million. If a company with free assets of £600,000 was writing a gross account of £20 million and reinsuring 75%, its solvency margin would be within the statutory limit (i.e. 12% against the minimum 10%). Should the value of its free assets fall to £400,000 for some reason, such as bad loss experience or a fall in security prices, the company could remain technically solvent and thus continue in business by ceding an additional 5% of its premium income to its reinsurers.

Forms and methods of placing reinsurances

The detailed analysis and comparison of the various types of reinsurance available, the methods of placing employed, and their usage in relation to the different classes of insurance business, are the subject of later chapters. Therefore, only a brief description will be given here of the main features.

Forms of reinsurance

The main characteristics of the various forms of reinsurance used in non-life reinsurance are set out briefly in Figure 3.6. Some life reinsurance is written on an excess of loss basis, but mostly a special type of proportional reinsurance is used (see Chapter 13).

All reinsurances can be classified into two types—proportional and non-proportional. Under a proportional reinsurance the reinsurer accepts a fixed share of the liabilities assumed by the primary insurer under the original contract of insurance, whereas under a non-proportional reinsurance he only becomes liable to pay if the losses incurred by the ceding company exceed some predetermined figure. Proportional reinsurances were the first to appear, having developed from the system of coinsurance where a number of insurers each take a share of a direct insurance.

Figure 3.6 Forms and types of reinsurance

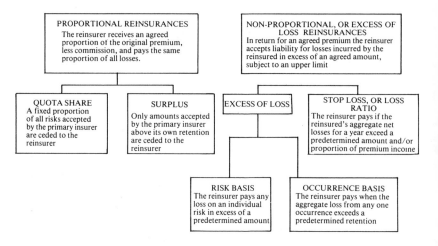

Under both forms the reinsurer can expect to incur a higher claims ratio (that is, claims : premiums) on each class of insurance written than a primary insurer. Taken alone this does not mean that reinsurers suffer poorer loss experiences than direct insurers, because allowance must be made for the relatively lower administrative costs of reinsurance business. Moreover in some cases (notably excess of loss covers), the average delay in claims settlements is longer under the reinsurance contract than under the underlying direct-insurance portfolio, so that the reinsurer will enjoy relatively higher investment earnings, though especially in a period of inflation and floating currencies the reinsurer may be exposed to offsetting claims development costs.[6] It is invalid, therefore, to make simple direct comparisons of claims ratios. What matters is the overall operating result, so the following remarks must be interpreted accordingly.

Proportional reinsurances: as the reinsurer accepts liability for a proportionate share of each risk ceded, his loss experience on individual risks will exactly follow that of the primary insurer. It is appropriate, therefore, that he should receive a corresponding proportionate share of the original premium, less an overriding commission to compensate the primary insurer for expenses incurred for their mutual benefit, such as survey and claims investigation costs.

The respective loss experiences of a ceding company and its reinsurers do differ, however, between quota-share and surplus treaty arrangements. Under a quota share the retained and reinsured portfolios will incur the same loss ratios in relation to original premiums. In the case of surplus reinsurances where the ceding company reinsures only those amounts which it does not wish to retain for its own account, the reinsurer's loss experience on the total portfolio of business ceded may differ significantly from the primary insurer's net retained account. Such differences may be due to various causes, such as:

(1) The reinsurer may receive a badly balanced account, only a few very large risks being ceded, so leaving the reinsurance portfolio heavily exposed to random fluctuations in loss experience from year to year.

(2) Although a reasonable spread of risks may be ceded, the ceded portion of the gross direct account may prove to be subject to either larger random fluctuations in losses or to a poorer experience than the retained part.

(3) The primary insurer may cede a larger proportion of the poorer (i.e. inadequately rated) risks it has written.

The random fluctuations associated with (1) or (2) do not necessarily call for remedial action by the reinsurer; like a direct insurer, what matters is not the fluctuations in the loss experience of business received from any one individual client but the stability of the total reinsurance portfolio. If, however, it is apparent that the expected long-run results of the business received from any ceding company are adverse, then the reinsurer has two possible remedies (apart from cancelling it)—he can either press his reinsured to increase premium rates, or he can reduce the reinsurance commission.

6 See pages 97 et seq.

Non-proportional reinsurances have become far more popular in recent years. Whereas proportional reinsurances, and particularly surplus reinsurances, help to stabilize the ceding company's operating results by reducing its exposures on individual risks, excess of loss reinsurances can perform that task more efficiently (see Chapter 5) and can also be used to deal with the problem of accumulations and catastrophe risks. A further advantage of non-proportional reinsurances is the saving in administrative time and so expense. The continuing rise in administration costs has reinforced the swing from proportional to non-proportional reinsurances, even for classes of insurance, such as fire, which traditionally were reinsured on a proportional basis.

Frequently excess of loss reinsurances are placed in layers. Some reinsurers, notably Lloyd's underwriters, are not interested in writing reinsurances with relatively low limits which may produce a large volume of claims, so it is cheaper to seek their participation only for protection against the larger losses. Furthermore some saving in administration costs may be achieved by reducing the number of reinsurers involved with the smaller losses. So, for example, a primary insurer may arrange three separate excess of loss treaties for its motor insurance account as follows:

	Lower limit— reinsurer assumes liability	Upper limit to reinsurer's liability
Retain for own account all losses from any one accident up to £10,000.		
(1) First excess of loss layer	£ 10,001	£ 25,000
(2) Second excess of loss layer	£ 25,001	£100,000
(3) Third excess of loss layer	£100,001	£500,000

Whereas proportional and normal excess of loss reinsurances are designed to reduce the ceding company's net liability on individual risks (or with excess of loss reinsurances arranged on an occurrence basis, its net liability for all losses flowing from a single occurrence), *stop loss reinsurances* protect a company against its aggregate annual net loss experience on a particular underwriting account exceeding some tolerable figure. The reinsurer's liability is for losses exceeding in the aggregate either an agreed monetary amount or a fixed percentage of net premium income, subject to an upper limit expressed as a higher monetary sum or percentage of premium income or the lesser of the two. Also frequently the ceding company is required to retain for its own account a proportion (usually 10%) of the risk. So, for example, a stop-loss reinsurance may cover 90% of net (i.e. after other reinsurance recoveries) losses incurred during the year in excess of 70% of net retained premium income up to a further 40%: thus the ceding company would obtain 90% protection against suffering a loss ratio of between 70% and 110% in any one year.

The major difficulty with non-proportional reinsurance is to fix premiums which are fair to both parties. The reinsurer's loss experience is not so directly tied to the ceding company's gross account as in proportional reinsurances. Therefore some method is required which relates the reinsurance premium to the expected loss experience under the reinsurance contract. In the case of excess of loss upper layers and stop-loss reinsurances such a method is extremely difficult to achieve. Inflation also creates problems in that unless some method is devised to adjust excess-of-loss limits the reinsurer's loss experience will be subject to a higher rate of claims inflation than the underlying direct-insurance account.

In arranging its reinsurance programme a typical non-life direct-insurance company will make use of various types of reinsurance.

Methods of placing reinsurances

A brief explanation of the methods employed for placing the various types of reinsurances is given in Figure 3.7.

The facultative method was the first to be used, reinsurance originally being confined to the placing of individual risks between direct insurance companies. The word facultative signifies that the arrangement is optional in the sense that neither is the ceding office bound to offer the business nor is the reinsurer bound to accept it. Thus, like a prospective coinsurer in direct insurance, an underwriter offered a risk facultatively has the opportunity to exercise his underwriting skill and judgment. He can examine the facts of the case, the terms and conditions applying, decide whether or not to accept, and agree on the proportion of the risk he will underwrite. He can then, in theory, monitor the amount of his potential liability on any individual unit or interdependent groups of exposure units, such as properties located in an area exposed to some natural peril, whether such liabilities arise from business accepted by way of facultative reinsurance or by direct insurances. Finally, it also enables an underwriter to try to maintain a balance between the reinsurances he cedes to another company and those he receives in return.

Although the facultative method of placing reinsurances both between direct companies and with professonal reinsurers is still employed, its use has declined in most countries because of its high administration costs, and the constraint it places on a direct insurer who wishes to accept

Figure 3.7 Methods of placing reinsurances

Method	Facultative	Open cover (or facultative obligatory)	Treaty	Pool
Description	Each risk offered individually to reinsurers, who are free to accept what share they desire, or to reject	A reinsurer agrees to accept obligatorily a share of any business conforming to predetermined conditions regarding class of insurance, type of risk, country, etc. offered by either: (1) a ceding company; or (2) a broker (when it is known as a broker's open cover and can include insurances written by different ceding companies). There is no obligation on the ceding company or broker to offer any business	Subject to terms and conditions agreed between the parties and set out in the treaty, there is an obligation on the reinsured to cede and the reinsurer to accept risks of a class falling within the limitations of the treaty	Takes various forms but often a quota share or surplus reinsurance arrangement between participating members. According to the rules agreed, insurances accepted by members are ceded to the pool which in turn arranges retrocessions to members. The pool may retain some part of each risk for its own account
Types of reinsurances for which employed	Mainly proportional reinsurances	Mainly surplus		Proportional reinsurances. The pool may protect itself by purchasing non-proportional reinsurance from outside reinsurers

immediately a risk in excess of his own retention. Generally it is now limited to cases where either it is considered inappropriate by the insurer or reinsurer for cover to be provided on an automatic treaty basis or where the risk is too large for the capacity of the automatic treaties. Normally facultative reinsurances are placed on a proportional basis but there is a growing tendency for cover to be arranged on a non-proportional basis.

Sometimes in fire insurance circles the old term 'guarantee' is still used to describe a facultative reinsurance. The ceding office is then known as the 'reinsuring company' and the reinsurance as a 'guarantee obtained', while the reinsurer is called the 'accepting company' and the reinsurance is the 'guarantee granted'.

Treaties. All types of reinsurance are placed through the use of treaties so that individual treaties vary in detail, but the general principles are the same. A treaty is an agreement invariably (though not necessarily) in writing[7] between a ceding company and one or more reinsurers, whereby the ceding company agrees to cede and the reinsurer agrees to accept the reinsurances of all of the risks written by the ceding company which fall within the terms of the treaty, subject to the limits specified therein. Thus, once a treaty has been concluded, a direct insurer (or a reinsurer under a retrocession treaty) can obtain reinsurance automatically for risks accepted which fall within the terms of the treaty. Indeed the ceding insurer is bound in principle to give priority to the treaty reinsurers(s) and only if the cover required exceeds the treaty limits can any surplus reinsurance be placed elsewhere while the treaty remains in force, though usually special provision is made to the contrary. Conversely, treaty reinsurers are bound to accept reinsurances offered to them within the terms of the treaty.

The automatic character of treaties makes them cheap to operate, and even for surplus reinsurance treaties, which involve the most administration, streamlining of procedures has helped to reduce costs. Originally through the provision of detailed bordereaux, treaty reinsurers were kept fully informed by ceding companies of all proportional reinsurances ceded. So in the case of, say, a fire surplus treaty, each reinsurer would receive information about the individual risks ceded, sums insured, the ceding company's own retention, premium rates and so forth. In the interests of economy such practices have long ago disappeared for the bulk of the reinsurance business handled by treaties, and reinsurers have to operate blind in relation to their commitments on individual or possibly associated risks[8]

7 The written contract is not always signed by both parties.
8 Lance La Bianca in writing of the Darwin cyclone disaster in 1974 said that 'some reinsurers were alarmed to note that their commitments were considerably greater than first suspected', 'Reinsurance, private insurance and the state', *Post Magazine and Insurance Monitor*, 27 May 1976.

75

Thus treaties have overcome, for ceding companies, the disadvantages associated with the facultative method and so have replaced it as the main method of handling reinsurance business.

The treaty method has its advantages for the reinsurer too, notably the lower administrative costs and the certainty of receiving a substantial volume of business from the ceding company, whether it be in the form of a guaranteed flow of cessions under a proportional treaty or the whole of the account underlying a working excess of loss reinsurance. The disadvantage is that the reinsurer forfeits his right to select the risks he reinsures: under a proportional reinsurance he cannot accept some of the risks the ceding company wants to reinsure and reject others, but must take good and bad alike. Treaty business must be judged on its overall results, and therefore before entering into the contract the prospective reinsurer will want to know all about the ceding company's portfolio and management because it is the nature of the business accepted and the skill of the management in underwriting and handling claims which will determine whether in the long run the treaty will produce a reasonable profit or consistently run at a loss.

Facultative obligatory arrangements and open covers lie midway between the facultative and treaty methods. Like a treaty, a reinsurer enters into an agreement with another insurer, or (in the case of brokers' open covers) with a broker, to accept all reinsurances offered to him that conform with the conditions set out in the agreement. The important difference is that there is no obligation on the ceding company or broker to offer any risk for reinsurance during the currency of the agreement.

The demand for such covers has arisen from the continuing growth in the size of individual risks that affects all types of property insurance. The concentration of manufacturing plants into larger units, and the development of more capital-intensive methods of production, means that increasingly direct insurers have difficulty in fully absorbing the whole risk within the constraints imposed by their reinsurance treaty arrangements. Consequently facultative obligatory and open cover arrangements have grown in popularity throughout the 1960s and 1970s because they offer companies and brokers a means of immediately being able to reinsure any remaining surplus instead of having to delay 100% acceptance of a risk until sufficient facultative reinsurance cover can be found.

Both types of arrangement are confined to the placing of surplus reinsurances, and the prospective reinsurer places a limit on his potential acceptances expressed either in terms of the ceding company's retention or as a monetary limit per risk. Also the type of business that will be accepted is defined in the agreement. Arrangements vary considerably—

examples are property insurances written for a particular industrial or commercial group, perhaps a multinational company; the insurances of any company falling within a certain type of industry; or any reinsurance required for a particular class of insurance in a certain territory.

Apart from such restrictions the prospective reinsurer can exercise no control over the business ceded, and the resulting portfolio of reinsurances inevitably tends to be even less balanced than that received under a normal surplus treaty. Indeed if the ceding company has several facultative obligatory agreements in force with different reinsurers, there is frequently no clear understanding of the order in which they should be used, thus leading to the possibility of adverse selection against certain reinsurers. Consequently not all underwriters regard such business favourably; in particular, underwriters of direct-writing companies sometimes argue that by agreeing to accept facultative obligatory business they are deprived of the opportunity to accept or reject business that otherwise would be offered to them direct on a coinsurance basis. In so far as brokers use open covers to limit the number of coinsurers interested on any risk no doubt there is some substance in that argument, and thus the skill of the underwriter is relegated to assessing the quality of the total portfolio of reinsurances ceded rather than reviewing each risk on the strength of its individual merits.

A further potential source of conflict lies in the uncertainty that exists regarding the position of a facultative obligatory reinsurer if a loss occurs before a ceding company has completed all of its reinsurance arrangements. Could it be assumed that the facultative obligatory reinsurer would automatically be liable up to his limit (like a treaty reinsurer) even though at the time of the loss no part of the risk had been specifically ceded to him?

Reinsurance pools may be organized in a variety of ways. As noted in Chapter 2, each participating company may subscribe part of the capital required to establish a separate reinsurance corporation, which will reinsure some agreed part of the risks underwritten by the companies, perhaps in turn retroceding part of the risks accepted back to member companies. Alternatively the management of the pool may be undertaken by one of the member companies or by a jointly established organization, its task being to share between all of the members in agreed proportions reinsurances ceded to the pool by individual member companies.

A pool may be formed to handle some specific, possibly hazardous, class of insurance, such as life insurance for substandard lives or aviation insurance, or it may be more broadly based. Similarly it may be restricted to risks situated in one country or include members drawn from several countries like the regional reinsurance pools.

Normally, pooling arrangements are based on some form of proportional reinsurance, each member either ceding a fixed proportion of all of the 'pool-type' business it writes, or the whole or a predetermined part of any surplus above its own retention limits. Sometimes a pool may handle excess of loss covers, but more frequently any involvement in non-proportional reinsurances arises from the pool purchasing catastrophe excess of loss reinsurance from the international reinsurance market to provide overall protection for its members.

Although the objectives and organization of reinsurance pools do differ there are common to all a number of problems which the following example illustrates. Assume six companies decide to form a pool to reinsure business of a particular class, their respective average results on a gross basis over the last five years being as in Table 3.2.

The business of the six companies displays marked differences in terms of their expense and claims ratios and their underwriting results. Therefore, if the total business was pooled the companies would be faced with very difficult problems in trying to decide upon an acceptable method (or methods) of allocating shares and profits in the pool. For example, would companies B and F, who produce well-above-average underwriting profits, be content with a share of the total profit of ₡103,000 equal to their share of the total premium income? An additional complication would arise with the allocation of the reinsurance costs of catastrophe protection for the pool, particularly

Table 3.2 ₡ = Monetary units (thousands).

Company	Gross direct premiums	Expenses and commission		Claims		Underwriting profit or loss	
	₡	₡	%	₡	%	₡	%
A	500	180	36.0	325	65.0	− 5	− 1.0
B	800	280	35.0	480	60.0	40	5.0
C	650	240	36.9	400	61.5	10	1.5
D	1,000	340	34.0	660	66.0	0	0
E	800	260	32.5	560	70.0	− 20	− 2.5
F	1,250	380	30.4	792	63.4	78	6.2
Total	5,000	1,680	33.6	3,217	64.3	103	2.1

Percentages are a ratio to premiums.

It is assumed that the cash-flow characteristics of the companies' businesses are identical, so that differences in investment earnings will be attributed only to variations in the investment policies pursued. Therefore investment earnings can be ignored for the purpose of this example.

following a sharp rise in the reinsurance premium due to the occurrence of a major loss involving only one or two members of the pool.

Such problems are present whether a pool accepts reinsurances from members on a quota share or a surplus basis, though the smaller the proportion of direct business ceded by each company the less likelihood there is of serious dispute in that each member's results will be less affected by the pool's experience. The size of individual retentions also has a bearing on another contentious issue—underwriting discipline. A company which retains very little business for its own account may be tempted either to accept risks or to agree terms which it would have refused in the absence of the pool. Such a danger can only be avoided by close cooperation between the participating companies, or by the business of the pool being managed by a separate centralized organization.[9]

Whatever form of organization is adopted, companies with highly profitable portfolios of business may have to accept the fact that part of the cost of participating in a reinsurance pool is a certain loss of profit. If such a company placed its reinsurances conventionally it could probably obtain above-average overriding reinsurance commissions and/or profitable reciprocal inwards reinsurances.

Another danger associated with national pools, or even in some cases regional pools, is the accumulation risk, particularly where there is a danger of catastrophes due to natural perils or the concentration of a country's productive assets on a relatively few very large industrial or extractive plants. Under such circumstances the losses resulting from a single event may be beyond the capacity of the whole insurance market of any one country or even of several countries,[10] especially if the underlying security for the insurers' invested funds are the assets exposed to loss. Moreover if the loss does occur the national economy would not receive the benefit of an inflow of funds from foreign reinsurers. It is important, therefore, that external reinsurance protection should be obtained to protect pools from catastrophe losses, even though it would involve extra expense which, as the UNCTAD study report adds, 'may put a heavy burden on some small participating companies'.[11]

---

9 *Reinsurance Problems in Developing Countries*, p.33.
10 Maurice Greenberg in referring to the Managua and Guatemalan earthquake disasters commented, 'To talk about self-sufficiency ... under these circumstances is nonsense ... All of Central America could not have handled these losses.' 'International problems and possible solutions', a paper read to the International Insurance Seminar, San Francisco, 1976.
11 *Reinsurance Problems in Developing Countries*, p.33.

Reinsurance practices and problems

Disputes regarding reinsurance contracts

A feature of reinsurance contracts is that provision is invariably made for any disputes which may arise between the parties to be settled by arbitration rather than by recourse to the courts. One important reason in the past for the inclusion of arbitration clauses in reinsurance treaties written in Britain was the unenforceability of marine reinsurance treaties before the repeal in 1959 of the relevant clauses of the Stamp Act 1891 and sections 23(2) – (5) and 25(2) of the Marine Insurance Act 1906. As Mr H.E. Gumbel explains, roundabout ways were available to enforce the provisions of a marine reinsurance treaty with a non-UK party through the use of arbitration in a country where the Queen's writ did not run, but generally arbitration offered the only means of dealing with disputes[12].

Other arguments no doubt were advanced favouring arbitration rather than litigation. Referring to the inclusion of arbitration clauses in insurance policies generally, the Master of the Rolls, Lord Jessel, said they were to prevent the delay and expense of litigation,[13] and in the case of *Russell* v *Russell* (1880)[14] he added that quarrels on policies can thus be kept from the public eye, and discussion in public avoided, which might be painful and injurious even to a successful litigant. Furthermore persons with an expert knowledge of the subject can be appointed to act as arbitrators, and foreign arbitration awards can be enforced more easily in many countries than the judgments of foreign courts.

Apart from the last point, it is arguable that nowadays arbitration in England is no more advantageous than litigation in the Commercial Court,[15] and the judgments of the court possess the merit of establishing rules for the settlement of similar issues in future disputes. Nevertheless arbitration clauses remain a universal feature of reinsurance contracts, whether issued in Britain or elsewhere.

Reciprocity

It was noted in Chapter 2 that ceding insurers frequently demand an exchange of reinsurance business in return for their own cessions, particularly when their own treaties are profitable. There are various reasons for such a practice, notably the desire of companies:

---

12 H. Edward Gumbel, 'Arbitration under reinsurance contracts' in *Festschrift für Reimer Schmidt*, F. Reichert-Facilades *et al.* (Verlag Versicherungswirtschaft eV, 1976), pp.886 – 7.
13 *Piercy* v *Young* (1879), 14 Ch.D. 200, 208.
14 14 Ch.D. 471, 477.
15 Gumbel, 'Arbitration under reinsurance contracts', p.884.

(1) To increase their net premium income by adding to the premiums retained from their direct business the premiums for reinsurances accepted.

(2) To obtain a more diversified portfolio of business which would help to stabilize underwriting results.

(3) To gain access to insurance business from other countries where the establishment of a direct-insurance operation may either be prohibited or too costly.

(4) To reduce the ratio of adminstrative expenses to net premiums.

(5) To increase total profits.

State-controlled insurance corporations may also see reciprocity as a means of reducing the foreign-exchange costs of buying reinsurance from abroad and improving the nation's balance-of-payments position.

Points (1), (4) and (5) may be illustrated by a simple example. Assume that a direct insurer:

(1) Writes a gross direct premium income of £1,000,000.

(2) Incurs a loss ratio of 62%, and acquisition and administration expenses of 35%.

(3) Earns underwriting profits of 3%.

(4) Reinsures 60% of all risks accepted on a quota share basis, receiving a reinsurance commission of 35%.

Its results would be as follows (a) without and (b) with exactly equivalent reciprocal reinsurance exchange.

	(a) without reciprocity £	(b) with reciprocity £
Direct premium income	1,000,000	1,000,000
− 60% ceded, less reinsurance commission	390,000	390,000
	610,000	610,000
− 62% losses on retained business	248,000	248,000
	362,000	362,000
− Acquisition and administration expenses	350,000	350,000
	12,000	12,000
+ Reinsurance premiums accepted, less commission	—	390,000
		402,000
− 62% losses	—	372,000
	12,000	30,000

Thus, in theory, through the reciprocal exchange of reinsurances the company could restore its profits to the level it could have achieved if it had been able to retain for its own account all of the direct business it had accepted and, provided there was a high degree of stochastic independence between the direct and inwards reinsurance portfolios, it would also achieve a reduction in risk. In reality things may be very different.

As noted earlier, reinsurance may be purchased to provide a company with additional underwriting capacity, and to assist in financing its business. The supervisory regulations applying in most countries tie the amount of business a company is permitted to write (as measured by premium income) to its capital and free reserves, so that a company operating near to its limit could not afford to seek reciprocity without expanding its capital base. Even for a company not so constrained there are other factors to be considered — the above example is open to criticism on a number of points.

Not all types of treaty nor all classes of insurance business lend themselves to the reciprocal exchange of reinsurance business. Basically only reinsurances yielding reasonably predictable results are suitable. Therefore reciprocity is usually confined to proportional treaties, and in particular fire quota share and first surplus treaties which are not subject to wide fluctuations in results from year to year. On the other hand insurers, instead of placing their reinsurance treaties individually, may offer all of their business for consideration as a whole, so that the merits of the more stable and profitable treaties perhaps can help to offset the less attractive features of other reinsurances. Furthermore, Professor Borch has demonstrated that the best form of reciprocal reinsurance exchange between two insurers will depend upon the (utility) value they respectively place on profits versus the risk of losses, so that under certain conditions a form of reciprocal stop-loss reinsurance may be preferred[16]. Borch admits, however, that his model *may* be too simple to have direct practical application, so that apart from noting what may be more of a theoretical rather than a practical comment on reciprocity, such ideas will not be pursued further here.

Reciprocity does not necessarily mean the exchange of treaties covering the same class of business. Also there is the question of which is the more important consideration — premium income or operating results: Wilko H. Börner explains this issue as follows:[17]

---

16 Borch, *Mathematical Theory of Insurance*, ch. 4.
17 W.H. Börner, 'An appraisal of the alternatives to the practice of reciprocity in reinsurance', a Bolesaw Monic Fund prize essay abridged in the *Quarterly Letter of the Nederlandse Reassurantie Groep*, March 1970, No. XVI/61.

In the former case, the theory is that one selects partners with portfolios of comparable quality, with whom one exchanges an equal volume of premium income. Although the technical results may vary in individual years, in the long run the profits for both sides should be more or less the same. The exchange will have fulfilled its purpose of increasing and balancing better the net retained account of both parties. The same effect is aimed at when reciprocity is exchanged on the basis of results: only in this case the partners take into account the differing qualities of their treaties and the one with the more profitable portfolio cedes less premium income than the one with the lower profit margin business gives in return.

A direct-writing company may particularly benefit from the reciprocal exchange of reinsurance business if thereby it can write a more diversified portfolio of risks, including different classes of business and with a geographical spread which it otherwise could not obtain. Thus reciprocity between two direct-writing companies can be mutually beneficial, especially when they operate in different territories so that there is no risk of either picking up under inwards reinsurance additional commitments on risks already covered by direct insurance: under such conditions both companies will reduce the probability of incurring losses on their total net portfolios. [18] The only parties then to suffer are the professional reinsurance companies that are denied the opportunity of competing for the reinsurance business of direct offices simply on the strength of price and quality of service.

Not surprisingly the system of reciprocity has been strongly criticised, not least by professional reinsurers. One writer has suggested that it adversely affects the performance of direct companies as sellers of reinsurance because in seeking reciprocal exchanges: [19]

> their objective is thus more aimed at finding the best possible quality of business for the exchange than with the technicalities of reinsurance and the provision of appropriate cover in the circumstances concerned.

More fundamentally one can point to the possible disadvantages for direct companies themselves which have been summed up as follows: [20]

(1) If the companies concerned in reciprocity business operate in the same field they do not obtain a better spread of business and in the event of a catastrophe loss may find that their position has not been improved at all.
(2) The business ceded by one of the companies may be more profitable than that

---

18 As UNCTAD point out the 'probability (per annum) that an overall adverse result emanating from the reciprocal exchanges accepted from various territories may coincide in time with adverse results in the company's own net business is evidently small.' *Reinsurance Problems in Developing Countries*, p.20.
19 Neave, 'Reinsurance today', p.61.
20 'Dangers inherent in reciprocity systems', *The Review*, vol. 69 (25 November 1938).

ceded by the other. If this turns out to be the case, the reciprocal relations are usually terminated after a short trial.

(3) Commission rates and experience differ in various parts of the world, and it is usually difficult for a company to convince itself that it should pay a larger commission for the business it receives than it secures in return from the other company.

(4) Exchange of reinsurance between direct-writing companies means disclosure of expirations and other trade secrets to competitors.

(5) There are various schools of thought so far as underwriting is concerned as regards the size of net lines, the desirability of different types of risks, etc. It is often difficult for the managers of one direct-writing company to convince themselves that the wholly different underwriting methods employed by another direct-writing company are sound.

(6) The underwriting departments of direct-writing companies are often inclined to spend as much time and expense in underwriting reinsurance offered by another company as if the risks were offered to them by their agents. This results in an increased expense ratio.

(7) The managers of direct-writing companies are usually not as skilled in drawing reinsurance contracts and appraising reinsurance arrangements as the managers of professional reinsurance companies.

Points (4) to (6) are far less valid today because most treaties tend to be operated blind so that there is little opportunity for the underwriting of individual risks, even if the underwriter was inclined to do so. Nevertheless, the problem remains that the management of small direct-writing companies, and of insurance corporations in developing countries, may lack the knowledge and expertise to assess such factors as the technical nature of the risks, the market conditions, the risk of accumulations and so forth associated with the overseas reinsurances they are offered, and to undertake an analysis of the results before negotiating renewals. There is too the cost of handling the incoming reinsurance business, and here a company needs to consider not only the administrative costs but also the opportunity cost of the management time which otherwise could have been devoted to the development of the company's direct insurance business.

The demands on management time may be considerable. If a company attempts to place all of its reinsurances with other direct insurers in exchange for a share in their treaties, it is likely to increase substantially the number of reinsurers with whom it deals because it will wish to spread its own business widely in order to acquire a well-diversified portfolio of inwards reinsurances in return. Every reciprocal exchange will need to be negotiated individually, and thereafter separate accounts must be kept for each one. Even if much of the work is undertaken by a reinsurance broker, reciprocal reinsurance exchanges inevitably cause some increase in a company's administrative burden. It may also encounter new types of administrative problems: for example, a company that writes only domestic business may for the first time run into all of the difficulties of exchange control if it obtains a reciprocal exchange of business with a company operating in another currency.

The question of profitability (point (2)) has already been discussed, and a company can find little satisfaction in exchanging its own reinsurances for business that proves unprofitable. Consequently whenever there is a general tendency for underwriting profits to decline the demand for reciprocity likewise falls. The substitute for reciprocity for direct companies that still have profitable reinsurance business to offer is an increase in overriding reinsurance commissions or profit commission, perhaps on a sliding scale. Such a change in market conditions offers professional reinsurance companies the opportunity to expand their share of the business. Writing in a period of unprecedented losses on fire insurance in many parts of the world, J.A.S. Neave summarized the situation as follows: [21]

> The recent unfavourable results of fire business in the more industrialized countries has inevitably brought this well established vogue of reciprocity into the limelight and under searching review, since fire is the branch most favoured for reciprocal exchanges. Certainly these exchanges will not be looked upon in quite the same light again, and a compromise seems probable between the post war attitude of reciprocity at any price and the previous cautious preference for retaining one's own business and exercising complete control over it. Already there is a demand for special terms from non-reciprocating reinsurers, and since this involves a guaranteed profit it is bound to find favour with companies who have been at the receiving end of unprofitable business in reciprocal exchanges.

The possibility of exchanging profitable for unprofitable business is one side of the coin. The other is what happens when a company itself goes through a bad period. Robert Reinarz stresses the danger of reciprocal arrangements being cancelled.[22] He makes the point that however much care is exercised in controlling the direct portfolio, there will always be someone who is unhappy. It is when a company experiences a serious deterioration in its underwriting results that the real problems arise, because then it can least afford to have shares of its treaties cancelled. Its bargaining powers will be at their lowest and valuable time will have to be devoted to finding replacements, probably on less advantageous terms, so that the company's reinsurance costs will rise.

The benefits of exchanging reinsurance business can only be judged in the long term, and only companies with adequate underwriting capacity

---

21 Neave, 'Reinsurance today', p.61.
22 Robert C. Reinarz, *Property and Liability Reinsurance Management* (Greenwich, Conn: Mission Publishing Co., 1969), p.141.

and reserve funds can afford to take such a view. In other cases the short-term costs may prove too high a price to pay, especially when the incoming reinsurances are ill-balanced and subject to fluctuations in annual results beyond the capacity of a company to absorb.

Therefore, professional reinsurers claim that though they expect to be compensated for the services they provide, they do offer in return a number of advantages compared with reciprocal reinsurance exchanges. Besides the technical and administrative services they provide for clients, both Börner and Reinarz claim that professional reinsurers are more willing to provide continuity of cover during a period when the ceding insurer's own experience is adverse. Furthermore the major professional reinsurers possess the capacity to absorb large amounts of business which direct insurers are reluctant to entertain. Therefore Börner concludes that:[23]

> Reciprocity will probably remain an important factor in the relationships between large direct groups well equipped also to handle reinsurance. Many companies, however, will find it to their advantage to eschew incoming reinsurance and to concentrate on maximizing their profits from their own direct underwriting. Professional reinsurers will be able to provide them with a package of services meeting all their reasonable needs.

Yet despite all of the reservations about the wisdom of reciprocity and the dislike of it by reinsurers, the practice persists, and even professional reinsurance companies cannot always escape from the demands for reprocity. All that a professional reinsurer can offer, however, is a share in the retrocession of reinsurances he has himself written.

Therefore, a reinsurer may arrange a quota share retrocession treaty covering his own inwards reinsurance treaties of a specified type. For example, ceding companies may be offered a share of such a retrocession treaty covering worldwide fire and special-perils treaties, excluding non-proportional treaties, hail reinsurances, and North American business on the same terms as the original reinsurances, less a small overriding commission. The advantages to a ceding company are threefold:
(1) It can thereby participate in a portfolio which probably will be more widely diversified than it could obtain from many direct insurers.
(2) It can rely on the expertise of the reinsurer in having negotiated and in managing the underlying reinsurances.
(3) Subject to the retrocession treaty's inner limits and its own share of the treaty, its maximum possible loss on any one risk is likely to be very small.

Provided retrocession treaties are used to increase a professional reinsurer's own underwriting capacity they can play a useful role, but if

23 Ibid., p.8.

they result in the unnecessary further spreading of business, they simply add another stage to the insurance production process and increase total administration costs.

Reinsurance commissions

Reinsurance commission is the commission paid by a reinsurer to a ceding company, and is expressed as a proportion of the premiums ceded. It should not be confused with the brokerage which is paid by a reinsurer when an intermediary introduces the business.

Reinsurance commission is not normally paid on excess-of-loss reinsurances so the following discussion relates only to proportional reinsurances.

Essentially the reinsurer should pay sufficient commission to cover the costs incurred by the ceding company in acquiring and administering the business ceded. Normally, however, the amount of commission allowed is adjusted to take account of the anticipated loss ratio on the business, so that the actual reinsurance commission paid to a ceding company may be more or less than its costs.

The practice of allowing high commission rates as a means of acquiring business that is expected to produce good results is inherently risky. It has two effects:[24]

(1) It increases the ceding company's expected underwriting profit at the expense of the reinsurer, and if results should prove worse than expected it may enable the ceding company still to earn a profit though the reinsurer suffers a loss.

(2) It has a gearing effect on the reinsurer's results, fluctuations in losses having a larger impact on the treaty results relative to the expected profit.

Although in order to compete for a highly profitable portfolio a reinsurer may be prepared to accept a lower rate of profit than that being earned by the ceding company, there are better ways of rewarding a reinsured than paying a high flat rate of reinsurance commission. The two alternative systems in use are the payment of either (*a*) a reinsurance commission determined according to a sliding scale related to the account's loss ratio, or (*b*) a separate profit commission.

It is often said that some direct companies use reinsurance as a means of increasing their profits. Such a statement deserves closer scrutiny because in fixing the reinsurance commission allowed on any business a reinsurer must always pay regard to his own administrative costs. So, for example, take the case of a direct insurance company which writes a gross account that produces the following underwriting results.

24 These points are examined in more detail and illustrated with an example in Appendix 3.1.

	£	£
Gross premiums		2,000,000
less commission and expenses	700,000	
claims	1,100,000	
		1,800,000
Underwriting profit		200,000 = 10% of premiums

The only way in which the company could use reinsurance to increase its *aggregate* underwriting profit would be to find a reinsurer sufficiently foolish to reinsure all or part of the business at a net reinsurance premium less than the claims costs of the business ceded.

Alternatively one can consider *relative* profits. If the rate of reinsurance commission is less than the ceding company's ratio of combined commission and expenses to gross premiums, the underwriting profit expressed as a percentage of net premiums will be lower than if the company wholly retained its business. Only by obtaining a rate of reinsurance commission (including profit commission) greater than its combined commission and expense ratio can a company increase its *relative* underwriting profits. Sometimes competition for business is so keen that companies earning exceptionally large profits on their gross accounts can obtain such high rates of commission, and thereby acquire a risk-free profit on the business ceded. The danger is that it may encourage a company to operate more like a broker than as an insurer, and live off the overriding commission plus possibly the investment income obtainable on retained premium reserves.

The calculation of the reinsurance commission for a proportional reinsurance is usually obtained by simply applying the agreed rate per cent to the reinsurer's share of the original gross premiums. The difficulties lie in agreeing on the rate of commission which, in principle, should be sufficient to reimburse the ceding company for the costs it incurs in acquiring the business plus some contribution towards its management expenses. There are no hard and fast rules for deciding exactly what is an appropriate rate of commission; as stated above, it is a matter for bargaining between the parties. However the following important factors will be taken into account.

(1) *The type of reinsurance and method of placing employed. Facultative reinsurances* involve the reinsurer in relatively higher administrative expenses than treaty business, do not provide him with the same sort of balanced account, and the risks concerned are often more hazardous than average. Therefore, invariably the rates of

commission allowed on facultative reinsurances are lower than on proportional treaties for comparable business. For example, a UK fire reinsurance may carry a rate of 20% to 25% for a facultative reinsurance and of 32½% on a first surplus treaty. *Quota-share* treaties usually carry higher rates of commission than *surplus* treaties not only because under the former the reinsurer receives an agreed proportion of all of the business written by the ceding company and so should bear his proportion of the original acquisition and administration costs, but also because the degree of selection exercised against the reinsurer under surplus treaties tends to result in a higher loss ratio. The commissions payable under second and third surplus treaties and under facultative obligatory reinsurances are progressively less than under first surplus treaties.

(2) *Whether the premiums are ceded to the reinsurer on an original gross premium basis or are subject to deductions.* For example, marine premiums are commonly ceded net of all acquisition costs. This point can present problems when dealing with overseas business in that it is not always clear what brokerages are to be deducted. Although the intention originally may have been to allow only for brokerages payable over and above the ordinary commission paid to agents, unless the treaty wording is tightly drafted, it is easy for other items to creep in with the result that the reinsurer may not receive his fair share of the original premium. Therefore, great care must be taken during the initial negotiations to ascertain precisely what are the ceding company's acquisition costs, and usually treaty wordings nowadays only allow the deduction of brokerage payable to local brokers in accordance with a recognized tariff rule or local custom. The rate of reinsurance premium then allowed on the balance of the premium would be reduced accordingly.

(3) *In some countries it is common practice to grant substantial rebates on the gross insurance premium rates to direct insured.* The reinsurer can handle the situation either by accepting a lower reinsurance premium rate or by increasing the rate of reinsurance commission accordingly. Companies operating in some countries record rebates such as no claims bonuses (NCB) or good record returns (GRR) as a separate item in their reinsurance accounts, usually net of commission.

(4) *The acquisition and administration costs of the ceding company.* In some developing countries the volume of insurance business available is so small that handling costs are relatively high. Consequently

reinsurance commission rates can be far higher than for UK business.

(5) *The claims experience of the business over the years.* Although claims costs have little or no bearing on an insurer's acquisition costs, a reinsurer may be willing to concede a higher rate of commission on classes of business that produce relatively stable results which are consistently better than average.

(6) *The prospective investment earnings of the business.* Such earnings depend not only upon the cash-flow characteristics of the business (notably the average claims settlement delays), but also upon the proportion of the funds available to the reinsurer for investment in view of any treaty provisions regarding the retention by the reinsured of premium reserves, regulations regarding the compulsory localization and investment of funds, etc.

Sliding-scale commission rates.

The use of sliding-scale commission rates provides a means whereby a treaty reinsurer can automatically reward a ceding company which uses its skill to write a profitable account, without incurring the risks discussed above, and conversely penalize a company for a bad loss experience.

Instead of the rate of reinsurance commission having to be renegotiated periodically in the light of the claims' experience, the commission clause provides for the rate payable to be determined each year according to a sliding scale related to the treaty's loss ratio. Either the rate may be based on the loss ratio for the year in question (see the specimen clause in Appendix 3.2.) or provision may be made for both losses in excess of a maximum loss ratio, and profits resulting from losses falling below a minimum loss ratio, to be carried forward for a number of years. Thus the ceding company knows in advance the prospective rewards (and penalties) for good (or bad) underwriting.

The way in which the basic system works is as follows:

(1) During the year the reinsured debits the reinsurer with a provisional commission on premiums paid under the treaty, usually calculated at the agreed minimum rate of commission so that any possible adjustment can only be one way—from the reinsurer to the reinsured.

(2) At the end of the period the commission is adjusted according to the rate of commission obtained by applying the loss ratio for the year to the sliding scale set out in the treaty. Loss ratios are calculated on earned premiums as follows, though the resulting rate is then applied to written premiums:

$$\frac{\text{incurred loss}}{\text{earned premium}} \times 100$$

where incurred loss = losses plus loss expenses paid by the reinsurer during the current year (plus in some cases any excess losses or profits carried forward from previous years)

+ provision for outstanding losses at the end of the current year

− provision for outstanding losses at the beginning of the current year

earned premium = premiums for the current year

+ unearned premium reserve at the beginning of the current year

− unearned premium reserve at the end of the current year.

Premiums and loss portfolios may wholly or partially replace the unearned premium and outstanding loss reserves.

There are advantages in calculating earned premiums without any deduction for commission.

(3) The precise terms of the sliding scale of commission rates will be negotiated by the two parties concerned. They will be influenced by the factors discussed above regarding reinsurance commissions in general, but may take the form, for example of a ½ — 1% increase in the commission rate for every 1% reduction in the loss ratio with limits of, say:

32% if the loss ratio is 60% or more; to

47% if the loss ratio is 40% or less.

Actual limits vary according to individual circumstances.

Essentially the ceding company should receive in a normal year the same rate of commission as if a flat rate applied. The upper and lower limits should then balance out in the sense that in a good year the reinsurer should be able to retain sufficient premium to provide a contingency fund related to the risk of losses exceeding the upper loss ratio. A portfolio subject to periodic catastrophe losses merits a less generous sliding scale than more stable portfolios unless provision is made to carry forward losses in excess of a specified loss ratio into the calculation of the loss ratios for subsequent years.

The carrying forward of 'excess' losses and profits takes various forms, but one example will show the principles involved.

Example. Losses exceeding a loss ratio of 75% are to be carried forward for not more than two years.

1st year

$$\frac{\text{incurred losses}}{\text{earned premiums}} = \frac{£21,250}{£25,000} \times 100 = 85\%$$

Losses exceeding 75% to be carried forward $= 10\% \times £25,000$
$$= £2,500$$

2nd year

Provisional calculation: $\dfrac{£18,900}{£27,000} \times 100 = 70\%$

Definite calculation: $\dfrac{£18,900 + £2,500}{£27,000} \times 100 = 79\%$

Overall loss to be carried forward to third year:

From first year:	loss	£2,500
From second year:	profit	£1,350 $\quad(=5\%$ of £27,000)
	loss	£1,150

3rd year

Provisional calculation: $\dfrac{£24,000}{£30,000} \times 100 = 80\%$

Definite calculation: $\dfrac{£24,000 + £1,150}{£30,000} \times 100 = 84\%$

Overall loss to be carried forward to fourth year:

From first year:	nil
From second year:	nil (eliminated by first-year loss)
From third year:	£1,500 $(=5\%$ of £30,000)

Upon the cancellation of the treaty, the commission for the year of cancellation would be subject to subsequent adjustment until the final settlement of outstanding claims.

An alternative method of calculation is on an underwriting year basis. For example, if the commission clause provided for the adjustment of the commission rate in accordance with the development of the results of each underwriting year, at the end of year 2 the commission payable in respect of underwriting year 1 would be based on the loss ratio calculated as follows:

$$\frac{\text{incurred losses for underwriting year}}{\text{earned premiums for underwriting year}} \times 100$$

where: incurred losses = losses paid in years 1 and 2 for underwriting year 1 plus reserve for losses which occurred in year 1 and are outstanding at the end of year 2

earned premiums = written premiums accounted for in years 1 and 2 for underwriting year 1.

The commission would continue to be recalculated until the final settlement of all claims which occurred in underwriting year 1.

A profit commission payable in addition to a flat-rate reinsurance commission is an alternative method of rewarding a ceding company for better-than-average claims experience, and it is found in the majority of surplus and quota share treaties. The idea is simply that the ceding company is given a share of any profit earned by the reinsurer on the reinsurances it cedes under its treaty. The difficulties lie in arriving at a fair basis for calculating the results of the treaty. Moreover the combined flat rate of commission and the profit commission must be pitched at a level which will enable the reinsurance company to retain for its own account sufficient profit in the good years to contribute towards the dividends for its shareholders and to set aside reserve funds to cover the deficits of bad years. Like the sliding-scale basis, the aim is to provide a reasonable profit for the reinsurer taken over the long term. If the results of the business are subject to considerable variability with periodic heavy deficits, the ceding company cannot expect to take a large share of any profit, and indeed profit commission is normally only paid under treaties which are expected to produce reasonably stable loss ratios.

The treaty result for any one year is generally taken as the difference between the reinsurer's income and outgo for the year, where:

income = premium included in the account for the year
+ unearned premium reserve at the end of the preceding year
+ outstanding loss reserve at the end of the preceding year

outgo = losses and loss expenses paid by the reinsurer during the current year
+ commission included in the account for the year
+ any other deductions (e.g. premium taxes, fire brigade charges, etc.)
+ unearned premium reserve at the end of the current year
+ outstanding loss reserve at the end of the current year

The items for incoming and outgoing premium and loss reserves may be totally or partially replaced by premium and loss portfolios.

Also included in outgo ought to be an item for the reinsurer's own management expenses, calculated at a rate of between 2¼% and 5% of the year's premiums. Inevitably a reinsurer will incur costs in operating his business, and therefore some allowance should be made for this when calculating the results of any individual portfolio of business. The counter-argument is that the bulk of a reinsurer's expenses are fixed in the sense that they would be unaffected by the acquisition or loss of an individual account so that they should be ignored when calculating the results thereof. The case for taking the reinsurer's expenses into account is, however, the stronger despite the problems involved in fairly allocating fixed costs.

Profit is thus defined as the excess of income over outgo, and the profit commission payable by the reinsurer is generally fixed at between 10% and 20%. These figures can, however, only be taken as a broad guide, and sometimes a higher percentage may be agreed, the matter being entirely one for negotiation between the parties in the light of the prevailing circumstances.

Three points may be noted:

(1) Like the sliding-scale method, premiums are brought into account on an 'earned' basis. The treaty will specify the method of calculating the unearned premium reserve which will usually be expressed as a fixed percentage of the year's premiums, so that accuracy is traded off against the benefit of ease of calculation. The method of calculating claims costs brings into account adjustments to outstanding claims reserves for claims occurring in previous years, so that the treaty result will be affected by over- or under estimating in previous years.

(2) The treaty result, therefore, is dependent not only upon actual payments but also the valuation of liabilities.

(3) The flat rate of reinsurance commission payable by the reinsurer will itself critically influence the emergence of 'profit'. Therefore, as indicated above, both rates of commission must be considered together in the light of the results (exclusive of reinsurance and profit commission) which may be expected from the treaty.

It is in the nature of reinsurance business that results fluctuate from year to year, and therefore it is not usual practice to calculate profit commission on only one year's results. The state of competition in most insurance and reinsurance markets is such that underwriting losses tend to occur with greater frequency than profits, and though theoretically this could be allowed for in fixing the rates of commission, there is the risk that one exceptionally bad year to which the ceding company would make no additional premium contribution would more than wipe out any profits in which the reinsured would be entitled to share. Consequently two basic methods are in use to deal with the problem of fluctuations.

Three-year average system. The most important method, which is in general use for United Kingdom fire treaties, is the three-year average system. The aggregate profit for the current and the two preceding years, ascertained in the manner described above, is divided by 3 to obtain the average profit for the last three years to which the agreed percentage is applied to obtain the commission payable. Each year the oldest year's result drops out of the calculation so that the system works on a three-year moving average, with special provision being made for the first two years of the treaty's life.

In the first year the commission is calculated on the result for that year; in the second year on half the aggregate profit for the first and second years; and thereafter it is based on one-third of the aggregate profit for the last three years. If the aggregate result is a loss, then no profit commission is payable even if the treaty produced a profit in any of the three individual years under review.

Changes in the ceding company's retentions and in individual reinsurers' shares of a treaty mean that it is not sufficient to produce only one profit commission statement for the whole treaty. Separate statements must be produced for each reinsurer, so that profit commission is calculated on the income and outgo of each reinsurer over the three years.

Losses to extinction. The second method is termed the losses to extinction basis whereby a loss disclosed by one year's calculation is debited to the next year, thereby reducing any profit or increasing any loss arising from that year's results. So long as the profit statement for any year is in deficit, the loss(es) will continue to be carried forward to the next year until sufficient profit has been earned to extinguish past losses. Theoretically this method would be suitable for accident treaties and poorly balanced fire treaties where the degree of fluctuation in the results is such that losses are unlikely to be averaged out over three years. In practice if a ceding company suffered a major loss which would impair its results for several years, it would be inclined to look for another reinsurer so that it could make a fresh start for the purpose of calculating profit commission.

It is normal practice to employ a variation on the latter method where under a fire treaty the profit commission is based on one year's results. Instead of losses being carried forward to extinction they are carried forward for a maximum of only two or three years as in the specimen included in Appendix 3.2.

Marine and aviation treaties in particular usually employ a system of calculating profit commission on an *underwriting year* basis. The profit statement is drawn up one or two years after the close of the underwriting year in question, with provision for annual adjustment thereafter for a fixed number of years before transfer to the next open year or alternatively to extinction. A specimen calculation is given in Appendix 3.3.

Instead of the parties agreeing to a fixed rate of profit commission, the practice is growing of using more flexible methods, notably *sliding scales or stepped scales of profit commission.* Briefly, the profit is calculated in accordance with one of the methods described above. The profit is then expressed as a percentage of the written or earned premiums for the year, and that percentage determines the rate of profit commission which is payable. The sliding-scale method operates like the sliding scales used for calculating reinsurance commission rates, the profit commission rate increasing in proportion to the relative profit, perhaps at a rate of one percentage point increase in the commission rate for every one per cent increase in the profit ratio. A typical example of a stepped scale would be:

On the part of the profit	Rate of profit commission
up to 5%	20%
between 5% and 10%	25%
over 10%	40%

So, for example, if the treaty produced a profit of £6,000 on a premium income of £20,000 the commission would be:

$$
\begin{array}{llll}
20\% \text{ on } £1000 & = & £\ 200 \\
25\% \text{ on } £1000 & = & £\ 250 \\
40\% \text{ on } \underline{£4000} & = & \underline{£1600} \\
£6000 & & £2050 & = \text{ total profit commission}
\end{array}
$$

Finally, and for purely commercial reasons, a *super profit commission* may be payable. This is employed in respect of contracts carrying a flat rate of profit commission and takes the form normally of an additional percentage of the profit over and above the basic rate indicated in the treaty terms. Super profit commission is usually granted by those reinsurers who are not offering reciprocity to the ceding company, or in cases of exceptionally high profitability which the reinsurer wishes to recognize. Super profit commission may be paid only by some of the reinsurers to a treaty and then only in respect of an established contract which is well balanced and of proven quality. It is a feature largely confined to property reinsurance.

Often one of the flexible methods is used instead of the reinsurer allowing a higher flat rate of profit commission in return for the ceding company placing its reinsurances without claiming a reciprocal exchange of business. It is preferable to a straightforward increase in the rate of profit commission in that the ceding company will only benefit if its business in fact proves to be highly profitable.

Finally, whichever of the methods of calculating profit commission is employed, special provision has to be made for the calculation of profit following the termination of a treaty in order to deal with the items relating to future liabilities. So long as a treaty remains in force the reserves for unearned premiums and outstanding claims roll forward from year to year, and any under- or over-estimating of such liabilities creates no real problem because it will be corrected automatically in the accounts of subsequent years. When a treaty is cancelled, however, it is necessary to ensure, before the last profit commission statement is finalized, that the reserves are adequate to run off all outstanding liabilities, some of which may not be settled for perhaps several years. Two systems are employed for dealing with this. Under the first the final year's profit commission statement is prepared in the normal way, and the reserves at the end of that year are carried forward to a special account against which future claims are debited as they are settled. When all of the outstanding items have been settled the account is closed and a final profit commission adjustment is made. The second system is simply to delay the profit commission statement for the final year until all outstanding liabilities have been settled. Although the final settlement will be the same whichever system is used, the timings of the payments will differ, which can be a matter of some importance in a period of high interest rates.

Inflation and floating exchange rates

Since the end of the 1960s the problems of conducting reinsurance business, especially on an international scale, have considerably increased because of the rise that has occurred in domestic rates of inflation, and the abandonment of the International Monetary Fund's system of fixed parities between currencies.

Inflation influences all classes of insurance and reinsurance business, though some are more adversely affected than others. Like all insurers, reinsurers suffer not only from rising administrative expenses but also from a tendency for increases in premium rates to lag behind the rise in the cost of property, liability and most other non-life claims, so reducing underwriting profits[25]. If profits are insufficient to enable free reserves to be increased in step with premiums then solvency margins must inevitably fall, which adversely affects financial stability and/or underwriting capacity.[26]

The Table 3.3 shows how delay in the settlement of a type of claim where the policyholder is entitled to an indemnity based on values or costs prevailing at the date of settlement may result in a substantial increase in the final claims cost during a period of inflation.

Table 3.3 Cost of settling a liability claim for bodily injury occurring mid-1970

Settlement date (mid-year)	*Claims cost increasing at an annual rate of*			
	2½%	*5%*	*10%*	*in line with the UK index of average earnings*
1970	100.0	100.0	100.0	100.0
1971	102.5	105.0	110.0	111.5
1972	105.1	110.3	121.0	126.3
1973	107.7	115.8	133.1	143.6
1974	110.4	121.6	146.4	169.4
1975	113.1	127.6	161.1	214.5
1976	116.0	134.0	177.2	248.0
1977	118.9	140.7	194.9	273.1

Reinsurers tend to be even more exposed to the effects of inflation on claims costs than direct insurers for two reasons:

(1) Apart from quota share treaties where the loss experiences of the direct and reinsurance portfolios are identical, the average settlement delays on reinsured losses tend to be longer than on the underlying direct insurance portfolios. Generally under both surplus and non-proportional reinsurances, reinsurers are involved in the larger losses which tend to take longer to settle than small claims. So, for example, if on a liability insurance portfolio the respective average settlement delays (by payments) were, say, two years for all original claims and four years for reinsured losses, the average cost of settling claims occurring in 1973 would have been as follows:

	Claims cost increasing at			
	2½% p.a.	*5% p.a.*	*10% p.a.*	*the UK rate*
Direct insurer	+ 5.1%	+10.3%	+21.0%	+49.4%
Reinsurer	+10.4%	+21.6%	+46.4%	+90.2%

25 Munich Reinsurance Co., *The Influence of Inflation on Insurance* (1971); R.L. Carter, *Economics and Insurance* (London: P.H. Press, 1972).
26 R.L. Carter, 'Insuring for the future', *Policy*, December 1976, and P.H. Bartrum, 'Solvency and profitability', *Policy*, December 1977.

(2) Under excess of loss reinsurances, inflation may *(a)* raise more claims above the lower excess limit, and *(b)* for losses falling within the excess of loss reinsurance band, the reinsurer will bear the full impact of inflation. Consequently the rate of increase of claims costs suffered by the reinsurer will be higher than that of the underlying direct claims. Over the last decade many reinsurers have had to increase by substantial amounts their provisions for outstanding claims on long-tail excess of loss reinsurances to cover liabilities inflated in such a manner.

Today in most countries direct insurers have devised ways of dealing with the problem of inflation by indexing sums insured or premiums, building inflation factors into premium rates (after allowing for the expected effect of inflation on investment earnings), etc., in the hope that the additional premium income plus investment earnings will take care of their extra costs. The relationship between the rate of inflation and investment yields is of critical importance. If an increase in the rate of inflation is matched by an equivalent rise in investment yield, then the higher cost of claims will be covered by extra investment earnings on the insurer's technical reserves. It is when inflation is accelerating and outpacing the rise in investment earnings that an insurer may find that, despite the measures he has taken, claims costs exceed income. Reinsurers, however, have further problems.

Under surplus reinsurances, even if the ceding company is successful in raising its average level of premiums sufficiently to cover the increase in the total costs of direct claims, the reinsurer may still suffer a shortfall in income for two reasons. First, the ceding company may not have allowed for the possibility that the average claims settlement delay on the larger risks ceded to the reinsurer is longer than on its total portfolio of business. Secondly, the reinsurer may not be able to obtain as large a rise in investment earnings as the ceding company; this may happen if the ceding company holds the treaty technical reserves and credits the reinsurer with interest. All that reinsurers can do is to try to ensure that their ceding companies keep direct premiums in line with inflation, and stipulate that the rate of interest paid on reserves held by a ceding company is related to the yield it can obtain on investments.

In the case of excess of loss reinsurances, an increase in premium rates by the ceding company in line with forecast rates of inflation, and thus an increase in its gross net premium income on which the reinsurance premium is based, can compensate the reinsurer only partially for his increased liability.[27] Either the reinsurer must obtain a further increase in the reinsurance premium, or the ceding company's retention must rise

---

27 See Gunnar Benktander, 'The effect of inflation on excess layers', *The Review*, 12 January 1968.

in proportion to the rate of inflation so that it shares in the increased claims liability. The solutions which have been adopted by reinsurers will be examined in Chapter 5.

The one advantage the international reinsurer possesses compared with a direct insurance company operating in only one country is flexibility. The reinsurer can be more selective in the business he underwrites; he can afford to reduce his commitments on reinsurances from countries suffering from high rates of inflation and switch his marketing efforts elsewhere, whereas the direct insurer must either continue to service the needs of his clients whatever the rate of domestic inflation or lose ground to competitors.

Fluctuating foreign-exchange rates have always posed problems for international reinsurers, but for over a quarter of a century following the ending of the Second World War they enjoyed the relative security of the IMF Bretton Woods system of fixed exchange rates. The American decision in August 1971 to float the dollar plunged reinsurers into a new era of uncertainty.

There are several facets to the problem of writing foreign reinsurance in a period of fluctuating exchange rates.

When a treaty covers risks written in foreign currencies the effect of movements in exchange rates on the respective financial positions of the ceding company and the reinsurer will depend upon:

(1) The provisions regarding the currency or currencies in which accounts are to be rendered and settled.
(2) The ability of the reinsurer to match liabilities with assets in the same currency (or currencies).

The reinsurer's liability under an excess of loss treaty will also depend upon how the treaty limits are designated. If they are fixed in original currencies his potential liability will be unaffected by exchange-rate movements during the currency of the treaty. However if the limits are designated in one main currency, any change in the rate of exchange used to convert the limits into other currencies may significantly affect the reinsurer's liability for any loss.

Market practice regarding the settlement of accounts and the designation of the monetary limits under excess of loss treaties is discussed in Chapters 5 and 7 respectively, which leaves the question of currency matching for consideration now.

If a reinsurer could exactly match liabilities with assets in the same currency then a change in the currency's value on the foreign-exchange markets could result in neither a profit nor a loss being incurred. In practice currency matching is usually an unattainable, and not infrequently an undesired, objective for several reasons:

(1) Although the reinsurance contract may specify that premiums and losses shall be paid in the original currency, the reinsurer may not either be able, or want, to retain all of the premiums in the original currency, so that the time lag between receipt of the premiums and payment of the claims opens up the possibility of exchange-rate losses or gains.

(2) There is a case for the localization of technical reserves, but sometimes local capital-market conditions may be so unfavourable that, even if the local market offers high rates of return, it may still be thought worthwhile to invest the funds elsewhere despite the exchange-rate risk. Moreover a reinsurer's free reserves need to be kept in a central fund immediately available to cover any deficit in local reserves. It is inevitable that centralized funds are exposed to exchange-rate fluctuations, though a reinsurer with a strong home currency will view the situation differently from one whose currency is weak.

(3) The degree of variability in claims costs generally precludes a reinsurer from achieving perfect currency matching even if desired. The smaller the volume of business obtained from any country the greater will tend to be the degree of variability in its results.

(4) Frequently the freedom international reinsurers possess to move funds at will and to retain foreign currencies is severely restricted by the exchange-control and insurance supervisory regulations.

Whatever the reason for imperfect currency matching the result is the same. For example, assume that a reinsurance is written in francs and the premium of F100,000 is converted to sterling at a rate of F10 = £1. Losses occur amounting to F88,000 which if converted at the same rate as the premium will cost the reinsurer £8800 leaving a surplus of £1200. However, if in the meantime the rate of exchange falls to F8 = £1 the cost of settlement in sterling will rise to £11,000 resulting in a deficit of £1000. On the other hand if the premium is retained in francs until all losses have been settled, the sterling value of the balance of F12,000 will rise from £1200 to £1500.

Apart from such real exchange-rate losses and gains that may fall on an international reinsurer, there is a further technical dimension to the problem which has been described by J.A.S. Neave as follows:[28]

> Let us assume that five reinsurers resident, say, in Zurich, Munich, Paris, New York and London, each have a portfolio of business which is identical in content, comprising the same shares of the same contracts from the same ceding companies in a number of different

28 J.A.S. Neave, 'The effect on international reinsurance of changing patterns in economic interrelationships', Mercantile & General, 1976.

countries all over the world. It would be logical to suppose that the technical results for each of these five reinsuring companies, committed on identical business, would be the same. Indeed inescapably this is so. But each company is required by law to publish its balance sheet in its own local currency. If we now make the further assumption that each company has a similar accounting system, it is a suprising fact that because of currency instability, the results of our five reinsurers when converted into their own domestic currency will each be significantly different.

Fluctuating exchange rates can thus have an entirely capricious effect upon the results of a business which consists in the collection of premiums and the settlement of claims in the currencies of the countries where the risks are situated, but which will be expressed eventually in the currency of the country where the reinsurer himself is registered.

This apparent accounting paradox can be illustrated by the following example.

Example. Five reinsurers in London, Munich, Paris, New York and Zurich each took an equal share in some Dutch excess of loss business in 1972. By the end of 1975 all the claims for the 1972 underwriting year were settled and it was found that the account in florins had broken even as follows:

Year	Premiums	Claims paid	Balance
1972	40,000	10,000	30,000
1973	50,000	30,000	20,000
1974	10,000	40,000	− 30,000
1975	—	20,000	− 20,000

Each reinsurer decided that it would bring its balances home each year thus involving a currency conversion. This operation took place at the end of each year.

The transactions were as follows:

Date	Amount in D. Florins	Florins to £	Florins to Marks	Florins to F. Francs	Florins to Dollars	Florins to S. Francs
31.12.72	30,000	3,963	29,703	47,619	9,317	34,884
31.12.73	20,000	3,049	19,230	34,483	7,067	22,989
31.12.74	− 30,000	− 5,102	− 28,846	− 53,571	− 12,000	− 30,303
21.12.75	− 20,000	− 3,683	− 19,608	− 33,333	− 7,435	− 19,608
		− 1,773	479	− 4,802	− 3,051	7,962
Sterling equivalent at 31.12.75		− 1,773	90	− 531	− 1,510	1,502

If each reinsurer had left the balances in Dutch florins each would have ended up with zero profit, but on paper the results would still have been the same as above. The apparent paradox arises from the need for the purpose of preparing year-end accounts to convert overseas balances into the home currency.

Appendix 3.1 The effect on a reinsurer's results of increasing the rate of reinsurance commission

On page 87 it was stated that by increasing the rate of reinsurance commission allowed on a treaty:

(1) A ceding company's underwriting profit will be increased at the expense of the reinsurer.

(2) The reinsurer's results will be exposed to larger fluctuations relative to his expected profit.

These points can be proved quite simply. If investment earnings on funds and possible changes in administrative expenses due to fluctuations in claims are ignored, the expected profit on a treaty $\bar{\pi}$ will be the premium income P less expected losses $\bar{L}$, commission C and expenses E, i.e.:

$$\bar{\pi}_1 = P - \bar{L} - C_1 - E$$

If commission was *increased from* C_1 to C_2, then:

$$\bar{\pi}_2 = P - \bar{L} - C_2 - E$$

$$\text{and } \bar{\pi}_2 < \bar{\pi}_1$$

In both cases, any variation in actual losses L from the expected losses would alter *absolute* profits by the same amount $(\bar{L} - L)$, but the respective changes in *relative* profits would be:

$$(\bar{L} - L) / \bar{\pi}_1 < (\bar{L} - L) / \bar{\pi}_2$$

The following simple example illustrates the same points numerically. Again investment earnings and any change in administrative expenses due to a change in claims are ignored.

Example. A 50% quota share reinsurance is arranged on a portfolio with an annual gross direct-premium income of £2 million.

On the basis of past claims experience the gross direct claims for the year are expected to be £1,100,000.

The ceding insurer's agency commission and administrative expenses amount to 35% of the gross direct premiums.

The reinsurer's administration costs amount to £40,000.

If the actual claims cost increased by 10% and 20% the results of the business would be as shown in Table 3.4.

Table 3.4

	£000's	£000's	£000's
Actual gross claims	1100	1210	1320
SITUATION 1:			
REINSURANCE COMMISSION 33%			
Ceding insurer's results			
Gross premiums	2000	2000	2000
less Commissions and expenses net			
of reinsurance commission	370	370	370
Reinsurance premium	1000	1000	1000
Net claims cost	550	605	660
Underwriting result =	80	25	− 30
Underwriting result as percentage of net			
(of reinsurance) premiums	8.0%	2.5%	− 3.0%
Reinsurer's results			
Reinsurance premium	1000	1000	1000
less Commission	330	330	330
Administrative costs	40	40	40
Claims cost	550	605	660
Underwriting result	80	25	− 30
Underwriting result as percentage			
of net premium =	8.0%	2.5%	− 3.0%
SITUATION 2:			
REINSURANCE COMMISSION 37½%			
Ceding insurer's results			
Gross premiums	2000	2000	2000
less Net of commissions and expenses			
and net claims costs	875	930	985
Net reinsurance premium	1000	1000	1000
Underwriting result	125	70	15
Underwriting result as percentage of net premiums	12.5%	7.0%	1.5%
Reinsurer's results			
Net reinsurance premium	1000	1000	1000
less Commission	375	375	375
Administrative costs and claims cost	590	645	700
Underwriting result	35	− 20	− 75
Underwriting result as percentage of net premium	3.5%	− 2.0%	− 7.5%

Appendix 3.2   Commission Clauses

Sliding-Scale Commission

(a)   The REINSURED shall receive a commission on the premiums ceded to the REINSURER in the accounts for each annual period of this Agreement calculated at a rate determined in accordance with the following scale:
        per cent where the loss ratio is   per cent or above increasing by   per cent for each   per cent decrease in the loss ratio up to a maximum of   per cent where the loss ratio is less than   per cent the loss ratio being the percentage which the Incurred Loss bears to the Earned Premium.

Incurred loss   shall be all paid losses and loss expenses included in the accounts for the current year including cash losses paid by the REINSURER during the current year and not brought into account, plus the outstanding loss reserve as at the end of the current year less the outstanding loss reserve as at the end of the previous year.

Earned premium shall be all premiums included in the accounts for the current year, plus the previous year's unearned premium reserve less the current year's unearned premium reserve calculated at the percentage shown in the Schedule.

(b)   For the first annual period the calculation will not include a previous year's unearned premium reserve or outstanding loss reserve.
(c)   Any premiums and loss recoveries under reinsurances which inure to the benefit of this Agreement shall be included in the calculation.
(d)   The REINSURED will debit the REINSURER in the accounts during each year with a provisional commission of   per cent.
(e)   The final account for each annual period shall be rendered to the REINSURER together with a statement of the annual commission adjustment calculation and this final account shall include the amount due to either party in respect of annual commission taking into consideration provisional commission payments already made.
(f)   Upon termination of this Agreement no adjustment of the commission will be made in respect of the annual period ending at that date until all liability of the REINSURER has ceased and a final statement shall then be rendered.

Profit Commission: three year average basis

(a)   The REINSURER shall pay to the REINSURED a profit commission on a three years average basis as stated in the Schedule calculated on the profit arising from all business ceded under this Agreement and included in the accounts for each annual period of this Agreement in accordance with the following formula:

Income

1.   Release of preceding year's Unearned Premium Reserve.
2.   Release of the Outstanding Loss Reserve as at the end of the preceding year.

3. Premium included in the accounts for the current year.
   Items 1 and 2 will not apply to the first Profit Commission Statement.

Outgo

1. Commission included in the accounts for the current year.
2. Paid Losses and Loss Expenses included in the accounts for the current year including cash losses paid by the REINSURER during the current year and not brought into account.
3. Unearned Premium Reserve calculated at   per cent of the Premium Income for the current year.
4. The Outstanding Loss Reserve as at the end of the current year.
5. REINSURER's Management Expenses calculated at   per cent of the Premium Income for the current year.

(b) Any excess of Income over Outgo shall be deemed to be the profit for the annual period, it being understood that any Premium and Loss recoveries under reinsurances which inure to the benefit of this Agreement shall be taken into consideration.

(c) In the first year the REINSURER shall pay profit commission on 100% of that year's profit and in the second year on one-half of the aggregate profit of the first and second years. Thereafter the REINSURER shall pay profit commission calculated on one-third of the aggregate net profit of the current and two preceding years.

(d) The REINSURED shall render to the REINSURER a statement for each annual period in accordance with the above formula and any profit commission due shall be included in account.

(e) The Profit Commission Statement shall be drawn up for the first time in respect of the period ending   and annually thereafter.

(f) On termination of this Agreement no Profit Commission Statement will be rendered until all liability of the REINSURER has ceased. All entries appearing in accounts rendered to the REINSURER after the date of termination together with the appropriate entries relating to the last period this Agreement was in force shall be included in a final statement.

Profit Commission: losses carried forward to extinction

(a) The REINSURER shall pay to the REINSURED a profit commission as stated in the Schedule calculated on the profit arising from all business ceded under this Agreement and included in the accounts for each annual period of this Agreement in accordance with the following formula:

Income

1. Release of preceding year's Unearned Premium Reserve.
2. Release of the Outstanding Loss Reserve as at the end of the preceding year.
3. Premium included in the accounts for the current year.
   Items 1 and 2 will not apply to the first Profit Commission Statement.

Outgo

1. Commission included in the accounts for the current year.
2. Paid Losses and Loss Expenses included in the accounts for the current year including cash losses paid by the REINSURER during the current year and not brought into account.
3. Unearned Premium Reserve calculated at   per cent of the Premium Income for the current year.
4. The Outstanding Loss Reserve as at the end of the current year.
5. REINSURER's Management Expenses calculated at   per cent of the Premium Income for the current year.
6. Aggregate Loss (if any) brought forward from the previous year's statement.

(b) Any excess of Income over Outgo shall be deemed to be the profit for the annual period it being understood that any Premium and Loss recoveries under reinsurances which inure to the benefit of this Agreement shall be taken into consideration.

(c) The REINSURED shall render to the REINSURER a statement for each annual period in accordance with the above formula and any profit commission due shall be included in account.

(d) The Profit Commission Statement shall be drawn up for the first time in respect of the period ending   and annually thereafter.

(e) On termination of this Agreement no Profit Commission Statement will be rendered until all liability of the REINSURER has ceased. All entries appearing in accounts rendered to the REINSURER after the date of termination together with the appropriate entries relating to the last period this Agreement was in force shall be included in a final statement.

Profit Commission: losses carried forward for three years

(a) The REINSURER shall pay to the REINSURED a profit commission as stated in the Schedule calculated on the profit arising from all business ceded under this Agreement and included in the accounts for each annual period of this Agreement in accordance with the following formula:

Income

1. Release of preceding year's Unearned Premium Reserve.
2. Release of the Outstanding Loss Reserve as at the end of the preceding year.
3. Premium included in the accounts for the current year.
   Items 1 and 2 will not apply to the first Profit Commission Statement.

Outgo

1. Commission included in the accounts for the current year.
2. Paid Losses and Loss Expenses included in the accounts for the current year including cash losses paid by the REINSURER during the current year and not brought into account.
3. Unearned Premium Reserve calculated at   per cent of the Premium Income for the current year.
4. The Outstanding Loss Reserve as at the end of the current year.

5. REINSURER's Management Expenses calculated at   per cent of the Premium Income for the current year.

6. Aggregate Loss (if any) brought forward and calculated in accordance with the provision shown in the first paragraph below.

(b) Any loss resulting from each year's profit commission calculated shall be carried forward and offset against the profit of the next two years. If at the end of the third year the overall result is still a loss then the loss of the first year and the profits for the second or third years shall be eliminated from any further profit commission calculations. Where the second year is also a loss then the loss carried forward to the fourth year shall be the full loss of the second year less any profit resulting from the combined result of the third year's profit less the first year's loss. Where the third year is a loss then the full loss of that year will be carried forward and offset against the profit of the next two years in the same manner.

(c) Any excess of Income over Outgo shall be deemed to be the profit for the annual period it being understood that any Premium and Loss recoveries under reinsurances which inure to the benefit of this Agreement shall be taken into consideration.

(d) The REINSURED shall render to the REINSURER a statement for each annual period in accordance with the above formula and any profit commission due shall be included in account.

(e) The Profit Commission Statement shall be drawn up for the first time in respect of the period ending   and annually thereafter.

(f) On termination of this Agreement no Profit Commission Statement will be rendered until all liability of the REINSURER has ceased. All entries appearing in accounts rendered to the REINSURER after the date of termination together with the appropriate entries relating to the last period this Agreement was in force shall be included in a final statement.

Profit Commission: on an underwriting-year basis

(a) The REINSURER shall pay to the REINSURED a profit commission as stated in the Schedule calculated on the profit arising from all business ceded under this Agreement in respect of each underwriting year in accordance with the following formula:

Income

1. Premium included in the accounts for the underwriting year.

Outgo

1. Commission included in the accounts for the underwriting year.
2. Paid Losses and Loss Expenses included in the accounts for the underwriting year including cash losses paid by the REINSURER and not brought into account.
3. The Outstanding Loss Reserve for the underwriting year.
4. REINSURER's Management Expenses calculated at   per cent of the Premium Income for the Underwriting Year.

(b) Any excess of Income over Outgo shall be deemed to be the profit for the underwriting year it being understood that any Premium and Loss recoveries under reinsurances which inure to the benefit of this Agreement shall be taken into consideration.

(c) The REINSURED shall render to the REINSURER twenty-four months after the last calendar day of each underwriting year a statement in accordance with the above formula and any profit commission shall be payable to the REINSURED accordingly. Thereafter the REINSURED shall render to the REINSURER annually a separate readjustment statement for each underwriting year reflecting changes in the above items for such underwriting year and any additional or return profit commission shall be included in the next account.

(d) The Profit Commission Statement shall be drawn up for the first time in respect of the underwriting period ending   and annually thereafter.

Appendix 3.3 Calculation of profit commission on an underwriting-year basis

Calculation for underwriting year 1 at the end of year 2

	£		£
Commissions	6,000	Premiums	20,000
Other deductions	200		
Losses paid	4,000		
Loss reserve	3,000		
Management expenses at 5% =	1,000		
Profit	5,800		
	20,000		20,000

10% profit commission = £580

Adjustment for underwriting year 1 at the end of year 3

	£		£
Losses paid	2,000	Return of loss reserve	3,000
Loss reserve	2,500	Loss	1,500
	4,500		4,500

		£
Underwriting year 1 in year 3:	Loss	1,500
Underwriting year 1 at end of year 2:	Profit	5,800
Underwriting year 1 at end of year 3:	Profit	4,300

Adjustment of 10% profit commission for underwriting year 1 at end of year 3:

		£
10% of £4,300	=	430
− already paid at end of year 2		580
Refund of commission due		150

Notes

Adjusted profit commission statements for this underwriting year would be rendered until all liability has ceased.

In the event of an overall loss, the loss is usually carried forward and compensated with the overall result of the next underwriting year. It is important that the result for each underwriting year is established first before any previous underwriting year losses are brought forward for compensation.

REINSURANCE

4
Legal principles applying to reinsurance contracts

REINSURANCE

4
Legal principles applying to reinsurance contracts

The nature of reinsurance contracts

It was established in Chapter 1 that reinsurance is a contract whereby one party, known as the reinsurer, undertakes to indemnify the other party for liabilities he may incur under a contract of insurance. Such was the view of Lord Mansfield, who in *Delver* v *Barnes*, defined reinsurance as:[1]

> A new assurance, effected by a new policy, on the same risk which was before insured in order to indemnify the underwriters from their previous subscriptions; and both policies are in existence at the same time.

More recently an American court has construed a contract of reinsurance as being:[2]

> A contract whereby one for a consideration agrees to indemnify another wholly or partially against loss or liability by a risk the latter has assumed under a separate and distinct contract as insurer of a third party.

These two judgments highlight three features of reinsurance contracts:
(1) The reinsurer's undertaking to indemnify the primary insurer itself constitutes a contract of insurance.
(2) The reinsurance may provide a complete or only partial indemnity against the liabilities the primary insurer may incur under the head policy.
(3) The reinsurance is a separate contract between the reinsurer and his reinsured to which the original insured is not a party.

It has also been held that the risks covered by a reinsurance contract may be in a narrower or even wider form than those assumed by the

1 (1807) 1 Taunt. 48, 51.
2 *Stickel* v *Excess Insurance Company of America*, Ohio Supreme Court, 22 November 1939, 23 N.E. (2nd) 839, 136 Ohio St. 49.

reinsured under the original insurance.[1] If a reinsurance contract did provide cover for, say, a wider range of perils than an underlying original insurance, the reinsurer's liabilities thereunder would be no wider in extent than those incurred by the primary insurer. An American decision on this point held that:[2]

> While a contract of reinsurance implies the same subject matter of insurance as the original policy, and runs against perils of the same kind, it need not be for the identical hazard insured against in the first policy, but may be for a less, though not for a greater risk.

Like other insurances, a contract of reinsurance does not necessarily provide a full and perfect indemnity. Normally there are not the same difficulties of establishing the amount of the insured loss as occur in direct insurance where the concept of a perfect indemnity can be no more than a theoretical ideal. Nevertheless problems may arise in fixing the amount of compensation to which the reinsured is entitled[3] and only in a small proportion of cases are reinsurances arranged to compensate the reinsured fully for losses incurred.

Is reinsurance a contract of insurance?

The characteristics of a reinsurance contract clearly fit accepted definitions of a contract of insurance. The reinsurer undertakes to pay should a specified uncertain event occur which involves the ceding insurer suffering a loss under an original contract of insurance, and obviously such a loss adversely affects the interest of the insurer. Therefore the courts have followed the judgment of Lord Mansfield virtually without question in treating reinsurance contracts as contracts of insurance,[4] at least where the point at issue concerned facultative reinsurances.

English law is far less certain in the case of reinsurance treaties. One interpretation of the position is that: 'A treaty does not constitute a partnership between the parties, but is a form of reinsurance.'[5]

---

1 *Traders and General* v *Bankers & General Insurances* (1921), 38 T.L.R. 94.
2 *London Assurance Corporation* v *Thompson*, 170 N.Y. 94.
3 See, for example, *Versicherungs und Transport Aktiengesellschaft Daugava* v *Henderson* (1934), p.131 *infra,* regarding appropriate rates of exchange.
4 See, for example, *Australian Widows Fund Life Assurance Society Limited* v *National Mutual Life Association of Australasia Limited,* [1914] A.C. 634 and *Re London County Commercial Reinsurance Office,* [1922] 2 Ch. 67.
5 Colinvaux *Law of Insurance,* p.180, who in support quotes *English Insurance* v *National Benefit Assurance,* [1929] A.C. 114; *Motor Union* v *Mannheimer, etc.,* [1933] 1 K.B.812; *Re Norwich Equitable Fire* (1887), 3 T.L.R. 781, *per* Kay J.

The fact that a treaty is not a partnership agreement was firmly established in the case of *Re Norwich Equitable Fire*,[1] it being held that the treaty in question constituted a contract of agency between the reinsurer and the ceding company. The reports of Mr Justice Kay's judgment are less certain about whether it was also a contract of insurance.[2] Relatively few cases concerning treaties have come before the courts but in those where the issue was specifically considered some emphasis was placed on the role of bordereaux by which the business was actually ceded to the reinsurer. Arguably the courts were following the same principles as have been laid down in America where it has been held:[3]

> A reinsurance treaty is merely an agreement between two insurance companies whereby one agrees to cede and the other to accept reinsurance business pursuant to the provisions specified in the treaty. Reinsurance treaties and reinsurance policies are not synonymous: reinsurance treaties are contracts for insurance, and reinsurance policies or cessions are contracts of insurance.

Consequently it has been suggested by the legal correspondent[4] of *Reinsurance* that three distinct situations need to be distinguished, as follows:[5]

(1) Open covers which are clearly only an agreement to make future reinsurances.
(2) Treaties where the ceding company needs to take some action before its liabilities (or part thereof) under some policy or policies are reinsured, i.e. the need to cede surplus lines by an entry on a bordereau.
(3) Quota share and non-proportional reinsurance treaties where the risks accepted by the ceding office are automatically reinsured according to the terms of the treaty without any further action having to be taken by the reinsured.

Only the last type of treaty would qualify *per se* as a contract of insurance. In the first two situations the open cover and the treaty would rank as contracts to enter into contracts of insurance, the reinsurances being effected when the cessions were made.

---

1 (1887) 3 T.L.R. 781.
2 'Are reinsurance agreements contracts of insurance?', *Reinsurance*, February 1974.
3 *Pioneer Life Ins. Co. v Alliance Life Ins. Co.*, 30 N.E. 2d 66, Ill, 576.
4 J.S. Butler, who is also the author of the other articles from *Reinsurance* cited in this chapter.
5 'Treaties: agreements to enter into future reinsurances?', *Reinsurance*, March 1974.

The subject-matter of reinsurance

The subject-matter of insurance of a direct insurance is something exposed to loss or damage, or some potential liability which the policyholder insures, and the subject matter of the contract is the policyholder's financial interest in that property, chose in action or liability. Where a direct insurer reinsures then it would seem logical that the subject-matter of the insurance should be the liability which the insurer has accepted under the original contract of insurance, so that all contracts of reinsurance would be contracts of liability insurance. In those cases where this has been considered by the courts, however, it has been held that the subject-matter of the insurance under the reinsurance contract is the same as the subject-matter of the underlying insurance.[1] So if an original policy insures, say, a ship or some other property, or some liability which the insured may incur, then the subject-matter of insurance of a reinsurance contract effected by the insurer will be the same ship, property or liability. However, it is arguable that all these cases do no more than establish that the subject-matter of insurance may be the subject-matter of reinsurance if it is so described in a reinsurance contract and that they do not decide that the subject-matter of reinsurance must be the subject-matter of the original contract of insurance. The reasoning of Mr Justice Blackburn's judgment in *Mackenzie* v *Whitworth* could be interpreted as indicating that in some circumstances the subject-matter of insurance under the reinsurance contract may differ from that under the original insurance, depending upon how it is actually described in the contract. Consequently it has been suggested:[2]

(1) That, so far as facultative reinsurances are concerned, they are usually so worded that it can be taken that the subject-matter of insurance of the original policies are described as the subject-matters of insurance of the contracts of reinsurance.

(2) That, so far as proportional treaty reinsurances are concerned, they are, as a rule, so ambiguously worded that it would be possible to construe them as defining the subject-matters of insurance of the original policies as the subject-matters of insurance of the treaties.

(3) That, so far as non-proportional treaties are concerned, they are often so worded that it would be difficult to construe them as defining subject-matters of insurance of the original policies as the subject-matters of insurance of the treaties ... It is the possible liability of the ceding

---

1 *Mackenzie* v *Whitworth* (1875), 45 L.J.Q.B.233; *Uzielli & Co.* v *Boston Marine Insurance Co.* (1884), 54 L.J.Q.B.162; *Glasgow Assurance Corporation (Liquidators)* v *Welsh Insurance Corporation* (1914)S.C.320; *Forsikringsakabet National (of Copenhagen)* v *Attorney-General* (1929), 93 L.J.K.B.679 and [1925] A.C.639.

2 'Looking at the reinsurance contract', *Reinsurance*, April 1972.

company to make payments to its assureds which is actually defined in non-proportional treaties as being the subject-matter of insurance.

However, for the purposes of United Kingdom insurance supervision a reinsurance effected to protect a direct insurer is treated as an insurance of the same class as the direct business reinsured.[1] The courts would appear to have reached this conclusion on two separate grounds: some judges considered that it was a consequence of the identity of the subject-matter of insurance and reinsurance while others based their decisions on the wording of the relevant statutes.

Although the courts have held that the subject-matter of insurance is identical under both an original insurance and its associated reinsurance, the subject-matters of the two contracts differ. The distinction has been expressed as follows:[2]

> . . . a policy of reinsurance is a policy of interest in the subject-matter of the insurance, that interest being different from that protected by the original policy and acquired by the fact that the assured is the underwriter under the original policy.

Thus the contract of reinsurance is independent of the contract of insurance, and the original insured obtains no rights (or responsibilities) thereunder.

The law applicable to reinsurance contracts

English law has developed no special rules relating to reinsurance contracts, *qua* reinsurance contracts. They are subject to the general law of contract and the rules applicable to insurance contracts in particular.[3] US law has developed in a similar manner.

Consequently the provisions of contract law relating to such matters as an intention to create a legal relationship, offer and acceptance, consideration, capacity to enter into contracts, legality, assignment and so forth apply in general to the formation, construction, performance and validity of reinsurance contracts. In addition they are subject to the special rules governing insurance contracts, notably:

(1) There must be insurable interest.
(2) The contract is one of utmost good faith.
(3) The contract is one of indemnity.

---

1 *Glasgow Assurance Corporation (Liquidators)* v *Welsh Insurance Corporation* [1914] S.C. 320; and *Forsikringsakabet National (of Copenhagen)* v *Attorney General* (1929), 93 L.J.K.B. 679 and [1925] A.C. 639.
2 Quoted by Scrutton LJ in *Forsikringsakabet National (of Copenhagen)* v *Attorney General,*, (1929), 93 L.J.K.B. 679 and [1925] A.C. 639.
3 *Norwich Union Fire Insurance* v *Colonial Mutual Fire Insurance Co.,* [1922] 2 K.B. 461, 466.

Of necessity the reader must be referred to standard works on contract law in general and insurance law in particular. It is only possible in the scope of this chapter to outline briefly the law as it specifically affects reinsurance contracts.

The form of the contract

There is no general requirement in English law that reinsurance contracts take any special form, or even be in writing. To be valid a reinsurance contract need only comply with the basic requirements of a simple contract, that is (1) the parties have capacity to contract; (2) there is an intention to create a legal relationship; (3) there has been an offer and acceptance; and (4) consideration has passed.

It follows that in general in Great Britain, as in most other Common Law jurisdictions, a purely oral contract of reinsurance would be valid. The two exceptions are life and marine reinsurances. The Life Assurance Act 1774, s.2, while not directly stipulating that a policy shall be issued, does require that the person with the insurable interest (or for whose benefit the insurance is effected) shall be named in the policy. Section 22 of the Marine Insurance Act 1906 provides that a contract of marine insurance shall be inadmissible in evidence unless embodied in a marine policy in accordance with the Act.

Many countries require all contracts of insurance to be in writing, but it is not clear to what extent such provisions would apply to reinsurance contracts because reinsurance is generally excluded from the regulatory provisions of the relevant insurance codes. For example, in France the law of 13 July 1930, which requires non-marine insurance contracts to be made in writing, is specifically stated not to apply to reinsurance so that oral contracts of reinsurance do not offend against that statute.

Likewise in America, as 'a general rule a contract of reinsurance is not regarded as a promise to pay the debt of another and accordingly need not be in writing'.[1]

In practice it is preferable that reinsurance contracts, like direct insurances, should be embodied in documentary form signed by the reinsurer. Furthermore when there are reciprocal obligations on both parties, as in reinsurance treaties, it is conventional for the document to be issued in duplicate, both copies being signed by both parties. In the nature of things not only is it far easier to prove the terms of a written contract than of an oral contract but also in committing an agreement to writing it is more likely that greater care will be exercised in defining the detailed terms and conditions.

1 Kenneth R. Thompson, *Reinsurance*, 4th ed., p.249, op cit.

Often reinsurance agreements involve intermediaries and/or the parties are of different nationalities, so increasing the likelihood of misunderstanding and dispute. By expressing the terms of the agreement in writing the possibility will be removed of the reinsurer being involved, for example, in any dispute between a broker and the ceding company about the scope of the former's authority in arranging the contract or about the terms of the contract that had been arranged.

Insurable interest

'There is nothing in the *common law* of England which prohibits insurance, even if no interest exists.'[1] Statute law, however, renders illegal and void most insurances where the insured has no interest at the time of taking out a policy. Any insurance effected without interest is deemed a wagering contract and is unenforceable at law. In broad terms, an insured is deemed to have an insurable interest if he stands in some legal or equitable relationship to the subject matter of the insurance that will be prejudiced by the happening of the insured event.

In life insurance the interest must subsist at the time the policy is effected, though not necessarily at the time a claim is made.[2] Under the terms of the Marine Insurance Act 1906 (ss.4 – 8) the insured must be interested at the time of the loss, though not necessarily so at the time the insurance was effected.

Interest of the ceding company

The validity of a reinsurance contract likewise rests on the ceding company possessing an insurable interest in the subject-matter of the insurance. The nature of that interest was described by Lord Brett in *Uzielli* v *Boston Marine Insurance Company,*[3] as follows:

> They were not the owners [of the ship], and therefore they had none as owners. But they have an insurable interest of some kind, and that insurable interest is the loss which they might or would suffer under the policy, upon which they themselves were liable.

Another definition which more precisely explains the extent of the ceding company's interest is:[4]

1 *Williams* v *Baltic*, [1924] 2 K.B. 282, 288.
2 Life Assurance Act 1774; *Dalby* v *India and London Life Assurance Co.* (1854), 15 C.B.365.
3 (1884) 15 Q.B.D.11.
4 *Arnould on Marine Insurance,* 10th ed., vol.1, p.323, quoted by McCardie J. in *Norwich Union Fire Insurance Society* v *Colonial Mutual Fire Insurance Co.* [1922] 2 K.B.461, 466.

> The thing which the reassured insures is the thing originally insured. In this thing he has an insurable interest to the extent of the liability which he may incur under and by reason of his original contract of insurance.

Thus the insurable interest of a primary insurer (or a retrocessionaire) is limited to the extent of the losses he may incur under the policy, or policies, he has issued, his liability thereunder being dependent on:

(1) The sum(s) insured, or limit(s) of indemnity.
(2) The things or liabilities insured.
(3) The perils covered.

Golding summarizes the position as follows: [1]

> So a company which has undertaken to insure property against fire, would not thereby acquire an insurable interest which would enable it to reinsure against loss by burglary, for that is a loss by which it could not be prejudiced.

If an original insured possesses no insurable interest then his policy is void, and the direct insurer has no interest to support a contract of reinsurance. [2] However, it has been observed in a case involving marine insurance arranged on a PPI (policy proof of interest) basis, where all of the parties knew that there was no insurable interest in the strict sense, that insurers who in practice 'pay losses on such policies are usually indemnified by their reinsurers.' [3]

There is little scope in practice for dispute about the time when the ceding company's insurable interest must exist. In order to establish a claim against a reinsurer a ceding company must either have paid, or have outstanding, a valid claim under the underlying policies which are the subject of the reinsurance, so clearly an insurable interest must exist at that time. Under reinsurance treaties and open covers the reinsurance of any particular risk only becomes operative from the time the ceding company itself accepts the risk, so insurable interest exists from the inception of the reinsurance. In a case where the reinsurer agreed to reinsure fire insurance written by the ceding company at a future date, an American court held that an insurable interest subsisting during the risk and at the time of the loss was sufficient to support a reinsurance policy insuring against loss by fire. [4] Only with a facultative reinsurance might the ceding company not possess an insurable interest at the time the

---

1 Golding, *Law and Practice of Reinsurance,* p.9.
2 *Colonial Insurance Co. of New Zealand* v *Adelaide Marine Insurance Co.* (1886), 12 App. Cas. 128, 135.
3 N. Legh-Jones, *MacGillivray and Parkinson on Insurance Law*, 6th ed. (London, Sweet & Maxwell, 1975), p.25, who cites *Re London County Commercial Reinsurance Office*, [1922] 2 Ch.67.
4 *Sun Insurance Office* v *Merz*, 64 N.J.L. 301.

reinsurance is effected, but that is unlikely as enquiries for cover probably would be on the basis that the reinsurance attached only on completion of the underlying contract of insurance.

Utmost good faith

Reinsurance contracts, like other forms of insurance, are subject to the principle *uberrimae fidei* - of utmost good faith.[1] It is not sufficient that the parties merely refrain from making misrepresentations, they have a duty to disclose fully all material facts in the same way as the duty applies to contracts of direct insurance. This duty falls on both parties; as Lord Mansfield said:[2]

> Good faith forbids either party by concealing what he privately knows, to draw the other into a bargain, from his ignorance of that fact, and his believing the contrary ... The policy would be equally void, against the underwriters; if he concealed; as, if he insured a ship on her voyage which he privately knew to be arrived; and an action would be to recover the premium.

Likewise Farwell LJ said:[3]

> Contracts of insurance are contracts in which *uberrima fides* is required, not only from the assured, but also from the company assuring.

However, the duty of disclosure falls mainly on the party applying for the insurance, that is the proposer. As Scrutton LJ explained in *Rozanes v Bowen:*[4]

> It is the duty of the assured, the man who desired to have a policy, to make full disclosure to the underwriters without being asked of all the material circumstances, because the underwriters know nothing and the assured knows everything.

A test of what is material can be found in section 18(2) of the Marine Insurance Act 1906:

> Every circumstance is material which would influence the judgement of a prudent insurer in fixing the premium or determining whether he will take the risk.

---

1 See Lord Blackburn in *Brownlie v Campbell (1880), 5 App. Cas. 925, 954.*
2 *Carter v Boehm* (1766), 3 Burr. 1905, p.1909.
3 *Re Bradley and Essex and Suffolk Accident Indemnity Society*, [1912] 1 K.B.415, C.A.
4 (1928) 32 Ll. L.R. 98.

Whether a particular fact is material is a question of fact to be decided in the light of the particular circumstances prevailing at the time the fact should have been disclosed: it is no defence to show that subsequent events rendered the fact immaterial. At common law the duty of disclosure continues throughout the negotiations until with a marine insurance the slip is issued or in other classes of insurance a binding contract is concluded[1] (although direct insurers frequently insert in policies a condition which imposes a continuing duty on the insured). The test of 'a prudent insurer' is purely objective in the sense that it is immaterial whether the particular insurer would or would not have been influenced by the disclosure of a fact.

An insured is not bound to disclose any of the following facts, unless he is expressly asked about them.[2]

(1) Facts which he does not know, and which in the ordinary course of his business he could not be expected to know.

(2) Facts which diminish the risk.

(3) Facts which are known or can be presumed to be known to the insurer; that is facts which are either of common notoriety or knowledge, or which an insurer carrying on that particular class of insurance could be expected to know.

The duty of disclosure extends to any agent employed to make a contract of insurance on his principal's behalf. He must disclose all of the facts which the principal knows or ought to know, and any facts which he has discovered in the course of his agency. However, in the case of *Blackburn* v *Vigors*,[3] it was held that just because a reinsurance broker had received notice of a matter it could not be implied that his principal also knew of it unless the knowledge came to the broker in the course of his employment and it was the broker's duty to communicate such knowledge to his principal.

Application to reinsurance

Applying these general principles to reinsurance, the same duty of disclosure which rests on the original insured during the negotiations leading up to the conclusion of an insurance contract, now falls on the ceding company. The main difference is that both parties can be assumed to be experts, equally knowledgeable about the business they are transacting.

A reinsured cannot avail himself of the defence that he passed on incorrect or inadequate information supplied to him by the original

---

1 N. Legh-Jones, *MacGillivray and Parkington on Insurance Law*, p.294.
2 Marine Insurance Act 1906, s.18.
3 (1897) 12 App. Cas. 531, 541.

insured.[1] Furthermore whereas the latter may not be bound to disclose anything about his character which may adversely affect the risk, the ceding company must disclose to the reinsurer all that it knows about its insured.[2] Disclosure of information regarding past criminal activities of British policyholders is, however, limited by statute. The Rehabilitation of Offenders Act 1974 provides that after a specified rehabilitation period all details of any person's convictions for criminal (including motoring) offences can be removed from the records, and penalties are imposed on any one who passes information about 'spent' convictions to a third party. There is no reason to doubt that the Act applies to communications between insurers and reinsurers.

Whether representations made by an original insured are relevant to the validity of a reinsurance contract depends on its terms. If an original insured before the conclusion of his insurance makes incorrect statements which are warranted true in the original policy and in turn are clearly stated to form the basis of the reinsurance contract, the reinsurer on discovering the truth is entitled to repudiate liability.[3] Similarly the terms of a reinsurance contract may indicate that the original insurer adopted its insured's statements and warranted their accuracy at the time the reinsurance was effected, so rendering the latter contract void (or voidable) if at that time the statements were untrue. Alternatively the recital of the original declaration may be interpreted as simply informing the reinsurers of the declaration which formed the basis of the original policy.[4]

The nature of the facts which should be disclosed by a ceding company have been expressed by Golding as follows:[5]

> The foundation of a reinsurance is:
> (1) Full information, so far as possessed by the ceding company as to the risk on which the reinsurance is requested.[6]
> (2) Full information as to the amount retained by the ceding company on the identical property on which the reinsurance is requested.

A ceding company will be held to have knowledge of those facts which

---

1 *Equitable Life Assurance Socy* v *General Accident Assurance Corp.*, (1904) 12 S.L.T. 348.
2 *Ionides* v *Pender* (1874), L.R. 9 Q.B. 531. An American decision on the same point was *New York B.F. Insurance Co.* v *New York Fire Insurance Co.*, 17 Wend. 359.
3 *Australian Widows Fund Life* v *National Mutual Life Association of Australia Ltd.*, [1914] A.C. 634.
4 Legh-Jones, *MacGillivray and Parkington on Insurance Law*, p.295, who cites the divided opinion of the court as to the correct interpretation of the declaration in *Foster* v *Mentor Life* (1854), 3 E. & B. 48.
5 Golding, *Law and Practice of Reinsurance*, p.9.
6 For example, in *Equitable Life Assurance Socy* v *General Accident Assurance Corp.*, (1904) 12 S.L.T. 348 it was held that where a proposer for a life insurance stated that his occupation was 'driving motor cars' and the insurers in applying for reinsurance produced their policy showing the occupation as 'gentleman' without disclosing that he occasionally drove in races, the reinsurers were able to repudiate the reinsurance contract.

in the ordinary course of its business it ought to know.[1] It may be presumed by the reinsurer that the original insurances are subject to all of the terms and conditions usually applying to that class of business, and the ceding company must disclose any unusual omissions or additions.[2]

It is necessary, however, to distinguish facultative reinsurance from treaty reinsurances both in relation to the facts which should be disclosed and the duration of the duty.

Facultative reinsurances

The duty of a ceding company in relation to the facultative reinsurance of individual risks is analogous to that of the original insured, both as to the nature of the facts which must be disclosed and the duration of the duty of disclosure. The business is normally offered to the reinsurer by means of a slip on which all of the material particulars of the risk must be shown, including:

(1) Details of any losses incurred by the ceding company on that business. Ignorance of the details or significance of the loss experience is no excuse for non-disclosure where the relevant facts are either already in the possession of, or are available, to the ceding company.[3]

(2) The prospective ceding company's own retention. If the company revises its proposed retention before the reinsurance is concluded the fact must be disclosed.[4]

Treaty reinsurances

Of necessity the principle of utmost good faith is substantially modified for treaty reinsurances. Treaties were devised to eliminate the need for ceding companies to submit details of each particular risk and retention to the reinsurer for individual acceptance. Furthermore the use of bordereaux has so declined that often under proportional reinsurance treaties the reinsurer receives little or no information about the individual risks ceded, and under non-proportional reinsurances he has no direct interest in the individual risks written by the ceding company.

---

1 *London General Insurance Co.* v *General Marine Underwriters' Association,* [1921] 1 K.B. 104.
2 *Charlesworth* v *Faber* (1900), 5 Com. Cas. 408; *Vallance* v *Dewar* (1808), 1 Camp. 503.
3 *London General Insurance Co.* v *General Marine Underwriters' Association* [1921] 1 K.B. 104: 4 LP.L Rep.382 where details of a casualty had been reported in *Lloyd's List*, though the plaintiffs had not read it before reinsuring the risk. *General Accident, Fire and Life Assurance Corporation Ltd* v *Campbell* (1925) 21 LC, L.R.151 where the defendant, having asked for more information before agreeing to accept a reinsurance, was given information about losses already reported to the plaintiff which amounted to a misstatement or led to a non-disclosure of material facts.
4 *Traill* v *Baring* (1864), 33 L.J.Ch.521.

Nevertheless, the duty of utmost good faith still remains.

The type of information which must be supplied to the reinsurer(s) under a treaty will be dealt with more fully in later chapters. As will be seen much depends on the class of reinsurance concerned. One distinction between facultative and treaty reinsurances is the time when the duty of disclosure ceases. Golding says that:[1]

> The ordinary rule as to disclosure of material facts operates only up to the time the contract is concluded, but it may be submitted that under a treaty something more may be required. The mere completion of the contract is but the beginning, not the end of the reinsurance operations which are contemplated thereunder. Every time a cession is made under a treaty this initiates an actual reinsurance, and though the details which have to be communicated to the reinsurer are limited, yet in the general operation of the treaty the ceding company is bound to exercise the utmost good faith towards its reinsurer, even though this must occur after the contract was completed.

Exactly what Golding had in mind can only be conjectured. Under quota share and non-proportional reinsurance treaties any risks accepted by the reinsured are ceded automatically to the reinsurer, provided they fall within the terms of the treaty, so the duty of disclosure imposed by the principle of utmost good faith does not apply after the treaty has been concluded. Likewise with surplus treaties and open covers, as the reinsurer is obliged to accept risks ceded in accordance with the reinsurance agreement there can be no question of the underwriter being influenced in deciding what to accept or what terms to apply. The one element of good faith that does remain in such cases is that the reinsured should not try to cheat his reinsurer by making fraudulent claims or deliberately incurring a loss. For example, it would not be open to a ceding company to make a cession under a treaty after a loss had already occurred under the original policy, although often a clause is inserted in treaties permitting such action provided the ceding company keeps its normal retention.

Waiver of common law duty

The parties to a reinsurance contract may agree to waive their rights to be informed of material facts. In the case of *Property Insurance Company Ltd* v *National Protector Insurance Company Ltd*,[2] the plaintiff had reinsured a hull policy and retroceded part to the defendants. The original policy and the reinsurance contract both contained a clause

1 Golding, *Law and Practice of Reinsurance*, p.10.
2 (1913), 108 L.T.104.

permitting the ship to operate on the Canadian lakes at an additional premium, and the retrocession contract contained a written clause reading: 'Subject without notice to the same clauses and conditions'. The court held that although liberty to navigate the Canadian lakes was a material fact that ought to have been disclosed under normal circumstances, the defendants, under the terms of the clause and in particular the words 'Subject without notice', had waived their rights to such disclosure.

Closely related to waiver by the terms of the agreement is the position of errors and omissions clauses in the case of surplus treaties (see below).

Remedies for breach of duty

When a reinsurer can prove that there has been a breach of utmost good faith he has the same options available as a direct insurer. Upon becoming aware of a breach, whether of non-disclosure or misrepresentation, and whether innocent or fraudulent, the reinsurer has the right to avoid the contract *ab initio*. If he fails to exercise that right within a reasonable time he will be held to have waived his right to do so and the contract will remain in force.

Variations in the duty of disclosure

A ceding company can only be expected to disclose what it has been told by its own insured or such facts as, in the ordinary course of its business, it ought to know about the risk to be reinsured. The duty placed on an original insured by English law, however, is more stringent than that imposed in many other countries. Consequently the rights of a reinsurer following the discovery of an innocent non-disclosure by the original insured must be influenced by the proper law of the reinsurance contract.

It is possible that in Britain before long the duty will be relaxed somewhat. The existing law has been criticized in various quarters and by the Law Reform Committee.[1] Also discussions taking place within the European Economic Community regarding the law of contract relating to insurance contracts are expected to lead to the adoption of common rules throughout the Community. However it would appear that such rules are not intended to apply to reinsurance contracts.

---

1 See Legh-Jones, *MacGillivray and Parkinson on Insurance Law*, pp.336-8 for a discussion of the issue.

Indemnity

All reinsurance contracts are contracts of indemnity, the general principle being that the liability of the reinsurer is restricted to the actual loss which the ceding company has suffered, subject to the limit of the contract of reinsurance.[1] Even if the original insurance is not one of indemnity, as with life and other insurances on human life, the principle will apply to any reinsurance contract on the same subject-matter of insurance.

Limitations to the reinsured's rights to an indemnity

A ceding company must be able to prove that the loss for which it claims an indemnity from its reinsurer(s) falls within the terms of the reinsurance contract, and that it was itself liable to pay the loss.[2] Thus if a ceding company makes an *ex gratia* payment for a loss suffered by its insured, it will have no right to an indemnity from its reinsurer(s); in *Chippendale* v *Holt*,[3] it was held that the term in the reinsurance contract 'to pay as may be paid thereon' should be construed to mean 'to be properly paid thereon'. Likewise the indemnity provided by a reinsurance does not include costs incurred by the ceding company without the reinsurer's consent in resisting or defending a claim for which otherwise the reinsurer would have been liable.[4] However, where an original liability policy contained a clause indemnifying the original insured against costs incurred in defending a claim and entitled the insurer to take over the defence of their insured, the reinsurers who had reinsured 'liability under the policy' were held liable to indemnify the original insurer for costs incurred.[5]

In practice a ceding company usually wishes to bind its reinsurer(s) by its settlements. Therefore the strict rules of common law are often overridden by the incorporation into reinsurance contracts of conditions giving the primary insurer the right to settle all claims at his discretion and look to the reinsurer for an indemnity.

A number of cases have come before the courts where words similar to those used in the case of *Chippendale* v *Holt* have been included in the reinsurance contract.[6] In *Western Assurance Company of Toronto* v

---

1 American law follows the same principle: *Hone* v *Mutual Safety Insurance Co.,* 3 N.Y. Super 137; affd. 2 N.Y. 235.
2 *St. Paul Fire & Marine Company* v *Morice* (1906), 22 T.L.R. 449; and *Merchants Marine Insurance Co.* v *Liverpool Marine & General Insurance Co.* (1928), 44 T.L.R. 512.
3 (1895) 73 L.T. 472.
4 *Scottish Metropolitan Insurance Co.* v *Groom* (1924), 40 T.L.R. 676.
5 *British General Insurance Co.* v *Mountain* (1919), 1 Lloyd's L.R. 605; 36 T.L.R. 171.
6 See 'Compromose settlement', *Reinsurance,* July 1970.

Poole,[1] where the same words were used, Bingham J. agreed that the reinsurer could only be liable for losses for which the primary insurer was liable under the original insurance and which fell within the terms of the reinsurance contract but added:

> So long as liability exists, the mere fact of some honest mistake having occurred in fixing the amount of it will afford (the reinsurer) no excuse for not paying.

Thus the reinsurer was held liable for a compromise settlement as to the amount of the loss. In *Excess Insurance Company Ltd* v *Mathews*[2] the reinsurance contract included a clause which read, 'and to pay as may be paid thereon and to follow their settlements'. Branson J held that the words 'to follow their settlements' extended to cover compromise settlements where the liability of the primary insurer was in doubt.

So depending on the exact words of the contract a reinsurer may have to pay on compromise settlements as to amount and liability, provided the settlements were made honestly and with due care. In neither of the above cases, however, were the words used sufficiently wide as to bind the reinsurer to indemnify the reinsured for *ex gratia* settlements (i.e. a payment made with no question of legal liability to do so). Whether a 'follow the fortune' clause in a reinsurance contract would embrace *ex gratia* settlements is not clear. In the American case of *Insurance Company of North America* v *US Fire Insurance Company* it was held by the Supreme Court of the State of New York that 'follow the fortune' had the same meaning as 'pay as may be paid'. However, again it would appear that each case must be judged according to the precise wording of the clause. If the intention of the parties to the reinsurance contract is to give the reinsured absolute discretion in handling claims, including the right to make *ex gratia* payments and to bind the reinsurer to follow, then the agreement must be made clear as in the following specimen clause typically inserted into reinsurance treaties:[3]

1 [1903] K.B.376.
2 (1925) 31 Com. Cas.43.
3 See 'Follow the fortune', *Reinsurance*, October 1971. Dr Golding appears to have agreed with this interpretation of the position. In speaking of 'follow the fortune' clauses he says:
> In the opinion of the writer their intention is to set up a kind of partnership in treaty matters, so that whatever fortune, good or bad, should befall the ceding company should be shared by the reinsurer and whatever the ceding company should decide to do in relation to any treaty matter should be equally binding on the reinsurer, even though it had not been consulted. This would clearly cover such things as mistakes or omissions in ceding, contesting of claims or making *ex gratia* payments and compromises of all kinds which the ceding company may see fit to make with its own insured.

Later he adds:
> Whatever is to be done must be within the four walls of the contract. Therein the ceding company is to have freedom to conduct the affairs of the treaty as it deems best, but not to stray outside them. It would not even give the power to make *ex gratia* payments so as to bind the reinsurer unless such a power were expressly reserved by the terms of the contract. (*Law and Practice of Reinsurance*, p.63).

The ceding company have the sole right to settle claims either by way of compromise 'ex gratia' payments, or otherwise, and all settlements are binding on the reinsurers. The reinsurers should be liable for their share of any costs incurred in resisting or defending any claim.

Clauses dealing with compromise and *ex gratia* settlements are not so common in facultative business, though since the rules of the Fire Offices' Committee contain similar provisions, they are by implication imported into facultative reinsurances arranged between members of that association.

A reinsurer is always entitled to call for proof of the original loss.[1] In view of the rulings regarding *ex gratia* payments it is not sufficient for a ceding company to show that it has paid a claim under the original policy.[2]

Time and extent of a reinsurer's liability

The precise manner in which the principle of indemnity is applied to reinsurance contracts is less clear regarding both the timing and extent of the reinsurer's liability. It would seem that a contract of reinsurance may be interpreted in three possible ways:[3]

(1) As a contract of indemnity against actual payment by the reinsured.[4] In this case the reinsurer would not be required to indemnify the ceding company until the latter had made a payment to its insured.

(2) As a contract of indemnity against liability in the sense that the liability is the final amount for which the ceding company settles a claim brought within the terms of the original policy. Then the reinsurer would be required to pay as soon as the final settlement had been agreed or the ceding company had been found liable to make payment by due process of law.[5] Thus it was held that where a reinsurance claim was payable in a foreign currency and the rate of exchange changed between the date of the loss and when the ceding insurer agreed a final settlement with the original insured, the reinsurer was liable at the rate prevailing at the date of settlement.[6]

(3) As a contract to pay on the happening of a contingency, so that the reinsurer becomes liable to pay as soon as the contingency occurs,

---

1 Mathew L.J. in *Nelson v Empress Assurance*, [1905] 2 K.B. 281, 285.
2 Bateson J. in *Fireman's Fund Insurance Co. v Western Australian Insurance Co. and Atlantic Insurance Co.* (1928), 138 L.T. 108.
3 'Contracts of indemnity', *Reinsurance*, August 1969.
4 In the *Fireman's Fund Insurance Co.* case (*supra*), Bateson J. said: 'As I understand it, a contract of reinsurance is a contract to indemnify against liability and a payment. There must be both liability and payment, and the precise liability must be covered in each case.'
5 *Re Eddystone Marine Insurance Company*, 66 L.T. Rep 370; [1892] 2 Ch.423.
6 *Versicherungs und Transport Aktiengesellschaft Daugava v Henderson* (1934), 151 L.T. 392.

even if the ceding company suffers no loss or subsequently secures a reduction in its loss.[1]

The manner in which the courts would construe a particular contract of reinsurance would seem to depend upon the words employed by the parties to express their agreement.[2] The Legal Correspondent of *Reinsurance* concludes, however, that:[3]

> It is not very probable that the courts would hold a reinsurance contract to be a contract for payment on a contingency unless this was clearly called for by the wording of the contract, other than in cases where the liquidation of the reinsured was concerned and the original policies were policies of contingency or near contingency insurance themselves.

The distinction in practice between the first two types of contract in general is not significant. Usually there is little delay between a final settlement being agreed with the original insured and the insurer paying the claim. However, if the contract were construed as one of indemnity against liability, the ceding company would be entitled to receive the reinsurance monies even if it did not pay its insured the agreed sum, and it could retain them so long as its liability subsisted.

Reinsurer's rights of recovery

Whether the reinsurance contract be construed as one of indemnity against payment or against liability, the reinsurer is equally entitled to recover his share of any amount by which the reinsured's liability is reduced.[4] Thus a reinsurer, having indemnified his reinsured, is entitled to benefit from any recovery which the primary insurer obtains by the succesful exercise of his rights to subrogation or contribution arising from the loss.[5] The American courts have also held that a reinsurer not only has 'an interest in the disposition of salvage but also a right to ask

---

1 See in *Re Law Guarantee Trust & Accident Society Ltd, Godson's Claim,* [1915] 1 Ch.341, Neville J.'s comments on the judgments given in the Court of Appeal in *Re Law Guarantee Trust & Accident Society Limited, Liverpool Mortgage Company's Case,* [1914] 2 Ch. 617.

2 In the United States Supreme Court case of *Fidelity & Deposit Co.* v *Pink*, 302 U.S. 224, 229 (1937) it was held that the liabilities under a reinsurance contract must 'be determined upon consideration of the words employed, read in the light of attending circumstances'.

3 'Contracts of indemnity', *Reinsurance*, August 1969.

4 Lord Blackburn in *Burnard* v *Rodocanachi*, 7 App. Cas.333, expressed the principle as follows, 'The general rule of law (and it is obvious justice) is that where there is a contract of indemnity (it matters not whether it is a marine policy, or a policy against fire on land, or any other contract of indemnity) and a loss happens, anything which reduces or diminishes that loss reduces or diminishes the amount which the indemnifier is bound to pay; and if the indemnifier has already paid it, then, if anything which diminishes the loss comes into the hands of the person to whom he has paid it, it becomes an equity that the person who has already paid the full indemnity is entitled to be recouped by having that amount back.'

5 For subrogation rights see *Assicurazioni Generali di Trieste* v *Empress Assurance Corporation* (1907) 2 K.B.L.R. 814; and in the United States *Universal Insurance Co.* v *Old Time Molasses Co. et al*, 46 Fed (2d) 925. For contribution rights see *Union Marine Insurance Co.* v *Martin* (1866), 35 L.J.C.P.181.

that it be prudently and carefully managed'.[1]

Where the ceding company incurs any reasonable expenses in pursuing its subrogation rights, it is entitled to deduct such expenses from the resulting sum it recovers for the benefit of its reinsurer(s).[2] Usually, treaties contain a clause dealing with expenses and recoveries. Under excess of loss treaties an 'ultimate net loss' clause normally provides that the net recovery (that is, the amount recovered less expenses incurred) shall be applied first in reduction of the ultimate net loss reinsured. In the case of proportional reinsurances it is usual for the clause to apply net recoveries in agreed proportions between the ceding company and the reinsurer(s).

The reinsurer's right to share in any recovery which reduces the ceding company's loss is limited to any action which the latter party could have brought under the reinsured portion of the original insurance.

Construction of a reinsurance policy

English courts follow the same general rules for construing reinsurance contracts as apply to other contracts, including other policies of insurance. American courts have followed the same principle. In the case of *Stickel* v *Excess Insurance Co. of America* (*supra* p.115) it was said of the reinsurance policy:

> It has long been an established rule that contracts of insurance should be construed like other contracts, so as to give effect to the intention of the parties expressed by the language of the parties ... And a court cannot extend or enlarge the contract by implication so as to embrace an object distinct from that originally contemplated.[3]

The courts in other cases added:

> The language used is given its usual and ordinary meaning.[4]

> ... taking into account, when the meaning is doubtful, the surrounding circumstances. Custom or usage is presumed to enter into the intention when it is found as a fact, not only that it existed, but was uniform

---

1 Thompson, *Reinsurance*, p.366, who cites *Maryland Casualty Co.* v *City of Cincinnati et al.* 291 Fed. 825
2 *Assicurazioni Generali di Trieste* (*supra*).
3 In *Norwich Union Fire Insurance* v *Colonial Mutual Fire Insurance Co.* [1922] 2 K.B. 461, 466, a case concerning marine insurance, McCardie J. said, 'a policy of insurance and its attendant burdens and rights must, subject to any special rules of law, and to any statutory provisions applicable to insurance, be construed upon the normal principles of contract which prevail in the English courts. Insurance, after all, is a mere branch of the general body of contracts. The question here (i.e. under the policy of reinsurance) must be tested with that consideration in mind.'
4 *Justice* v *Stuyvesant Insurance Company*, 265 F. Supp. 63.

and either known to the parties when the contract was made, or so generally known as to raise a presumption that they had it in mind at the time.[1]

Regrettably it is not always clear exactly what is intended by words and phrases used in reinsurance contracts. In the case of *Law Guarantee Trust and Accident Society Ltd* v *Munich Reinsurance Company*,[2] Eve J. described the contract as:

made up ... of paragraphs culled from several different precedents and strung together without any accurate estimate of their relative consistency.

Likewise Justice O'Brien in the *Continental Insurance Company* v *Aetna Insurance Company*[3] case said:

But we know that the multifarious transactions of businessmen are not always preceded by carefully and accurately measuring their words, nor are their ordinary agreements or contracts always drawn by persons skilled in the use of the language.

Inevitably, imprecision in recording the terms of the agreement between the parties leads to disputes involving the wording of reinsurance contracts, and examples of the manner in which English courts have applied the normal rules of construction to reinsurance policies in order to ascertain the intentions of the parties can be seen in three cases. In the case of *Excess Insurance Company Ltd* v *Mathews*[4] Branson J. recognized that the word 'settlement' has a technical meaning at Lloyd's but held that:

The use of the word 'follow' with the word 'settlements' indicates that the latter word is used in the sense of 'compromise' and not a mere settlement in account.

Where a reinsurance was expressed in a typewritten slip attached to an ordinary fire policy, it was held that the writing overrode the printed policy.[5] Finally, in the case of *Western Assurance Company of Toronto* v *Poole*,[6] the court sought to ascertain the intention of the parties to a contract of reinsurance in order to reconcile an inconsistency in its terms.

---

1 *Continental Insurance Co.* v *Aetna Insurance Co.*, 138 N.Y. 16.
2 (1915) 31 L.T.R. 572.
3 138 N.Y.16.
4 (1925) 31 Com Cas. 43.
5 *Home Insurance Company of New York* v *Victoria-Montreal Fire Insurance Co.* [1907] A.C. 59, P.C.
6 [1903] 1 K.B. 376.

134

Incorporating the terms of the original policy

A question of construction relevant only to reinsurance contracts is to what extent the parties may intend that the terms and conditions of the original insurance shall apply to the reinsurance policy. Frequently clauses are inserted in reinsurance policies incorporating the terms of the original policy by reference; for example:

> Every reinsurance ceded hereby is subject to all the conditions of the original insurance.
> Subject to the same clauses and conditions as the original policies.

In the marine-cargo insurance case of *Joyce* v *The Realm Marine Insurance Company*, [1] the plaintiff had reinsured with the defendants the homeward part of a round voyage he had insured, and the reinsurance policy contained a clause reading:

> being a reinsurance subject to all of the clauses and conditions of the original policy, and to pay, as may be paid thereon.

One of the clauses in the original policy provided that any part of the outward cargo that remained on board for twenty-four hours after the vessel arrived on the coast of Africa should be deemed to have been shipped upon the homeward journey. It was held that the defendants were liable to pay for loss to such cargo although under the terms of the outward reinsurance policy the risk upon the goods was to commence, 'From the loading thereof on board the said ship,'

The case of *Home Insurance Company of New York* v *Victoria-Montreal Fire Insurance Company*[2] concerned a retrocession of a fire insurance effected by affixing to a printed fire policy a typewritten slip containing the special terms relating to the retrocession which was stated to attach to and form part of the policy. One of the printed conditions of the policy read:

> No suit or action on this policy for the recovery of any claims shall be sustainable in any court of law or equity until after full compliance by the insured with all of the foregoing requirements nor unless commenced within twelve months next after the fire.

The court criticized the careless manner in which the reinsurance policy had been prepared but held that a condition which it was reasonable for an original insured to observe could not reasonably be held to bind the

1 (1872) L.R. 7 Q.B. 580.
2 [1907] A.C. 59.

retrocessionaire who could not sue on the reinsurance policy until the direct loss was ascertained between parties over whom he could exercise no control.

In the case of Australian Widows Life Assurance Society v *Life Association of Australia Ltd,*[1] the contract of reinsurance included a clause that 'The proposal for reinsurance was deemed to be part of, and incorporated in, the reinsurance contract.' The reinsurance proposal contained a clause reading:

> It is understood that in accepting the risk under this reinsurance the Australian Widows Fund Life Assurance Society Limited does so on the same terms and conditions on which the National Mutual Life Association of Australia Limited, have granted a policy and by whom, in the event of claims, the settlement will be made.

The court held that the clause in question could not be held to contradict the express provisions of the reinsurance policy.

It would seem, therefore, that the effect of such clauses is to incorporate into the reinsurance policy such terms and conditions of the original policy as are 'reasonably applicable to such a contract of reinsurance between the parties and such terms and conditions, therefore, as the parties may be presumed to have had in mind when the contract was made.' Such was the view expressed by an American court in the case of *Homan* v *Employers Reinsurance Corporation*[2] where a clause in the reinsurance contract made it subject to 'all of the general and special conditions of such (original) policies and endorsements', copies of which were supplied to the reinsurer. The primary insurer became insolvent and the court held that an express provision in the original policy enabled the insured to bring an action directly against the reinsurer to recover the reinsured portion of a loss he had suffered.

Although the legal principles may be reasonably clear, the effect of the clauses in practice is far from certain. As argued by the Legal Correspondent of *Reinsurance,*[3] there are almost bound to be some conditions in any particular original policy about which it is impossible to be certain whether or not the intention of the parties was to incorporate them into the reinsurance contract. Furthermore, in the cases cited above, the reinsurer either had the opportunity to discover the actual terms of the original policies because the reinsurance was facultative or, as in the *Homan* case, he had had copies sent to him. Often where treaty reinsurances are concerned the reinsurer has no detailed knowledge of the terms of the original policies and so does not

1 [1914] A.C. 634.
2 136 S.W.(2d) 289.
3 'The intent of the parties', *Reinsurance*, July 1972.

know what may be incorporated into the reinsurance contract so that the consequences of using such clauses becomes unpredictable. [1]

Errors and omissions clauses

Frequently reinsurance treaties contain errors and omissions clauses and it seems likely that these clauses had their origins in the reinsured's obligation to supply the reinsurer with various bordereaux; for example, the following clause is taken from a surplus treaty: [2]

> Error delay or omission on the part of the company in rendering any account or furnishing any bordereau or making any entry in the reinsurance books or bordereau or notifying any claims or giving any information which ought under the provisions hereof to be given shall not invalidate any obligation imposed on the reinsurer hereunder.

Under a surplus treaty (though, arguably, not under a quota share treaty) the reinsured has to take further action after the treaty agreement has been concluded to make it complete; that is, he has to decide what proportion of the risk he shall retain, and he may be required to record such decisions in writing in bordereaux. In the absence of an errors and omissions clause the failure of the reinsured to record such information may place him in the situation where, depending upon the legal status of the bordereaux, he could either ask for rectification of the contract or be held in breach of a condition. The clauses in surplus treaties dealing with the supply of bordereaux usually indicate that they are to be merely regarded as records of what *has been* ceded and not of what is to be ceded, so that failure to complete a bordereau correctly would amount to a breach of condition entitling the reinsurer to damages for the loss he has suffered, and the reinsured would then be able to recover his loss. It would seem, however, that the original purpose of such clauses was to provide an easy remedy only where the reinsured had failed to record correctly his intentions at the time, so that if a reinsured subsequently changed his mind about a retention (for example, after a loss had occurred) he would not be able to claim rectification at the expense of the reinsurer. [3] In practice the wording of clauses differs substantially so that exactly how any particular clause would be construed by the courts must depend upon its precise wording and the terms of the clause dealing with the supply of bordereaux. In no case though would fraudulent behaviour, such as deliberate concealment or misdescription of any risk, be excused.

1 Ibid.
2 'Errors and omissions clause', *Reinsurance*, February 1970.
3 Ibid.

Once it is discovered that an entry has not been made in the reinsured's books or on a bordereau so that by error or omission a risk has not been properly ceded, the reinsurer normally becomes entitled to receive the appropriate premium from the time the reinsurance is deemed to have run.

The scope of errors and omissions clauses is not restricted simply to the completion of bordereaux under proportional reinsurances. The clause quoted above also includes, *inter alia*, the notification of claims, and as excess of loss treaties do not require the completion of bordereaux, the following clause taken from an excess of loss treaty presumably applies to the claims-reporting provisions of the treaty:

> No error or inadvertent omission on the part of the company shall relieve the reinsurer of liability in respect of losses hereunder provided that such errors and/or omissions are rectified as soon after discovery as possible.

The consequences of such a clause could be to vitiate the provisions of the claims-reporting clause,[1] with all of the implications that has for the reinsurer by way of exercising control over claims, reserving for outstanding claims and calculating premiums.

Rights of the reinsured's policyholders

In English law the reinsured's policyholders, whether they be the original insured or in the case of a retrocession an insurer, have no interest in, and therefore neither obtain any rights nor incur any liabilities under, a reinsurance contract.[2] As Bingham J. said in *Western Assurance Company of Toronto v Poole*:

> There is no privity between the original assured and the reinsurer. The liability of the latter is only to indemnify the insurer, the reassured, in respect of a loss for which he is liable to the assured by reason of his insurance policy.[3]

The same general principle applies in American law too,[4] the general rule being that 'A reinsurer has no contractual obligations with the original insured and is not liable to him.'[5]

---

[1] Ibid.

[2] Golding, *Law and Practice of Reinsurance*, p.5.

[3] (1903) K.B. 13, 376.

[4] Thompson, *Reinsurance*, p.334, who cites *Republic Metalware Company v General Reinsurance Corporation*, 245 App. Div. 232, 281, N.Y.S.5, 282, N.Y.S.993.

[5] Ibid., p.337, citing *Morrow v Burlington Basket Co.*, 66 S.W. 2(d) 746; and *Hoffman v North British & Mercantile Insurance Co.* 70 N.Y.S.106, 35 Misc.40.

A major difference between the two systems of law lies in the effect of the parties incorporating into a reinsurance contract special provisions giving the reinsured's policyholders an interest therein. American courts have held that a clause in a reinsurance contract giving an original insured the right to claim direct against the reinsurer is enforceable in the insured's favour even though he is not a party to the contract. In the case of *Bruckner-Mitchell* v *Sun Indemnity Co. of New York*,[1] the court said:

> It is true that typical reinsurance agreements do not operate in favour of the original insured. They are merely contracts of indemnity of the insurer and there is no privity between the original insured and the reinsurer. But nothing in law forbids drafting reinsurance agreements in special terms so that they will operate in favor of the original insured.

It was noted above (page 136) that in the *Homan* v *Employers Reinsurance Corporation* case it was held that the original insured, unable to obtain an indemnity from his insurers because of their insolvency, was entitled to take advantage of such a special provision in the reinsurance contract to claim direct from the reinsurers for their share of the loss. Therefore, to avoid the difficulties that, following the insolvency of the reinsured, can arise in connection with such matters as the extent of the reinsurer's liabilities, persons entitled to payment and so forth, it is often the practice in America to insert in reinsurance contracts 'cut-through' or 'loss-assumption' clauses whereas in Britain they are used only in retrocession contracts. Such clauses permit the reinsurer, in the event of the ceding company's insolvency, to pay the company's policyholders direct for the reinsured portion of losses they have suffered and to obtain from them a full discharge from any further liability.

Thompson also points out that in certain circumstances an original insured in America may be given a statutory right by a state to sue a reinsurer direct.[2]

Under English law it is very doubtful whether any special agreement between the parties to a reinsurance contract, that is the ceding company and the reinsurer, could confer such rights on the reinsured's policyholders in that it would conflict with the fundamental principle of privity of contract.[3] It is very uncertain whether the policyholder has a right either to bring an action at common law against the reinsurer to

---

1 82 Fed.(2d) 434, 444; 298 U.S. 677.
2 Thompson, *Reinsurance*, p.339.
3 Lord Haldane in *Dunlop* v *Selfridge*, [1915] A.C. 847, said: 'In the law of England certain principles are fundamental. One is that only a person who is a party to a contract can sue on it. Our law knows nothing of a *jus quaesitum tertio* arising by way of contract. Such a right may be conferred by way of property, as, for example, under a trust, but it cannot be conferred on a stranger to a contract as a right to enforce the contract *in personam*.'

enforce him to make a payment for the policyholder's benefit,[1] or to establish in equity that the contracting parties entered into a contract as a trustee on his behalf so that he could sue the reinsurer as a trustee.[2] It would be possible, however, for a reinsurer to create a trust for the benefit of the original policyholders, but this would require an express declaration of trust in the proper form.

Therefore, J.S. Butler concludes that in English law the validity of cut-through clauses is extremely dubious, and if the parties to a reinsurance contract wish to ensure that in the event of the reinsured's insolvency his policyholders will be able to recover direct from the reinsurer the reinsured portion of any losses they suffer then other methods would have to be used.[3]

Insolvency of the reinsured

Rights of the the reinsured's policyholders and third parties

As noted above, the general principle of English law is that only the parties to a reinsurance contract, that is the ceding insurer and the reinsurer, have any rights thereunder and so can sue for the payment of any benefit due thereunder. Consequently in the event of a ceding company becoming insolvent and thus being unable to meet in full liabilities it has incurred to policyholders or third parties under policies it has issued, such policyholders or third parties have no right to sue the reinsurer in order to recover the reinsured part of such loss.[4] The provisions of the Third Parties (Rights against Insurers) Act 1930 which confer on third parties the rights to claim directly against liability insurers in the event of the insured becoming insolvent do not extend to contracts of reinsurance (s.1(5)).

Generally the same principle that an original insured or a third party cannot proceed against a reinsurer in the event of the reinsured's insolvency also holds in American law.[5]

Normally, therefore, following the insolvency of the reinsured any sums due from the reinsurer, including sums due in respect of reinsured losses, will go to swell the reinsured company's general assets, and the

---

1 See Lord Reid's comments on the views expressed by Lord Denning on this principle in *Beswick* v *Beswick*, [1966] 3 All E.R. 1, when the case went to the House of Lords.

2 See *Green* v *Russell*, [1959] 2 All E.R. 525, where it was held that an employer by effecting a personal accident policy for the benefit of his employees did not create a trusteeship.

3 'Cut-through clauses are no short cut', *Reinsurance*, November 1972.

4 See Marine Insurance Act 1906, s.9 (2).

5 See *Insurance Company of Pennsylvania* v *Park & Pollard Co.*, 190 App. Div. 388; *Greenman* v *General Reinsurance Corporation* 237 App. Div. 648, 262 N.Y.S 569; *Gutride* v *General Reinsurance Corporation* 167 Misc. 608; and Thompson, *Reinsurance*, pp. 339-43.

original insured or third parties will only have the right to prove as ordinary creditors for their share of the general assets.[1]

It is permissible, however, under American law for the parties to a reinsurance contract to make special provision for the reinsured's policyholders to recover direct from the reinsurer in the event of the reinsured's insolvency.[2] For example, the requirements of New York state and most other American states regarding the admissibility of reinsurance as an asset of the ceding company may be met by including a liquidation clause in the reinsurance contract. Such a clause would provide that one way in which the reinsurer's liabilities may be discharged is for payment to be made directly to the original insured.[3]

Effect on the amount and the timing of the reinsurer's liability

In considering the principle of indemnity it was suggested that, depending upon the words used, a contract of reinsurance could be interpreted in three possible ways.[4]

Considerable difficulties would arise in the event of the insolvency of the reinsured if the principle established in the case of *Fireman's Fund Insurance Co.*[5] was held to apply; that is, that the reinsurer's liability for losses was conditional on the original insured having first been paid.

Possibly it would mean that if the insurer possessed insufficient assets to pay policyholders' claims in full the reinsurer's liability would be reduced proportionately. However, there do not appear to have been any cases involving liquidation of the reinsured where English courts have construed a contract of reinsurance as being a contract of indemnity against payment. Therefore it may be concluded that a court would be prepared to follow that principle in a case of insolvency only if that were the obvious intention of the parties clearly expressed in the policy.

Two cases have come before the American courts where the wording of the contract expressed such an intention. The relevant clauses read:

> The Reinsurer's proportionate share of a loss ... shall be paid to the Reinsured upon proof of the payment of such items by the Reinsured.[6]
> The term 'ultimate net loss' shall be understood to mean ... the sum actually paid in cash in settlement of losses.[7]

---

1 *Re Law Guarantee Trust*, [1915] 1 Ch. 340; *Re Harrington Motor Co.*, [1928] Ch. 105.
2 See *Homan* v *Employers Reinsurance Corporation*, page 136 *supra*.
3 See page 144 *infra*.
4 See page 129 *supra*.
5 (1928) 138 L.T. 108.
6 *Fidelity and Deposit Company* v *Pink*, 302 U.S. 224, 230 (1937).
7 *Stickel* v *Excess Insurance Company*, Ohio Supreme Court, 22 November 1939, 23 N.E. (2nd) 839, 136 Ohio St. 49.

In both cases payment of a loss by the reinsured was held to be a condition precedent to the liability of the reinsurer. These judgments were contrary to that in *Allemannia Insurance Company* v *Firemen's Insurance Company*,[1] where the words in the reinsurance contract read:

> ... and losses, if any, shall be payable *pro rata* with, in the same manner, and upon the same terms and conditions as paid by the said reinsurance company (the reinsured) under its contracts hereby reinsured.

The court held that the reinsured did not first need to pay a loss before proceeding against the reinsurer, the latter being bound to indemnify the reinsured against his liability to his policyholders which was unaffected by the reinsured's insolvency.

English courts likewise would tend to construe reinsurance contracts as ones of indemnity against liability unless the contrary was called for by the terms of the contract. In such cases the liability of the reinsurer would in no way be diminished by the reinsured's insolvency; the reinsurer would remain liable to indemnify fully the ceding company for the reinsured portion of all claims settlements even though the latter company was unable to meet its policyholder's claims in full.[2] The reinsurer, however, may be able to set off against his total liability amounts owed by the reinsured.

Provided the reinsurance contract could be interpreted as either one of indemnity against liability or as a contract to pay on the happening of a contingency, the timing of the reinsurer's liability to pay for losses under a single facultative reinsurance likewise would not be affected by the reinsured becoming insolvent. Once the final settlement had been agreed (or in the second case the contingency had happened) the reinsurer would be liable to pay in full his share of the loss even though the original insured had not been paid or, because of the insufficiency of the reinsured's assets, there was no prospect of his claim being fully paid. However, where there may be a question of set-off, the reinsurer will only be liable to pay the liquidator when the amount of his final net liability under all of his contracts with the ceding company has been determined.

---

1 209 U.S. 326.
2 See *Re Eddystone Marine Insurance Company* (1892), 166 L.T. 370 and [1892] 2 Ch. 423, and *British Dominions General Insurance Company Limited* v *Duder*, [1915] 2 K.B. 394, regarding liability under contracts of indemnity against liability; and *Re Law Guarantee Trust and Accident Society*, [1914] 2 Ch. 617, on contracts to pay on a contingency. In the *British Dominions General* case Pickford L.J. said: 'The reinsurer has to pay the original insurer his liability, whether he had discharged it or not, and that it is immaterial to him what the original insurer does with the money. But there is no diminution of the liability; the original insurer, though bankrupt, is still liable for the full amount; if assets were to come in in time he could be made to pay; and even in his insolvent state, if the creditor could get judgment, he could be made to pay this particular creditor, if it were not for the bankruptcy laws, which compel an equal distribution of his assets.'

The American courts have similarly held in such circumstances that the liability of a reinsurer is not diminished or deferred merely because the ceding company has insufficient assets to pay its insureds' losses in full. In the case of *Ex parte Norwood*,[1] Judge Blodgett said of a clause in the reinsurance contract which read, 'loss, if any, payable at the same time and *pro rata* with the insured':

> Now it is to my mind absurd to say, if a loss occurs on one of those reinsured policies, that the company primarily liable is to have its claim against the reinsuring company limited by its ability to meet its obligations to its original policyholders. The very object of making the policy of reinsurance was to place the company in funds with which to make its policyholders whole, and that is defeated if the construction which is insisted upon by the assignee is the true one.
>
> I am of the opinion that the *Republic* is liable on these policies to the extent of the adjusted losses, even if the *Lorillard* had not been paid a cent.

The court in considering a similar clause said:[2]

> The condition in that policy that 'in case of loss the company shall pay *pro rata* at and in the same time and manner as the reinsured', cannot mean that in case of the insolvency of the Fulton Company the defendant shall only be obliged to pay the *pro rata* of the dividends of the assets of said company upon the claim of the first insured.

In the case of *Providence-Washington Fire Insurance Company* v *Atlanta-Birmingham Fire Insurance Company*,[3] it was held that the agreement of the policyholders of an insolvent insurance company to accept 30 per cent of their proved claims in full settlement did not reduce the reinsurer's share of those losses by 70 per cent; the reinsurer remained liable to pay in full.

The position of a liquidator

The liquidator of an insolvent ceding company possesses no greater rights with respect to a claim against the reinsurer than those possessed by the reinsured at the time of his appointment.[4]

When a winding-up order is made in Britain in respect of an insurance

---

1 3 Biss 504.
2 *Cashau* v *The Northwestern etc. Insurance Co.*, 5 Biss. 476.
3 166 Fed. 548.
4 The liquidator occupies the position of a trustee for the creditors (or the contributories in a solvent company) *per* Lord Selborne in *Re Black & Co's Case* (1872) L.R. 8 Ch. App. 254, or possibly an agent of the company with the special duty of applying the company's assets in paying creditors, *per* Romer J. in *Knowles & Scott*, [1891] 1 Ch. 717. His first duty is to take into custody or control all of the property, effects and things in action to which the company is or appears to be entitled (Companies Act 1948, s.243(1)). He is given no greater rights than those possessed by the company.

company transacting non-life insurance all outstanding policies are terminated and, apart from outstanding claims, the liability of the insolvent company is reduced to the repayment of unexpired premiums.[1] Consequently the liquidator is not called upon to enter into new reinsurance arrangements. In the case of a company carrying on long-term insurances, unless the court otherwise directs, the liquidator must carry on the long-term business with the view to transferring it as a going concern to another company.[2] Thus, although the liquidator may not effect new direct insurance contracts he may deem it necessary to alter existing, or arrange new, reinsurances in which case any agreement between the liquidator would be an expense of the liquidation payable in full.[3]

American law follows the same basic principles in relation to both the rights of a liquidator[4] and reinsurances arranged by him.[5]

Winding up and set-off

Insurance companies, including reinsurance companies, are subject in Britain to the normal rules applying to the winding up of companies, as modified by special statutory regulations relating to insurance companies.[6] It is not proposed here to review those rules but only to consider the relationship of reinsurers and reinsured in the event of the insolvency of either party.

At any point in time either party may have outstanding financial commitments to the other consisting of both outstanding balances on account, and of special funds held under the terms of the reinsurance contract. Examples of outstanding balances would be reinsurance premiums owed by the ceding company less payments for reinsured claims owed by the reinsurer, and typical of funds held under treaties would be the retention by the ceding company of funds to cover the technical reserves for reinsured risks. Consequently in the event of insolvency either party may stand in the position of a debtor or creditor. It is also possible that there may be more than one reinsurance contract in force between the parties with, say, the reinsurer simultaneously being a creditor under one and a debtor under another. Consequently questions of set-off may involve amounts owed by the parties under more than one contract.

1 Companies Act 1948, s.365; Insurance Companies Act 1974, s.51(1).
2 Insurance Companies Act 1974, s.48(1).
3 Companies Act 1948, s.245(1)(b).
4 See *Keehn* v *Excess Insurance Co.* 129 F 2d. 503.
5 See *Garris* v *Carpenter*, 1939 92P. 2d 688, 33 Col. App. 2d 649.
6 Insurance Companies Act 1974, ss.44 – 51.

Set-off is the process whereby either a debtor deducts any amounts owed to him by a creditor from the sum of his debt to that creditor and renders the balance in satisfaction, or a creditor deducts any amount owed by him to his debtor from the amount he is owed by that debtor and claims for the balance.

English law provides that where insolvent companies are concerned, the rights of a party to set-off are governed by section 317 of the Companies Act 1948, which provides that section 31 of the Bankruptcy Act 1914 (which itself reproduces section 39 of the Bankruptcy Act 1869), shall be applicable in the winding up of an insolvent company in the same manner as it is applicable to the administration of the estate of a person adjudged bankrupt. Section 31 of the Bankruptcy Act provides that where there have been mutual debts or other mutual dealings between the parties, the sum due from one party shall be set off against any sum due from the other party, and only the balance shall be claimed. Dealings covered by one contract clearly fall within the term 'mutual dealings', even if they consist of a number of separate transactions. Transactions under two or more contracts between the same persons may not necessarily amount to mutual dealings;[1] the test seems to be whether 'The dealings are so related that they can be fairly said to form part of a connected series of business transactions between the parties acting in the same right.'[2]

In the case of *Re City Equitable Fire Insurance Company Ltd (No.2)*,[3] the question of mutual reinsurance dealings between two parties involved both outstanding balances under a number of reinsurance contracts between the two parties, and a special deposit held by the reinsured under the terms of one treaty as security against the failure of the reinsurer to pay balances due under that treaty, the reinsured being required to pay the reinsurer interest at $3\frac{1}{2}$ per cent on any part of the deposit not used to compensate the reinsured for unpaid balances. Lord Hanworth held that:

(1) Any sum due under one reinsurance contract could be set off against any sum owed on any other reinsurance contract between the parties.

(2) The interest payable on the deposit should also be brought into account.

(3) But the deposit was held for a specific purpose and any balance remaining after that purpose was satisfied could not be brought into any set-off.

---

1 *Lee v Chapman* (1885), 30 Ch.D.216.
2 N. Legh-Jones, *MacGillivray and Parkington on Insurance Law*, p.173, who cites *Re Eagle Insurance* (1872), Alb. Arb. 16 S. J.483; *Peat v Jones* (1881), 8 Q.B.D. 147; *Jack v Kipping* (1882), 9 Q.B.D. 113; *Tilley v Bowman*, [1910] 1 K.B. 745.
3 [1930] 2 Ch. 293.

It may be concluded that where one of the parties to a reinsurance contract holds any reserves, if it is clear from the wording of the contract that they are held for some specific purpose, the funds cannot be brought into account in set-off against amounts owed under other contracts. Moreover if 'A liquidator holds such a premium reserve, as a trustee by way of security, the depositor will be entitled to recover the full amount of any balance left after the satisfaction of the security, rather than a mere dividend on the amount of such balance.'[1]

Disputes between the parties

The relatively small number of cases which have come before English courts involving disputes arising out of reinsurance contracts is attributable in no small measure to the use made of arbitration. Whatever may be its merits compared with recourse to litigation,[2] in practice arbitration clauses are universally included in reinsurance contracts,whether effected in Britain or elsewhere, as laying down an agreed means of settling disputes arising out of the contract.

British courts long ago recognized the validity of arbitration clauses, and the principles laid down governing their usage in contracts in general and insurance contracts in particular equally apply to reinsurance contracts. It is not possible within the scope of this chapter to deal in detail with all of the principles governing arbitration clauses and the conduct of arbitration proceedings. Therefore the following paragraphs should be seen as outlining only some of the main principles of English law.

The courts have held that the parties to a contract may agree that no action shall be brought in the courts until any dispute has been submitted to arbitration and an award made.[3] In the case of insurance contracts both questions of amount[4] and liability[5] relating to claims can be subject to reference to arbitration. The parties may also agree that in the event of dispute all claims will be barred unless arbitration is commenced within a certain time.[6] An English court will not, however, uphold an arbitration clause which seeks to remove its jurisdiction altogether.[7]

Under section 4(1) of the Arbitration Act 1950, if one party to a

---

1 'Winding-up and set-off', *Reinsurance*, May 1971.
2 See H. Edward Gumbel, 'Arbitration under reinsurance contracts', in *Festschrift für Reimer Schmidt*, ed. F. Reichert-Facilides *et al.* (Verlag Versicherungs wirtschaft eV, 1976), pp.884 – 6; and Chapter 3 *supra*.
3 *Scott* v *Avery* (1856), 5 H.L. Cas. 811; *Jureidini* v *National British & Irish Millers' Insurance Co.*, (1915) A.C. 499, 504, *per* Lord Haldane.
4 *Viney* v *Bignold* (1887), 20 Q.B.D. 172.
5 *Trainor* v *Phoenix Assurance* (1891), 65 L.T. 825.
6 *Atlantic Shipping and Trading Co.* v *Louis Dreyfus & Co.*, [1922] 2 A.C. 250.
7 *Heyman* v *Darwins*, [1942] A.C. 356.

contract brings legal proceedings in respect of any matter which it had been agreed should be referred to arbitration, the other party may make an application to the court for a stay of proceedings. The court can exercise its discretion in deciding whether to stay the action, and where (1) a question of fraud by either party arises, the court may order that an arbitration clause shall have no effect;[1] but (2) it may also refuse to stay any action brought in such circumstances in breach of the agreement.[2] If an action in the courts has not been so halted its decision will be binding on the parties regardless of the terms of the arbitration clause.[3]

Arbitrators in making their awards must in general abide by some fixed and recognizable system of law. Sometimes arbitration clauses inserted in reinsurance contracts contain words such as the following which appear to relieve the arbitrator(s) of such a duty:

> The arbitrator or umpire, as the case may be, shall interpret this treaty rather as an honourable engagement than as a merely legal obligation.[4]
> The arbitrators and umpire are relieved from all judicial formalities and may abstain from following the strict rules of the law.[5]

Although in both of the cases cited the offending words were not upheld by the court, there is the risk that the court may regard such words as invalidating the whole contract on the grounds that the parties did not intend it to have legal effect. If it is merely the intention of the parties that arbitrators shall take into account reinsurance custom and practice when making their awards, that intention can be achieved without incorporating such potentially dangerous phrases as those quoted above.[6]

American law also recognizes the right of the parties to agree to refer disputes to arbitration. The Federal Arbitration Act (U.S.C.A., title 9), which applies only to agreements which may be carried out in the United States, provides that written agreements to that effect shall be valid, irrevocable and enforceable, except upon such grounds as exist at law or in equity for the revocation of any contract. As in England, a court has power to stay any action upon the application of a party to an agreement which provides for the referral of disputes to arbitration.

Under the provisions of the Federal Arbitration Act on the application of one party a court may set aside an arbitration award only where:
(1) It was procured by corruption, fraud or undue means.
(2) There was evident partiality or corruption in the arbitrator(s).

---

1 Arbitration Act 1950, s.24(2).
2 Arbitration Act 1950, s.24(3).
3 *Dolman & Sons* v *Ossett Corporation*, [1912] 3 K.B. 251.
4 *Maritime Insurance Co. Ltd* v *Assecuranz-Union von 1865*, 1935] L1.L.L.B.16.
5 *Orion Cia Española de Seguros* v *Belfort Maatschappij voor Algemene Verzekeringen* (1962) 2 U.L.R. 257.
6 See Gumbel, 'Arbitration under reinsurance contracts', p.889f.

(3) There is misconduct by the arbitrators in the conduct of the arbitration proceedings by which the rights of any party are prejudiced.

(4) The arbitrators exceeded their powers, or so imperfectly executed them that a mutual, final and definite award was not made.

If an award is set aside the court has discretion to direct a rehearing by the arbitrators if the time specified by the agreement for making the award has not expired.[1]

In addition to federal law there are also state laws governing arbitration. As a general statement, American courts are more reluctant than English courts to re-examine arbitration awards and 'will not set aside arbitration awards for error in either law or fact.'[2]

Reference has already been made to the use of objectionable phrases in arbitration clauses in reinsurance contracts, and in 1975 the Institute of London Underwriters, after discussions with the Reinsurance Offices' Association and Lloyd's Insurance Brokers' Association published a proposed standard arbitration clause (see appendix to this chapter). The clause deals with the scope of the arbitration, the constitution and appointment of the arbitration tribunal, the place and law of the arbitration proceedings, and the payment of costs.

Conflict of laws

The international character of reinsurance business means that contracts are often effected between companies domiciled in different countries and not infrequently dealing with the reinsurance of a risk situate in a third country. Consequently the question may arise as to which system of law is to be applied to resolve any dispute concerning the contract, though the answer may be found within the terms of the contract itself, possibly being specified in an arbitration clause. In the absence of such agreement between the parties it is necessary to turn to the principles of private international law to determine which system of law shall govern the contract.

The differences of opinion that exist on those principles and the highly specialist nature of the subject are such that the reader must be referred to current textbooks on the conflict of laws.[3] It must suffice here to say that where the contract does not expressly select the proper law

---

1 Thompson, *Reinsurance*, p.141.
2 Gumbel, 'Arbitration under reinsurance contracts', p.888.
3 For example, A.V. Dicey and J.C. Morris, *Conflict of Laws*, 9th ed. (London: Stevens & Sons, 1973); G.C. Cheshire, *Private International Law*, 9th ed. by P.M. North (London: Butterworth, 1974); M. Wolff, *Private International Law*, 2nd ed. (1950).

governing the contract English courts have established a number of principles for determining it having regard to the presumed intention of the parties as evidenced by the contract and the circumstances of its formation. Where it is decided that the proper law is that of a foreign country, an English court will apply that law, if necessary with the help of experts in it.[1]

Reinsurance brokers

The legal position of a reinsurance broker is basically the same as that of an insurance broker. Whereas the latter is an agent who is authorized to negotiate and effect policies of insurance on behalf of his principal, a reinsurance broker performs the same duties in respect of reinsurance contracts. In both English and American law the legal relationships and responsibilities that arise from the performance of such duties are governed in general by the law of agency, and the particular application of that law to insurance agents and brokers basically applies to reinsurance brokers too. There are ample sources of reference to such law,[2] and therefore the aim here will simply be to highlight issues of particular relevance to reinsurance brokers.

The broker's principal

It is a long-established principle that an insurance broker is *prima facie* the agent of the insured not the insurer,[3] so by the same token the principal of a reinsurance broker is the ceding insurer not the reinsurer. Not infrequently, however, a reinsurance broker is appointed to obtain business for a reinsurer and possibly to act as an underwriting agent with powers to accept reinsurance business on behalf of the reinsurer. Consequently a broker may find himself in a position where he has two principals in respect of the same transaction. English law in such circumstances is quite clear, and has been expressed as follows:[4]

> [the broker] may not act for both parties to a transaction unless he ensures that he fully discloses all the material facts to both parties and obtains their

1 A short explanation of generally accepted principles as they affect insurance contracts can be found in Legh-Jones, *MacGillivray and Parkington on Insurance Law*, ch. 18.
2 See, for example, F.M.B. Reynolds and B.J. Davenport, *Bowstead on Agency*, 14th ed. (London: Sweet & Maxwell, 1976) and Legh-Jones, *MacGillivray and Parkington on Insurance Law* and Colinvaux, *Law of Insurance*.
3 *Rozanes v Bowen* (1928), 32 Ll. L.R. 98; *Newsholme Bros v Road Transport and General Insurance Co.*, [1929] 2 K.B. 356; and in American law *Condon v Exton-Hall Brokerage and Vessel Agency*, 144 N.Y. and 760, 83 Misc. Rep. 130.
4 Reynolds and Davenport, *Bowstead on Agency*, p.143.

> informed consent to his so acting ... Any custom to the contrary will not be upheld.

In the absence of such consent the broker would be in a breach of his duty to his principal(s). A non-assenting principal could in such circumstances either treat the contract as void or sue the broker for damages in respect of any loss or damage suffered as a consequence of the failure to make disclosure.[1]

Similarly the American courts have held that where a broker had been employed as agent for both an insurer and a reinsurer he was not entitled without the assent of both to make a contract between them in a matter in which he was invested with discretion. Only in a case where an agent has no discretion to exercise for either party would a contract arranged on behalf of and between two principals be enforceable.[2]

Even more commonly a broker who has placed an insurance for his principal, the insured, may subsequently find himself being asked to act as the agent of the insurer. It is common practice in London in both the Lloyd's and non-Lloyd's insurance markets when a claim is made under a policy for the underwriter to instruct the broker to obtain an assessor's report. In two cases relating to direct insurances the underwriters subsequently disputed liability and the broker refused the request of his principal, the insured, to furnish a copy of the assessor's report on the grounds that it belonged to the insurer.[3] Although the broker had acted according to market custom, Donaldson J. in the *North and South Trust Co.* case described it as an unreasonable custom which could not of itself bind the insured to acquiesce in the dual role of the broker. Therefore, one authority concludes:[4]

> If Lloyd's brokers wish to accept instructions from underwriters as well as from the assured, they must obtain the consent of the assured before accepting instructions to make a claim under his policy ... Otherwise, unless the assured knows of the custom and his acquiescence can safely be presumed, the broker acts at his peril in following the usual practice at Lloyd's.

Reinsurance contracts involve only persons who it may be assumed are well versed in market practice, and so a reinsurance broker may argue that it is reasonable to presume that a ceding insurer gives his acquiescence unless there are good reasons to believe the contrary.

---

1 *North and South Trust Co.* v *Berkeley*, [1971] 1 All E.R. 980 at page 993.
2 *The Empire State Insurance Co.* v *American Central Insurance Co.* 138 N.Y. 446.
3 *Anglo-African Merchants Ltd* v *Bayley*, [1970] 1 Q.B. 311, and *North and South Trust Co.* v *Berkeley*, [1971] 1 All E.R. 980.
4 Legh-Jones, *MacGillivray and Parkington on Insurance Law*, p.191.

However, unless the particular practice concerned had already been proved in a court of law, the broker would have the difficult task of establishing that it is general, notorious and certain, and that it is not unreasonable.[1] Even that may prove insufficient: the Legal Correspondent of *Reinsurance* goes on to argue that:[2]

> A custom will not be upheld by the courts of this country if it contradicts the vital principle that an agent may not at the same time serve two masters—two principals—in actual or potential opposition to one another: unless, indeed, he has the explicit, informed, consent of both principals. An insurance broker is in no privileged position in this respect.

Therefore, the safest course for a reinsurance broker who may find himself in the position of acting for two principals is to make full disclosure to both and obtain their written consent.

A broker's duty of disclosure

The employment of a broker or other agent raises two issues in relation to the disclosure of information during the negotiations leading to the formation of a contract of reinsurance.

First, there is the broker's duty of disclosure to the reinsurer. Here the position in English law is quite clear. A broker who arranges an insurance has a duty to disclose to the insurer all material facts known to him. This principle is clearly stated in section 19 of the Marine Insurance Act 1906 which provides that an agent must disclose:

> Every material circumstance which is known to himself and an agent for the assured is deemed to know every circumstance which in the ordinary course of business ought to be known by, or to have been communicated to him.

Thus a broker has a duty which is independent of that of his principal, extending beyond the mere transmitting to the insurer of facts supplied to him by his principal. If a broker fails to convey to the insurer any fact supplied by his principal or misrepresents any such fact, the question then arises as to whether at the time the broker was acting as the proposer's agent for the purpose of effecting the insurance or reinsurance, or was acting as the insurer's (or reinsurer's) agent for the purpose of obtaining the business. If he was acting in the latter capacity, then the information supplied by the proposer may be imputed to the

---

1 *Anglo-African Merchants Ltd* v *Bayley*, [1970] 1 Q.B. 311, and *North and South Trust Co.* v *Berkeley*, [1971] All E.R. 980.
2 'Agency-trade usages and customs', *Reinsurance*, December 1970.

insurer, and the validity of the contract would not be affected.[1] Should the contract be invalidated due to a breach of the duty of disclosure by a broker then his principal will have the same remedies as would apply to any failure by an expert agent to carry out his duties, i.e. the right to sue for damages.

The second issue is the extent to which an agent's knowledge may be imputed to his principal. The general rule has been stated as follows:[2]

> (1) When any fact or circumstance, material to any transaction, business or matter in respect of which an agent is employed, comes to his knowledge in the course of such employment, and is of such a nature that it is his duty to communicate it to his principal, the principal is deemed to have notice thereof as from the time when he would have received such notice if the agent had performed his duty, and taken such steps to communicate the fact or circumstances as he ought reasonably to have taken.
> (2) Knowledge acquired by the agent otherwise than in the course of his employment on the principal's behalf, or of any fact or circumstance which is not material to the business in respect of which he is employed, is not imputed to the principal.

In two interrelated cases, marine reinsurances had been effected after a broker employed by underwriters Blackburn, Low and Company had heard in the course of his business that the vessel in question had been lost but had failed to report the fact to his principals. The broker proceeded to negotiate a reinsurance without informing the reinsurers of the fact, and it was held that Blackburn, Low and Company could not recover on grounds of non-disclosure.[3] After the first reinsurance had been arranged the plaintiffs themselves proceeded to place a second reinsurance with other reinsurers, still unaware of the loss of the vessel. It was held on appeal to the House of Lords that the knowledge of the broker could not be imputed to Blackburn, Low and Company who could recover from those second reinsurers.[4]

Therefore, it may be concluded that the knowledge of an insurance broker of material facts can only be imputed to his principal if:
(1) He had a *legal duty* to communicate it to his principal, and in many cases although a broker may have a moral duty to inform his principal of facts which come to his knowledge it will not amount to a legal duty; and
(2) The knowledge had been acquired in the course of the broker's employment.[5]

---

1 *Newsholme Bros. v Road Transport and General Insurance Co.*, [1929] 2 K.B. 356.
2 Reynolds and Davenport, *Bowstead on Agency*, p.355.
3 *Blackburn Low & Co. v Haslam* (1888), Q.B.D. 144.
4 *Blackburn Low & Co. v Vigors* (1887), 12 App. Cas. 531.
5 For a fuller discussion of the two cases see 'Imputation of an agent's knowledge to his principal', *Reinsurance*, July 1974.

The broker's duty to account

It is customary for reinsurance brokers to receive payments for both premiums and claims for transmission to reinsurers and ceding companies respectively. In handling such funds the duties of an insurance broker as laid down by English law are clear, namely:

(1) To act with due diligence in collecting amounts and to pay over any sum received in his employment in accordance with the arrangements agreed with his principal.

(2) To render an account when required.

(3) To keep his principal's property distinct from his own.

(4) Not to make any profit beyond the commission or remuneration paid by his principal.

There is no reason to doubt that the same general rules apply to reinsurance brokers. However, in the United States where the insurance statutes of many of the states deal specifically with the fiduciary nature of the funds representing premiums and claims monies collected by insurance brokers, the supervisory authorities have taken the view that reinsurance brokers are exempt from the regulations.[1] Following the failure of a major reinsurance broker, in 1976 the New York legislature enacted para. 122a of the New York Insurance Law which laid down that every reinsurance intermediary should have a fiduciary responsibility for funds which he receives or collects in that capacity. It is expected that the National Association of Insurance Commissioners will eventually recommend that all states enact legislation dealing with funds held by reinsurance brokers.[2]

In one respect insurance and reinsurance market practice runs contrary to the normal rules of agency. It is customary for insurance and reinsurance brokers to use funds at their disposal to earn interest *for their own benefit* until the monies are remitted to the respective parties. Whether the courts would uphold the practice as a long-recognized market custom is an open question. A factor that would have to be taken into account is that on occasions a broker may have to withstand a negative balance on his account due to having paid a large claim before receiving payment from all insurers or reinsurers: then he does not expect his principal to recompense him for lost interest.

Another issue which is open to doubt is who bears the loss if a broker absconds with premiums or claims payments he has received. In the case of marine insurance, the Marine Insurance Act 1906 stipulates that:

---

1 Harold M. Tract, 'Accounting for reinsurance premiums by reinsurance brokers', *Best's Review*, vol. 78 No. 8, December 1977.

2 Ibid.

> Unless otherwise agreed, where a marine policy is effected on behalf of the assured by a broker, the broker is directly responsible to the insurer for the premium. (S.53(1).)
>
> Where a marine policy effected on behalf of the assured by a broker acknowledges the receipt of the premium, such acknowledgement is, in the absence of fraud, conclusive as between the insurer and the assured. (S.54.)

Although premiums paid to a broker for facultative reinsurance may qualify for such treatment, the position regarding treaty premiums and balances is uncertain.

In regard to claims it has been held that an assured is bound by a settlement of a loss in account between his insurer and broker where he expressly authorizes the broker to receive payment by way of a settlement, or he impliedly gives such authorization by employing a broker in full knowledge of the custom.[1] Most, if not all, ceding companies would be in the latter position.

Following the failure of the American reinsurance broker referred to above, it has become the practice to include in treaties covering American business the following intermediary clause.

> _____ is hereby recognized as the Intermediary negotiating this Agreement for all business hereunder. All communications (including but not limited to notices, statements, premiums, return premiums, commissions, taxes, losses, loss adjustment expense, salvages, and loss settlements) relating thereto shall be transmitted to the Reinsured or the Reinsurer through _____.
> Payments by the Reinsured to the Intermediary shall constitute payment to the Reinsurer but payment by the Reinsurer to the Intermediary shall only constitute payment to the Reinsured to the extent that such payments are actually received by the Reinsured.

Thus responsibility for the credit risk associated with dealing through a broker is placed on the reinsurer. Consequently there has been some tightening up of the terms of credit applying to the payment of reinsurance balances by brokers, and some reinsurers require more information regarding the financial status and accounting procedures of brokers with whom they deal.

---

[1] _Scott_ v _Irving_ (1830) B. & Ad. 605; 9 L.J.O.S.K.B. 89; _Stewart_ v _Aberdein_ (1838), 4 M. & W. 211.

Appendix 4.1 Standard Arbitration Clause

(Institute of London Underwriters, Reinsurance Offices' Association, Lloyd's Insurance Brokers' Association).

1. All matters in difference between the reassured and the reinsurer (hereinafter referred to as 'the parties') in relation to this agreement, including its formation and validity, and whether arising during or after the period of this agreement, shall be referred to an arbitration tribunal in the manner hereinafter set out.

2. Unless the parties agree upon a single arbitrator within 30 days of one receiving a written request from the other for arbitration, the claimant (the party requesting arbitration) shall appoint his arbitrator and give written notice thereof to the respondent. Within 30 days of receiving such notice the respondent shall appoint his arbitrator and give written notice thereof to the claimant, failing which the claimant may apply to the appointor hereinafter named to nominate an arbitrator on behalf of the respondent.

3. Should the arbitrators fail to agree, then they shall within 30 days of such disagreement appoint an umpire to whom the matter in difference shall be referred. Should the arbitrators fail within such period to appoint an umpire, then either of them or either of the parties may apply to the appointor for the appointment of the umpire.

4. Unless the parties otherwise agree, the arbitration tribunal shall consist of persons employed or engaged in a senior position in insurance or reinsurance underwriting.

5. The arbitration tribunal shall have power to fix all procedural rules for the holding of the arbitration including discretionary power to make orders as to any matters which it may consider proper in the circumstances of the case with regard to pleadings, discovery, inspection of documents, examination of witnesses and any other matter whatsoever relating to the conduct of the arbitration and may receive and act upon such evidence whether oral or written strictly admissible or not as it shall in its discretion think fit.

6. The appointor shall be ____.

7. All costs of the arbitration shall be in the discretion of the arbitration tribunal who may direct to and by whom and in what manner they shall be paid.

8. (a) The seat of the arbitration shall be in ____ and the arbitration tribunal shall apply the laws of ____ as the proper law of this agreement.

(b) The award of the arbitration tribunal shall be in writing and binding upon the parties who covenant to carry out the same. If either of the parties should fail to carry out any award the other may apply for its enforcement to a court of competent jurisdiction in any territory in which the party in default is domiciled or has assets or carries on business.

REINSURANCE

5
Forms of reinsurance

REINSURANCE

5
Forms of reinsurance

The main forms of reinsurance were briefly described in Chapter 3, the purpose of this chapter is to examine in more detail their characteristics, advantages and disadvantages. Then the following three chapters will deal with their methods of operation as laid down in the various types of reinsurance contract.

I QUOTA SHARE REINSURANCE

Simplest of all forms of treaty reinsurance is the quota share contract whereby the reinsurer agrees to reinsure a fixed proportion of every risk accepted by the ceding company, sharing proportionately in all losses and receiving in return the same proportion of all direct premiums less the agreed reinsurance commission. The treaty will specify, *inter alia*, the class(es) of insurance covered; the geographical limits and any other restrictions such as any specific types of risk excluded from the treaty; and whether a monetary limit applies to any one risk. The treaty will provide that the ceding company automatically will cede and the reinsurer accept the agreed share of every risk underwritten which falls within the contract.

Simplicity is perhaps the major advantage offered by quota share reinsurance. Once the treaty has been arranged, its operation calls for very little administration and accounting. Provided all risks accepted by the ceding company fall within the terms of the treaty no special effort need be devoted to the reinsurance of any individual risk or to the apportionment of premiums and claims. Experienced staff therefore will be able to devote their time to other aspects of the business: in a small new company, perhaps short of such people, that may be a considerable benefit.

There are, however, other advantages for both parties. The ceding company is able to write business safe in the knowledge that reinsurance is available automatically to contain potential losses within an acceptable limit, while the reinsurer receives a share of every risk so obtaining a more balanced portfolio of business than could be obtained from reinsuring the particular account by any other form of reinsurance. Such participation creates an identity of interest between reinsured and reinsurer, often inducing the reinsurer to provide for the ceding company technical training facilities and other services which are of particular value to new companies in developing countries.

It was noted in Chapter 3 that the favourable view which reinsurers take of quota share business leads to higher rates of reinsurance commission being paid than on surplus treaties covering comparable original portfolios. On a very profitable account a ceding company may be able to obtain both reinsurance commission at a rate sufficiently high to cover its acquisition costs plus a contribution towards administrative expenses, and a profit commission which would effectively provide it with a risk-free profit. In any event the retention of premium and possibly loss reserves, and the payment of reinsurance premiums after the receipt of the original premiums, may provide a ceding company with a source of investment income in excess of any interest payable to the reinsurer, thereby assisting in the expansion of the company's own business. Over time as a company builds up its gross premium income and reserves, so it will be able to increase its retention limits and reduce the share ceded if it so desires.

On the other hand, quota share reinsurance does suffer from substantial disadvantages. Notably the ceding company cannot select the risks it cedes so that the reinsurer will take a share of the premium for risks which lie well within the company's own financial capacity. Moreover, although the company will gain from being able to accept larger risks than otherwise would be possible, by reinsuring the same proportion of every risk underwritten, the relative variability of expected losses on the retained portfolio will be the same as on the total portfolio. Therefore, judged in terms of its impact on the risk borne by the ceding company, a quota-share reinsurance fails to reduce:

(1) the incurred loss ratio on the retained account; and
(2) the possible variation in actual retained losses incurred during one year from the expected retained losses (i.e. it will not reduce the coefficient of variation of retained losses).

On the other hand, by reinsuring a fixed proportion of all insurances written a company will reduce its probability of ruin[1] because it will

---

1 I.e. the probability that losses will exceed the company's resources. See Chapter 9.

achieve a smaller absolute variation in retained losses (i.e. the standard deviation) relative to its capital and free reserves.

It is for such reasons that limited use is made of quota share as the sole form of reinsurance employed by a company for protecting any particular class of business. Generally it is restricted to new companies or to when a company is entering into a new class of business or a new area of operation. Then the offer of a quota share treaty may entice a reinsurer to provide essential reinsurance protection. Although initially the portfolio of business may be small and limited in its spread, and the ceding company inexperienced in handling such business, the reinsurer can at least be assured that there will be no selection so that he will obtain a share of the good as well as the bad.

Quota share reinsurance may also form an appropriate part of a reinsurance programme for more specialized uses, notably:

(1) Where the ceding company wishes to arrange reciprocal exchanges of business.
(2) For classes of business where it is difficult to define a single risk, e.g. crop hail insurances.
(3) For reducing a ceding company's exposure under policies covering natural perils.
(4) For classes of business where, although there may be policy limits, the incidence and size of losses are uncertain, e.g. liability business.

Despite its disadvantages, quota share does possess the great merit of simplicity and thus cheap administration. At times of financial difficulty, or perhaps following the implementation of more stringent solvency regulations, it also provides an easy and effective means whereby a company can quickly reduce its retained premium income so that it can continue to meet a prescribed ratio of net income to capital and free reserves.

Finally, quota share arrangements may also form part of a group-underwriting practice whereby all members of a group, instead of participating directly in an insurance written by one member, share it by means of quota share reinsurance up to agreed limits before interesting outside reinsurers.

II SURPLUS REINSURANCE

The advantages

Surplus reinsurance is the most common form of treaty reinsurance. Like quota share it is a form of proportional reinsurance whereby the reinsurer accepts a certain share of a risk, receiving an equivalent proportion of the gross premium (less reinsurance commission) and paying the same portion of all claims. The basic difference between the two is that under surplus reinsurance arrangements the ceding company only reinsures that portion of any risk which exceeds its own retention.

Under a surplus treaty normally the ceding company will adopt varying retention limits directly related to the degree of risk associated with different types of exposure units. For example, a fire underwriter may fix a higher retention for, say, engineering factories of fire-resistant construction than for timber-built woodworking shops because not only will the former be subject to a lower probability of a fire occurring but also the extent of loss relative to value at risk will probably be smaller too. In other words, in fixing its retention limits a company will pay regard to the same factors as are taken into account in calculating premium rates, and some companies draw up their tables of retentions on the basis of the premium rates applied to the original insurances.

Thus surplus treaties overcome the disadvantages of quota share.

The ceding company is able to keep for its own account all of the premium for risks underwritten which fall within the scope of its own retention, differentiating for some portfolios between classes of risk.

Also, by ceding amounts in excess of its retention limits, but retaining for its own account 100% of risks falling below those limits, the ceding company reduces the range of possible losses on its retained portfolio, thereby reducing the potential relative variability of its claim costs. Robert Reinarz[1] says on this point that a surplus treaty enables 'The law of large numbers to operate with maximum efficiency', and adds:

> The surplus treaty imparts a limit of size homogeneity to the primary insurer through the working of the retention. The retention effectively cuts off all variance above a certain level of liability in each class, thereby definitely limiting the variance to a smaller margin. The reinsurers absorb the wide variances in size.

The same point is illustrated in Figures 5.1, 5.2 and 5.3. The first diagram shows the distribution of an original portfolio by sums insured. A 50% quota share treaty would reduce the ceding company's retentions as shown in Figure 5.2: although its maximum liability would be halved, the relative variations remain unchanged. The effect of a surplus reinsurance is shown in Figure 5.3: for the sake of simplicity it is assumed that the company fixes a flat retention of M instead of having differing retentions according to category of risk, as would be more usual in practice. As can be seen, the retained portfolio distribution is contained within narrower limits giving a lower coefficient of variation.

1 Robert C. Reinarz, *Property and Liability Reinsurance Management* (Greenwich, Conn: Mission Publishing Co., 1968), p.29.

Figure 5.1 Original portfolio

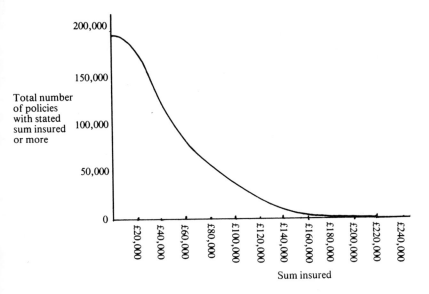

Figure 5.2 Retained portfolio: 50% Quota share

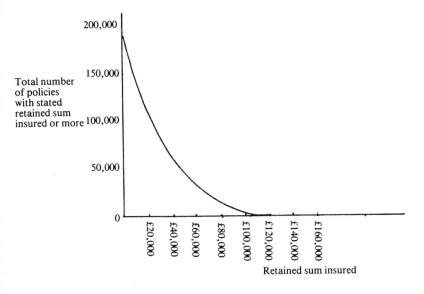

Figure 5.3 Retained portfolio: Surplus reinsurance with retention limit of £M

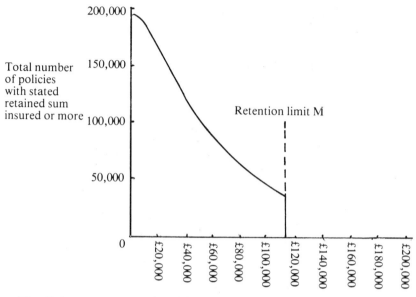

The Reinarz argument is subject to the important qualification that there is no change in the distribution of the reinsured's retained portfolio by size of risk. If the company used its surplus reinsurance facilities to enable it to write a larger proportion of large risks it would tend to counterbalance the favourable impact of the surplus reinsurance arrangements on the loss variance of the retained portfolio.

Besides those special advantages, surplus reinsurance fulfils the other functions of reinsurance discussed in Chapter 3. In particular it enables a direct company to handle larger risks than otherwise would be possible given the constraints imposed by its financial resources. By providing the company with a more stable portfolio of retained business it reduces the probability of suffering random large losses which may badly strain the company's finances. Moreover like quota share, provided the company can provide its reinsurers with a profitable portfolio of business, by reinsuring it may be able to increase its own profits relative to retained premium income and thus over time build up its reserves and underwriting capacity.

The disadvantages

There are, however, substantial disadvantages associated with surplus reinsurance which have encouraged the swing towards the use of non-proportional reinsurances. Some of the disadvantages apply equally to the reinsured and the reinsurer, others represent a disadvantage to one party but an advantage to another.

For example, the advantages discussed above which the ceding company obtains from being able to reinsure only the larger risks it accepts conversely present several disadvantages for the reinsurer. Inevitably the ceding company will tend to retain for its own account a large part of the less hazardous class(es) of business it writes so that, *ceteris paribus*, a disproportionate amount of its heavier-risk business will be ceded to the reinsurer(s). It does not follow, however, that this practice leaves the reinsurer carrying a disproportionate share of poor business written by the ceding company.[1] Such a result only holds true if original premium rates are unfairly discriminatory in the sense that the rates charged on the low-risk business are sufficient to yield profits while those on the more hazardous risks are inadequate. The unavoidable disadvantage to the reinsurer (and conversely the advantage to the ceding company) lies in the imbalance of the portfolio ceded which:

(1) will contain a narrower spread of business, so that if the loss experience of a high-risk group deteriorates the reinsurer probably will suffer more than the ceding company because of a higher concentration of such business being included in the reinsured portfolio; and

(2) the distribution of the reinsured business by size of risk will tend to be wider, so exposing the loss experience to greater variability.

The costs incurred by both ceding companies and reinsurers in administering surplus treaties tend to be higher than for other forms of reinsurance.

A ceding company needs to compare its acceptance on each risk underwritten with its retention limit for that class of risk to determine the amount, if any, to be ceded; an entry has to be made in the reinsurance register both at inception and when any alteration is made to the sum(s) insured or premium rate(s); and the correct portions of all premium receipts or returns and claims payments have to be included in the quarterly reinsurance accounts. The use of computers can reduce the administrative burden for both ceding companies and reinsurers, but there remains the need to undertake work not required for other forms of reinsurance.

Generally very little information is now supplied by ceding companies to their reinsurers regarding individual risks ceded so reducing costs for both parties. On the other hand the reinsurer suffers the disadvantage of not being able to exercise the same watch over the business ceded and

---

1 Reinarz, *Property and Liability Reinsurance Management*, p.30.

thus his own acceptances, as in the days when detailed bordereaux were common practice.

Finally neither surplus nor quota share reinsurances can provide perfect protection against the accidental accumulation of losses, however carefully a company monitors its business and sets its retention limits. For example, even a well controlled fire account will always be exposed in some degree to major conflagrations or wide-ranging windstorms.

Controls exercised by reinsurers

In order to keep his portfolio risk within acceptable limits the reinsurer needs to exercise some control over the business ceded; it would be against his interests to enter into an open-ended commitment to accept anything the ceding company wished to reinsure. Therefore, every surplus treaty invariably contains:
(1) A precise definition of its scope, i.e. class(es) of insurance covered, territorial limits and so forth.
(2) The limit of the reinsurer's liability for any one risk.
The reinsurer's limit of liability is usually expressed in relation to the ceding company's own retention, though sometimes a maximum monetary limit may be imposed too. Thus in, say, a five-line treaty (where a line is defined as being equal to the reinsured's own retention) the reinsurer's maximum liability would be five times the amount retained by the ceding company, subject to any lower monetary limit. How the limit operates is illustrated in the following example of a five-line fire surplus treaty where the ceding company is offered the six risks A to F:

Risk	Sum insured £	Ceding company's retention limit £	Amount reinsured £	As a multiple of the amount retained	Balance £
A	48,000	10,000	38,000	3.8	—
B	70,000	15,000	55,000	3.7	—
C	45,000	7,000	35,000	5.0	3,000
D	35,000	5,000	25,000	5.0	5,000
E	12,000	5,000	7,000	1.4	—
F	14,000	15,000	—	—	—

The sum insured for F is below the ceding company's retention limit and so could be retained wholly for its own account. Out of the remaining five cases the sum insured in excess of the company's retention is less than the treaty limit for A, B and E, so that the business could be accepted. The sums insured for C and D exhaust the capacity of the treaty and if the company wished to be interested in the business it would either offer to take a smaller share or obtain additional reinsurance in the facultative market for the amounts shown in the final column; it could not cede more than the five lines to its treaty reinsurers.

The example also illustrates the points made above that the reinsurers obtain a narrower spread of business being only interested in five of the risks; they are more heavily interested in the poorer risks; and there is a relatively greater dispersion in the sums insured than those retained by the ceding company. A critical factor in determining what business is ceded under a surplus treaty is the retention policy of the reinsured. The wider is the spread of retention limits the more unbalanced will tend to be the business ceded unless the sum insured on every case written by the ceding company approaches its acceptance limit, so that after keeping its retention it fills the treaty limits too. Therefore in considering whether to accept a share of a surplus treaty a reinsurer will be interested in seeing that the ceding company maintains a reasonable relationship between its minimum and maximum retention limits. Generally the market is reluctant to accept a ratio exceeding 1 : 10. As can be seen from the above example where the minimum retention shown is £5,000, to raise the higher limits from £10,000 and £15,000 to, say, £33,000 and £50,000 would deprive the reinsurers of most of the better class of business.

Another factor to be considered is the number of lines to be provided, whether by a first surplus treaty or by a combination of first, second and possibly third surplus treaties.[1] If a company has access to a large number of lines of reinsurance so that it need retain for its own account only a small share of any insurance written, it may be tempted to accept a far larger proportion of high-risk business than it otherwise would be willing to write. In other words, there is the danger that underwriting standards may be allowed to slip if the resulting losses are mainly transferred to the reinsurers.

If a company does require a large number of lines of reinsurance to accommodate its policyholders and agents, and perhaps thereby withstand competition from other insurers, the tendency this has to unbalance a treaty may be corrected partially by ensuring that the company's retentions for low-risk insurances are not disproportionately large. Thus the reinsurers can expect to receive a reasonable share of all of the business written by the reinsured. Alternatively the imbalance may be reflected in the allowance of a lower rate of reinsurance commission.

---

1 See Chapter 7 for an explanation of how such an arrangement operates.

The capacity of a surplus treaty

It is impossible to speak of a typical surplus treaty. The variations that can be found in the number of lines of reinsurance provided by reinsurers is as great as the difference in ceding companies' retentions, ranging from two or three lines up to, exceptionally, two hundred. Although the number of lines required by a direct insurer tends to be inversely related to its size, plenty of exceptions can be found to prove that such a relationship cannot be taken as a universal rule. Everything depends upon the needs of the insurer, in particular (1) the nature of its business and the size of risk it must be able to accept in order to compete successfully in the market, and (2) its own retention limits.

Generally as a company expands its premium income and reserves it will be able to increase its retentions, so reducing the number of lines of reinsurance it will need in order to underwrite a given sum insured. For example, if a company is able to double its retention on a particular class of risk from, say, £5,000 to £10,000, the number of lines of reinsurance it will need in order to accept a sum insured of £80,000 can be halved from 15 to seven. On the other hand, as a company grows it may be able to compete for the larger industrial and commercial insurances and so need to retain substantial reinsurance facilities in order to handle sufficiently large amounts to act as the leading company on coinsured risks.

Local companies operating in markets where the number of insurers allowed to transact insurance business is limited by government regulation may have a special need for exceptionally large reinsurance facilities which will not reduce over time. Values at risk, often becoming concentrated on fewer exposure units as the result of technological progress, may increase as fast or faster than the financial resources of local insurance companies which will therefore require a commensurate increase in their reinsurance facilities in order to continue to meet all of the insurance needs of residents.

Clearly the needs of a company will depend upon a set of circumstances which do not lend themselves to strict rules. The most that can be said was summarized by Golding as follows:[1]

> The purpose of the first surplus treaty is completely to cover the normal needs of the ceding company and to leave nothing to be disposed of elsewhere. The second surplus treaty if required at all is only for the occasional abnormally large case, or for special groups of risks in particular areas.

---

1 Golding, *Law and Practice of Reinsurance*, p.49.

Even such a rule of thumb, of course, begs the question of what should be construed as 'normal needs', and that cannot be answered without knowledge of individual circumstances. What may be regarded as reasonable for one company may seem as encouraging another to engage recklessly in business well beyond its own technical competence and financial resources. Reasonableness therefore is a question for underwriting judgment based on experience plus a knowledge of the management of a ceding company and the market conditions in which it operates.

It is for such reasons that the following comments regarding the number of lines of reinsurance that are encountered in practice today must be treated as generalizations to which many exceptions can be found. Futhermore, practice varies between the different classes of insurance; for example, a large insurance company may arrange up to ten lines of reinsurance for its fire account (though the average number is probably around five) whereas it may prefer to rely on excess of loss reinsurance for its accident account. Similarly a small company may effect anything between 20 and 60 lines for its fire account, but restrict its accident surplus reinsurance to between 9 and 14 lines, though some companies effect combined quota share and surplus treaties. There are some fire surplus reinsurances in existence providing up to 200 lines, though numbers in excess of 60 are unusual: the maximum number for accident treaties is about 20 lines.

Scope of a surplus treaty

The scope of a treaty in terms of the classes of insurance covered, its geographical limits, and the commencement of liability by the reinsurer are all matters of practical detail rather than of basic principle. Therefore they will be discussed in Chapter 7 when dealing with the details of proportional treaties, together with the other mechanics of their operation such as what information is supplied by the ceding company, claims handling, the settlement of disputes, etc.

Pricing surplus reinsurances

As the reinsurer accepts liability for a certain proportion of each risk ceded and pays the same proportion of any loss which occurs, the starting point for the price required by the reinsurer for the protection provided is an equivalent share of the original premium. The ceding company will have incurred the costs of acquiring and administering the business ceded, and therefore it is the universal practice for reinsurers who bear no part of those costs to allow a deduction in the form of a reinsurance commission. Often an additional commission in the form of a profit commission is provided as a reward to the ceding company for ceding profitable business to the reinsurer. The principles determining the size of the commission allowed have been discussed already in Chapter 3 so that it is sufficient to note here that the rate(s) allowed will depend upon:

(1) What deductions, if any, have been taken from the original premium credited to the reinsurer.

(2) The claims ratio of the reinsured portfolio.

(3) The composition of the reinsured portfolio.

The reinsurer will tend to compensate for a poorly balanced portfolio with a preponderance of hazardous risks by reducing the rate of commission allowed, so second or third surplus treaties carry lower commission rates than the first surplus treaty. On the other hand it is not unusual for treaties to pay rates of commission in excess of the ceding company's total expense ratio if the claims ratio on the original business is very low, so enabling the reinsured to obtain an extra risk-free profit.

Combined quota share and surplus reinsurances

Sometimes treaties are arranged to provide quota-share reinsurance for all insurances of a specified class (or classes) written by the ceding company, plus a surplus reinsurance on its gross line. The following example will illustrate how such an arrangement operates.

Example. A ceding company fixes a retention limit of £4,000 on any one risk accepted for its property account but wishes to be able to accept any one risk up to £100,000. It arranges a combined quota share and surplus treaty, the reinsurer providing:

(1) 80% quota share reinsurance, subject to a monetary limit any one risk of £20,000; and

(2) four-line surplus reinsurance for amounts in excess of the ceding company's gross line of £20,000.

If the ceding company was offered three insurances for sums insured of £10,000, £50,000 and £100,000 its retentions and the amounts ceded would be:

Gross line accepted £	Retention £	Ceding company's Share of gross premium %	Ceded to reinsurer Quota share £	Surplus £
10,000	2,000	20	8,000	—
50,000	4,000	8	16,000	30,000
100,000	4,000	4	16,000	80,000

The reinsurer's share of the original premium and of any losses would be calculated in proportion to the amount ceded in the normal way.

Such treaties are particularly suited to the requirements of newly established companies where the company probably cannot offer a sufficiently balanced portfolio to obtain a surplus treaty to provide automatic cover for the large risks which periodically it may be called upon to write. On the one hand it is cumbersome and administratively expensive to arrange separate facultative reinsurance for each large risk, but the alternative of a ceding company fixing its share of a quota share treaty so low as to keep its retention on large risks within its underwriting capacity may not be acceptable to either party. The reinsurer may worry about the lack of incentive that the ceding company would then have to exercise underwriting discipline, while the ceding company may object to passing on an unnecessarily large proportion of its gross premium income to the reinsurer; for example, if a primary insurer fixed its maximum retention at £4,000 it would require a 96% quota share treaty to handle a sum insured of £100,000. A combined quota share and surplus treaty offers a compromise solution. Not only can the ceding company retain a larger share of its gross premium income, but also over time, as it builds up its reserves, it will be able gradually to phase out the quota share reinsurance.

Frequently, combined quota share and surplus treaties are also used by well established companies to supplement the protection provided by a 'working' excess of loss cover for their property accounts. In such cases, the main purpose of the quota share would be to attain a reciprocal exchange of business, with the surplus element providing additional capacity.

III EXCESS OF LOSS REINSURANCE

General principles

Whether an excess of loss reinsurance is arranged on an individual risk or an occurrence basis the fundamental principle is the same. Instead of the reinsurer assuming liability for an agreed share of all losses occurring on individual risks ceded by the reinsured as with proportional reinsurances, he undertakes to indemnify the reinsured against any loss occurring on the reinsured portfolio of business in excess of an agreed amount, subject to an upper limit. Except for excess of loss reinsurances arranged facultatively for very large individual risks, this form of reinsurance essentially is concerned with the spreading of losses incurred on a portfolio of business rather than with the spreading of the original risks.

Frequently excess of loss reinsurances are arranged in layers for the reasons already outlined in Chapter 3. Although such arrangements obviously affect the administration of a reinsurance programme and may help to cut its cost, they do not alter the principles stated above.

The advantages of excess of loss reinsurances

It can be deduced from the above that from the standpoint of a ceding company excess of loss reinsurances have three major advantages over proportional reinsurances:
(1) The ceding company obtains protection only against the large losses which could strain its financial capacity, but, within the excess limits, that protection is 100% protection. Thus the company can cut off its liability at the chosen monetary limit. Theoretically the variability of retained losses would be smaller on a portfolio protected by excess of loss reinsurance than on an identical portfolio protected by surplus reinsurance which transferred the same aggregate annual expected loss to the reinsurer. (Conversely the reinsurer would be exposed to a higher variability of outcomes, which influences attitudes towards the provision of 'working' excess of loss covers and the premium loading required.)
(2) Because the reinsurer has no liability for the more frequent small losses costing less than the excess of loss reinsurance lower limit, the ceding company retains for its own account a higher proportion of its gross premium income.
(3) Administration costs are far lower for both parties. The ceding company no longer needs to classify each risk it underwrites to fix its retention, arrange reinsurance for any balance, apportion premiums

and losses, etc. Instead, after arranging the excess of loss cover, the reinsurance administration will be confined to paying the initial premium, calculating and paying any adjustment premium, and notifying and settling with the reinsurer any losses which fall within the treaty limits. At the same time it will be able to carry on its business in the knowledge that it has automatic protection against any losses falling within the reinsurance excess limits, though that should not lead to any change in its underwriting policy. Most excess of loss treaties are subject to exclusion clauses and limits which effectively require the ceding company to maintain the same underwriting standards etc. as before.

The extent to which excess of loss reinsurance reduces the variability of a ceding company's claims costs as compared with surplus reinsurance can be illustrated by considering a single risk with a probability distribution of losses by size as shown in Figure 5.4: for simplicity it may

Figure 5.4

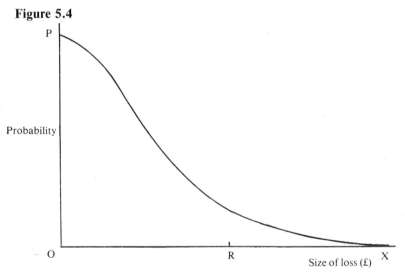

be assumed that only one loss may occur in any one year. Thus the insurer's annual loss experience may range from nil to a maximum loss of £X, with an annual loss expectancy given by

$$\sum_{j=0}^{X} P_j Z_j$$

where P_j = the probability of a loss of size Z_j
Z_j = losses of varying size j up to size X.

A measure of the variability of claims costs would be given by the standard deviation of the distribution.

If the company wished to limit its liability to R, which is half the maximum possible loss, it can either (1) cede half the risk by a surplus reinsurance, or (2) effect an excess of loss reinsurance providing cover up to X in excess of R. Thus by both methods the company can limit its maximum possible loss to the chosen amount, but the loss expectancies transferred to the reinsurer would differ as shown in Figure 5.5. With the excess of loss reinsurance the value transferred would be equal to the shaded area under the curve PX to the right of R (i.e. the area RSX) whereas for the surplus reinsurance the company would transfer the risk of half of every possible loss, i.e. the whole of the shaded area under curve PX.

Figure 5.5

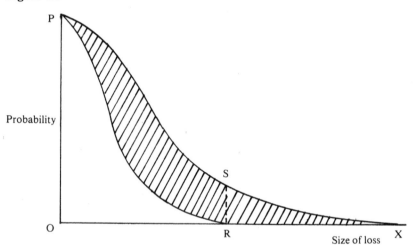

If investment earnings on the insurance fund and administration costs are ignored, it being assumed that the company charges its insured, and in turn pays to its reinsurer, a premium equal to the actuarial value of the risk transferred in each case, then Figure 5.5 shows that:

(1) The premium charged for the original insurance will be equal to the area OPX.

(2) With the surplus reinsurance the company retains 50% of the original premium, its net premium being equal to the area OPR, and with excess of loss reinsurance the retained premium is a larger sum equal to $OPSR$.

(3) The range of potential retained losses $O-R$ is smaller relative to the net retained premium with excess of loss cover than with surplus reinsurance.

174

Table 5.1

Size of loss z		(2) Probability of a loss of size z	Loss expectancy (Col 1 × col 2)
Range £	Midpoint £		£
0	0	0.900	0
1 – 100	50.5	0.050	2.525
101 – 500	300.5	0.025	7.513
501 – 1000	730.5	0.011	8.036
1001 – 2500	1750.5	0.008	14.004
2501 – 5000	3750.5	0.003	11.252
5001 – 7500	6250.5	0.002	12.501
7501 – 10000	8750.5	0.001	8.751
		1.000	z = 64.582

Expressing the same idea using a numerical example, if the probability distribution was as shown in table 5.1, then:

(1) The annual loss expectancy of the original insurance (and thus the premium) would be £64.58, with a standard deviation of £470.91.

(2) If half the risk was reinsured by means of a surplus reinsurance the retained loss expectancy (and so the premium) would also be half of the above, i.e. £32.29, and the standard deviation likewise would be halved.

(3) If the company effected an excess of loss reinsurance of £5,000 in excess of £5,000, its retained loss expectancy (and premium) would be £58.33, and the standard deviation would be £378.81, which is smaller relative to its retained premium than with the surplus reinsurance.

This analysis can be criticized on two grounds. First, the assumption that premiums are equal to loss expectancies obviously is highly unrealistic. Insurers and reinsurers not only load their risk premiums to allow for expenses and profit, but the variability of losses must also be taken into account. Consequently some of the advantage the ceding company gains by effecting excess of loss cover rather than proportional reinsurance will tend to be lost because of the relatively larger allowance the reinsurer will need to make for loss variability when pricing the cover provided. In the above example the reinsurer's loss expectancy on the excess of loss reinsurance would be £6.25 with a standard deviation of £130.83 and obviously he would be unwilling to enter into the reinsurance contract unless a substantial allowance was made in the premium for the loss variance.

Secondly, both ceding companies and reinsurers are not so much concerned about individual risks as with their expected experience on a portfolio of business. However, the conclusion regarding the superiority of excess of loss reinsurance over surplus reinsurance in reducing the variability of losses relative to retained premium income still holds. Indeed Professor Karl Borch in discussing optimal reinsurance contracts has demonstrated that stop loss covers protecting a total portfolio of risks are even better than any other form of excess of loss reinsurance, stop loss reinsurances being the 'most efficient' in the sense that, for a given net premium, they 'maximize the reduction of the variance in the claim distribution of the ceding company'.[1] However, as Borch has pointed out, the parties to a reinsurance contract have conflicting interests and in comparing different reinsurances a key factor is the premium loading required by the reinsurer to provide, *inter alia*, for variance, so that the optimal contract must appear as a reasonable compromise between those interests.[2]

The disadvantages

The rating problems associated with non-proportional reinsurances can be the major demerit of that class of reinsurances. Unlike proportional reinsurances where original premiums can normally be taken as a firm base from which the reinsurer can operate, adjusting the reinsurance commission he allows according to the loss experience and balance of the reinsured portfolio, the non-proportional reinsurer lacks such a direct relationship. On the other hand at times it may prove to be a blessing. If the original insurance has been inadequately rated, the excess of loss reinsurer does possess the advantage of having the freedom to quote rates for the reinsurance cover he provides on the basis of his own experience of such business.

Even so, premium rating poses many problems. Past loss experience may provide a reasonable base for rating working excess of loss reinsurances involving a sizeable number of reinsured losses each year but often is of little help in calculating the premiums for catastrophe and stop loss covers. Given all of the information that could be made available by brokers and ceding companies to arrive at a fair assessment of the risk, the rating of most non-proportional reinsurances must still involve a large measure of subjective judgment concerning the impact of various possible events on future loss experience. These problems will be explored more fully when rating methods are examined in detail later.

1 Borch, 'An attempt to determine the optimal amount of stop-loss reinsurance', in *Transactions of the XVI International Congress of Actuaries*, vol. 1 (1960), pp 597-610.
2 Borch, *Mathematical Theory of Insurance*, ch.2.

The other main disadvantages which may be cited are:

(1) Normal excess of loss reinsurances provide a ceding company with protection mainly against severity of loss: the company has to bear itself any increase in the frequency of losses below its chosen retention limit. Only a stop loss reinsurance offers protection against an increase in either or both elements of a company's loss experience.

(2) If a company seeks to protect itself against an increase in the expected frequency of losses by selecting a low retention limit, more losses will have to be processed by the reinsurer so that both parties will incur higher administration costs, thereby negating one of the advantages of excess of loss reinsurance.

(3) Special arrangements often have to be made for target and peak risks because their inclusion in an excess of loss treaty will tend to increase the variance of its results to a degree which may be unacceptable to the reinsurer and ceding company alike.

(4) Unlike proportional reinsurances, non-proportional reinsurances provide little or no assistance in financing the expansion of a ceding company's business. Generally a deposit reinsurance premium is payable by the ceding company before it has received its premium income for the year or the period of cover, although the reinsurer may be willing to relieve the strain somewhat by either charging a deposit premium lower than the anticipated final premium or by spreading it over four quarters.

(5) Under fire and marine excess of loss treaties subject to reinstatement clauses the ceding company is faced with the possibility of having to pay an additional premium if any losses occur during the year. Should experience be particularly bad the reinsured may be faced with having to pay two or three premiums during the year under the terms of an automatic reinstatement clause.

Types of non-proportional reinsurances

Non-proportional reinsurances can be classified in at least two ways.

In Figure 3.6 of Chapter 3 the class is broken down into stop loss or excess of loss ratio reinsurances, and excess of loss reinsurances with a further subdivision between excess of loss covers arranged on a risk basis or an occurrence basis. Each type differs in the nature of the protection it offers the ceding company, particularly against the risk of an accumulation of losses.

An excess of loss reinsurance arranged on a risk basis protects an insurer against a loss affecting an individual exposure unit where the company's liability exceeds what it regards as a tolerable sum. Like a

177

proportional reinsurance treaty, such an excess of loss treaty provides no protection against either an accumulation of losses arising from a single incident (such as a natural disaster), or from an abnormal number of losses occurring during one financial year.

Protection against an accumulation of losses due to a single incident affecting more than one policy is provided by an excess of loss cover arranged on an occurrence basis. The reinsurer's liability is determined not in relation to the cost of individual claims but according to the aggregate net retained loss sustained by the ceding company as a result of a single occurrence. Thus such a reinsurance is desirable whenever a portfolio of risks is exposed to a catastrophe which may involve a substantial number of exposure units.

A stop loss (or excess of loss-ratio) reinsurance provides a ceding company with protection against an unacceptable degree of variance in the aggregate loss experience of a reinsured portfolio of business during any one financial year. The reinsurer's liability is no longer tied to losses sustained on individual risks or to an accumulation of losses attributable to one occurrence, though one catastrophe may be so serious as to push up the ceding company's annual claims cost above the stop-loss or loss-ratio limit. Instead these two types of cover offer protection against an accumulation of losses, whether attributable to a greater severity or frequency of loss or a combination of both, which raises the ceding company's net retained losses above a financially tolerable level expressed either as a monetary limit (stop loss) or in terms of a target loss ratio. Such a contract theoretically could provide a company with an absolute guarantee against the risk of ruin if, after paying the reinsurance premium, the company was left with sufficient reserves to meet all losses up to the stop-loss limit. Unfortunately from the standpoint of ceding companies, practice does not coincide with theory because:

(1) The premium loading required by a reinsurer to compensate for the risk he assumes may adversely affect the company's reserves — or at least its ability to service those reserves — relative to retained liabilities.

And more importantly because:

(2) the reinsurer invariably limits his liability so that (*a*) the reinsured is required to take a share of losses falling within the reinsurance cover, and (*b*) an upper limit is placed on the cover provided.

Table 5.2 summarizes the scope of the cover provided by the three types of non-proportional reinsurance.

Table 5.2

Type of reinsurance	Single loss in excess of company's retention	Accumulation of losses arising from a single occurrence exceeding in the aggregate the company's retention	Total net retained losses over a year exceeding a certain amount or loss ratio
(1) Excess of loss (a) risk basis (b) occurrence basis	Protected Unlikely to be protected	No protection Protected	No protection No protection
(2) Stop loss or excess of loss ratio	Not relevant	Not relevant	Protected

The size of a ceding company's retention obviously differs according to the type of cover, and in each case the reinsurer's liability generally is subject to an upper limit, though sometimes reinsurers are prepared to give unlimited cover, notably for motor and employers' liability excess of loss treaties. Retentions are expressed in terms of the ultimate net loss incurred by the ceding company; that is, the company's share of the original claims cost less recoveries including recoveries from reinsurances effected in priority to the excess of loss cover.

Under most *excess of loss covers* the reinsurer assumes 100 per cent liability up to a specified amount for the balance of any ultimate net loss incurred on the reinsured portfolio in excess of a certain sum. For example, under an excess of loss reinsurance of £35,000 in excess of £15,000 the reinsurer's liability for losses of varying size would be as shown in Table 5.3.

Table 5.3

Ultimate net loss £	Ceding company's liability £	Reinsurer's liability £
12,000	12,000	nil
25,000	15,000	10,000
60,000	15,000 + 10,000	35,000

Thus, if in the above circumstances the ceding company incurred an ultimate net loss exceeding £50,000 it would have to carry the balance itself in addition to its basic retention. There are many occasions, however, where the ceding company carries a self-participation in an excess of loss cover, such as a 10% share of the losses falling under a catastrophe cover.

It was mentioned in Chapter 3 that excess of loss covers are frequently arranged in layers. If in the above case the ceding company had arranged a second layer for, say, £50,000 in excess of £50,000, the second reinsurer would become interested in any ultimate net loss exceeding £50,000 so that he would be liable for the balance of £10,000 on the £60,000 loss.

The same principles apply to *stop loss and excess of loss ratio covers* but with the latter the ceding company's retention is expressed as an annual loss ratio (that is the ratio of claims incurred to earned premiums or of claims arising to premiums written) for a particular class of insurance business. Normally the loss ratio is fixed sufficiently high to leave the ceding company with no profit on its net retained account. Therefore, retentions vary according to individual circumstances, including the class of insurance concerned — the different levels of acquisition and administrative costs being a major factor in determining the excess point. The reinsurer only becomes liable to indemnify the ceding company when its aggregate retained losses in any year exceed the agreed loss ratio, but thereafter the reinsurance pays for all losses, both large and small, up to an agreed limit of liability, expressed either as a loss ratio or an absolute amount, or the lower of the two figures. For example, a treaty may cover losses incurred in excess of 75% of earned premiums up to 125%, i.e. the reinsurer's liability being up to 50% or £1 million, whichever is the less. Thus so long as the ceding company's annual earned premium income remains below £2 million the loss ratio limit of 50% in excess of 75% applies, but if it expands its business beyond that figure the reinsurer's potential liability will be restricted to the absolute sum of £1 million. Rapid premium growth is often accompanied by a serious deterioration in the quality of business written, and the imposition of an absolute limit of liability is one way in which a reinsurer can safeguard his own interests.

Almost invariably stop loss and excess of loss-ratio treaties contain another safeguard. The ceding company may be required to carry a share of the losses falling within the reinsurance limits; normally the reinsurer limits his liability to 90% or 95% of the losses, leaving the ceding company to carry 5% or 10% itself. Thus a ceding company is not relieved entirely of the consequences of lax underwriting. The knowledge that it will incur a continuing, even if reduced, liability should its retained losses exceed the selected loss ratio is likely to be more effective in persuading a ceding company to maintain underwriting discipline than the threat that any marked deterioration in its loss experience will lead to a review of its reinsurance terms.

A special form of excess of loss ratio reinsurance which is sometimes used in the fire department, particularly for the protection of crop hail insurance, likewise requires self-participation by the reinsured in the excess layer. Known as 'excess-of-average-loss' cover, the excess point is recalculated each year as a moving average of the loss ratio experienced on the account over an agreed number of preceding years, and the ceding company is required to retain for its own account an agreed share of any loss in excess of that average.

It would be wrong to view stop loss covers as providing a ceding company with a means whereby it can guarantee a profit each year without any risk of incurring an underwriting loss. The lower the retained loss ratio and so the larger the liabilities transferred to the reinsurer, the larger too will be the proportion of the premium income required as a reinsurance premium. Unless the underlying direct gross account is soundly underwritten to produce an expected profit from year to year, there is no way in which any form of reinsurance can transform losses into profits. Indeed reinsurance adds another link to the production chain and thus additional costs, and the reinsurer too must have a reasonable expectation of earning a profit on the risk he assumes. Therefore, the object of a stop loss cover is to protect a company against random fluctuations in its annual loss experience on a class of business that, taken over a period of years, can be expected to yield a profit, and its main use is for classes of insurance, such as hail and livestock epidemic risks, subject to wide fluctuations in loss experience from year to year.

The scope of excess of loss reinsurances

Although increasingly excess of loss reinsurances for very large risks are being placed on a facultative basis, most of the business is handled by treaties. Like surplus treaties, an excess of loss treaty may embrace more than one class of insurance and include business written in more than one country.[1]

Frequently so-called *whole-account covers* are arranged to cover some or all of the types of accident insurance written by a direct insurer. Sometimes risks written by a fire department may also be included, and in special cases the cover may extend to marine risks too. Apart from treaties arranged for very small companies, the cover may be tailored to meet the special needs of the ceding company with differential underlying retentions, limits and premium rates applying to each main class of insurance included in the treaty.

---

1 For a discussion of the merits and demerits of including more than one class of business and/or territory in the same treaty see page 251.

Treaties arranged to cover a single class of insurance also sometimes provide for different underlying retentions and excess limits to apply to different classes of risk. Although such an arrangement is very unusual for fire and accident business it is fairly common for excess of loss reinsurances covering a marine account.

Even after an insurance company has arranged reinsurance protection in some form for each class of insurance it underwrites there remains the possibility that it may suffer an exceptionally heavy loss due to a single event affecting several classes of business. A mid-air collision of two aircraft over a town, for example, could result in losses affecting each of the following classes of business, each with its own separate retention(s):

(1) Aviation — hull and liability.
(2) Fire — damage to property on the ground.
(3) Motor — damage to vehicles.
(4) Personal accident — involving both passengers and persons on the ground.
(5) Products liability — due to some defect in the navigational equipment of one of the aircraft.

Sometimes a company will arrange an *umbrella cover* to protect itself against an accumulation of net retained losses under one or more classes of insurances arising out of a single event, including occasionally losses under life policies.

Normally excess of loss treaties exclude any liability for losses arising under excess of loss reinsurances accepted by the ceding company. Also it is now quite common for property 'working' covers to limit the reinsurer's liability for losses arising out of a single event, such accumulations being the subject of 'catastrophe' covers.

Professional reinsurers (and direct insurers writing inwards reinsurances) effect retrocession excess of loss covers to protect their overall net retained account. Normally separate retrocession arrangements are made for the protection of proportional and non-proportional portfolios, although it may be possible to include both within one retrocession treaty. Generally the retroceding company will have little information to guide either itself or the retrocessionaire in the potential accumulations of loss apart from its sources and types of business underwritten.

Defining the reinsurer's liability

Great care is required in defining the reinsurer's liability. An excess of loss reinsurance may be arranged either as the sole form of reinsurance for an individual risk or class of insurance, or in conjunction with some form of proportional reinsurance. The intention in every case is that the reinsurer shall only be liable if the amount of a loss actually borne by the ceding company itself exceeds some agreed figure. Therefore the reinsurer's liability is usually expressed as relating to the 'ultimate net loss' sustained by the ceding company *net of all recoveries, including recoveries from underlying insurances.*[1] Only if the ceding company's ultimate net loss exceeds the lower excess limit will the reinsurer become liable to contribute.

Although most reinsurers prefer to make their own retrocession arrangements, some excess of loss treaties are arranged to protect both the ceding company and all or some of its participating underlying treaty reinsurers. Such a cover is said to be for the *common account* of the reinsured and its reinsurers, and the excess-of-loss reinsurance would apply to their net losses. Where the underlying treaty is a quota share there should be no great difficulty in applying a single excess of loss cover to the net and treaty losses combined. Underlying surplus treaties pose more problems because the treaty loss experience may differ substantially from that of the ceding company's net retained account. Therefore it is then usually both fairer and more practical to arrange separate limits and excess points to treaty and net accounts, though in effect the excess of loss treaty would no longer be for the common account.

Aggregating losses

In addition to relating the reinsurer's liability to the net losses retained by the ceding company, it is also necessary to specify what losses can be aggregated for the purpose of applying the excess limits. Here one must look to the intention of the parties, and a distinction can be drawn between excess of loss reinsurances arranged on a risk basis or on an occurrence basis. In other words, is it the intention to protect the ceding company's account against the impact of large losses affecting one exposure unit, or against a series of losses attributable to the occurrence of a single event affecting a number of exposure units which collectively assume catastrophic proportions?

Although the parties to a treaty may be clear about their own intentions, the precise expression of such intentions in the wording of a treaty can pose enormous problems. On more than one occasion English courts have been required to decide on the meaning of words such as

---

1 Determination of the 'ultimate net loss', including the treatment of recoveries and claims-settlement costs, and the respective rights of the two parties regarding the contesting of claims, is discussed more fully in Chapter 8.

'accident' used in insurance policies, but there is nothing germane in their decisions to such terms as used in reinsurance contracts.

Golding illustrates how market thought and practice have developed in this area with the example of a motor insurance involving the collision of two cars insured by the same company. At one time the collision would have been treated *prima facie* as two events in that if two insurers had been involved each would have had to bear its own underlying excess of loss reinsurance retention. If the reinsurer's liability were defined as applying to 'any one event' or 'any one occurrence', such an interpretation would penalize the ceding company through the double application of the excess, i.e. it would be applied separately to the loss sustained by (or attributable to) each vehicle. As the intention of the parties to a motor reinsurance treaty nowadays is to treat such circumstances as a single event they may be content to define the reinsurer's liability as applying to 'any one event' and rely on market practice for the correct construction of the words used. Alternatively they may prefer to clarify their intention by using such words as 'any one event or series of events due to the same cause'.

When an excess of loss reinsurance is used as the sole form of protection for a fire account, instead of the reinsurer's liability being based on any one event it may be applied to 'any one risk'; that is, to individual risks included in the reinsured's portfolio. Thus in the event of loss the underlying retention and the upper reinsurance limit are applied separately to each individual risk, however many such risks are involved in the one event. It is important that the two parties to the treaty should be in agreement as to what is 'one risk' otherwise disputes may arise regarding, say, mercantile risks where the property of several policyholders is stored in one warehouse.

Essentially where excess of loss reinsurances are used as the sole form of reinsurance for a particular class of insurance, perhaps in lieu of surplus reinsurance, the main object will be to obtain protection against large losses which may be incurred under individual policies. Then the size of the underlying retention will usually be such that in the ordinary course of events the reinsurer can expect to be liable on a number of losses each year. Such reinsurances are known as *underwriting* or *working* covers. Additional layers of reinsurance may be arranged, if necessary, to protect the ceding company against the occasional exceptionally large single loss, such layers being described as 'top layers.'

The term *catastrophe cover* is used essentially to describe excess of loss reinsurances designed to protect the reinsured against an accumulation of losses arising from one event (or occurrences) of a particularly severe or catastrophic nature. Frequently such reinsurances are arranged to protect property insurance accounts covering natural perils and marine accounts where a large number of policyholders may suffer loss at the same time. In the case of motor and liability accounts where injuries or damage sustained by a large number of third parties may be attributable to the same cause, the loss may fall either under a top-layer working cover if only one policy is involved, or under a catastrophe cover if several policies are affected by the same event (e.g. motor claims arising from a multiple crash). Both property and liability insurances present ample scope for dispute over the interpretation of phrases such as 'one event' or 'a single occurrence.' For example, would a large number of property losses occurring over a period of, say, 24 hours due to a series of earthquakes, or similarly extensive damage spread over a far wider area caused by winds gusting in places to hurricane force, constitute one occurrence?

Professional indemnity and products liability risks present similar problems with the added complication that losses may be spread over a number of years. Is a series of claims occurring over two or three years for injuries which are traced to a defective drug produced in several batches one or more events? This question arose with the drug thalidomide where in England the direct insurers claimed that the birth of each deformed child was a separate occurrence; regardless of the outcome of that particular case, the issue remains to be decided by the courts. As excess of loss reinsurances are usually written on a 'losses occurring' basis,[1] delays in the emergence of claims allegedly attributable to the same event doubly complicate the issue.

Special wordings defining in more detail the meaning of an 'occurrence' by inserting time and/or geographical limits, and special agreements about the application of the excess limits, have been developed to deal with these difficulties; examples are provided in later chapters.

The limitations of written language probably make it impossible to express the intentions of the parties in words which are sufficiently flexible to cover all possible circumstances while at the same time totally avoiding any possible ambiguity. Therefore market custom must play an important role in the construction of the terms used to define the reinsurer's liability, and if dispute arises regarding the cause(s) of a loss the doctrine of proximate cause will apply. Where doubt exists about whether a number of losses are attributable to one or more events, the onus of proof will rest with the ceding company.

---

1 See page 290: basically the reinsurer accepts responsibility for all losses arising on policies attributable to one event occurring during the contract year.

Annuities

Finally, special consideration needs to be given to classes of insurance where the ceding company may incur a liability to pay the claimant an annuity; for example, a motor insurance covering countries where the courts may award an annuity to an injured third party, or when workmen's compensation statutes provide for the payment of annuities.

There are two possible ways of determining the reinsurer's liability. Under the first method the reinsurer becomes liable when the aggregate annual payments exceed the ceding company's retention. So, for example, under a treaty for £45,000 in excess of £15,000, if an annuity for life of £3,000 per annum was awarded the reinsurer would be liable to pay after the fifth payment had been made. Thereafter the reinsurer would be solely responsible for future payments, subject to the upper limit; in this case 15 further payments of the annuity would exhaust the reinsurer's limit of liability leaving the ceding company solely responsible for any further payments.

Although many treaties operate in this manner, arguably it is unduly favourable to the ceding company. It ignores the extra investment earnings the reinsured can obtain on the funds set aside to pay the annuity. In the above example, if it is assumed that the first payment is made immediately, followed by subsequent instalments at yearly intervals, and that the market interest rate is 8%, between the date the annuity is awarded and the fifth annual instalment the company could earn £2,807.76 in interest on its retention of £15,000.

Therefore one author has suggested that the ceding company should be responsible for the first x number of instalments which could be financed by investing its retention at the current rate of interest: in the above example it would pay the first 6.01 instalments.[1] He further argued that the reinsurer should then be responsible for subsequent instalments, the limit of his liability being determined by dividing the excess cover by the value of the annuity — in this case 45,000/3,000 = 15 instalments.

Such a method of determining the limit to the reinsurer's liability would be unfair in that it ignores the interest earnings accruing to the reinsurer. Equity would demand that as the reinsurer pays each instalment its value also should be discounted to its present value at the date of the award, so that the limit to the excess cover could be ascertained in terms of the aggregate present value of the annuity instalments. Using the same discount rate of 8% the present values of the instalments payable in years 8 and 9 would thus be £1,750.47 and £1,620.81 respectively and so on until the aggregate present value of the

---

1 'Apportionment of liability excess of loss claims', *Quarterly Letter from the Nederlandse Reassurantie Groep*, No. XIX/73, December 1973.

instalments paid reached the excess cover of £45,000: in this case the reinsurer would probably pay all remaining instalments because the present values of instalments 8 to 30 amount to only £19,905.

Another objection that could be raised to this first method is that with the award of a lifetime annuity the ultimate liability of both the ceding company and the reinsurer is dependent upon the size of the annuity and the number of years the claimant lives. Thus the reinsurer's liability (a) will be determined by a stochastic process, and (b) may not arise for several years and then extend over many more. Therefore, an alternative method of dealing with an annuity is to calculate when the award is made the capital sum required to purchase such an annuity. If that capital sum exceeds the ceding company's retention the reinsurer would pay the balance immediately, subject to his monetary limit, leaving the ceding company to decide whether to accept the mortality and investment risks involved in paying the annuity out of the fund it would thus hold, or whether to transfer such risks by purchasing an annuity from a life insurer.

Although there are strong reasons in favour of this second method its market usage is fairly limited. Generally only workmen's compensation and motor excess of loss treaties are made subject to a commutation clause for determining the reinsurer's liability for annuity payments.

Whichever method is employed, if the reinsurance cover is arranged in layers it is essential that all of the treaties are subject to the same provisions.

The award of indexed annuities in a period of inflation creates additional problems, as will be discussed later.

Underwriting considerations

An Advanced Study Group of the Insurance Institute of London identified the nub of the problem in underwriting excess of loss reinsurance treaties as follows:[1]

> In the case of excess of loss reinsurance the interests and fortunes of the reinsured and his excess of loss reinsurer may vary considerably and .... the principle which is applicable under proportional reinsurance (quota share, surplus, etc.), that the reinsurer shall follow the fortunes of the reinsured, can only be applied in a very limited sense. With these divergent interests, it is even more important that the reinsured should underwrite and handle his business with the interests of his reinsurers as much in mind as his own.

1 Report by Advanced Study Group No 201, *Excess of Loss Methods of Reinsurance* (Insurance Institute of London, 1975).

Under an excess of loss reinsurance treaty, even more than under a surplus treaty, basically a reinsurer is backing the underwriting judgment and integrity of his reinsured. He has no interest in the individual risks written by the reinsured; his concern is with the spread and profitability of the total reinsured portfolio. Consequently to ensure that the reinsured exercises the degree of underwriting discipline which is necessary to protect the reinsurer's interest, the company will be made to retain a reasonable stake in the business it accepts, and not infrequently it may also be required to bear a small share of the losses falling within the treaty limits.

There must exist a high degree of mutual confidence between the two parties, and a willingness to cooperate in the running of the business, including prompt notification to the reinsurer of all claims and cooperation in their settlement. At inception the reinsurer will want as much information as possible regarding the nature of the business written by the reinsured, local conditions which may have a bearing on future loss experience, the reinsured's underwriting policy (including details of retentions, underlying reinsurances, etc.), and the experience and ability of the company's staff. All of that can be summed up simply in the duty of a prospective reinsured to comply fully with the principle of *uberrima fides*, and throughout the currency of the treaty to inform the reinsurer of any actual or proposed changes that may affect the results of the treaty. Some of the requirements of the reinsurer may be given contractual force by the insertion in the treaty of claims notification, change of underwriting policy, change of law, and similar clauses, and risks which the reinsurer regards as unacceptable may be excluded from the scope of the treaty.

In practice a great deal of the information the reinsurer requires will be obtained through personal contact between the parties, and when the business is handled by a broker through his personal involvement too.

Unfortunately practice does not, and due to the pressures of work often cannot, accord with theory. Reference has been made already in Chapter 2 to the complaints that brokers do not always provide reinsurers with all of the information they require. Inadequacy of information apparently is not confined solely to broker-controlled cases. Three papers to the 1977 Reinsurance Offices' Association International Seminar were devoted to the problem, and three questionnaires which it was proposed should be used generally by reinsurers are shown in Appendixes 10.3 and 11.2.[1] Though not denying the desirability of obtaining such a wealth of information, some delegates argued that

---

1 Three papers by A. Taylor, J. Lavers, and G.W. Croton on the general subject 'Underwriting information and the non-proportional account', in *Papers presented at the Third International Reinsurance Seminar* (Reinsurance Offices' Association, 1977).

during the last hectic quarter of the year when most reinsurance contracts fall due for renewal, even if the information were made available it would not be possible to analyse and utilize it at the time. That view is too pessimistic: once a system has been set up to handle information, in the majority of cases it would have to accommodate only marginal changes most years.

A study of the three questionnaires will reveal that they seek to elicit information regarding the ceding company's underwriting policy, its exposure on target risks, its loss experience, and so forth. Additionally the reinsurer will need to know as much as possible about local conditions, including social, economic and political conditions. For example, political instability may lead to strikes and riots resulting in physical damage and business interruption, while economic pressures may produce inflation and the imposition of exchange controls preventing the remittance of premiums by the ceding company. The reinsured equally will be concerned about economic or political developments which may impede the ability of the reinsurer to carry out his side of the contract.

Premium rating

Like any other insurer, the aim of a non-proportional reinsurer must be to obtain from each reinsured a premium which after covering expected claims costs, plus acquisition and administrative expenses, will leave a sufficient contribution towards the reserve funds set up to provide for the catastrophe losses that may occur on that or other cases included in the reinsurer's portfolio and to yield a profit. The manner in which a reinsurer can set about calculating such a premium will depend upon a number of factors, notably:

(1) The form of non-proportional reinsurance required; i.e. whether excess of loss or stop loss.
(2) Whether it is a working excess of loss cover or a catastrophe cover.
(3) The size of the portfolio to be reinsured.
(4) The practice of the underwriter making the quotation.

Whatever method is employed the basic factors to be taken into consideration are:

(1) Past loss experience and loss trends.
(2) Any factors likely to affect future loss experience.
(3) The catastrophe potential of the business to be reinsured.
(4) The ceding company's retention and the reinsurance limits.
(5) The cost to the reinsurer of acquiring and administering the business.

189

Loss experience

Although the past loss experience of the ceding company is a major consideration, the reinsurer will be influenced too by his own experience of the class of insurance and the area concerned, and of the general history of losses of the type to be reinsured.

The significance of the ceding company's own experience will depend on how long it has written the business to be reinsured, the size of its account, the frequency of losses, the number of losses larger than the company's proposed retention, and whether there has been any change of circumstances which could substantially affect future loss experience. Though the reinsurer will only be liable to contribute to losses exceeding the ceding company's retention, it is useful to know the experience of the gross account or at least the account net of any underlying reinsurances. Such a presentation of the loss data is referred to as 'from the ground up' ('FGU'). It has the merit of appraising the reinsurer of the total distribution of losses, enabling him to estimate the effect that a small deterioration in experience would have on reinsured losses. For example, a portfolio of business with a large number of net retained losses lying just below the lower treaty limit would be decidedly less attractive to a reinsurer than one with few losses anywhere near to that point.

An increase in the portfolio of business underwritten will tend to be accompanied by an increase in the number of losses, including large losses. Therefore, in looking at the loss experience of a company over a number of years allowance must be made for changes in the volume of business written. Conventionally this is achieved by preparing the loss experience on a so-called 'burning cost' basis[1] whereby the loss experience is expressed as a percentage of premium income. The calculation of a burning cost will be explained in detail later; it is sufficient to note here that a reinsurer will want to see a statement covering usually the previous three or five years showing the losses for which he would have been liable expressed as a percentage of the ceding company's original premium income. Ideally losses occurring each year should be related to earned premium income to avoid any possible distortion in the calculated burning cost due to the expansion or contraction of the volume of business written. In practice this ideal is often not achieved; frequently excess of loss treaties are rated on the basis of written premiums, so losses have to be related to whatever premium base is used for rating purposes.

---

1 The use of the word 'burning' does not mean that the term is confined to fire insurance; indeed it originated in motor and liability departments.

If lengthy delays are likely between the occurrence and settlement of claims, the reinsurer will require from the ceding company so-called 'development statistics'. Such statistics show details of each individual claim falling within the proposed reinsurance limits, together with separate figures for the amounts paid and outstanding at the end of each year from the date of occurrence until final settlement (see page 539). Only with such information can the reinsurer form a judgment about the accuracy of the ceding company's claims-estimating methods and the size of loading to be applied to the burning cost for IBNR (incurred but not reported) claims. Development statistics also reveal the cash-flow characteristics and so investment-earnings potential of a portfolio.

Burning cost is of most value for working covers arranged for a substantial portfolio of business on which a reasonably stable number of losses can be expected each year. At the other extreme are top-layer and catastrophe covers where, to date, the ceding company may never have experienced a loss on which the reinsurer would have been liable - a zero burning cost obviously would be no justification for a zero reinsurance premium. Between the two extremes are many cases where adjustments must be made to the burning cost obtained from the company's records.

When the ceding company's loss experience fluctuates substantially from year to year the reinsurer must decide what confidence can be placed on an average rate obtained from several years' data. The first step is to look for the possible reasons for the fluctuations. One possible cause may be the random occurrence of a few large claims on a small portfolio, or of the odd exceptionally large loss on a sizeable, well spread block of business. Alternatively the account may be unbalanced and suffer in some years from an unusually high incidence of large losses. Whatever the reason, allowance must be made for it in the reinsurance premium, and the reinsurer may obtain some guidance from his own experience or market data covering the same type of business.

Amongst other factors which may undermine the value of a ceding company's past loss data are the effects of inflation, legal developments, changes in the company's underwriting policy, and also, in the case of portfolios covering overseas risks, changes in foreign-exchange rates. The impact of inflation has already been discussed in Chapter 3. Legal developments may have a similar effect; for example, a mandatory increase in workmen's compensation benefits could push more settlements above the ceding company's retention.

A company must always be responsive to changing conditions and adjust its underwriting policy accordingly. Consequently past loss experience can rarely if ever provide a perfect guide for the future because of changes in the size and composition of underwriting portfolios. The reinsurer must distinguish between marginal changes and major shifts in a ceding company's underwriting policy relating to the types of risks accepted or its retentions. A material alteration in underwriting policy either after or during the later years of the period covered by the burning cost statistics would call into question the validity of those statistics as a rating base for the changed portfolio.

Catastrophe potential

The catastrophe potential of the business covered by the proposed treaty may warrant a premium loading. Amongst the factors to be considered are:
(1) The nature of the risks covered; for example, does a fire excess of loss treaty include natural perils, and, if so, is the ceding company heavily committed in areas exposed to natural disaster?
(2) The form of reinsurance required and any exclusions. To what extent may the reinsurer be involved in accumulations of losses arising from the same event? The reinsurer's potential catastrophe loss obviously is far lower under a geographically widely spread property portfolio covering natural perils than one heavily concentrated in a potential disaster area. If a ceding company is willing to accept more restricted geographical and/or time limits in the definition of an 'occurrence', or to exclude particularly hazardous risks from top-layer working covers, the reinsurer's potential liability will be reduced and so a lower premium will be warranted.
(3) The treaty limits, including inner limits placed on the ceding company's net retentions for individual risks.
   The purpose of a 'catastrophe' cover is to protect the ceding company against occasional very large losses. Therefore, as reinsurers expect claims to be few and far between under such covers, it is now normal practice for fire and marine catastrophe treaties (and occasionally also the higher layers of working covers) to be subject to an automatic reinstatement clause which may require the reinsured to pay an additional premium to reinstate the cover in the event of any claim being incurred under the treaty. The details are discussed more fully in the relevant chapters. Only rarely are such provisions applied to accident treaties.

Administrative expenses

The costs for a working excess of loss treaty, or at least the lower layers of such a cover, will tend to be larger than for either a catastrophe cover or a stop loss treaty which should incur far fewer claims.

If a treaty is handled by a broker the cost of brokerage must be brought into account, though some offsetting savings may be achieved by taking full advantage of the services the broker can provide. The level of service expected of the reinsurer (e.g. help in training the ceding company's personnel or in handling claims), and the amount of contact requiring travelling to see the reinsured, must also be allowed for in the premium loading.

Continuity

Continuity of treaty arrangements between a ceding company and a reinsurer is still regarded as an important factor worthy of special consideration when fixing a reinsurance premium. It has been said that

> Excess of loss reinsurance to a greater extent than other forms of reinsurance ought to be a long-term relationship.[1]

Over recent years, however, perhaps the value placed on continuity has declined somewhat. Partly this is because the volume of supporting proportional reinsurance available for professional reinsurers has been falling, but perhaps of greater importance has been the widespread deterioration in the results of direct insurers throughout the world, both in terms of the average profitability of their business and in the variance of their results caused by a higher frequency of very large losses in many classes of business.

The deterioration in underwriting results makes both ceding companies and particularly reinsurers more reluctant to enter into long-term binding treaty agreements. A ceding company seeing its profits squeezed by rising claims costs, and in a period of inflation mounting administrative expenses too, will be more inclined to look around each year to secure the most favourable terms, even though over the long term it may fare worse than if it had stuck to one reinsurer. On the other hand a reinsurer may be reluctant to bind himself to continue a treaty for three or five years when the level and stability of results are deteriorating. Consequently instead of reinsurers being willing to grant premium concessions for treaties written on a three or five year basis they are more likely to look for a higher premium rate as with fire working excess of loss treaties which are still often written on a long-term basis. It has been market practice for many years for reinsurers to write marine and liability treaties on an annual basis, or at least to reserve the right to terminate the treaty at any year end.

---

1 Report of the Advanced Study Group of the London Insurance Institute, p.13.

Methods of premium rating

There are three basic methods of rating non-proportional reinsurances, namely:
(1) The *flat premium*, where the reinsurer charges a fixed sum of money.
(2) An adjustable premium where a *fixed premium rate* is applied to the subject premium income.
(3) An adjustable premium where a *variable premium rate* is applied to the subject premium income.

When an excess of loss cover is arranged facultatively for an individual risk the reinsurer may either quote a flat premium or, more usually, a premium rate may be applied to the original premium which itself may be subject to adjustment.

Flat premium

Usually a flat premium is quoted when the reinsurer can obtain no guidance from the loss experience of the ceding company. In particular flat premiums are charged for:
(1) Catastrophe covers where little confidence can be placed on the ceding company's past experience as a guide to future losses: a similar problem arises with top layer working covers. In both cases the reinsurer is being asked to cover the tail of the reinsured's claims distributions where one is dealing with large losses with very low frequencies of occurrence.
(2) New accounts for companies just commencing underwriting, or with total portfolios so small that (*a*) past loss experience cannot provide a guide to the future, and (*b*) the reinsurer may require a certain minimum premium to cover administrative costs and make the business worthwhile. As the ceding company's business develops sufficient information may become available to permit the use of a more flexible method of rating.

The major weakness of flat premiums is their failure to respond automatically to changes in either the ceding company's business or underwriting conditions which may be reflected in its loss experience. Therefore flat premiums must be reviewed each year, especially when used for treaties covering new, quite possibly rapidly expanding, companies.

Although the same principles govern the rating of any risk, exactly how a reinsurer will approach the calculation of a flat premium for a particular treaty will depend upon the individual circumstances. In every case theoretically he needs a reliable estimate of the ceding company's claims distributions from which to calculate the annual expected (i.e.

average) cost of reinsured losses and of their variance.

One, possibly cynical, view of the rating process in practice is that 'By far the most popular method is based on pure guesswork', and that 'Actuaries require too much information from ceding companies and produce formulas that underwriters cannot understand.'[1] The estimation of claims distributions probably falls within the scope of the latter comment.

The actuarial approach has been summarized by Dr B. Benjamin as follows:[2]

> From an examination of the claim rate and the claim amount distribution it would be possible to calculate $H(X)$ = the expected number of claims that will exceed the retention X and $M(X)$ = the average excess claim over retention, giving a net premium $P(X) = H(X) \times M(X)$.

Such a process would require data drawn either from the whole market or from a number of large offices, in order to obtain reliable estimates of low-frequency claims. Several actuaries have worked on the problem of fitting curves to available data. G. Benktander and C.O. Segerdahl in particular have studied the estimation of claims distributions in excess of loss reinsurance, and have found the Pareto and sometimes the lognormal distributions to be appropriate.[3] Using formulas derived from distributions it is possible to calculate the risk premium for an excess of loss treaty which then has to be loaded for contingencies, etc.

Although such formulas may be complex, and data obtained from market experience may not be perfectly representative of a ceding company's business, they are likely to produce more accurate flat premiums than pure guesswork - or even inspired guesswork.

Adjustable premiums

No insurance portfolio is static. Changes occur in both the population of policies and their associated risk factors so that the risk accepted by a direct insurer may alter considerably over time. In turn a reinsurer's exposure under an excess of loss treaty will change. Ideally therefore some method is required to ensure that the reinsurance premium will adjust to changes in the treaty exposure. Probably the best *single*

---

1 'Excess of loss rating science', *Reinsurance*, January 1977.

2 B. Benjamin, *General Insurance* (London: Heinemann, 1977), pp.218–19.

3 G. Benktander and C.O. Segerdahl, 'On the analytical representation of claims distributions with special reference to excess of loss reinsurance', *Transactions of the 16th International Congress of Actuaries*. See also G. Benktander 'The calculation of a fluctuating loading for excess of loss reinsurance', *The ASTIN Bulletin*, 1975/2, VIII, 272.

measure of that exposure is the ceding company's gross net annual premium income (i.e. gross original premiums less returns and cancellations and less premiums paid for reinsurances which inure for the benefit of the treaty). It is a measure of the aggregate loss expectancy of the various risks insured under the original portfolio less any part of those risks ceded under proportional reinsurances. An increase in the gross net premium income will indicate that the company has either:

—insured a larger number of exposure units; or

—that sums insured on smaller cases have been increased nearer to or above its retention limit; or

—altered its portfolio mix to include a larger proportion of more hazardous, more highly rated risks; or

—increased its net retentions (though under the terms of the treaty this probably could not be done without reference to the reinsurer).

In each case the reinsurer's loss expectancy would also tend to increase.

Thus by linking the reinsurance premium to the ceding company's gross net premium income the reinsurer is automatically compensated for any change in his potential liability. Two basic methods are employed:

(1) By applying a fixed premium rate to the reinsured's gross net premium income during the treaty year. Over time because the relationship between the degree of risk borne by the reinsurer and the gross net premium income may change, the premium rate may need to be adjusted.

(2) By applying to the reinsured's gross net premium income a premium rate which is adjusted automatically each year on the basis of the treaty loss experience.

Fixed premium rates

Normally at the beginning of each year the ceding company pays a deposit premium. Then at the end of the year the final premium is calculated by applying the agreed premium rate to the company's gross net premium income for the year.

Where the reinsurer's liability is for losses occuring on policies in force on the ceding company's books during the year, the correct measure of exposure is the reinsured's earned premium income which:

(1) brings into account that portion of the premiums paid on policies written during previous accounting periods which apply to the periods of insurance run during the current year; and

(2) deducts that portion of the premiums written during the year applying to the periods of insurance unexpired at the end of the year and so may give rise to claims in future years.

196

As can be seen from the following example, if an account is expanding the written premium income for the year will be greater than earned premium income, whereas if the business is contracting the reverse situation will occur. Therefore if the reinsurance premium is based on the ceding company's gross net written premium income it may over- or under-compensate the reinsurer for his exposure during the year.

	Year 1 £000's	Year 2 £000's	Year 3 £000's	Year 4 £000's
Gross net written premium income	1,000	1,200	1,500	1,400
+ unearned premium reserve at beginning of year at 40%	340	400	480	600
	1,340	1,600	1,980	2,000
− unearned premium reserve at end of year at 40%	400	480	600	560
Gross net earned premium income	940	1,120	1,380	1,440

Nevertheless despite the distortion produced by use of written premiums, in practice written premium income or accounted premium income is normally used for ease of calculation.

Fixed rate premiums are charged for all types of non-proportional reinsurance treaties, including working excess of loss covers, though under the latter type of contract where the reinsurer is exposed to a relatively large number of claims each year a variable premium rate may be used.

The reinsurer has little choice in calculating the premium for a catastrophe cover. It would be unsound to adjust the premium in response to loss fluctuations. The object must be to arrive at a premium sufficient to absorb the (hopefully) occasional losses and confine adjustments to any changes in exposure or other factors that indicate an increase in the treaty's loss expectancy. Therefore the reinsurer will try to fix a premium rate which when applied to the ceding company's expected gross net premium income for the forthcoming year will produce a reinsurance premium approximately equal to the appropriate flat premium for the risk insured. However, the fixed-rate method has the advantage that if the ceding company's premium income, and so the reinsurer's exposure, vary from what is expected at inception the reinsurance premium will be adjusted accordingly.

Essentially the same considerations enter into the determination of the premium rate as apply to the calculation of a flat premium. The only additional points for negotiation are the size of the deposit premium, whether the deposit is paid in full at inception or is spread over four quarters, and whether earned, written or accounting premiums are to be used. Sometimes special refinements on the fixed rate may be agreed, notably:

(i) *The coded excesses method.* Various classes of business lend themselves to rating on the basis of exposures revealed by an analysis of the original portfolio by size of sum insured, e.g. working covers for personal accident and burglary risks. In the fire department the 'coded excesses' method is a formalized system of rating designed to adjust automatically the premiums for working excess of loss covers arranged on an individual-risk basis in line with changes in the reinsurer's exposure revealed by changes in the size of the ceding company's portfolio and its distribution by size of sum insured. The reinsurer fixes premium rates expressed as a percentage of the gross net premiums for risks falling within agreed bands of sums insured, higher premium rates being charged for the higher bands. The total reinsurance premium is then calculated as the sum of the premiums for each band. A deposit premium is paid at the beginning of the year and at the end it is adjusted according to the volume of business written by the ceding company in each size band.

(ii) An increased limit premium method may be used for rating liability business, though in practice it is rare. Again the objective is to link the reinsurance premium more closely to the ceding company's potential liability under individual policies, and thus to the reinsurer's own exposure. Here the factor to be considered is the basic limit of liabiity any one occurrence under the original policy. In the same way as the ceding company will apply higher premium rates to higher limits, so likewise the reinsurance premium will be calculated by applying differential rates to the reinsured's portfolio broken down into bands of limits any one occurrence — the higher the limit the higher the premium rate charged by the reinsurer.

(iii) *A special records clause* may be inserted in a treaty when the portfolio of business to be reinsured has produced a sufficient number of losses in the past to provide a basis for the rating of the risk, but the reinsurer disagrees with the ceding company about the adequacy of its estimates for outstanding claims. The clause will stipulate that if the total value of the claims falling within the excess of loss limits during the x number of years immediately preceding the inception of the treaty exceed a stated amount, the premium rate for the current year will be increased accordingly. The rate may be increased either:

— in the same proportion as the excess balance bears to the stated amount; or

— to a higher rate stated in the clause.

Generally the proportionate adjustment of the rate is the preferred method.

In practice it is more common simply to insert in a treaty a clause stating that the amount to be included for outstanding claims shall be agreed by the parties. If the sum included subsequently proves to be inadequate future premiums are adjusted accordingly.

While it is in the interest of both parties to agree on a rate which can remain stable for several years, in an era of technological, economic and social change, inevitably loss expectancies also change and reinsurance premiums must be adjusted accordingly. Therefore fixed rates must be reviewed periodically.

As an incentive to the ceding company to accept what it may regard as a high fixed premium rate, the reinsurer may offer to pay a *profit commission* or, very rarely, a *no claims bonus*. Thus, if incurred claims in any year are less than an agreed figure the reinsured will be entitled to a premium refund.

When a profit commission is allowed normally:

(1) The maximum rate of commission allowed is 50%.

(2) For purposes of calculating the commission the gross profit (i.e. reinsurance premiums paid minus claims) is reduced by an allowance for the reinsurer's expenses and a contribution to a catastrophe reserve.

(3) Provision is made either to carry forward past losses or to calculate the commission only on the aggregate results of a number of years.

(4) The profit commission is subject to annual adjustment until all claims included in the calculations are settled.

Variable premium rates offer a means whereby the reinsurance premium can be adjusted regularly and gradually to changes in the reinsurer's loss expectancy as revealed by the ceding company's loss experience. The starting point for this method of premium rating is the treaty's 'burning cost'. As the aim is to adjust the premium only to the underlying trend of losses, the method is suitable only for working excess of loss treaties that produce a regular flow of reinsured losses each year. Even then to avoid violent fluctuations in the reinsurance premium rate various precautions are necessary, notably the imposition of lower and upper adjustment limits, and possibly the averaging of losses over a number of years.

When the method is used correctly, variable premium rates offer advantages for both parties. A ceding company knows that it will benefit by way of a lower reinsurance premium rate if it is successful in improving its loss experience, but at the same time it will still be able to budget within limits each year for the cost of its reinsurance protection because of the premium adjustment limits. Conversely the reinsurer can be sure that if the reinsured's loss experience does deteriorate the premium rate will increase automatically.

Whichever of the methods explained below is used for calculating the 'pure burning cost' of the ceding company's loss experience, it must be recognized that past experience is often not a perfect guide to the future. Conditions change and due allowance may need to be made in the premium to be charged. Also the reinsurer needs to allow for his own acquisition and administrative costs and to provide a contribution to the contingency reserve to cover claims fluctuations in his total portfolio. Therefore 'burning costs' (or 'pure burning costs', the terms are synonymous) are loaded by some percentage to produce a 'loaded burning cost' which gives the rate used to calculate the reinsurance premium. Before considering the loading factor, methods of calculating 'pure burning costs' will be examined.

There are conflicting considerations in choosing the number of years to be included in the burning cost calculations. One line of argument is that the predictive value of such statistics is directly related to the number of years included because:

(1) for many classes of insurance the figures for immediate past years are largely based on estimates because of delays in the reporting and settlement of claims; and

(2) the longer the period taken the less sensitive will be the average loss experience to annual random fluctuations.

On the other hand if substantial changes have occurred in either the reinsured portfolio or its risk factors, the loss results of past years may no longer provide a reliable guide to the future. Insurers operate under dynamic conditions and therefore the older the data the less reliable they are likely to be for rating purposes. Consequently it is the practice to base burning cost statistics on no more than five years and possibly three years' loss figures. Some treaties are rated on a so-called 'year of account' only basis, the reinsurance premium required for one year being tied to claims occurring during that year.

The figures in Table 5.4 will illustrate how burning costs are calculated by the various methods in use - the limits to the size of the reinsurance premium charged in any one year as given by agreed minimum and maximum rates will be ignored until later.

Table 5.4

Year	Gross net premium income	Losses payable by reinsurer as known at end of year 5	Pure burning cost
	£	£	
1	1,000,000	15,500	1.550%
2	1,200,000	26,700	2.225%
3	1,380,000	70,770	5.128%
4	1,600,000	58,160	3.635%
5	1,900,000	79,380	4.178%
	7,080,000	250,510	3.538%

(1) *Year of account basis.* If it was agreed to base the reinsurance premium on the claims results for the year of account only, the pure burning cost for year 5 as calculated at the end of that year would be 4.178%. However, at that time the ceding company's final gross net premium income for the year would not be known, and a large part of the losses would still be outstanding. Therefore, provision must be made for the burning cost to be recalculated at the end of each subsequent year until all claims are finally settled, and for the reinsurance premium to be adjusted accordingly. So, for example, given a loading factor of 100/70, the premium for year 5 would be adjusted as follows, assuming all claims are finally settled at the end of the fourth year of account and ignoring minimum and maximum rates.

Year	Gross net premium income for year 5	Year 5 claims paid and outstanding to end of year	Pure burning cost	Loaded burning cost
	£	£		
5	1,900,000	79,380	4.178%	5.969%
6	1,950,000	84,500	4.333%	6.190%
7	1,950,000	85,650	4.392%	6.274%
8	1,950,000	83,780	4.296%	6.138%

Year	Reinsurance premium for year 5 as calculated at end of year £	Adjustment premium £
5	£1,900,000 × 5.969% = 113,411	—
6	£1,950,000 × 6.190% = 120,705	+ 7294
7	£1,950,000 × 6.274% = 122,343	+ 1638
8	£1,950,000 × 6.138% = 119,691	− 2652

(2) *Average of previous three (or five) years.* This method bases the reinsurance premium rate on the burning cost of the previous three (or five) years.

Again using the data in Table 5.4, the premium rate to be applied to the ceding company's gross net premium income to produce the reinsurance premium for year 6 would be based (depending on whether a three- or five-year average was used) on the results of years 3 – 5, or 1 – 5. The hypothetical individual year burning cost figures used in these examples would raise doubts regarding the trend of the reinsured's experience. Losses in the first two years are substantially lower than in years 3 – 5, and the variance in the results of the last three years is much smaller than for all five years. Therefore, before including the figures for years 1 and 2 in the calculations far more information would be needed regarding the numbers and sizes of losses incurred in each of the five years, whether the ceding company had substantially changed its underwriting policy during the period under review, and so forth. At first sight the experience for the last three years would seem more reliable, and so an average of years 3 – 5 may be preferred. The calculations would be as follows, again using a loading factor of 100/70.

Year	Gross net premium income £	Losses payable by reinsurer £	Burning cost	Loaded burning cost
3	1,380,000	70,770		
4	1,600,000	58,160		
5	1,900,000	79,380		
	4,880,000	208,310	4. 269%	6.098%

Thus, if the ceding company's gross net premium income for year 6 was £2,150,000, its total reinsurance premium for the year would be £131,107. Even the use of a three-year average does not overcome the objection that it is weighted by the growth of the business. Therefore, if an average is to be used, there is a strong case for calculating the burning cost for each year and taking the average of the annual rates.

In this instance the average burning cost for years $3-5$ would be 4.314%, so producing a loaded burning cost of 6.163% and a reinsurance premium for year 6 of £132,501.

(3) *Three (or five) year spread loss.* This method is similar to the preceding one. The difference is that the current underwriting year's loss experience is brought into the calculation. Obviously the rate to be charged cannot be calculated until some time after the end of the year, allowing time for the notification and estimation of losses incurred during the year: at the beginning of each year the reinsured pays a deposit premium geared to past premiums. Thus if losses incurred during year 6 were estimated at £83,250, the reinsurance premium for that year (with the 100/70 loading factor) based on the average burning cost for the year of account plus the two previous years would be:

Year	Gross net premium income £	Losses payable by reinsurer £	Burning cost	Loaded burning cost
4	1,600,000	58,160		
5	1,900,000	79,380		
6	2,150,000	83,250		
	5,650,000	220,790	3.908%	5.583%

£2,150,000 × 5.583% = £120,034

(4) *Three year block (triennial slide).* This method is very similar to the preceding one. Essentially it is used for a long-term reinsurance treaty covering a three-year period where the premium is built up over three years. The premium for the first year is fixed at the end of the year on a burning cost calculated on that year's experience, the second year's rate is then based on the average of two years' experience, and so on until the full three-year average is obtained.

Like method (1), the reinsurance premiums payable under methods (2), (3) and (4) are subject to annual adjustment until the final settlement of all claims included in the burning cost calculations for that year.

Essentially methods (2), (3) and (4) work on the moving-average principle. Therefore the terms of the treaty will also stipulate that each year the latest year's figures are to be brought into the calculation of the average burning cost, replacing those of the oldest year. However, because of the problems involved in using more than one year's experience none of the methods is commonly used other than for property reinsurance.

Minimum and maximum premium rates. Whichever of the variable-rate methods is used, the reinsurance premium for any year must be subject to lower and upper adjustment limits to avoid either:

(1) the reinsured over time simply repaying the reinsurer in full for losses incurred plus the loading factor; or

(2) if losses were low for several years, the reinsurer receiving insufficient premium to cover his administration costs and to contribute to reserves and profits.

The size of the minimum and maximum rates must be determined principally by the variance of the reinsured's loss experience, the reinsurer's costs of administering the treaty, and the loading factor. The adjustment limits and the loading factor are interdependent and the more stable the loss experience the simpler it is to arrive at appropriate figures for both. Consider the following two cases where the reinsurance premium is fixed on a year of account burning cost basis:

Pure burning-cost data

Year	Treaty A %	Treaty B %
1	2.3	1.2
2	3.0	4.3
3	2.7	2.3
4	2.5	0.9
5	3.2	5.0
Unweighted mean	2.74	2.74
Standard deviation	0.36	1.83

Although the average burning cost is identical in both cases, treaty A has produced far more stable results than B. Also the figures suggest that whereas the results of A are normally distributed around the mean, for B they are positively skewed, i.e. the average of 2.74 for B is pulled up by the occasional bad year, and that in most years the loss experience would be better than average. If under both treaties the reinsured wanted to keep premium costs as stable as possible and (ignoring at present the loading) asked for adjustment limits to the pure burning cost of 2.5% and 3.0%, in three out of the five years the individual year's results of treaty A would have fallen within the limits. Treaty B presents a different picture: in no single year did the experience lie within the limits. Moreover B is likely to produce a far larger loss (in terms of burning cost) than A, as shown by the standard deviations. Therefore, by accepting narrow adjustment limits the reinsurer would run little risk under A and his loading for the risk of aggregate losses greatly exceeding expected amounts could be small. On the other hand, under B the pure burning cost rate in most years would be below that required to cover the treaty's expected losses, the risk of incurring very large losses would be much larger, so that a far larger loading factor would be justified. Later other aspects of loading factors will be considered.

Rebate systems. Another means of adjusting premiums to the treaty loss experience is through rebates if loss experience in any year proves better than some agreed standard. Various methods have been devised, though none are in common use: notable examples are the rebate rating scheme and the use of advance deposit premiums.

In a *rebate rating scheme*, at the beginning of each year the reinsurer quotes a premium rate divided between (1) expected claims costs and (2) the loading for administrative expenses, profit and contingency reserves. If the final actual claims cost for the year of account is less than the premium applicable to the expected claims, the difference is returned to the reinsured.

With an *advance deposit premium*, at inception the reinsurer fixes a rate of premium which is divided into two components - part to establish a claims fund which he will hold and administer, and the balance to provide a 'reinsurance premium' to cover the expected cost of the residual risk he assumes, his administrative expenses and a profit margin. Each year the agreed part of the total premium paid by the ceding company is credited to the claims fund and claims incurred are debited against the fund. If losses are sufficiently low that at the end of any year the claims fund has built up to an agreed maximum amount, then the premium rate payable by the reinsured for the following year(s) will be reduced to provide only the 'reinsurance premium', and it will remain at that level until more incurred claims reduce the claims fund below the agreed maximum. The risk assumed by the reinsurer is that incurred claims may exceed the amount available in the claims fund.

A treaty arranged on such a basis would normally be expected to run for several years. However, it is market practice to include an annual cancellation clause entitling the reinsured to receive the following proportions of the claims fund which at the date of termination is free (i.e. not earmarked to pay outstanding claims):

— if cancelled at the end of the first year: $33\frac{1}{3}\%$
— if cancelled at the end of the second year: $66\frac{2}{3}\%$
— if cancelled at the end of the third or later years: 100%

The 100% refund would take place when all claims had been settled.

Nowadays both ceding companies and reinsurers tend to avoid long-term commitments and prefer to review treaty terms annually.

The loading factor

Throughout the above examples a constant loading factor of 100/70 has been used to calculate the reinsurance premium but in practice the size of the factor will depend upon the individual circumstances of each case. The loading factor can be broken down into three elements:

(1) a charge to cover the reinsurer's acquisition and administrative expenses;

(2) a safety loading to cover the risk accepted by the reinsurer (i.e. the fluctuations in claims costs); and

(3) a contribution to profit.

The calculation of the *expenses loading* requires the reinsurer to estimate (1) the expected total cost of administering the treaty, (2) the pure premium rate, and (3) the reinsured's gross net premium income. A reinsurer's total costs are composed of fixed and variable costs and so in calculating the cost of running a treaty he must decide how his fixed costs shall be allocated over individual treaties. As the charge to the ceding company for administrative expenses takes the form of a proportionate loading of the premium rate instead of a lump sum, in order to recoup the estimated cost the reinsurer must take a view of the reinsured's likely gross net premium income and the pure premium rate. If that rate is based on and adjustable according to burning cost, then the variability of the claims experience and the size of the adjustment limits must also be taken into account.

Various views have been expressed regarding the calculation of *safety* loadings for non-proportional reinsurances. There are persuasive arguments in favour of fixing loadings proportional to the standard deviation of the probability distribution of the claims which may be made under the treaty in that such a method would give the reinsurer a fair price for the risk he assumes.[1] Professor Borch, however, has argued that such an approach ignores the realities of the market where companies both cede and accept reinsurances, and where the price the buyer is prepared to pay may not match what the seller would regard as 'fair'. He demonstrates that there is some justification for making the safety loading proportional to the pure premium.[2]

Professor Borch's observations about market conditions are also relevant to the loading for profit. In a competitive market the reactions of competitors cannot be ignored. Whatever method is used to calculate a premium rate which may be regarded as actuarially correct, it will

[1] H. Ammeter, 'The calculation of premium rates for excess of loss and stop loss reinsurance treaties', in *Non-proportional Reinsurance*, ed. S.Vajda (Arithbel SA, 1955).

[2] 'The safety loading of reinsurance premiums', in *The Mathematical Theory of Insurance*.

usually need to be modified in the light of prevailing market conditions. Also burning cost alone is only a partial measure of expected claims costs — allowance must be made too for the cash-flow characteristics of the treaty (that is, the timing of premium receipts and claims payments, what part of the technical reserves is held by the ceding company and the rate of interest, if any, paid thereon); what constraints are placed on investments; and money and capital market conditions.

Stability or index clauses

Brief reference was made in Chapter 3 to the disproportionate impact of inflation on an excess of loss reinsurer's liability due to:
(1) more claims falling within the monetary limits as inflation pushes their cost above the lower limit; and
(2) the reinsurer having to bear in full the additional cost of claims falling within the monetary limits.
A simple example will illustrate the latter point, showing how the reinsurer's claims liability increases far faster than the underlying rate of inflation.
    Assume: — Excess of loss reinsurance £50,000 excess of £10,000
                — Estimated cost of settling claim in year t is £11,000.
                — Rate of inflation of claims costs is 10% per annum.

| | Direct claims cost | | Reinsurer's liability | |
Year	Estimated cost of settlement	Cumulative percentage increase since inception	Amount payable	Cumulative percentage increase since inception
	£	%	£	%
t	11,000	—	1,000	—
$t+1$	12,100	10.0	2,100	110
$t+2$	13,310	21.0	3,310	231
$t+3$	14,641	33.1	4,641	364
$t+4$	16,105	46.4	6,105	511
$t+5$	17,716	61.1	7,716	672

Several writers have pointed out that for liability covers such disproportionate increases in a reinsurer's liability are not just caused by inflation. Awards for personal injury are related to earnings which during periods of economic expansion rise even if prices remain stable. Moreover there is a tendency throughout the world for courts to be more generous towards claimants in extending the principles of liability, in the levels of compensation awarded, and in admitted heads of damages, while advances in medical knowledge are both helping to keep alive more seriously injured persons and increasing the costs of treatment. The combined effect of these factors on claims costs has been called 'superimposed inflation'.[1]

When a direct insurer writes an insurance he must recognize that inflation, changes in the law, and other developments may raise the cost of claims and administrative expenses above past levels. Therefore original premiums need to be adjusted accordingly. It may be argued that excess of loss reinsurers should provide for their potentially larger liabilities in the same way but that is easier said than done. The estimation of required premium increases is difficult enough for direct insurers[2] but it is considerably more so for reinsurers. The problem is particularly acute for the so-called 'long-tail' classes of insurance where claims often remain outstanding for five or more years while their potential costs of settlement continue to rise through inflation.

Using data drawn from the experience of a motor account Gunnar Benktander has demonstrated that, as shown above, inflation will increase the cost to the reinsurer of the excess of loss claims by a larger multiplier than the increase in the total original claims.[3] Moreover even if the ceding company increased its premiums by the rate of inflation the burning cost of the treaty would still increase; in other words the increase in the reinsurance premium obtained from the increase in the reinsured's gross net premium income would be insufficient to cover the reinsurer's additional claims cost. The higher the excess layer the greater would tend to be the deficiency.

The same results can be observed from the following hypothetical simplified example using pure premiums (i.e. premiums equal to expected losses):

Ceding company's claims distribution £

Size of loss (£)	0 – 1,000	1,000 – 2,000	2,000 – 3,000	3,001 – 4,000	4,001 – 5,000	5,000 and over
Mid-point £	500	1,500	2,500	3,500	4,500	10,000
Numbers of losses	400	200	160	120	70	50

1 G. Benktander, op cit; 'The principle of stability clauses in excess of loss reinsurance', *Quarterly letter from the Nederlandse Reassurantie Groep*, August 1974 No. XIX/75.
2 See, for example, J-M Belloy & A. Gabus, 'A model for measuring the impacts of inflation on motor insurance business', *The Geneva Papers* No. 1 (January 1976), and *The influence of inflation on insurance* (Munich Reinsurance Co., 1971).
3 Benktander, op cit.

Assume:

— Losses occur on average mid-year.
— Average settlement delay for losses up to £4,000 is six months and for losses of £4,001 and over is 18 months.
— Interest earned on funds is 5%.
— An excess of loss cover is arranged for £45,000 in excess of £5,000.

In the absence of inflation (and ignoring interest on technical reserves) the expected claims costs based on mid-point values, and therefore the pure premiums, would be:

Total original claims	£2,135,000
Reinsured excess losses	£500,000

so producing a 'pure' reinsurance burning cost of 23.42%.

If inflation caused claims costs to increase at a constant rate of 8% per annum the mid-point values up to £4,000 would increase by a factor of 1.08, and those of £4,001 and above by 1.08^2. Assuming that the 70 claims in the original £4,001 – £5,000 band were evenly distributed by size, a 16.64% rise in settlement costs would take 50 of them over the £5,000 retention limit. Therefore the expected claims costs would become:

Total original claims	£2,376,215
Reinsured excess losses	£604,000

so increasing the reinsurance burning cost to 25.42%.

Therefore to cover the increase in the total original claims cost the ceding company would have needed to have raised its pure premiums by 11.3%. Although by applying the original burning-cost rate of 23.42% to the ceding company's revised premium income the reinsurer would have obtained a higher premium of £556,510, it would have been insufficient to have covered his increased expected claims liability of £604,000.

If an allowance for investment earnings on technical reserves is introduced into the calculation of the ceding company's premiums, the situation gets somewhat more complex, but usually the basic result will remain the same. Under the usual conditions experienced in a period of inflation, an increase in the ceding company's premiums sufficient to cover the increase in the present value of expected total claims will not be enough to compensate the reinsurer for the increase in his claims costs.[1]

Benktander points out that in practice neither party possesses sufficient information to calculate current burning costs with any degree of accuracy. To do so means estimating the run-off of claims at forecasted rates of inflation. Even then if inflation is accelerating or decelerating the adjustment of burning cost rates to current experience may still result in the reinsurer being under- or over-compensated for the cover he provides. Consequently, with the long-tail classes of insurance, i.e. liability and motor, and to a far lesser degree property covers where the original sums insured rather than the premiums are index linked (e.g. household insurances and other fire insurances in France and some other countries), the market has adopted the alternative solution of stability (or index) clauses.

A typical clause is included in Appendix 5.1. The opening words express the principle that the ceding company's retention and the liability of the reinsurer shall retain the same relative values as existed at the inception of the treaty. The method employed is to tie the treaty monetary limits to an agreed index which it is hoped will prove a reasonable proxy for the rate of inflation of claims costs. Usually some form of wage index provides the best fit for motor and liability reinsurances, particularly if the stability clause is only applied to bodily injury claims.[2] If such an index is not available for the country concerned, then a retail price or some other price index may have to be used. The way in which the clause operates can be illustrated by reference to the example on page 207 where it was shown that the effect of 10 per cent inflation on a claim outstanding for six years was to increase the ceding company's retained liability by 61.1% and the reinsurer's liability

---

1 For example, if in the absence of inflation the ceding company in calculating its pure premium assumed that a rate of 5% could be earned on funds, the present (i.e. discounted) values of the expected cost of claims shown in the above distribution would be:

Present value of total original claims	£1,996,372
Present value of reinsured excess losses	£453,515

The burning cost (as conventionally calculated) would be $\frac{500,000}{1,996,372} \times 100 = 25.05\%$, and the reinsurance premium would be £500,000. If interest rates rose to 10% when inflation was running at a rate of 8%, the present values of the expected claims would be as follows and the ceding company would adjust its premiums accordingly:

Present value of total original claims	£2,081,645
Present value of reinsured excess losses	£496,000

Applying the burning cost rate of 25.05% to a gross premium of £2,081,645 would provide the reinsurer with a premium of £521,452.

In the non-inflationary situation, after allowing for the interest earned by the reinsurer on his funds, the reinsurance premium of £500,000 would yield a surplus of £46,485 which, presumably, would be allowed for when fixing the burning cost loading. With inflation at 8% and interest at 10% the surplus would be reduced to £25,072.

2 'The principle of stability clauses in excess of loss reinsurances - a brief outline,' *N.R.G. Quarterly Letter*, August 1974 No. XIX/75. An analysis of UK court awards for bodily injury over a fifteen-year period has shown that there is a strong relationship between levels of earnings and the size of awards; see 'Problems of liability insurance', *Post Magazine and Insurance Monitor*, 7 and 14 April 1977.

by 672%. If the reinsurance had been subject to a stability clause where the chosen index had also shown a steady rise of 10% per annum the adjusted result would have been as follows:

Year	Direct claims cost £	% increase	Treaty limits Reinsured's retention £	Reinsurer's liability £	Liabilities Reinsured	Reinsurer
t	11,000	—	10,000	50,000	10,000	1,000
$t+5$	17,716	61.055	16,105	80,528	16,105	1,611

Instead of the full impact of inflation falling on the reinsurer the additional claims cost is shared proportionately, the cost to each party increasing by 61.055%.

The indexing of the reinsured's retention also avoids the reinsurer picking up liability for claims which, in the absence of inflation, would have been settled for less than the lower excess point at the inception of the reinsurance. So, for example, if inflation running at an annual rate of 10% raised the cost of a claim from £9,500 at the date of occurrence to £15,300 five years later, it would still fall below the ceding company's adjusted retention limit of £16,105.

In the clause quoted in Appendix 5.1, the indexation takes place at the date of the settlement of losses. However, some reinsurers prefer for ease of administration to operate on the basis of just an annual adjustment of the treaty limits.

When several claimants are involved in the same event so that a loss under an original insurance is settled in instalments, the reinsurer's liability should not be ascertained by adjusting the reinsured's retention on each occasion by the index value at that time. A more equitable method is:
(1) to discount the payments to commencement-of-treaty values and so ascertain what would have been the excess loss at that date;
(2) to calculate the ratio of that excess loss to the adjusted claims value; and
(3) to apply that ratio to the total actual payments to ascertain the reinsurer's liability.

The following example illustrates this point: it is assumed that the same treaty limits and constant 10% rate of inflation apply as before.

	£
Instalment 1 of claims paid end of year $t+3$	8,000
Instalment 2 of claims paid end of year $t+5$	12,500
	20,500

Claims value adjusted to year t:

Instalment 1 $£8,000 \times \dfrac{100}{133.1}$ $=$ 6,011

Instalment 2 $£12,500 \times \dfrac{100}{161.05}$ $=$ 7,762

                                                      13,773

Reinsurer's liability in year t values $= £13,773 - £10,000 = £3,773$

Reinsurer's liability $\dfrac{3773}{13773} \times £20,500 = £5,616$

A more detailed example using an alternative method of arriving at the same result is given in Appendix 5.2, illustration (1).

Sometimes only part of the cover provided by an excess of loss contract may be subject to the provisions of a stability clause — for example, only the liability sections of a motor treaty or a combined hull and liability aviation treaty. It is then necessary to determine the reinsurer's liability in two stages. First the ceding company's retention must be apportioned between the two components of any loss in proportion to the respective payments. Secondly the reinsurer's liability for the indexed component needs to be deflated in accordance with the terms of the clause. An example of such split indexation is given in Appendix 5.2, illustration (2).

Variations on the standard clause

Besides the standard type of stability clause discussed above there are a number of variations in use. They fall into four categories:
(1) A fixed amount of reinsurance cover is given in excess of an indexed retention limit.
(2) Indexation is applied only to the ceding company's retention but not to the upper treaty limit, so that over time the reinsurer has a narrowing liability.
(3) Indexation takes the form of a franchise of, say, 10% so that any rise in the index of less than 10% is ignored but beyond that the standard stability clause provisions operate.
(4) The 'severe inflation clause', which only applies if the index has increased by more than, say, 30% and then only in respect of any rise in excess of 30%.

Indexed annuities

Further complications arise when injured third parties or their dependants are awarded annuities with payments tied to a wage or price index. Although developments in France in relation to awards for persons severely injured or killed in motor accidents brought the issue to a head, the award of indexed annuities is not confined to that country alone.[1] Moreover, as stated in a recent report, 'There would appear to be no reason why indexed awards may not be given for non-motor injuries and even in cases not involving bodily injury at all.'[2]

Although such awards may accord with social justice they mean that insurers and reinsurers are left to pick up potentially far greater liabilities due to the failure of governments to control inflation. They may face the prospect of incurring a liability to make payments 20 or more years hence rising in value at an uncertain rate each year. As stated earlier, apart from motor and workmen's compensation excess of loss reinsurances, it is not normal market practice to include in treaties a claims-commutation clause but in cases where such a clause is used reinsurers are not prepared to accept liability for future inflation. Therefore the clause will stipulate that the actuarial value of the annuity will be calculated on the assumption of stable prices, and the ceding company will be left to decide how to invest the capital sum it receives from the reinsurer. Only if it can invest in an index-linked security of some kind will future inflation pose no problem. If the government does not make available such securities, the ceding company is left to carry the risk that investment earnings will be insufficient to cover the additional annuity payments due to inflation, and presumably try to recoup the costs by charging higher premiums to future generations of policyholders.

Market views differ about the most equitable manner of treating indexed annuities where the treaty does not include a commutation clause. Some treaties are written without an index clause so that the

---

1 For details of other countries see the report by an international sub committee of the Reinsurance Offices' Association, *Indexed Annuities and the Reinsurer*, (ROA, 1978). In 1978 the Pearson Commission recommended that awards of inflation-proofed payments should be introduced in Britain for the most serious cases of personal injury. *Report of the Royal Commission on Civil Liability and Compensation for Personal Injury*, Vol.1 (London: HMSO, 1978).
The award of indexed annuities in France involved not only domestic insurers but also the insurers of foreign motorists driving in France. In 1974 a scheme was arranged whereby, in consideration of a levy on motor premiums, the Caisse Centrale de Réassurance undertook to reimburse domestic insurers for the indexed element of annuities awarded under the terms of the law of 27 December 1974. It was announced in October 1977 that in cases involving foreign motorists insured by companies not established in France, the insurer would be allowed to take advantage of the scheme too: it would be required to deposit with a French insurer or reinsurer that acted as its correspondent, or with the Caisse Centrale de Réassurance, a sum equal to the capitalized value of the annuity at the date of the award, and the Caisse Centrale would assume responsibility for additional liabilities due to the indexing of the annuity. (See *Indexed Annuities and the Reinsurer*).
2 See *Indexed Annuities and the Reinsurer*.

reinsurer obtains no relief from the impact of inflation on either lump-sum claims payments or indexed annuities. The result is that any inflationary increases in the annuity payments reduce the number of payments the ceding company has to make before the reinsurer becomes liable to pay: using the earlier example on page 186, the effect of a 10% annual rate of inflation on the amount payable at the beginning of each year would be as follows:

Year	*No inflation*		*10% inflation*	
	Annual payments £	*Cumulative payments* £	*Annual payments* £	*Cumulative payments* £
1	3,000	3,000	3,000	3,000
2	3,000	6,000	3,300	6,300
3	3,000	9,000	3,630	9,930
4	3,000	12,000	3,993	13,923
5	3,000	15,000	4,392	18,315
6	3,000	18,000	4,832	23,147
7	3,000	21,000	5,315	28,462
8	3,000	24,000	5,846	34,308

Given the retention limit of 15,000, instead of the ceding company being solely responsible for the first five payments the reinsurer would become liable to contribute £3,315 towards the fifth and after the eighth payment his total claims cost would have increased to £19,308 compared with only £9,000 in the absence of inflation.

Under such conditions the reinsurer merely has the consolation that his limit of liability will be reached that much sooner! It is more sensible, however, to deal with the apportionment of the additional liability by means of a form of stability clause, even if no such provisions are applied to the payment of capital sums. Again there are varying views on how a stability clause should operate.

The most sophisticated method that has been advocated is an extension of the system of calculating the present value of the annual annuity payments outlined on page 186 above, but with further adjustment for inflation.[1] Essentially the annuity payments would be apportioned between the ceding company and the reinsurer by:
(1) calculating the capital required to make each payment at the commencement of the underwriting year, using an agreed discount rate; and
(2) deflating the resulting figure to strip out the effects of inflation

---

1 'Indexed annuities - apportionment of claims between cedant and reinsurer', *Quarterly Letter from the Nederlandse Reassurantie Groep*, May 1974, No. XIX/74.

between the commencement of the treaty and the date of the annuity payment.

The calculations would be made at the time each annuity payment was made.

Although such a method theoretically has a great deal to commend it, the type of stability clause in general use on the London market is far simpler in that it ignores investment earnings on the funds. Under the terms of the clause all payments arising out of one occurrence are adjusted by means of an appropriate index to the base value operative at the commencement of the treaty. The retention of the ceding company and the liability of the reinsurer are then revalued by multiplying the monetary limits stated in the treaty by the following ratio:

$$\frac{\text{total actual payments}}{\text{total adjusted values of payments}}$$

An example will illustrate how the clause operates:

Assume:

(1) Excess of loss cover £50,000 excess of £25,000, indexed at beginning of year t.

(2) Indexes to be applied:
   (a) For indexed annuity payments - the index used in the calculation of the annuity.
   (b) For all other payments - the Average Earnings index.
   Both indexes have a value of 100 at base date t.

(3) Claims payments:

Claimant		Payment	Year of payment	Latest index at date of payment	Payment revalued to base date
		£			£
A	Property damage	Capital sum 3,000	t	102	2,941
B	Personal injury	Capital sum 15,000	$t+1$	108	13,889
C	Personal injury	Capital sum 28,000	$t+2$	117	23,932
D	Personal injury	Capital sum 30,000	$t+3$	127	23,622
		Indexed annuity			
		3,000	$t+3$	129	2,326
		3,256	$t+4$	140	2,326
		3,558	$t+5$	153	2,326
		3,953	$t+6$	170	2,326
		4,209	$t+7$	181	2,326

After the fourth payment of the annuity in year $t+6$ the loss would be apportioned as follows:

$$\frac{\Sigma \quad \text{actual payments}}{\Sigma \quad \text{adjusted payments}} = \frac{89{,}767}{73{,}688} = 1.2182$$

Adjusted ceding company's retention = £25,000 × 1.2182 = £30,455
Adjusted reinsurer's liability = £50,000 × 1.2182 = £60,910

Apportionment of actual payments:
Ceding company   £30,455
Reinsurer   £59,312   (i.e. £89,767 − £30,455)

The fifth payment of the annuity would exhaust the reinsurer's liability, as follows:

$$\frac{\Sigma \quad \text{actual payments}}{\Sigma \quad \text{adjusted payments}} = \frac{93{,}976}{76{,}014} = 1.2363$$

Adjusted retention   £25,000 × 1.2363 = £30,908
Adjusted liability   £50,000 × 1.2363 = £61,815

Apportionment of actual payments:
Ceding company   £30,908 + £1,253
Reinsurer   £61,815

The French market has approached the problem in another way, making use of the commutation principle whereby losses are apportioned between the ceding company and its reinsurer(s) on the basis of the purchase price of a fixed annuity deflated to the index level at the inception of the contract.[1] The method operates as follows:

Step 1   Following the award of an indexed annuity, the parties ascertain the purchase price of an ordinary annuity for the same amount as that payable under the indexed annuity at the date of the award.

Step 2   That purchase price is deflated by the agreed index to the index level prevailing at the inception of the contract.

Step 3   The deflated purchase price plus any other payments (adjusted, if necessary) relative to the ceding company's retention limit determines the proportions in which the capital sums and the initial indexed annuity instalment are apportioned between the reinsured and reinsurer(s). All future instalments of the initial annuity are then divided

---

[1] The ROA sub committee ended their report by expressing a strong preference for this type of scheme -*Indexed Annuities and the Reinsurer*, p.30.

between them in the same proportions until the death of the annuitant.

Step 4   The reinsurer also pays the same proportion of the additional (indexed) cost of each annuity instalment, subject to the total purchase price of additional ordinary annuities not exceeding the reinsurer's share of the purchase price of the initial annuity.

Thus, using the same example as before, the reinsurer's liability would be calculated as follows:

Step 1   The parties obtain a purchase price of £27,000 for a £3,000 annuity for the injured claimant.

Step 2   That purchase price revalued to the inception of the reinsurance contract would be:

$$£27,000 \times \frac{100}{129} = £20,930$$

Step 3   Total revalued 'payments' (i.e. capital sums + annuity
purchase price)   = £85,314

Apportionment: £

Ceding company £25,000 + £10,314 =   35,314 = 41.4%
Reinsurer   =   50,000 = 58.6%
                                     ‾‾‾‾‾‾
                                     85,314

So the reinsurer pays:

58.6% of the capital payments of £76,000 = £44,536

+ 58.6% of an annuity of £3,000 (= £1,758 p.a.) until the death of the annuitant.

Step 4   The reinsurer also pays 58.6% of the indexed part of future instalments up to the point where the aggregate purchase price of the additional annuities equals the reinsurer's share of the purchase price of the initial annuity (i.e. 58.6% of £27,000 = £15,822).

Selecting the index

In practice a major difficulty with stability clauses is to select an index which will move reasonably in line with the rate of increase of claims costs. The above examples have assumed a perfect match but usually real-life experience is not as good as that: for example, during the period 1973 – 6 the rate of increase of UK court awards tended to lag behind the rise in average earnings. Countries like the UK, USA and France publish a variety of indexes from which reinsurers can select an appropriate index, but when dealing with business from some countries the choice is far more restricted and it may be necessary to make use of whatever is available, such as an index of consumer prices.

When business written in several countries is covered by one treaty, it is necessary to apply a separate index to losses occurring in each country.

Currency fluctuation clause

Unless special provision is made in non-proportional reinsurance contracts covering portfolios which may result in losses being incurred in several currencies, fluctuations in foreign exchange rates may easily lead to dispute regarding the extent of the reinsurer's liability. Two matters need to be dealt with in the contract — the rates of exchange to be used:

(1) for determining the monetary limits (i.e. the ceding company's retention and the reinsurer's liability) unless they are listed in the contract for each currency.

(2) for converting losses into the main currency (or currencies) in which accounts are to be rendered.

The following example illustrates the scope for disagreement in the absence of any provisions in the contract.

Assume:—A treaty covers risks written in Britain and Tranzonia.

—The reinsurer's liability is expressed in £ sterling as £75,000 in excess of £25,000.

—An original claim is settled for 400,000 francs.

—Rate of exchange at inception of treaty is 10 francs = £1.

—Rate of exchange at settlement of claim:
Situation (1)   8 francs = £1
Situation (2)   10 francs = £1
Situation (3)   12 francs = £1

Reinsurer's liability in francs

	Situation (1)	Situation (2)	Situation (3)
Case 1. Monetary limits in francs determined at date of settlement			
Limits	600,000/200,000 Fr	750,000/250,000 Fr	900,000/300,000 Fr
Reinsurer's liability	200,000 Fr	150,000 Fr	100,000 Fr
Case 2. Monetary limits in francs determined at inception of treaty			
Limits	750,000/250,000 Fr	750,000/250,000 Fr	750,000/250,000 Fr
Reinsurer's liability	150,000 Fr	150,000 Fr	150,000 Fr

Reinsurer's liability as accounted in £

A. If liability converted at rate of exchange at date of settlement			
Case 1 above	£25,000	£15,000	£8,133
Case 2 above	£18,750	£15,000	£12,500

B. If liability converted at rate of exchange at inception of treaty

Case 1 above	£20,000	£15,000	£10,000
Case 2 above	£15,000	£15,000	£15,000

It is impossible to eliminate totally the effects of exchange-rate fluctuations, but it is possible to minimize the scope for disagreement between the parties. If the ceding company had the right to choose which rate of exchange to use then:

(1) if the franc appreciated against the £ (situation (1)), it would pay the reinsured to convert both the monetary limits and the resulting reinsurer's liability into £ at the rate of exchange prevailing at the date of settlement, but

(2) if the franc depreciated against the £ (situation (3)), it would pay to convert both at the rate of exchange at the inception date of the treaty.

Clearly such a situation would not be in accord with the intention of the parties to a reinsurance contract. As reinsured losses are accounted for and settled soon after settlement by the ceding company, the rate of exchange prevailing at the date of settlement is the appropriate rate for accounting purposes. Regarding the reinsurance monetary limits, the aim of the parties is to maintain a stable level in each currency, so that rates of exchange applying at the inception date of the contract should be used. It is the practice, therefore, to include in non-proportional treaties a currency fluctuation clause to give effect to those objectives: a specimen clause as used on the London market is included in Appendix 5.3.

The second part of the clause deals with the position where losses in several currencies are involved. Appendix 5.4 gives an example of how the clause then operates.

Appendix 5.1   Stability clause

(a)   It is agreed that the retention of the Reinsured and the liability of the Reinsurer as set out in the Schedule shall retain the relative values existing at the date of commencement of this Agreement.

(b)   Any change in relative monetary value shall be ascertained from the latest available index of basic hourly wage rates of all workers in manufacturing industries issued by the Department of Employment and published by Her Majesty's Stationery Office in the *Monthly Digest of Statistics.*

(c)   On payment of any claim the retention of the Reinsured and the liability of the Reinsurer shall be increased or decreased in proportion to the increase or decrease in the above index from the date of commencement of the Agreement to the time of payment of the claim.

(d)   The time of payment of any claim for the purpose of this Agreement shall be deemed to be as follows:

    (i) Where no award is made by the courts the actual date upon which payment is made by the Reinsured.

    (ii) The date an award is made by a court (if no appeal is made).

    (iii) The date an award is made on final appeal.

    (iv) Notwithstanding anything to the contrary contained herein it is understood that in the event of a loss being settled by more than one payment, all advance payments in respect of any one claimant shall be added to the final payment to that claimant and the index at the time of the final payment shall be that used to calculate the Reinsurer's liability hereunder in respect of such payments.

Appendix 5.2 Illustrations of excess of loss reinsurance loss settlements subject to stability clauses

Illustration 1: basic index

Contract limits: $100,000 excess of $100,000.
Contract base date: 1st January 1974.
Contract base rate: 100 (this is the index applying at the inception date of the contract—for this example 100 has been used but it could be any figure).

Dates of payments	Loss amounts $	Index applying on day of settlement by ceding company	Adjusted loss $
10. 3.74	20,000	102	19,608
5.10.74	20,000	106	18,868
1. 2.75	20,000	112	17,857
6. 6.75	20,000	122	16,393
7.12.75	20,000	130	15,384
1.11.76	20,000	136	14,706
14. 4.77	20,000	142	14,084
	140,000		116,900

Each payment having been deflated, the following equation can be used to calculate the reinsurer's liability:

$$\text{Gross loss} = \$140,000$$

Original payments = $\dfrac{\$140,000}{116,900} \times$ deductible $100,000 = $ 119,760

Indexed loss to reinsurer $ 20,240

An unindexed contract would have produced a loss of $40,000.

Illustration 2: split indexation for combined Hull and Liability reinsurance

Contract limits: $100,000 excess of $100,000.
Liabilities: indexed.
Hulls: unindexed.

Base date: 1st January 1974.
Base rate: 100.

Dates of payments	Loss amounts $	Index applying on day of settlement by ceding company	Adjusted loss $
Liability payments			
10. 3.74	20,000	102	19,608
5.10.74	20,000	106	18,868
1. 2.75	20,000	112	17,857
6. 6.75	20,000	122	16,393
7.12.75	20,000	130	15,384
1.11.76	20,000	136	14,706
14. 4.77	20,000	142	14,084
	140,000		116,900
Hull payment			
30. 6.74	15,000	N.A.	15,000

Total loss

Hull	$ 15,000
Liability	$140,000
	$155,000

Deductible in proportion

Hull $\dfrac{15,000}{155,000} \times 100,000$ = $ 9,677

Liability $\dfrac{140,000}{155,000} \times 100,000$ = $ 90,323

Reinsurer's liability

Hull	$ 15,000		
Deductible (in proportion)	$ 9,677		
		=	$ 5,323
Liability	$140,000		
deductible (in proportion) indexed			

$\dfrac{140,000}{116,900} \times 90,323 =$ $108,171 = $ 31,829

$ 37,152

Appendix 5.3   Currency fluctuation clause

In the event the Reinsured sustains losses in a currency other than ____[1] the Reinsurer's liability shall be calculated as follows:

(a) The retention of the Reinsured and the liability of the Reinsurer as expressed in ____[2] shall be converted into the currency concerned at the rate of exchange ruling on the ____[3] in accordance with ____[4]

and

(b) The balance of any loss payment in excess of the Reinsured's retention shall be converted from the currency in which the loss was settled into ____[2] at the rate of exchange as used by the Reinsured and ruling on the date or dates of settlement of the loss by the Reinsured.

In the event losses are sustained by the Reinsured in respect of the same loss occurrence in more than one currency the retention of the Reinsured and the limit of liability of the Reinsurers shall be apportioned between the various currencies in the proportion that each currency bears to the total loss calculated by converting each currency into ____[2] at the rates of exchange ruling at ____.[3] The balance of any loss payment in each original currency in excess of the Reinsured's retention in each currency apportioned as above shall be converted into ____[2] at the rate of exchange used by the Reinsured and ruling on the date or dates of settlement of the loss by the Reinsured.

1 Sterling, US dollars or currency as stated in schedule.
2 Main currency of contract, e.g. £ for UK, francs for France or as negotiated.
3 1 January or inception or as negotiated.
4 Rates of exchange ruling on date specified above (note 3), either as in company's books, specified attached schedule, or the *Financial Times*.

Appendix 5.4   Application of currency fluctuation clause

Reinsurance contract limits: £1,000,000 excess of £500,000

Loss:
$$
\begin{aligned}
\text{A\$} &\ 1,000,000 \\
\text{US\$} &\ \ \ 800,000 \\
\text{Swiss francs} &\ 1,200,000 \\
\pounds &\ \ \ 500,000
\end{aligned}
$$

Currency conversion rates at inception:

$$
\begin{aligned}
\text{A\$ } 1.6 &= \pounds 1 \\
\text{US\$ } 1.7 &= \pounds 1 \\
\text{Swiss francs } 4.3 &= \pounds 1 \\
\pounds \text{ par} &
\end{aligned}
$$

Therefore contract limits expressed in individual currencies are:

A$ 1,600,000   excess of   A$ 800,000
US$ 1,700,000   excess of   US$ 850,000
Swiss francs 4,300,000   excess of   Swiss francs 2,150,000
£ 1,000,000   excess of   £   500,000

Apportionment of the deductible and limit to reinsurer's liability

(a) Loss converted at rates of exchange at inception

	£	% of total
A$ 1,000,000 at 1.6 =	625,000	33.339
US$ 800,000 at 1.7 =	470,588	25.103
Swiss francs 1,200,000 at 4.3 =	279,070	14.886
Plus sterling	500,000	26.672
	1,874,658	100.000

(b) Allocation of the deductible and the limit to the reinsurer's liability for the original currency losses calculated in proportion to losses converted into sterling

Contract limits	x	Percentage	= Reinsurer's liability	= Deductible
A$ 1,600,000 excess of 800,000		33.339	A$533,424	A$266,712
US$ 1,700,000 excess of 850,000		25.103	US$426,752	US$213,376
SFr 4,300,000 excess of 2,150,000		14.886	SFr640,098	SFr320,049
£ 1,000,000 excess of 500,000		26.672	£266,720	£133,360

Calculation of the reinsurer's liability

In this case the loss in the original currency less the apportioned deductible in each case exceeds the limit of the reinsurer's liability as apportioned in (b) above.

Therefore the loss payable by the reinsurer in sterling is the sum of the apportioned limit of liability converted at the following rates of exchange prevailing at the time of the settlement of the original losses.

$$A\$ \ 1.657 = £1$$
$$US\$ \ 1.765 = £1$$
$$SFr \ 3.890 = £1$$

Loss calculation

A$ 533,424	÷ 1.657	=	£321,922
US$ 426,752	÷ 1.765	=	£241,786
SFr 640,098	÷ 3.890	=	£164,550
£ 266,720			£266,720
			£994,978

REINSURANCE

6
Facultative reinsurance

REINSURANCE

6
Facultative reinsurance

The preceding chapters have dealt at some length with the general principles of law applying to reinsurance contracts and the various types of reinsurance that are available. Now attention can be turned to the two main ways of handling reinsurance business, their merits and demerits, and the terms of the contracts employed in the market. For ease of exposition this section is divided into three chapters, the first dealing with the facultative method and the next two chapters respectively covering proportional and non-proportional treaties. Also to avoid confusion the discussion will exclude practice relating to life reassurance, which is the subject of a separate chapter.

The use of facultative reinsurance

Although the facultative method of placing reinsurance has largely been superseded by the extensive use of treaties, it still plays a useful role in reinsurance markets in four circumstances:
(1) Where the required reinsurances would be unattractive to reinsurers if offered on a treaty basis. For example, if a company requires very little reinsurance each year for a particular class of insurance, the loss potential on any one reinsured risk may be so high in relation to the total annual reinsurance premiums that a treaty would be very unstable in the sense of being exposed to highly variable total claims costs in any one year.
(2) Where:
  (a) the risk to be reinsured would fall outside the company's existing treaties, for example, because the insured risk is located outside the geographical limits or is a (possibly hazardous) excluded class of risk; or
  (b) the sum insured exceeds the treaty limits; or

  (c) the risk is of such a nature that the ceding company would not
      want to cede it to its treaty, perhaps because of its potentially
      destabilizing effect.

So a ceding company may decide to seek facultative reinsurance for
peak and/or especially hazardous risks it may have accepted, or
separately reinsure the target risk on a fire schedule, provided the
terms of its treaties do not prohibit such arrangements.

(3) Where, to accommodate a special case, a company wishes to increase
    its gross acceptance capacity, perhaps in order to retain or to acquire
    the lead on a coinsured insurance.

(4) Where a company wishes to increase its net account by offering
    business in exchange for inwards facultative reinsurance.

Sometimes facultative reinsurance may be used for property insurance
as a means of interesting an insurance company in a large case where for
some reason or other it is unable to participate directly as a coinsurer.

Essential characteristics

The two basic features of the facultative method of handling
reinsurances are: (1) its optional character, with the ceding insurer and
the prospective reinsurer being free respectively to offer and to accept or
reject the reinsurance; and (2) its use for placing individual risks. Thus
for direct insurers it provides a greater degree of flexibility in their
reinsurance arrangements than otherwise would be possible, while it
remains the one area where the reinsurer can exercise his underwriting
judgment in relation to individual risks, in that he retains the right to
accept or reject each risk offered.

Most of the reinsurances placed facultatively are still of the
proportional type, but increasingly the method is used for individual
excess of loss reinsurances (e.g. for certain kinds of property risks and in
the aviation market where an airline itself may insure 'excess liabilities'
— see page 452). In both cases the two parties to the reinsurance contract
are mutually involved in the experience of an individual risk, and thus
both are interested in the quality of the business accepted and in taking
remedial measures if it produces adverse results. There is, however, a
complete community of interest between ceding company and reinsurer
in all proportional facultative covers which may not exist with excess of
loss. Apart from odd cases where a reinsurer may take a proportional
share of an excess of loss insurance written by the ceding company,
under a normal excess of loss reinsurance the reinsurer will only become
interested in losses which exceed the reinsured's deductible limit, whereas
under proportional reinsurances the two parties to the contract together
share *pro-rata* in the same direct premium and losses.

The disadvantages

There are three main disadvantages with the facultative method.

First, despite the considerable streamlining of administrative procedures that has taken place since the Second World War, some delay inevitably occurs in the placing of reinsurances facultatively because each case must be negotiated individually with the prospective reinsurer(s). Consequently final acceptance of the original insurance may be prolonged too. The provision made in treaties for the automatic ceding of reinsurances avoids such delay.

Secondly, the administrative costs both parties incur in individually negotiating and accounting for facultative reinsurances, and subsequently dealing with individual renewals, are far higher than for treaty reinsurances. Moreover a ceding company is likely to suffer some loss of reinsurance commission. Rates of commission on facultative reinsurances tend to be lower than for treaties in that they reflect both the higher costs incurred by the reinsurer and the fact that a ceding company's expenses on big cases will tend to be relatively lower than on the total portfolio reinsured under a treaty. Generally, moreover, no profit commission is allowed on facultative reinsurances.

Finally, there is the ever-present danger that a ceding company will overlook the need to place or to renew a facultative reinsurance.

Given such disadvantages it may seem surprising that use of the facultative method not only continues but has tended to grow in recent years, at least in terms of the absolute amount of business placed. Part of the reason lies in the advance of modern technology resulting in larger, and sometimes more hazardous, production units, products and means of transport, so that direct insurers increasingly find that they are presented with business which either exceeds their treaty capacity or for which they wish to obtain other reinsurance in order to protect their treaties.

Usage of facultative reinsurance

The extent to which facultative reinsurance arrangements are used not only varies considerably between the various classes of insurance, but also tends to alter over time as market conditions and the nature of the demand for insurance change. For example, given the impact of both technological progress on unit size and of inflation, property values at risk have tended to rise faster over the last decade than the increase in insurers' free reserves. Consequently the demand for facultative reinsurance cover for industrial fire risks has been revitalized over the last few years.

A similar trend has occurred in the marine market too where the sizes and carrying capacity of ships seem to grow almost at a geometric rate. Indeed an insurer who seeks additional facultative reinsurance for the very large risks which strain total market capacity may be faced with the prospect of either having to pay a premium rate higher than the original or of obtaining a low rate of reinsurance commission.

Marine facultative reinsurances and retrocessions are often placed on more restricted terms than the original insurance. An insurer, for example, may be content to retain in full the risk of partial losses but may wish to protect his account against the full impact of a total loss. Therefore reinsurance may be sought on a TLO (total loss only) basis for hull risks or an FPA (free of particular average) basis for cárgo, when it is necessary to agree a special premium rate for the reinsurance. Facultative reinsurance may also be arranged for cargo where an insurer has had to accept an abnormally large line or an exceptionally hazardous risk.

A special highly speculative feature of the marine facultative reinsurance scene is the market, mainly confined to Lloyd's, for overdue vessels. When a vessel is reported overdue at a port of destination the original insurers or their reinsurers may seek to transfer the risk of loss by wholly reinsuring their liability. Such reinsurances may be placed at any time until the vessel is either confirmed as lost or is posted as missing presumed lost when a total loss claim would be payable to the owners. Obviously the longer a vessel is overdue the higher will be the rate of premium that the reinsurer(s) will require. Rates for overdue risks are still quoted in guineas (= £1.05) per cent of the sum to be insured, the gross premium being divided between the reinsurer and the broker in the proportions £.1.00 net premium and 5p commission. Usually rates commence at around 10 guineas (= £10.50) and may rise to 85 guineas (= £89.25) per cent.

The situation in aviation insurance is somewhat different in that there are still relatively few underwriters who possess the considerable skill and knowledge required to write such business successfully. The London market possesses such underwriting expertise and attracts a lot of overseas business in the form of facultative reinsurance. Often this provides the means whereby an inexperienced local insurance company that is required to handle the business of a domestic airline can obtain the assistance it requires in underwriting and dealing with claims, besides ceding a large proportion of the business to reinsurers who would probably be reluctant to provide treaty cover in such circumstances. In such cases the terms for the original direct insurance may be fixed in consultation with the leading reinsurers, and the reinsurance policy may specify that the reinsurer shall handle the investigation and settlement of all losses (see page 452).

Facultative reinsurances are also arranged by experienced aviation insurers for the general reasons outlined above.

Generally the use of facultative reinsurance has tended to decline in the accident department since most direct insurers have adequate treaty arrangements to handle almost all of the business they accept, especially in view of the ever-growing popularity of non-proportional reinsurance treaties. On the other hand the practice of excluding certain risks from automatic treaty arrangements generates a large amount of facultative business.

Inflation, larger risks, and the escalation of court awards which have adversely affected liability insurance, also have meant that in some cases normal accident excess of loss treaty limits are insufficient. Then extra layers may be arranged facultatively, though at relatively higher premiums than if the whole of the account was protected by an additional treaty.

Frequently too insurers resort to facultative reinsurance cover when exceptionally large sums insured are arranged under personal accident policies.

Procedures for placing facultative reinsurances

The pressures that are exerted on insurers by competition, public opinion, and in some cases supervisory authorities, to economize on their administrative costs have led to a streamlining of the procedures for handling facultative reinsurances.

Traditionally the placing of a facultative reinsurance commences with the ceding company or its broker preparing a slip providing brief details of the original sum insured and the risk to be placed, including the total sum insured; perils covered; premium and conditions; its own retention and the amount (if any) ceded to treaties. The last items have an important bearing on a reinsurer's judgment and when the ceding company is part of a group that employs group underwriting the group retention must be disclosed too.

The reinsurance may relate to a part or the whole of the original insurance accepted by the ceding company. In the case of fire insurance for example, provided the cover is not arranged as a 'blanket insurance' in which property at risk at different locations is insured as one item without any breakdown of the total sum insured, the ceding company may choose to reinsure only certain items.

Next the slip is taken to prospective reinsurers who, if they are prepared to accept, will initial it indicating the proportion of the risk each is prepared to underwrite. If there is a substantial sum to be placed it may be necessary to obtain the acceptance of several reinsurers, and as a reinsurer's liability only commences from the time the slip is initialled, sometimes there can be considerable delay before a risk is fully reinsured. However, facultative reinsurers are usually willing to backdate their cover provided no loss is known to have occurred. Normally for a proportional reinsurance the reinsurer(s) will accept the risk offered at the original premium rate less an agreed reinsurance commission. Sometimes special terms will need to be agreed, e.g. marine reinsurances on more restricted terms than the original insurance, or where a fire insurer may seek to reinsure only certain hazardous items selected from a specification with an average premium rate applying to all items.

When full details of the risk to be insured are not available (for example, where an insurer is asked to grant cover before a survey can be arranged or other vital information obtained) a reinsurer in the past would agree to go on risk provisionally, perhaps initialling the slip accordingly, e.g. 'subject to survey'. Nowadays the reinsurer will often either reject or firmly accept the risk, relying on the judgment of the direct insurer to agree appropriate terms with the original insured.

Fire insurers frequently have standing arrangements with a number of other companies, including professional reinsurers, for handling their facultative reinsurances. One arrangement dispenses with the issue of a slip, the offer being made by telephone, and the reinsurer likewise accepts or rejects the offer verbally.

After the initialling of the slip it was the practice for the ceding office to issue a 'request' note, again briefly setting out the details of the risk to be reinsured including the dates of commencement and termination of the cover, and the reinsurer would respond by sending a 'take' note formally accepting the reinsurance in accordance with the details on the request note. Nowadays the two documents are usually combined in a single 'offer and acceptance' note issued by the ceding office in duplicate, which the reinsurer accepts by signing and returning one copy to the ceding office. Indeed quite often no formal guarantee note is issued, the risk being accepted simply by an exchange of letters.

As part of the streamlining procedures now in use companies frequently enter into arrangements to provide cover in course of post for particular classes of insurance, subject to territorial and possibly other restrictions. Instead of issuing a slip, the ceding company short-circuits the proceedings by first sending by post an offer and acceptance note for any reinsurance required up to an agreed limit. Although prospective reinsurers retain the right to reject any risk so offered, each agrees to be bound for its share unless the ceding company is notified to the contrary within an agreed period after the receipt of the note. Usually a period of

Figure 6.1 Specimen facultative slip

XYZ Reinsurance Company Limited

Accident Department Guarantee No. ....

Ceding company

Insured

Policy No.

Description of risk
and sum insured

Amount retained by
ceding company

Reinsurance hereon

From ... to ...   Renewal date

Present premium   Commission   %

Future premium

The XYZ Reinsurance Company Limited hereby
guarantees the ceding company to the extent shown
subject to the terms and conditions of the original
insurance.

Signed for and on behalf of the company this ...... day
of .... 19 ....

---

48 hours is allowed for refusal, though a longer period may be agreed.

The final stage would be for the ceding company to supply the reinsurer with a copy of the original policy or specification, and for the reinsurer to issue a reinsurance policy expressly incorporating the specification and terms and conditions of the original insurance.

When there is a regular flow of facultative reinsurance business passing between companies it is now usual to dispense with the issue of reinsurance policies. Upon receipt of the final closing details the reinsurer will prepare a slip, like the specimen shown in Figure 6.1, and the companies may agree that the initialling of the slip shall constitute evidence of the existence of a reinsurance contract. Then at weekly or monthly intervals the ceding company enters on a bordereau brief details of all reinsurances completed during the period. The bordereau is sent in duplicate to the reinsurer who signs and returns one copy in lieu of issuing separate policies, and retains the other copy for his own records. The bordereaux provide part of the information from which the ceding company will prepare the reinsurance accounts. A specimen premium bordereau is shown in Figure 6.2.

Renewals

The renewal of facultative reinsurances also requires individual consideration: if the original insurance is renewed, then the reinsurance will need to be renewed too.

Some facultative reinsurances are accepted only for one year. If the original insurance provides for annual renewal, then the ceding company must agree terms with the reinsurer before inviting renewal. In all other cases the renewal procedure has the following pattern.

Because of the days of grace allowed for the renewal of original policies, delays in the settlement of brokers' accounts, etc., it is often several weeks after the renewal date of a non-marine policy before a direct insurer knows whether it has been renewed, during which time a claim may occur. Therefore, where an underlying original fire or accident policy is renewable, unless either party has given prior notice of an intention to terminate the reinsurance as from renewal, it is market practice for the reinsurer automatically to extend the cover beyond renewal date unless and until notification is received from the ceding company that the original insurance has not been renewed. It is understood in all such cases that the existing terms, conditions and limits of the reinsurance contract continue unchanged. If either party wishes to terminate the reinsurance at renewal date due notice must be given as specified in the reinsurance policy, or in cases where policies are not issued, in accordance with the terms of the agreement between the parties. Normally the period of notice is fixed at 30 days prior to renewal date.

At quarterly (or more rarely, monthly) intervals the reinsurer will prepare in duplicate and send to the ceding company a list of reinsurances that have fallen due for renewal. The ceding company will then mark the individual items 'renewed' or 'cancelled' and return one copy of the list to the reinsurer.

Marine and aviation reinsurance practice follows renewal procedures in the direct market. Notice of cancellation is not normally given, and the reinsurer(s) will decide whether to continue on the risk when presented with the renewal slip on or before the renewal date. If for some reason the renewal arrangements for a direct insurance are not completed on time it is customary for the reinsurer(s) to write the reinsurance subject to warranty 'held covered at terms and conditions to be agreed'. The number of days allowed for the presentation of the final renewal details normally would be indicated. The premiums for reinsurances renewed appear on the next quarterly account like new cases.

Figure 6.2 Premium bordereau

SHEET No ....   YEAR .... QUARTER ....

Cession No.	Policy No.	Class	Ref.	Comm	Insured	Description	Period From	Period To	Curr	Original Sum Insured	M.P.L. or Exposure	Acceptance on Sum Insured	Retention on Sum Insured	Amount Reinsured	Reinsurance Premium	(a)	Stg.	Treaty Premium
																	B/F	

Alterations

Amendments to the cover provided by underlying original insurances (e.g. changes in sums insured or in the property or perils covered) or any other material fact (e.g. change of interest, or any change of circumstances affecting a premium rate) have to be notified to the reinsurer. Where necessary as with an addition to the list of perils insured or the substitution or addition of new properties to a fire insurance, the consent of the reinsurer must be obtained. Any alteration to a fire reinsurance would be notified initially by a preliminary alterations form to be followed subsequently by more detailed information regarding sum(s) insured, premium changes, etc.

Marine and aviation practice differs somewhat from non-marine. With non-marine insurance reinsurers only accept liability for alterations from the time they are notified by the ceding company. Generally marine reinsurers accept automatic liability from the date the alteration occurs provided it neither breaches any market agreement nor makes the reinsurance illegal; the ceding company is still under a duty to notify any change immediately it comes to the company's notice.

If an alteration results in an addition to or return of premium, the reinsurer will be credited or debited accordingly for his share in the next quarterly account.

Claims

Although the direct insurer is responsible for the settlement of claims arising under the original insurance, normally the reinsurer will want notification of all losses which occur irrespective of their size. The British fire tariff companies use a standard reporting form recording the:
—Acceptance number.
—Policy number.
—Name of the insured.
—Loss number.
—Date of loss.
—Gross estimated loss expressed as both an absolute sum and as a percentage of the sum insured.
—Estimated amount of the net loss to the ceding company.
—Estimated amount of the loss payable by the reinsurer.

By notifying the reinsurer of a loss the ceding company does not relinquish its sole right to arrange a settlement with the original insured, and as a general rule reinsurers do not seek to be involved.[1] However,

1 Aviation reinsurers sometimes take a different view (see page 232).

when a British tariff company retains on a fire insurance only a small proportion of the sum insured it is the practice that, as a matter of courtesy, it will consult its reinsurers regarding the adjustment and/or settlement of losses.

The timing and extent of the reinsurer's liability will depend upon the precise wording of the reinsurance contract, and the reader is referred to Chapter 4 for a full discussion of this point. Normally the reinsurer will be liable for his share of the final settlement with the original policyholder, though the reinsurer will incur no liability in respect of any *ex gratia* payment unless either the reinsurance contract expressly states that the reinsurer shall be so bound to pay his share, or he was consulted beforehand by the reinsured and agreed to follow. The rules of the Fire Office's Committee deal with compromise and *ex gratia* settlements, and are usually incorporated by reference into facultative reinsurances for UK business arranged between FOC members. Marine facultative reinsurance slips normally contain a condition along the following lines:

Being a reinsurance and subject to all terms, clauses, conditions, returns, additional premiums, warranties as original and to pay as may be paid thereon. To follow in every respect all settlements of original Underwriters.

It has been noted in Chapter 4 that expressions such as 'to pay as may be paid thereon' are not so wide as they may seem, the liability of the reinsurer being limited to those losses properly paid under the original policy. Although *ex gratia* or 'without prejudice' loss settlements cannot be recovered from the reinsurer as of right, in practice such claims often are paid, particularly in the case of 'without prejudice' settlements where a doubt may exist concerning liability but the original insurer is able to reach a reasonable compromise with the policyholder. Strictly the reinsurer should always be consulted if later difficulty is to be avoided.

Although the reinsurer will normally be liable to pay immediately settlement of the original claim has been agreed, it is usually the practice for small losses to be charged to the quarterly account with the reinsurer, leaving only large claims to be paid immediately by cheque or banker's order. The parties will agree at the outset the size of loss which merits immediate cash payment.

Accounts

The accounting arrangements for facultative reinsurances are dealt with in Chapter 13.

Facultative obligatory agreements and open covers

General characteristics

It will be recalled from Chapter 3 that the term facultative obligatory is derived from the nature of such an agreement in that the ceding company can choose whether or not to offer, as with a facultative reinsurance, any risk falling within the terms of the agreement, whereas the reinsurer is obliged to accept any business offered.

The term 'open cover' is applied to various types of contract. In the marine market it is used to describe contracts arranged between direct insurers and their insured to provide automatic insurance cover for consignments of cargo. The reinsurance market employs it to describe facultative obligatory type contracts arranged either between a ceding company and reinsurer, or, more usually, between a broker and a reinsurer: in each case the essential feature is the obligation placed on the reinsurer to accept reinsurances voluntarily ceded by the other party to the contract.

A broker's open cover provides a broker with automatic access to additional reinsurance facilities for any risk he is endeavouring to place which falls within the terms of the agreement. Sometimes when placing a large direct insurance a broker may find that the insurers he is trying to interest require additional reinsurance protection. He can then turn to his open cover to provide the reinsurance cover required within the limits of that agreement.

The demand for both facultative obligatory agreements and open covers is increasing, though their usage is still confined to surplus reinsurances, mainly for fire and marine business.

Direct insurers look to facultative obligatory arrangements to supplement automatically their normal treaty facilities or to provide reinsurance cover for the occasional risk which could upset the balance of a treaty. An open cover provides a broker with a facility for rapidly placing insurances he is handling in that effectively it can increase the acceptance limits of the direct companies with which he deals. In both cases the primary purpose is to provide an automatic means of dealing with risks which are either irregular in their incidence, or which for some reason are unsuitable for normal reinsurance treatment, or are so large as to exhaust a company's treaty reinsurance facilities. So, for example, in fire insurance a facultative obligatory agreement may provide a direct insurer with the means of dealing with the seasonal increases in value at risk that occur in some trades, or the occasional exceptionally large insurance which is offered to the company. Similar situations can occur in marine insurance where for various reasons an underwriter periodically may find himself heavily committed on one vessel or at a particular location.

Although facultative obligatory reinsurances and open covers meet a need that exists in the market, they are not popular with reinsurers because they present the disadvantages of treaties without the compensating advantages. The reinsurer, subject to the scope and acceptance limits of the agreement, can be committed as automatically as under a treaty, whereas the ceding company (or broker) is under no corresponding obligation to cede business. Consequently the risk of selection against the reinsurer is far higher than under a treaty, and there is unlikely to be a sufficient volume of business ceded to provide the degree of balance that can be expected from a surplus treaty. Therefore, before entering into any agreement the reinsurer will need to be satisfied on a number of points, notably:

(1) In the case of a facultative obligatory agreement:
    (a) The nature of the ceding company's business and its underwriting standards.
    (b) That a reasonable number of risks will be ceded.
    (c) That the company will use the reinsurance facility provided for the purpose envisaged and not to discriminate haphazardly against him.

(2) For a broker's open cover:
    (a) The type and volume of business likely to be ceded.
    (b) Of even more importance, the broker's reputation and market standing.

Reinsurers can, and do, also build into the agreements some protection for themselves by limiting the scope (e.g. restricting a fire agreement to business emanating from certain territories) and by specific exclusions. For example, risks accepted by a ceding company under inwards facultative reinsurances, and target risks, are commonly excluded from fire covers; and marine covers may exclude specific types of vessels, such as tankers or fishing boats.

Contract conditions

There is no standard form of contract setting out the terms of such agreements which, like surplus treaties, are not reinsurance policies but agreements to enter into contracts of reinsurance. Essentially, contract wordings follow those of surplus treaties which are discussed in the following chapter, the only fundamental difference being that the ceding company (or broker) retains the freedom to select the risks to be reinsured.

The agreement, therefore, will deal with such matters as its scope, its commencement and termination, provision of bordereaux, reporting and handling of claims, calculation of premium and reinsurance commission, accounting procedures, settlement of disputes, and so forth. As practice follows that relating to surplus treaties only the following points need special mention.

The agreement will need to specify exactly its territorial scope and what risks may be reinsured; including special exclusions from any general class of risk.

The commencement date and duration of the agreement must be stated. Usually agreements run until cancelled by either party giving proper notice or the occurrence of some exceptional circumstance which automatically cancels the agreement. Some agreements arranged to cover the needs of, say, a seasonal trade may be for a short, fixed duration but usually such an arrangement is not very satisfactory in that a new cover must be taken out each year or each time the need arises.

Because the results of the business may prove very uneven the reinsurer may reserve the right to revise the terms at short notice, and will require the ceding company to notify any change in underwriting practice or retentions.

Generally when an agreement is terminated by either party, existing cessions are allowed to run off until expiry or next renewal date unless the parties agree to the contrary. However, provision may be made for the ceding company unilaterally to make a clean break, cancelling all unexpired cessions and taking over liability for outstanding losses, the reinsurer in return paying the agreed premium portfolio and loss portfolio consideration.

The maximum share of any risk which may be ceded to the reinsurer will be expressed in terms of the ceding company's own retention, subject possibly to a monetary limit on any one risk. Usually in fire covers the ceding company is left free to fix its own retentions: it may be required to interest its treaties before ceding any business under the agreement, and it may be allowed to arrange prior facultative reinsurance too. In marine covers the ceding company's retention may be specified as fixed amounts.

Invariably the ceding company (or broker) is required to advise by bordereau every individual risk ceded. Not only is this essential because of the optional nature of the agreement from the standpoint of the ceding company (or broker) but also because the reinsurer will want to know what liabilities he is assuming.

The method of calculating the premium and reinsurance commission must be specified. Premiums for fire covers normally follow the original insurance but for marine covers arranged on a more restricted basis than the original insurance special rates(s) must be agreed. The rate of reinsurance commission allowed is usually higher than for individual facultative reinsurances (for fire covers generally it is between 2½% and 5% higher), though somewhat lower than for surplus treaties.

7
Proportional reinsurance treaties

7
Proportional reinsurance treaties

This chapter and the next will be concerned with the general features of non-life reinsurance treaties, and in particular with the forms of contract wording employed to embody the agreement between the parties. The suitability of the various types of treaty to the different classes of insurance business will form the subject of later chapters; for the time being the discussion will be confined to issues and practices common to all classes of business.

Most reinsurances nowadays are handled by various forms of treaty, and despite the growing popularity of excess of loss reinsurances, the surplus treaty remains the most widely used method. Therefore it is proposed to deal first with proportional treaties though some parts of the wordings employed apply equally to non-proportional treaties.

The form of reinsurance treaties

One of the difficulties in trying to describe reinsurance treaties and procedures is the absence of standard forms of contract wordings. Partly this is because of ·the differences between the various forms of reinsurance, but it also reflects the differing needs of ceding companies and, to a lesser degree, of reinsurers, sometimes arising from local supervisory and exchange control regulations. For example, the retention by the ceding company of premium and loss deposits may be settled not according to the wishes of the two parties but by local regulations.

Major reinsurers usually have standard sets of treaty wordings already prepared for use covering the various forms of reinsurance, including alternative wordings to meet particular circumstances. However when a reinsurance is being arranged by a large direct insurer or a broker they may take the initiative in proposing the form of wording to be used.

247

Therefore, even for the same kind of treaty many variations in wordings are employed. Nevertheless every treaty whether of a proportional or non-proportional type contains certain common elements, notably:

(1) The details of the two parties.

(2) The commencement date of the treaty.

(3) An operative clause defining the form of reinsurance; the classes of insurance covered; the territorial scope; and the treaty limits.

(4) Exclusions.

(5) A premium clause specifying the basis on which reinsurance premiums shall be calculated, including such taxes and other charges which shall be recoverable by the ceding company from the reinsurer.

(6) A commission clause stipulating what profit commission, if any, shall be payable, and in the case of proportional treaties the reinsurance commission to be deducted from the reinsurer's share of the original premiums.

(7) A claims clause, dealing with the notification of claims to the reinsurer and their payment.

(8) An accounts clause dealing with the preparation and settlement of accounts.

(9) An arbitration clause laying down the procedure to be followed in the event of any dispute.

(10) A termination clause dealing with notice of termination of the treaty and the run-off of liabilities.

Where a treaty covers business written in two or more currencies there will be:

(11) A currency clause specifying the currency in which premiums and losses are to be paid, and the rates of exchange used for settlements.

Other clauses will be included to deal with the special requirements of the particular class of reinsurance involved (e.g. the provision of bordereaux under surplus treaties) or other special circumstances (e.g. the retention or deposit of premium and loss reserves). Many treaties are prepared in a scheduled form, the details of the individual contract (e.g. the names and addresses of the parties, the scope of the treaty, the treaty limits, and the commencement date) being inserted in the schedule.

Sometimes there are combined in one treaty different forms of reinsurance (e.g. quota share and surplus), or two excess of loss layers. Such a situation would be accommodated by preparing separate schedules for each form or layer.

Commencement of a proportional reinsurance

When a new treaty is arranged it is important that there shall be no doubt regarding the commencement of the liabilities assumed by the reinsurer. Apart from treaties arranged by new insurers or by companies on the point of writing a new class of insurance, care must be taken to avoid either any gap in or overlapping of the cover provided by a new treaty and the treaty (or facultative reinsurances) it replaces. Therefore the precise terms of the commencement clause must be drafted to match the termination clause of any reinsurance contract it replaces.

When a proportional reinsurance treaty is terminated the cessions may be allowed to run on until the annual renewal date or the expiry of the underlying direct insurances, subject perhaps to a limit of 12 months from the date of termination. If so, although any new treaty will be dated to come into force at a certain time, provision must be made for its application to the individual insurances written by the ceding company by means of a commencement clause along the following lines:

> This agreement shall take effect in respect of all insurances relating to risks covered hereunder issued or renewed on and after the date as stated in the schedule.

Many treaties still so provide for the reinsurer to assume liability for risks ceded only as from the date of issue or renewal of the underlying insurances. In particular the method is extensively used for marine and aviation treaties which are normally written on an underwriting-year basis (see page 430). However, upon the termination of fire (and to a lesser degree accident) treaties it is now more common for the parties to make a clean break — that leaves two quite distinct types of liability to be dealt with by the new treaty.

First, the new reinsurer may agree to take over responsibility for losses occurring during the unexpired period of cessions still in force when the old treaty is terminated. The commencement clause of the new treaty will then need to read as follows:

> This agreement shall take effect in respect of all losses occurring on or after the _____ under policies in force, issued or renewed.

The terms used may be modified according to the class of insurance concerned. For example, the words 'losses discovered' may be substituted for 'losses occurring' for Fidelity Guarantee business.

The great merit of this 'losses occurring' method is its simplicity of operation. In the event of a new treaty being arranged there is no question of the old reinsurer remaining on risk to run off his liabilities under cessions still in force when the treaty is terminated. Thus it avoids any administrative complications due to an underlying direct portfolio of business being protected for a time partly by an old treaty and partly by its replacement. In return for the liabilities he assumes under reinsurances in force, the new reinsurer is entitled to an additional portfolio consideration equivalent to the reserve for unexpired risks (see page 274): normally that consideration is equal to the premium portfolio withdrawal from the old reinsurer.

Secondly, at the date of termination of the treaty the reinsurer is likely to be interested in a number of outstanding claims awaiting settlement. It may be agreed that the new reinsurer shall assume liability for the reinsured share of the final settlement costs in return for an additional loss portfolio consideration based on the estimated settlement cost of the outstanding losses (see page 279).

The operative clause

The obligations placed on the two parties respectively to cede and to accept all reinsurances falling within the terms of the treaty will be expressed in this clause, as follows:

> The Reinsured shall cede and the Reinsurer shall accept by way of reinsurance the proportion stated in the Schedule (hereinafter called the Reinsurer's proportion) of those insurances stated in the Schedule.

The clause thus encapsulates the essential differences between the facultative and treaty methods of placing reinsurance business. Under a quota share treaty the risks to be reinsured will consist of all of the business written by the ceding company. A surplus treaty, however, must specify exactly what risks the reinsured shall cede; that is, basically the surplus on any insurance it writes above its own net retention, subject to the treaty limit.

In order to protect a quota share or surplus treaty from the potentially destabilizing effect of very large or hazardous risks, often the reinsurer may agree to individual facultative reinsurances being effected in front of the treaty. The reinsurer may also allow the ceding company to obtain further protection against the risk of catastrophe losses on its net account by effecting appropriate excess of loss reinsurance. Both concessions are set out in the following clauses:

The Reinsured may in the interest of the Reinsurer reduce the amount to be ceded in respect of any risk by effecting individual facultative reinsurances. The Reinsured may also effect catastrophe reinsurance to protect its net retained account.

The use of excess of loss reinsurance in addition to quota share or surplus obviously has the effect of limiting the ceding company's net retained liability in respect of either individual losses or the aggregate net losses from one occurrence, and is a material fact which should be disclosed to the reinsurer at the inception of a treaty or when the excess of loss reinsurance is subsequently effected. This point arose in an American case,[1] where unknown to its proportional reinsurer a ceding company had a catastrophe excess of loss treaty with Lloyd's which provided 90% reinsurance for all of the company's retained losses in excess of $30,000. The proportional treaty obliged the ceding company to retain a stake in every insurance not less than the amount ceded to the reinsurer, and as the existence of the excess of loss cover was contrary to that obligation the court held that the reinsurer's liability could be reduced equivalently. Although it is not certain that an English court would follow that ruling there is little doubt that the existence of an excess of loss reinsurance would be regarded as a material fact which should be disclosed to a proportional reinsurer, and such is the recognized practice of the London market.

Besides defining the type of reinsurance involved and the respective obligations of both parties, the treaty also must clearly specify in either the operative clause or an annexed schedule:

(1) The class(es) of insurance business to which the treaty applies.
(2) The geographical area(s) from which such business is obtained.
(3) The nature of and limit to the reinsurer's liability.

The class(es) of insurance

Although there are good reasons for restricting a treaty to one class of insurance business, treaties covering several classes of accident insurance (other than motor and liability) are quite common. Treaties combining both fire and accident risks are also becoming more popular, but marine or aviation reinsurances are rarely combined with other classes of insurance.

When a treaty is issued embracing several classes of business, separate retention and treaty limits may be applied to each class of insurance. Usually, unless it is impractical to do so, reinsurers prefer to have either:

---

1 *North-Western Mutual Fire Association* v *Union Mutual Fire Insurance Co.*, 144 Fed. (2d) 274.

(1) separate reinsurance accounts prepared for each main class of insurance covered by the treaty; or

(2) a supporting technical recapitulation, i.e. an analysis of premiums, claims, etc., for each class of business.

Their aim in seeking such information is to monitor the performance of each class, and to facilitate the preparation of their own accounts.

The objections to mixing several classes of insurance in the same treaty lie mainly in the way it further restricts the reinsurer in exercising his underwriting judgment. It is unlikely that the results of two or more classes will be identical. If one deteriorates badly there is the danger that either it will not be identified quickly so that remedial measures can be taken to improve the underlying direct business, or the ceding company will try to defer such action, pointing to the profits being earned on the other class(es). On the other hand a small company may not be able to produce enough premium income to make separate treaties for individual classes of insurance self-supporting.

Whether it is the intention that the treaty should cover one or more classes of insurance, it is vital that there should be no doubt regarding its scope. It is dangerous to use terms which may be construed more widely, or more narrowly, than the parties intended. Whenever the terms of a contract are open to doubt, English courts will follow the *contra proferentem* rule which, if the contract has been drafted by the reinsurer, means that the words will be construed in favour of the ceding company. So, for example, terms such as 'fire insurances' or 'liability insurances' lack the degree of precision which is needed. While it is likely that the words 'fire insurances' would be construed to include the extra perils commonly insured under a fire policy, a direct company will usually want wider reinsurance protection to embrace all of the perils which may be insured through its fire department whether they be covered as an extension of a fire policy or otherwise. Conversely the term 'liability insurance' may be construed too widely, embracing all forms of liability insurance, whereas the intention of the parties may be to limit the reinsurance contract to cover only certain forms of liability insurance, such as products liability, excluding aviation products. Therefore, the wording of a treaty should express precisely the intention of the parties. Examples of the wordings used for various classes of reinsurance are included in the relevant following chapters.

Geographical scope

When a ceding company operates in only one country and writes no foreign business either direct or through reinsurances accepted, the geographical scope of its treaties presents no problems. The company will only need to ensure that for those classes of insurance in which the terms of the orginal policy may provide cover for losses occurring elsewhere in the world (e.g. products liability, life, personal accident and travel insurances) the reinsurance treaty follows suit.

Companies that operate or accept business from abroad must decide whether to combine their reinsurances for particular classes of insurance in world-wide treaties or arrange separate treaties for different territories. The decision may not lie entirely with the company.[2] An ever-growing number of governments nowadays require any insurers operating in their country to cede all or at least a part of their reinsurances to a state reinsurance corporation, or to place their reinsurances only with reinsurers licensed to operate in the country. Alternatively it may be difficult to obtain permission to remit the premiums for any reinsurances effected abroad. Even when no such restrictions apply there are still several reasons why a company may prefer to make separate reinsurance arrangements for business emanating from some countries. For example, centralized reinsurance arrangements may conflict with decentralized management policies or with the cultivation of good relationships in local markets. Also because of the special market conditions applying in North America it is the practice of British and European companies to effect separate treaties for American and Canadian business, though it is not unknown for Canadian risks to be included in a world-wide treaty.

The normal practice of British insurers is to arrange both their fire and accident treaties on a world-wide basis combining home and overseas business in the same treaty with the exception of North American risks which would usually be covered by separate treaties. The terms applying to the reinsurance may discriminate, however, between the various territories included in the scope of the treaty. Likewise marine and aviation treaties are normally arranged on a world-wide basis, though frequently they are restricted to cover only business written in specified territories. Quite often reinsurers are prepared to provide cover under a hull treaty only for vessels under the flag or management of the country where the ceding company is domiciled (see page 426).

The main advantage of combining home and foreign business in the same treaty is that it will help to stabilize the reinsurer's results. The underwriting results of insurance business in every country fluctuate from year to year as the result of competition and the random occurrence of catastrophe losses. By geographically diversifying its business an insurance company reduces the chance of incurring disastrous losses in

2 For a fuller discussion see Chapter 15 and R.L. Carter and G.M. Dickinson, 'Economic effects of restrictions on international trade in reinsurance', in *Papers presented to the Third International Reinsurance Seminar at Cambridge April 1977* (Reinsurance Offices' Association).

any year because the probability of several countries simultaneously experiencing bad results is lower than that for one country. Therefore, if its reinsurance business is placed on a world-wide basis its reinsurers too will enjoy the benefit of such risk reduction through diversification, in that in any one year bad results of one country (hopefully) will be compensated by profits from another.

There are dangers, however, in combining in one treaty business derived from more than one country. Not only may reinsurers be induced to accept business which on its own merits would be unacceptable, but also there is less pressure on a ceding company to take remedial action to improve its business in a country which consistently produces poor results. Thus policyholders in one country may be subsidized for years by those elsewhere.

Nature and extent of the reinsurer's liability

Lastly, the liability being undertaken by the reinsurer must be defined either in the treaty wording or in the schedule attached.

The provisions of a *quota share* reinsurance are straightforward: the ceding company will undertake to cede and the reinsurer to accept a fixed percentage of each and every insurance written by the company which falls within the scope of the treaty, subject to an agreed monetary limit for any one risk.

Surplus reinsurances are more complicated in that they must specify:
(1) The reinsurer's share of any surplus ceded by the reinsured in respect of any risk it writes which falls within the treaty.
(2) The limit to the amount which the reinsurer will accept on any risk expressed as a certain proportion of the net amount retained by the ceding company for its own account, subject sometimes to an upper monetary limit on the amount (i.e. sum insured) ceded.
(3) How the ceding company shall fix its net retention for any risk.

Usually the treaty will provide reinsurance facilities for up to a certain number of lines (i.e. an agreed multiple of the reinsured's own net retention), with a number of reinsurers participating in the treaty: to avoid any doubt it is customary to refer in the treaty to the ceding company's table of retentions which is often incorporated in the treaty or at least supplied to the reinsurer(s). Nowadays each reinsurer's share is usually expressed as a certain percentage of the surplus ceded so that in a five-line treaty a reinsurer that accepts 10% of the surplus would have a maximum liability equal to half a line subject also to any monetary limit.

When a second surplus treaty is arranged the operative clause *may* specify that the reinsurer(s) shall only be entitled to an agreed share of any surplus which remains after the first surplus reinsurers have received their full share, subject to the 'line' and monetary limits expressed in the treaty. However in many cases ceding companies interest second treaties before filling the first surplus. Similarly in the relatively few cases where a third surplus treaty is arranged the reinsurer(s) *may* only become entitled to a share when the first and second surplus treaties have received their full shares, though again the third surplus reinsurers may be interested before the underlying treaties are filled. The following example illustrates how three surplus treaties work when the first and then the second treaties must be filled before any business is ceded to the third.

Assume:

—The ceding company's own retention for a particular type of risk is £5,000.

—The company arranges:

(1) A first surplus treaty for eight lines.
(2) A second surplus treaty for four lines.
(3) A third surplus treaty for two lines.

Allocation of original sum insured of

| | £5,000 | £10,000 | £25,000 | £60,000 | £75,000 |
	£	£	£	£	£
Company's own retention	5,000	5,000	5,000	5,000	5,000
First surplus treaty	—	5,000	20,000	40,000	40,000
Second surplus treaty	—	—	—	15,000	20,000
Third surplus treaty	—	—	—	—	10,000
	5,000	10,000	25,000	60,000	75,000

The ceding company would retain £5,000 of any business accepted, leaving the first surplus treaty to absorb up to £40,000 of any surplus in excess of £5,000. The second surplus treaty would only become interested on any risks where the sum insured accepted exceeded £45,000 and could then absorb up to another £20,000. Finally no more than an additional £10,000 could be ceded to the third treaty. Thus for the particular type of risk the ceding company's acceptance limit would be £75,000; the acceptance of any larger sum would necessitate the placing of additional facultative reinsurances. If the ceding company accepted a risk with a sum insured less than the amount required to fill a treaty, each reinsurer's share of the surplus would be scaled down accordingly. Thus in this example, a first treaty reinsurer with a maximum acceptance limit of one line would receive one-eighth of any surplus up to £40,000 ceded to the treaty — on a cession of, say, £20,000 its share would be £2,500.

The extent of a reinsurer's liability clearly depends upon the number of lines included in a treaty and the ceding company's own retention, both of which are matters for discussion when a treaty is being arranged.[3] Therefore once the treaty becomes operative the company will be expected to abide by its usual retention limits. When a ceding company wishes to take advantage of an 'errors and omissions' clause to cede, or to correct an earlier cession of, some risk after a loss has occurred, it will be required to observe its usual limit for that type of risk as in the following clause:

> The Reinsured shall decide what constitutes one risk hereunder and unless otherwise hereinafter provided shall fix its net retention without reference to the Reinsurer in accordance with the usual net retentions of the Reinsured. If however the Reinsured shall know of the probability of a loss affecting this agreement prior to either the fixing or revision of its net retention then the retention shall be not less than that shown by its records and practices to be its usual net retention for similar risks. The usual net retentions of the Reinsured shall not be altered without the prior consent of the Reinsurer.

Changes in underwriting policy, retentions, etc.

A reinsurer negotiating a new treaty will want full details of all factors that could affect his potential liability, e.g. the types of business accepted by the ceding company, any special local conditions or practices, its general underwriting policy, and its retentions for different types of risk. The latter factor is of particular importance for surplus treaties because of the relationship between the original sum insured, the ceding company's retention, and the reinsurer's share of the insurances accepted.

Likewise during the currency of a treaty the reinsurer will want notice of any change of policy by the ceding company which may affect the character of the business ceded. Therefore it is usual to insert in treaties a clause along the following lines:

> The Reinsured undertakes not to introduce, without the prior approval of the Reinsurer, any change in its established acceptance and underwriting policy in respect of those insurances to which this agreement relates.

In an era of rapid political and social change the reinsurer may also deem it expedient to obtain some protection against external changes which may adversely affect the business ceded. Undoubtedly liability excess of loss reinsurances are most exposed to the effects of changes in statute or other law, both because of the nature of the underlying risk

---

3 For a discussion of these issues see Chapter 5.

and because all of the additional liability may fall upon the reinsurer. However, other classes of insurance and any proportional reinsurances arranged to cover them may be affected to some extent too. For example, a government may decide to relieve public authorities of liability to pay compensation for damage to property caused by rioters, and insurers covering riot risks may be powerless to adjust to such a change until policies fall due for renewal. If, however, at renewal a ceding company decides to assume liabilities which previously it did not cover, then it is only equitable that its reinsurers should also have the opportunity to review their position. Consequently although clauses such as the one quoted below have been designed primarily to protect excess of loss reinsurers against the effect of changes in law, sometimes they are inserted in proportional treaties too.

> In the event of any change in the law by which the Reinsurer's liability hereunder is materially increased or extended the parties hereto agree to take up for immediate discussion a suitable revision in the terms of the agreement. In the event of failure to agree a suitable revision this agreement shall operate from the effective date of the change of law as if the change had not occurred or upon its termination the Reinsurer's liability will not be increased or extended by any change of law affecting this agreement which has not been agreed by the Reinsurer.

Bordereaux

Under a surplus treaty the reinsurer's liability only attaches to risks that have been specifically ceded, and in the early days of treaties reinsurers required regular and frequent notification of every risk ceded: the forms used for that purpose came to be known by the French word *bordereaux*. At weekly intervals the ceding company would prepare from the entries made in its reinsurance register a *preliminary bordereau* providing brief details of every cession made during the week listing:
—The cession number.
—The policy number.
—The name of the insured.
—A description of the risk including location.
—The sum insured or maximum possible loss.
—The company's own retention.
—The amount reinsured.

The preliminary bordereaux would be followed at longer intervals, generally once a month, by *definite bordereaux* listing the final details of all preliminary cessions where the original insurance had been completed by the issue of a policy during the month. Most of the information supplied would simply duplicate that listed on the preliminary bordereau though in the event of any discrepancy between the two the particulars contained in the definite bordereau would be taken as correct. In addition the definite bordereau would cite (1) the preliminary cession number so that the reinsurer could link the two together in his records, and (2) details of the original and reinsurance premiums required for the preparation of the quarterly accounts.

Any alterations to a cession involving a change of premium or the cancellation of a preliminary cession which was not completed for any reason, would be listed on an *alterations bordereau*. Again sufficient information would be provided to enable the reinsurer to identify the original cession in his records and for additional or return of premium to be included in the next quarterly account.

Easy access to such information about every risk ceded is obviously of benefit to a reinsurer, and it can be beneficial to a ceding company too. The advantages have been neatly summarised as follows:[4]

> Detailed bordereaux ... enable the reinsurer to examine the underwriting and the rating policy followed by the ceding company, to check the cessions and the apportionment of risks between the retention and the amount reinsured, to have some insight into the structure and distribution of the business ceded under the treaty and to check the apportionment of claims when they arise. They also provide the reinsurer with the material he utilizes to index risks, investigate accumulation and compile the information required for his retrocession plans. On the other hand, bordereaux are very useful instruments for a newly established direct writing company, because they promote orderly registration of business and facilitate analysis of the portfolio whenever required.

Weighing heavily against those benefits are the costs of preparing and analysing such a mass of detail. Consequently over the last 40 years the notification by bordereaux of risks ceded has declined considerably. Today many treaties are operated blind, the reinsurer learning little about the business apart from what can be gleaned from the quarterly accounts and the individual notification of large losses, unless he cares to exercise any right provided by the treaty to inspect the reinsured's books. Preliminary bordereaux have almost disappeared from reinsurance practice and the use of definite bordereaux is virtually limited to:
(1) cases where either the reinsured is a new company or is embarking on a new class of insurance business;
(2) 'top' covers, such as second and third surplus treaties and facultative obligatory reinsurances; and
(3) occasions when a reinsurer requests details of cessions exceeding a certain amount to enable him to arrange his own retrocessions on an individual risk rather than a whole treaty basis.

4 UNCTAD, *Reinsurance Problems in Developing Countries*, p.18.

When definite bordereaux are supplied, apart from those cases where they are sent purely for information purposes, provision must also be made to deal with alterations.

The ever-growing size and complexity of fire and marine risks is again causing attitudes to change. Many reinsurers would now like to see bordereaux generally reintroduced for the very large risks where, because the original insurance is widely coinsured, a reinsurer may pick up liability for the same risk under cessions from several direct insurers. Provision of such information would enable the reinsurer to monitor his commitment on peak risks and, if necessary, to retrocede part of the liability accepted. Occasionally treaties do provide for the supply of such information but to date it has not become general practice. A different approach to the problem of accumulations has been adopted by the German fire insurance market.[5] Under the Codex system almost all German insurers supply to a central computer record details of their commitments on industrial risks over a certain size. Thus reinsurers, who have access to the central records, can check potential accumulations of liability.

When it is agreed that bordereaux shall be supplied, the frequency of supply is a matter for negotiation. Market practice is not rigid on this point: monthly or quarterly intervals may be equally acceptable depending on individual circumstances.

The decline in the supply of bordereaux has extended to loss bordereaux too. Apart from requiring immediate notification of large losses (see page 261), generally treaties only require the ceding company to supply individual loss details in respect of losses where cash settlement is wanted, or where premium bordereaux have been rendered.

Inspection of records

When a treaty is operated blind it is imperative that the ceding company should maintain precise records containing all of the details of risks ceded and of any losses thereunder necessary for the preparation of the quarterly accounts. It is general practice to include in the treaty authority for the reinsurer to inspect the ceding company's records at any reasonable time, or upon giving notice. The ceding company may also be required to supply copies of such records or other documents relating to the operation of the treaty upon request from the reinsurer, as in the following specimen clause:

---

5 *1971 Monte Carlo Panel Discussion Papers* (Reinsurance Offices' Association, 1971), p.31.

After prior advice to the Reinsured the Reinsurer may by an authorized representative inspect at any reasonable time all records and documents relating to the business hereunder.

Copies of policies, records or documents of any kind relating to any business covered by this agreement shall be supplied by the Reinsured to the Reinsurer immediately on request.

Errors and omissions

Almost inevitably, however much care is exercised, mistakes are likely to creep into the operation of any surplus treaty. Cessions may be recorded incorrectly or totally omitted from the records, or an error may be made in calculating the company's own retention so that the amount ceded is either too large or too small. It is in neither party's interest that mistakes should be binding, and invariably provision is made in treaties for the rectification of genuine errors even after a loss has occurred.

Care must be taken, however, to ensure that an errors and omissions clause is not so wide as to excuse mistakes which amount to a fundamental breach of the express or implied terms of a treaty, such as a breach of the general duty of good faith or a specific treaty requirement to advise the reinsurer of changes in underwriting practice. If a clause could be so construed it could override the reinsurer's right to cancel the treaty under the 'sudden death' section of the termination clause because of a breach of the terms of the treaty. Thus a clause as wide as the following could have unfortunate consequences for the reinsurer.

Error delay or omission on the part of the Reinsured in rendering any account or furnishing any bordereau or making any entry in the reinsurance books or bordereaux or notifying any claims or giving any information which ought under the provisions hereof to be given or doing any of the acts or things provided by the terms hereof shall not invalidate any obligation imposed on the Reinsurer hereunder.

A far safer practice is to include separate errors and omissions clauses in those provisions of the treaty to which it is intended that the clause should relate, notably the recording of cessions, and the preparation and supply of the quarterly accounts.

Calculation of the reinsurance premium

The method agreed between the parties for the calculation of the reinsurance premium must be set out in the treaty. Apart from exceptional cases such as marine reinsurances arranged on more restricted terms than the original insurances, proportional treaties simply need a clause entitling the reinsurer to receive in respect of each reinsurance ceded the same proportion of the original gross premium as the amount ceded bears to the original sum insured. Where premiums are subject to local taxes or other charges (e.g. fire brigade levies), or locally recognised deductions for brokerages and such like, the treaty will need to define exactly how such items are to be treated for the purpose of calculating the reinsurance premium. It is becoming increasingly common to stipulate that the deductions allowed shall be limited to the rates in force when the treaty is negotiated so that the reinsurer is protected against the arbitrary actions of governments in raising or imposing charges, particularly taxes on reinsurance premiums.

Reinsurance commissions

The treaty must also state the amount of commission which the reinsured may deduct from the premiums ceded. Only the rate of commission needs to be shown if the flat-rate method is employed. If the reinsurance commission is to be determined according to a sliding scale, or if an additional profit commission is allowed, precise details of the method of calculation must be set out in the treaty: specimen clauses are included in Appendix 3.2.

Claims notification and claims cooperation

It is a universally accepted principle that the primary responsibility for the handling of losses shall rest with the ceding company. Yet at the same time treaty reinsurers need prompt advice of losses which may involve them in a substantial liability, and at each stage of the claims negotiations they require sufficient information to understand the nature of the loss, to form a view of liability, to assess the probable cost, and to keep their own retrocessionaires informed about large losses. Quite possibly the original insurance may be extensively coinsured or heavily reinsured facultatively, so that a reinsurer may be involved in a large loss under cessions from several sources. Therefore, without early notice and periodic information regarding the progress of such losses, the calculation by a reinsurer of its outstanding claims reserves could become little more than guesswork and it would be impossible to monitor the performance of treaties. A reinsurer may also wish to exercise some control over the negotiation of large claims, or at least to watch developments and consult with the ceding company when thought desirable. Invariably, therefore, proportional treaties stipulate that the reinsurer(s) shall be notified of the occurrence of large losses.

Sometimes quite a long time elapses before original insurers are themselves notified of events which may give rise to·a claim. Even then the potential size of the loss may be open to considerable doubt: for example, liability may be disputed or some time may elapse before the extent of the loss can reasonably be established. The ceding company thus must be given some latitude in the timing of notification to the reinsurer and so the treaty clause may stipulate that the ceding company shall notify the reinsurer as soon as is *reasonably practicable* of any occurrence which may *reasonably* be considered as giving rise to a loss exceeding £x.

Occasionally reinsurers take a firmer line, the ceding company being required to advise the reinsurer *immediately* it becomes aware of any loss which *may* cost a specified sum—the following clause is taken from a fire surplus treaty.

> All potential claims under this agreement which equal or exceed the amount stated in the schedule shall be individually advised immediately to the Reinsurer together with relevant details and an estimate of the probable cost of such claims. The Reinsured shall keep the Reinsurer informed of all developments likely to affect the cost of any such claims and undertakes in so far as is reasonably possible to consult the Reinsurer or its representatives with regard to the settlement of such claims.

Possibly even then the probability of a loss attaining such proportions may be so minute that the ceding company may be justified in waiting for the position to become somewhat clearer before notifying the reinsurer.

The size of claim for which immediate notification will be required is a matter for agreement between the parties. A low figure will serve little purpose but add considerably to administrative costs. The criterion depends upon individual circumstances—not infrequently the chosen figure is related to the volume of premiums ceded under the treaty, a limit of between 5% and 10% of the expected annual reinsurance premium income being quite common for some classes of business. Where a treaty is shared between a number of reinsurers the loss advice limit applies to the treaty and not to the liability of the individual reinsurers, all of whom would be entitled to notification of the loss regardless of the size of their own participation.

The information required by reinsurers for large losses is the same as that supplied for facultative reinsurances (see page 238).

Conduct of claims

In the absence of any provision to the contrary the ceding company is alone responsible for the conduct of all claims negotiations with the original insured and any other interested parties, and the reinsurer will be liable for his share of all payments properly made by the reinsured under the terms of the original policy (or policies). A ceding company cannot assume that the reinsurer will be liable for any payment it cares to make. The position regarding *ex gratia* payments has been discussed already (Chapter 4). It could also be argued that costs incurred by the ceding company in contesting the validity of an insurance contract on which a claim is made cannot be regarded as payments properly made under the policy, the existence of which the company seeks to deny. However, if the reinsured's conduct has been approved by the reinsurer, such payments certainly would be admissible as part of the treaty claim. Also, it is market practice in Britain for the reinsurer to accept liability for payments made by the ceding company for which it has no legal liability but are incurred under certain market agreements. For example, under the terms of the Motor Insurers' Bureau Domestic Agreement an insurer in certain circumstances will accept liability for personal injuries suffered by a third party even though the company has no legal liability to indemnify its policyholder.

On the other hand circumstances may arise where the reinsurer would not be liable for payments made by the ceding company although the original policyholder's claim was based on the existence of the original policy. In the United States, for example, an insurer may be liable, as a result of the way in which it has handled a claim brought against a policyholder, for damages awarded against the policyholder in excess of the limit of indemnity contained in a liability policy. In addition a policyholder may be able to recover damages, including punitive damages, in respect of a number of torts which may be committed by the insurer in connection with the effecting of a policy as well as in the settlement of claims.[6] Unless in such circumstances the reinsurer clearly was associated with the conduct of the ceding company he would have no liability under the treaty for what is essentially a malpractice claim brought against the reinsured. In order to make their position clear American reinsurers are now inserting in reinsurance contracts various types of exclusion clauses such as the following:[7]

6 For the distinction between the so called 'excess verdicts' and punitive damages as well as related matters, see J.S. Butler, *Punitive Damages and Reinsurance* (Reinsurance Offices' Association, 1977), pp.31 *et seq.*

7 Anthony M. Lanzone, 'Punitive damages: Insurer and reinsurer, adversaries or partners?', *Best's Review*, Property/Casualty Edition, vol. 78, No. 9, January 1978. The author quotes five other examples of such exclusion clauses and discusses other ways in which American insurers and reinsurers are seeking to deal with the problem of 'excess verdicts' and punitive damages.

> Regardless of the terms and conditions of the company's policy the reinsurer shall not be liable for claims arising out of bad faith or outrage judgment against the company.

The general principles regarding the conduct of claims are usually modified by the insertion into treaties of special provisions relating to cooperation in the conduct and settlement of large claims, *ex gratia* payments and litigation expenses.

Cooperation

The ceding company may be required to keep the reinsurer informed of all developments likely to affect the cost of claims already notified to him under the provisions discussed above, and so far as is reasonably possible to cooperate with the reinsurer in the conduct and settlement of such claims. Especially when the ceding company has little experience in handling a particular sort of loss it may be in the interests of both parties for the reinsurer to take over the conduct of the claims negotiations, or for the two parties at least to agree on a course of action. Of course, when a treaty covers overseas risks normally the ceding company will be more familiar than the reinsurer with local conditions, law and practices.

Ex gratia payments

The reinsurer's liability for his share of any *ex gratia* payment may be made conditional on his prior consent to the payment having been obtained.

Litigation expenses

Although a decision by a ceding company to contest a claim means embarking on what may prove to be a very costly exercise, under a proportional reinsurance treaty the reinsurer does have the assurance that if the proceedings prove successful he will obtain his share of the benefit. It is normal practice, therefore, to allow the ceding company to exercise its discretion in commencing or defending any legal proceedings and to commit the reinsurer to pay his share of the expenses incurred. A typical clause reads as follows:

> The Reinsured may at its sole discretion commence continue defend compromise settle or withdraw from actions suits and proceedings and generally do all such things relating to any claim or loss which in its judgment may be expedient and the Reinsurer shall pay its due share of expenses connected therewith.

Payment of claims

The procedure for the payment of claims under the treaty must also be agreed. Practice with proportional treaties normally follows that of facultative reinsurances whereby small losses are dealt with in the quarterly account leaving larger losses to be settled individually. If the reinsurers had to pay their share of every loss at the time of settlement with the original insured there would be a ceaseless flow of cheques, mostly for trifling sums. On the other hand to delay the payment of large losses for three months or so could place a serious cash strain on a ceding company. Therefore for any claim where the total loss under the treaty exceeds an agreed sum provision is either made for the loss to be paid automatically by the reinsurers within a period of usually 15 days after notification, or immediately upon the request of the reinsured. Two examples of such clauses are as follows:

> The share of the Reinsurer in each loss settlement shall be debited in account but when the total sum recoverable in respect of any one loss from all the Reinsurers participating herein exceeds   payment in   for its share shall be made by the Reinsurer within fifteen days after communication of the particulars.

> The Reinsured shall maintain a record of all losses paid hereunder and these shall be advised as stated in the schedule to the Reinsurer on a bordereau form together with or prior to the account for that quarter. The Reinsured shall have the right to request immediate payment from the Reinsurer of its proportion of any loss settlement which equals or exceeds the amount as stated in the schedule.

The size of the cash loss limit must depend on individual circumstances. Ideally it should be fixed sufficiently high to avoid the reinsurers having to make a large number of individual payments during any normal year but not so high as to cause possible financial embarrassment to the ceding company. Where a treaty is fragmented between a large number of reinsurers the payment of such losses may still involve the reinsurers with small shares paying trifling sums, but from the ceding company's viewpoint it is essential that each reinsurer contributes its share, however small that may be, of each cash loss settlement.

Normally the treaty provisions will also entitle the ceding company to ask its reinsurers to make a cash payment if it has itself made an interim claims payment exceeding the treaty's cash loss limit. In practice ceding companies usually ask for substantial sums to be paid but allow small amounts to accumulate. When ceding companies are themselves on the point of rendering a quarterly account showing a balance due to the reinsurer, sometimes they will agree to a cash loss simply being deducted from the account balance.

Statements of outstanding claims

It is normal practice for treaty reinsurers to stipulate that within, say, three months of the end of each year the ceding company shall supply a statement of all outstanding claims showing the amounts for which the reinsurer may be liable. Such information would, of course, supplement that provided for large losses, and further assist the reinsurer in fixing his own loss reserves and in checking the performance of the treaty.

Premium reserve

Despite resistance from reinsurers, for many classes of business it is now fairly common for the ceding company to retain a certain proportion of the premiums payable to the reinsurer as a security for the performance by the reinsurer of his obligations under the treaty, often to meet conditions imposed by local legislation.

The reasons for the growth of this practice can partly be explained as caution on the part of ceding companies; if a reinsurer fails the reinsured will have access to earmarked funds which are excluded from the reinsurer's general assets available to meet the claims of all creditors in the winding-up of the company. The retention of premium reserves therefore is a means of obtaining collateral security for the fulfilment of a reinsurer's obligations under a treaty.

It is unlikely, however, that ceding companies' doubts about the financial standing of their reinsurers have played a major role. Probably of far greater importance has been the action of governments concerned about the balance-of-payments effects of reinsurances ceded to foreign reinsurers, and the relationship between the security provided by reinsurers and the solvency of ceding companies.[8] Some supervisory authorities require foreign reinsurers to deposit locally their technical reserves, sometimes with the ceding company when they may be treated as the property of the latter for the purpose of testing its solvency. Other countries deal with the solvency aspect by means of gross reserving regulations for direct insurers. The exact details of such regulations vary between countries, but in essence under the gross reserving system a supervisory authority when checking the solvency of an insurance company will not allow premiums ceded to unauthorized (i.e. usually foreign) reinsurers to be wholly or partially deducted from the

---

8 For a fuller discussion see Chapter 15.

company's own liabilities. Therefore, the only way to ease the strain on the company's financial position is for it to hold the treaty premium and loss reserves.

The retention of reserves by a ceding company is, however, disadvantageous for the reinsurer for reasons considered later and therefore will only be agreed if there are sound reasons for doing so. If agreed, then theoretically the calculation of the premium reserve should be based on the same principles as apply to the valuation of portfolio consideration following the withdrawal of a portfolio of unexpired risks on the termination of a treaty (see pages 274-5). In practice, however, the amount of the premium reserve is always calculated as a fixed percentage of the premiums ceded. Usually the figure ranges between 35% and 40% of the reinsurance premiums (before deduction of reinsurance commission).

When a reinsurer takes over a new treaty the procedure adopted will depend upon whether the reinsurance will apply to cessions for insurances issued or renewed on and after the commencement date of the treaty, or whether the reinsurer also takes over the portfolio of unexpired risks. In the former case the premium reserve will be built up over the year, the ceding company withholding the agreed percentage of premiums payable to the reinsurer each quarter. Thereafter the premium reserve held by the reinsurer will be based on the total premiums ceded in the last four quarters; a simple illustration of the method is given below:

Quarter	Premiums ceded	Premium reserve retained at 40%	Premium reserve released	Total premium reserve
	£	£	£	£
Year 1: 1	80,000	32,000	—	32,000
2	120,000	48,000	—	80,000
3	110,000	44,000	—	124,000
4	130,000	52,000	—	176,000
Year 2: 1	120,000	48,000	32,000	192,000
2	115,000	46,000	48,000	190,000

The premiums ceded over the first four quarters total £440,000, the total premium reserve for the year calculated at 40% therefore being £176,000. At the end of the next quarter the total premiums ceded over the last four quarters amount to £480,000, an increase of £40,000 which is the difference between the fifth quarter's premiums now brought into account and the premiums for the first quarter which are omitted; thus the premium reserve needs to be increased by £16,000. The premiums for the sixth quarter are £5,000 less than for the second quarter, so the reinsurer is entitled to an equivalent return of the premium reserve, that is £2,000.

When the reinsurer takes over the portfolio of unexpired risks the portfolio consideration is treated as the previous year's premium reserve and is wholly retained by the ceding company as the deposit. Then during the first year of the treaty the premium reserve for each quarter is calculated and retained as above, 25% of the portfolio consideration being released each quarter. So, for example, if in the above case the reinsurer had been credited with a portfolio consideration of £100,000, the additional premium reserve retained commencing at quarter 1 would be £7,000 (i.e. £32,000 – £25,000), and in subsequent quarters, £23,000, £19,000 and £27,000. If the reinsurer had accepted a portfolio consideration calculated as a proportion of underlying premiums less than the percentage laid down for the premium reserve, he would have had to deposit an additional sum in the first quarter to augment the portfolio consideration which then would be released over succeeding quarters in the normal way.

Sometimes when a treaty is cancelled the reinsurer will allow the ceding company to use the premium reserve to cover the run-off of losses.

If a ceding company is allowed to withhold premiums to build up a premium reserve not only will the reinsurer's cash inflow be reduced but also he will suffer a loss of investment income. Invariably, therefore, when ceding companies are allowed to hold premium reserves in the form of a cash deposit reinsurers require some compensation through the payment of interest on funds held by the reinsured. The rate of interest payable will be a matter for negotiation by the parties in the light of prevailing investment conditions in the country or countries concerned. Often a fixed rate is agreed upon as in the following specimen clause, but in a period of economic instability when market interest rates are subject to considerable fluctuations over relatively short periods (for example, between February 1975 and October 1976 the redemption yield on British government short-dated stocks ranged between 10.55% and 15.56%) there is a case for agreeing on a flexible rate tied to some recognized market rate of interest. If a flexible rate is agreed then it may also be desirable to agree to upper and lower limits. Essentially the aim should be to fix a rate which fairly reflects the yield which the ceding company itself can earn on the funds it holds so as to avoid the possibility of substantial gratuitous profits or losses being made out of the reserving operation, though it is accepted that ceding companies usually do earn more than they pay as interest on deposits.

Provided a ceding company's reason for seeking the deposit of premium reserves is simply to safeguard its own solvency or to comply with supervisory regulations, it may agree to accept the deposit of suitable securities equivalent in value to the premium reserve. A fall in the market values of the securities deposited or an increase in the size of the premium reserve would necessitate the deposit of additional securities, but such an arrangement would remove any grounds for dispute regarding investment income because the reinsurer would continue to receive in full interest and dividends earned on the securities. An advantage for the ceding company is that by agreeing to the deposit of securities it is relieved of the investment risk involved in guaranteeing to pay a certain rate of interest on cash deposits.

The following specimen clause provides for the premium reserve to be held by the ceding company either as a cash deposit or by the deposit of securities.

Premium reserve deposit clause

(a) The Reinsured shall retain from the Reinsurer a premium reserve deposit in cash calculated at ____ per cent on the premium ceded to the Reinsurer in the accounts rendered hereunder. Such retained deposit shall be released to the Reinsurer in the corresponding account of the following year.

(b) The Reinsurer may at any time request the release of the premium reserve deposit retained in cash and its replacement with bonds and/or securities acceptable to both parties and the reinsurer shall receive all dividends interest and other rights accruing thereon. When a deposit is constituted in bonds and/or securities the Reinsured shall have the right to debit the Reinsurer and retain in cash any deficiency between the premium reserve deposit required and the market value of the bonds and/or securities held. The cash deposit so retained shall be held by the Reinsured until covered by bonds and/or securities deposited by the Reinsurer.

(c) The Reinsured shall credit the Reinsurer in the accounts rendered hereunder with interest calculated at the rate of ____ per cent per annum on the amount of premium reserve deposit retained at any time throughout the relevant period in cash.

(d) It is hereby expressly agreed and declared that all sums of cash bonds or securities held by the Reinsured in accordance with the provisions of this clause remain the property of the Reinsurer and are held by the Reinsured as trustee for the Reinsurer and may only be utilized by the Reinsured in the event and up to the amount of the Reinsurer's failure to discharge its liability under this agreement.

The deposit of securities should not be regarded as a perfect solution to the problem of premium reserves free from any disadvantage, and the reader is referred to Chapter 14 for a further discussion of the subject, including a third alternative—the use of letters of credit.

Outstanding loss reserve

Besides depositing with the ceding company the premium reserve, on occasions reinsurers are also obliged to deposit a loss reserve to cover the estimated cost of outstanding claims.

The method of calculation follows that for the portfolio loss consideration paid by a reinsurer upon the withdrawal of outstanding losses following the termination of a treaty (see page 274). Normally the reserve is fixed at 100% of the estimated value of outstanding losses attaching under the treaty, with provision for adjustment annually or, if the ceding company can provide the necessary information, quarterly.

A quarterly adjustment is preferable for two reasons. Unless it is agreed that large losses which fall within the cash-loss provision shall be paid out of the loss reserve, the ceding company may gain from receiving payment in cash while still holding on to the relevant loss reserve for, perhaps, nearly 12 months until the annual adjustment takes place. Secondly, there is the problem of accurately assessing outstanding losses, particularly for classes of business such as liability where both liability and quantum may be in dispute.

Outstanding-loss reserve clauses follow the same format as a premium reserve clause, including provision for:

(1) The deposit to be either in cash or securities.
(2) The payment of interest at an agreed rate by the ceding company on cash deposits.
(3) Cash losses to be paid by the reinsurer out of the loss reserve deposit, except that following the cancellation of a treaty the reinsurer may become liable to pay cash losses in cash to avoid running down the loss-reserve deposit before the periodic review of the estimated value of losses still outstanding.

Preparation and settlement of accounts

The obligations of each party regarding the preparation, checking and settlement of accounts, including in the case of overseas treaties the currencies and rates of exchange to be employed, need to be defined carefully in every treaty. A discussion of such matters is contained in Chapter 14.

Arbitration clause

The universal use of arbitration as a means of settling disputes between the parties to a reinsurance contract has already been discussed in Chapters 3 and 4, and Appendix 4.1 contains a copy of a standard arbitration clause which has been proposed by the Institute of London Underwriters.

Termination of the reinsurance

There are many reasons why one or both parties may deem it desirable, or even necessary, to terminate a treaty. The reinsurer, for example, may be dissatisfied with the loss experience and may decide that there is little hope of ever earning a profit. On the other hand the ceding company may have discovered that better terms can be obtained elsewhere or that its reinsurance arrangements need a drastic overhaul. If the decision to terminate is a voluntary act it is only reasonable that the other party should be given early notice of the intention to bring the treaty to a close.

Conversely there are occasions when there is little or no option but to bring a treaty to an immediate end, such as the insolvency of one of the parties or some extraneous event like the imposition of new exchange control regulations which prohibit the remittance of settlements between them.

The rights of both parties to terminate the contract must be set out in the treaty with the two types of circumstances clearly distinguished. A specimen termination clause taken from a surplus reinsurance treaty is given below.

> Either party shall be at liberty to terminate this treaty as at midnight of the thirty first day of December of any year upon giving not less than three months' previous notice in writing.
>
> If either party gives notice to terminate any contract in consideration of which this treaty has been granted, such notice shall be regarded as applying equally to this treaty. Either party shall have the right to determine this treaty forthwith or at such date as the Reinsured shall specify by notice in writing:
>
> (a) If a petition be presented for the winding-up of the Reinsured or the Reinsurer or if the Reinsured or Reinsurer pass a resolution for voluntary liquidation.
>
> (b) If the business of either party be acquired controlled or administered by any other company corporation or authority *de facto,* or if there is a material change in the management.
>
> (c) If in the country in which either party resides or carries on business or is incorporated any regulation whether by decree or otherwise be enforced by the government *de facto* which shall restrict or prohibit the performance by either party of any or all of its obligations under this treaty or any contract in consideration of which this treaty has been granted.
>
> (d) If the country in which either party resides or carries on business or is incorporated be in a state of war whether war be declared or not.
>
> In the event of any law or regulation becoming operative so as to prohibit or render illegal the whole or any part of the arrangements made herein this treaty or that part of it which relates to any particular district affected may be determined forthwith by the Reinsured.

Both the time when notice must be given and the period of notice required are matters for agreement between the parties, though the provisions of the above clause are typical of present-day practice. It is in neither party's interest to allow notice to be given at any time. The reinsurer needs to plan his business and having secured a new treaty will not want to see it cancelled shortly thereafter. Conversely the ceding company will wish to avoid the prospect of having to arrange new cover, perhaps at an inconvenient time, for possibly a series of reinsurances that have unexpectedly been cancelled from differing dates. Therefore, the common practice now is to stipulate that a treaty can be cancelled at the desire of either party only as from a specified date, usually to coincide with the end of the ceding company's financial year.

Although a longer period of notice may be chosen, perhaps up to six months, a period of three months is probably a fair compromise between giving a ceding company sufficient time to arrange a fresh treaty and the reinsurer being able to see how the business for any particular year is developing.

Turning now to the so called 'sudden-death' section of the clause which sets out the circumstances under which either party may give notice of immediate cancellation, basically it deals with three situations:

(1) where there is a change in the ownership, financial position or the management of either party;

(2) where a change in the law or other circumstances prevents either party from honouring its obligations under the treaty; and

(3) the outbreak of war or hostilities affecting either party. Sometimes the outbreak of civil war or occupation by a foreign power are also specified as grounds for termination.

The insolvency of either party may involve the other in loss, but the possible inability of a reinsurer to meet claims is a matter of major concern for a ceding company. Therefore, as in the above clause, it may be deemed expedient not to wait until the reinsurer's insolvency has been proved but to give the ceding company the option to cancel and arrange cover elsewhere as soon as a petition for winding-up is presented. The circumstances in which an insurance company may be wound up vary from country to country; for example, in Britain and other countries where the supervisory regulations require a non-life insurance company to maintain a minimum margin of solvency, the supervisory authority may petition for its winding-up if it is technically insolvent, although judged by normal standards the company may still be able to pay its debts. In some other countries less stringent regulations apply. Therefore, the treaty provisions may also stipulate that notice of termination may be given if either party loses the whole or part of its paid-up share capital.

Amongst the many facts each party will consider before entering into a reinsurance treaty is the ownership and management of the other company. Therefore any change therein will also usually appear in the termination clause as permitting the other party to cancel the treaty forthwith.

The ability of a company to honour its obligations under a treaty may be impaired for many reasons beyond its own control. Not infrequently governments prohibit the remittance of funds overseas or effectively make it impossible to obtain the requisite foreign exchange; or a government may decree that reinsurances shall not be placed with unauthorized foreign reinsurers; or a company's authority to transact particular classes of insurance (or reinsurance) business may be withdrawn by a supervisory authority. Again the other party to a treaty must be permitted to cancel immediately in order to protect its own interests.

Under English law, immediately upon the outbreak of hostilities contracts with enemy aliens become illegal and thus void, so that a clause dealing with that position only restates the law. However, in view of the international character of reinsurance business and possible differences in law between countries, it is normal practice to make the position clear by an express clause. Also the rights of either party to terminate the treaty are usually extended to cover the situation where the country in which either party resides or carries on business or is incorporated becomes involved in armed hostilities with another country. Very occasionally it may further be agreed that if the treaty is not terminated under the latter circumstances the reinsurer will undertake not to retrocede any of the treaty business to any company in the country with which the ceding company's country is at war.

It used to be thought that the devaluation of either party's currency ought to be included in the termination clause as providing the right to cancel a treaty.[9] Given the changes that have occurred in international monetary arrangements, devaluation no longer appears in treaties amongst the list of reasons for termination.

When either party has given notice to terminate a proportional reinsurance treaty at the specified time, the ceding company is entitled to make, and the reinsurer to receive, cessions under the treaty in the normal manner until the date of termination. When the 'sudden-death' provision is invoked so that the treaty is terminated immediately the question of future cessions does not arise.

9 Golding, *Law and Practice of Reinsurance*, p.85.

Unexpired risks

Usually when a treaty is terminated there will be a large number of individual cessions still in force with varying periods to run until expiry. As a general rule the reinsurer will remain liable thereon until expiry or renewal of the underlying direct insurances, unless either the treaty has been brought to an end because continuation would be illegal or the parties agree to cancel the unexpired cessions.

When a fundamental change of conditions warrants a ceding company immediately terminating a treaty under the 'sudden-death' provisions, it may be equally prudent at the same time to transfer existing cessions to a new reinsurer. Under other circumstances although there may be no such urgency, a ceding company may still prefer to terminate simultaneously both the treaty and existing cessions in order to avoid administrative difficulties. If cessions are allowed to run off, the reinsured for a time will have two or more treaties running in parallel requiring separate records of cessions made under each treaty in order to deal with subsequent alterations and losses. Moreover because of the delays in the reporting and settling of losses, such records will need to be preserved carefully for several years so that for every loss occurring during the period of overlap the records can be checked to ensure that the reinsurer's share is assigned to the correct treaty. Such procedures are possible but will increase both administrative costs and the risk of error. If a company regularly changes its treaties the administrative arrangements can become very complex and confused. Therefore, apart from marine and aviation reinsurances and other treaties written on an underwriting year basis, the practice of making a clean break as opposed to allowing cessions to run off has become increasingly popular, particularly for fire and other property treaties. The following specimen clause permits the ceding company to ask for a clean break.

> In the event of this treaty being determined the Reinsured shall have the option to cancel all reinsurances allotted hereunder and then in force and to debit the reinsurer with ____% (net of commission) of the premiums in the accounts for the last four quarters otherwise all reinsurances shall continue in force until the expiry of their current terms unless previously cancelled by the Reinsured.

Portfolio withdrawal and assumption

Occasionally termination clauses give both parties the right to request the withdrawal of existing cessions upon cancellation of a treaty, though Golding rightly stresses the importance of confining that right only to the ceding company.[10] If the reinsurer is allowed to demand withdrawal the ceding company may be unable to reinsure the run-off risk and thus become exposed to potential losses substantially larger than its normal retention(s).

Explicit in the withdrawal of a portfolio is the right of the ceding company to receive the unexpired premiums on existing cessions held by the reinsurer. As the company will then require fresh reinsurance protection against potential losses there has developed the 'portfolio system' whereby the withdrawn unexpired risks are accepted by a new reinsurer who, in return for an appropriate premium consideration, assumes liability for claims occurring during their run-off. This system necessitates some procedure for the valuation of the unexpired risks under the old treaty and the payment of an agreed sum to the new reinsurer.

Ideally, unless there is a marked seasonal pattern to claims, the reinsurer should return a *pro rata* share of the premiums received equal to the unexpired period of insurance for each risk ceded, i.e.

$$\text{return of premium} = \sum \frac{U_i}{T_i} P_i$$

where U_i = unexpired period of insurance

T_i = the total period of insurance

P_i = the reinsurance premium
less reinsurance commission

for the ith risk ceded

The return of premium would be net of reinsurance commission at the same rate as allowed by the reinsurer on the premiums he received. For a company with a fully computerized accounting system the calculation of individual unexpired periods of insurance and proportionate returns of premium should be relatively easy but in practice the estimating methods laid down in treaties are usually far cruder. Often the treaty will simply provide for the return of a stated percentage of the premium received by the reinsurer over the preceding 12 months.

For UK treaties the commonest figure used for calculating the return of premium is probably 40%, though it may go as low as 35% of the last year's reinsurance premiums. Such figures are based on the assumption that if the business ceded under a treaty is evenly distributed throughout the year and the underlying direct insurances are all annual policies, then on average one-half of the periods of insurance will be unexpired at the

10 Golding, *Law and Practice of Reinsurance*, p.87.

end of the year. Historically commission rates on original business were around 20%, so discounting the 50% of premiums for their share of commission already paid produces a figure of 40% and discounting original premiums at a rate of 30% for reinsurance commission gives a figure of 35%. Therefore a return of 40% would err on the generous side and allow for more business having been ceded in the second half of the year, as would tend to occur with an expanding account. If the business included a substantial volume of longer-term insurances the figure would need to be increased accordingly, whereas a large amount of short-term business or a higher rate of reinsurance commission would call for a reduction in the proportion of premiums returned. Sometimes instead of providing for a fixed percentage of premiums to be returned, it may be agreed to return 50% less the current rate of reinsurance commission. This method accommodates changes in the rate of commission paid under sliding-scale provisions. When original premiums include premium taxes and such like which are deducted in arriving at the reinsurance premium, returns of reinsurance premiums must be adjusted likewise.

Even if such factors as seasonal patterns in the distribution of business ceded are taken fully into account in fixing the percentage figure, there is the possibility of the pattern of business ceded varying from year to year. Therefore various methods have been devised to try to produce more accurate values without the need to calculate a *pro rata* return for each individual risk. The use, for example, of 'eighth' and 'twenty-fourth' systems represents attempts to deal with changes in the distribution of risks ceded over the year. Under the eighths system the reinsurance premiums are analysed by quarters, each risk being allocated to the quarter of the year when ceded to the reinsurer, whereas under the twenty-fourths system the premiums are analysed on a monthly basis. It is assumed that the business is written evenly throughout each quarter (or month) so that on average cessions will commence halfway through the quarter (or month) and terminate 12 months later. Thus the values for each quarter under the eighths system are:

Date of cession	Unexpired risk at the 31 December expressed as a fraction of a year	Mid-value
1 January – 31 March	0 2/8	1/8
1 April – 30 June	2/8 4/8	3/8
1 July – 30 September	4/8 6/8	5/8
1 October – 31 December	6/8 8/8	7/8

The mid-value fractions would then be applied to the total premiums for the risks ceded each quarter to produce the value of the unexpired risks at the end of the year. A simple example will illustrate how the system works.

Assume that under two treaties the total reinsurance premiums for risks ceded during the year amounted to £100,000, but were distributed as follows:

	Treaty A £	Treaty B £
1st quarter	25,000	20,000
2nd quarter	25,000	23,000
3rd quarter	25,000	27,000
4th quarter	25,000	30,000
	100,000	100,000

The respective valuations of the unexpired risks at the end of the year would be:

Treaty A	Treaty B
£25,000 × 1/8 = £ 3,125	£20,000 × 1/8 = £ 2,500
£25,000 × 3/8 = £ 9,375	£23,000 × 3/8 = £ 8,625
£25,000 × 5/8 = £15,625	£27,000 × 5/8 = £16,875
£25,000 × 7/8 = £21,875	£30,000 × 7/8 = £26,250
£50,000	£54,250

If the business had been concentrated more heavily in the earlier instead of the later part of the year, the value would be less than 50% of the total premiums ceded during the year.

Under the twenty-fourths system, the unexpired period of insurance for cessions made during the first month of the treaty year is taken as 1/24th (premiums for policies with a period of insurance which exactly coincides with the treaty year are normally excluded), for cessions during the second month 3/24ths, and so on. If the business is evenly distributed through the year this system, like the eighths system, produces a value equal to 50% of the total premiums ceded during the year. The advantage of using the twenty-fourths method is simply that it will cater more accurately for an uneven distribution of cessions during each quarter.

Whichever method is employed the resulting value must be reduced by the same rate of reinsurance commission as that allowed on the original cessions, with appropriate adjustment for sliding-scale rates of commission and charges such as premium taxes. Neither system allows for the distorting effects of long-term or short-period insurances: if they amount to a substantial part of the business ceded the value of the portfolio of unexpired risks will need to be increased or reduced accordingly.

When a portfolio of unexpired risks is to be taken over by new reinsurer(s) the ceding company will normally pay a consideration equal to the value returned by the original treaty reinsurer(s). It is possible that a larger sum may be demanded; for example, if the reinsurer in terminating the treaty because of bad loss experience had also been able to exercise the right to cancel existing cessions, the new reinsurer may be unwilling to assume the liability of running off unexpired risks in return for a proportionate share of premiums which are known to be too low. Obviously under such circumstances a ceding company is not likely to withdraw the portfolio.

The premium base on which the portfolio consideration is calculated deserves some thought. If it is based on premiums accounted for in the last four quarterly accounts, they may not coincide exactly with the premiums for the risks ceded during the last 12 months because of accounting delays. Premiums for some of the risks ceded towards the end of a quarter tend to be carried over to the next quarter. Therefore some of the premiums included in the first quarter's account will relate to risks ceded in the previous year, while the premiums for some of the risks ceded during the last three months of the year will not appear in the fourth quarter's account but will be held over to the next year. When a

278

ceding company breaks down its accounts between underwriting years, i.e. belated premiums are assigned to the relevant underwriting year, it is possible to identify the premium income relating to the current year. Then the portfolio consideration can be calculated accordingly, with subsequent adjustments as belated premiums work through the accounts. Most companies, however, do not follow that practice, though lags in the payment of premiums are of no great consequence so long as a treaty continues in force, provided the delays are not so lengthy that the reinsurer suffers a substantial loss of investment income. The problem arises when a treaty is terminated because it will leave some items still to be paid after the settlement of the fourth quarter's account. Even so, as the ceding company will have already received a portfolio consideration based on 12 months' premiums, the payment of the belated premiums generally should not entitle the company to any additional consideration. The only circumstances under which a case could be made for the return of additional consideration would be if the belated premiums were substantially larger than the previous year's premiums which had been included in the first quarter's account.

Finally, it may be noted that the same questions of portfolio consideration arise in the case of portfolio changes where either one reinsurer alters his share of a treaty, or the ceding company increases its retention.

Outstanding losses

At the date of termination of a treaty there may be a number of losses outstanding in which the reinsurer is interested. As final settlement of those losses may take months or even years, the reinsurer will face the prospect of a lengthy continuing liability. Moreover when the ceding company is entitled to hold the technical reserves until all losses are finally extinguished and is obliged to credit the reinsurer with only a low rate of interest, significant overestimating of provisions for outstanding claims may involve the reinsurer in a considerable loss of investment income. Therefore it has become increasingly common to insert in fire and property (though not accident) proportional treaties provision for the reinsurer to discharge his liability for losses outstanding at the date of termination of the treaty either by payment to the ceding company of an appropriate lump sum, or at least allowing it to retain that part of any premium-reserve deposit which is equivalent to known outstanding losses.

Usually, however, only the ceding company is given the option to withdraw the loss portfolio and upon doing so assumes sole liability for the ultimate loss settlements (though normally that liability would be transferred to the incoming reinsurer as mentioned below). Thus there can be a 'clean-cut' termination of the treaty, the reinsurer paying a consideration for both the withdrawal of the portfolio of unexpired risks and for the loss portfolio.

The consideration for a loss portfolio is normally calculated as a fixed percentage of the reinsurer's share of the aggregate estimated value of outstanding losses, the amount being negotiated by the parties. The agreed percentage will depend upon a number of factors. Loss of potential investment earnings may be a significant factor that the reinsurer should consider, and available evidence indicates that some classes of insurance generally tend to be more prone to the over- or underestimating of claims provisions than others. Also the ceding company's own claims-estimating practice and record need to be considered—should the company make a practice of overestimating outstanding claims (possibly due to ignoring potential salvage) then a figure as low as 90% may be agreed to restore the balance. Conversely if there is a tendency to underestimate, a figure in excess of 100%, and in very exceptional cases as high as 110% may be considered equitable. 90% tends to be the normal figure, mainly in recognition of the fact that the reinsurer forfeits investment income by effectively paying its share of claims immediately.

Questions of investment income and the impact of inflation on loss settlements have become more important in recent years. When the reinsurer pays the loss portfolio consideration the ceding company obtains a lump sum available for investment until the losses are settled. On the other hand the company will assume the whole risk that the aggregate final settlements will vary from the amount estimated. Possibly the ceding company may benefit by being able to settle the outstanding claims for a lower sum, but nowadays the reverse is more likely to occur. Rates of inflation tend to be higher than the best forecasts; changes in the law usually adversely affect claims costs particularly for liability insurances; and universally members of the public become increasingly claims conscious. Therefore in most countries claims costs have tended to increase faster than investment earnings. Nevertheless it should not be assumed that the two automatically cancel out, and in examining the ceding company's loss-estimating procedures close attention should be paid to the forecasts of what has been called 'superimposed inflation' (see Chapter 5).

Because of the degree of uncertainty in claims estimating both parties to a treaty may reserve the right to review the position and perhaps ask for a revision of the agreed loss portfolio percentage in the light of a change in conditions.

Instead of the ceding company assuming liability for the reinsured share of the outstanding claims, agreement may be reached whereby the new reinsurer takes over the liability in return for the loss portfolio consideration paid by the previous reinsurer. The loss portfolio consideration would be accounted for in the same manner as the portfolio consideration for unexpired risks. This method has come to be known as the clean-cut system of terminating and commencing treaties.

Appendix 7.1 Specimen surplus reinsurance agreement

SURPLUS REINSURANCE AGREEMENT made between ____ (hereinafter called the 'REINSURED') of the one part and ____ (hereinafter called the 'REINSURER') of the other part.

IN CONSIDERATION of the payment of the premium as hereinafter provided it is agreed:

ARTICLE I

(a) The REINSURED shall cede and the REINSURER shall accept by way of reinsurance the proportion stated in the Schedule (hereinafter called the REINSURER'S proportion) of those insurances stated in the Schedule.

(b) The REINSURED shall decide what constitutes one risk hereunder and unless otherwise hereinafter provided shall fix its net retention without reference to the REINSURER in accordance with the usual net retentions of the REINSURED. If however the REINSURED shall know of the probability of a loss affecting this Agreement prior to either the fixing or revision of its net retention then the retention shall be not less than that shown by its records and practices to be its usual net retention for similar risks. The usual net retentions of the REINSURED shall not be altered without the prior consent of the REINSURER.

(c) The REINSURED may in the interest of the REINSURER reduce the amount to be ceded in respect of any risk by effecting individual facultative reinsurances. The REINSURED may also effect catastrophe reinsurance to protect its net retained account.

(d) An insurance granted by the REINSURED wherein the REINSURED is named as the Insured either alone or jointly with another party or parties shall not be excluded from this Agreement merely because no legal liability may arise in respect thereof by reason of the fact that the REINSURED be the Insured or one of the Insureds.

ARTICLE II

(a) The liability of the REINSURER in respect of each cession hereunder shall be subject to all the stipulations, clauses, waivers and modifications of the original policy and of any endorsement thereto except in so far as they are contrary to the terms of this Agreement.

(b) However, the liability of the REINSURER hereunder in respect of each claim shall not be increased by reason of the inability of the REINSURED to recover amounts from any other Reinsurers for any reason whatsoever.

ARTICLE III

(a) The REINSURED undertakes not to introduce, without the prior approval of the REINSURER, any change in its established acceptance and underwriting policy in respect of those insurances to which this Agreement relates.

ARTICLE IV

(a) The REINSURED shall maintain a record of all cessions hereunder and of all renewals and alterations thereto and these shall be advised as stated in the Schedule to the REINSURER on a bordereau form. Any error and/or inadvertent omission in this connection shall not prejudice the rights of either party but shall be corrected retrospectively upon discovery so that the parties hereto shall be placed in the same position as if the error and/or inadvertent omission had not occurred.

ARTICLE V

(a) The REINSURED shall pay to the REINSURER the REINSURER'S proportion of the original gross premium due to the REINSURED in respect of all risks ceded hereto. The REINSURER shall allow commission as stated in the Schedule, but unless otherwise provided no other deduction will be made.

ARTICLE VI

(a) All potential claims under this Agreement which equal or exceed the amount stated in the Schedule shall be individually advised immediately to the REINSURER together with relevant details and an estimate of the probable cost of such claims. The REINSURED shall keep the REINSURER informed of all developments likely to affect the cost of any such claims and undertakes in so far as is reasonably possible to consult the REINSURER or its representatives with regard to the settlement of such claims.

(b) All loss payments made by the REINSURED within the conditions of the original insurance and falling within the scope of this Agreement shall be binding on the REINSURER. The REINSURER shall also be bound by *ex gratia* payments made with its consent. All legal costs and professional fees and expenses (excluding salaries of all employees and office expenses of the REINSURED) which are reasonably incurred in connection therewith shall form part of such loss payment. The REINSURER shall be liable for its proportion of such loss payment in respect of any risks ceded hereto less its proportion of any recoveries applicable thereto made by the REINSURED whether as salvage or otherwise.

(c) The REINSURED shall maintain a record of all losses paid hereunder and these shall be advised as stated in the Schedule to the REINSURER on a bordereau form together with or prior to the account for that quarter. The REINSURED shall have the right to request immediate payment from the REINSURER of its proportion of any loss settlement which equals or exceeds the amount as stated in the Schedule.

(d) The REINSURED shall as soon as practicable and in any event not later than three months after the date or dates as stated in the Schedule send to the REINSURER a statement of unsettled claims as at the date of such statement showing the amount for which the REINSURER may be liable in respect of each individual claim.

ARTICLE VII

(a) The accounts between the REINSURED and the REINSURER in respect of the business under this Agreement shall be closed quarterly and rendered by the REINSURED as soon as possible thereafter but in any event not later than two months after the end of each quarter. The conversion of currencies into the currency of payment of this Agreement will be at the rates of exchange ruling at the time they were entered in the books of the REINSURED.

(b) Accounts shall be confirmed by the REINSURER within one month of receipt but inadvertent errors or omissions in the quarterly accounts shall not delay the payment of any balance due hereunder unless such errors or omissions have a major effect on the remittable balance. Any necessary correction shall be made in the next quarterly account rendered hereunder (except in those cases where the error or omission has a major effect on the remittable balance necessitating an immediate adjustment).

(c) Balances due to the REINSURED shall be paid at the time of confirmation and balances due to the REINSURER shall be paid by the REINSURED at the same time as the accounts are rendered.

ARTICLE VIII

(a) Any amounts due by either party under this Agreement which are outstanding one month after the date on which settlement is due shall be subject to the payment of interest by the debtor as from the expiry of that one month's period of grace. Interest shall be calculated at the rate stated in the Schedule and remain payable up to the day of the debtor effecting settlement unless the creditor shall amend or extend the one month period of grace.

ARTICLE IX

(a) Any payment hereunder shall be in the currency stated in the Schedule unless otherwise agreed in which event such payment shall be made at the rates of exchange ruling on the date of remittance.

ARTICLE X

(a) In the event of any change in the law by which the REINSURER'S liability hereunder is materially increased or extended the parties hereto agree to take up for immediate discussion a suitable revision in the terms of the Agreement. Failing agreement on a revision this Agreement shall operate from the effective date of the change of law as if the change had not occurred.

ARTICLE XI

(a) This agreement shall take effect in respect of all insurances relating to risks covered hereunder issued or renewed on and after the date as stated in the Schedule and shall be terminated on the basis set out in the Schedule. In the event of either party giving notice of termination in accordance with the provisions set out in the Schedule then such notice shall be automatically deemed to have been given by both parties. During the period of notice the REINSURER shall continue to participate in all cessions covered by the terms of this Agreement.

(b) Either party shall have the right to terminate this Agreement by giving the other party written notice by the quickest means available which shall be deemed to be served upon dispatch or where communications between the parties are interrupted upon attempted dispatch where:

    (1) The performance of the whole or any part of this Agreement be prohibited or rendered impossible *de jure* or *de facto* in particular and without prejudice to the generality of the preceding words in consequence of any law or regulation which is or shall be in force in any country or territory or if any law or regulation shall prevent directly or indirectly the remittance of any or all or any part of the balance or payments due to or from either party.

(2) The other party has become insolvent or unable to pay its debts or has lost the whole or any part of its paid-up capital or has had its authority to transact any class of insurance withdrawn, suspended or made conditional.

(3) There is any material change in the management or control of the other party.

(4) The country or territory in which the other party resides or has its head office or is incorporated shall be involved in armed hostilities with any other country whether war be declared or not or is partly or wholly occupied by another power or be in a state of civil war.

(5) The other party shall have failed to comply with any of the terms and conditions of this Agreement.

(c) the REINSURER shall (unless specifically agreed otherwise) remain liable for its share of all cessions hereunder in force on the effective date of termination until their next annual renewal date or natural expiry or for a period not exceeding 12 months whichever shall occur first.

ARTICLE XII

(a) After prior advice to the REINSURED the REINSURER may by an authorized representative inspect at any reasonable time all records and documents relating to the business hereunder.

(b) Copies of policies, records or documents of any kind relating to any business covered by this Agreement shall be supplied by the REINSURED to the REINSURER immediately on request.

(c) The provisions of this Article shall continue to apply for as long as either party has any liability hereunder.

ARTICLE XIII

(a) All communications and notices served in accordance with any of the provisions of this Agreement shall be addressed to the party concerned at its head office or at any other address previously designated by the other party.

(b) All postal, cable, remittance and other similar charges shall be paid by the sender.

ARTICLE XIV

(a) Any alterations to this Agreement which may be agreed in writing between the parties hereto shall be considered as part hereof and equally binding.

ARTICLE XV

(a) Either party may at its discretion set off against any amounts due from the other party hereunder or under any other Agreements between the parties hereto any amounts which are due under this or those other Agreements.

ARTICLE XVI

(a) All disputes arising out of the above Agreement or concerning its interpretation or validity whether arising before or after its termination shall be referred to two Arbitrators in accordance with the provisions of the Arbitration Act 1950, or any statutory re-enactment or modification thereof for the time being in force.

(b) The Arbitrators and Umpire shall be officials of insurance or reinsurance organizations and the venue of the arbitration shall be in London.

(c) The Arbitrators and Umpire are relieved of all judicial formalities and they may abstain from following strict rules of law. They shall settle any dispute under the above Agreement according to an equitable rather than a strictly legal interpretation of its terms.

(d) This arbitration agreement shall be construed as a separate and independent contract between the REINSURED and the REINSURER and arbitration hereunder shall be a condition precedent to the commencement of any action at law.

The Schedule together with any Appendix thereto is deemed to form an integral part of this Agreement.

IN WITNESS WHEREOF this Agreement has been signed in duplicate on behalf of and by the authority of each contracting party.

At ＿＿ this ＿＿day of ＿＿ 197＿ for and on behalf of ＿＿.

and at ＿＿ this ＿＿ day of ＿＿ 197＿ for and on behalf of ＿＿.

THE SCHEDULE

attaching to and forming part of the SURPLUS REINSURANCE AGREEMENT made between the REINSURED and the REINSURER.

ITEM

1. BUSINESS COVERED AND TERRITORIAL SCOPE (Article I(*a*))
2. LIMITS (Article I(*a*))
3. PREMIUM BORDEREAU (Article IV(*a*))
4. COMMISSION (Article V(*a*))
5. PRELIMINARY LOSS ADVICE (Article VI(*a*))
6. LOSS BORDEREAU (Article VI(*c*))
7. CASH LOSS LIMIT (Article VI(*c*))
8. OUTSTANDING LOSS BORDEREAU (Article VI(*d*))
9. INTEREST ON BALANCES (Article VIII(*a*))
10. CURRENCY (Article IX(*a*))
11. COMMENCEMENT (Article XI(*a*))
12. TERMINATION (Article XI(*a*))

REINSURER'S SHARE: ＿＿ of all amounts appearing in the Schedule.

IN WITNESS WHEREOF this Schedule has been signed in duplicate on behalf of and by the authority of each contracting party.

At ＿＿ this ＿＿ day of ＿＿ 197＿ for and on behalf of ＿＿.

and at ＿＿ this ＿＿ day of ＿＿ 197＿ for and on behalf of ＿＿.

8
Non-proportional treaties

REINSURANCE

8
Non-proportional treaties

The matters which have to be covered by treaty wordings are largely the same regardless of the type of reinsurance involved. Therefore, some of the general comments made in the previous chapter are equally applicable to non-proportional treaties, and the various items to be found in an excess of loss treaty will be dealt with in the same order as in the last chapter.

Whereas it is arguable that a surplus treaty strictly is only an agreement between the two parties respectively to cede and to accept all reinsurances falling within the terms of the agreement, the cessions themselves being the contracts of reinsurance, with non-proportional treaties the treaty itself is the contract of reinsurance. Under a non-proportional treaty there is no question of the reinsured having to cede part of the liability arising under individual policies; the reinsurer automatically accepts responsibility for all losses in excess of an agreed sum (subject to an upper limit) arising under any policy issued by the reinsured within the scope of the reinsurance contract. It follows that the comments made in Chapter 7 regarding the supply of bordereaux do not apply to non-proportional treaties.

Commencement of a non-proportional treaty

Accounting difficulties are considerably eased if the commencement date of an excess of loss treaty is arranged to coincide with the begining of the ceding company's financial year, because the reinsurance premium will be based on its total premium income obtained from the reinsured portfolio of business. Then the treaty can run from year to year for an indefinite period until brought to an end by either party giving notice of termination or some event occurring that automatically terminates the agreement.

There are two distinct systems in use for applying a treaty to the ceding company's business—the 'issued and renewed' and the 'losses occurring' systems. Each has its merits and demerits though the losses occurring method is the one most frequently used.

Issued and renewed

Under such a cover the reinsurer is liable for all claims occurring under policies issued and renewed by the ceding company during one year. Thus the reinsurer has a continuing liability for claims which may occur during the following year under policies which are still in force at the end of the year. The wording of the treaty commencement clause would follow that shown for a proportional reinsurance (Chapter 7).

When a treaty is arranged on an 'issued and renewed' basis usually the reinsurance premium is calculated on the ceding company's written premium income for the year net of refunds and reinsurance premiums ceded for reinsurances which inure to the benefit of the excess of loss reinsurer by reducing the net retained losses. Strictly speaking the resulting premium will not exactly measure the reinsurer's exposure because of the deduction from written premiums of refunds paid in respect of policies effected during the previous year. However the margin of error arising from that factor normally will be of no real significance.

Losses occurring

Under this system the reinsurer assumes liability for all claims occurring during the year under all policies in force, regardless of their inception dates, but he has no responsibility for any claims which occur after the end of the year.

The use of written premiums as a base for the calculation of the reinsurance premium is less satisfactory in this case, though the premiums for most fire and accident treaties are so calculated in practice. Because the reinsurer is liable for losses occurring during the year he will pick up claims arising (1) on the unexpired portion of policies written in the previous year, and (2) on that portion of the periods of insurance which fall within the current year of policies issued and renewed during the year. Written premiums, however, make no allowance for unexpired risks brought forward at the begining of the year or carried forward at its end. In other words, unless the unearned premium reserves at the begining and end of the year are equal, the reinsurance premium payable by the ceding company will not exactly match the liability it transfers to the reinsurer. If the underlying account is expanding the premiums received will exceed premiums earned, and vice versa. However, provided the amount of business written by the ceding company does not either fluctuate violently or continuously expand or contract, over a period of years any difference(s) should even out. Therefore, though from a theoretical point of view earned premiums (adjusted for underlying reinsurances) provide a sounder base for the calculation of excess of loss treaties arranged on a losses-occurring basis, usually the extra effort involved in producing such figures is not considered worthwhile, particularly bearing in mind that the reinsurer will base his quotation on the subject premium income whether written or earned premiums are used.

As for the difficulty associated with the two systems, in many cases the 'issued and renewed' method could create intractable problems under excess of loss reinsurances. Consider, for example, an excess of loss catastrophe reinsurance arranged to protect a property insurance account against aggregate retained losses in excess of £250,000 arising from any one occurrence, the reinsured perils being windstorm and flood. As the result of an extensive flood occurring some months after a new treaty has been arranged the ceding company suffers an aggregate net retained loss of £450,000 of which £240,000 relates to policies issued or renewed since the commencement of the new treaty while the balance falls under the old treaty. No recovery could be obtained from either reinsurer because the aggregate loss applicable to each treaty is below the treaty limit. Therefore, net account catastrophe covers can only be arranged on a 'losses-occurring' basis. Golding cites a similar example of excess of loss reinsurances arranged for a motor account where two policyholders insured by the same ceding company under policies effected at different times are involved in the same accident.[1] If the two vehicles also collided with a third party's building or other static property there would be the added complication that the ceding company would have to apportion the compensation payable to the third party between the two motor policies in order to determine the liability of the respective excess of loss reinsurers.

Under the 'losses-occurring' method problems can arise if for any reason the reinsurer decides to terminate the reinsurance. The reinsurer's liability would then end, leaving the ceding company without any protection for the remaining unexpired periods of insurance of the business on his books. Normally this should present no difficulty in that another reinsurer could be found to take over the reinsurance, albeit at a higher rate. If, however, the reinsurance had been cancelled because of a disastrously poor claims experience then even if it proved possible to find a reinsurer prepared to take over the business, subject to the ceding company undertaking whatever measures were required to improve its experience, the new reinsurer might not be willing to pick up the potentially high liabilities on the unexpired risks. Normally such problems should not arise in that the reinsurer could be expected to act before the situation got so bad. Moreover most reinsurers on entering

1 Golding, *Law and Practice of Reinsurance*, p.129.

into an excess of loss treaty arranged on a losses-occurring basis would agree to include an optional extension clause whereby they undertake to run off their liabilities following cancellation of the treaty, subject to the payment of an additional premium to be mutually agreed at the time.

If an optional extension clause cannot be negotiated, the only alternative left to a ceding company unwilling to accept the risk of being left with unprotected liabilities is to arrange its treaty on an issued and renewed basis when on cancellation the reinsurer would be obliged to run off his liabilities. If the worst then happened the ceding company could refuse to renew the offending direct insurances.

The operative clause

The following clause expresses in a typical manner the obligatory nature of an excess-of-loss treaty.

> In respect of each ultimate net loss (as hereinafter defined) sustained by the Reinsured under those insurances specified in the Schedule the Reinsurer shall indemnify the Reinsured by way of excess of loss reinsurance within the limits set out in the Schedule.

The obligation placed on the reinsurer to provide an indemnity for losses sustained calls for no counter-obligation on the reinsured to cede any risk because the treaty will automatically cover the whole of the reinsured account. What must be added, either as part of the operative clause or in a schedule incorporated into the treaty, is a statement defining precisely the extent of the reinsurer's liability.

All of the comments made in Chapter 7 regarding the class(es) of insurance and the geographical scope of the business included in a reinsurance treaty apply equally to non-proportional treaties. For example, in a treaty combining several classes of insurance different excess limits may be applied to each class of insurance in the same way as the ceding company may fix different retentions under a surplus treaty. The difference between the two main forms of treaty lies in the nature of the reinsurer's liability.

Nature and extent of the reinsurer's liability

The key factors which determine the extent of a reinsurer's liability under an excess of loss treaty, and therefore need to be defined in the treaty, are:

(1) The volume and type of business accepted by the reinsured.
(2) The reinsured's net retention on each risk accepted (i.e. after allowing for any underlying reinsurances).
(3) Whether the treaty is arranged on an individual risk, occurrence, or stop loss basis.
(4) The lower and upper excess limits, and whether the reinsured is required to participate in the losses which fall within those limits.

The reinsurer's liability under excess of loss treaties

'Ultimate net loss'. As noted in Chapter 5, the reinsurer's liability is normally related to the 'ultimate net loss' sustained by the ceding company. The intention is that the reinsurer shall only be liable when the amount (including legal costs and similar claims-settlement expenses) actually paid by the ceding company, less all recoveries from underlying reinsurances or other sources, exceeds the lower excess limit. It is necessary, however, to qualify the terms of the treaty to deal with two situations which may arise.

Firstly, the reinsured's ultimate net loss calculated for purposes of the excess of loss treaty should not be increased by any amount which the company for any reason is unable to recover from an underlying reinsurer. If this contingency is not dealt with in the treaty provisions the reinsurer in effect insures the reinsured against losses sustained due to the failure of other reinsurers and for which he has received no premium.

Secondly, with marine hull and particularly liability insurances it is quite common for several years to elapse before the final cost of a claim is known. Settlement of personal injury claims can be very protracted. Often it can take several months to establish the full extent of lasting injuries, and whenever the circumstances of a loss indicate possible negligence by a third party, years may elapse before liability is finally established and a recovery effected. If in the meantime the ceding company has made substantial payments it would be inequitable for the reinsurer to delay settlement until the reinsured's ultimate net loss was known.

The following specimen clause taken from an accident excess of loss treaty deals with both of the above situations:

> *(a)* The term 'ultimate net loss' shall be understood to mean the total amount which the Reinsured has actually paid in settlement of all claims or series of claims arising out of any one accident or event which may occur during the period set out in the Schedule including any legal costs and professional fees and expenses (excluding salaries of all employees and office expenses of the Reinsured) reasonably incurred in connection therewith. Recoveries including amounts under reinsurances which inure to the benefit

of this agreement shall be first deducted from such amount to arrive at the amount of liability, if any, attaching hereunder. Any recoveries effected subsequent to a settlement of any such ultimate net loss shall be applied as if effected prior to such settlement and such adjustment as may be necessary shall be made forthwith. Nothing in this article however shall be construed to mean that claims are not recoverable hereunder until the ultimate net loss of the Reinsured has been ascertained.

(b) The liability of the Reinsured hereunder in respect of each ultimate net loss shall not be increased by reason of the inability of the Reinsured to recover amounts from any other Reinsurers for any reason whatsoever.

Besides payments made to policyholders or third parties, legal fees and other costs incurred in the settlement of claims are also allowed in calculating the reinsured's net retained loss but the reinsurer is entitled to the full benefit of any recoveries by way of salvage, the exercise of subrogation rights or contributions from underlying reinsurances. Generally legal and other costs incurred in defending claims will only be recoverable from the excess of loss reinsurer if his consent was obtained to legal proceedings being taken.

The loss event. The treaty wording must also clearly show whether the cover is on an individual risk or on an occurrence basis. In the former case the ceding company when calculating its ultimate net loss is allowed to aggregate only losses affecting an individual risk so the words used must leave no doubt as to what constitutes one risk. Sometimes that poses no great problems; for example, for marine cargo treaties the term 'any one vessel' is unambiguous (though goods stored on quays or in warehouses pose problems (see Chapter 12). In other cases, such as fire treaties (see Chapter 10) it is far harder to provide a precise definition.

Like most excess-of-loss treaties, the clause quoted above ties the reinsurer's liability to 'all claims or series of claims arising out of any one accident or event'. When the interpretation of such words was discussed in Chapter 5 it was pointed out that sometimes it may be highly desirable for the parties to spell out in the treaty their intentions as to the meaning of one 'event', 'happening', 'occurrence' or whatever other phrase is used.

Each class of insurance presents its own peculiar features in relation to what may constitute 'one event'. Property portfolios covering natural perils are exposed to the risk of claims arising for properties damaged over a wide area due to, say, storms or a series of earthquake shocks perhaps occurring over several hours or days. Therefore, as explained in Chapter 10, fire reinsurers tie down the definition of 'one event' by imposing time and/or geographical limits on the accumulation of losses attributable to the operation of a particular peril.

Marine reinsurers on the other hand accept that a ceding company may suffer losses extending over both time and place due to one climatic event (e.g. a windstorm that blows for several days over a very wide area) and normally impose no time or geographical limits in their treaties.

Other classes of insurance present different features. For example, claims may occur under products liability policies over a period of several years for injuries sustained as the result of a defective product which itself may have been in production for a substantial period of time. Whether such a series of claims arise out of one or more events is open to dispute so direct insurers normally restrict their potential liability by undertaking to indemnify the policyholder (subject to agreed limits of indemnity) for claims for injury, etc., happening during the period of insurance, regardless of when the offending goods were manufactured or supplied.[2] Therefore normally reinsurers similarly restrict their liability to losses arising under individual policies written by the reinsured, so taking advantage of the annual aggregate limit of indemnity in the original policy (see Chapter 11).

The treaty limits. Whatever form the excess of loss reinsurance takes the treaty must specify the point at which the reinsurer becomes liable to contribute towards the claims incurred by the ceding company, and the limit to the reinsurer's liability. The two most common ways of dealing with this are to stipulate that the liability of the reinsurer(s) is to pay:

(1) Up to £y in respect of each ultimate net loss in excess of the first £x; or

(2) Excluding the first £x, any ultimate net loss up to £y.

So, for example, if the treaty is arranged to cover ultimate net losses of up to £100,000, the reinsured retaining the first £10,000, the limits in each case would be:

(1) £90,000 in excess of £10,000.

(2) £10,000/£100,000.

Method (1) has the merit of clearly stating the amount of cover provided by the reinsurer in excess of the reinsured's own retention.

Where the excess of loss cover is arranged in layers care must be taken to ensure that the deductible applying to each cover takes account of the underlying layer(s). For example, where two layers are arranged the respective monetary limits may appear as follows:

(1) £90,000 in excess of the first £10,000 each ultimate net loss.

(2) £100,000 in excess of the first £100,000 each ultimate net loss.

Thus the reinsured would retain the first £10,000 of each ultimate net loss and then have reinsurance protection up to £200,000, the reinsurers' combined maximum liability being £190,000.

---

2 P. Madge, 'Products liability insurance', in *Handbook of Insurance*, ed. R.L. Carter, ch. 4.3.

When a treaty covers two or more classes of insurance or two or more territories separate limits may be applied to each class and/or territory.

If the treaty is subject to any sort of aggregate liability, that limit too must be shown. For example, under an excess-of-loss treaty covering a personal accident account there is always the risk of accumulations due to, say, several policyholders being aboard the same aircraft or train. Therefore, the reinsurer may wish to contain his potential liability by placing a limit on the reinsured's maximum net retention, such as:

(1) £3,000 original principal sum insured on any one life.

(2) £9,000 known accumulation any one aircraft.

If in exceptional circumstances the reinsured then wished to write larger amounts he would need to arrange either surplus reinsurance or specific facultative reinsurance.

Under property catastrophe treaties the reinsured is often required to retain a share of any losses falling within the excess limits. For example, the cover may be limited so that the reinsurer pays only 90% of losses exceeding £x up to a limit of £y.

Reinstatement. As noted in Chapter 5, it is normal practice for property and marine catastrophe treaties to contain a reinstatement clause which:

(1) limits the reinsurer's liability in any one year to x times the treaty monetary limit; plus (sometimes)

(2) makes provision for the ceding company to reinstate all or part of the cover in return for the payment of an additional premium. [3]

Stability and currency fluctuation clauses. The influences on an excess of loss reinsurer's potential liability of domestic inflation and, in the case of treaties covering risks outside the reinsurer's own country, of international monetary movements have been fully discussed in Chapter 5. Therefore the reader's attention will only be drawn here to the case for including a stability (or index) clause in excess of loss treaties, particularly those covering motor or other liability risks. Likewise when a treaty covers risks in several territories and the treaty monetary limits are expressed in one currency, so that foreign-exchange rates need to be used to determine limits in other currencies, it is essential that a currency fluctuation clause should be included in the treaty.

The reinsurer's liability under stop loss and excess of loss ratio treaties. Under such treaties the term 'ultimate net loss' takes on a special meaning. Instead of relating to the losses paid by the ceding company for individual risks, or the aggregate losses arising from one occurrence, the

---

3 See Chapters 10 and 12 for fuller details.

ultimate net loss is expressed in terms of the company's loss ratio during any treaty year on the insurance business which is the subject of the reinsurance. The treaty will set out the method of calculating the loss ratio which may either be the ratio of incurred losses to earned premiums, or the ratio of incurred losses to written premiums.

The treaty limits are then expressed in terms of loss ratios, and are almost invariably subject to an upper monetary limit as in the following example:

> To pay 90% of all losses in excess of a loss ratio of 75% up to a further 30% or £500,000 whichever is the lesser.

As noted in Chapter 5, the reinsured normally is required to participate in losses falling within the treaty limits.

Changes in underwriting policy, retentions, and the law

The comments in Chapter 7 under this heading apply with double force to excess of loss treaties. Treaties covering liability risks are particularly exposed to the effects of legal changes. For example, during the currency of a treaty a decision of the legislature or the judiciary may result in liability for certain types of loss or accident being extended or even introduced where no such liability existed before. Also the severity of losses may be increased; for example, in Australia, the United States and other countries workmen's compensation benefits are regularly increased by government order.

Consequently the change in underwriting policy and change in law clauses quoted in Chaper 7 are invariably applied to non-proportional treaties.

Calculation of the reinsurance premium

Apart from treaties written at a flat premium where only the amount needs to be shown, the treaty wording must (1) specify the premium rate to be charged; and (2) define the ceding company's 'annual premium income' to which the rate is to be applied in order to calculate the reinsurance premium.

If the treaty is rated on a burning-cost basis the precise formula to be employed must be stated in the treaty. A specimen clause is included in the appendix to Chapter 5.

The definition of the ceding company's annual premium income must make clear (1) what deductions, if any, are to be allowed from original gross premium income, and (2) whether premiums are to be counted on a written, accounted or earned basis. Normally no deduction is allowed for brokerage, commission or other acquisition costs incurred by the reinsured, though there are exceptions, such as reinsurances effected by Lloyd's syndicates. Premiums paid for underlying reinsurances which reduce the company's ultimate net losses and so the reinsurer's potential liability would usually be deducted. Therefore the 'annual premium income' would consist of:

Total gross premiums
less returns
less cancellations
less premiums paid for reinsurances which inure to the benefit of the treaty
less premiums relating to risks excluded from the treaty.

Although theoretically it is sounder to apply the reinsurance premium rate to earned premiums, in practice written or accounted premiums are normally employed. Whichever basis is used it must be shown in the premium clause; the specimen clause below employs accounted premium income.

When a treaty embraces both home and foreign insurances special provision will need to be made for conversion of currencies for the purpose of determining the ceding company's annual premium income. The following is a typical clause:

> The Reinsured shall pay to the Reinsurer premium at the net rate stated in the Schedule calculated on the annual premium income of the Reinsured in respect of insurances covered hereunder less premiums paid for reinsurances which inure to the benefit of this agreement. The term 'annual premium income' shall mean gross original premiums less returns and cancellations under the terms and conditions of the original insurances accounted for during each annual period hereof.
>
> In respect of the Reinsured's gross original premium in currencies other than as stated in the Schedule the Reinsured shall, for the purpose of determining the aforementioned annual premium income, convert such premiums at the rates of exchange ruling in the Reinsured's books at the end of each annual period of the agreement, or if the agreement is terminated in any year prior to the end of the annual period, then in respect of that year, at the rates of exchange ruling on the date of termination.

Normally all original premiums are converted into one currency such as the £ sterling, and the reinsurance premium would then be calculated and settled in that currency. The floating of exchange rates and the degree of monetary instability that has occurred in the 1970s has led, however, to some change in practice. Occasionally when a treaty covers original business written in two or more major currencies the reinsurance premium may also be calculated in those same currencies, leaving only business written in minor currencies to be converted. This change in practice is part of the wider problem of currency instability which will be discussed more fully in Chapter 14.

Claims notification and cooperation

Non-proportional reinsurers, for the same reasons as were outlined in Chapter 7, invariably require from ceding companies prompt notification of any claim if it appears that the company's ultimate net loss may exceed the treaty lower limit. Particularly with treaties covering liability risks, the reinsurer may not be content to rely on the notification of claims only when it becomes reasonably clear that they may give rise to a loss under the treaty. Initially a ceding company may have good reason to believe that, say, a third party will substantially recover from his injuries or that a claim can be defended successfully, only to discover later that the claim is going to cost much more to settle than originally estimated. Consequently the reinsurer may impose a far more stringent duty on the ceding company as in the following extract from a clause taken from a liability excess of loss treaty.

(a) The Reinsured shall notify the Reinsurer immediately of each accident or event with all relevant details where either the sums claimed or the potential loss amounts to or exceeds the sum stated in the Schedule whether or not the Reinsured considers that it has an adequate defence or that there may be any contribution by a third party, and the Reinsured shall advise the Reinsurer of its estimate of the probable cost of the loss.

(b) In addition, the following categories of claims or potential claims shall be reported to the Reinsurer immediately, regardless of any questions of the liability of the insured or the Reinsured:

(1) Fatal injuries unless it is known that there is no dependency.

(2) Bodily injuries as specified below:
  — brain injuries
  — spinal injuries resulting in partial or total paralysis
  — total or partial amputations or permanent loss of use of a limb or limbs
  — severe burn injuries
  — total or partial blindness
  — extensive scarring or severe facial disfigurement
  — all other injuries likely to result in a permanent disability rating of 50% or more.

(3) Bodily injuries resulting in payment of an annuity.

(4) Bodily injuries or property damage for which suit has been filed if the amounts claimed by the plaintiff or plaintiffs exceed the sum stated in the Schedule.

Unlike proportional treaties where the ceding company is only required to notify the reinsurers of losses on which their aggregate liability is likely to exceed some agreed sum, excess of loss treaties normally stipulate that the reinsured shall inform the reinsurer immediately of any loss to which he may be liable to contribute, or which otherwise falls within a category listed in the clause, regardless of its size. The difference in practice is due to the fact that any loss which is likely to involve an excess of loss reinsurer will be relatively large.

Stop loss treaties likewise contain claims notification clauses. Thus the reinsurer will receive early warning should it appear that the reinsured's retained losses are likely to exceed the agreed loss ratio.

The comments made in Chapter 7 regarding the rights of the ceding company to conduct all claims negotiations and the liability of the reinsurer to contribute to all payments properly made which fall within the treaty limits, equally apply to non-proportional treaties. Likewise special provision is made in treaties to ensure that the ceding company cooperates with the reinsurer in the conduct and settlement of claims to which the latter is, or may become, liable to contribute, and to make the reinsurer's liability for *ex gratia* payments conditional on his prior consent to payment having been obtained.

It is well accepted practice that expenses incurred by the ceding company in commencing or defending any legal proceedings in connection with any claim, plus costs of a sucessful claimant, shall be included in the calculation of the ultimate net loss. However the decision whether to engage in litigation is not normally left to the sole discretion of the reinsured. Whereas the ceding company and reinsurer(s) proportionately share in the costs and benefits of litigation under quota share and surplus reinsurance treaties, with excess of loss treaties there is not the same identity of interest. The benefit of a successful defence will accrue solely to the ceding company if the amount of the disputed claim is within its own retention limit, but if the case is lost the reinsurer may become liable for some of the extra costs incurred. Therefore the reinsurer may seek to protect himself against the ceding company unreasonably contesting claims which may result in losses being incurred under the treaty by inserting a clause requiring the ceding company to obtain his consent before either commencing an action or contesting a claim which may give rise to a claim under the treaty, though at the same time stipulating that such consent shall not be withheld unreasonably.

Alternatively the ceding company may be subjected to an express duty to 'conduct or consent to the settlement or resistance of claims as conscientiously as if it were liable for the whole amount of the claim', or to take such action as it deems beneficial to both parties, as in the following clause:

> The company may commence, continue, defend, settle or withdraw from actions, suits or prosecutions and generally do all such things relating to any loss occurrence in which the reinsurers are interested as, in the company's judgment, may be beneficial or expedient to both parties.

Although there is much to be said in favour of a reinsurer endeavouring to exercise close control over the conduct of large claims and especially over possible litigation, like so many other aspects of reinsurance practice the ideal frequently has to give way in face of competition. Normally the best that can be achieved is the inclusion of a claims cooperation clause along the following lines, though in practice most ceding companies are only too happy to obtain the advice of a major professional reinsurer when it comes to handling large claims.

> The Reinsured shall keep the Reinsurer informed of all developments likely to affect the cost of any claims hereunder and undertakes in so far as is reasonably possible to cooperate with the Reinsurer or its representative in the conduct and settlement of such claim or claims and in the estimating of claims reserves.

In the past it was the practice to stipulate in non-proportional treaties that the ceding company should not only obtain the reinsurer's consent before commencing legal proceedings but also was only entitled to recover from the reinsurer that proportion of the legal costs which the reinsurer's share of the loss bore to the total damages awarded (or agreed if settled out of court). So, for example, if the ceding company's retention was £15,000 and the loss amounted to £20,000 damages plus costs amounting to £2,400 the reinsurer's liability would be:

$$\text{Damages:} \quad £20,000 - £15,000 = £5,000$$

$$\text{Costs:} \quad £\ 2,400 \times \frac{£5,000}{£20,000} = \frac{£600}{£5,600}$$

Although there is considerable merit in the principle involved such clauses have disappeared from use.

Payment of claims

Normally excess of loss treaties provide for all losses to be payable by the reinsurer upon receipt of a statement of the settlement of the original loss or within two weeks or so thereafter. Many ceding companies and brokers are content, however, to bring relatively small sums into the quarterly accounts.

On the other hand, because of the many payments involved under both motor and liability working covers and property catastrophe covers it is fairly common practice for reinsurers to be asked to make payments on account once the ceding company's retention has been exceeded. Also under motor and liability treaties the reinsurer may well be asked to contribute to a payment into court, though if he does so he should be entitled to his share of any interest earned.

Statements of outstanding claims

Excess of loss treaties, like proportional treaties, require the ceding company to supply within three months after the end of each year a statement of all outstanding claims.

Premium and loss reserve deposits

Only very rarely when required by local legislation is provision made under non-proportional treaties for the deposit with the ceding company of premium reserves. The vast majority of treaties are written on a losses-occurring basis under which the reinsurance premium is fully earned at the end of the year, there being no reserve to carry into the following year.

Even for treaties on an issued and renewed basis the need for ceding companies to obtain premium deposits is not so pressing as for proportional treaties. The premiums ceded for excess-of-loss reinsurances tend to be far smaller in relation to a ceding company's gross direct premiums and so constitute less of a financial problem for companies subject to gross reserving regulations. When a deposit is agreed the same type of clause would be used as for proportional reinsurances with provision for the deposit of securities or the payment of interest on cash deposits, the deposit usually being between 40 and 50% of the reinsurance premium.[4]

4 See Chapter 7 for clauses used in proportional treaties.

Loss reserve deposits are even rarer, being used only where they are required by local regulations. The same principles may apply as for proportional reinsurances (see Chapter 7); in particular if the deposit has to be made in cash it is important that provision be made for the payment of interest, especially for liability and other 'long-tail' classes of business where claims may remain outstanding for several years.

Preparation and settlement of accounts

Accounting procedures for non-proportional treaties are relatively simple though, as explained in Chapter 13, they need to be set out in the treaty. In particular the provisions regarding the payment of deposit and adjustment premiums, and the treatment of foreign currencies when a treaty covers overseas risks, need to be specified.

Arbitration clause

Excess of loss reinsurers follow normal reinsurance practice of using arbitration as the means of settling any disputes arising in connection with treaties, and invariably treaties include an arbitration clause.[5]

Termination clause

Even though in many cases the performance of an excess of loss treaty will be subject to annual review, most treaties are effected for an indefinite period with provision for cancellation. The provisions that are incorporated in the termination clause are of the same type as for proportional treaties and for the same reasons. Therefore the reader should turn to Chapter 7 for details.

The major difference arises in connection with treaties arranged on a losses-occurring basis. There is no question of any continuing liability for losses occurring after the termination of the treaty, and this fact may be emphasized by a statement to that effect in the termination clause, such as:

> After the date of termination the liability of the reinsurer shall cease outright other than in respect of claims which have occurred during the period of the agreement and are not settled at that date.

5 See Chapters 3 and 4 for a full discussion of arbitration.

Occasionally, however, provision may be made to provide for the run-off of liabilities under the direct portfolio after the cancellation of a 'losses-occurring treaty at a premium to be agreed. Obviously the additional premium required cannot be agreed in advance, and would be quoted by the reinsurer at the time of cancellation.

Appendix 8.1 Specimen fire excess of loss reinsurance agreement

FIRE EXCESS OF LOSS REINSURANCE AGREEMENT made between ____ (hereinafter called the 'REINSURED') of the one part and ____ (hereinafter called the 'REINSURER') of the other part.

IN CONSIDERATION of the payment of the premium hereinafter provided it is agreed:

ARTICLE I

(a) In respect of each ultimate net loss (as hereinafter defined) sustained by the REINSURED under those insurances specified in the Schedule the REINSURER shall indemnify the REINSURED by way of excess of loss reinsurance within the limits set out in the Schedule.

(b) The REINSURED shall be the sole judge as to what constitutes one risk, it being understood and agreed that one risk shall mean all property or interest at any one location and designated by the REINSURED in its records as subject to one risk retention.

(c) It is warranted that the REINSURED undertakes not to retain on one risk an amount greater than that stated in the Schedule.

(d) An insurance granted by the REINSURED wherein the REINSURED is named as the Insured either alone or jointly with another party or parties shall not be excluded from this Agreement merely because no legal liability may arise in respect thereof by reason of the fact that the REINSURED be the Insured or one of the Insureds.

ARTICLE II

(a) The term 'ultimate net loss' shall be understood to mean the total amount which the REINSURED has actually paid in settlement of any one claim any one risk which may occur during the period set out in the Schedule including any legal costs and professional fees and expenses (excluding salaries of all employees and office expenses of the REINSURED) reasonably incurred in connection therewith. Recoveries including amounts under reinsurances which inure to the benefit of this Agreement shall be first deducted from such amount to arrive at the amount of liability, if any, attaching hereunder. Any recoveries effected subsequent to a settlement of any such ultimate net loss shall be applied as if effected prior to such settlement and such adjustment as may be necessary shall be made forthwith. Nothing in this Article however shall be construed to mean that claims are not recoverable hereunder until the ultimate net loss of the REINSURED has been ascertained.

(b) The liability of the REINSURER hereunder in respect of each ultimate net loss shall not be increased by reason of the inability of the REINSURED to recover amounts from any other Reinsurers for any reason whatsoever.

ARTICLE III

(a) The REINSURED shall pay to the REINSURER premium at the net rate stated in the Schedule calculated on the Gross Net Premium Income of the REINSURED in respect of insurances covered hereunder. The term 'Gross Net Premium Income' shall mean gross original premiums less returns and

cancellations under the terms and conditions of the original insurances and less premiums paid for reinsurances which inure for the benefit of this Agreement during each annual period hereof.

(b) In respect of the REINSURED's Gross Net Premium Income in currencies other than as stated in the Schedule the REINSURED shall, for the purpose of determining the aforementioned Gross Net Premium Income, convert such premiums at the rates of exchange ruling in the REINSURED's books at the end of each annual period of the Agreement, or if the Agreement is terminated in any year prior to the end of the annual period, then in respect of that year, at the rates of exchange ruling on the date of termination.

ARTICLE IV

(a) The REINSURED shall pay to the REINSURER a Deposit Premium as provided for in the Schedule.

(b) As soon as possible after the end of each annual period of this Agreement as stated in the Schedule but in any event within three months thereof, the REINSURED shall supply to the REINSURER a declaration of its Gross Net Premium Income as defined in Article III. The annual premium due to the REINSURER under this Agreement shall be calculated in accordance with Article III and after taking into consideration the deposit premium already paid in respect of the same period any premium adjustment due by the REINSURED shall be paid to the REINSURER at the same time as the premium declaration is rendered.

(c) The premium adjustments shall be confirmed by the REINSURER within one month of receipt and any premium adjustments due to the REINSURED shall be paid by the REINSURER at the time of confirmation.

ARTICLE V

(a) The REINSURED shall notify the REINSURER immediately of each claim with all relevant details where there is a potential loss which may affect this Agreement together with an estimate of the probable cost of the loss.

(b) The REINSURED shall keep the REINSURER informed of all developments likely to affect the cost of any claim hereunder and undertakes in so far as is reasonably possible to cooperate with the REINSURER or its representative in the conduct and settlement of such claim.

(c) In calculating the liability of the REINSURER hereunder all loss payments made by the REINSURED within the conditions of the original insurance and falling within the scope of this Agreement shall be binding on the REINSURER. The REINSURER shall be bound also by *ex gratia* payments made with its consent.

(d) The REINSURER shall remit its share of all loss payments within 14 days of receiving a request from the REINSURED so to do.

(e) The REINSURED shall as soon as practicable and in any event not later than three months after the date or dates stated in the Schedule send to the REINSURER a statement of unsettled claims as at the date of submission of such statement showing the amount for which the REINSURER may be liable in respect of each individual claim.

ARTICLE VI

(a) Any amounts due by either party under this Agreement which are outstanding one month after the date on which settlement is due shall be subject to the payment of interest by the debtor as from the expiry of that one month's

period of grace. Interest shall be calculated at the rate stated in the Schedule and remain payable up to the date of the debtor effecting settlement unless the creditor shall amend or extend the one month period of grace.

ARTICLE VII

(a) In respect of losses in a currency other than that in which the monetary limits of the Agreement are stated in the Schedule, the REINSURER's liability shall be calculated as follows:

(1) The retention of the REINSURED and the liability of the REINSURER as expressed in the relevant part of the Schedule shall be converted into the currency concerned at the rate of exchange ruling on the Commencement Date of this Agreement in accordance with the attached Currency List; and

(2) The balance of any loss payment in excess of the REINSURED's retention shall be converted from the currency in which the loss was settled into the main currency appearing in the Schedule at the rate or average rates of exchange as used by the REINSURED and ruling on the date or dates of settlement of the loss by the REINSURED.

ARTICLE VIII

(a) Any payment hereunder shall be in the currency stated in the Schedule unless otherwise agreed in which event such payment shall be made at the rates of exchange ruling on the date of remittance.

ARTICLE IX

(a) The REINSURED undertakes not to introduce without the prior approval of the REINSURER any change in its established acceptance and underwriting policy which is potentially capable of increasing or extending the liability or exposure of the REINSURER hereunder in respect of those insurances to which this Agreement relates.

ARTICLE X

(a) This Agreement shall take effect and shall be terminated on the basis set out in the Schedule. In the event of either party giving notice of termination in accordance with the provisions set out in the Schedule then such notice shall be automatically deemed to have been given by both parties.

(b) Either party shall have the right to terminate this Agreement by giving the other party written notice by the quickest means available which shall be deemed to be served upon dispatch or where communications between the parties are interrupted upon attempted dispatch, where:

(1) The performance of the whole or any part of this Agreement be prohibited or rendered impossible *de jure* or *de facto* in particular and without prejudice to the generality of the preceding words in consequence of any law or regulation which is or shall be in force in any country or territory or if any law or regulation shall prevent directly or indirectly the remittance of any payments due to or from either party.

(2) The other party has become insolvent or unable to pay its debts or has lost the whole or any part of its paid-up capital or has had any authority to transact any class of insurance withdrawn suspended or made conditional.

(3) There is any material change in the management or control of the other party.

(4) The country or territory in which the other party resides or has its head office or is incorporated shall be involved in armed hostilities with any other country whether war be declared or not or is partly or wholly occupied by another power or be in a state of civil war.

(5) The other party shall have failed to comply with any of the terms and conditions of this Agreement.

(c) After the date of termination the liability of the REINSURER shall cease outright other than in respect of claims which have occurred during the period of the Agreement and are not settled at that date.

(d) The REINSURER shall be under no liability for losses caused by events which are in progress at the commencement of this Agreement to the extent that the REINSURED may claim in respect of such losses under any other reinsurance contract.

(e) The liability of the REINSURER hereunder shall extend to losses occurring after the termination of this Agreement provided such losses are caused by an event which commenced before termination.

ARTICLE XI

(a) After prior advice to the REINSURED the REINSURER may by an authorized representative inspect at any reasonable time all records and documents relating to the business hereunder.

(b) Copies of policies, records or documents of any kind relating to any business covered by this Agreement shall be supplied by the REINSURED to the REINSURER immediately on request.

(c) The provisions of this Article shall continue to apply for as long as either party has any liability hereunder.

ARTICLE XII

(a) All communications and notices served in accordance with any of the provisions of this Agreement shall be addressed to the party concerned at its head office or at any other address previously designated by the other party.

(b) All postal, cable, remittance or other similar charges shall be paid by the sender.

ARTICLE XIII

(a) Any alterations to this Agreement which may be agreed in writing between the parties hereto shall be considered as part hereof and equally binding.

ARTICLE XIV

(a) Either party may at its discretion set off against any amounts due from the other party hereunder or under any other Agreements between the parties hereto any amounts which are due under this or those other Agreements.

ARTICLE XV

(a) All disputes arising out of the above Agreement or concerning its interpretation or validity whether arising before or after its termination shall be referred to two Arbitrators in accordance with the provisions of the Arbitration Act 1950, or any statutory re-enactment or modification thereof for the time being in force.

(b) The Arbitrators and Umpire shall be officials of insurance or reinsurance organizations and the venue of the arbitration shall be in London.

(c) The Arbitrators and Umpire are relieved of all judicial formalities and they may abstain from following strict rules of law. They shall settle any dispute under the above Agreement according to an equitable rather than a strictly legal interpretation of its terms.

(d) This Arbitration Agreement shall be construed as a separate and independent contract between the REINSURED and the REINSURER and arbitration hereunder shall be a condition precedent to the commencement of any action at law.

The Schedule together with any Appendix thereto is deemed to form an integral part of this Agreement.

IN WITNESS WHEREOF this Agreement has been signed in duplicate on behalf of and by the authority of each contracting party.

At ＿＿ this ＿＿ day of ＿＿ 197＿
for and on behalf of ＿＿.

And at ＿＿ this ＿＿ day of ＿＿ 197＿
for and on behalf of ＿＿.

THE SCHEDULE

Attaching to and forming part of the EXCESS OF LOSS REINSURANCE AGREEMENT made between the REINSURED and the REINSURER.

IN WITNESS WHEREOF this Schedule has been signed in duplicate on behalf of and by the authority of each contracting party.

At ＿＿ this ＿＿ day of ＿＿ 197＿
for and on behalf of ＿＿.

And at ＿＿ this ＿＿ day of ＿＿ 197＿
for and on behalf of ＿＿.

REINSURANCE

9
Fixing retentions

9
Fixing retentions

Probably the most difficult part of formulating a reinsurance programme is the fixing of retention limits. A number of attempts have been made to tackle the problem with the help of mathematical models, but to date no entirely satisfactory method has been devised, so that decisions are still based largely on rules of thumb. The object of this chapter is to identify the key elements in the decision-making process which it is hoped will be of some value to readers even though at present it is impossible to provide any definitive formula for the calculation of optimal retention limits.

The pragmatic approach

All of the theoretical methods that have been developed so far for determining retentions are too simplistic for practical use.[1] Consequently retention limits for both proportional and non-proportional reinsurances tend to be fixed on the basis of market practices that have stood the test of time.

It is reasonable to assume that there is a relationship between the size of a company's business and the amount of loss it can safely absorb either on any one risk or in respect of the aggregate losses arising from one event or in any one year. Dr B. Benjamin has observed that:[2]

> In general, given sound rating and reserving practice, the higher the premium income, the higher the retention of the direct insurer because the relative variance of the larger claims experience will be less and the need for reinsurance will be less. Indeed an arrangement of offices by retention and premium income shows a marked positive linear relationship.

That such a relationship exists is confirmed by an investigation conducted by the Mercantile and General Reinsurance Company into the retentions of some of its ceding companies under fire surplus treaties.

---

1 A major limitation is the assumption that loss exposures are stochastically independent. See, for example, H. Bühlmann, *Mathematical Methods in Risk Theory* (Berlin: Springer-Verlag, 1970), ch. 5.
2 Benjamin, *General Insurance*, p.227.

The results of that study are given in Figure 9.1, which shows the relationship between a company's net premium income X and its retention Y. Most of the points lie close to a regression line which has a value of $\log Y = 1.7034 + 0.449 \log X$. If companies A and B are excluded then a regression line with an approximate value of $\log Y = \frac{1}{2} \log 1000X$ can be drawn which indicates that as companies double their net premium incomes their retention limits tend to be increased by a factor of 1.4, and a quadrupling of premium income is associated with a doubling of retention limits[3]. There is no reason to believe that the same general relationship does not also hold both for other classes of insurance, and for retentions under non-proportional treaties, though the proportionate increases in retentions relative to increases in premium incomes may vary. However, so far as is known, there have been no other detailed studies undertaken to confirm or refute such relationships between retentions and either premium incomes or other measures of company size such as capital and free reserves.

The evidence that is available regarding retentions can be interpreted in two ways—either that by experiment the majority of companies have discovered the right levels of retentions relative to the amount of business they transact, or that they are either reinsuring too much or too little. Whichever interpretation is correct, and at least companies may claim that the test of time has shown that they are not badly under-reinsured, there remains the fact that some companies, such as A and B on the scatter diagram, have retentions which substantially diverge from the norm. What are the characteristics of their businesses or their financial situations that may explain such differences? It is not possible here to look at those individual cases but such differences do indicate that before a company simply follows general market practice in the fixing of retentions it should consider the basic factors involved.

The factors determining retentions

When the needs of insurers for reinsurance were considered in Chapter 3 it was shown that at the heart of the problem lies the potential variation in aggregate claims costs from the amount expected in any period due to random fluctuations in either the number or average cost of claims. Moreover at the limit the size of adverse fluctuation which a company can tolerate during any period is determined by its initial reserves plus its premium income. If both sales and administration expenses and

---

3 The precise value of the regression line is $\log Y = 1.68 + 0.466 \log X$ and it has a coefficient of correlation of 0.9251 which shows that there is a close positive relationship between the two variables.

Figure 9.1 Fire retentions in relation to net premium incomes

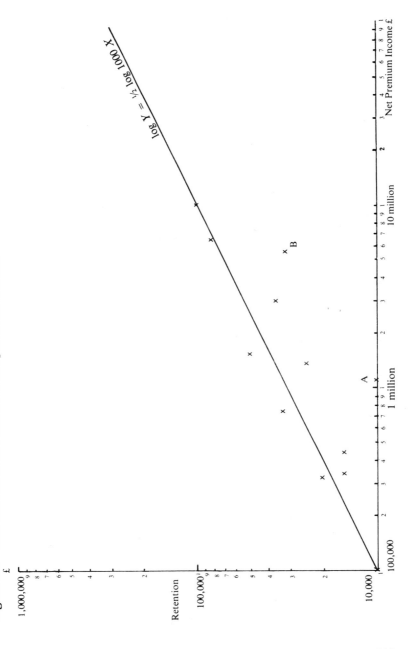

investment income are ignored then this point can be illustrated simply by means of Figure 9.2.

The figure shows a company's claims distribution function F for a particular period of time, its maximum possible aggregate claims cost being X. Point A is equal to the company's reserves R_0 plus its aggregate risk premiums for the period P: thus if aggregate claims exceeded A the company would be ruined, so that the area under the claims curve to the right of A gives its probability of ruin. By building a contingency loading λ into its premiums the company would increase its resources to, say, B which consists of:

$$R_0 + P(1 + \lambda)$$

and thereby reduce its probability of ruin. Nevertheless the company is left with the risk of aggregate claims during the period under review exceeding B. The role of reinsurance is to reduce that risk at a price which is acceptable to the company.

Figure 9.2 can be modified to show how reinsurance operates to achieve that objective. As explained in Chaper 5, the effect of surplus or excess of loss reinsurance would be to modify the claims distribution function, in particular by shortening the tail as in Figure 9.3, the distribution of retained losses being given by curve F_m. Point B is identical to B on Figure 9.2. The company would be required to pay a reinsurance premium which can be expressed as a percentage ω of gross premiums. Therefore its resources would be reduced to C which is given by:

$$C = R_0 + P(1 + \lambda)(1 - \omega)$$

Thus it may be deemed worthwhile buying reinsurance if the premium required relative to the risk transferred is such that the net effect is to reduce the company's probability of ruin.

Professor R.E. Beard has illustrated this reinsurance process and the fixing of retentions with the simple example of a life assurer that writes 1,000 one-year term assurances each with a £100 sum assured and all for lives aged 50 years with an expected mortality rate of 0.00700. If expenses and interest are ignored the company will need to charge a risk premium of £0.7, to obtain a total premium income of £700 which is sufficient to pay the seven expected claims. If less than seven lives insured die during the year the company will earn a mortality profit whereas if more than seven die the company would be insolvent unless it had sufficient reserves to cover the extra claims.[4] Thus the ability of the company to withstand fluctuations in its mortality experience is a

---

4 R.E. Beard, 'Three R's of insurance: risk, retention and reinsurance', *Journal of the Institute of Actuaries Students Society*, vol. 15, part 6 (1959).

function of the size of its reserves, which must be provided either by policyholders in the form of a premium loading or by the shareholders as share capital. Moreover the size of reserves a company will need is related to the probability distribution of its expected claims which will depend on the nature and size of its portfolio of business.

Figure 9.2

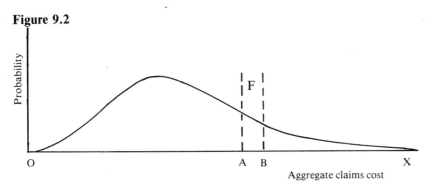

Figure 9.3

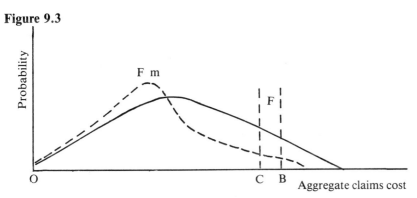

This latter fact may be illustrated by considering the relative variability of claims costs that may be expected on two portfolios of insurance business differing only in terms of the number of insured risks. A measure of such variability is the coefficient of variation V, where $V = s/E(x)$ (s being the standard deviation and $E(x)$ the expected ((i.e. average)) claims cost). Taking the above example, and assuming all lives to be independent, V measured in terms of numbers of claims would be:

$$V = \frac{\sqrt{(pqn)}}{E(x)} = \frac{\sqrt{(0.993 \times 0.007 \times 1000)}}{7}$$

$$= \frac{2.6365}{7}$$

$$= 0.3766$$

If the company doubled its portfolio by insuring 2,000 lives instead of 1,000, the coefficient of variation would become:

$$V = \frac{\sqrt{(0.993 \times 0.007 \times 2000)}}{14} = \frac{3.7285}{14} = 0.2663$$

So as a company increases the size of its business, provided its portfolio is composed of independent risk units, its claims results will tend to become more stable and the smaller will become its probability of ruin for any given level of reserves.[5] Beard illustrates the relationship between size of business, level of reserves and the probability of ruin by means of the data in Table 9.1.

Table 9.1 Probability of n claims from a portfolio of x lives =
$\binom{1,000}{n} 0.007^n(0.993)^{x-n}$

On a portfolio of 1,000 lives			On a portfolio of 2,000 lives		
Number of claims		Cumulative	Number of claims		Cumulative
Number	As % of expected number	probability	Number	As % of expected number	probability
7	100	0.59871	14	100	0.57044
8	114.3	0.72954	16	114.3	0.75653
9	128.6	0.83121	18	128.6	0.88342
10	142.9	0.90222	20	142.9	0.95269
11	157.1	0.94728	22	157.1	0.98363
12	171.4	0.97346	24	171.4	0.99513
13	185.7	0.98748	26	185.7	0.99874
14	200.0	0.99445	28	200.0	0.99972
15	214.3	0.99768	30	214.3	0.99994

The occurrence of less claims than the expected number will cause an underwriter no loss of sleep, but he will be concerned about claims in excess of the number expected, so Table 9.1 concentrates on just that situation. If the company's only resources for the payment of claims were its premiums, then in both cases it would face a probability of ruin somewhat in excess of 40%. In order to reduce that probability to around 0.5%, given a portfolio of 1,000 lives it would need sufficient additional reserves (i.e. £700) to cover double the expected number of claims, but with a portfolio of 2,000 lives only an extra £1,000 would be needed to cover 24 claims, i.e. only 71.4% more than the number expected. If it is further assumed that the additional reserves are

5 Even if a portfolio is composed of heterogeneous exposure units, as the number is increased loss experience will tend to become more stable *provided* loss exposures are independent. See G.M. Dickinson, 'Risk and the law of large numbers', in *Handbook of Risk Management*, ed. R.L. Carter and N. Doherty (Brentford: Kluwer, 1974), pp.2.7 – 18.

obtained by borrowing, on which a rate of interest of 10% is payable, the company would need to load its premium rates by 10.0% on a portfolio of 1,000 lives or by 7.14% on a portfolio of 2,000 lives in order to service the loan. The same principle applies if the reserves are provided in the form of share capital: shareholders too expect a rate of return on their funds.

In practice companies are constrained in the size of premium loading they can charge by competition and/or by government control over premium rates. If a company tries to reduce its probability of ruin by increasing its premium loadings, then in a competitive market it is likely to lose business to competitors. Moreover, as shown above, small companies are in a less favourable competitive position than large companies. So how can reinsurance help?

Again Beard identifies some of the key points by developing the above example of a company with capital of £700 writing 1,000 one-year term policies. It loads its premiums by 10% to yield sufficient revenue to pay a service charge on its capital of £70. If it retains all of the business for its own account its probability of ruin is 0.00555 but if it effects a 50% quota share reinsurance on original terms its position changes as follows:

	100% retention £	50% retention £
Total resources		
Capital	700	700
+ retained risk premium income	700	350
	1,400	1,050
Expected claims cost	700	350
Balance	700	700

The company's total resources of £1,050 after payment of the reinsurance premium are sufficient to pay up to 21 claims, which reduces its probability of ruin to 0.00001. On the other hand if the reinsurer also takes one half of the premium loading the company will have available only £35 to service its capital compared with the £70 required. Reinsurance, however, may still assist in two ways.

First, if a reinsurer has a large and thus more stable portfolio of such business he may be prepared to accept a smaller loading. So, for example, if market conditions are such that the company could write 1,000 policies with a 10% premium loading but could obtain a 50% quota share with only, say, a 5.71% loading, its retained premium income would be £400 (i.e. £770—£370) which would be sufficient to service a capital of £500 after allowing for the expected net claims cost of £350. Thus the company would be able to pay up to 17 claims which would leave it with a probability of ruin of 0.00034 against the original probability of 0.00555.

Even if a reinsurer could not be found that was willing to accept a smaller loading than that charged by the ceding company, reinsurance may still be used to attain a desired probability of ruin. If the company wanted to reduce its probability of ruin to 0.00001, in the absence of reinsurance it would require reserves of £1,400 on which the service charge would be £140, which is equal to a premium loading of 20%. Given only reserves of £700 its actual ruin probability would be 0.00555 but with a premium loading of 20% it would have more than sufficient income to meet its service charge of £70. Now a 50% quota share on original terms would reduce its probability of ruin to 0.00001 and enable it to service its capital of £700.

The second possibility is that the company may be able to obtain reciprocity. If the reinsurer agreed to cede 1,000 cases of £50 each on the same terms as the company's own cessions then it would acquire a portfolio of 2,000 lives and obtain a net retained premium income sufficient to service a capital of £700, thereby enabling it to meet up to a total of 28 claims. Thus its probability of ruin would be reduced to 0.00028.[6]

Although the simplest form of proportional reinsurance has been used above, the same basic factors apply to the determination of retentions for other types of reinsurance too. Expressing them formally we may say that retentions are a function of the following variables:

$$R_t = f(N, p(x), C(z), A, r, \lambda, P_r, W, I)$$

where R_t = retention in time period t

N = size of the portfolio = $\Sigma\ S_{(xn)}$

$S_{(xn)}$ = the number n of exposure units of size x included in the portfolio

$p(x)$ = probability of an exposure unit of size x incurring a loss in time t

$C(z)$ = the size of loss z if a loss occurs

A = ratio of capital and reserves to N

r = rate of return payable on A

λ = premium loading

P_r = selected probability of ruin

W = price payable for reinsurance

I = the company's investment policy

Now that the variables have been identified it is possible to explore more fully each of the relationships assuming the others remain constant.

6 Beard, 'Three R's of insurance', p.404.

Size of the portfolio

A further examination of the example used above will establish more clearly the fact that as a portfolio increases in size, provided the claims distribution $C_{(z)}$ remains unaltered, the retention level can be raised while maintaining the same probability of ruin. As shown, if the company could load its premiums by 10% but purchase quota-share reinsurance with a loading of only 5.71%, then given a capital of £500 requiring a servicing charge of £50, it could achieve a probability of ruin of 0.00034 on a portfolio of 1,000 lives by retaining only 50% of each insurance written. If the company could double its portfolio and its reserves (i.e. to £1,000 to maintain the same ratio to portfolio size) then, *ceteris paribus,* it would be able to retain 72½% of each risk written and pay up to 28 claims so that its probability of ruin (0.00028) would remain at around the same level as before.

Probability of loss

This is directly related to the time period under review. Normally a company will fix its retentions in relation to losses occurring over a period of 12 months, but if, for example, a facultative reinsurance is arranged for an individual insurance contract with a period of indemnity shorter or longer than one year the ceding company may wish to fix its retention for losses occurring during that period. The probability of loss will usually be directly related to the length of the period under review.

Normally a portfolio of insurance business will comprise a collection of heterogeneous exposure units with differing probabilities of loss.[7] This factor is to be borne in mind not only when fixing retentions for proportional reinsurances but also for excess of loss treaties covering a portfolio of business in that a change in portfolio mix may significantly change the mean probability of loss.

Size of loss

There are two variables in an insurer's risk process, the number of claims which is given by $\Sigma\, p(x)N_x$ and the size of the claim $C(z)$.[8] Generally, apart from contracts of guarantee (notably life assurance) where $C(z)$ is equal to the sum insured, the sizes of individual losses may fall within a range of values. Therefore, although a ceding company when fixing its

---

7 Furthermore such probabilities may not only be subject to secular change over time but they may also fluctuate around the basic probabilities within short time periods (see page 327).
8 See R.E. Beard *et al.*, *Risk Theory: The Stochastic Basis of Insurance*, 2nd ed. (London: Chapman and Hall, 1977), Ch. 3.

retentions must pay regard to total values or amounts at risk, the probability distributions of losses by size of loss also merit consideration. This latter factor is of particular importance for portfolios with very skew probability distributions because the occurrence of a very large loss, though possibly remote, may have a disastrous impact on total claims costs.

The fixing of retentions for property insurances on the basis of total sums insured may lead to over-reinsuring in that the probability of a total loss may be zero. Therefore retentions for large insurances are frequently fixed according to the underwriter's judgment regarding potential sizes of loss rather than the sum insured. Essentially underwriters work to some notion of the largest loss that may occur under normal conditions, an idea that is expressed in a variety of terms such as maximum possible loss (MPL), probable maximum loss (PML) and estimated maximum loss (EML). The danger is that (1) all of these terms lack precision of definition, often meaning different things to different people which may lead to confusion between a ceding company and its reinsurer; and (2) such estimates often prove unreliable, not least because periodically abnormal events do occur. In order to deal with the first point the Reinsurance Offices' Association has produced a report which recommends the use of a single term—estimated maximum loss—which it defines, in relation to material damage from fire and explosion, as follows:[9]

> An estimate of the monetary loss which could be sustained by insurers on a single risk as a result of a single fire or explosion considered by the underwriter to be within the realms of probability. The estimate ignores such remote coincidences and catastrophes as may be possibilities but which still remain unlikely.

The report goes on to discuss the factors which underwriters should and should not take into account when assessing EMLs and the definition of a 'single risk'. There still remains, however, the second problem which is partly attributable to differing ideas about the dividing line between probabilities and possibilities. Can a potential loss greater than the EML be regarded only as a possibility if one thinks it is likely to occur less frequently than every 20 years (i.e. a 5% probability) or every 100 years ($=1\%$) or only every 1,000 years ($=0.1\%$)? Even if a standard could be agreed, lack of data would still mean that subjective judgment would play a large role in fixing EMLs.

Liability insurances pose even greater problems. With a property insurance the sum insured is an upper limit to the insurer's liability and,

---

9 Reinsurance Offices' Association, *Definition of Estimated Maximum Loss.*

subject to under-insurance, says something about the nature of that liability. However, with liability insurance, even if a limit is placed on the insurer's liability in the form of a limit of indemnity, the size of the portfolio [$\Sigma S_{(xn)}$] has far less meaning as a guide to a company's loss exposure. Far more relevant is the probability distribution of losses by size of loss $C(z)$, though if such data are drawn from the company's past claims experience they may need adjustment for such factors as past inflation and the exclusion from the claims data of settlements in excess of limits of indemnity then in force. Finally a comprehensive picture of the company's exposure under its portfolio of liability business may be obtained by examining to what extent limits of indemnity currently in force may possibly exclude losses towards the tail of the loss distribution.

Although the size of loss under a life policy is for a given sum, a portfolio of life business will be composed of policies with differing sums assured. Therefore claims results will be subject to a larger degree of variability than in the above example which used constant sums assured. Most life policies are long-term insurances written with level annual premiums so that over time reserves are accumulated. Therefore the amount at risk under each policy is the sum assured less the reserves attaching to that policy: this aspect of life assurance and its relevance to retentions will be dealt with in the life chapter.

Whatever the class of business, ideally the insurer needs to identify the risk profile of the portfolio in order to determine retentions for either proportional or non-proportional reinsurance. The following example is given by F.E. Guaschi for a life portfolio.[10]

Size of sum at risk £	Number of risks
1,000	250,000
2,000	150,000
5,000	75,000
10,000	10,000
20,000	1,000
50,000	50
100,000	10
200,000	3
Total:	486,063

From such a table it is possible to calculate the type of information necessary for fixing retentions. Assuming that the probability of a claim

10 F.E. Guaschi, 'Non-proportional reinsurance', *Journal of the Institute of Actuaries Students Society*, vol. 19, part 1, (January 1970).

occurring under any one policy during the year is either 0.001 or 0.005, and that there is independence between claims, the risk characteristics of the portfolio would be as follows:

	Probability of loss	
	0.001	*0.005*
Expected number of claims in a year $\bar{N}$	486	2430
Standard deviation of number of claims	22	49
Average size of claim	£2,158.4	£2,158.4
Standard deviation of size of claim	£2,130.2	£2,130.2
Expected amount of claims		
$= \bar{N} \times £2,158.4$	£1,048,982	£5,244,912
Standard deviation of amount of claims	£66,825	£149,386

If the company effected a quota share reinsurance it would not affect the expected number of claims but it would reduce proportionately the size of its retained claims. Thus the expected retained amount of claims and the standard deviation would also reduce proportionately, though the coefficient of variation would remain unchanged.

Surplus or excess of loss reinsurance on the other hand would confine the company's retained losses (both individual and aggregate) within narrower limits. Guaschi illustrates the results as follows, assuming a probability of loss of 0.001.

The effect on the retained portfolio of reinsuring all amounts in excess of £R is:

R = £5,000		R = £10,000	
Size of sum at risk £	*Number of risks*	*Size of sum at risk* £	*Number of risks*
1,000	250,000	1,000	250,000
2,000	150,000	2,000	150,000
5,000	86,063	5,000	75,000
		10,000	11,063
	486,063		486,063

Thus the mean and standard deviations of the retained portfolio given different retention levels would be as follows:

Retention	Expected number of claims to ceding company	Expected size of claim	Expected total claims	Standard deviation of total claims	Maximum claim
£		£	£	£	£
1,000	486	1000.0	486,000	22,036	1,000
2,000	486	1485.7	722,032	34,544	2,000
5,000	486	2016.9	980,213	54,759	5,000
10,000	486	2130.6	1,035,472	61,866	10,000
20,000	486	2152.5	1,046,115	64,389	20,000
50,000	486	2156.4	1,048,010	65,408	50,000
All	486	2158.4	1,048,982	66,825	200,000

Unless the retention is fixed at a very low level, given such a highly skewed distribution of amounts at risk, the size of the retention does not substantially affect either the expected total retained claims or their standard deviations. It would be fallacious, however, to argue from this fact that the company should fully retain all risks written. The possibility of incurring a £100,000 or £200,000 claim, though remote, cannot be ignored. The impact of one such claim on the total claims costs could be disastrous—one £200,000 claim would be a 19% increase on top of an expected claims cost of £1,048,942. Moreover the possible adverse effect of fluctuations in basic probabilities must be considered too. Conceivably some temporary change in risk conditions (e.g. a particularly severe winter) could cause a larger fluctuation in mortality rates amongst older persons who tend to have higher sums insured than amongst younger age groups. Similar remarks regarding skewed distributions equally apply to non-life portfolios.

Capital, reserves and rate of return

There is a direct relationship between the size of a company's reserves relative to volume of business written and the amounts it can retain for its own account. However, as shown above, in fixing retentions regard must also be paid to the cost of servicing capital and this factor introduces the complex interaction between the return a company must pay its own shareholders and other suppliers of finance, the size of loading it can build into its premium structures, and the price it must pay for reinsurance.

Premium loading

Retention levels are directly related to the size of contingency loading which a company can build into its premium rates: the higher the loading the larger the capital reserves it is able to service relative to volume of business written and/or the larger its expected profits which, if retained, will enable it to build up reserves over the years. Benjamin demonstrates this formally as follows.[11]

As a very approximate but practical rule the solvency of a company u_1 (expressed as an amount of free reserves) may be assumed to be

$$u_1 = 2\sqrt{(P_tM)} - \lambda P_t$$

where P_t = the premiums required to time t, i.e. an amount equal to expected claims = $Np_xC(z)$

M = the retention limit

λ = the premium loading

Thus an increase in the amount of business written P_t without any increase in the reserves u will necessitate a reduction in the retention limit. If the equation is rewritten as

$$u_1 + \lambda P_t = 2\sqrt{(P_tM)}$$

then it is clear that, *ceteris paribus,* an increase in the premium loading will allow the retention limit M to be increased.

The constraint imposed by competition on the size of loading a company can charge has been noted already, and even a monopoly company cannot wholly ignore the effect of high loadings on the demand for insurance. Yet the strength of competition, and therefore the size of loading a company can charge, is likely to vary between different classes of business so that an optimal reinsurance programme will accordingly provide for different retentions to be applied to the different classes of insurance which the company writes. The same point also holds for different types of risk within a class. For example, in considering a fire portfolio the first point a company must decide is the maximum loss which it can afford to withstand on any one risk. Then in arranging a surplus treaty it may go on to compile a line sheet of retentions with the retentions on different types of risk reduced in proportion to the relative premium loadings. Usually, however, underwriters have little idea of the relative loadings built into gross premium rates, so that decisions on differential retention limits are very subjective allowing plenty of scope for underwriting flair. Further formal explanation of the direct relationship between the expected profit of a class of business and the

11 Benjamin, *General Insurance*, p.224.

size of the optimal retention is given by G Taylor.[12]

The selected probability of ruin

The nature of insurance business is such that though a company may arrange its affairs so that its probability of ruin approaches zero, no form of reinsurance available on the market will totally eliminate risk. Even non-proportional reinsurances are subject to upper limits of indemnity which may be exceeded given the worst conceivable combination of circumstances. Given the other factors—size of reserves, expected size and risk characteristics of the portfolio of business, etc—a company may either decide how much reinsurance it can afford to buy and so determine its probability of ruin, or it may aim for a certain probability of ruin and fix its retentions accordingly, even though the cost of the necessary reinsurance may severely eat into its profit margins. In other words, there is a trade-off between security and profit.

The price of reinsurance

No reinsurer is prepared to accept business at a price only sufficient to cover the actuarial value of the expected losses transferred by the ceding company. An additional loading will be required to cover the costs of administering the business, and to provide for fluctuations in loss experience and, it is hoped, a profit, after also allowing for expected investment earnings derived from the business. If the coefficient of variation of the amount of claims on the reinsured portfolio is large, as may occur on a catastrophe excess-of-loss reinsurance, it is possible that the loading may exceed the risk premium.

Thus what may be an optimal retention programme on the basis of direct and reinsurance premiums based solely on the actuarial values of risks transferred, may not be optimal after allowing for premium loadings.[13] As illustrated in Figure 9.3 and in the first example above, the higher the loading in the reinsurance premium the less reinsurance can a ceding company afford and still achieve a target rate of return on its capital employed.

Investment policy

An insurance company's ability to meet claims as they fall due for payment without incurring additional financing costs depends upon the

---

12 G. Taylor, 'A survey of the principal results of risk theory', a note deposited with the Institute of Actuaries Library.
13 Borch, *Mathematical Theory of Insurance*, ch. 2.

size and liquidity of the funds at its disposal. If a company is forced to sell long-term securities at unplanned dates to meet its commitments, then it may incur both a transactions cost and a capital loss on realization. On the other hand, by holding funds in cash and short-dated securities, it will normally have to accept a lower rate of return and forgo the possibility of capital gains.

Therefore, in deciding upon its investment policy an insurance company needs to consider the cash-flow characteristics of the types of insurance it is writing, and in particular its retained claims distribution function. Thus insurers transacting non-life business normally tend to keep a higher proportion of liquid funds than life offices because of the larger fluctuations in claims costs incurred in non-life business. Through reinsurance, however, a company can modify its retained claims distribution functions, so that decisions on investment policy and on reinsurance should be taken jointly:[14] if a company is not to impair its security a decision to hold a lower proportion of liquid assets will necessitate a reduction in its retentions.

Time horizons in reinsurance planning

The discussion so far has not explicitly dealt with time horizons in the reinsurance planning process, though implicitly a one-year view has been adopted in both the Beard and Guaschi examples. The relevance of the planner's time horizon lies in the nature of the risk under review. Provided that risk factors do not change over time, and there is no undue fluctuation in basic probabilities, the coefficient of variation in losses on a given portfolio of insurance business will be inversely related to the length of the time period under review. The limiting case is the infinitely long period when the actual losses incurred would equal the sum of the expected losses.

In practice, however, no company can afford to take a very long view. Not only are insurers subject to solvency constraints imposed by supervisory authorities, but also proprietary companies normally have a dividend policy which is dependent upon maintaining a minimum level of profits from year to year. Consequently in planning its retentions a company will normally be concerned with the annual fluctuations in loss experience which may imperil its solvency position or its ability to service its capital each year. Conceivably a company may be required to take an even shorter view; for example, if solvency margins are continuously monitored by a supervisory authority rather than being subject to annual

---

14 K.H. Borch, 'The optimal portfolio of assets in an insurance company', *Transactions of the XVIII International Congress of Actuaries*, Munich 1968.

scrutiny, a company may need to adopt smaller retentions to protect itself against a loss or accumulation of losses which temporarily could impair its solvency. Likewise, if solvency margins are subject to periodic revision a company may adopt a conservative retention policy so that it will be in a position to comply with any anticipated increase in the required solvency margin. Many UK and European companies probably had to reduce their retention levels in 1978 in order to meet the higher solvency margin provisions of the EEC Non-Life Establishment Directive.

The risk of fluctuations in basic probabilities needs to be considered too. Even a temporary increase in the frequency and/or severity of losses of only short duration may place an intolerable strain on the cash flow and possibly the solvency of a company at the time. Unless basic probabilities change such an increase in claims costs should be counterbalanced over the long run by fluctuations in the other direction, but such a reduction in claims costs may occur too late to save the company from severe financial strain or even insolvency. Every class of insurance is exposed to such fluctuations.

On the other hand, an insurance company that has guaranteed access to extra funds if required to tide it over a period of financial difficulty may be prepared to take a longer view than just one year. Companies that are subsidiaries of a large group may fall into that category.

Yet even companies that have access to sufficient resources to take a long-term view have an incentive to review their reinsurance programmes each year or so. The keen competition that exists between reinsurers can lead to a ceding company sometimes being able to obtain a sufficiently large cut in its reinsurance premiums, perhaps in exchange for a relatively small change in its retention(s), to offset the disadvantage of switching reinsurers.

Summary

The above determinants of retention limits may be summarized in an equation which concentrates attention on seven factors, i.e.

ε = the probability of ruin

F_m = the claims distribution function as modified by the purchase of reinsurance

R_0 = the reserves at the beginning of the time period

n = the total number of expected claims

m = the expected value of each claim

λ = the contingency (security) loading in the premium

ω = the reinsurance premium expressed as a decimal fraction of the risk premium.

The probability of the company not being ruined during the period under review can then be expressed as:[15]

$$1 - \varepsilon = F_m [R_0 + nm(1 + \lambda)(1 - \omega), n]$$

One application of the equation is to highlight the issues involved in the adjustment of retention limits to allow for inflation. On the one hand a company's resources should increase during a period of inflation due to a rise in premium income produced by higher sums insured or the adjustment of premium rates to allow for the impact of inflation on claims costs. At the same time its claims distribution function F will change too as inflation increases the expected value of each claim m. Thus with non-proportional reinsurances a ceding company will need to review both its deductible and the upper limit to the cover. In the case of surplus reinsurances unless it raises its retention limits, thereby extending the tail of its retained claims distribution F_m, over time it will find itself ceding an increasing proportion of its gross premium income to reinsurers.

A company's ability to raise retention limits without increasing its probability of ruin will depend, however, upon its ability to earn sufficient to increase its reserves out of retained profits or to supplement them by raising more capital, and to maintain its premium loadings in order to service that additional capital.

The use of stability clauses partially takes care of adjusting excess-of-loss retentions in line with inflation, but ceding companies need to be aware of the dangers. Unless a company can meet the conditions mentioned above for safely raising retentions, the automatic operation of a stability clause will increase its probability of ruin.

As for the general application of the formula, every underwriter should possess firm information about two of the variables, R_0 and ω. What is so often lacking is reliable data regarding either the gross claims distribution function or the function as modified by reinsurance. Until that deficiency is remedied the fixing of retentions will inevitably remain dependent upon a large measure of subjective judgment.

Interdependence between exposure units

It is doubtful whether any insurance portfolio fully meets the condition

15 R.E. Beard, 'A mathematical model for motor insurance', in *Mathematical Modelling*, ed. J.G. Andrews and R.R. McClone (London: Butterworth, 1976).

of absolute independence between exposure units, though in some cases the degree of interdependence may be so small that retentions can be fixed on the assumption of statistical independence. Other types of portfolio are heavily exposed to accumulations of losses due to high degrees of interdependence between insured risks. Notable examples are insurances against natural perils, credit insurance, products and certain other types of liability risks, though portfolios covering other types of peril may be exposed quite severely to accumulations of losses, e.g. portfolios composed of group accident and group life insurances. In such cases portfolio risk is composed of two elements:

(1) The expected loss per individual exposure.

(2) The probability of two or more individual exposures simultaneously suffering loss.

The value of past loss experience in evaluating the portfolio risk varies between classes of insurance but even when it can provide a reasonable guide to future individual loss frequencies and severities, rarely, if ever, does it yield any reliable information for forecasting future catastrophe losses. D.G. Friedman has pointed out that in the case of property insurance portfolios covering natural perils, damage experience is:[16]

> A resultant of an interaction of (1) the natural hazard (frequency and severity of geophysical events—storms, earthquakes, floods) with (2) the character and distribution of insured properties.

Possibly past experience for a particular territory may reveal (1) a certain relationship between the severity of natural perils and the degree of damage suffered by different types of exposure units, and (2) a regularity of occurrence of such events. However, an insurer's loss experience over the same period will have been affected by other factors some of which are subject to substantial changes over time, notably whether the events affected densely or sparsely populated areas and the distribution of the insurer's portfolio by area and types of property insured: the extent of insurance coverage provided (notably first loss and deductible limits); the cost of repairs; etc. Therefore past claims experience on multiple losses is highly unlikely to provide a credible guide to an insurer's future exposure to such events, particularly when the probabilities of occurrence are very small.

Insurers' loss experience for other classes of insurance subject to substantial interdependencies between individual exposure units suffer from the same types of defects. Aggregate losses are the result of the interplay of many complex relationships which cannot be reduced to any

16 D.G. Friedman, 'Insurance and the natural hazards', *The Astin Bulletin*, vol. 7, part 1 (December 1972).

relatively simple mathematical formula. Yet underwriters need reliable estimates of the loss potentials of the portfolios they write for rating, acceptance and retention purposes. Friedman suggests the use of simulation models using Monte Carlo methods as opposed to the analytical methods developed in the theory of risk as a technique for evaluating the portfolio risk for natural perils. There is no reason why such models should not be extended to other classes of insurance and to the fixing of retentions.

It is not possible to deal here with the techniques of computer simulation, but it is hoped that sufficient will be said to explain its value as a risk-evaluation and decision-making tool.[17] Basically a simulation model is an analogue designed to represent the way in which the real world behaves. It is particularly useful for dealing with situations where outcomes depend upon the random occurrence of uncertain events and the interaction between a number of variables in that it is possible to simulate a very large number of actions and observe the outcomes. So, for example, in the case of an area exposed to damage by hurricanes one can simulate damage experience over several hundred years resulting from hurricanes of varying intensity, duration and paths, and analyse the results to produce such information as mean losses, minimum and maximum losses, measures of variability, etc. The analogue is achieved by a series of mathematical equations linked by logical relationships, the occurrence of random events being achieved by drawing numbers at random. Thus it is also possible to test the effect of changing assumptions regarding the values of the variables; so, for example, in the case of a hurricane-damage model it would be possible to test the effect of assuming different probability distributions for frequency and severity of occurrences. Computers have made it possible to build very complex models which could be used for solving reinsurance problems by rapidly showing the results of many simulated years of experience and levels of retention.

Friedman uses natural-hazard simulation to provide measures of both of the risk components of an insured portfolio covering natural perils using the types of models illustrated in Figures 9.4 and 9.5.[18] The natural-hazard model in both diagrams represents the physical mechanism which produces at irregular intervals the impulse into the

17 A number of general texts are available on simulation such as G.T. Jones, *Simulation and Business Decisions* (Harmondsworth: Penguin, 1972) and a brief introduction to its use in insurance and risk management can be found in M.H. Atkins, 'Simulation models in risk management', in *Handbook of Risk Management*, ed. R.L. Carter and N.H. Doherty (Brentford: Kluwer, 1974). An excellent detailed description of five models developed to assist in the calculation of premiums for group life contracts which depend on mortality fluctuations, such as stop-loss contracts and group life assurances with rebate of premiums, can be found in S. Benjamin, 'Simulating mortality fluctuations', *Transactions of the XVII International Congress of Actuaries*, vol. III, Pt. II, 1964.
18 Friedman, 'Insurance and the natural hazards', p.33.

Figure 9.4

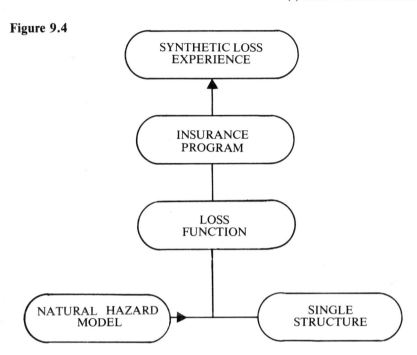

Figure 9.5

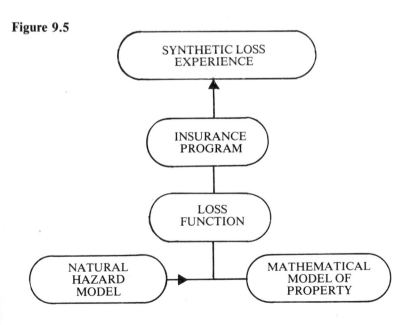

system—the storm, flood or earthquake. Records maintained by meterological services, etc., can provide the data for the frequency, duration, severity, location and geographical extent of such occurrences. The natural hazard interacts in Figure 9.4 with the physical characteristic of an individual property to determine the extent of the damage shown as the loss function. How far this will correspond with the insurer's loss experience will then depend upon the insurance cover provided, e.g. the size of any deductible, which thus acts as a filter to the synthesized losses included in the loss function.

The potential loss per individual structure shown in Figure 9.4 would provide a guide to the actuarial premium required to cover the expected annual loss per structure, but it is insufficient to evaluate the second risk component of an insurance portfolio, i.e. the catastrophe potential. Therefore the model in Figure 9.5 is extended to take account of the geographical distribution of the different types and values of insured properties. Again the character of the insurance provided would act as a filter on the synthesized losses to generate the insurer's expected loss experience.

Thus by running the program a large number of times it would be possible to see a pattern of loss experience over very many years showing the mean loss experience and the variation around the mean, including the largest aggregate losses in any one year. It would be possible to extend the model further by introducing an extra filter into the loss experience in the form of different forms of reinsurance and retention limits. Then the effect on retained losses could be compared with the likely cost of reinsurance to determine the optimal form and amount of reinsurance purchased.

A company's ability to construct such a model depends upon a detailed indexing of insured risks. Friedman, for example, divided Metropolitan San Francisco into 130 grid areas each representing 36 square miles.[19] Likewise realistic estimation of the values of other variables required to simulate the impact of losses on a ceding company's financial position or a reinsurer's exposure under any form of treaty requires reliable information regarding distributions of losses by size and claims-settlement delays, and the size and loss experience of the portfolio of business to be reinsured.[20] It may be objected that indexing and the detailed recording and analysis of loss data are very costly processes for both ceding companies and reinsurers. Unfortunately there is no simple, cheap solution. Simulation models offer the only satisfactory means of measuring exposures when there exists a substantial interdependence

19 Ibid.
20 See F.E. Guaschi, *Accident Excess of Loss: An Actuarial Approach to the Rating Problem* (Mercantile and General Reinsurance Co., 1969).

between exposure units, and the predictive value of any model is dependent upon the quality of its data.

General application of simulation models

The usefulness of simulation models for improving the information required to take decisions regarding the most suitable form of reinsurance and retention levels is not limited to portfolios exposed to the risk of accumulations of losses. It may be applied to solving such problems in general.

Rarely does a ceding company or reinsurer possess fully reliable data regarding all of the variables involved. Although past experience may provide a good guide to the frequency of small to medium losses, usually information regarding the tail of loss distributions is far less reliable. Likewise available evidence may identify a trend in losses but it may be insufficient to predict future loss experience with any high degree of confidence; for example the forecasting of inflation perhaps several years ahead is notoriously error prone. Also, as shown above, such factors as the cost of servicing capital, which is related to current market interest rates and dividend yields; required solvency margins; and the price of reinsurance, which may vary between reinsurers in a competitive market, play an important part in fixing retention levels. Before seeking quotations for its business a ceding company may wish to ascertain how possible differences in required reinsurance premiums may affect its decisions. The simulation method enables outcomes to be tested given the specified interrelationships between variables using differing assumptions about their values.

Conclusions

Inevitably, empirical methods and underwriting judgment will continue to play an important role in the fixing of retention levels. Nevertheless risk theory can help to illuminate the decision-making of ceding companies and reinsurers, even if so far there is no sufficiently comprehensive mathematical model to provide with certainty the retention levels necessary to achieve solvency and profitability.

The potentially most useful tool now available is the simulation method, though its application will require ceding companies and reinsurers to keep far more comprehensive records than at present. Moreover such models need to be handled with great care. Results depend very much upon the data input, with the claims distribution being a key function in any retention model. If, for example, the data provided by a small sample of claims are fed directly into a computer without any preliminary consideration of whether they are likely to be representative of the total population of claims, then quite probably the results of the model will be atypical. If a simulation model is used, the limitations of the data input must always be kept very much in mind.

10
Fire reinsurance

Scope of fire reinsurance

Previous chapters have discussed reinsurance in general terms. Now attention can be concentrated on the special features of the main classes of insurance business, starting with fire reinsurance.

Although market practice in the main follows certain general lines it is not rigid, with the result that, to some degree, classification of reinsurance business must be arbitrary. Fire reinsurance is a case in point. Essentially it is concerned with the insurance of property and may extend to cover all of those perils and risks to which property is exposed. In Britain following the reclassification of insurance business by the Companies Act 1967, which required insurers to submit to the supervisory authority a separate return for 'property business', many companies rearranged their reinsurances to coincide with the statutory classes. Consequently their 'fire' treaties now cover not only those perils traditionally insured in the fire department, i.e. fire, explosion, aircraft, riot, malicious damage, windstorm, flood, impact and earthquake, but also theft, plate glass, etc. Other companies, however, still prefer to confine their fire reinsurance arrangements to those insurances traditionally handled by the fire department, but embracing, besides material damage covers, their exposures under business interruption (other than engineering interruption) policies, including interruption losses arising from the occurrence of infectious diseases in the case of hotel, catering and similar trades.

The pattern is, however, more complicated. A considerable amount of household and small trade property insurance is written under 'comprehensive' policies that besides insuring fire and allied perils extend to include property (e.g. theft) and liability risks that are regarded as accident (casualty) business. Likewise companies operating in some countries may seek to include in a fire treaty insurances against liabilities for material damage caused by fire and associated perils. For example, the inclusion of the fire risk on motor vehicles is common, and French insurers will include all third-party liability risks written in conjunction with fire insurance, such as *Recours de Voisins, Risques Locatifs,* and *Risques Locataires.* [1] Thus in practice the scope of a fire treaty may extend well beyond the types of loss conventionally thought of in Britain or America as fire business so that a reinsurer must be careful to ascertain precisely what sort of liabilities he is being asked to accept. It must be emphasized that though a fire treaty may embrace liability risks no cover is ever provided for liability in respect of bodily injury.

When a ceding company trades in, or obtains business from, more than one country, either separate fire treaties may be arranged for each major area of its operations, or the treaty cover may be arranged on a world-wide basis subject only to the exclusion of the United States. The merits and demerits of multi-territory treaties have been discussed in Chapter 7 and so need not be repeated here.

The following two clauses taken from fire surplus treaties illustrate the various points discussed above. Both clauses include business interruption (consequential loss) risks, but whereas the second restricts cover to United Kingdom business only, it does make provision for the inclusion of various classes of accident business. The exclusion of war, civil war, atomic and nuclear energy risks is normal market practice, and the exclusion of obligatory reinsurances is to avoid the reinsurer being exposed to possible unknown accumulations of risk over which the ceding company has no control.

CLAUSE A

Business covered and territorial scope
Fire and allied perils, including consequential loss, insurances written anywhere in the world (excluding the United States of America and Canada) subject to the exclusions set out in appendix 1 attached hereto

APPENDIX 1

The reinsurer shall not be liable under this agreement for claims arising from:
(1) War and civil war.
(2) Atomic or nuclear energy risks.
(3) Obligatory reinsurances.
(4) Excess of loss insurances and reinsurances.

CLAUSE B

Class of business
This agreement refers to the liability of the company under each and every policy and facultative reinsurance written by the company against direct

---

1 Report by the Advanced Study Group of the Insurance Institute of London, p.30.

and/or consequential loss by fire and/or allied perils and various classes of accident business specified in the schedule attached hereto on risks situated in the United Kingdom of Great Britain and Northern Ireland (including the Channel Islands and the Isle of Man), and on risks situated outside thereof which may be included in such insurances or reinsurances of which are insured by policyholders resident therein.

General exclusions
(1) *War and civil war exclusion clause*
   Any loss or damage occasioned by or through or in consequence directly or indirectly of war, invasion, act of foreign enemy, hostilities or warlike operations (whether war be declared or not), civil war, rebellion, revolution, insurrection or military or usurped power.
(2) *Nuclear energy and atomic pools exclusion clause*
   Any loss or liability accruing to the company directly or indirectly and whether as insurer or reinsurer, from any pool of insurers or reinsurers formed for the purpose of covering atomic or nuclear energy risks.

Exposure to loss

A fire underwriter in formulating his reinsurance programme needs to recognize his exposure to losses arising on:
(1) one risk;
(2) from one event; and
(3) in the aggregate during a year.

Although he will need to limit his exposure on any one individual risk, i.e. a building or range of adjoining buildings, the possibility of an accumulation of losses arising from one event cannot be ignored; fire risks are not perfectly independent. A fire may spread or an explosion may damage adjacent property which the underwriter may also insure, and a far higher interdependence between exposure units is present in a portfolio containing insurances against natural perils—windstorm, flood and earthquake. Also if business interruption insurances are written, allowance must be made for the exposure to both material damage and interruption claims arising from a loss involving only one insured. Finally, the annual loss experience of certain types of insurance which a fire underwriter may handle, notably hail damage to growing crops, is subject to wide variability from year to year.

The reinsurance programme will need to cope with all of these exposures.

Arranging the reinsurance programme

Traditionally throughout the world wherever competitive fire insurance markets exist large fire risks have been spread between insurers either on a direct basis by means of coinsurance or, in many markets, through

341

facultative reinsurance. Individual insurers then have arranged to reinsure any amount accepted surplus to their own retentions on a proportional basis. The large diversity in the size of individual risks insured means that not only small direct insurers have a need for reinsurance. It is usually the large companies that take the lead and are asked to accept the largest shares of the major industrial and commercial risks. These provide them with a sufficiently large stream of business requiring reinsurance protection to make a treaty arrangement practicable so that only the exceptional cases will need to be handled wholly or partially on a facultative basis.

Three trends in underwriting conditions are to some degree changing the traditional picture. First the impact of technology on the size of individual risks has resulted in a revival in facultative reinsurances. Often major manufacturing complexes, particularly in high-risk industries such as petrochemicals and oil refineries, are too large for local markets to handle, and *ad hoc* assistance is required from international reinsurers. Secondly, in many parts of the world, including developing countries, there are growing concentrations of values at risk in areas exposed to natural disasters. Consequently there is an increased demand for catastrophe excess of loss reinsurances with ever higher upper limits to protect the whole account. Thirdly, fire insurers are under the same pressures to reduce their administrative expenses as are other insurers and this has had two effects. There has been a streamlining of direct underwriting practices: instead of each separate fire risk in a large fire insurance schedule being covered by a separate item with individual sums insured for buildings and contents, they are amalgamated in one blanket insurance so that the underwriter cannot be so selective in his reinsurance arrangements. The drive for economy has also resulted in a swing towards using excess of loss reinsurance as the main form of protection for fire accounts.

Before considering the suitability of the various forms of reinsurance it is desirable to look more closely at the factors determining an insurer's exposure to loss.

Individual risks

There are two basic factors to be considered:
(1) The company's commitment on the property concerned; that is, its total sum insured under one or more policies covering one or more interests. Normally there is only one policyholder to consider, but in the case of, say, public warehouses an insurer may be interested under several policies.
(2) The nature of the risk concerned.

The probability of a loss occurring and the potential maximum loss relative to the value at risk will depend on a variety of factors which will be reflected in the premium rate charged. Fire loss potential is affected notably by the construction, height, and size of a building; whether it is subdivided by fire-resistant walls and floors; the methods of heating and lighting; the trade(s) carried on and the materials used and stored in the building; its proximity to other buildings and their fire characteristics; internal and external fire-fighting facilities; and so forth. When an insurance is arranged on a blanket basis so that separate sums insured are not available for the individual fire risks, the underwriter will be dependent upon whatever breakdown he can obtain from the original insured of the distribution of the total value between the various buildings, and his surveyor's estimate of the estimated maximum loss.

The underwriter must consider too the loss potential from other insured perils. For example, the Flixborough chemical plant disaster dramatically demonstrated that the loss potential of an explosion was far greater than of fire spreading through the plant. And a plant or materials that may be relatively resistant to fire or smoke damage may be highly sensitive to water damage, especially if flood water contains chemical solutions.

Although the loss potentials of various insured perils may differ very considerably, normally reinsurers prefer ceding companies to carry the same net retention on extraneous perils (i.e. storm, water damage, earthquake, subsidence, etc.) as on the fire risk to avoid anti-selection. However, sometimes separate reinsurance arrangements are made for certain specified perils; for example, a quota share treaty may be arranged for earthquake risks when the corresponding fire business is reinsured on a surplus basis.

Besides the material damage insurance separate consideration needs to be given to the loss potential of business interruption policies. Attention must be paid to such factors as the indemnity period (i.e. the length of time after damage has occurred during which the insurer is liable to indemnify the policyholder for losses sustained); whether the trade is seasonal; the interdependencies between processes within the same or other plants; the vulnerability of sources of power and possible alternative supplies; and, where an insurance is extended to cover losses due to damage occurring at suppliers' and/or customers' premises, the degree of dependence on any one supplier/customer. Although the probability and severity of property damage is obviously of importance, business interruption losses are hardly ever proportional to the extent of any property damage. Also where an insurance is extended to cover suppliers'/customers' premises, an insurer must recognize the possibility of incurring losses under two (or more) policies covering different policyholders.

Sometimes separate treaties are arranged for business interruption insurances, but normally such business is included in the fire treaty. Whichever method is adopted, ceding companies usually fix separate retentions for material damage and interruption insurances, but limit their combined retention for any one risk to a maximum sum, a common figure being 150% of the fire retention.

Though a direct underwriter will need to consider individually each risk that he is offered, in the same way as different types of risks are classified for premium rating, so too insurers classify risks according to their loss potentials for the purpose of fixing retentions and thus acceptance limits. A class retention limit is in effect the norm for a typical risk of its class, and the retentions for individual cases are adjusted according to their individual features; for example, a retention lower than the norm would be fixed for a building largely constructed of combustible materials, whereas a building of superior construction protected by automatic sprinklers would warrant a higher retention.

Accumulations of losses due to one event involving more than one risk

Catastrophe risks are a particularly important feature of the various natural perils. A direct underwriter can exercise a certain amount of control over his total exposure by a careful indexing and thus limitation of insurances covering properties within areas exposed to natural disasters, such as known earthquake zones, flood plains, or hurricane belts. There are limits, however, to indexing. Although advancing computer technology may overcome the problem of the high labour cost of manually maintaining a comprehensive index of all insured property, an underwriter may be forced to accept more of such business than he desires in order to compete for other classes of insurance. Furthermore there is the perennial problem that nature does not conform to standard patterns of behaviour. There are, for example, an infinite number of combinations of wind pressures and paths that a hurricane can take in passing through a particular region, and the same sort of comment can be made about earthquakes or floods.

Consequently, even if an underwriter has been successful in limiting both his retentions on individual risks and the volume of business he has written within any region to levels which would enable him to cope within his own financial resources with any accumulation of losses attributable to normal occurrences, he is still sure to need some protection against the exceptional losses that infrequently do occur. Such protection can only be obtained by effecting non-proportional reinsurance.

The amount that a company can afford to retain on any one fire risk and in the aggregate on an accumulation of losses from any one event depends on the factors discussed in Chapter 9, notably its capital and free reserves relative to premium income and the relative size of the contingency loading it can build into its premiums.

Forms of reinsurance

Exactly what sort of reinsurance programme a direct company arranges will depend upon individual circumstances and preferences. Much of the fire reinsurance placed by companies operating in both developed and developing countries still takes the form of proportional, usually surplus, treaties.

Only rarely are quota share treaties effected as the main form of reinsurance. The wide disparities in the size of fire sums insured and the large number of individual risk units available for insurance mean that even small companies are capable of fully retaining a significant proportion of the cases they accept. Therefore companies that want to build up their net retained accounts do not look with favour on the idea of ceding a fixed proportion of all of the business they write. Though a combined quota share/surplus treaty may be less objectionable in that it would enable the company to retain a larger share and obtain automatic reinsurance for sums insured in excess of the quota share limits, quota share treaties have tended to find a place in fire reinsurance programmes only for:

(1) New companies until they have gained some underwriting experience.
(2) Companies whose treaty results have been so poor that they have been forced to offer their reinsurers a share of all of their business in order to retain some reinsurance protection.
(3) The reinsurance of special perils, such as hail and earthquake, where quota share enables the reinsurer to obtain a better balanced portfolio of reinsured business, particularly if the ceding company's fire retention limits are high relative to the business it is writing.

There has, however, been a certain change of attitude in recent years to quota share reinsurance, largely in response to the rising cost of administering surplus reinsurances. The trend has been for companies to increase substantially the level of their net retentions, thus absorbing a large part of the premiums previously ceded to first surplus treaties, and then to protect the enlarged net account by an excess of loss cover. Occasionally companies also then arrange quota share treaties but usually the motive is to maintain reciprocal exchanges rather than to increase their gross capacity. In either event the company will still retain a surplus reinsurance treaty to deal with the reduced number of larger risks accepted for sums insured above its enlarged net retention limit.

Regardless of the method used to limit a company's exposure on any one risk, it will also need reinsurance protection against the risk of accumulations of losses from one event involving several—and possibly a large number of—policyholders. Thus catastrophe excess of loss treaties form a normal part of a company's reinsurance programme.

Finally there is the question of a company's aggregate loss exposure during any one year. Reinsurers are unwilling to provide stop-loss reinsurance as a substitute for other forms of reinsurance cover for normal fire business and at best will only consider it as a final supplementary level of protection. However, as noted earlier, there are certain classes of business written by fire insurers, notably hail damage to growing crops and windstorm, where, because of the seasonal nature of the cover and the fluctuations in underwriting results, stop loss cover is considered suitable as the primary form of reinsurance protection.

Facultative and facultative obligatory reinsurances

As far as fire reinsurance is concerned, little needs to be added to the comments made in Chapter 6 regarding the use and the procedures for dealing with facultative and facultative obligatory reinsurances. The only special feature is that in Britain members of the Fire Offices' Committee are required to observe certain rules relating to the administration of facultative reinsurances covering UK business. The rules, which are confidental to members, cover such matters as the form of the offer, the form of acceptance, documentation, and the method of premium and claims payments.

Surplus treaties

The discussion of the surplus form of reinsurance in Chapter 5 and of the formation, administration and termination of surplus treaties in Chapter 7 largely cover the position regarding fire surplus treaties. There are, however, certain aspects of fire business that call for special treatment.

Scope of the treaty

As noted earlier, a reinsurer must take steps to ascertain at inception precisely what types of business are to be included in a treaty and word it accordingly. Now that bordereaux are not normally supplied (except possibly for very large risks or top covers, or by new companies (see Chapter 7) initial enquiries and careful treaty drafting are the only means left to a reinsurer to avoid being exposed to unacceptable, or at least unexpected, risks.

The reinsurer's exposure

Given the growth of conurbations and the concentrations of property values in relatively small areas in many parts of the world, reinsurers have begun to demand far more information regarding their exposures to losses due to natural perils. For example, a ceding company writing earthquake insurance in Japan would be required to supply details of the distribution of its exposures between the various zones, and possibly the reinsurer may ask for bordereaux to be supplied too. The next step has been for reinsurers to introduce aggregate zone limits into some surplus treaties.

Mercantile risks

Normally in fixing its retention for an individual risk a ceding company only has to take account of the insurance arranged by one policyholder. However, docks, wharves, public warehouses, bonded stores and similar locations present special difficulties. Not only does the total value at risk fluctuate as goods are moved into and out of such premises perhaps daily, but also an insurer may be interested under policies arranged by different insureds, running for different periods of time, for values at risk that may be changed frequently and, in the case of floating policies on stocks, without any precise knowledge of where the goods may be located at any one time. Obviously it would be very difficult to arrange reinsurances for goods insured at such locations in the normal manner. The company would have to fix its aggregate retention for each location, and keep a check on values at risk for different policyholders. When the aggregate value at risk exceeded its retention it would have to reinsure a proportion of each insurance and adjust all of the individual cessions when any policyholder moved goods into or out of the premises. Not only would such an arrangement be very costly to operate but also very difficult, if not impossible with floating policies on a declaration basis.

To avoid such complications it is usual to include in fire surplus treaties a clause along the following lines which allows the ceding company to fix an aggregate retention, and usually also for any one name insured. Then, according to the build-up of the company's gross commitment, the sums insured under some policies might be wholly retained whereas others might be 100% reinsured. Thus in the event of loss the reinsurer will be liable for the following proportion of the loss under each policy:

$$\frac{\text{aggregate amount ceded}}{\text{total gross commitment}} \times \text{ loss under individual policy}$$

In effect, the clause operates like a quota share arrangement for policies covering warehouse risks.

> In the case of insurances on the contents of bonded stores, elevators, public warehouses, general storage warehouses, wharves and timber yards, it shall not be obligatory for the Company to cede a proportionate amount of each policy to the Reinsurer and the retention of the Company shall not be held to apply to the identical property on which an amount has been ceded to the Reinsurer. In the event of loss, however, all cessions on the risk affected, though made under specified policies, shall, provided name limits are not thereby exceeded, be deemed to cover proportionately all policies in force on such risks.

Non-proportional reinsurances

As in other branches of insurance, the types of non-proportional reinsurance employed in the fire branch fall into three main divisions, namely:

(1) Working excess of loss treaties arranged to cover losses affecting one risk.

(2) Catastrophe excess of loss treaties designed to cover accumulations of losses arising out of one event.

(3) Excess of loss ratio or stop loss treaties to cover aggregate losses during any one year in excess of a specified loss ratio or amount.

The comments already made regarding the scope of surplus treaties in terms of geographical area, the classes of insurance covered, and agreed exclusions, equally apply to non-proportional treaties and so will not be repeated. Instead, this section of the chapter will concentrate on the particular features of the three types of non-proportional treaty as applied to fire and other property insurances.

Working excess of loss treaties

Working excess of loss covers are a fairly new development in the fire department, being designed to replace *pro rata* reinsurances as a method of reinsuring individual risks which exceed the ceding company's net retention.

Besides excess of loss treaties arranged in conjunction with a quota share treaty, the emergence in the direct market of large groups capable of retaining for their own combined account substantial sums insured has reduced the need for proportional reinsurance as a means of providing adequate basic underwriting capacity, and has created a demand for excess of loss reinsurances as the sole form of reinsurance protection for reasons common to other classes of insurance.

Other market developments have also played a part in the growing popularity of working excess of loss treaties, notably the practice of basing retentions on assessments of EML (estimated maximum loss) or MPL (maximum probable loss).[2] A working cover, whether arranged in one or more layers, is then designed to protect the ceding company against expected losses on any one risk, the reinsurer's liability for the ceding company's 'ultimate net loss' being defined in terms of 'any one claim any one risk'.

Normally working treaties cover direct insurances and facultative reinsurances written by the ceding company, but inwards treaty reinsurances are usually excluded. The replacement of surplus reinsurance by a working excess of loss treaty should mean no general change in a ceding company's underwriting policy. It will be expected to continue to use a table of gross retention limits for individual risks which may be incorporated in the treaty, and reinsurers are reluctant to provide working covers unless the ceding company can retain a reasonable deductible (say 10%) in relation to the gross retention.

'One risk'

Exactly what constitutes 'one risk' may be defined in the treaty, for example:

> A building or group of buildings under one and the same roof and/or buildings within 30 feet of each other not separated by unbroken parapet walls.

---

2 See Chapter 9 for definitions of these terms.

And in the case of agricultural insurances: [3]

> All property belonging to one insured and situate on one farm or the land attached to the one homestead, and in the case of goods stored in the open any one risk shall include all the stocks or dumps within one compound.

On the other hand, quite frequently the ceding company is left to decide for itself what constitutes one risk, as in the following clauses.

> The Reinsured shall be the sole judge as to what constitutes one risk, it being understood and agreed that one risk shall mean all property or interest at any one location and designated by the Reinsured in its records as subject to one risk retention.
>
> It is warranted that the Reinsured undertakes not to retain on one risk an amount greater than that stated in the Schedule.

Retentions based on EMLs

The danger of operating on the basis of EMLs is that sometimes estimates go badly wrong. [4] Business interruption insurances can add to that risk if such an insurance is wholly or partially retained in addition to the property insurance. There is the temptation to underestimate the combined EML on the grounds that even fairly serious property damage need not result in a prolonged disruption of the business, only then to discover that a loss occurs at the worst possible time from a production/trading point of view.

If, following normal practice, a ceding company has effected a catastrophe excess of loss cover in addition to its working cover, the consequences of underestimation of an EML could fall entirely on the catastrophe reinsurer (subject to the adequacy of the treaty's upper limit). Such a situation is neither fair nor in accord with the purpose of a catastrophe cover. Therefore reinsurers usually try to ensure that ceding companies retain a financial involvement in the consequences of their errors of judgment. One way which is often used is to arrange the treaty limits so that a gap is left in the cover provided. The following example shows how it works.

---

3 Advanced Study Group Report of the Insurance Institute of London, pp.33 – 34.
4 The estimated maximum loss for the Flixborough plant was 20% but the explosion resulted in an 80% property damage loss, G. Hickmott, *Flixborough Disaster* (Mercantile and General Reinsurance Co., 1977).

Total sum insured on one risk:	£1,000,000.
Estimated maximum loss:	£250,000.

Working excess of loss cover (any one risk):
£250,000 in excess of £50,000.

Catastrophe excess of loss cover (any one event):
£1,000,000 in excess of £200,000.

	£
Loss	1,000,000
Paid by 'working cover'	250,000
∴ 'Ultimate net loss' for catastrophe cover	750,000
less catastrophe deductible	200,000
∴ Amount payable under catastrophe cover	550,000
Total reinsurance recoveries	800,000
Total retained loss	200,000
	1,000,000

Thus by fixing the deductible under the catastrophe cover at well above the ceding company's retention limit of £50,000, it will be penalized for any loss in excess of the EML for any one risk.

Another safeguard now commonly used is to insert in catastrophe treaties a 'two risks' warranty specifying that the reinsurer will be liable only in respect of claims where at least two risks are involved in one event. Thus the ceding company can obtain no relief under the catastrophe cover if, due to underestimation of an EML, it incurs a large net loss on one risk.

Rating

The rating of working covers depends upon a number of factors. In every case the reinsurer needs to consider:
(1) The ceding company's past claims experience on its gross and net portfolios, and of individual large claims.
(2) The size of risk profile of the portfolio.
(3) The size of the portfolio and its rate of growth.
(4) What restrictions, if any, are placed on reinstatement of cover following claims under the treaty. Since the Darwin disaster it has become common for reinsurers to insert a limit on losses arising from one event: such a restriction may take the form of either a limit on the maximum number of reinstatements of cover or, more usually, an

351

aggregate cash limit in respect of accumulations of losses arising from one event. So, for example, if the treaty cover was for £250,000 in excess of £50,000 although no limit may be placed on the number of reinstatements for individual losses, an aggregate limit of, say, £750,000 may be imposed for any one event.

These factors will determine the size of the risk premium and the loading required. A flat premium may be charged for very small portfolios to provide an adequate sum. In other cases either a fixed rate may be applied to the ceding company's relevant premium income or a variable premium rate may be quoted calculated on either an annual or a longer-term burning cost. Many treaties now employ a method (which was pioneered mainly in America) of exposure rating by size of risk. In many cases the burning cost is calculated automatically by computer to produce a pure burning cost rate which is applied to the subject premium income. The resulting figure is then loaded in the normal manner. [5]

Catastrophe treaties

The object of a catastrophe excess of loss treaty is to protect the reinsured against unexpectedly large losses due to the occurrence of some event causing an accumulation of losses from more than one insured risk. Invariably the cover provided is on an 'any one event' basis, and it is additional to the protection provided by either a proportional or a working excess of loss treaty.

Emphasis is placed on *unexpectedly* large; that is losses beyond the ceding company's normal expectations. In the case of loss caused by natural perils the idea is not to provide cover for normal seasonal conditions, even if they may prove unexpectedly severe. So, for example, if a company chooses to provide flood insurance in an area that regularly suffers from seasonal flooding, it is the underwriter's own responsibility to control exposures and fix individual retentions at a sufficiently low level to be able to withstand the expected seasonal accumulation of losses. Therefore reinsurers try to ensure that by providing a catastrophe cover the ceding company is not given an excuse for reckless underwriting or for abandoning control over exposures. Control can be exercised in four ways:

(1) By fixing the treaty deductible sufficiently high to leave the reinsured unprotected for the first slice of any losses in excess of what may normally be expected.

(2) By requiring the ceding company to participate up to, say, 10% in the

---

5 See Chapters 5 and 10 for fuller descriptions of exposure rating by means of coded excesses.

excess cover provided.

(3) By limiting the number of reinstatements of cover allowed.

(4) By charging a realistic premium, including an additional premium for reinstatements.

'Any one event'

Reference was made in Chapter 8 to the need to define in property catastrophe excess of loss treaties the meaning of 'any one event'. A portfolio covering natural perils and riot, strike and malicious damage is exposed to the risk of accumulations of losses which may occur over a wide area during a period of perhaps several days. Therefore reinsurers operating on the London market normally impose time and/or geographical limits for the purpose of determining what constitutes an event or occurrence: the following 'hours clause' is a typical example of the definitions employed.

> The term 'loss occurrence' shall mean all individual losses arising out of and directly occasioned by one catastrophe.
>
> However, the duration and extent of any 'loss occurrence' so defined shall be limited to:
> — 72 consecutive hours as regards hurricane, typhoon, windstorm, rainstorm, hailstorm and/or tornado.
> — 72 consecutive hours as regards earthquake, seaquake, tidal wave and/or volcanic eruption.
> — 72 consecutive hours and within the limits of one city, town or village as regards riots, civil commotions and malicious damage.
> — 168 consecutive hours for any other catastrophe of whatsoever nature.
> And no individual loss from whatever insured peril which occurs outside these periods or areas shall be included in that 'loss occurrence'.
>
> The Reinsured may choose the time and date when any such period of consecutive hours commences and if any catastrophe is of greater duration than the above periods, the reinsured may divide that catastrophe into two or more 'loss occurrences', provided no two periods overlap and provided no period commences earlier than the time and date of the happening of the first recorded individual loss to the Reinsured in that catastrophe.

Though the exact terms of such a clause are a matter for individual negotiation (for example, a 72 hour period is shown for windstorms and similar atmospheric disturbances whereas a 48 hour period is equally common), the market adheres to the following general principles in defining 'one event' for the purpose of aggregating losses:

(1) No geographical limitation is placed on losses caused by windstorm, etc., but they must be caused by the same atmospheric disturbance within the specified time period. Likewise earthquake losses must be attributable to an earthquake or seaquake having the same epicentre.

353

(2) Besides the hours restriction, riot and strike damage are subject to geographical limits. For the purpose of aggregating losses, riot and strike damage are limited to losses occurring within the limits of one city, town or village.

(3) In applying the hours limit, usually the ceding company is permitted to chose the time when the period shall commence, provided it is not before the first recorded damage.

(4) If the event lasts longer than the time specified the ceding company is permitted to divide it into two or more periods in the manner most favourable to itself subject to each period being of the specified length and not overlapping with another.

However precise and detailed the wording of such a clause it is impossible to cover every possible contingency and some room for dispute is always certain to remain. The London Insurance Institute's Advanced Study Group cited two examples.[6] The first concerns earthquake where two shocks occur, the second sufficiently long after the first to be considered as a separate event but before the damage caused by the first could have been fully assessed, so that it is impossible to say with any accuracy how much of the total damage could be attributed to each event. The second example cited is of fire damage which normally is not specifically dealt with in an hours clause. Forest fire, or bush fires in, say, Australia are often caused by separate deliberately or accidentally caused fires spreading and merging to become a major conflagration. Under such circumstances it is difficult if not impossible to say with certainty what is 'one event', and one solution reinsurers have adopted is to include in excess of loss treaties an annual aggregate limit for bush and forest fires. An alternative which is more favoured today is to extend the hours clause to limit losses not otherwise specifically mentioned to a seven-day (or 168-hour) aggregate time limit.

Given the difficulties of (1) devising wordings which are capable of covering all possible circumstances, and (2) sorting out a series of losses into different time periods, in practice a great deal of common sense rather than legal precision is necessary in apportioning losses. The purpose of hours clauses is simply to try to ensure that all damage due to the same event is treated as such. Inevitably the parties must be prepared to try to reach a mutually agreeable apportionment of losses, particularly when it is very difficult, if not impossible, to specify precisely the time and extent of the damage sustained by individual properties.

Moreover, although the selection of time periods may be important when a ceding company's aggregate losses exceed the treaty upper limit, often in practice the question of whether one or two events occurred is more likely to be a matter of dispute between reinsurers on different

6 p.31.

layers of a catastrophe cover than between the reinsurers and the ceding company.

An example will show how an hours clause operates in theory. In particular it will show how the distribution of losses between the various interests will depend upon the length of period chosen, the build-up of losses, and the excess limits.

Example

Excess of loss reinsurances are arranged on an event basis for:
(1) £100,000 in excess of £100,000 any one event.
(2) £500,000 in excess of £200,000 any one event.
Two windstorms, A and B, cause ultimate net losses as follows:

Losses during period				*Cumulative losses*		
Hours	*Event A*	*Event B*		*Hours*	*Event A*	*Event B*
	£	£			£	£
0 – 24	50,000	80,000		0 – 24	50,000	80,000
25 – 48	70,000	130,000		0 – 48	120,000	210,000
49 – 72	110,000	120,000		0 – 72	230,000	330,000
73 – 96	40,000	130,000		0 – 96	270,000	460,000

Loss apportionment:
(1) If the reinsurances operate with a 48-hour limit:

	Event A	*Event B*
	£	£
Reinsured's liability	190,000	200,000
Reinsurer's liability under first layer	80,000	200,000
Reinsurer's liability under second layer	—	60,000
	270,000	460,000

In the case of event A it would pay the ceding company to select the period commencing 24 hours after the first damage occurred. If it chose to take two 48-hour periods commencing from the first damage, it would be able to recover from its reinsurers only £70,000 (i.e. £20,000 for period 0 – 48 hours, plus £50,000 for period 48 – 96 hours).

For event B the company would obtain the largest recovery by taking two 48-hour periods commencing from the first damage.

(2) If the reinsurances operate with a 72-hour limit:

	Event A £	Event B £
Reinsured's liability	140,000	180,000
Reinsurer's liability under first layer	100,000	100,000
Reinsurer's liability under second layer	30,000	180,000
	270,000	460,000

In the case of event A the ceding company would benefit by taking the 72 hours commencing with the first damage, whereas with event B it would pay to take the period commencing after the first 24 hours.

It can be seen that the longer is the chosen period the greater is the likelihood that the top layer(s) of catastrophe covers will be involved, with a commensurate reduction in the liability under the lower layer(s).

Further complications may arise if (as is usual) only a limited number of reinstatements are allowed under the treaties and more than one catastrophe occurs during one year. This point is illustrated in Appendix 10.1.

Rating

The rating of catastrophe treaties does not lend itself to any of the burning-cost methods described in Chapter 5. Either a flat premium must be charged or a premium rate may be applied to the reinsured's premium income. The latter method is the more desirable in that it ensures that the reinsurance premium is tied to changes in the reinsurer's exposure as measured, albeit imperfectly, by the amount of business written by the ceding company during the year.

Whether the reinsurance premium is fixed or adjustable, reinsurers usually determine the size of premium required by a process of objective and subjective evaluation aimed at producing a sum which will cover the losses anticipated over a number of years. American reinsurers use the fairly self-explanatory term 'payback' to describe the process; that is if the reinsurer expects to pay a claim equal or near to his total liability, say, every 10 years, then he will want an annual premium which will repay any loss over 10 years. On the London market the term 'rate on line' is used, it being a rate which if applied to the liability accepted by the reinsurer will produce an annual premium sufficient to meet the losses expected over a number of years. So, for example, if a cover was arranged for £500,000 excess of £250,000, and the reinsurer after examining all of the available facts concluded that he would be likely to be called upon to pay one major loss every eight years then he would want an annual premium capable of yielding an eight-year payback

$$= \text{£}500,000 \div 8 = \text{£}62,500$$

or a rate on line of 12½% so giving an annual premium of:

$$\text{£}500,000 \times 12\tfrac{1}{2}\% = \text{£}62,500$$

In both cases the required premium would be loaded to cover the reinsurer's administration costs, profit and contingencies, and adjusted to allow for investment earnings on the fund, to produce a premium rate to be applied to the ceding company's subject premium income. Provided the premium base to be used is made perfectly clear in the treaty, it does not matter greatly whether the reinsurance premium rate is applied to the ceding company's written or earned, or gross or retained, premiums, though earned retained premium income theoretically provides the soundest base.

The higher the reinsurance layer, the lower its exposure. Therefore payback periods will be longer (and rates on line lower) for higher layers than bottom layers, and rates on line may range from, say, 25% of retained premium income at the lower end to 1% at the top end of catastrophe covers.

The simplicity of such methods has an obvious appeal to underwriters, but the results are not always so satisfactory for reasons considered below.

Underwriting and rating excess of loss reinsurance

The adverse underwriting experience suffered by insurers and reinsurers world-wide since the mid-1960s, including the occurrence of a number of major disasters, has increased the pressure for more 'scientific' underwriting and rating of property excess-of-loss reinsurances. The nature of the business and the need for administrative economy ensure that 'underwriting flair' and relatively simple procedures will always retain a place in underwriting, but the need for more detailed and more accurate information is now well recognized.

Working covers

Often reinsurers have been content to rate working covers on a crude burning cost, obtaining from the ceding company:

(1) details of losses for perhaps the last five years which would have fallen within the proposed treaty limits; and

(2) forecasts of future premium growth.

Now not only is a more detailed analysis of the figures usually required so that adjustments may be made for such factors as inflation, but also a reinsurer may seek additional information such as:

(1) An analysis of the company's past experience on both its gross and net retained accounts.

(2) Details of the gross account broken down by size of risk so that the 'risk profile' of the portfolio to be reinsured can be ascertained.

Table 10.1 shows such a breakdown for a company that limits its acceptances to a maximum sum insured of £100,000.[7]

If the company was negotiating a treaty on an 'any one risk' basis with a deductible of, say, £20,000, the figures in Table 10.1 reveal that only 74% of the ceding company's premium income relate to risks on which the reinsurer could incur any liability. Moreover, if the proposed treaty was for £40,000 in excess of £60,000, the reinsurer's liability would be restricted to less than a total loss in 1,500 cases commanding 30.0% of the premium income. It is quite conceivable that the risk profile of an account may change substantially though the total premium income hardly alters, and it may take some time for the change in the reinsurer's exposure to be reflected in his loss experience. The 'coded excesses' method of rating working covers automatically deals with such changes (Chapter 5).

(3) Other data particular to the account to be protected, notably details of the company's underwriting limits, retention limits and underlying reinsurances, perils insured, and sources and types of business included in the account.

(4) Data general to the area of operation of the account to be reinsured, including local underwriting practice (e.g. premium rate levels, whether cover is freely given for catastrophe-type perils, whether cover for certain perils is subject to compulsory deductibles, etc.).

Catastrophe covers

Similarly there is an increasing awareness of the need to obtain more information than just a ceding company's past experience, plus possibly loss data for comparable companies, in order to calculate payback figures for catastrophe treaties. When negotiating a new treaty a reinsurer may ask for:

7 A. Taylor, 'The property account: the truth, the whole truth and nothing but the truth', in *Papers presented at the Third International Reinsurance Seminar* (Reinsurance Offices' Association, 1977).

Table 10.1

Sum insured by range	Number of policies within range		Premium income relating to those policies		Total sum insured relating to those policies	
£		% of total	£	% of total	£	% of total
0 – 20,000	5,000	50	150,000	25.6	75,000,000	21.7
20,001 – 40,000	2,000	20	140,000	23.9	70,000,000	20.3
40,001 – 60,000	1,500	15	120,000	20.5	80,000,000	23.2
60,001 – 80,000	1,000	10	112,500	19.2	75,000,000	21.7
80,001 – 100,000	500	5	63,000	10.8	45,000,000	13.0
	10,000		585,500		345,000,000	

(1) Details of the ceding company's loss experience over a period extending possibly up to 25 years in order to smooth out the random fluctuations, and to identify any trends in relation to the amount of business written and changes in the company's basic underwriting policy and acceptance limits. The company may be asked to analyse its experience on both its gross and net accounts and identify the causes and locations of major losses.

(2) A forecast of future premium growth.

(3) Facts about the account to be protected. Besides the sort of information required for working covers, a prospective reinsured may be asked to supply:

(a) details of any inwards treaty reinsurances to be included in the portfolio; and

(b) the distribution of the net retained premium income by type of risk and geographical area; and its exposure to natural perils in agreed zones (e.g. the recognized earthquake zones of Japan).

(4) Data general to the area of operation of the account to be reinsured, including local loss experience from natural perils.

Taylor has suggested that reinsurers should cooperate in preparing standard questionnaires which could be used throughout the market to elicit the detailed information required by underwriters.[8] He presented his own ideas of what should be asked for in the specimen questionnaire reproduced in Appendix 10.2.

The demand for more information does presuppose that reinsurers possess the technical knowledge and skill to interpret it. Thus the underwriting of property reinsurances calls for a knowledge of both technology, seismology and other climatic sciences, and of the social sciences, i.e. economics, sociology and politics. Moreover premium

8 Ibid.

rating, like retention decisions, involves a probabilistic process, especially for catastrophe covers where natural disasters are (it is hoped) few and far between. The use of standard rates on line for calculating catastrophe premiums, whereby a uniform rate is applied depending on whether the cover is a first, second, third or higher layer, suffers from many shortcomings.[9] Given better information, the computer simulation techniques described in Chaper 9 could be used to arrive at more soundly based reinsurance premiums.[10]

Ceding companies may object that the production of so much detailed information is far too costly. An alternative view is that they need the same information themselves to measure their own exposures and so formulate an efficient reinsurance programme.

Given the number of variables and uncertainties involved, it is inevitable that there are differing ideas about retentions, the amount of reinsurance cover required, and the premiums to be charged. However, in an attempt to show how decisions may be reached, two practical case studies are included in the appendix to this chapter.

Exclusions and limitations

Apart from war risks, fire excess of loss treaties usually contain few exclusions.[11] The exact terms of the contract are a matter for negotiation in the light of the nature of the business transacted by the ceding company, but common exclusions from both working and catastrophe treaties are:

(1) War and civil war risks.
(2) Classes of business, such as hail, that are more appropriately reinsured separately.
(3) Any liability the ceding company may incur as a member of an atomic or nuclear energy risk pool.
(4) Excess of loss insurances and reinsurances.

Under *working covers* it is also market practice:

(1) To exclude liabilities accepted under all types of inwards reinsurance treaties.
(2) To place an 'event limit' on the reinsurer's liability for losses affecting two or more individual risks arising from any one event.

If a ceding company accepts reinsurance business it will need to arrange a separate retrocession treaty. American treaties also frequently exclude under the terms of a 'target risk' clause any liability accepted by the

9 Ibid.
10 D.G. Friedman, 'Insurance and the natural hazards'.
11 Advanced Study Group report of the Insurance Institute of London, p.34.

ceding company on a number of specified major risks. The object of the clause is to enable reinsurers to control their exposures on exceptionally large risks, the insurance of which is, by necessity, widely spread across the American market.

For *catastrophe covers* reinsurers usually insist on the ceding company participating to some degree in losses falling within the excess cover. The reinsurer's liability may be fixed as low as 90% of reinsured losses but figures of 95% or even 97½% are more usual. Furthermore such treaties are normally subject to restrictive reinstatement provisions (see below).

There are sound reasons for all of these exclusions and limitations. The reinsurer expects the ceding company to exercise the same degree of control over its potential liabilities as if it were not reinsured. Thus the reason for generally excluding excess-of-loss insurances and reinsurances, and for excluding all other inwards reinsurances under working covers, lies in the inability of the ceding company to exercise the same degree of control over its potential liability as is possible with normal direct insurances.

Quite frequently by mutual agreement separate reinsurances are arranged for particularly hazardous risks such as growing and standing crops, or for catastrophe perils such as earthquake, especially if the ceding company writes such business in high-risk areas (e.g. earthquake cover in Japan). By excluding such risks from the excess of loss reinsurance arranged for the main account, the ceding company avoids the possibility of a bad loss experience on the hazardous part of its account adversely affecting the terms for the rest of its business.

Reinstatement

Normally, apart from an event limit, no restriction is placed on the number of claims that may be made in any one year under working covers. Sometimes, however, when working covers are split into two layers, the upper layer may be restricted to two or three reinstatements subject to the payment of a *pro rata* additional premium.

It is now general practice for UK, European, American and other catastrophe treaties, whether effected with Lloyd's or in the company market, to be subject to restrictive reinstatement provisions. Most treaties are limited to only one full reinstatement of the cover, subject to the payment of an additional premium. Many ceding companies, however, would prefer to pay a commensurately higher initial premium in return for the right to claim one, or perhaps two, reinstatements during any one year without payment of further premium.

The method of calculation of the additional premium is negotiable, the normal options ranging between a premium:

(1) *pro rata* as to amount and period; and

(2) *pro rata* as to amount only.

So, for example, if three-quarters of the way through the year the reinsurer paid a loss of £150,000 under a treaty for £300,000 excess of £200,000, the additional premium required to reinstate the cover would be:

(1) $\quad \dfrac{150,000}{300,000} \times \dfrac{3}{12} = 0.125$ of the annual premium; or

(2) $\quad \dfrac{150,000}{300,000} = 0.5$ of the annual premium.

Thus whereas in both cases the size of the additional premium required is proportionate to the amount of the loss to be reinstated, under method (1) it also depends on the date of occurrence. Normally reinstatement of cover is automatic, so that if under method (2) the loss occurred towards the end of the treaty year the ceding company could not choose to take the risk of another loss occurring rather than pay the reinstatement premium for the sake of only a few days' protection.

Sometimes, as a compromise between equity and ease of calculation, it is agreed that any reinstatement premium shall be based on 50% of the annual rate, the assumption being that losses occur on average in the middle of the period. If past loss experience indicates that losses are highly seasonal, such an assumption may be unfair to one party.

The following specimen reinstatement clause provides for additional premiums to be calculated according to method (1).

(a) In the event of the whole or any portion of the liability hereunder being exhausted by loss the amount so exhausted shall be automatically reinstated from the time of occurrence of the loss provided that the liability of the Reinsurer shall never be more than the amounts specified in the Schedule in respect of each ultimate net loss and all ultimate net losses occurring during any 12-month period commencing on the date at which this agreement either takes effect or is renewed.

(b) Reinstatement shall take effect in consideration of additional premium calculated on the premium earned hereon for the 12-month period during which the loss occurred being *pro rata* as to the proportion of the total liability hereunder reinstated and the portion of the 12-month period of this agreement unexpired at the time of occurrence of the loss.

(c) If the loss payment is made prior to the adjustment of the premium the reinstatement premium shall be calculated provisionally on the annual deposit premium.

A series of losses which exhausted both the basic reinsurance cover and the one permitted reinstatement could place a ceding company in a difficult position. Not only would it need to seek further reinsurance protection at an unpropitious time, but also having already made two payments of its underlying retention any further large losses could prove financially embarrassing. For example, if a company with a net retained premium income of £10 million arranged catastrophe excess of loss cover of £800,000 excess of £200,000, two payments of its underlying retention would absorb 4% of its premium income. Such difficulties may be alleviated by arranging either:

(1) A second reinstatement cover, which in the event of the primary cover being exhausted by a series of losses would automatically provide new cover on the same terms as the primary cover, including provision for one reinstatement. Thus the ceding company would obtain full first-layer cover for four total losses of the layer though, as noted above, its resulting aggregate retained losses could be embarrassingly large; or

(2) A contingency excess of loss reinsurance which would provide some additional relief against the net retained losses for the third and fourth losses covered by the contingency reinsurance. For example, in the above case the reinsurer may also accept liability for, say, £150,000 excess of £50,000 in respect of the ceding company's net retained loss of £200,000.

Contingency covers are fairly uncommon and pose considerable rating problems.

Sometimes umbrella covers are arranged to cover the aggregate net retained losses in excess of a specified amount which a company may incur under two or more branches of insurance as the result of the occurrence of some event.

Facultative excess of loss reinsurances

There has been a growth in the number of individual risks reinsured facultatively on an excess of loss basis. Partly this has been due to the rapid growth in the number of captive insurance companies which generally wish to arrange their reinsurances on an excess of loss basis. Also other companies that employ working excess of loss treaties as their primary reinsurance cover find it advantageous to place their facultative reinsurances on an excess of loss basis too.

The other main occasions when this form of reinsurance is employed for fire accounts are:

(1) to facilitate the placing of very large risks; and
(2) as a protection against errors in calculating EMLs.

Such reinsurances have a certain attraction for reinsurers too. It gives them a greater control over the premium they can obtain for a given risk, so that a reinsurer can circumvent any apparent under-rating of the original risk. On the other hand, the reinsurer receives a smaller premium than under proportional facultative reinsurances though he may be accepting liability for a catastrophe exposure.

The normal approach to premium rating is for the reinsurer to consider his exposure relative to the total amount at risk. For example, if reinsurance cover is required for £500,000 excess of £500,000 for a risk with a total sum insured of £1,000,000 the reinsurer's exposure is 50% excess of 50%. Various tables have been produced based on probability distributions of losses by relative size of loss which thereby show the distribution of the gross premium for each percentage of the sum insured. It should be noted, however, that even if the probability distribution of losses is correctly estimated:

(1) Allowance needs to be made in the reinsurance premium for:
    (a) administration expenses not being proportional to the risk transferred; and
    (b) the higher variance of loss experience on excess-of-loss covers.
(2) The original gross premium may itself be inadequate.

Excess of loss ratio and stop loss reinsurances

Such reinsurances present so many undesirable features from the standpoint of reinsurers that there is no ready market for them as a substitute for other forms of reinsurance for normal fire business. At best they will be provided only as an additional and final protection after other forms of reinsurance.

However, stop loss reinsurance is considered a suitable form of primary reinsurance protection for certain specialized classes of business. The notable examples are hail on crops, and storm insurances because:

(1) There are problems of defining either individual risks or events.
(2) The cover required is seasonal.
(3) There is considerable fluctuation in underwriting results from year to year.

Stop loss reinsurance then provides a convenient way of providing the ceding company with a more stable experience.

Scope and limitations

When such cover is provided normally it is for the protection of the ceding company's net retained account after deduction of all other proportional and non-proportional reinsurances. Liabilities accepted under inwards reinsurance treaties are generally excluded.

The cover may be expressed in terms of the excess of either an agreed loss ratio or aggregate losses incurred during one year, which itself may be defined as an underwriting year or calender year. Invariably the reinsured is required to retain for its own account at least 5% of all losses falling within the cover provided, and an upper monetary as well as a loss-ratio limit is normally placed on the reinsurer's liability.

Underwriting and rating

Reinsurers usually require fairly simple information, consisting primarily of a detailed statement of the past experience of the portfolio to be reinsured, and of the expected business and premium income for the coming year.

Because the cover provided is a form of financial guarantee, reinsurers normally insist that the deductible carried by the ceding company is sufficiently high to ensure that it will incur an underwriting loss before the cover operates. The amount of the deductible required in any individual case therefore will depend upon the ceding company's acquisition and administration expense ratio.

Many stop loss treaties are written on some form of burning-cost or automatic rating basis which reflects their purpose of spreading the cost of a bad year over a number of good years. In such cases the rating adjustments are subject to minimum and maximum rates. When a flat-rate basis is appropriate then the payback method used for catastrophe excess of loss treaties is employed.

Appendix 10.1 Application of the hours clause to a catastrophe treaty, subject to only one full reinstatement

Assume an excess of loss reinsurance is arranged on an event basis for:
(1) £100,000 in excess of £100,000 any one event.
(2) £500,000 in excess of £200,000 any one event.
Two windstorms occur during the year and on each occasion the build-up of ultimate net losses is as follows:

Hours	Losses during period £	Hours	Cumulative losses £
0 – 24	80,000	0 – 24	80,000
25 – 48	130,000	0 – 48	210,000
49 – 72	120,000	0 – 72	330,000
73 – 96	30,000	0 – 96	360,000

Following the first storm the ceding company would be best advised to take two 48-hour periods commencing from the first damage, and the losses would be apportioned as follows:

	£
Reinsured's liability	200,000
Reinsurer's liability under first layer	150,000
Reinsurer's liability under second layer	10,000
	360,000

This settlement would leave only £50,000 cover remaining under the first layer.

If following the second windstorm the ceding company again took two 48-hour periods apportionment would be as shown in column (1). By selecting the period commencing 24 hours after the first damage it could increase its reinsurance recoveries as shown in column (2).

	(1) £	(2) £
Reinsured's liability	300,000	260,000
Reinsurer's liability under first layer	50,000	50,000
Reinsurer's liability under second layer	10,000	50,000
	360,000	360,000

Appendix 10.2 Catastrophe questionnaire: world-wide, excluding the USA [12]

A. Direct and facultative reinsurance portfolio

(1) Breakdown of property premium income by territory, split:
 (a) Dwellings including all special forms covering Household business (referred to herein as 'dwellings').
 (b) All other Property and consequential loss business (excluding C.A.R.).
 (c) C.A.R. (if to be protected hereunder).
(2) Maximum net retention to be protected:
 (a) Which of the following methods do you employ to fix your maximum net retentions:
  (i) Sum insured any one risk.
  (ii) EML as defined by the Reinsurance Offices' Association.
  (iii) PML, Amount subject, loss ratio or any other method.
 (b) Please advise how the method or methods you employ are applied to the underwriting of:
  (i) High-rise buildings.
  (ii) Major industrial complexes, e.g. petrochemical plants.
  (iii) Any one project in respect of C.A.R. business.
  (iv) Risks where perils other than fire (e.g. explosion, earthquake) are a potential cause of serious loss.
 (c) What are your present maximum net retentions under the method or methods used and indicate any alteration by comparison with recent years.
(3) Please give brief details of any reinsurance treaties, *pro rata* or excess, which will inure to the benefit of this protection, i.e. quota share/surplus or risk excess covers, and which have been taken into account in the answers to question 2*(c)*. If risk excess covers are effected, please state any catastrophe limitation which is imposed by them.
(4) In the event that you accept business of a type or on a form different from the normal tariff form with full average (coinsurance) condition or equivalent, give details of the type, volume, and net retention of each such other special class underwritten. Particularly could we have details of contracts or risks of either facultative or direct excess of loss or first loss insurance?
(5) *Earthquake*
 Please advise total earthquake insurance in force in the following territories. These totals should include the aggregate earthquake shock and fire following liability (where shock liability only reported please indicate accordingly) on fixed properties under whatever original policy form this peril is accepted.
 (a) Japan
  (i) By zone.
  (ii) In zones 5, 6 and 8 by prefecture.
 (b) Mexico
  (i) Mexico City—zones C, T and 2 separately.
  (ii) Acapulco—zones 3 and R separately.
  (iii) Rest of Mexico.

12 Taylor, 'The property account: the truth, the whole truth and nothing but the truth.'

(c) Puerto Rico
(d) Jamaica
(e) Israel
(f) South Africa
(g) New Zealand
(h) Philippines
(i) Australia—as per specific Australian Questionnaire.
(j) Any other territory in which you operate where there is a major earthquake potential, e.g. Central America, South America, the Mediterranean and Middle Eastern areas.

Is it contemplated that these figures will change substantially for the coming year. If so, by how much?

Please indicate whether (and, if so, how) policy forms and conditions on which earthquake is written differ from the local tariff (or equivalent) form of the territory.

(6) *Windstorm*
Please advise the following details of your writings in the territories listed below:
(a) Australia—as per specific Australian Questionnaire.
(b) Caribbean area

	Total insurance in force for dwellings	Total property P.I. (ex. dwellings) or total insurance in force for property (ex. dwellings)
(i) Puerto Rico		
(ii) Jamaica		
(iii) The Bahamas		
(iv) Any other island or group of islands where aggregate liabilities exceed proposed deductible.		

(c) Philippines

(7) *Flood*
(a) Please give details of your underwriting policy regarding the granting of flood coverage in respect of:
(i) Dwellings.
(ii) All other business.
(b) Please identify the areas which you consider represent the major flood hazard to your catastrophe programme. For those areas please advise how you record your flood liabilities and control your aggregate accumulations, advising current aggregate liabilities.
(c) If C.A.R. business is to be protected hereunder, please comment specifically on how you control accumulations under this portfolio.

(8) *Loss Record.* Please give details of major past losses, both 'actual' and 'as if', based on your proposed reinsurance programme for the coming year.

B. Inwards treaty portfolio
(Only to be answered if this business is to be protected hereunder.)

(1) Please advise the breakdown of your premium income by territory, split:
(a) Reciprocal writings.

(b) Non-reciprocal writings.

(2) In the territories listed in A5 and A6 please identify the number of treaties and the applicable premium income, divided as follows:

	Solely in respect of dwellings business		*In respect of any other business*	
	No.	*P.I.*	*No.*	*P.I.*

(a) Quota Share

(b) All other treaties

Please state aggregate liabilities by catastrophe peril per territory/zone where known.

*If any treaties are not 'solely' in respect of dwellings but contain a substantial volume of such business please allocate the income to each section as accurately as possible.

(3) Please confirm that no *pro rata* treaties are accepted that comprise retrocessions of excess of loss reinsurance business or are mixed portfolios where excess of loss reinsurance business might be included.

(4) Do you consider that your inward treaty portfolio permits any substantial cession to you of business written on forms other than the normal tariff form with full average clause?

(5) Please give details of actual losses sustained from this portfolio in respect of:

(a) those losses listed in section A8 above.

(b) any other major losses to this portfolio.

If there has been any alteration in your acceptance and/or retention programme, please estimate 'as if' loss figure.

Appendix 10.3 Arranging a fire working excess of loss treaty

The following information is supplied by the ABC Insurance Company Limited.

Annual gross fire premium income

		£
Current year t		2,000,000
	year $t-1$	1,818,000
	year $t-2$	1,653,000
	year $t-3$	1,503,000
	year $t-4$	1,366,000
Total 5 years		8,340,000

Existing reinsurance arrangements. The company's table of retentions provides for six classes of risk with retention limits ranging from £2,000 to £20,000.
The existing surplus treaty arrangements are as follows:

First surplus	4 lines
Second surplus	5 lines

This gives the company a *maximum* automatic capacity of 10 × £20,000 = £200,000 sum insured any one risk.

Analysis of portfolio. An analysis of the current portfolio is shown in table 10.2, the portfolio being broken down into groups according to the proportion reinsured, and not according to retention limits.

Table 10.2

Group	Number of policies	Gross premium	Percentage of business reinsured
		£'000	%
1	4,000	150	Nil
2	3,000	250	50.0
3	2,000	300	66.7
4	1,000	300	75.0
5	750	300	80.0
6	500	250	83.3
7	400	200	85.7
8	300	100	87.5
9	200	100	88.9
10	100	50	90.0
	12,250	2,000	

Past claims. Table 10.3 shows details of the claims in the previous five years that have exceeded £20,000 gross.

Table 10.3

Year	Claim No.	Amount of gross claim £	Gross sum insured under policy £	Net retained share of company %
t	A	20,000	50,000	40
t	B	50,000	80,000	20
$t-1$	C	30,000	60,000	15
$t-1$	D	80,000	200,000	10
$t-2$	E	40,000	100,000	15
$t-3$	F	150,000	200,000	10
$t-3$	G	80,000	100,000	20
$t-4$	H	70,000	150,000	10
$t-4$	I	20,000	20,000	100

Notes. The percentage of the gross premium income currently retained by the company is approximately 30%, as shown in Table 10.4.

Table 10.4

Group	Gross premiums £'000	Percentage retained %	Net retained premiums £'000
1	150	100	150
2	250	50	125
3	300	33.3	100
4	300	25	75
5	300	20	60
6	250	16.7	42
7	200	14.3	29
8	100	12.5	12
9	100	11.1	11
10	50	10	5
	2,000		609 = 30.45%

If the company increased all retentions five-fold to produce a minimum limit of £10,000 to a maximum of £100,000 it would fully retain all of the business in groups 1 – 5, and increase the proportions retained in the remaining groups as shown in Table 10.5.

Table 10.5 Revised retentions

Group	Gross premiums £'000	Percentage retained %	Net retained premiums £'000
1	150	100	150
2	250	100	250
3	300	100	300
4	300	100	300
5	300	100	300
6	250	83.3	208
7	200	71.5	143
8	100	62.5	62
9	100	55.5	56
10	50	50	25
	2,000		1,794 = 89.7%

If such a five-fold increase in retentions had been applied five years ago the distribution of gross claims over £20,000 would have been as shown in Table 10.6.

Table 10.6

Year	Claim No.	Net retained share %	Amount £	Surplus share %	Amount £
t	A	100	20,000	Nil	Nil
t	B	100	50,000	Nil	Nil
t − 1	C	75	22,500	25	7,500
t − 1	D	50	40,000	50	40,000
t − 2	E	75	30,000	25	10,000
t − 3	F	50	75,000	50	75,000
t − 3	G	100	80,000	Nil	Nil
t − 4	H	50	35,000	50	35,000
t − 4	I	100	20,000	Nil	Nil

It may be assumed that inflation was insignificant over the five years so that there is no need to adjust premiums and losses to place them on a common price level.

Changeover to working excess of loss reinsurance

The working excess of loss cover. If the company increased its retentions five-fold, and provided it adhered to the same acceptance limits as before then it could reduce its surplus cover to one line but it would be exposed to retained losses ranging up to £100,000. Therefore in order to protect itself against the possibility of individual retained losses in excess of £20,000 it could arrange working excess of loss covers for:

First layer	£30,000 excess of £20,000
Second layer	£50,000 excess of £50,000

(If the company fixes its retentions on the basis of EMLs it may wish to arrange a higher limit in order to take care of any increase in its retained losses due to an underestimation of an EML.)

So, for example, if it accepted an insurance for £120,000 on a risk with a retention limit of £60,000, its reinsurance arrangements would be:

Retention	£ 60,000	with losses in excess of £20,000 protected by excess of loss reinsurance
Surplus 1 line	60,000	
	£120,000	

Calculation of the excess of loss premiums

The reinsurer may choose to calculate the premium on the basis of his exposure as revealed by Table 10.5 (see Chapters 5 and 10 for the method). However, it will be assumed that he prefers to base premiums on the five years' burning cost using the information in Table 10.6, i.e.:

	Losses	
Year	First layer £	Second layer £
t	30,000	—
t − 1	22,500	—
t − 2	10,000	—
t − 3	60,000	55,000
t − 4	15,000	—
	137,500	55,000

First layer. If it is assumed that in each of the past five years the company's gross net premium income would have been approximately 89.7% of its gross premium income (see Table 10.5),its burning costs would have been as shown in Table 10.7.

Table 10.7

Year	Losses £	Gross net premium income £	Pure burning cost %
t	30,000	1,794,000	1.672
t − 1	22,500	1,630,746	1.380
t − 2	10,000	1,482,741	0.674
t − 3	60,000	1,348,191	4.450
t − 4	15,000	1,225,302	1.224
	137,500	7,480,980	1.838

Unweighted mean = 1.880
Standard deviation = 1.482

In deciding upon the size of the loading factor to be applied to the pure burning cost rate of 1.838% the reinsurer would need to consider the following factors:

(1) The estimated cost of administering the treaty, and the size of contribution needed towards providing a return on capital employed.
(2) The cash flow generated by the treaty, i.e. when premiums will be received and claims are likely to be paid.
(3) The rate of interest that can be earned on the treaty funds.
(4) The loading required to provide for claims fluctuations.
(5) The adjustment limits to be applied to the loaded burning cost rate.
(6) The size of the reinsurer's existing portfolio of such contracts.
(7) The terms likely to be quoted by competitors.

As shown above, annual burning costs have fluctuated quite widely. The ABC Company may rightly point out that the fluctuations occur around both sides of the mean, and that the reinsurer is writing a portfolio of business so that in any one year adverse experience on one treaty may be balanced by good experience on another. Nevertheless the adverse fluctuation in year $t-3$ is twice as large as that of the best year $t-2$, so some additional loading is warranted.

If the reinsurer estimated that, after allowing for items (2) and (3) above he would need £3,500 to cover his administration and capital-servicing costs, a loading of the pure burning cost rate of 1.838% by a factor of 100/91 would produce the required sum on the current gross net premium income.

Ideas about the size of contingency loading required to cover claims fluctuations may differ considerably, but essentially three factors need to be taken into account:

(1) The degree of fluctuation in the claims experience.
(2) Whether a fixed or variable premium rate is to be charged.
(3) The size of the reinsurer's portfolio of such business measured in terms of the number of fairly similar treaties he has on his books.

A case can be made for charging a loading taken as a proportion of the standard deviation of the pure burning costs. For a reinsurer with a medium to large-sized portfolio of identical business it may be considered appropriate to fix the contingency loading within the range of one-third down to perhaps as low as one-tenth of the standard deviation. So the reinsurer may be thinking in terms of a final loading factor of up to, say, 100/75 calculated as follows:

$$\text{pure burning cost rate} = 1.838\% \text{ of gross net premium income}$$

Therefore: pure premium based on current year

=	£2,000,000 × 1.838%	=	£36,760
plus loading for administration, etc.			£ 3,500
plus contingency loading (⅓ of standard deviation			
=	⅓ × 1.482% × £2,000,000)	=	£ 9,880
			£50,140

$$1 \div \frac{50,140}{36,760} \qquad = \qquad 0.733$$

Therefore, loading factor $\qquad = \qquad \dfrac{100}{73.3}$

If the premium rate is to be subject to annual adjustment in accordance with burning costs, then the larger the spread between the agreed minimum and maximum premium rates, the smaller need be the contingency loading.

Finally the reinsurer must compare what he regards as the appropriate premium rate and terms with current market terms for that class of business. If most other reinsurers could be expected to charge less then he must decide whether to write the business at a possibly inadequate premium or quote what he regards as adequate and risk losing the business.

Second layer. The pure burning cost rate based on five years' experience would be:

$$\frac{55,000}{7,480,980} \times 100 = 0.735\%$$

Given that the reinsurer would have been involved in only one out of the five years, despite what was said earlier the burning cost method is not suitable for rating this layer. The reinsurer would need to try to obtain some measures of his potential exposure, such as:
(1) the number of policies under which the ABC Company could incur an ultimate net loss of between £50,000 and £100,000; and
(2) the proportion of the gross net premium income attributable thereto.
Ideally the data should be broken down into size bands. So, for example, the ABC Company may be able to produce the information given in Table 10.8.

Table 10.8

Maximum ultimate net loss £	Number of policies	Gross net premium income attributable to these policies £
50,001 – 60,000	400	88,000
60,001 – 70,000	450	111,150
70,001 – 80,000	350	90,000
80,001 – 90,000	220	76,500
90,001 – 100,000	60	17,100
	1,510	382,750

Even that amount of information, however, would not be sufficient to permit a purely statistical approach to fixing a premium rate. Consequently unless far more information could be made available (and in practice usually it cannot be produced), the underwriter would be forced to rely largely on his own judgment as to an appropriate premium. He would pay regard to the rates he charges for similar portfolios of business, rates currently being quoted in the market, and finally seek to arrive at a premium rate which would not be inconsistent with the rate quoted for the underlying layer.

Appendix 10.4　A catastrophe excess of loss treaty in the fire department

The following background information is provided regarding the XYZ Insurance Company Limited which is seeking a catastrophe excess of loss reinsurance to cover all of the business written by its fire department.

Portfolio to be protected. Net retained share of direct insurances and facultative reinsurances written in the fire department covering commercial, industrial and simple risks.

Perils covered. Fire, explosion, lightning, cyclone, earthquake, flood.

Geographical scope. Tranzonia only.

Gross net retained premium income for previous five years.

Year	Fr000's
t	15,000
$t-1$	12,500
$t-2$	11,000
$t-3$	10,000
$t-4$	850

Note: Fr10 = £1.

Company's net retention. For industrial and commercial risks the company retains a maximum of Fr500,000 sum insured and a minimum of Fr100,000 any one risk. Amounts above retention are ceded to a surplus treaty.

For simple risks (dwelling risks) the company has a 50% quota share reinsurance and the maximum exposure any one risk (building and contents combined) for its 50% net retention is Fr300,000.

Past losses. During the previous 25 years the net losses in excess of Fr500,000 suffered by the company are as shown in Table 10.9.

Table 10.9

Year	Region	Occurrence	Net loss Fr	As percentage of local values at risk
3	C	Earthquake	700,000	1.0
16	A	Bush Fires	1,600,000	2.6
20	B	Cyclone	1,500,000	1.4
23	B	Floods	900,000	9.9
24	E	Cyclone	10,500,000	19.5

Note: The cyclone in year 24 was far more severe than any other recorded in the area over the last 100 years.

376

Geographical distribution of business and exposures. The company's premium income is spread as follows; there have been no significant changes in the proportions over the years.

Region	Percentage
A	40
B	20
C	15
D	15
E	10
	100

The company's net aggregate exposures in respect of Cyclone are as shown in Table 10.10.

Table 10.10

Area	Dwellings	Commercial and industrial	Total
	Fr'000	Fr'000	Fr'000
Region B			
Area 1	110,000	50,500	160,500
Area 2	50,500	11,800	62,300
Area 3	6,000	4,000	10,000
Area 4	6,000	6,000	12,000
	172,500	72,300	244,800
Region E			
Area 1	3,000	4,000	7,000
Area 2	10,000	5,000	15,000
Area 3	2,000	1,500	3,500
Area 4	17,500	10,000	27,500
Area 5	500	2,000	2,500
	33,000	22,500	55,500

The company's net aggregate exposures in respect of Earthquake are as follows:

Area	Dwellings Fr'000	Commercial and industrial Fr'000	Total Fr'000
Region A, Area 1	180,000	120,000	300,000
Region C, Area 1	200,000	20,000	220,000
Region D, Area 2	100,000	45,000	145,000

The only area of important exposure in respect of flood is in Area 1 of Region B where the company estimate that their total net retained exposure would not exceed Fr10,000,000 of which not more than 50% is situated in flood-prone areas.

Premium income and capital. The company's premium income (net of all reinsurances ceded) from all non-life insurance business in year *t* is Fr37 million. Its capital and free reserves are Fr12.8 million and it has a separate Extreme Natural Peril Reserve of Fr3 million.

The suggested terms

The company's retention limit any one event. Normally reinsurers are unwilling to accept a deductible of less than 10% of a company's net retained premium income. For the ceding company there is a trade-off between the amount of reinsurance protection it should buy and the cost thereof. Reinsurers would also ensure that the deductible in respect of any one event would be significantly greater than the retention per risk. They would also insist, in all but the smallest cases, on a self-participation of 2½% or 5% in each layer, thus giving the company a further involvement in catastrophe losses.

In this case, given XYZ's retained premium income, the level of net retentions and the past loss experience, the deductible would need to be not less than Fr1,500,000 and possibly up to Fr2,500,000 or a little more. The company should consider the deductible under the catastrophe programme as its ultimate retention and this should bear a reasonably modest relationship to the size of the company's free reserves, especially in a country subject to frequent natural disasters.

The treaty cover. Protection must be balanced against cost, and the following factors need to be considered.

Given its solvency requirements and current capital and reserves (including the Extreme Natural Peril Reserve), the XYZ Company could not afford to withstand a loss (including the deductible) larger than Fr5.5 million.

If the company accepted a deductible of Fr1.5 million, an excess of loss cover of Fr30 million excess of Fr1.5 million would provide the levels of protection against the company's total exposures shown in Table 10.11.

Table 10.11

	Deductible	Excess of loss cover
	%	%
Cyclone		
Region B, Area 1 (target area)	0.9	18.7
Region B, whole region	0.6	12.3
Region E, Area 4 (target area)	5.5	109.1
Region E, whole region	2.7	54.1
Earthquake		
Region A - Area 1	0.5	10.0
Region C - Area 1	0.7	13.6
Region D - Area 2	1.0	20.7
Flood		
Region B - Area 1	15.0	300.0

Excess of loss cover of Fr30 million would be equal to 200% of the company's gross net premium income in year t. A deductible of Fr1.5 million would leave the company with 'free' reserves of Fr4 million to provide additional protection if a loss should exhaust the excess of loss cover.

The company's own loss experience, a more detailed analysis of its exposures, and weather/earthquake records indicate that an excess of loss cover of Fr30 million would provide an ample margin over EMLs even for cyclone damage in Region E. Also one automatic reinstatement (at an additional premium) should take care of the risk of two events occurring in any one year. If two events were to occur the XYZ Company would, however, have to carry two deductibles, so it may be reluctant to increase the size of the deductible.

Therefore it is suggested that catastrophe excess of loss cover is arranged for Fr30 million in excess of Fr1.5 million any one event.

Arranging the cover

Usually catastrophe covers are arranged in layers in order to mobilize market capacity and reduce premium cost. In this case the following layering would be appropriate for the cover sought:

First layer	Fr5,000,000 excess of Fr1,500,000
Second layer	Fr10,000,000 excess of Fr6,500,000
Third layer	Fr15,000,000 excess of Fr16,500,000

Apart from the advantages of placing different layers in the most suitable markets a further reason for layering is the reduced impact of reinstatement premiums for losses only involving a small part of the cover provided.

The cost of reinsurance

Reinsurers will relate reinsurance premiums to the ceding company's net retailed premium income and for such catastrophe covers would fix rates on pay-back assumptions based on past experience (both of the company and of the areas concerned), and of estimates of future exposures.

If the XYZ Company had affected excess of loss cover over the past 25 years and had adjusted the deductible and the reinsurance limits to maintain the same levels of protection as shown above, only the ultimate net losses in years 3, 20 and 24 would have involved the first layer of the excess of loss cover, and the second layer would have incurred a liability only in respect of the cyclone loss in year 24. There are, however, other factors to be considered which are not revealed by the information given above. For example:

(1) Far more information should be sought regarding past occurrences of the different perils. For earthquakes the underwriter needs to know dates of occurrences, their epicentres, depth, magnitude and distance from given areas: given such information it is possible to convert earthquakes measured on the Richter scale into Modified Mercalli Intensities. Likewise for hurricanes information is needed about wind intensities, direction and duration. In reality records in many parts of the world do not extend over sufficiently long periods to make possible reliable statistical evaluation of probabilities of occurrence, especially for occurrences of low or medium severity.

(2) Topographical data: areas need to be zoned according to degree of exposure, which necessitates identifying subsoils, heights above sea-level, water courses, etc. Then the insured portfolio can be broken down into zones.

(3) Building codes: have there been any changes in building codes since past occurrences? What proportion of the property insured conforms to the newer codes? Coupled with seismological records converted into Modified Mercalli Intensities, such information would enable the underwriter to estimate degrees of destruction for earthquakes of given intensities.

(4) Insurance conditions: have there been any changes in the conditions applying to the insurance of the various perils, e.g. the imposition of compulsory excesses?

It is on the strength of such information that the reinsurer should attempt to arrive at his pay-back assumptions, and not just on the strength of the ceding company's past experience.

11
Accident reinsurance

REINSURANCE

382

11
Accident reinsurance

The term accident insurance (known in North America as casualty business) embraces all types of insurance not conventionally handled by fire, marine and aviation, or life departments. Thus it includes a heterogeneous collection of risks such as theft, liability, personal accident, fidelity guarantee, motor, engineering, credit, livestock, and various contingency insurances. Given such diversity in the nature of the risks involved, together with the wide range of size and experience of companies writing such insurances throughout the world, it is impossible to lay down any hard rules regarding reinsurance practice in relation to accident business. A further complicating factor is that frequently property (e.g. theft) insurances are included in fire reinsurance treaties (see Chapter 10). Therefore the following comments should be interpreted as only a broad indication of practice in this field.

Facultative reinsurance

The treaty method of handling accident reinsurances is now so widely used that normally the only risks placed facultatively are those that:
(1) are specifically excluded from the treaty arrangements, such as jewellers, furriers and such like under a theft reinsurance; or
(2) could upset the balance of a treaty so that the ceding company wishes to reinsure them separately; or
(3) are so large as to exceed the capacity of the treaty; or
(4) are of a type not normally written by the ceding company (e.g. contingency insurances) and which, therefore, are outside the scope of its treaty arrangements.
Many reinsurers also prefer to deal with contractors' all risks business on a facultative basis. The insurances are long-term and, more important, they need to be underwritten individually by both the ceding company and the reinsurer because of the very complex nature of the risks involved.

Facultative cover for individual risks is arranged on both a proportional basis, and as excess of loss reinsurance. There is nothing special about the arrangements for the placing of accident facultative reinsurances, and for the handling of claims, accounting, etc., so that the reader can be referred back to Chapter 6 for a general discussion of the various procedures.

Treaty reinsurances

The reinsurance market

All sections of the London market participate in the underwriting of accident treaties—i.e. professional reinsurers, Lloyd's and the direct companies—and frequently representatives of all three groups may take a share of a large treaty. Although there are exceptions, the writing of excess of loss business is largely confined to the professional reinsurers and Lloyd's, the reinsurance departments of the direct companies tending to limit their acceptances to proportional reinsurances. A similar situation exists in other countries too. There is little demand for reciprocity by ceding companies, mainly because of the more heterogeneous nature of the business included in accident treaties and the greater instability of underwriting results.

Type of treaty

There are no rigid rules regarding the type of treaty reinsurance that is best for the protection of accident business. Various factors need to be considered:

(1) The classes of insurance involved. Some classes lend themselves more readily to a particular type of reinsurance than others; for example, surplus reinsurance cannot be used when the reinsurer's liability is open-ended, such as under various forms of liability insurance.
(2) The ceding company's:
    (a) experience of the class(es) of business to be reinsured.
    (b) size of account.
    (c) retention limits relative to the amounts it normally insures.

Factors 2*(b)* and *(c)* together with the classes of insurance concerned, have an important bearing on the reinsurance premium income and stability of claims experience that a reinsurer can expect from particular types of treaty, and so upon his willingness to provide such cover.

The scope and administration of treaties

Over the last 20 or so years the emphasis that has been placed on minimizing administrative costs has operated against the interests of accident reinsurers in many ways. Although when first offered a new treaty reinsurers now make far more extensive enquiries about the nature and composition of the direct insurer's portfolio, generally they know less about the details of the risks ceded than in the past. Apart from the cases cited on pages 387 and 390, only very rarely are bordereaux supplied for proportional reinsurances. Also, as noted in Chapter 7, it is now common practice for several classes of accident business to be included in the same treaty and for the reinsurer to be supplied with only the barest information to monitor the results of each class.

All types of treaty are normally arranged for an unlimited period but with provision for cancellation by either party. Reinsurers review the performance of accident treaties annually and, if necessary, negotiate fresh terms.

The general provisions regarding the commencement, scope, claims administration, accounting, termination, etc., of different types of treaty have been discussed already in Chapters 7 and 8, so need not be repeated here.

Quota share treaties

Usage

Apart from those classes of accident insurance for which quota share is the most suitable form of reinsurance (notably contract guarantee), the use of quota share treaties for the protection of accident accounts tends to be confined to three situations:

(1) For new companies, when a quota share treaty provides the reinsured with additional underwriting capacity while enabling the reinsurer to participate in all of the business written.

(2) When a company is writing a very small account for which some reinsurance protection may be required (e.g. to reduce a company's exposure to large accumulations of liability under travel insurances) but the volume of business would be too small to support either a surplus or an excess of loss treaty.

(3) For some specialist types of business, notably credit insurance written on a 'whole-turnover' basis (see page 389).

However, even in situations (1) and (2) it is common market practice when dealing with the conventional classes of accident business (i.e.

theft, personal accident, fidelity guarantee and livestock) for reinsurers to provide ceding companies with a mixed quota and gross line surplus treaty (see page 388).

Over recent years there has been a perceptible change of attitude by reinsurers towards quota share covers for new motor insurers. Far too often in the 1960s quota share treaties were used to enable new companies to expand rapidly and write a disproportionate volume of business relative to their own capital and free reserves, or to obtain a profit with very little risk. Therefore there is now a resistance to providing such facilities unless the company is prepared to retain a substantial share for its own account.

Whenever a ceding company is exposed to the risk that it may incur either a single net retained loss, or an unknown accumulation of such losses, beyond its own capacity, an excess of loss cover may be arranged to supplement the protection provided by a quota share treaty. If desired by the quota share reinsurer the excess of loss reinsurance may be arranged for the common account to protect his interest too.

Scope

A quota share treaty may be effected to cover all classes of accident insurance business, other than motor and liability insurances for which it is market practice to make separate arrangements. There is a strong case too for excluding credit insurance and surety bonds from a general accident treaty. Credit insurance in particular is largely confined to one or two specialist insurers in each country: if a general insurer does write either credit or surety business it is very difficult to decline unsatisfactory risks offered by policyholders who provide an important volume of other insurances, so that it is better for both ceding companies and reinsurers that such risks should be reinsured separately.

Considerable care is necessary in the drafting of an accident treaty to avoid any ground for dispute regarding the cover provided. It is preferable to list both the classes of insurance included and the types of risks specially excluded from the scope of those classes: likewise the geographical scope of the treaty needs to be specified. The practice of defining the scope by the use of such words as 'all risks written by the accident department other than...' followed by a list of the exclusions has now gone out of fashion because with the development of new types of insurance and the absence of bordereaux a reinsurer could unwittingly find himself accepting liabilities never envisaged when the treaty was arranged. Thus by clearly listing exactly what is covered by the treaty the reinsurer can restore some of the control which was lost with the abandonment of bordereaux.

386

Ceding company's retention

To ensure that a quota share treaty does not become merely a form of financing arrangement and that the ceding company will exercise underwriting discipline, it is normal market practice to require the reinsured to retain for its own account a reasonable proportion of the business, the percentage varying according to the class of business involved and individual circumstances.

Limits and exclusions

At inception the reinsurer will require detailed information regarding the ceding company's underwriting policy, including its proposed acceptance limits, its policy towards the acceptance of hazardous classes of risk, and whether inwards facultative reinsurances are to be included in the scope of the treaty. For example, jewellers, furriers, banks, tobacco and spirit warehouses are obvious target theft risks, while motor racing, motor coaches, taxis, private hire and self-drive hire fleets are regarded as unattractive motor business. Having established the character of the ceding company's business, the reinsurer will protect himself from any radical change in underwriting policy during the currency of the treaty by:
(1) imposing maximum limits on the amounts that the reinsured may cede; and
(2) excluding from the scope of the treaty certain types of risk. A specimen list of exclusions that may be applied to treaties covering personal accident, employers' liability and public liability insurances are included in Appendix 11.1. If a ceding company regularly writes any of the normally excluded risks the manner in which the reinsurance is to be handled will be a matter for negotiation.

Once the treaty terms have been agreed the ceding company will need to arrange facultative reinsurance if it wishes to accept any risk which exceeds the treaty limits or is an excluded risk. When two or more classes of insurance are included in the same treaty different limits may be applied to each class.

Administration

The administration and terms of accident quota share treaties closely follow the general lines discussed in Chapters 5 and 7. Therefore it is sufficient to note here that:
(1) Premium and claims bordereaux are now normally only supplied for
 (a) large risks and *(b)* claims on those large risks.

(2) Reinsurance commission may be arranged on either a sliding-scale basis, or a flat rate. In the latter case often a profit commission is paid using one of the methods of calculation discussed in Chapter 3.

(3) Usually premiums and claims are settled in quarterly accounts, though a cash loss clause may be included in a treaty to provide for the immediate settlement of losses in excess of an agreed figure.

(4) Provision may be made for the ceding company to retain a proportion of the reinsurance premiums as an unearned premium reserve, though reinsurers may resist requests for deposits unless required by law. Normally interest is payable by the ceding company on the reserve if the deposit is in cash.

Combined quota share and surplus treaties

When because of the smallness of a company's account it is necessary to arrange a quota-share treaty, problems may arise if the ceding company expects to write some large risks fairly regularly. As explained in Chapter 5, in such circumstances the best way in which the company may obtain the required protection without having either to have recourse to facultative reinsurance or to cede an unnecessarily large proportion of its gross premium income to a reinsurer, may be to effect a combined quota-share and surplus treaty. Such treaties are fairly common for the reinsurance by new companies of standard accident risks such as theft, fidelity guarantee and livestock.

Surplus reinsurance treaties

Surplus treaties are arranged by all types and sizes of direct insurers for the protection of their accident accounts, though the surplus method of reinsurance is of limited application to accident business. Basically its usage is confined to those classes of insurance where the maximum liability of the ceding company is known: as stated above, it cannot be employed for liability insurances which are not subject to a limit of liability, such as UK motor and employers' liability insurances.

The classes of insurance normally included in surplus treaties consist of fidelity guarantee, livestock, personal accident and theft risks. Contractors' All Risks insurances are rarely included: normally surplus reinsurance facilities are restricted to companies that have a proven experience of writing such business and are subject to underwriting limits which would require very large risks to be reinsured facultatively.

Exceptionally surplus reinsurance is used for the accidental damage section of motor and engineering insurances and very rarely liability insurances are so reinsured, the retention and treaty limits then being fixed in terms of limits of indemnity.

The use of surplus reinsurance for the protection of credit insurance accounts has declined somewhat over recent years because of the development of whole-turnover policies in place of specific-account policies covering a single contract or a series of transactions with one or more named buyers.[1] Under the whole-turnover policy all of the insured's business is covered up to a discretionary credit limit, so that the insurance may embrace a large number of separate accounts for widely differing sums. As policyholders do not supply the insurer with details of individual values at risk it is not feasible to reinsure such business on a surplus basis which therefore is restricted in its application to specific-account policies. Consequently combinations of quota share treaties plus excess of loss reinsurance covering the company's net retention are now more highly favoured than surplus reinsurance for the protection of credit insurance accounts.

Either quota share or surplus reinsurance may be employed for surety and bonding business.

Method of operation

An accident surplus treaty operates in the manner described in Chapters 5 and 7. The ceding company will decide on its maximum retention limits for the different types of risk within each class of insurance transacted and, subject to the treaty limits, cede to the reinsurer(s) any sum accepted in excess of its own retention. When the treaty covers more than one class of insurance, the ceding company may fix different retentions for each class. Frequently schedules of retention limits are included in treaties, and it is general practice to insert a maximum limit.

The treaty will provide the ceding company with several lines of reinsurance cover, with a number of reinsurers each taking an agreed share. As noted earlier in Chapter 5 it would be unusual for an accident surplus treaty to be arranged for more than 20 lines, and a maximum figure of 9 to 14 would be more usual.

If the ceding company wishes to accept a risk for an amount in excess of its gross acceptance limits (i.e. its own retention plus the maximum number of lines of reinsurance), additional facultative reinsurance will be required. Accident treaties normally also permit a ceding company to arrange facultative cover in front of the treaty if considered advisable by the company.

Sometimes accident surplus reinsurances for some classes of insurance, notably contractors' all risks, engineering and theft

---

1 For fuller details see P.A. Dawson and Martin Roberts, 'Credit Insurance', in *Handbook of Insurance*, ed. R.L. Carter.

insurances, are arranged on an estimated maximum loss (EML) or maximum probable loss (MPL) basis, the sharing of a risk between ceding company and reinsurer then being based on the estimated maximum loss instead of the sum insured. For example, a food warehouse may contain stocks valued at £500,000, but the direct insurer may conclude that it would be impossible to lose more than, say, £50,000 in any one raid. Therefore, if the property is insured for its full value, instead of the insurer relating its normal retention of, say, £20,000 to the sum insured it would apply it to the EML of £50,000, so retaining 40% of the risk and reinsuring the balance of 60%. If the original insurance is itself written on a first-loss basis the retention is applied to the sum insured.

Scope and administration of surplus treaties

Like quota share treaties, the scope of the treaty in terms of class(es) of insurance included, any specially excluded risks, and geographical limits, needs to be defined carefully. Market practice regarding the commencement of accident treaties, inspection of records, claims procedures, calculation of premiums, accounting, termination, arbitration, etc., is usually in accord with the description given in Chapter 7. Normally bordereaux are required only for:
(1) Large risks (which the reinsurer may wish to retrocede).
(2) Risks accepted by way of coinsurance or reinsurance, when bordereau details are necessary to enable the reinsurer to control his own accumulations.
(3) From new companies.

Reinsurance commission is normally payable either according to a sliding scale, or on a flat percentage basis plus profit commission. The rates allowed usually are marginally lower than for comparable quota share treaties.

Excess of loss reinsurance

This form of cover, which was developed originally for the protection of liability insurance accounts, is now becoming the most widely used method of reinsuring accident accounts because of its ease of operation and low administrative costs. It is however wholly unsuitable for certain classes of insurance, and proportional reinsurances, rather than working excess of loss treaties, still remain preferable for the primary protection of some other classes. Space precludes a detailed consideration of each of the many types of insurance handled by accident departments but by looking at the characteristics of the major classes it should be possible to derive some general principles regarding the applicability of excess of loss reinsurance.

All risks, burglary and theft (from premises) insurance

This class of business is akin to fire and allied property insurances for which proportional reinsurances (notably surplus) provide a satisfactory method of reinsurance. Normally there is little risk of accumulations, though bank raids including attacks on safe-deposit boxes, demonstrate that huge losses can occur.

When excess of loss cover is arranged for such business it is normally as part of a multi-class treaty.

Money and goods in transit

Theft is again the major peril but both of these classes of insurance are exposed to the risk of accumulations which, often, neither the original insured nor insurer can control. In cases where original insureds employ security firms to collect and/or deliver cash there is the ever present risk of money belonging to several firms insured with the same insurance company being loaded on board the same vehicle. Likewise goods belonging to several insureds may be collected and housed in the same warehouse, garage or lorry park awaiting delivery next day. There is a similar risk of accumulations in public warehouses, etc., in connection with transit policies extended to cover a period after delivery into store. Even when individual consignments are reinsured on a surplus basis, catastrophe excess of loss cover is required to provide protection against the accumulation risk.

When policyholders require cover providing high limits for individual consignments the insurer may arrange surplus reinsurance for sums in excess of his own retention limit but protection will still be required in the form of excess of loss reinsurance against the accumulation risk. Arguably a combination of working and catastrophe excess of loss treaties is the best way of dealing with transit insurances because even on policies with high limits many consignments may be well below the ceding company's retention.

Contingency insurances

Most of these insurances, which undertake to indemnify the original insurers against the risk of loss arising from such causes as the breach of restrictive covenants, the reappearance of missing beneficiaries, missing documents of title, the birth of children affecting the provisions of trusts, and so forth, are usually issued for very long or even unlimited periods of insurance on payment of a single premium.[2] They are, therefore, unsuitable for excess of loss reinsurance. Whichever form of proportional reinsurance is employed such insurances should be excluded from general accident treaties and be reinsured either facultatively or, if there is a sufficient volume of business, under a separate treaty.

Guarantee insurances

Indemnities against various types of risk fall under this heading—fidelity guarantee, court and various government bonds, and performance guarantees, including advance payment bonds.[3]

An original insurer's liability under *fidelity guarantee and local government guarantee policies* (which indemnify employers against defalcations of money or property by employees) is subject to a limit of guarantee, often relatively small in amount. Apart from the possibility of collusion between two or more employees, a risk which should be allowed for in underwriting and fixing the guarantee limits for each insurance, the probability of an accumulation of losses is normally remote. Therefore if instead of the normal surplus reinsurance arrangements excess of loss cover is arranged, usually it is as an any one event working form of cover forming part of a miscellaneous accident excess of loss treaty.[4]

The nature of the losses arising under such contracts poses a problem for excess of loss covers. The original insurer's liability is normally expressed in terms such as:[5]

> The company will indemnify the employer against all such direct pecuniary loss that he may sustain... caused by the fraud or dishonesty of the employee... committed during the period of indemnity... and discovered during the period of indemnity or within 12 months of the termination of employment whichever shall happen first.

Thus the insurer accepts the risk of losses arising from a fraud spread over several years during which the policy has been in force, and perhaps only discovered within 12 months of its cancellation. Normally because of the difficulties of apportioning over time the losses arising from a fraud extending over a long period, when an excess of loss cover is arranged the reinsurer accepts liability for losses discovered during the

2 For fuller details see F. de Carteret-Bisson, 'Contingency insurance', in *Handbook of Insurance*, ed. R.L. Carter, ch. 5.4.
3 Ibid., ch. 5.2, 5.3 and 5.5.
4 Report of the Advanced Study Group of the Insurance Institute of London, p.40.
5 F. de Carteret-Bisson, in *Handbook of Insurance*, ed. R.L. Carter, pp. 5.2-06 – 7.

period of reinsurance regardless of whether the particular fraud commenced beforehand.

Court of protection and similar bonds required of administrators appointed to look after the affairs of incapable persons involve two difficulties in relation to excess of loss covers: (1) the long-term nature of the guarantee; and (2) an accumulation risk where one administrator may handle several estates when any irregularity may result in the affairs of the different estates becoming inextricably mixed up so that it is difficult to establish what is 'one event'. Both working and catastrophe covers are appropriate for these types of bonds, and frequently the term 'any one event' will be defined in terms of all defalcations made by one person or by two or more persons acting in collusion.

Other types of bonds likewise may carry an accumulation risk. A firm of accountants may hold several *bankruptcy* (i.e. trustee or liquidator) bonds if it is involved in the winding-up of a number of companies. Similarly more than one *customs and excise* bond may be arranged by a company group, perhaps for stocks held in different warehouses or for subsidiaries as well as the parent company.

Performance guarantees issued in the UK by a guarantee or surety company to provide a surety against the failure of a contractor or exporter (including exporters of services) to carry out work properly according to the terms of a contract, usually carry an indemnity limit between 10% and 25% of the contract price, though in the Americas a 100% guarantee is common.[6] The difference is fundamental from the standpoint of an excess of loss reinsurer in that if the guarantee is fixed at only a fraction of the contract price there is a high probability that if the original insurer is called upon to pay the guarantee it will be for the full amount. Thus an excess of loss reinsurance becomes almost the same as quota share cover. When a 100% guarantee is issued the probability of a total loss claim becomes far more remote though not impossible: for example, if a major construction fault is discovered during the late stages or upon completion of a construction project the entire structure may have to be demolished and wholly rebuilt in the event of the contractor being held responsible. Reinsurers do not look with favour upon either type of cover, and are resistant to providing working covers when guarantees are issued for a fraction of contract values.

The largest accumulation risk arises out of the insolvency of a single contractor for whom several contract guarantees (including tender, retention monies and maintenance bonds[7]) may be in force. Such losses do not conform to the normal concept of a catastrophe for purposes of a catastrophe excess of loss cover. An added dimension to the

6 Ibid., p.5.5-02.
7 For descriptions see ibid.

393

accumulation risk arises from the increasing popularity of joint ventures where two or more contractors jointly tender for a very large project; then the failure of one partner may result in the other(s) also being unable to fulfil their contractual obligations.

Most performance guarantees for very large contractors now tend to be reinsured facultatively, but regardless of the form of reinsurance it is essential that the original insurer should obtain and make available to reinsurers full details of such matters as:

(1) The history and activities of the contractor.
(2) Its financial position, overdraft facilities and securities provided, and its dependence upon individual contracts.
(3) The background to the particular contract to be guaranteed, including partners, major subcontractors, etc.

As an additional protection it is normal for excess of loss treaties to carry an underwriting limit any one contractor as well as any one bond.

Credit insurance

Under this class of insurance an original insurer is exposed to the risks of:

(1) An accumulation of losses under individual (notably whole-turnover) policies during any one year, subject to the policy limit.
(2) An accumulation of losses arising under the whole portfolio during the year. Although the major risks probably arise from a deterioration in the general economic climate causing an increase in the number of bankruptcies, or a severe slump in a particular industry, the failure of a major company may have a domino effect on its customers and suppliers.

Export credit guarantee insurance is exposed to additional risks of a political character, e.g. the imposition of new and more stringent exchange control regulations by a country, or the sequestration of foreign-owned assets. Such business is so specialized, however, that it is not proposed to deal with it here.

It is arguable that some form of excess of loss ratio or stop loss reinsurance is the ideal method of reinsuring a credit insurance account. However, due to the cyclical nature of the business and the difficulties of fixing reinsurance premiums, such covers are not attractive to reinsurers and normal excess of loss cover is the only form of non-proportional reinsurance available on the market. However, even excess of loss reinsurance on a single risk basis is not regarded as attractive business by reinsurers, and is normally provided only if linked to a quota share treaty with the excess of loss cover protecting the ceding company's retentions. The original underwriter's experience in writing credit insurance is a major consideration, and reinsurers generally require five years' satisfactory experience on a quota share treaty before being prepared to grant excess of loss cover. Until an underwriter possesses such experience he must rely on either facultative reinsurance, or possibly a combined quota share and surplus treaty to deal with any cases above the quota share limits. Increasingly it is market practice for both credit and guarantee treaties to specify that in the event of a change of underwriter no further business shall be ceded until the new underwriter has been approved by the reinsurer: if such approval is not given, the treaty is terminated though existing business is run off to natural expiry.

It is normal practice to describe a single risk as a company or group of companies with a common parentage. Thus if separate credit policies have been issued to a parent company and its subsidiaries, the claims incurred as the result of the failure of a customer dealing with various members of the group will be aggregated together for purposes of the excess of loss treaty limits. On the other hand it precludes the aggregation of claims incurred by a number of independent companies due to a single event, such as the domino effect of the failure of a major firm—the treaty limits would apply separately to the ceding company's retained loss for each company or group of companies.

No limit is applied to the number of claims that may be made in any one year under a credit excess of loss treaty, it not being market practice to require reinstatement premiums. Therefore some measure of protection is afforded against the accumulation risk due to a general fall in the level of business activity or the domino effect.

Livestock and bloodstock insurance

An original insurer's portfolio will be exposed to:
(1) Large losses for very valuable animals, i.e. bloodstock and prize cattle.
(2) Catastrophe losses due either to many animals belonging to one insured being housed or transported together, or to widespread epidemics causing the death of animals belonging to two or more insured.

Although surplus reinsurance provides an appropriate method for dealing with animals valued at more than an original insurer's normal retention limit it cannot be used by many companies which write only a small, unbalanced livestock account. Consequently, the only feasible way in which such companies can obtain reinsurance protection against individual large losses is either to arrange a quota share treaty or to deal with individual large risks facultatively. If a company hopes to write an expanding account, a combined quota share and surplus treaty would be desirable, subject possibly to a limit applying to any one herd.

Excess of loss reinsurance for individual animals is not very suitable for the protection of even large livestock portfolios, not least because of the premium-rating difficulties. Nevertheless, although still rare, a few working covers have been arranged particularly for bloodstock but with a lower excess point sufficiently high to exclude most if not all losses involving only one animal.

Excess of loss reinsurance is unquestionably the most suitable way of protecting a company's net retained account against catastrophe losses involving several animals. 'One event' would be defined to exclude losses involving only one animal.

There are the two distinct aspects of the catastrophe risk—the risk arising from several animals being housed or conveyed together; and the epidemic risk. Frequently the two types of risk are separately insured and reinsured, special policies being issued for foot-and-mouth disease, brucellosis or swine vesicular disease, including losses due to compulsory slaughtering of animals.

Excess of loss treaties arranged to cover non-epidemic catastrophes may be restricted to losses caused by named perils, such as fire, explosion, accidents to vehicles, etc., with inner limits on any one animal and/or conveyance.[8]

The growth of demand for insurances covering the various types of epidemical 'disease' involving potential claims for the large-scale slaughter of animals belonging to several insureds has led to an increasing demand for excess of loss reinsurance to protect total portfolios against 'all risks'.[9] When such cover is provided, agreement on what constitutes 'any one event' may create difficulties. Possibly scientific evidence may be able to establish whether two or more outbreaks of disease separated by time and/or distance constitute 'one event', but it may be considered preferable to agree on some mutually acceptable definition at the outset.

Great care is needed in controlling exposures if foot-and-mouth, etc., insurances are written because of the potentially rapid spread of virulent diseases to other farms in the same region. The most suitable form of non-proportional reinsurance is stop loss or excess of loss ratio: not only does it help to spread the cost of losses which tend to fluctuate widely from year to year, but also it avoids the difficulties of deciding whether several outbreaks within a short period constitute one event. Frequently a quota share treaty is used to provide the first-line protection for a portfolio, with a specific limit per herd and possibly a limit per county or other defined geographical area, the ceding company then arranging the

8 Report of the Advanced Study Group of the Insurance Institute of London, p.41.
9 Ibid.

occasional facultative reinsurance to provide extra cover when required. An excess of loss ratio or stop loss cover may then be arranged to protect the ceding company's net retained account.

Personal accident

Proportional insurance is suitable for providing a ceding company with protection against individual cases with sums insured in excess of its normal retention, or even against known accumulations such as a number of insured persons on board the same aircraft. Excess of loss reinsurance is required, however, to provide protection against unknown accumulations which may involve a company in catastrophe losses involving more than one insured life.

Consequently the demand for excess of loss reinsurance is mainly for 'catastrophe' covers designed to protect the ceding company from losses involving more than one insured life and in excess of its retention for known accumulations. Occasionally working treaties are arranged on a per-life basis, but the portfolios of most direct insurers are too small to support such a cover in view of the degree to which a working treaty is exposed to total losses.

The accumulation risk is heavily influenced by the nature of the business underwritten by a company. A portfolio including group policies will have a higher degree of exposure than a portfolio composed solely of individual policies, in that there is a greater probability of several members of a group travelling together or being injured in the same industrial accident. Likewise the risk of unknown accumulations will be high for a company that sells travel policies from automatic machines at airports. Therefore, when excess-of-loss reinsurance is sought the reinsurer will need to know about the nature and sources of the company's business, and may wish to exclude certain classes from the main treaty.

Motor and other liability insurances

Excess of loss reinsurance is the most widely used form of protection for such business. Even when a company effects proportional reinsurance (notably quota share) for such classes of insurance, it is normal to arrange excess of loss reinsurance either to protect its own net retained account or, if preferred by the proportional reinsurer, for the common account.

Motor, employers' liability and public liability insurances all share certain common features. Notably an insurer's liability under individual liability policies is not tied to a fixed sum insured, as in the case of property, guarantee and personal accident insurances. Also claims-settlement delays tend to be far longer than under other classes of insurance so that liability insurances are frequently referred to as 'long-tail' business. On the other hand there are significant differences between the three classes of liability insurance so that even if they are combined together in one excess of loss treaty the reinsurer should consider the three components separately when deciding upon the treaty terms. Moreover the possibility of a ceding company incurring liabilities under two or even all three classes of business as the result of a single incident should not be overlooked because if such an incident occurs the definitions of the ceding company's ultimate net loss and the treaty limits may significantly affect the reinsurer's liability.

Motor

A reinsurer's potential liability under an excess of loss treaty covering motor business will depend upon a number of factors, notably:
(1) The types of vehicles insured by the ceding company. Not only are commercial vehicles more expensive on average than private cars, but also because of their size, weight and cargo they tend to result in larger third-party claims. Moreover certain types of commercial vehicles, such as buses, coaches, petrol tankers and other vehicles used for the carriage of volatile gases and liquids or other explosive substances, are far more likely to give rise to losses of catastrophic proportions, though the possibility of a car being the cause of an accident involving such a vehicle must never be overlooked.
(2) The nature of the liabilities and extent of the awards for personal injury and damage to property applying to owners and drivers of motor vehicles in those countries where the ceding company operates. For example, is liability based on proof of negligence, strict liability or some form of no-fault system, and are courts able to award only capital sums or may they under certain circumstances award annuities linked to the cost of living or some other price index?[10]
(3) The extent of compulsory insurance provisions, including limits of indemnity, applying in the country, (or countries) in which the ceding company operates and market practice in relation thereto.[11]
It must be remembered in connection with points (2) and (3) that with the growing volume of international traffic and the 'green card' system operating in Europe an insurer can be exposed to more stringent liabilities than those applying in the country from which it derives its

10 See *Indexed Annuities and the Reinsurer*.
11 For details see 'International survey of regulations governing motor insurance', *Sigma* (Swiss Reinsurance Co. (UK) Ltd), No. 11/12 (November/December 1977).

business.

Although all motor policies provide insurance against third-party liabilities, often the cover extends to include the risks of fire, theft and accidental damage to the insured vehicle, personal accident cover for the policyholder and spouse, theft of personal baggage, etc., i.e. so-called comprehensive cover. A motor excess of loss treaty may include or exclude such additional risks and in either case the reinsurer will need to know the breakdown of the gross premium income between third-party only and comprehensive policies in that the proportion of gross claims that will fall within the excess limits will be far lower in relation to the gross premium income of a portfolio composed mainly of comprehensive policies than one consisting almost exclusively of third-party insurances.

Employers' liability

An excess of loss reinsurer's exposure under a treaty covering employers' liability insurances likewise will depend to a large degree upon the nature of the legal liabilities imposed on employers for injuries sustained, or diseases contracted, by employees in the course of and arising out of their employment. The important distinction between employers' liability insurance as provided in the United Kingdom and *workmen's compensation* insurance which still operates in many countries (e.g. the United States and Australia) is that whereas an employers' liability insurance only provides an indemnity against claims for damages brought by injured employees on grounds of negligence and/or a breach of statutory duty, workmen's compensation schemes provide all injured employees with an automatic right to compensation according to legally prescribed scales of benefit either in lieu of or in addition to any claim for damages. This factor, together with other aspects of workmen's compensation insurance discussed below, make it highly desirable to reinsure such business separately from other liability insurances.

The other important points to be considered in the reinsurance of employers' liability insurance are:
(1) The scope of the cover provided by the original insurances. Under the terms of the Employers' Liability (Compulsory Insurance) Act 1969 employers in Britain are required to insure their liability for a minimum of £2 million but in practice policies are issued without any limit of indemnity.
(2) The nature of the portfolio written by the ceding company. Some companies specialize in writing business for certain trades, and others obtain their business predominantly from small traders. The hazards and the frequency and severity of industrial accidents vary substantially between occupations and industries, and the larger the

number of people employed in a plant, workshop, construction site, etc., obviously the higher will be the catastrophe risk.

General public liability and products liability

The content of a general public liability portfolio also needs careful analysis in view of the differences in the nature of the liabilities associated with different classes of liability business, ranging from individual personal liability policies to products liability insurances for high-risk industries, such as pharmaceuticals and agricultural chemicals, with very high limits of indemnity. Potential liabilities under professional indemnity policies also vary widely, certain professions such as architects, consulting engineers and medical personnel being particularly exposed to very large claims. However, as members of the public become more claims conscious the number of professions exposed to the risk of substantial claims grows.

An increasingly important aspect of all types of liability insurance is the extent to which an original portfolio is exposed to claims for accidents occurring outside the country. It is increasingly common in many industries to find not only sales staff being sent abroad, but also installation, construction and maintenance engineers, etc. More holidaymakers and other persons also travel abroad in their private capacity, and exporters may find themselves exposed to far severer liabilities abroad for accidents involving their products than they may incur at home.[12] Therefore, the geographical limits applying to original policies and jurisdiction clauses have an important bearing on both a ceding company's and its reinsurer's exposures.

Reference has been made already in Chapter 8 to the difficulty of defining what constitutes an 'event' or an 'occurrence' for products liability.[13] Unless a treaty is carefully worded, the danger exists of a reinsurer picking up liability for an accumulation of claims perhaps spread over several years and possibly arising from a product that itself was in production over a considerable period of time. Therefore reinsurers normally restrict their potential liability by:

(1) Applying the treaty limits to the ceding company's ultimate net loss under each individual policy written during the year. It is normal practice for direct insurers to undertake to indemnify policyholders for all claims for injury, etc., happening during the period of insurance (but subject to an annual aggregate limit of indemnity) regardless of when the offending goods were manufactured or

12 This is particularly true of exports to the United States: see Mark R. Greene, 'Trends in American liability insurance', *Sigma* (Swiss Reinsurance Co. (UK) Ltd), No. 9 (September 1977).
13 P. Madge, 'Products liability insurance', *Handbook of Insurance*, ed. R.L. Carter, ch. 4.3.

supplied. Thus the reinsurer's liability in respect of multiple claims under one policy will itself be limited by the aggregate limit under the original policy.

(2) Further specifying that if claims arise in the course of more than one policy period during one treaty underwriting year, the reinsurer's liability shall be limited to twice his liability for any one year.

The following clause is a typical example of such a definition of the reinsurer's liability.

In respect of products liability it is understood and agreed that where any policy of insurance or reinsurance provides for a limit of indemnity during the period of insurance or reinsurance the Reinsurer shall indemnify the Reinsured up to the amount of each ultimate net loss specified in the Schedule in excess of the retention of the Reinsured by aggregating all claims arising during the period of such policy of insurance or reinsurance having commenced in the current treaty underwriting year and expiring within 12 months of its end.

If such claims become manifest in the course of more than one policy period during one treaty underwriting year the Reinsured shall assume its retention for each policy period in respect of claims falling thereto and the Reinsurer shall assume all excess liability up to its maximum liability any one policy period but not more than twice the maximum amount of its liability any one policy period.

Bearing in mind all the above factors, although excess of loss reinsurance undoubtedly is the most satisfactory way of reinsuring a general liability account, it is imperative that the reinsurer should:

(1) Obtain very full details of the types of business being written, and the extent of the indemnities provided, both in amount and scope.

(2) Take great care in drawing up the terms of the treaty.

(3) If necessary, exclude from the scope of the treaty particularly hazardous risks for which special provision should be made.

Workmen's compensation insurance

Reference was made above to the differences between workmen's compensation and other classes of liability insurance. Besides an employee's automatic right under workmen's compensation statutes to compensation for industrial injuries according to prescribed scales of benefit, two other features of such schemes pose problems for excess of loss reinsurers.

(1) Benefits usually take the form of both capital sums and weekly or monthly benefits payable during periods of incapacity and possibly for the rest of a man's life. Consequently individual claims may remain outstanding for several years: the problem of court awards in

the form of annuities has been discussed in Chapter 5 so that it is sufficient to note here that a treaty covering workmen's compensation insurances would normally include a commutation clause.

(2) Some governments, notably Australia, have passed legislation in recent years retroactively increasing the statutory benefits to both the newly injured and those already in receipt of weekly or monthly benefits for past injuries. The effect of such legislation on excess of loss reinsurers has been *(a)* to increase their liability for claims falling within the treaty limits already in course of payment; *(b)* to bring within the treaty claims previously below the lower limit; and *(c)* to increase their potential exposure for new claims occurring during the remainder of the treaty year and for which no additional premium has been received. Sometimes the increase in benefits is sufficient to bring within a treaty's limits claims which the ceding company has been paying for several years: in a few cases excess of loss reinsurers have been notified that they have become liable some 25 years after the date of the accident, and a 10-year lag is not uncommon.[14] Of course, direct insurers too are adversely affected by such legislation. However they are in a more favourable position than reinsurers in that an increase in benefits has the same sort of gearing effect as general inflation on the claims experience of an excess of loss treaty (see Chapter 5). Moreover because of this fact it is easier for a direct insurer to recoup the extra cost of the higher benefits payable to past generations of claimants by increasing at next renewal the premiums of the present generation of policyholders than it is for a reinsurer to obtain a commensurately higher increase in the premiums on his contracts. Therefore it is usual to include in treaties covering workmen's compensation an 'Acts in force' clause designed to restrict the reinsurer's liability to such amounts as would be payable in accordance with the laws in force at the commencement of the treaty unless an extension of his liability be agreed with the reinsured.

In other respects workmen's compensation insurance is much like employers' liability business. A reinsurer's exposure is substantially affected by the type of business being written by the reinsured, and even if individual benefits are relatively low, the possibility of catastrophe losses cannot be ignored. Therefore excess of loss reinsurance is required, possibly arranged in layers, to provide protection against losses involving the death of, or serious injury to, more than one employee arising from one event.

---

14 Report of the Advanced Study Group of the Insurance Institute of London, p.54.

Engineering

There has been a considerable expansion of this class of insurance over the last few years beyond the traditional engineering policies covering pressure vessels, lifting equipment and the breakdown of electrical equipment. It now also embraces business interruption and advanced loss of profits insurances associated with the explosion or breakdown of plant; and computer insurances. Most of these insurances include within the one package cover against two or more types of loss, e.g. property damage and liabilities to third parties, and/or loss of revenue or increased cost of working. Thus an insurer is usually exposed to a possible accumulation of losses arising out of one event, and in many cases very high values are at risk.

Much of the direct business is handled by specialist engineering insurance companies that can afford to employ qualified engineers to carry out plant inspections, advise on plant design, etc. Generally their portfolios of business are sufficiently large to warrant the use of excess of loss reinsurance as the sole means of protection. The reinsurance is then arranged in layers, the lowest layer being a working treaty to cover losses in excess of the ceding company's retention under any one policy. Several additional layers are usually necessary to provide the very high limits required to protect the company against major catastrophes.

Companies writing small portfolios may have neither enough experience nor a wide enough spread of business to provide a reinsurer with a sufficiently stable base for granting a working excess of loss cover. Therefore, their reinsurance arrangements often consist of a proportional treaty to reduce liabilities under individual policies plus a catastrophe excess of loss cover on an 'any one event' basis to provide protection against losses exceeding EMLs or an accumulation of net retained losses under several policies. Small, inexperienced companies typically reinsure individual liabilities by means of a quota share treaty, although many reinsure the liability sections through their public liability accounts. Surplus reinsurance may be used for larger accounts, with the liability sections again possibly being reinsured with other liability risks. As noted earlier, the limits imposed on both types of proportional treaty require specific facultative reinsurances to be arranged for larger risks.

A special feature of engineering reinsurance is the technical assistance with underwriting and claims handling which can be provided by a few of the major professional reinsurance companies.

Contractors' All Risks

As noted already, large C.A.R. insurances are normally individually insured and reinsured, generally on a proportional basis. Excess of loss reinsurance is usually arranged only to provide protection on a catastrophe basis for various types of loss arising from one event.

Applicability of excess of loss reinsurance

Three factors to emerge from the above examination of the characteristics of the main classes of accident insurance are:

(1) Only catastrophe excess of loss reinsurance offers adequate protection for classes of insurance which present a risk of unknown or uncontrollable accumulations of losses arising from a single event whether involving several exposure units covered by a single policy or a number of policyholders. Known accumulations can be handled by proportional reinsurance.

(2) Although working excess of loss covers are becoming more popular they are not suitable for:

(a) portfolios which are too small to provide the reinsurer with an adequate premium and reasonably stable loss experience; or

(b) new companies and companies commencing writing new classes of business, particularly specialist companies, who therefore do not possess a proven underwriting record; or

(c) certain types of specialist classes of business (e.g. performance guarantees).

(3) Excess of loss ratio, or stop loss, reinsurance is arguably the best form of protection for classes of accident business which are exposed:

(a) to cyclical fluctuations in annual aggregate loss experience (e.g. credit risks); or

(b) periodically to losses occurring during a short time over a wide area where it may be difficult to decide what is one event (notably livestock epidemic risks).

However reinsurers may be resistant to granting such cover.

Comprehensive and combined policies

A feature of accident business is the volume of business written in the form of 'comprehensive', 'combined' or 'package' policies both for individuals and householders, and for business risks. Reference has been made already to the various types of risks included in engineering and contractors' policies; the same position applies with many other insurances. With some schemes the insured is allowed to choose what cover he requires from a list of insurable risks (e.g. traders' combined policies) whereas in other cases he is offered an inclusive package (e.g. package travel policies for holidaymakers, and householders' comprehensive policies).

When the insured is given a choice, an identifiable part of the total premium is allocated to each class of insurance. Consequently each section of the policy can be reinsured as part of the company's proportional or excess-of-loss reinsurance arrangements for that class of insurance. Alternatively the whole policy may be reinsured under a miscellaneous accident treaty.

Reinsurance arrangements for inclusive policies can be handled in two ways. As separate premiums are not charged for each section it is not feasible to allocate the reinsurance for each section to specific treaties for the individual classes of insurance. Consequently the business must be dealt with as a whole in a miscellaneous accident treaty or alternatively specific reinsurance can be arranged for such policies. In view of the catastrophe exposure on all types of inclusive policies a catastrophe excess of loss reinsurance will be required, and if the cover includes liability insurance a working excess of loss cover may be needed to protect individual risks, though usually the amounts insured under property, business interruption, and personal accident sections are relatively low and well below a company's retention limits. On the other hand most companies deal with the liability risks covered under their householders' comprehensive policies by allocating a fixed percentage (usually 5%) of the total premium income to their Public Liability Employers' Liability account. Only if a company writes a large volume of 'inclusive' policies will a separate treaty be warranted.

Combined excess of loss treaties

Given the diversity of business written in the accident department it is not surprising that many insurers prefer to embody several classes of insurance in one treaty. Common examples are treaties covering all classes of liability insurance. Such treaties are easy to administer and also take care of the possibility of several types of loss being caused by one event. For example, an explosion in a factory may injure both employees and members of the public so giving rise to claims under the firm's employers' liability (or workmen's compensation) policy and its general third-party policy too.

Similarly some very large direct insurers prefer to reinsure all of their accident business (excluding credit and contract guarantee insurances) under a combined accident excess of loss treaty, possibly with separate treaty limits applying to the different classes of insurance. In any event reinsurers ask for details of a ceding company's underwriting limits which may be incorporated in the treaty. Cover is arranged in layers in the normal way, though the upper layers may apply only to motor and employers' liability risks for which UK insurers provide unlimited cover for policyholders.

Underwriting and rating of excess of loss reinsurances

Whenever excess of loss cover is sought for an account embracing several classes of insurance, because their risk characteristics differ it is important that the reinsurer should obtain a breakdown of the ceding company's gross net premium income and past loss experience for each class.

Besides distinguishing those classes of business for which working excess of loss covers are not suitable as a primary protection, a reinsurer may think of accident business as falling into three groups:
(1) The standard classes of accident business, e.g. theft, fidelity guarantee and livestock.
(2) The specialist classes such as credit, guarantee and Contractors' All Risks.
(3) Liability risks.
Within each group some risks are far more hazardous than others. Though reinsurers apply the same sort of exclusions to excess of loss treaties as to proportional treaties (see Appendix 11.1), it is not sufficient to rely solely on excluding the more obvious, highly hazardous risks. As explained earlier, the reinsurer must try to gather as much information as possible regarding the types of business written within each class (e.g. the private-car and various types of commercial-vehicle components of a motor account), the sources of such business, and its geographical spread. Dealing with practice in relation to accident reinsurance, one underwriter commented:[15]

> In the past we have as reinsurers been guilty of attempting to underwrite on a very limited information base. This certainly has improved over the last 10 years but we still do not in my opinion go as deeply into the portfolio we are protecting as we should.

Liability (including motor) excess of loss covers are particularly hazardous from a reinsurer's standpoint for reasons that have been mentioned already and will be further considered below. Therefore, such insurances are normally excluded from general accident treaties, and are reinsured separately.

It is common practice to exclude from all accident excess of loss treaties:

15 J. Lavers, 'Underwriting information and the non-proportional account', in *Papers Presented at the Third International Reinsurance Seminar* (Reinsurance Offices' Association, 1977).

(1) Liabilities arising under excess of loss insurances or reinsurances accepted by the ceding company.

(2) War risks.

(3) Atomic energy risks.

Rating

The rating of accident treaties follows the methods described in Chapter 5. In particular, working covers are normally rated on the basis of burning cost (usually year of account only), provided that the premium income is sufficiently large and there is an actual claims experience. The rating of all accident excess of loss treaties is subject to annual review.

Treaty terms

Accident reinsurance practice follows the general principles set out in Chapters 5 and 8.

Motor and liability risks

These risks are probably the most difficult for an excess of loss reinsurer to underwrite successfully. Reference has been made (in Chapters 3 and 5) to the disproportionate impact of economic (notably inflation), social, legal and political developments on a reinsurer's liability, and therefore of the need for the inclusion of stability (or index) and change-of-law clauses in all treaties covering liability risks.

The need for a stability clause is particularly acute for liability treaties. Not only is there a direct relationship between inflation and the cost of claims settlements, but also liability claims tend to remain outstanding for longer periods than claims arising on most other classes of insurance. The experience of one large reinsurer showed the following delays on liability excess of loss treaties:[16]

| | Average delays (in years): | | | |
| | in notification of claims | | in settlement of claims | |
	by numbers	by amount	by numbers	by amount
All classes	2.4	2.2	5.1	5.7
Motor only	2.0	N.A.	4.7	N.A.

A later study showed that out of 4,379 claims incurred in a particular year, 13.3% were still outstanding after 10 years, and 4.1% were settled after 15 years.[17]

16 F.E. Guaschi, *Accident Excess of Loss* (Mercantile & General Reinsurance Co Ltd, November 1972).

Delays in the notification and settlement of claims also have important implications for the calculation of burning costs. In the early years of the claims development of any one underwriting year IBNR claims will be an important element in the estimated value of outstanding claims. Moreover, given the uncertainties surrounding the eventual settlement costs of potentially large claims, many years may elapse before even a reliable estimate can be obtained regarding the final cost of claims occurring in a particular underwriting year.

These problems have led accident reinsurers to employ 'claims development' statistics (i.e. analyses of claims by delays in settlement) for the estimation of IBNR and outstanding claims values for the purpose of calculating burning costs. [17] The Advanced Study Group cites some of the dangers inherent in such methods (e.g. the failure to take into account the combined effects of settlement periods and inflation; inadequate information, etc.)[18] J. Lavers also points out that the crude use of ratios derived from past claims run-off data to project final settlement costs for later years may prove inaccurate, simply because of a change in the ceding company's claims manager. One man may optimistically underestimate outstanding claims whereas another more cautious man may consistently tend to overestimate.[19]

This whole question of outstanding claims estimation will be considered in more detail in Chapter 14.

Finally the need for detailed information regarding the ceding company's business must be doubly emphasized for liability reinsurances. Appendix 11.2 contains two questionnaires recommended by Lavers. Some classes of products liability, professional indemnity and public liability business (e.g. dam construction, chemical manufacturers, oil and petro-chemical installations) fall into the category of 'target risks', which may be extensively coinsured or facultatively reinsured. To avoid the possibility of incurring accumulations of losses on such risks, reinsurers sometimes either specifically exclude particular types of potential target risks or exclude reinsurances or 'coinsurances', or 'insurances in respect of which the company does not write 100% of the policy unless specially agreed with the reinsurer'.[20]

17 F.E. Guaschi, *Accident Excess of Loss* (Mercantile & General Reinsurance Co. Ltd, February 1975).
18 See the Report of the Advanced Study Group of the Insurance Institute of London, p.49.
19 Lavers, 'Underwriting information and the non-proportional account' in *Papers presented at the Third International Reinsurance Seminar* (Reinsurance Offices' Association, 1977).
20 Report of the Advanced Study Group, p.55.

Appendix 11.1   Normal exclusions from accident treaties

Personal accident

(1) Coupon insurance and/or automatic vending machine business.
(2) Aviation risks other than as a passenger mounting into, travelling in or dismounting from any fully licensed passenger-carrying aircraft and not being a member of the crew nor for the purpose of engaging in any trade or technical operation therein.
(3) Automatic passenger liability covers granted to airline operators or ticket agencies in respect of flying risks.
(4) Permanent (i.e. non-cancellable) health business.
(5) Personal accident benefits under motor policies.
(6) Personal accident benefits under life policies.
(7) Professional racing risks of any kind.
(8) Excess of loss insurances or reinsurance.
(9) War and civil war.

Employers' liability and Workmen's Compensation Act insurances

(1) Mines and collieries; quarries using explosives.
(2) Seamen and shipping risks.
(3) Shipbuilding, ship-breaking or ship-repairing risks.
(4) Stevedores and dockside risks.
(5) Demolition risks.
(6) Tunnelling risks and sewer contractors.
(7) Work on towers, steeples, chimney shafts, or steel-erectors.
(8) Aircrew, being any trade or occupation which involves employees flying in aircraft except as a passenger not engaged in any trade or technical operation therein.
(9) Manufacturers of celluloid and pyroxylin.
(10) The manufacture, storage, filling, breaking down or transport of explosives (including fireworks and ammunition) and/or air under pressure in containers.

Public liability

(1) Railways, tramways and trolley-buses.
(2) Mechanically propelled vehicles used on a public road in such a manner as to render the insured responsible under the Road Traffic Acts.
(3) Mines and collieries; quarries using explosives.
(4) Shipbuilding, ship-breaking or ship-repairing risks.
(5) The working and navigation of any vessel other than light craft on inland waterways.
(6) Aviation risks including liability of any airport owner or any concern or corporation maintaining or operating an airline and any risks involving the refuelling of aircraft.

(7) Manufacture of celluloid and pyroxylin.

(8) The manufacture, storage, filling, breaking down and transport of explosives (including fireworks and ammunition) and gas and/or air under pressure in containers.

(9) Electricity and gas undertakings.

(10) Chemical manufacturers.

(11) Oil-storage installations, refineries (other than retail garages and petrol-filling stations).

(12) Tunnelling risks, hydroelectric works, construction and maintenance of dams or any subaqueous work.

(13) Spectator stands.

(14) Professional indemnity.

(15) Products liability risks.

Appendix 11.2   Accident reinsurance questionnaires[2][1]

Motor excess of loss questionnaire

Premium

(1) Gross premium income for the last six completed years:
    19..
    19..
    19..
    19..
    19..
    19..
(2) Estimated gross premium income:
    Current year:
    Year to be rated:
(3) Do you operate overseas (other than Green Card)
    YES/NO
    If yes please give list of countries and estimated or actual premium incomes
    for current and six preceding years country by country in original currency.
(4) Please give details of rate increases for the past six years and estimates for
    current year and year to be rated.
(5) If Green Cards are issued please state:
    (a) Approximate number of Green Cards issued per annum.
    (b) Coverage afforded under Green Cards.
    (c) Premium charged for Green Cards.

Portfolio

(1) Please indicate the approximate breakdown of your portfolio as follows:

	Estimated OGPI		*Approximate number of vehicles*	
	Comprehensive	*Non-comprehensive*	*Comprehensive*	*Non-comprehensive*

(a) Private car
    Driver's age: Under 21
    21 – 25
    25 and over
(b) Public hire: Taxis
    Goods-carrying
    Self-hire
(c) Heavy goods
(d) Coaches/buses
(e) Tankers and vehicles
    carrying hazardous goods
(f) Contractors' equipment
(g) All other

---

21 Reproduced from J. Lavers, 'Underwriting information and the non-proportional account', in *Papers presented at the Third International Reinsurance Seminar* (Reinsurance Offices' Association, 1977).

(2) Has the breakdown materially altered in the past six years? If so give details.
(3) What types of vehicle are not written as a matter of policy and can be excluded from the scope of the proposed cover?

Third Party liability
(1) Please state your normal and maximum Third Party Property Damage limits on:

	Normal	Maximum

(a) Private cars
(b) Commercial vehicles
(c) Vehicles carrying hazardous goods
(d) Contractors' equipment

(2) If the law does not require statutory unlimited third-party bodily injury coverage please supply risk profile as follows:

Motor physical damage
(1) Please state average and maximum values on the following types of vehicles:

	Average	Maximum

(a) Private car
(b) Commercial vehicle
(c) Buses and coaches
(d) Contractors' equipment

(2) Please supply risk profile for vehicles which exceed the proposed deductible.
(3) If you have any known concentrations of vehicles exceeding   please give following details of each:
(a) Name of insured
(b) Location of known concentration
(c) Maximum value of concentration
(4) Do your policies cover the following perils? If so state percentage of total premium for each peril.
(a) Storm and flood   %
(b) Earthquake   %
(c) Strikes, riots and civil commotion   %

Motor personal accident
If you wish motor personal accident to be protected please state normal and maximum limits as follows:

	Normal	Maximum

Any one person
Any one vehicle

Claims

In respect of all claims occurring during the past six years which have cost or have been or are estimated to cost more than ____% of the proposed deductible please give the following details:
(1)   Name and age of insured and type of vehicle.

(2) Date of loss.
(3) Type of policy—comprehensive/non-comprehensive.
(4) Policy sum insured (if not limited).
(5) Details of Third Party Personal Injury.
(6) Details of Third Party Property Damage.
(7) Cost of own damage claims.
(8) Incurred claim split paid and outstanding from the ground.
(9) Incurred claim split paid and outstanding from the ground at 31 December each year subsequent to occurrence.
(10) If coverage is required on a 'policies incepting basis' please state inception of policy.

Reinsurance cover

(1) For what deductibles and cover are quotations required?
(2) Will protection be required on losses-occurring or policies-insured basis?
(3) Are quotations required with standard stability clause or severe inflation clause or both?

Original cover

(1) Please supply copies of your standard forms of policy for risks which will be protected hereunder.
(2) Please supply copy of your rating manual.

Employers' liability and workers' compensation excess of loss questionnaire

Premium

(1) Gross premium income for last six years:
   19..
   19..
   19..
   19..
   19..
   19..
(2) Estimated gross premium income:
   Current year
   Year to be rated
(3) Do you operate overseas?
   YES/NO
   If yes please give list of countries and estimated or actual premium incomes for current and six preceding years country by country in original currency.

Portfolio

(1) If in any country where you operate the maximum statutory benefits under workmen's compensation policies vary from state to state please give estimated premium income for that country state by state.
(2) If any industry, trade or occupation produces more than 5% of your total income please supply details of occupation and percentage of income derived.
(3) What are the normal and maximum benefits provided under employers' liability policies?
   N.B. If the account protected affects more than one country please state normal and maximum by country.
(4) Does the account to be protected include stated benefits? If so:
   (a) What is the estimated income?
   (b) What are the normal and maximum amounts of coverage given?
   (c) Do such policies only cover employees earning wages or salaries in excess of a certain figure, if so what is that figure?
   (d) Does the percentage of benefits exactly follow that provided under the Workmen's Compensation Act? If not please state in broad terms how it varies. Please give information by territory and by state if applicable.
   (e) Is coverage given on a 24-hour basis?
   (f) Do the policies cover sickness as well as accident?
(5) What types of risk are not written as a matter of policy and can be excluded from the proposed coverage?

Claims

In respect of all claims occurring during the past six years which have cost or have been or are estimated to cost more than ____% of the proposed deductible please give the following details:
(1) Name and occupation of insured.

(2) Date of loss.
(3) Trade(s) of injured party/parties.
(4) Policy sum insured (if applicable).
(5) Your share of original policy.
(6) Details of injuries.
(7) Incurred claim split paid and outstanding from the ground (your share).
(8) Incurred claim split paid and outstanding from ground at 31 December each year subsequent to occurrence.
(9) If coverage is required on 'policies incepting basis' please state inception date of policy.

Reinsurance cover

(1) For what deductibles and cover are quotations required?
(2) Will protection be required on losses occurring or policies issued basis?
(3) Are quotations required with standard stability clause or severe inflation clause or both?

Original cover

Please supply copies of your standard forms of policy for risks which will be protected hereunder.

General third party excess of loss questionnaire

Premium

(1) Gross premium income for last six completed years:
    19. .
    19. .
    19. .
    19. .
    19. .
    19. .
(2) Estimated gross premium income for:
    Current year
    Year to be rated
(3) Do you operate overseas?
    YES/NO
    If so please give a list of countries and estimated or actual premium incomes for current and six preceding years country by country in original currency.

Portfolio

(1) Please supply a risk profile by general public liability, professional indemnity and products liability, by occupation or profession of original insured as follows:
(2) As regards policies covering damage by fire to the property of third parties where hazardous equipment is being used (e.g. blowlamps, oxy-acetylene equipment, explosives; etc.):
    (a) What is the maximum limit of cover you are prepared to give?
    (b) To what extent are you prepared to effect facultative reinsurance to limit exposure to this treaty?
    (c) Do you incorporate burning and welding warranties into the original policy? If so please supply copy of standard warranty.
(3) With respect to products liability:
    (a) What are the usual and maximum amounts of coverage provided?
    (b) Is it your practice to insist on annual limits in the aggregate? If so what are the normal and maximum aggregate limits as a function of the limit of indemnity per event?
    (c) Are the following products liability risks written?
    Manufacturers or suppliers (other than retailers) of:
    (i)   Aircraft or component parts thereof
    (ii)   Vessels or component parts thereof
    (iii) Mechanically propelled vehicles or components parts thereof
    (iv)   Any fuel used in (i), (ii), or (iii) above
    (v)   Pharmaceutical products
    (vi)   Fertilizers
    (vii) Agricultural products
    (viii) Insecticides
    (ix)   Animal foodstuffs
    If so please give the following details by policy:
    (i)   Name of insured
    (ii)   Indemnity per event

(iii) Indemnity any one year
(iv) Occupation of original insured
(v)   Scope of coverage given
(4) What types of risk are not written as a matter of policy and can be excluded from the scope of the proposed cover?

Claims

In respect of all claims occurring during the last six years which have cost or have been or are estimated to cost more than ____% of the proposed deductible please give the following details:
(1) Name and occupation of insured.
(2) Date of loss.
(3) Sum insured and your share of the policy.
(4) Details of Third Party Personal Injuries.
(5) Details of Third Party Property Damage and its cause.
(6) Incurred claim split paid and outstanding from the ground (your share).
(7) Incurred claim split paid and outstanding from the ground at 31 December each year subsequent to occurrence.
(8) If coverage is required on policies incepting please state inception date of policy.

Reinsurance cover

(1) For what deductibles and cover are quotations required?
(2) Will protection be required on losses occurring or policies issued basis?
(3) Are quotations required with standard stability clause or severe inflation clause?

Original cover

Please supply copies of your standard forms of policy for risks which will be protected hereunder.

REINSURANCE

12
Marine and aviation reinsurances

12
Marine and aviation reinsurance

I MARINE REINSURANCE

Although there are many features in common between marine and other classes of non-life reinsurance, there are also significant differences due to the nature of marine insurance. First there are important differences between the underwriting of hull, cargo and other risks. For example, a hull account will contain far fewer individual exposure units and thus tend to be less stable than cargo or most non-life insurance accounts. On the other hand, though the mobile nature of the risks insured presents both hull and cargo underwriters with problems in controlling exposures, the cargo underwriter is particularly exposed to unknown accumulations of values at risk and may only learn of the full extent of his liability after a loss has occurred.

Secondly marine insurance lends itself less to standardization than most other classes of insurance because of the very individual nature of the risks insured. A certain degree of classification is possible, e.g. by type of vessel, type of cargo and method of packing, nature of voyage, scope of cover, etc., but each risk presented to an underwriter involves varying combinations of such factors, some of which are subject periodically to significant and sometimes rapid changes. For example, hardly a year goes by without the introduction of new products, methods of transportation, and types of vessels, and though an event like the oil crisis may appear to have little direct impact on marine insurers, the rise in oil prices enabled OPEC countries to embark on ambitious economic development projects leading to severe congestion in some ports. A marine underwriter therefore requires considerable technical knowledge, experience and judgment in order to evaluate and rate the business offered to him.

Consequently a reinsurer is very much in the hands of the direct underwriter and whenever any type of reinsurance is to be placed he will want to know the qualifications of the direct underwriter(s) and the ceding company's underwriting policy. Furthermore, in the case of treaties as opposed to a facultative reinsurance for an individual risk, he also needs two other crucial pieces of information:

(1) The composition of the company's portfolio of business. A company, for example, may specialize in hull business and quite possibly in certain types of vessels such as oil tankers or bulk carriers, or it may be predominantly a cargo insurer, perhaps with a large specialized account for certain commodities or valuables.

(2) The sources of the company's business. For example, are its activities confined to a local market where it mainly deals direct with domestic clients, or does it operate in one or more of the subscription markets (such as London, Paris, New York or Rotterdam) where risks are usually placed on a coinsurance basis and both national and international business is accepted, largely through the medium of brokers?

Reinsurance protection is sought in the London market not only by conventional direct companies but also by the protection and indemnity mutual clubs which provide protection for shipowners against liabilities not normally covered by the orthodox marine policies. Generally the clubs reinsure on an excess of loss basis, the business largely being written in the London market, often following a Lloyd's lead.

Development of a marine reinsurance programme

Ideas about the type of reinsurance programme a marine underwriter should assemble and the fixing of retentions vary according to personal preferences and circumstances. Therefore the following comments can only be taken as representing one line of thought current in the market about the manner in which a company may rearrange its reinsurances as it develops its marine account and gains experience. The general principles discussed in Chapter 9 apply to the fixing of retentions, notably the size, spread and profitability of a company's account, and its financial resources.

Exactly how a company arranges its reinsurance programme will depend largely on the structure and size of its marine account which, as indicated above, can vary considerably between companies. Generally companies tend to treat marine business as falling into four distinct classes—hull, cargo, excess of loss, and offshore oil and gas rigs and similar risks—and to make separate reinsurance arrangements for each. The last two classes are of a specialist nature, so the following comments relate only to hull and cargo business.

Whether a company is newly formed, or an established company about to commence the writing of marine insurances, a major consideration is likely to be the need to keep administration costs as low as possible. Therefore it will want a method of reinsurance that is cheap to operate. The obvious candidate is a quota share treaty whereby the company can fix its share at a sufficiently low level to enable it to handle the majority of the business it is likely to be offered without further reinsurance assistance. Its share, however, should not be so small that it merely channels business to the reinsurer while earning a virtually risk-free profit from reinsurance commission receivable: a 90% quota share is normally the maximum limit acceptable to reinsurers. Administration of such a treaty may be limited to the quarterly preparation of the reinsurance accounts, though a reinsurer may require bordereaux from a new company for the first few years in order to keep a check on the type of business being accepted, rates being charged and the company's underwriting policy generally. Additional facultative reinsurance could be obtained for the occasional case the company may receive in excess of the treaty capacity, though almost invariably reinsurers forbid ceding companies to reinsure facultatively in front of the treaty except for the common account.

Sometimes, with the approval of the quota share reinsurer(s), a new company may also arrange excess of loss cover on an 'any one event or occurrence' basis to protect itself against *unknown* accumulations. Known accumulations are a different matter: to allow a company to effect cover for known accumulations would effectively enable it to reduce its net retentions and so is rarely permitted. On occasions excess of loss cover is arranged to protect the interests of both the ceding company and its quota reinsurers who would contribute their share towards the premium.

State insurers and companies in local markets where relatively few insurers operate have special reinsurance needs. Unable to share original business through coinsurance, such companies need more than a quota share treaty to provide the capacity to absorb the size of risks they may be forced to underwrite. Therefore they need to supplement a quota share treaty with additional surplus reinsurance (known in marine circles as 'excess of line' cover) plus, possibly, facultative obligatory treaties.

After a few years of business expansion a company may be in a position to review both the size of its retentions and the type of reinsurance effected. One approach a company can adopt is to arrange (1) excess of line reinsurance to provide additional underwriting capacity while increasing the share of its direct premium income retained for its own account, plus (2) excess of loss cover to protect the net account against unknown accumulations.

It is unusual for companies to scrap their quota share treaties entirely in favour of excess of line, especially for hull business in subscription markets. Normally excess of line covers are effected just to provide extra capacity for larger risks. If a cargo quota treaty is scrapped, often it is replaced by a working excess of loss reinsurance.

Today the final stage in the development of the reinsurance programmes of a growing number of underwriters is to use excess of loss cover as the sole method of protecting both hull and cargo accounts. The trend world-wide is away from proportional to non-proportional treaties.

Reinsurance for restricted cover

As noted in Chapter 3, a distinctive feature of marine insurance is the number of reinsurances effected on a more restricted basis than the original cover. Sometimes when a facultative obligatory or an excess of line reinsurance is arranged to protect either a cargo or a hull account the ceding company will seek cover only for major losses, the cargo reinsurance then being placed on an FPA (free of particular average) and the hull reinsurance on a TLO (total loss only) basis. Possibly the explanation lies in the nature of marine losses. It may be that Figure 12.1 is a fair representation of the shape of probability distributions of losses by size of loss for both cargo and hull losses: not only are the majority of losses small relative to values at risk but also of the few losses that exceed a certain proportion of the value at risk the majority then become an actual or constructive total loss.

Figure 12.1

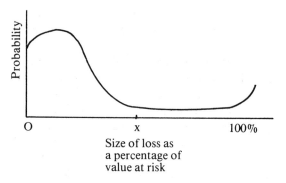

It has not been possible to obtain conclusive evidence to support this hypothesis, though statistics produced by the Liverpool Underwriters'

Association show that over the 15 years 1961 – 75 constructive total losses averaged around 50% of all total losses for tankers, bulk carriers and other types of vessels. Therefore a direct underwriter may conclude that he can afford to retain partial losses up to point x without recourse to reinsurance and will take a chance that he will not be so unlucky as to incur many losses exceeding that size other than those settled as actual or constructive total losses.

Special types of reinsurance cover

An account of marine reinsurance would not be complete without brief reference to highly specialized forms of marine reinsurance available on the London market, predominantly at Lloyd's.

Overdue risks

Before the days of good radio and telephone communications there was an active market for the facultative reinsurance of overdue vessels. Once a vessel was reported overdue the original underwriter's primary concern was to protect himself against a likely total loss, so reinsurance was sought on TLO terms at premium rates which approached 100% as the period overdue lengthened.

Now with instant world-wide communications such covers have become largely of historical interest, though they have not disappeared entirely from the Lloyd's market.

Tonners

Some underwriters, mainly at Lloyd's, are prepared to provide insurers with this peculiar form of protection against large losses. A policy is issued on p.p.i. (policy proof of interest) terms undertaking to pay the policyholder a fixed sum of money in respect of every vessel over a certain size which is reported a total loss, irrespective of whether the policyholder is interested in the loss. For example, the policy may undertake to pay £20,000 for the total loss of every vessel over 20,000 tons g.r.t.

Likewise 'tonner' policies are available in the aviation market when the underwriter undertakes to pay a certain sum in respect of every air crash resulting in a specified number of deaths.

Such policies are effected by insurers operating in the subscription markets where through coinsurance and/or reinsurance the probability of being interested in any large loss is high.

Hull and cargo reinsurance

Reference has been made above to the possibility that a direct insurer may tend to specialize in hull or cargo business. The two classes of marine business so differ in relation to their underwriting characteristics that normally separate reinsurance arrangements are made for each class, though sometimes treaties are arranged to cover both hull and cargo business but with separate limits.

Hull treaties

Hull treaties extend to cover the ancillary risks handled by a hull underwriter, namely machinery; construction and repair risks; disbursements; freight; dock-owners', shipowners' and charterers' liabilities, etc. In other words, the treaty will normally include all classes of risk which the ceding company treats as hull business.

Some proportional treaties are arranged on an excess-of-line basis, but the majority of hull treaties are still quota-share, though world-wide there is a trend towards excess-of-loss.

The scope of a hull treaty is a matter for negotiation in the light of the business being transacted by the ceding company. The reinsurer may wish to exclude certain hazardous types of risk: besides restrictions on vessels owned or managed in, or operating under flags of convenience of particular countries, normal exclusions are:

(1) Aviation hulls and liabilities.
(2) Oil or gas rig business.
(3) Cargo.
(4) 'Overdue' or 'tonner' risks.
(5) Treaty reinsurance business.

Other exclusions sometimes found relate to risks such as yachts, wooden vessels, vessels over 20 years old, fishing vessels, tows, loss of hire or earnings, TLO risks, liability risks not in conjunction with a hull policy or in excess of hull values.

War risks written in conjunction with marine risks may also be included in the same treaty, though it may be preferable to reinsure war, riot and strike risks separately. In cases where separate original insurances are effected for war, etc., risks (e.g. through specialist P and I clubs), separate arrangements are made for their reinsurance.

Cargo treaties

Cargo treaties likewise normally embrace all insurances written in the ceding company's cargo account, including all types of goods and specie and methods of transportation. Thus besides sendings by sea, the treaty will cover international consignments overland, and sendings by post or air. Few exclusions are applied, though the reinsurer may wish to exercise some control over liabilities accepted under automatic treaties (particularly excess of loss reinsurances) and a separate limit per location may be imposed in proportional treaties.

War risks cover for cargo is normally provided by the extension of original policies, and likewise is included in cargo treaties. In 1977 there was general agreement on the London market that all cargo reinsurance contracts and treaties covering war risks should be subject to a new Paramount War Clause (cargo). The clause is reproduced in Appendix 12.2. The object of London reinsurers was to limit reinsurance cover to terms and conditions no wider than the relevant London Institute war clauses. Two alternatives are, however, provided which require the ceding company to apply to original insurances the limitations of the revised United Kingdom Waterborne Agreement of August 1976 which essentially restricts cover to goods on board vessels, with a time limitation after arrival at the port of destination.

By the nature of marine business, treaty cover must be world-wide. Consequently the parties must agree regarding the currencies in which premiums and claims shall be paid, and the conversion rates to be employed. The nearest one gets to geographical limitations is that reinsurers may be wary about accepting liability for reinsurances accepted by a ceding company in London or other subscription markets or under master covers arranged by some of the major international brokers, and, as noted above, may exclude vessels operated under certain flags of convenience.

Accumulations of values at risk

The major accumulation hazard in respect of hulls arises when vessels are in port, though storms and hurricanes ranging over a large area may damage more than one vessel insured by an underwriter. Cargo presents more acute difficulties. Instead of arranging a separate policy for each consignment, firms regularly engaged in the import and/or export of goods normally effect either a floating policy or an open cover whereby the insurer agrees to cover automatically all consignments conforming to the terms of the agreement (e.g. type of vessel, destinations, etc.), subject to declarations of consignments. With exports the insurer soon learns of any consignment from the requests for, or copies of, certificates of insurance issued with the shipping documents, though for goods sent by container 'received for shipment' bills of lading give the operator the

427

right to ship the goods on a vessel other than the one named. The main problem, however, lies with imports where a considerable time can elapse after the commencement of an insurance before the insurer receives the details. An underwriter may eventually find himself overcommitted because several consignments in which he is interested have been loaded on the same vessel.

Unknown accumulations of cargo may occur also at ports where delay can cause large quantities of cargo to collect on the quays and in warehouses, and in vessels anchored in and around the harbour. The delays in certain Middle Eastern and African ports have led London underwriters to redefine 'arrival' and to introduce a voluntary Port Delay Clause.

Accordingly whatever indexing method an underwriter employs to maintain a check on his commitments so that additional facultative reinsurance can be arranged whenever necessary, there always remains the possibility that when a loss occurs his total commitments may exceed his normal retention. An excess of loss treaty provides protection against such an eventuality, subject to the limit of the reinsurer's liability.

There is a risk with cargo quota share and excess of line treaties written subject to the normal limit 'any one bottom' that unknown accumulations may result in a ceding company's gross commitments exceeding the treaty limits. Reinsurers, while recognizing the problem, must limit their own commitments and so deal with the situation by including in treaties a location clause along the lines of the following specimen which grants a limited extension to the cover provided. The extent of the additional liability a reinsurer will accept is a matter for negotiation at the commencement of a treaty: a doubling of the reinsurer's maximum liability as stated in the quoted clause is about the limit and a 50% increase is more usual. Furthermore the emphasis is on *unknown* accumulations—the clause does not permit the ceding company knowingly to accept more than its normal retention.

> Should it happen that, in case of a loss, the total interest of the Reinsured exceeds the maximum amount agreed upon, because of an unforeseen accumulation, the amount exceeding the contractual maximum liability shall be apportioned between the Reinsured and the Reinsurer up to 200% of the maximum agreed upon.
> All other terms and conditions remain unaltered.

A secondary advantage of negotiating such a clause is that it forces ceding companies to look more carefully at their potential share of risks and appreciate the nature of the liabilities they may be assuming.

Before leaving the subject of unknown accumulations a distinction needs to be drawn between accumulations which an insurer cannot possibly control and those which an efficient system of indexing ought to reveal. The demands placed on many insurers in developing countries to provide direct insurance for cargo has overwhelmed their administrative systems so that often they have no clear idea of their commitments on any one vessel. In such cases the reinsurance cannot be written with a limit 'any one bottom' and the only solution is to write the treaty with a relatively low limit for 'any one policy' in order to restrict potential aggregations of liabilities in any vessel or port. The reinsurer, however, will still be more heavily exposed than with an 'any one bottom' limit, so such a treaty will require a lot of investigation in the negotiation stage and regular checking thereafter.

Facultative reinsurance

It would be most unusual for a direct company to be without automatic treaty cover to take care of the normal run of risks for which it needs reinsurance protection, but a substantial amount of reinsurance business is still placed facultatively. Often, subject to the permission of its treaty reinsurer(s), a company will obtain facultative cover for their common account to reduce both its own and its reinsurer's net commitments on a known accumulation: obviously the facultative reinsurance must be obtained before the termination of a voyage and before any loss is known to have occurred.

As noted above, the reinsurance cover may be arranged on a more restrictive basis than the original insurance, such as TLO cover to enable the ceding company to reduce its liability in the event of an actual or constructive total loss involving a very large hull risk. In all such cases the rate to be charged is a matter for negotiation between the ceding company and the reinsurer.

Although most facultative reinsurance is of the proportional kind, there is a growing volume of excess of loss facultative reinsurances being placed, especially by American companies, mostly for hulls.

Finally, some war risks reinsurances are arranged facultatively. For example, if a treaty reinsurer exercises his right under the war cancellation clause to cancel the war cover, the ceding company needs to seek facultative cover for any remaining commitments to its own policyholders.

In all cases the arrangements for effecting facultative reinsurances, dealing with claims and paying accounts follow the procedures described in Chapter 6. For proportional reinsurances on original conditions a reinsurance commission reflecting the ceding company's own acquisition costs is allowed from the reinsurance premium.

Facultative obligatory and open covers

The high degree of selection involved in the operation of such agreements do not make them popular with marine reinsurers. Nevertheless in some markets they are being increasingly used, generally to supplement underlying quota share and/or surplus treaties in order to provide additional capacity for peak risks.

Their mode of operation is identical to that of proportional treaties, apart from the lack of any obligation on the part of the reinsured to cede risks to the reinsurer. Therefore the following discussion of proportional treaties should be taken to include facultative obligatory agreements.

Proportional treaties

The general comments made in Chapter 5 regarding the relative merits and demerits of quota share and excess of line (surplus) reinsurance treaties fully apply to marine business so they will not be repeated here. Also reference has been made already to the specific problem for the marine underwriter of often unknown accumulations of values at risk and the flexibility provided by the location clause. Therefore there will follow a discussion only of other matters peculiar to marine proportional treaties.

Period and basis of cover

Most proportional treaties are arranged on a permanent basis with provision to terminate in accordance with a cancellation clause. The basis of cover is normally for losses arising on insurance written during the currency of the treaty with reinsurances being run off to extinction in the event of the termination of a treaty.

Retentions and treaty limits

Under both quota share and excess of line treaties the ceding company's retention and the reinsurance cover are usually fixed in terms of the means of conveyance. Normally cargo treaties are subject to limits any one bottom, and will incorporate a table of limits, graded according to type and class of vessel, the limit applying to the ceding company's aggregate interest on cargo loaded on board the vessel, whether covered under one or more insurances. Occasionally the treaty limits are expressed in terms of any one policy (see page 429).

The usual practice with hull treaties is to fix a single retention/treaty limit. Some hull business is reinsured on an excess of line basis which is easier to operate than for cargo because there is not the same problem of accumulations, though several vessels may be involved in the same occurrence.

An important difference between marine excess of line and surplus reinsurances employed in other classes of insurance is that the reinsured's retention(s) stated in a marine treaty are mandatory. The ceding company is not permitted to retain more or less than the stated amount on any individual risk.

Cargo excess of line treaties arranged on an any-one-bottom basis present difficulties in operation that are peculiar to marine business. Frequently consignments of goods sent by different insureds may converge on the same vessel and though the value of each consignment may be less than the company's normal retention, in the aggregate they may exceed its limit and accordingly require reinsurance. It is customary to calculate the maximum value at risk as that applying during the main voyage, and that value is used to determine the ceding company's retention and the reinsurer's share. If reinsurance is required, the reinsurer will take a proportionate share of each individual insurance, receiving the same share of premiums and paying the same proportion of all losses. Not infrequently the individual consignments may have been insured on different terms, i.e. FPA (free of particular average), WA (with average) or all risks: by participating in each insurance complications regarding the reinsurer's liability for partial losses are avoided in that he pays his share of the ceding company's liability under each policy. Obviously in order to operate an excess of line reinsurance treaty an elaborate system of indexing is required but, as noted above, no system can avoid entirely the build-up of unknown accumulations.

Other problems arise in connection with enforced transhipment during a voyage, and with losses occurring prior to loading when it is not possible to prove that the goods had been allocated to any particular vessel. Both situations may be dealt with by including in the treaty an additional limit for 'any other risk' besides the limit applicable to any one bottom. Alternatively it may be agreed to deal with the reinsurance of 'unallocated risks' on a quota share basis subject to an appropriate additional premium.

Bordereaux

Usually the reinsurer is forced to operate proportional treaties with no more information than the quarterly accounts. Large direct insurers operating in the subscription marine markets do not normally provide their reinsurers with either premium or claims bordereaux. Moreover only rarely would such a treaty include a clause requiring notification of large claims, so that if the reinsurer has reason to believe that he may be interested in a major loss or series of losses the onus will rest on him to make enquiries. A reinsurer may get some idea of his total commitment in respect of a major loss from the requests he may receive from his clients for cash settlements, but the only way in which he can obtain full information in order to establish whether he in turn has a claim under his own retrocession excess of loss cover is to circularize all clients who may be interested in the loss occurrence.

Nowadays even treaties effected by small companies operating in less developed markets normally make no provision for the supply of bordereaux. New treaties are the only major exception: if the ceding company is just beginning to write marine business the reinsurer may try to insist on bordereaux being supplied for a time. Even then the reinsurer must be satisfied with whatever information he can obtain initially regarding the business and underwriting policy of the ceding company, the experience of its underwriters and so forth.

Reinsurance commission

The marine market follows the general practice of allowing reinsurance commission from the reinsurer's share of the original premiums ceded under proportional treaties, as discussed in Chapter 3.

Brief mention was made in Chapter 3 of the marine practice of reinsurance premiums being based on either gross original premiums or net premiums (i.e. net of commissions and brokerage), with the reinsurance commission being adjusted accordingly. The net basis is used for most of the business originally insured on the American and British markets whereas gross premiums are normally used for business emanating from the rest of the world.

Obviously the rates of reinsurance commission allowed on treaties placed on a net premium basis are lower than for cases where the reinsurer receives a share of the gross premiums. The marine market adheres to the general principle that a treaty reinsurer pays his share of the ceding company's acquisition costs (i.e. commission, brokerage and any discount paid to policyholders) plus some contribution towards administrative expenses. By basing the reinsurance premium on net premiums the ceding company automatically recoups its business acquisition costs so that only administrative expenses need to be taken into account in fixing the rate of reinsurance commission. Theoretically by adjusting the reinsurance commission rate the reinsurer aims to arrive at the same net reinsurance premium income for a particular portfolio of business whether it is based on gross or net premiums. The figures in

Table 12.1 give a broad idea of typical reinsurance commission rates for hull and cargo excess of line treaties for UK and similar accounts; the rates allowed for business emanating from some countries are far higher.

Table 12.1. *Reinsurance commission rates based on*

Excess of line	Gross premiums	Net premiums
Hull	20½% – 22½%	2½% – 5%
Cargo	27½%	7½%

The actual rate of commission allowed in individual cases will depend on such factors as the nature of the reinsured portfolio—i.e. its size, spread, etc.; premium rate levels; the ceding company's acquisition costs and expenses, and the profitability of the business. Essentially in every case the reinsurer will be aiming to obtain a net premium income adequate to cover expected claims plus his own administration costs and to leave a fair margin of profit. It is not marine practice to use sliding scales for the calculation of reinsurance commission, but a flat rate of profit commission is normally allowed on proportional treaties.

Profit commission

The long delays which occur in the notification and settlement of marine reinsurance claims, together with delays in accounting for premiums, mean that some time must elapse after the end of an underwriting year before a clear picture of the year's results emerges. It is normal for marine reinsurance accounts to follow the practice adopted for direct business of keeping separate accounts for individual underwriting years to which premiums can be credited and the claims run off over a period of several years. Therefore profit commission is normally calculated on the results of individual underwriting years, the first statement being prepared after the end of the second or third year following the close of the underwriting year. Because many claims may still be outstanding even after two or three years provision is often made for subsequent annual adjustment either for a specified number of years or until all claims have been run off. The reinsurer will always require losses arising on any one underwriting year to be carried forward into the accounts of subsequent years.

A specimen profit-commission clause is given in Appendix 12.1. It provides for (1) the run-off of claims to extinction, and (2) the carrying forward of deficits on the accounts of earlier underwriting years for a maximum of three years.

Excess of loss treaties

When dealing with excess of loss reinsurances for both hull and cargo business the marine market draws the usual broad distinction between working and catastrophe covers. It is impossible, however, to draw a fine dividing line between the two. Working covers have been defined as: [1]

> Those where the underlying retention is pitched at a relatively low level, thus exposing the covers to claims on single hulls of average value or, in terms of cargo, to limits which would normally be retained by the reinsured.

The London Insurance Institute's Advanced Study Group goes on to stress the point that although a catastrophe cover may be thought of as one where the reinsurer is not exposed to claims on single hulls of average value, such a claim on a vessel of unusually high value, or under a combined hull and cargo cover where there is an accumulation of cargo on board a vessel, may fall within a catastrophe cover. Nevertheless the notion that a catastrophe cover should only come into play for losses involving two or more vessels finds its expression in the incorporation into some hull excess of loss treaties of a 'two vessel warranty' or a 'two-rig warranty', which relieves the reinsurer of any liability unless two or more vessels or rigs are involved in the same loss occurrence. However, such clauses need careful drafting to reconcile the interests of the reinsurer and the ceding company. Therefore for both hull and cargo reinsurances a better arrangement is for the two parties to ensure that the ceding company's retentions on individual risks and the treaty excess point are so fixed that a treaty designed to provide 'catastrophe' protection does not pick up losses involving only one exposure unit. [2]

Period and basis of cover

Excess of loss treaties are normally effected for a 12 month period, but can be on a permanent basis, subject to a cancellation clause.

Cover may be arranged for losses in excess of the reinsured's retention either for 'losses occurring' or in respect of 'risks attaching' during the currency of the treaty. The former basis is the more popular in that it avoids the reinsurer incurring any liability for losses occurring after the termination of the treaty, thus shortening the claims-reporting and settlement tail. On the other hand, when an excess of loss account is arranged for the common account of the ceding company and its proportional treaty reinsurers, the risks attaching basis may be more

1 Report of the Advanced Study Group no. 201 of the Insurance Institute of London, p.59.
2 Ibid., pp.59 – 60.

convenient in that it will cover the same risks as those ceded to the proportional treaty during the year.

Loss occurrence

Although the treaty limits for some cargo treaties apply to any one vessel, marine excess of loss covers normally provide cover for all losses arising out of 'any one event or occurrence', without time or geographical limitation. So, for example, meteorological evidence clearly showed that windstorms that swept across Europe from eastern England to the North Sea coasts of Belgium, the Netherlands and Germany between 2 and 4 January 1976 were all part of the same weather disturbance. Consequently marine losses as far apart as England and Germany two days later were treated by reinsurers as arising out of one event for purposes of determining their liabilities under excess of loss covers. On the other hand a storm that raged simultaneously off the north-western coast of Britain was shown to be a separate event.

It is important that whichever basis is adopted, it should be clearly set out in the treaty because, as will be demonstrated later, the method employed can substantially affect the extent of the reinsurer's liability for losses involving two or more vessels. Occasionally a cargo treaty will give the ceding company the option of choosing whether a particular loss shall be adjusted on an 'any one event' or 'any one vessel' basis.

Normal terms and exclusions

Normally excess of loss treaties are effected on a 12 month basis; if continuous, the treaty would be reviewed annually.

The following classes of business may be excluded from treaties, though cover may be made available at an additional premium when required:
(1) Excess-of-loss reinsurance.
(2) Aircraft hulls and liabilities.
(3) Risks of capture, seizure, confiscation, etc.
(4) Oil-drilling insurances.
(5) Stevedores', warehousemen's, shipbuilders' and repairers' liability.

The exclusion of inwards excess of loss reinsurances, particularly from working covers, is because of the lack of control that a ceding company which accepts such business has over its total commitments. A demand does exist, however, for the inclusion of excess of loss reinsurances in the scope of treaties, especially for treaties effected by companies operating in the sophisticated marine markets.

Reinstatement

Since the 1960s it has become increasingly customary for reinsurers to limit the cover provided by excess of loss treaties through the insertion of reinstatement clauses into their treaty wordings.[3] Essentially such a clause limits the reinsurer's liability in any one year to x times the treaty monetary limit, plus sometimes provision for the ceding company to reinstate all or part of the cover in return for the payment of an additional premium.

This development was in response to the increasing number of large losses and the highly competitive conditions of both direct and reinsurance marine markets which have periodically led to premium rates being forced down to uneconomic levels. In particular reinsurers have tended to insist more on the inclusion of reinstatement conditions in catastrophe covers than for working excess of loss treaties. Partly this is because ceding companies are usually more willing to pay an adequate premium for the latter type of contract to ensure a reasonable degree of balance in the retained portfolio, and also because it is easier to calculate an adequate premium for working covers, there being more objective data on which to work. Adequacy of premium is the key factor, there being an observable trade-off between the level of premium the ceding company is prepared to pay and the stringency of the reinstatement conditions the reinsurer will seek to impose for any given aggregate limit.

The London Institute Advanced Study Group illustrate this point with the following example of the terms offered for a catastrophe excess of loss treaty providing cover for £250,000 excess of £500,000.

	Quotation A	Quotation B
Annual premium	£35,000	£40,000
Reinstatements allowed	1 at 100% of annual premium	2 at 50% of annual premium

Under A the ceding company would be able to recover from the reinsurer excess losses up to £500,000 during any one year for a total premium of £70,000. Under B the maximum recovery would be £750,000 for a total premium of £80,000.

Thus in return for a larger annual premium under B the ceding company could obtain, if required, extra cover during any one year of £500,000 for an additional premium of £40,000 (equal to a rate of 8%), whereas under quotation A the limited extra cover of £250,000 would cost £35,000 (equal to a rate of 14%). Endless permutations are possible. Often if the ceding company is prepared to pay a sufficiently high annual premium a certain amount of reinstatement may be provided free, which would have the advantage of avoiding the possible administrative costs

3 Ibid., p.66.

to both parties of calculating and paying additional premiums.

Specific reinsurance and third party recovery clauses

There is a duty on every ceding company to take all reasonable steps to minimize the losses for which the reinsurer may be liable, and to maintain existing underwriting policies. Therefore, it is arguable that an excess of loss reinsurer has the right to expect that a ceding company will continue to effect facultative reinsurance to reduce its commitments on individual large risks or known accumulations when judged necessary to maintain a reasonably balanced portfolio of business, and also that it will vigorously pursue its rights of recovery against third parties, although the benefit of both actions may accrue solely to the reinsurer. As an inducement to the ceding company to take such steps, reinsurers are sometimes willing to share the benefits. Under specific reinsurance and third party recovery clauses any sum recovered by the ceding company from an underlying facultative reinsurance and/or a third party has to be shared between the company and its reinsurer(s) in proportion to their respective liabilities. The following simple example will illustrate how a specific reinsurance clause works; a third-party recovery clause employs the same principle. Assume:

(1) Excess of loss cover for £80,000 in excess of £20,000.
(2) Insured value £60,000.
(3) Facultative reinsurance arranged for 50%.

If the insured property was a total loss the liabilities of the ceding company and the excess of loss reinsurer would be as in Table 12.2.

Table 12.2

Ceding company		Excess of loss reinsurer
Ultimate net loss £	After excess of loss recovery £	£
(a) in absence of facultative reinsurance		
60,000	20,000	40,000
(b) with 50% facultative reinsurance		
30,000	20,000	10,000
(c) with benefit of specific reinsurance clause		
	20,000	40,000
less share of facultative reinsurance recovery ⅓ =	10,000	⅔ = 20,000
	10,000	20,000

It must be recognized, however, that any sharing of the benefit which the reinsurer would otherwise have received will be reflected in the treaty results and thus in the premium required. Possibly because of this fact the clauses have now gone out of common use.

Hull treaties

Although there is a trend towards reinsuring hull accounts on an excess of loss basis, pure hull excess of loss treaties, as opposed to combined hull and cargo treaties, are still fairly uncommon. Many accounts are too small, but even when direct underwriters have established, well spread and balanced accounts which would be acceptable to excess of loss reinsurers, they may feel there is such a low risk of incurring unknown accumulations on hull business that it is not worth getting involved in the problems of negotiating the premium for an excess of loss cover. Certainly underwriters operating in purely local markets should encounter no great difficulties in keeping a check on their commitments on any one vessel, so that proportional reinsurance should be able to take care of acceptances in excess of the company's own capacity. Direct insurers writing business in the subscription marine markets on the other hand face greater difficulties in indexing their commitments because they may pick up liabilities not only through direct insurances but also under inwards facultative and treaty reinsurances. Therefore, there has been a demand from such markets for excess of loss treaties to protect ceding companies' net hull portfolios including inwards reinsurances: the excess of loss cover may be arranged in layers. Retrocession excess of loss treaties are also placed by reinsurers to protect themselves from accumulations of liabilities they may incur under proportional reinsurances they have accepted.

Excess of loss reinsurance normally would not be provided for a single vessel or even an individual fleet, proportional reinsurance being regarded as the more appropriate form of protection. Generally when an excess of loss treaty is effected it covers the whole of the ceding company's hull portfolio even though from the standpoint of a working cover the portfolio may contain only a relatively few hulls with values in excess of the company's retention limit.

Complications can arise when the ceding company has insured a fleet subject to an aggregate deductible, i.e. when the fleet · owner is responsible for the first £x of the total losses suffered by the fleet during any one underwriting year. If the fleet should suffer several losses during the year the method used to apportion the aggregate deductible between the original losses may substantially affect the excess of loss reinsurer's liability as shown in the following example.

Assume:

(1) Aggregate fleet deductible £10,000.

(2) Excess of loss reinsurance £100,000 in excess of £25,000.

(3) Losses during the year from four incidents are £8,000, £28,000, £4,000 and £30,000.

The various liabilities are shown in Table 12.3.

Table 12.3

Loss £	Fleet owner's liability £	Ceding company's net liability £	Reinsurer's liability £
(a) If deductible apportioned in chronological order of the losses			
8,000	8,000	0	0
28,000	2,000	25,000	1,000
4,000	—	4,000	0
30,000	—	25,000	5,000
70,000	10,000	54,000	6,000
(b) If deductible apportioned over all losses proportional to the size of loss			
8,000	1,143	6,857	0
28,000	4,000	24,000	0
4,000	571	3,429	0
30,000	4,286	25,000	714
70,000	10,000	59,286	714

The reinsurer may argue that method *(b)* is the fairer but it would be difficult to operate because of the long delays that often occur in the settlement of hull claims so that several years may elapse before the reinsurer's final liability could be established. Therefore in practice it is probably better for both parties if method *(a)* is adopted, particularly as it is becoming the practice in the London marine market to specify in the original hull policy that the aggregate deductible shall be absorbed in the order of the dates of the original claims settlements. Whichever method is adopted it is important that it should be clearly set out in the treaty wording to avoid the possibility of dispute between the ceding company and the reinsurer.

The rating of hull excess of loss treaties poses the sort of general problems discussed in Chapter 5, with the same broad distinction between working and catastrophe covers.

It may be argued that, especially for an insurer operating in the sophisticated international marine markets, the burning-cost method of calculating the premium is not very suitable for a working excess of loss hull treaty because the operating results of even well spread marine accounts are subject to severe cyclical fluctuations. Therefore, the London Advanced Study Group advocated a more direct method which bases the reinsurance premium on the exposure of the reinsured portfolio as follows: [4]

Step 1   Estimate the reinsurer's exposure by taking the sum of the individual values at risk in excess of the ceding company's retention, i.e.

$$E = \sum_{j=1}^{n} (v_j - r)$$

where E = total treaty exposure

v_j = individual values at risk

r = ceding company's retention (i.e. the treaty excess point)

and $(v_j - r) > 0$.

Step 2   Because the reinsurer becomes involved mainly in total losses, calculate the appropriate average Total Loss Only premium rate for the class(es) of vessels involved.

Step 3   Load the TLO rate to allow for:
(1) Possible contributions to large Particular Average and General Average losses.
(2) The reinsurer's administrative expenses and profit.
(3) A contribution to the reinsurer's contingency funds.

Step 4   Multiply E by the loaded rate to obtain the premium required.

Step 5   Express the premium as a percentage of the ceding company's current gross net premium income to obtain the reinsurance premium rate.

So, for example, if E = £1,000,000; gross net premium income = £250,000; average TLO rate = 0.6%; and the loading factor = 50%; then the required premium is:

$$£1,000,000 \times (0.6\% \times 1.5) = £9,000$$

and the reinsurance rate to be applied to the ceding company's gross net premium income is:

$$\frac{9,000}{250,000} \times 100 = 3.6\%$$

The calculation of the average TLO rate would need to be based more on the reinsurer's experience on the class of vessels involved than on current market rates and likewise the loading factor would be determined by the individual circumstances. Thus it would be hoped that the resultant reinsurance premium rate would be unaffected by the cyclical fluctuations in the direct marine market and so could be kept stable for a number of years. In reality this ideal is probably unattainable because no reinsurer is immune to prevailing competitive pressures and its premium rates have to be modified accordingly.

Premiums for hull catastrophe covers present the same problems as for other classes of insurance. Although reinsurers ask for details of the ceding company's past loss experience, such information is of very limited value because of the very low frequency of losses that fall within a catastrophe cover. Consequently the premium is more likely to be based on the reinsurer's estimate of his exposure obtained from information supplied about the portfolio to be reinsured, loss trends (i.e. the frequency of losses and, particularly in a period of inflation, the cost of repairs and of shipbuilding) and finally the current levels of premiums being quoted in the market for such covers.

Cargo excess of loss treaties

This method of handling cargo business is becoming increasingly popular because of the automatic cover provided for unknown accumulations and its economy of operation.

Cargo original insurances are arranged on a voyage basis; that is, the insurer provides cover for each consignment from the time of dispatch until delivery at destination, including storage in warehouses, wharves, etc., during the course of transit (subject to certain limitations). During any one underwriting year an insurer will be interested in many consignments: although most will commence and terminate their voyages during the year, many will lap over two underwriting years. Therefore, to avoid complications treaties are normally arranged on a 'losses occurring' basis.

The basis of cover. As stated earlier, cargo excess of loss treaties normally apply the treaty limits to 'any one event or occurrence', though some working covers are effected on an 'any one vessel' basis. Neither method has a clear advantage over the other: everything depends upon the particular circumstances of a loss and the treaty limits as the following examples show.

Assume:

(1) Excess of loss cover for £35,000 excess of £10,000.

(2) All losses arise out of the same event.

Table 12.4 shows the effects of two treaty bases on two sets of losses.

Table 12.4

Loss per vessel £	Treaty on 'any one vessel' basis		Treaty on 'any one event' basis	
	Ceding company's net liability £	Reinsurer's liability £	Ceding company's net liability £	Reinsurer's liability £
Example 1				
(a) 20,000	10,000	10,000		
(b) 8,000	8,000	0		
(c) 15,000	10,000	5,000	10,000	35,000
(d) 22,000	10,000	12,000	+ 20,000	
65,000	38,000	27,000	30,000	35,000
Example 2				
(a) 38,000	10,000	28,000		
(b) 22,000	10,000	12,000	10,000	
(c) 4,000	4,000	0	+ 20,000	35,000
(d) 1,000	1,000	0		
65,000	25,000	40,000	30,000	35,000

Although the total losses arising out of the one event are identical in both cases, in example 1 the ceding company would be better off with the excess of loss reinsurance arranged on an 'any one event' basis whereas in the second example it would benefit from the excess point being applied to the losses for each vessel.

Whichever method is adopted the ceding company must give considerable thought to the treaty limits. If the cover is arranged on an 'any one vessel' basis the occurrence of some event involving several vessels could leave the ceding company with a financially embarrassing accumulation of net retained losses. On the other hand the upper treaty limit for an excess of loss cover arranged on an 'any one event' basis must be sufficiently high to take care of such accumulations. When excess of loss cover is the only form of reinsurance effected, one possible compromise is to arrange a working cover on an 'any one vessel' basis and to supplement the cover with a catastrophe cover on an 'any one event' basis to cover the company's ultimate net losses.

One further difficulty with treaties arranged on an 'any one vessel' basis applies to consignments stored in warehouses, wharves, etc., which have not been allocated to a particular vessel. A possible solution is to apply a separate limit 'any one location' for such unallocated risks.

The rating of cargo covers follows the same methods as described for hull. Again the reinsurer should attempt to estimate his exposure by calculating the ceding company's aggregate liability according to the main trading routes covered by its portfolio of business and possible accumulations ashore; for example most of the consignments insured by a local company may pass through one or two ports. Then the reinsurer can calculate the premium rate to be applied to the ceding company's gross net premium income to produce the premium for a working cover. Instead of using a TLO rate the reinsurer would need to take a mean Free of Particular Average rate and also increase the loading factor to allow for accumulations ashore.

When dealing with large companies writing cargo business world-wide such a procedure is impractical and one of the burning-cost methods described in Chapter 5 must be used, despite the comments made earlier about the distortions produced by the fluctuating underwriting results of marine business.

Whole account (combined hull and cargo) excess of loss treaties

The disadvantage to a ceding company of arranging separate excess of loss treaties for its hull and cargo business is that it may find itself fully committed to the extent of its retentions under both accounts in respect of the same loss. One way an insurer may limit its aggregate liability is to fix lower individual retentions than it otherwise could afford to bear. A more satisfactory solution may be to arrange a combined hull and cargo treaty, often called a whole-account cover, where the monetary limits apply to all of the business accepted by the company.

The rating of combined covers works on the same principles as discussed for hull and cargo. For both working and catastrophe covers the reinsurer will try to obtain as much information as possible about the aggregate exposure under the hull and cargo sections of the account in order to assess his potential liability. The normal procedure with working covers is then to calculate separate rates for each section and apply the combined rate to the ceding company's total gross net premium income.

With catastrophe covers the reinsurer must take into account the increased probability of aggregate losses reaching the higher layers.

War risks

Following the Arab-Israeli War of June 1967 the leading excess of loss reinsurers operating on the London market agreed on a standard practice for dealing with war risks cover.[5] Now war risks are either excluded from

---

5 Ibid., p.67.

excess of loss treaties by the War Exclusion clause or included by the War Inclusion clause (see Appendix 12.3).

When, as generally happens, war risks are included in the treaty at one rate of premium, under the terms of the war inclusion clause:

(1) The war cover is restricted to the risks covered under the current Institute War Risk or similar clauses.

(2) There is no provision for cancellation mid-term.

(3) Only one reinstatement of cover is permitted, subject to the payment of an additional premium.

(4) The reinstatement provision applies jointly to both marine and war losses, so that in fixing the treaty limit regard must be paid to the potential losses from both marine and war risks.

In view of the restrictions imposed by (3) and (4) it is safer to deal with war risks by effecting a separate war risks excess of loss treaty at a separate rate, especially as it is then possible to negotiate, in return for a commensurately higher rate of premium, more than one reinstatement. The only other alternative is to reinsure war risks separately on a proportional basis so that there is no problem with reinstatement.

A major problem with the reinsurance of war risks by an excess of loss cover arranged on an any one event basis is the impossibility of defining in advance what is an event. For example, if a series of large-scale guerrilla attacks launched from country A on the ports of B over a period of, say, a fortnight provoke B into declaring war on A, would all losses occurring over that period constitute one event? Under such circumstances the parties to a treaty may have to wait several months or even years for an arbitration decision to establish the answer. Not suprisingly the London Institute Study Group concluded that:

> The moral may be that war risks do not lend themselves naturally to excess of loss protection. [6]

Reporting excess of loss treaties

Normally this type of cover is restricted to cargo business and is used when a ceding company is likely to insure only a few isolated risks for which reinsurance protection is required and there is little, if any, possibility of accumulations. In effect it is a form of facultative obligatory cover, the ceding company notifying the reinsurer of individual sums in excess of the agreed excess point.

There are two forms of reporting covers:

(1) Where the reinsurers receive prior advice of any exposure to the cover and are paid an agreed percentage of the original premium, plus normally 100% of the war premium and the over-age additional

6 Ibid., p.69.

premium, if any, on the amount exposed.

(2) Where the ceding company may make a monthly return totalling the sums exposed on the cover to which is applied an agreed rate. Normally a world-wide FPA plus war rate is agreed plus, if necessary, a flat premium per annum to cover storage risks where the original policies are extended beyond the terms of the Transit Clause of the Institute Cargo Clauses.

Specific excess of loss reinsurance

In some cases where an underwriter feels that his line on a particular contract is too large, he will arrange a specific excess-of-loss reinsurance to protect that contract alone. Normally such reinsurances are based on two-thirds excess of one-third of the line accepted by the ceding company, and the premium charged varies between 40% and 60% of the original net premium depending on the circumstances.

Stop loss and excess of loss ratio treaties

Aggregate excess of loss cover is a special limited form of stop loss cover employed in the marine market to protect an underwriter against the risk of a series of losses occurring during one year which, though individually falling within his retention limit, may in the aggregate cause financial embarrassment. The reinsurer provides cover on an excess of loss basis for losses arising from any one event (or any one vessel) in excess of the ceding company's retention up to an agreed limit, *but* the cover only operates when the claims otherwise recoverable under the treaty during any one year in the aggregate exceed some agreed amount.

The following example will illustrate how the cover operates.

Assume:

(1) A company has a gross premium income of £1 million.

(2) It arranges catastrophe excess of loss cover for £2 million excess of £100,000 any one event.

(3) Although it could afford to carry one or two losses of, say, £75,000 to £100,000 each, any more losses of such a size would cause financial strain.

(4) Reinsurers require a prohibitively high premium to lower the deductible on the excess of loss cover. Therefore the company arranges an aggregate excess of loss cover for £50,000 excess of £50,000 any one event, the company carrying the first £75,000 of losses otherwise recoverable under the treaty during one year.

(5) The company incurs the following losses during one year:

Loss 1	£120,000	(£20,000 recoverable under catastrophe cover)
Loss 2	£75,000	
Loss 3	£80,000	
Loss 4	£90,000	

The treaty would pay:

Loss	Retained loss in excess of £50,000 £	Treaty pays £	Aggregate retained loss £
1	50,000	—	50,000
2	25,000	—	75,000
3	30,000	30,000	—
4	40,000	20,000	—

If the treaty provided for one reinstatement of cover the whole £40,000 for loss 4 would have been payable too.

The term 'aggregate excess of loss cover' is also used to describe treaties arranged to provide additional reinstatements in the event of the main treaty being limited to, say, one reinstatement.

Excess of loss ratio treaties achieved a certain degree of popularity in the 1960s but now there is a very limited market for such business. Marine insurance is not the type of business which is exposed to the random occurrence of severe losses in any one year for which such treaties are ideally suited. Instead underwriting results tend to follow regular cycles associated more with the effects of competition than with the random incidence of severe losses, and a stop loss treaty would simply protect the ceding company from underwriting losses in those years when premium rates were forced down to uneconomic levels. Consequently rating poses considerable problems, and unless the excess point is fixed at a very high level it is difficult for a reinsurer to avoid incurring a loss.

Nevertheless there is a limited amount of excess of loss ratio business transacted on the London market, mainly at Lloyd's.

Excess of loss reinsurance and oil-rig accounts

Separate reinsurance programmes are normally arranged for both of these two particularly hazardous marine accounts with their high potential accumulations of liability. In both cases the market for such business is very limited, and the rates required are high. Because the rates required for such specific accounts are substantially higher than for treaties covering a ceding company's whole account, there is a tendency for companies seeking cover for top layers to obtain protection for the whole account though in fact cover is required only for the specific account. It is essential, therefore, that full information be obtained regarding a company's business when quoting for excess of loss covers, and especially top layers.

The relatively small number of offshore oil and gas rigs and production platforms operating thoughout the world, and the enormous values involved for some of the installations have created considerable capacity problems. One approach has been to organize master covers and other forms of pool whereby both direct insurers and professional reinsurers participate in the direct insurance of rigs and platforms for an agreed share based on net retentions.

II AVIATION REINSURANCE

Aviation as a separate class of business has developed out of insurances originally underwritten by insurers in their marine and accident departments which still handle a lot of insurance associated with air transport. For example, air cargo is normally insured under marine policies; many personal accident policies covering air travellers are issued by accident departments; and companies writing only a small amount of aviation business often have no separate aviation department. Over the last two decades, however, a distinctive aviation market has evolved in response to the rapid growth of air transport with its accompanying demand for insurance from air fleet operators, air charter and taxi operators, the owners of business and private aircraft, manufacturers of aircraft and components, passengers, crew, air cargo firms, and since the 1960s the manufacturers and operators of space satellites. The demand for insurance embraces property (hull and cargo), freight, personal accident, loss of licence, public liability and products liability risks. [7] Some of the insurances are for relatively small sums, but the level of protection required for other risks sometimes strains the capacity of international insurance markets, as witnessed by the hull and passenger liability losses arising from the collision of two jumbo jets at Tenerife airport in 1977.

Companies that write a substantial amount of aviation business have set up separate aviation departments or have cooperated in forming specialist aviation insurance companies, and alongside the local direct insurance markets there has evolved an international reinsurance market, largely centred on London. Following the considerable escalation of hull values and potential liabilities that has occurred over the last decade it has become necessary for insurers and reinsurers world-wide to participate in the provision of cover for the major risks.

So long as demand continues to develop as rapidly as at present, neither insurance and reinsurance practice, nor market conditions can be static. Until the early 1970s the acceptance of treaty business was confined mainly to the professional reinsurance companies and Lloyd's: now the aviation departments of many direct insurers have expanded their interest in such business too. Amongst the newer companies now participating in the international market are an increasing number of local companies operating in smaller countries that have been required by their governments to provide cover for national airlines. Some of the companies, in order to obtain a reasonably balanced portfolio of

---

[7] For a short account of the types of buyers of aviation insurance and the forms of cover available see W.C. Corbett, 'The insurance of aircraft and aviation risks', in *Handbook of Insurance*, ed. R.L. Carter.

business, have sought inwards international reinsurance business, which in turn has increased their underwriting capacity thereby enabling them to retain for their own account a larger share of the local direct business. Consequently 100% facultative reinsurances, often associated with national airline business, are becoming less common than in the past. Nevertheless because of government regulations a lot of business that otherwise would be placed direct comes on to the international aviation market as facultative reinsurances. Normally the lead on such business is taken by underwriters who mainly write direct business and who may fix the terms for the original insurance if the ceding company itself has little experience of aviation insurance.

Another feature of the aviation insurance market is the large volume of retrocession business that is placed internationally. The substantial liabilities involved for airlines and the major manufacturers requires both direct underwriters and reinsurers to spread the relatively limited number of individual risks as widely as possible. On the other hand, reciprocity as such is not of importance in aviation reinsurance practice. Direct insurers normally do not seek to obtain a reciprocal exchange of reinsurance business when placing their own reinsurances. The only general exchange of business occurs with individual risks, such as the business of national airlines.

Two special arrangements that have developed to spread risks and mobilize capacity more effectively are sharing agreements and the formation of national aviation pools. Generally pools have been set up in countries with large insurance industries but with little experience of writing aviation business. Sharing agreements may be between individual insurers or groups of insurers or pools, and are achieved by the normal type of reinsurance arrangement.

Finally, the predominance of American aircraft manufacturers and the role of US dollars in international monetary transactions, results in the majority of reinsurance contracts providing for all settlements to be in US dollars rather than local currencies.

Forms of aviation reinsurance business

All forms of reinsurance are used for the protection of aviation accounts. A substantial proportion of the total volume of business is still placed as proportional reinsurance, partly because of the relatively small number of individual risks—there are currently some 6,500 airline aircraft plus possibly 150,000 light aircraft in the United States and a further 60,000 in other parts of the world. The extent to which an underwriter can achieve a well-spread account clearly differs between one dealing with general aviation insurance and one covering airline business. Given the inherent instability of airline accounts, not unnaturally reinsurers prefer to participate in the whole account. Nevertheless, as in other classes of business there is a trend towards greater use of excess of loss covers.

The direction in which the business is developing can be seen in the insurance arrangements of airlines. At the end of the 1960s an airline would probably still have separate hull, hull war, passenger liability, third-party liability, freight liability, mail legal liability, and cargo liability policies. An insurer, therefore, could also make separate reinsurance arrangements for the separate classes of risk it accepted. Now in a drive to simplify insurance programmes and reduce administrative costs it is common to issue only two policies; a combined hull and liability insurance covering in one limit of indemnity all types of liability risk and a separate hull war policy. Consequently separate hull and liability reinsurances are becoming less usual—administratively it is easier to handle all of the business under one treaty.

Not all aviation business is for large amounts. Often limits of indemnity on the liability sections of policies covering small private aircraft operating in Britain are still only in the region of £100,000 and a substantial amount of personal accident business is written for small (e.g. £2,000) capital sums on individual lives. At the other end of the scale, in mid-1977 the values at risk for an airline operating only a small fleet could be $50 million or more for each hull, and an airline flying into the United States would require a limit of indemnity of up to $350 million on the combined liability section of its insurance. Similarly the limit on the products liability insurance of a large manufacturer could be $400 million. Although a leading underwriter will normally accept only between 5% and 10% of such major risks, the reinsurance arrangements for a company's direct insurance and reinsurance accounts must make provision for both the small and the large risks that it underwrites.

Given the considerable differences between companies engaged in the underwriting of aviation business it is impossible to speak of a typical reinsurance programme. The needs of aviation insurers range from a small company writing no airline or products liability business, to a state insurance corporation in a developing country whose business may consist largely of the insurances of a small national airline, to a major specialist company writing direct and reinsurance business on the London market. Therefore the distribution of reinsurances between the different forms of cover varies substantially, reflecting the differing circumstances of companies and their ideas regarding the most suitable arrangements. Nevertheless a certain pattern is discernible.

Generally companies operating in the major international markets tend to divide their aviation business into three separate accounts—hull and liability combined, hull war risks, and excess of loss reinsurances. Not all underwriters necessarily accept all of the classes of business, whereas others also engage in the provision of specialist insurances, such as airline personal accident insurances to provide automatic compensation for passengers, or loss of licence insurances for professional aircrew. Typically separate reinsurance arrangements are made to protect each account. The larger the account the more complicated the reinsurance arrangements are likely to be, but for a combined hull and liability account the reinsurance programme may consist of:

(1) A *quota share treaty* to provide the company with sufficient underwriting capacity to enable it to accept the normal run of business it is likely to be offered up to an agreed limit.

(2) A *surplus treaty* to take care of the larger risks above the quota treaty limit. Companies operating on the London and other major markets normally do not effect more than a 10-line treaty. Companies operating in more restricted markets where facilities do not exist for extensively spreading a risk among coinsurers often require commensurately larger reinsurance facilities. Normally two surplus treaties are then arranged. The first, for perhaps five lines, will provide protection for the normal run of relatively small business, while the second surplus treaty will provide the company with the capacity to handle the larger risks it is forced to write, including perhaps the insurances of a local airline.

(3) A *catastrophe excess of loss treaty* to protect the company against an accumulation of losses flowing from one event. The cover would be arranged in layers, five or more layers not being uncommon to provide protection against the very large liability that may arise from air disasters.

There has been a trend for the lower limits on excess of loss treaties to be brought down to levels where the cover takes on the characteristics of a working cover, but most of the business placed on the London market can still be classified as catastrophe protection.

Sometimes in addition to the above an insurer will arrange a facultative obligatory cover so that automatic proportional reinsurance is available for any risk offered in excess of its quota-share and surplus treaty limits.

Facultative reinsurance

A substantial amount of aviation reinsurance is placed facultatively, particularly on the London market. Though it mainly consists of proportional reinsurances, some excess of loss covers are placed facultatively too. In particular, when an airline has arranged its own liability insurance in layers, and has effected special 'excess liabilities' or 'remote exposure' insurance above its normal anticipated liability for protection against possible catastrophe losses, the direct insurer may in turn seek facultative excess of loss reinsurance to protect himself against part of the liability he has accepted. Generally such reinsurance follows the original insurance. Sometimes direct insurers reinsure only part of the liabilities they have accepted either by effecting a first loss or an excess cover: in such cases the facultative reinsurance is rated independently of the premium charged for the original insurance.

Aviation underwriters seek facultative cover for individual risks for the same reasons as apply in other classes of business, e.g. because the underwriter wants to accept some business in excess of, or of a type excluded from, his existing treaty facilities, or because he feels obliged to write some business which he normally prefers to avoid. Treaty reinsurers usually allow ceding companies to reinsure facultatively in front of the treaty, and thereby exercise their underwriting judgment for the benefit of both parties.

Besides what may be called the ordinary flow of facultative business, there is a special demand for facultative cover arising from the fairly common insistence of governments that the insurances of national airlines be placed with local insurers. Then recourse to the international insurance market through the use of facultative reinsurance may be the only way of dealing with the business. If the underwriting capacity of the local insurer(s) is low relative to the cover required, and particularly if the insured portfolio contains few, if any, other large risks, the airline business would be too unbalanced to be handled by normal treaty facilities. Given also that the local company may have little aviation insurance experience and thus lack the necessary underwriting and claims-handling expertise, the business offered to international insurers, though technically in the form of facultative reinsurance, is akin to direct insurance. Under such circumstances the ceding company's retention loses its normal significance, and the leading facultative reinsurer effectively assumes the role of leading underwriter. When such business is placed on the London market the lead is usually taken by one of the recognized leading direct underwriters who will quote the terms and conditions to be applied to the business, and the reinsurance will be made subject to a 'full reinsuring' clause along the following lines:[8]

Reinsurance Underwriting and Claims Control Clause

1. Being a reinsurance of the ____ Company and, except as provided by paragraph 2 hereof, warranted the same gross rate, terms and conditions as the said company has agreed at inception, and that the said company retains during the currency of this policy at least ____ on the identical subject-matter and risk and in identically the same proportion of each separate part thereof, but in the event of the retained line being less than as above, underwriters' lines to be proportionately reduced.

2. Subject to the foregoing, it is a condition precedent to any liability under this reinsurance that:

(a) No amendment to the terms or conditions or additions to or deletions from the original policy shall be binding upon Underwriters hereon unless prior agreement has been obtained from the said Underwriters.

(b) The Reassured shall upon knowledge of any loss or losses which may give rise to a claim under this policy, advise the Underwriters by cable within 72 hours.

(c) The Reassured shall furnish the Underwriters with all information available respecting such loss or losses, and the Underwriters shall have the sole right to appoint adjusters, assessors, surveyors and/or lawyers and to control all negotiations, adjustments and settlements in connection with such loss or losses.

As indicated in part (c) of clause 2, reinsurers usually want to exercise some control over claims. Notification of claims as received by the ceding insurer plus information regarding their progress is the normal minimum requirement so that the reinsurer can maintain a check on potential liabilities and reserve accordingly. If such information is not supplied, many months (or even years with liability claims) may elapse before the reinsurer becomes aware of a loss. At the same time the reinsurer may wish to be consulted regarding the handling of large claims; the following clause is a typical example of such a claims reporting and cooperation clause used on the London market.

Claims Cooperation Clause

Notwithstanding anything herein contained to the contrary, it is a condition precedent to any liability under this policy that:

(a) The reassured shall, upon knowledge of any loss or losses which may give rise to a claim under this policy, advise the underwriters thereof by cable within 72 hours.

(b) The reassured shall furnish the underwriters with all information available respecting such loss or losses, and the underwriters shall have the right to appoint adjusters, assessors and/or surveyors and to control all negotiations, adjustments and settlements in connection with such loss or losses.

---

8 This and the following two clauses are ones approved by Lloyd's Aviation Underwriters' Association.

Procedures

Procedures for placing facultative reinsurances on the London market, either direct by the ceding company or (more usually) through a broker, follow the general lines described in Chapter 6. Normally, pending the preparation of the policy a cover-note, or take-note, will be issued by the reinsurer or broker providing brief particulars of the risk reinsured and the terms and conditions applying.

Commissions

Sometimes premium rates for facultative reinsurances are quoted 'net absolute', when no reinsurance commission is allowed. Otherwise, reinsurance commission is allowed on aviation facultative reinsurances. Normally the same rate of commission is allowed as on the original insurance plus an overriding commission of up to 2½% on the net premium—a similar percentage is allowed as brokerage. It is not the practice for reinsurers to grant profit commission, but when a profit commission is allowed on the original insurance, the reinsurance premium will be based on the net original premium after deduction of the profit commission.

Proportional treaties

Quota share

Such treaties operate in the same way as for other classes of insurance, the reinsurer(s) accepting liability for an agreed share of all insurances (and reinsurances) written by the ceding company, and in return receiving the same share of the net original premiums, less overriding reinsurance commission.

Scope. The scope of the treaty may be defined broadly in such terms as:

> all original policies and agreements of Aviation Hull insurance issued by the reassured.

Alternatively a more detailed statement of the intention of the parties may be included by the use of clauses such as:

> It is further understood and agreed that whenever and wherever the word 'aircraft' appears herein, it shall be deemed to include spacecraft and/or satellites and/or hovercraft and/or any other business of a similar nature,

accepted or written by the Company in their Aviation Department as an aviation risk.

Limitations. Normally reinsurers wish to control the type of business that may fall within the scope of the treaty, and therefore will insert a list of exclusions relating to hazardous classes of risk, and inwards automatic reinsurances over which the ceding company can exercise no underwriting control. Some types of risk may be totally excluded; others may be excluded unless the reinsurer's prior consent has been obtained. The following list taken from an Aviation Hull quota share treaty gives a clear indication of the types of risk that reinsurers view with caution. In addition war risks would be excluded, the cover when required normally being arranged by a separate treaty.

EXCLUSIONS

This Agreement does not apply to:

(1) Reinsurances unless they be of a company managed by the Reassured.

(2) Coinsurances unless specially agreed by Reinsurers hereon prior to attachment.

(3) Scheduled and non-scheduled airlines and feeder-line operators. It is nevertheless agreed to include Assureds where scheduled flying forms only an incidental part of their operations.

(4) Agricultural risks except in respect of simulated crop dusting and spraying carried out by Assureds who operate demonstration and sales business.

(5) Helicopters unless forming part of a fleet of predominantly fixed-wing aircraft or where a helicopter is accepted by the Assured as a trade-in.

(6) Business, or renewals thereof, other than that already handled by ____ known to be already placed in the London market unless at the same rates terms and conditions or unless previously agreed by Reinsurers.

(7) Risks which have been written:

(a) On a first loss basis (unless it is warranted that no further insurance in excess of such first loss insurance will be effected).

(b) Complementary to or in excess of underlying insurances effected on such first loss basis.

(c) Subject to deductibles not borne net by the Assured.

It is agreed that the Reassured may underwrite risks in respect of 'Third Level Carriers' provided that they are submitted to and approved by reinsurers prior to attachment of the risk.

Also a restriction may be placed on the geographical sources of the ceding company's business, as in the following clause, and a maximum monetary limit will be placed on the size of individual insurance or reinsurance it may underwrite, e.g. a limit any one aircraft.

TERRITORIAL SCOPE

The territorial scope of policies covered by this agreement is world-wide provided that aircraft based outside of the Western Hemisphere are owned and/or operated by a Company based in the Western Hemisphere and/or any Subsidiary and/or Affiliated Company thereof and that the aircraft be registered in the country of the parent organization. If these conditions cannot be fulfilled then Assureds outside of the Western Hemisphere are only covered hereon subject to prior agreement by Reinsurers.

Period of cover. Normally aviation policies are issued for a period of insurance of 12 months but with provision for extension. Provision may be made in the treaty for cessions for longer periods, e.g. up to 36 months, though probably subject to the proviso that any such policy shall contain a cancellation clause, and provision for annual review.

Facultative reinsurances. It is normal market practice to include in treaties a clause along the following lines permitting the ceding company to arrange facultative reinsurance in front of the treaty. It would be unwise to allow a ceding company to reduce its own net retention unilaterally on selected risks, so when facultative reinsurance is arranged it must also protect the interest of the reinsurer(s). In return for the right to share in any claims recoveries, the clause requires the treaty reinsurer to pay his proportionate share of the premiums for facultative reinsurances arranged by the reinsured.

PERMITTED REINSURANCE

The Aviation Managers are at liberty, whenever they deem such a course to be advisable, to reinsure totally or in part any risk ceded under this agreement, such reinsurance being considered as for the common account of the Reinsured and the Reinsurers. The Reinsurers shall bear their proportionate share of any cost or risk attending such reinsurance and shall receive their proportionate share of any benefits, returns and/or claims collected thereunder.

Bordereaux. Almost invariably nowadays treaties are operated blind, the reinsurer being supplied with no details of the risks ceded, other than those special risks listed in an exclusions clause for which the prior approval of the reinsurer is required. The only control exercised by reinsurers is through the inclusion of a clause giving them the right to inspect the ceding company's books.

Claims bordereaux are sometimes still required, especially for small companies operating outside the main aviation insurance markets. In other cases the ceding company will be required to provide details of large losses expected to exceed an agreed sum (e.g. $100,000), and of the total estimated value of claims outstanding at the end of each quarter.

Commission. It is normal for reinsurers to pay both reinsurance commission and profit commission on aviation quota share treaties. The overriding rate of commission is normally between 2% and 5%, with brokerage between 1% and 2½%. Profit commission rates usually range from 5% to 10% with the commission being calculated on the results of individual underwriting years as for marine treaties.

Other provisions that are common to quota share treaties for other classes of non-life insurance, e.g. premium and claims reserves, the payment of interest on premium deposits, cash settlement of losses exceeding an agreed sum, cancellation, arbitration etc., similarly are inserted in aviation treaties.

Facultative obligatory and surplus treaties

Although quota share treaties are simple to administer and offer opportunities for the exchange of business between companies, they lack the flexibility which a company frequently requires as its business develops. One solution is for the ceding company to enter into a facultative obligatory agreement to take care of amounts accepted in excess of the monetary limit on its quota share treaty. Like a quota share treaty, the agreement will place restrictions on the types of risks which the reinsured may cede and will be subject to an upper monetary limit.

If there is a substantial volume of business requiring additional reinsurance support the company may enter into a surplus treaty, either in addition to or, far less frequently, in lieu of its quota treaty. As noted earlier, companies operating on the London or other major markets may arrange two surplus treaties.

Retentions. A table of retentions is incorporated into both facultative obligatory and surplus treaties. For a combined hull and liability treaty a maximum line limit is usually placed on both the combined limit of indemnity and a lower limit for separate hull covers, as in the following specimen clause taken from a combined hull and liability first surplus treaty.

> Aircraft Hulls and/or other business allocated by the Company to the Hull section of their account and/or Third Party Legal Liability and/or Passenger Legal Liability and/or Admitted Liability and/or Automatic Personal Accident and/or Baggage Liability and/or Products Liability and/or any other business allocated by the Company to the Liability section of their account. To take up to fifteen lines being the surplus of three lines subject to a maximum limit for one line of £222,222 or $400,000 any one aircraft/accident/occurrence in respect of any one policy and/or risk (or where any one aircraft not applicable) any one acceptance.
>
> BUT NOT EXCEEDING £27,778 or $50,000 any one aircraft thereof in respect of risks classified by the company as Hull Risks written in currencies other than United States or Canadian dollars shall be the equivalent of the

above pound sterling limits converted at the rate accepted by the Company when writing the risk.

The Company shall retain for their own account the three lines not declared hereunder, subject to excess of loss reinsurance, if any.

It is important that the treaty wording should state clearly how the retention limits are to be applied to fleet insurances (i.e. when two or more aircraft are provisionally insured together on the same original slip). The two options are:

(1) To apply the retention to the top insured amount of the fleet insurances, the reinsurance then applying *pro rata* to each aircraft; or

(2) To apply the retention to each aircraft.

A simple example will show how the two methods operate. Assume that an underwriter accepts a 1% share of the hull insurance of a fleet of two aircraft valued at $25 million and $10 million respectively. He has a four-line treaty and his own retention limit is one line of $50,000.

(1) Overall fleet retention:

Acceptance:	Reinsurance based on aircraft A:
Aircraft A = $250,000	Retention $ 50,000 $= \frac{1}{5}$
Aircraft B = $100,000	Reinsurance $200,000 $= \frac{4}{5}$

Reinsurance arrangements:

	Retention	Amount reinsured
Aircraft A	$ 50,000	$200,000
Aircraft B	$ 20,000	$ 80,000

(2) Individual aircraft retention:

	Retention	Amount reinsured
Aircraft A	$ 50,000	$200,000
Aircraft B	$ 50,000	$ 50,000

The disadvantage of the individual aircraft retention is that if two aircraft of different values belonging to the same fleet collide or are destroyed on the ground, the ceding company's net retained liability will be larger than if its retention had been based on the top insured value of the fleet, though excess of loss reinsurance would take care of that contingency. In practice the treaty may give the ceding company the option to adopt whichever method it desires, though it is important that the reinsurer should be aware of the basis on which cessions are made to the treaty.

Premium and claims bordereaux. The comments above regarding quota-share treaties equally apply to facultative obligatory agreements and surplus treaties. Reinsurers require the right to inspect the ceding company's books, and in turn an omissions clause is invariably included in surplus treaties to protect the reinsured against omissions or incorrect entries in the reinsurance register.

Rating and commission. The reinsurer normally follows the ceding company's rates, being entitled to a proportionate share of the original premium. Both reinsurance commission and profit commission are normally allowed on facultative obligatory agreements and surplus treaties along the same lines as for quota share treaties.

Excess of loss reinsurances

Until recently aviation underwriters have generally been satisfied to rely on proportional reinsurances to provide for their basic reinsurance needs, and to confine excess of loss reinsurances to catastrophe covers, designed to protect their accounts from losses involving two or more top-value aircraft or one such aircraft plus what may be a substantial passenger liability claim. However, despite the relatively small number of individual risks included in a typical aviation account which makes working excess of loss covers unattractive to reinsurers, the demand for such reinsurance is increasing.

Given the demand from airline operators for cover for 'excess liabilities', and the limits of indemnity sought by aircraft and aircraft-component manufacturers under their products liability insurances, aviation insurance accounts are inevitably exposed to potential catastrophe losses. Therefore, there is a substantial demand for catastrophe reinsurance covers, particularly for whole-account protection.

Both working covers and catastrophe covers are placed in layers.

Normally treaties are arranged for a 12-month period so that terms are subject to annual review. The usual practice is for net account covers to be placed on a 'losses occurring' basis, whereas the 'risks attaching' basis is used for treaties arranged for common account or for the protection of proportional reinsurances.

Although most excess of loss treaties now cover hull and liability combined, some underwriters still prefer separate reinsurances.

Hull excess of loss reinsurances

Generally working excess-of-loss covers are not provided for the separate reinsurance of hull risks, proportional reinsurance being considered a more appropriate form of protection against normal losses. Excess of loss reinsurance is usually confined to catastrophe risks.

Apart from war and allied perils which are usually reinsured separately, the severest exposure to catastrophe losses involving more than one top-value aircraft arises mainly as a ground risk at airports—mid-air collisions are rare, though with the growth of air traffic not so remote as in the past.

Liability excess of loss reinsurances

Treaties covering the liability section of a ceding company's account embrace all types of liability, i.e. passenger legal liability and/or automatic personal accident, general third party, baggage, mail and cargo liability, refuelling, crop spraying and similar risks, and product liability.

Working covers are common, with extra layers to provide the catastrophe protection. Exactly what constitutes a 'working' and a 'catastrophe' cover depends upon the nature of the ceding company's business. The increases that have occurred in both the seating capacity of aircraft and the size of court awards for personal injury have raised the upper limits of today's working covers to a size associated with 'sleep-easy' covers of yesteryear.

Combined hull and liability reinsurances

Besides hull and liability risks, combined treaties may embrace the whole range of business written in the aviation department, such as loss of licence and individual personal accident insurances. The precise scope of the cover provided must be defined in the treaty, but it may be drawn widely as follows, subject to specific exclusions set out in the treaty.

> _____ shall indemnify the Reassured in respect of all losses howsoever and wheresoever occurring in the world under binders, policies or contracts of insurance written in, or under aviation quota share and surplus treaties accepted by, its Aviation Department.

Common exclusions are:

(1) Any liability accepted under excess of loss reinsurances (other than, possibly, individual excess of loss reinsurances).

(2) Any liability accepted under other treaties written on the London market plus some other (notably USA) treaties.

(3) Hull War business.

(4) Directors' and officers' liability insurances.

The reinsurance may be arranged for:

(1) the ceding company's net retained account; or

(2) for the common account of the ceding company and its proportional reinsurers; or

(3) for treaty reinsurers only; or

(4) occasionally for the protection of an individual original contract.

Separate excess of loss treaties can be arranged to cover an excess of loss account, but at substantially higher premiums than for a whole account.

Sometimes combined covers are arranged on a 'working' basis, but generally proportional reinsurances are used for the basic protection, leaving excess of loss reinsurance to provide the catastrophe cover. A special version of the catastrophe cover is the so called 'two-plane warranty' which provides that the excess of loss reinsurer shall only be interested in losses involving at least two aircraft.

Retention and indemnity limits

Great care is required in determining the ceding company's retention (based on its ultimate net losses) and the treaty limits. Excess of loss reinsurances are arranged for so many diffferent types of account that each requires individual consideration.

When arranging a catastrophe cover the underlying retention must be fixed at a level which, in relation to the structure of the reinsured's portfolio of business, is sufficiently high to exclude the maximum likely cost of a 'primary' occurrence, i.e. a loss involving one major aircraft. Its size will depend on the nature of the reinsured's business including its net retentions (i.e. its gross acceptances less amounts ceded to proportional reinsurers). Sometimes reinsurers seek to include in treaties a warranty as to the ceding company's maximum net retention for any one aircraft or liability risk.

Most aviation excess of loss reinsurances are written on an 'any one event' basis, so that the underlying retention and the upper treaty limit(s) will apply to the aggregate losses flowing directly from the one event. In a small proportion of cases the limits are applied to 'any one event each aircraft' so that where, say, two aircraft are involved in the same loss the reinsurer will be liable to the extent of the treaty limit for each aircraft — but only in excess of the reinsured's retention for each.

A more complex method of controlling the reinsurer's exposure is to place limits on the amount of any claim under the treaty for specified classes of loss, notably (1) Hull and (2) Primary Liabilities. The lower limit for Hull would be fixed sufficiently high to exclude claims arising from the loss of a single aircraft, and for Liabilities it would be based on the claim for a full passenger load on one plane. Taken together the upper component limits should exceed the maximum limit on the treaty in order to leave the reinsured some flexibility in claims recoveries.

When war risks are reinsured it is necessary to define what constitutes an event. 'War Risks Hi-jacking (Losses in Flight) Excess Reinsurance

461

Clauses A or B define one event in terms of incidents occurring within 24 hours and within a 10-mile radius, the reinsured being allowed to select the time and area. The reinsured is also given the option of defining one hull loss on the basis of either 'each and every aircraft' or 'each and every event' so that the retention and indemnity limits apply either to one aircraft or to the aggregate loss rising from damage to two or more aircraft.

Underwriting and rating

The relatively narrow market for aviation insurance means that a reinsurer is more likely to be aware of the general nature of the business any insurer is writing than in other classes of insurance. Nevertheless, in order to underwrite excess of loss reinsurances successfully, far more detailed information is required regarding the underwriting policy and business of ceding companies. Frequently a questionnaire is used to elicit the information required, which will cover such matters as:

(1) The company's net premium income for each of the last five or six years either on an 'underwriting year' or 'accounted for' basis, and analysed by year of receipt.
(2) The company's loss experience over the same period analysed by year of occurrence, settled and outstanding claims, and by date of settlement.
(3) For combined covers, the proportion of the premium attributable to the main classes of business, i.e. hull, liability and non-automatic personal accident.
(4) Maximum commitments for hull and personal accident risks, and to any one insured, including liability risks.
(5) Maximum passenger liability commitments for airlines operating *(a)* within or into the USA and *(b)* elsewhere.
(6) Details of reinsurances accepted on the London market.

Sometimes the company will be asked to give details also of its participation in individual target risks.

The aim should be to establish the risk profile of the account to be reinsured. Various aspects of a company's underwriting policy will affect its potential liabilities, notably:

(1) The types of business accepted.
(2) The company's acceptance limits.
(3) The terms applying to original policies.

As an example of the latter point, passenger liabilities may be increased substantially by the failure of an airline to deliver passenger tickets and baggage checks stating the conditions of carriage *before* passengers board the aircraft. Therefore it needs to be established that a ceding company inserts in its original policies a 'Document of Carriage' clause imposing a duty on its insured to take all reasonable steps to ensure that tickets are delivered. A ceding company's procedures for controlling accumulations—including accumulations of different types of liabilities—needs to be checked too.

Regarding rating, essentially the same remarks apply as for marine business. Methods differ between working covers, low-level catastrophe covers, and high-level catastrophe reinsurances. For lower-layer working covers where a variable premium rate is used, burning-cost calculations are normally on a year of account only basis. For catastrophe covers the rate on line method is frequently used for calculating the premium.

The market for war risks is very restricted and it is impossible to say anything more than that premiums are a matter for negotiation in the light of individual and prevailing circumstances.

Stop loss and excess of loss ratio treaties

Reinsurers are generally reluctant to provide stop loss cover for the reasons already explained in connection with marine business, and the availability of cover is closely related to the underwriting cycle. When the market is in an unprofitable state few, if any, reinsurers are prepared to write the business; conversely during the upswing of the cycle there is little demand from insurers. Consequently, the amount of business transacted is relatively small.

When cover is arranged it may be for the protection of separate hull, liability or personal accident accounts or for a whole account. In view of the substantial fluctuations experienced in aviation insurance results, the ceding company's retention is normally fixed at a high level, so that a treaty may be arranged for something like 20% excess of 95% of the loss ratio for the underwriting year.

Appendix 12.1   Profit commission

Underwriting-year basis with losses carried forward three years

The Reinsurer shall pay to the Company a profit commission as stated in the Schedule calculated on the annual profit arising in respect of each underwriting year from all business ceded under this Agreement and prepared in accordance with the following procedure:

Income

(1) Premiums ceded for the respective underwriting year less returns of premiums and reinsurance which inure for the benefit of this Agreement.

Outgo

(1) Reinsurance commission as provided in the Schedule.
(2) Claims paid for the respective underwriting year less salvages and recoveries.
(3) Reserve for outstanding claims.
(4) ____% deduction on net premiums for the Reinsurer's management expenses.
(5) Deficit, if any, brought forward from the previous year's profit commission statement provided that no such deficit shall be carried forward for more than three years.

The Company shall compile and render to the Reinsurer profit commission statements with the fourth quarter's account of the second year following the close of the underwriting year. They shall be adjusted annually thereafter as may be necessary by supplementary income and/or outgo.

Appendix 12.2   Paramount War Clause (Cargo)

(1)   Notwithstanding anything to the contrary stated herein or subsequently added hereto, it is understood and agreed that if this contract/treaty provides that war risks may be ceded hereunder then the cover afforded by this reinsurance in respect of such war risks shall be subject to terms and conditions no wider than the relevant London Institute War Clauses current at the inception of the risk ceded hereunder or current at the later of either the inception date or the most recent anniversary date of this contract/treaty.

The acceptance of war risks under this contract/treaty is at all times subject to seven days' notice of cancellation given by either party; such period of notice to commence not later than three days from the date of notice given by the reinsurer.

Or (2)   War risks in respect of cargo interests are covered as in the original policy or policies, but subject to the reassured applying the limitations of the United Kingdom Waterborne Agreement dated 31 August 1976 and any subsequent amendment thereto.

The acceptance of war risks under this contract/treaty is at all times subject to seven days' notice of cancellation given by either party; such period of notice to commence not later than three days from the date of notice given by the reinsurer.

Or (3)   The reassured has given a written agreement, which forms part of this contract, to apply the limitations of the United Kingdom Waterborne Agreement dated 31 August 1976 and any subsequent amendment thereto.

The acceptance of war risks under this contract/treaty is at all times subject to seven days' notice of cancellation given by either party; such period of notice to commence not later than three days from the date of notice given by the reinsurer.

465

Appendix 12.3 War exclusion and inclusion clauses

War Exclusion Clause

Notwithstanding anything to the contrary contained in the foregoing part of this Clause this reinsurance expressly excludes any loss, damage, liability or expense:
(a) Caused by or resulting from the risks of War as specified in the original policy(ies).
(b) Which would be covered by the relevant Institute War Clauses or the War sections of the relevant Institute War and Strikes Clauses in current use at the inception of this reinsurance or at the time when the War risks cover would have commenced under the original insurance within the terms of these clauses, whichever is the earlier, if they were contained in or applied to the original policy(ies).
Provided that, if the risks of War are covered in the original policy(ies) under clauses approved by the London Hull War Risk Joint Sub-committee, or in respect of Cargo interests under the Standard War Risk Clause of any country which complies with the limitations of the United Kingdom Waterborne Agreement 31 August 1976, paragraph (b) above shall not apply.

War Inclusion Clause 1976

This Agreement includes loss, damage, liability or expense caused by or resulting from the risks of War as covered in the original policy/policies provided that such loss, damage, liability or expense would be recoverable under the terms and conditions of the relevant Institute War Clauses or the War sections of the relevant Institute War and Strikes Clause or relevant London aviation clauses in current use at the inception of this Agreement or at the time when War risks cover would have commenced under the original insurance within the terms of these clauses, whichever is the earlier, except that if the risks of War are covered in the original policy/policies under clauses approved by the London Hull War Risks Joint Sub-committee, or in respect of cargo interests under the Standard War Risk Clauses of any country which complies with the limitations of the United Kingdom Waterborne Agreement 31 August 1976 the foregoing proviso shall not apply.

In the event of loss or losses occurring under this section of this Agreement (War Inclusion Clause) the Agreement shall be automatically reinstated to its full amount from the time of such loss or losses until expiry of the Agreement in accordance with the general reinstatement conditions of the Agreement. Nevertheless, and irrespective of any other reinstatement conditions of the Agreement, the Reinsurers shall never be liable for more than (a)* in respect of any one loss nor for more than (b)* in respect of all losses coming within this section of the Agreement and which occur during the period of this Agreement, subject, however, to such overall limitation of cover as may be stipulated in the general reinstatement conditions of this Agreement.

Including Strikes, Riots, Civil Commotions and Malicious Damage Risks as original.

* The amount to be inserted at *(a)* would be the limit of the reinsurer's liability, and the amount *(b)* would be double that of *(a)* so providing the ceding company with one full reinstatement of cover.

13
Life reassurance

13
Life reassurance

Many of the comments made in earlier chapters regarding the reasons for effecting reinsurance and the use of facultative and treaty methods of placing reinsurances apply equally to life business. Throughout the world life reassurance practice is changing in various ways. A traditional feature of the business in most countries has been the reciprocal exchange of facultative life reassurances between direct companies. Although that practice continues, in Britain and elsewhere the pressure to reduce administration costs has substantially led to its replacement by the use of automatic treaties so that, taken world-wide, nowadays most life reassurance is placed with professional reinsurance companies. Also developments in the types of contracts offered by life assurers are reflected in changing demands for reassurance.

On the other hand, life reassurance differs in many important respects from other classes of reinsurance. The nature of the risks assumed by life offices has necessitated the development of forms of reassurance and methods of handling the business which are unique to life reassurance.

The life reassurance market

Compared with most classes of non-life insurance, the proportion of total life assurance premiums which is reassured is small, and most of the business is handled domestically. Some reassurance business is placed abroad with international professional reinsurance companies, but generally they play a smaller role than in non-life reinsurance.

The reciprocal exchange of reassurance business between the major direct companies remains an important feature of the British market. However, specialist life reassurers operate in both Britain and most other developed markets throughout the world, and in addition to providing the direct companies with reassurance protection they offer advice on all technical aspects of the business, including the underwriting of substandard lives.

Demand for life reassurance

Life assurance differs from non-life insurance in a number of important respects, notably:
(1) The long term, non-cancellable (by the life office) character of most life policies.
(2) The use of level annual premiums which:
    (i) spread the uneven mortality risk and business acquisition and administration costs evenly over the expected term of the policy; and
    (ii) result in reserves being built up over the policy term to meet the ultimate claims cost.
(3) The varying proportions of protection and savings elements in the different types of life policies.

The primary demand for reassurance is to provide protection against the mortality risk. Life underwriters are fortunate in possessing highly reliable loss frequency statistics in the form of mortality tables from which they can calculate how many of the lives insured in any given portfolio of business may be expected to die each year. Nevertheless the number of actual deaths in any year may vary significantly from the expected number for various reasons, though such fluctuations alone do not necessitate recourse to reassurance.

The cost to a life company of a claim arising from the death of a life insured is the sum assured (plus any bonuses attaching) less the reserve applicable to the policy. The difference is known as the death strain. Therefore, the impact of mortality on a life company's operating results over a given period depends not only on the divergence of the actual number of deaths from the number expected (and thus allowed for in the premium rates) but also 'upon the incidence of claims with respect to the amount of the death strain at risk'.[1]

Differences between actual and expected claims can arise from:
(1) Changes in the general level of mortality. Over the last few decades life offices in most countries have benefited from falling mortality rates, but if the trend should change the solution for direct insurers lies in adjusting premium rates not in reassurance.
(2) The occurrence of epidemics, natural disasters, war and so forth, all of which may result in substantial but temporary variations from the norm. Over periods longer than one year such fluctuations tend to iron out. One writer has suggested that in a country such as Britain life business is so widely spread that no 'single company is likely to be the victim of a catastrophe', and that the best defence against a

---

1 G.T. Foster, 'Some observations on life reassurance', *Journal of the Institute of Actuaries,* vol. 72, part 3, (1946), p. 340.

national catastrophe is a strong reserve position.[2] An earlier writer on the other hand argued that such temporary fluctuations could be covered by reassurance and that the most suitable form would be excess of loss ratio,[3] though many reinsurers and ceding companies have grave doubts about the suitability of the stop loss method for life business.[4]

(3) The total portfolio, or a particular part thereof, may consist of only a small number of insured lives with the result that experience will be subject to chance fluctuations.

The fluctuations attributable to (3) create the main demand for life reassurance. Every new company during its early years will tend to suffer from an uneven mortality experience on its total portfolio, but even large well established companies may encounter a similar experience on certain special classes of business where the numbers insured are relatively small, including assurances written on substandard lives. The main mortality risk for large companies, however, lies with large policies where adverse experience could reduce valuation surplus leading to a cut in the company's rate of bonus.

It is impossible to define in monetary terms 'a large policy': 'large' must be relative to the average sum assured of a company's portfolio of business, and that will vary from country to country. The effect of large policies on the stability of a portfolio depends on the numbers involved. Initially, as the number of such policies is increased, the portfolio will become more unstable until a point is reached when any further increase will improve the stability. Generally the distribution of sums assured will be such that there will be a relatively small number of large policies for which reassurance protection will be required.

The demand for reassurance for large policies is also enhanced by the tendency of actuaries to be conservative in fixing retentions.[5] Very heavy mortality was experienced in America on large cases in the period 1929-31, and though the continuing study published by the Society of Actuaries Mortality Committee shows that overall experience has tended to become closer to the expected[6], some actuaries probably still prefer to err on the side of caution. Certainly a company must expect a certain amount of self selection where sums assured are large, which cannot be

---

2 A.J. Steeds, 'Life Reassurance', *Journal of the Institute of Actuaries Students Society,* vol. 12, part 3, (March 1954).

3 Foster, 'Some observations on life reassurance'.

4 See page 481.

5 Steeds, 'Life reassurance'.

6 The study generally seems to indicate that (1) the experience on high-premium classes of policy is below that expected whereas for low-premium temporary assurances it is heavier than expected; and (2) on policies effected for credit reasons it is also heavier than expected. However, overall experience on large policies has tended to become closer to that expected for all business, possibly due to stricter underwriting of large cases and a relaxation of selection procedures for other business.

eliminated entirely by more stringent underwriting.

Finally, again it may be noted that the random fluctuations in claims costs due to a small number of policies become relatively larger the shorter the period considered. In Britain the trend over the last decade has been for life offices to reduce their valuation periods. Many offices now carry out an annual valuation and distribution of surplus, and given the competition both between life offices and with other savings institutions, claims stability has assumed greater importance than in the past. At the same time it must be recognized that there is a trade-off between claims stability achieved through the purchase of reassurance and expected profit.

Besides seeking protection against the mortality risk, some companies use reassurance to ease their new business strain. Generally the costs of acquiring new business, including agents' commissions, are so high that the balance of the first year's premium is insufficient to meet the mortality risk and, until the initial costs have been recouped out of subsequent premiums, the difference must be covered by the company's free reserves. Consequently a strain is imposed on the financial resources of any company that is writing a large volume of new policies relative to its existing business, such as a new company or a small company that embarks on a policy of rapid growth. Some relief can be obtained by reassuring a proportion of the new business on original terms (see page 475) whereby the reassurer allows the ceding company a rate of reassurance commission sufficiently high to cover not only the agent's commission paid on the share of the original premium ceded, but also to make some contribution towards the reassured's administrative expenses. Alternatively a block reassurance of part of a year's new business may be arranged, either to operate for a limited period or for a certain volume of business.

The Reassurance Agreement 1900

The Reassurance Agreement 1900 still regulates the transaction in Britain of facultative reassurances on original terms (see page 475) between most major direct companies. Although it does not apply to other forms of reassurance, and professional reassurers are not party to the agreement, its influence extends over the whole field of life reassurance, so details of its main provisions are included in Appendix 13.1. A.J. Steeds has summed up the agreement as follows:[7]

7 Ibid.

Perhaps the most interesting provision is that the reassurance may be effected on either the terms and conditions of the principal office (including following the principal office's bonus) or at the premiums used by the reassurer. The spirit of the agreement is that the reassurer should follow the fortune of the principal office and, indeed, this spirit should permeate all reassurance business. It is noteworthy, however, that the principal office has the power to surrender a reassurance though the original policy is still in force.

Forms of life reassurance

There are two main forms of reassurance—proportional and the reassurance of a part of the original contract. Under the latter the ceding company may reassure certain benefits, such as a family income benefit, while retaining for its own account the basic policy, but the most important form of a partial reassurance is the reassurance of all or a part of the death strain by the risk-premium method.

Proportional reassurance

Proportional reassurance may be arranged on either the terms applied by the ceding company to the original policy or on the premium scale that the reassurer would apply to direct business. The difference, however, is not just one of premium rates. In the former case the reassurer would follow the terms of the original policy, including surrender values, paid-up policy values, and the ceding company's bonus declarations for with-profit policies, whereas if the latter method is used the reassurer's own terms, conditions and, when applicable, bonuses apply to the reassurance. Obviously it is more satisfactory for the reassurance to follow the original policy, so normally proportional reassurances are arranged on original terms.

Reassurance on original terms.

This is the form of reassurance still favoured by many British life offices because of its ease of operation. Essentially it works in the same way as non-life proportional reinsurance—it can be placed either facultatively or by treaty, and in the latter case the treaty may operate as either a quota share or a surplus reassurance.

In return for accepting liability for an agreed share of an assurance on the same terms as applied by the ceding company to the original policy, the reassurer receives a proportionate share of the original premium. A

475

reassurance commission will normally be allowed, the rate depending upon the business concerned, whether the business is facultative or treaty, and the margin available in the original premium rate. Customarily the rate of commission allowed on facultative reinsurances is the same as that paid by the ceding company to its agent; in the case of companies that sell direct, not using agents or brokers, no reassurance commission is paid. A fixed rate of commission is usually allowed for treaty cessions irrespective of any differential rates paid by the ceding company to its agents. The reassurer determines the rate according to the maximum commission paid by the ceding company and the margin available in the original gross premiums compared with the pure premiums for the risks ceded; for ceding companies that pay no agents' commission the reassurance commission rate is scaled down to make roughly the same contribution to the company's administrative expenses. Under both facultative and treaty reassurances, initial and renewal commissions are identified separately and differential rates of reassurance commission are paid.

Normally treaties on original terms are arranged on a surplus basis. The only general use for quota share is for the reassurance of group life schemes where by reassuring a quota of the whole scheme the reassurer avoids adverse selection. If cover were arranged on a surplus basis the business ceded to the reassurer would tend to be concentrated on the older and/or less healthy members of the scheme. Apart from group life business, quota share treaties are rarely arranged because normally most of the business a company will obtain will lie within its own retention capacity.

Reassurance on the risk premium method

The risk premium method is designed to provide relief solely for the death strain. The basic idea is that the amount reassured each year shall be equal to the original sum assured in excess of the ceding company's retention less the reserves applicable thereto. Each year as the ceding company builds up the reserves attributable to a policy the amount at risk decreases and so the reassurance can be reduced accordingly.

The method is very flexible in its mode of operation. A ceding company can fix its retention in various ways to suit its own requirements; for example, it may:

(1) retain a certain share of the mortality risk under an original policy throughout its lifetime so that the amount reassured decreases each year by the increase in the value of the reserves relating to the initial sum reassured; or

(2) retain a constant amount at risk so that its net death strain in the

event of a claim will always be equal to its retention. Then the amount reassured will decrease each year by the increase in the reserves attributable to the whole policy, and the reassurance may be required only for part of the term of the policy: or

(3) arrange for the amount reassured to decrease by an arbitrary amount over an agreed period of years.

Generally method (1) is preferred but other methods are used to meet the special needs of ceding companies. For example, the sum retained may be increased by the value of the reserves already accrued under earlier policies effected on the same insured life, so reducing the amount to be assured.

Although risk premium reassurances are sometimes misleadingly called 'renewable term', they are permanent contracts which run for the life of the underlying original policy or such shorter term as may be agreed at the outset of the reassurance. Once effected neither party has a right to withdraw from the contract.

If the original policy is allowed to lapse the reassurer has no liability to contribute to any surrender value or paid-up policy value to which the original assured is entitled. Likewise the reassurer has no liability for maturity claims under endowment policies. In both cases the ceding company should be in a position to meet such liabilities from its accrued reserves. On the other hand, since the ceding company holds the reserves it is entitled to the benefit of any profit resulting from successful investment (but must also bear the risk of investment losses) or from the surrender or lapse of the original policy.

An advantage of the risk premium method is that the premiums payable to the reassurer are small relative to the original premiums so that the ceding company's fund will grow more rapidly than if a proportional method of reassurance is employed.

The risk premium method is traditionally used for reassurances placed internationally in that the outflow of premiums from a country is reduced to the bare minimum required to protect local life assurers against their mortality risk. Most governments are anxious to safeguard their balance of payments from capital outflows and to retain funds for investment in local capital markets. The risk premium method achieves such objectives by leaving the policy reserves in the hands of the ceding companies.

A disadvantage of the risk premium method is that the reassurance premium must be recalculated each year to reflect the reduction in the risk reassured. Nowadays, however, using computers reinsurers can undertake the calculations very speedily and at relatively little cost.

At the beginning of each policy year the risk premium is obtained by applying the risk premium rate for the attained age of the life reassured to the amount at risk for that year. Table 13.1 illustrates how the premium is calculated on the declining amount at risk as the ceding company builds up its actuarial reserve over the term of a policy.

Table 13.1. Specimen reassurance premiums on a risk premium basis. Endowment assurance, non profit, 20-year term, age at entry 45 years next birthday

Policy year	Age next birthday	Actuarial reserve	Amount at risk £	Rate ‰	Reassurance premium £
1	45	—	1000	3.58	3.58
2	46	41	959	3.98	3.82
3	47	82	918	4.43	4.07
4	48	125	875	4.93	4.31
5	49	168	832	5.49	4.57
6	50	213	787	6.11	4.81
7	51	259	741	6.80	5.04
8	52	305	695	7.57	5.26
9	53	353	647	8.42	5.45
10	54	403	597	9.36	5.59
11	55	453	547	10.40	5.69
12	56	505	495	11.60	5.74
13	57	559	441	12.80	5.64
14	58	615	385	14.20	5.47
15	59	672	328	15.70	5.15
16	60	732	268	17.40	4.66
17	61	794	206	19.10	3.93
18	62	860	140	21.00	2.94
19	63	928	72	23.00	1.66
20	64	1000	—	25.20	—

The net risk premium rate may be obtained from the formula:

$$P_x = v^{1/2} q_x$$

where $v^{1/2} = \dfrac{1}{1+i}$, i being the assumed rate of interest

q_x = the probability of a person aged x dying before his next birthday

The net rate must then be loaded to cover the reassurer's expenses, profit and a margin for mortality fluctuation so that the formula for the calculation of the gross risk premium becomes:

$$P^1_x = \frac{P_x + c}{1 - k}$$

where c = a lump sum expenses loading

k = an expenses loading proportional to the office premium.

A.J. Steeds suggests that the value of $v^{1/2}$ will be so trivial compared with the loading factor for the gross risk premium that it may be ignored.[8] He also points out that the above formula, which was developed by G.T. Foster, uses an ultimate rate of mortality and that some allowance must be made for selection. Although, therefore, the formula $(q_{[x] + t} + c)/(1 + k)$ is sometimes used (where $[x]$ = age at entry and t = duration in years since entry), it makes the schedule of risk premiums very complicated. Therefore in practice it is often assumed that selection need be considered only in the first year when the select rate is taken as 50% of the ultimate rate. The adjustment of risk premium rates to the reassurance of substandard lives will be considered later.

Reassurance commission is not allowed on risk premiums because the commissions paid to agents on original premiums have no direct bearing on the calculation of risk premium rates. However, virtually all automatic risk premium first surplus treaties now written in Britain provide for the payment of profit commission each year at rates varying between 25% and 50% of revealed profits. Normally profit commission is allowed only when there is a minimum number of cessions in force, usually 200, but if the stipulated number is reached within three years from the commencement of a treaty the calculation of profit commission may be back-dated to inception.

The calculation of profit commission requires the reassurer to prepare the account at the end of each year showing the following details:

Income	£	Outgo	£
Reserve brought forward from previous year		Commissions (less commission on retrocessions)	
Premium income less retrocessions		Expenses	
		Claims (less recoveries)	
		Reserve at end of year carried forward	
		Loss (if any) brought forward	
(Loss carried forward)		(Profit)	

The reserve for unexpired risks is conventionally taken as 50% of the year's premium income, and expenses are expressed as an agreed percentage either of premiums (usually 10% to 15%) or of sums assured in force (e.g. 1%). If a loss arises in any year it is carried forward to extinction in future years.

8 Ibid.

Excess of loss reassurances

The forms of non-proportional reinsurance increasingly favoured in the non-life markets — excess of loss and excess of loss ratio — have not made the same headway in life reassurance. In Britain this is partly due to the way in which insurance supervisory regulations have constrained the supply of non-proportional reassurances. The Department of Trade regulations regarding the valuation of life assurance companies' liabilities require details of each assured risk (e.g. sum assured, term and type of policy, the age of the life assured) to be identified separately. Such information is not made available to a reassurer under an excess of loss treaty.

There are also constraints on the demand for such cover. A major disadvantage to a ceding company is the short-term basis of excess of loss treaties. Occasionally an excess of loss treaty ia arranged to run for two or three years, but generally treaties are arranged on an annual basis. This is certainly so for large covers where the reassurer needs to retrocede part of the risk. If experience should prove worse than expected the reassurer may be unwilling to renew the treaty or, at best, require an increase in premium despite the fact that, unlike annually renewable non-life insurances, the additional cost cannot be passed on to existing policyholders whose premiums are fixed at inception. Conversely it is true that any improvement in a company's experience should be reflected in a reduction in its reinsurance premium rate. Yet even if claims outcomes are evenly distributed around the mean so that there are equal probabilities of being called upon to pay higher or lower reassurance premiums, a company may place a higher (utility) value on continuity and the maintenance of a known reassurance cost of existing business than on an equal expected but uncertain cost of reassurance. Such certainty can, of course, be obtained by reassuring on a proportional or risk premium basis where, apart from committing fraud or failing to pay its premiums, a ceding company knows that its existing business will continue to be protected at a known cost whatever may happen in the future.

Nevertheless with direct companies increasingly exposed to the risk of an accumulation of death claims arising out of one event, such as air crashes or natural disasters, there is a growing demand for excess of loss reassurances. Treaties normally provide cover only against the risk of at least a certain number of insured lives dying within a stated short time (e.g. 48 or 72 hours) of a particular event occurring, so that any protection the ceding company requires for large sums assured on individual lives must still be arranged by reassurance on original terms or by the risk premium method. Generally reassurers expect a ceding company to be able to retain an amount at least twice the size of its retention on any one life and, given the number of accidents causing two deaths, a limit of three lives is usually regarded as a minimum — the premium which would be required normally would rule out any smaller limit.

Treaty wording.

A specimen excess of loss treaty is shown in Appendix 13.2. Cover is only rarely arranged in layers. Some of the provisions are similar to those found in non-life treaties; notably the claims clause (article 3), the currency clause (article 6), and the inspection, alterations and arbitration clauses (articles 8, 9 and 11 respectively). The other clauses set out the essential characteristics of life excess of loss reassurances.

Cover is provided only against accidents and natural catastrophes (article 1). Reassurers are not prepared to provide cover for an accumulation of death claims due to natural causes, even if due to an epidemic. As noted above, the reassurer only accepts liability for claims in excess of an agreed amount (the ceding company's catastrophe retention) if at least a specified number of insured lives die in one event or series of related events. To avoid dispute, it is necessary to define in the case of death caused by natural perils what constitutes 'an event', and typical time limits are shown in article 1. The ceding company is always allowed to choose when any period shall be deemed to commence, provided it is not earlier than the first recorded death of an insured life, and that no two periods overlap.

Like non-life treaties, the *reassurer's liability* is based on the ultimate net losses incurred by the ceding company (article 2). However, in calculating the ultimate net loss, besides deducting any amount recovered from underlying reassurances, the sum assured paid under each policy is further reduced by the mathematical reserves held by the reassured in respect of such policies. Thus the excess of loss reassurance protects the ceding company against the net death strain due to multiple claims arising from one event, i.e. that part of the net sum at risk (as defined in article 1) payable by the company in respect of those claims.

Normally a number of limitations are placed in treaties to control the reassurer's potential exposure. The limitations fall into two categories:
(1) The excess limits, and an inner limit placed on the maximum sum assured retained by the ceding company on any one life (article 2). Any amendment of the company's retention on one life could significantly affect the reassurer's exposure, so invariably reassurers require immediate notification and the right to amend the treaty

terms accordingly.

Although the excess limits are usually fixed sufficiently high to provide for the payment in any one year of an amount between 1½ and 2 times the maximum retention per catastrophe, treaties normally make no provision for the reinstatement of cover, even at an additional premium. Thus if following one or more catastrophes the ceding company's aggregate ultimate net losses in excess of its catastrophe retention exhaust the treaty cover, then it will be necessary to negotiate fresh cover.

(2) Restrictions on potential concentrations of risk. Although group life schemes would normally be included in the reassured portfolio, because of their potential concentration and possible exposure to severe occupational accident hazards (e.g. in chemical and mining companies) which warrant special consideration when fixing the treaty rate, it is usual to place a limit on the membership of any one scheme (article 4). If the ceding company subsequently underwrites a larger scheme the reassurer's approval must be obtained to raise the limit. Occasionally very large group schemes are reassured separately, but normally they neither provide the reassurer with an adequate spread of risk nor are they large enough to absorb the fixed costs of administering a separate treaty.

Amongst the *list of exclusions* shown in article 4, war, riot and nuclear risks are commonly excluded from excess of loss treaties. The war and riot exclusion may be waived for 'safe' countries, and elsewhere sometimes war perils can be covered for an extra premium, particularly if the reassurance is placed with a foreign reassurer who would not be affected severely by any war likely to affect the ceding company's policyholders. The exclusion of flying is normally limited to flying in private aircraft (other than as passengers in company-owned aircraft for business purposes) and, like the exclusion of professional sports teams, can usually be deleted or modified in return for a suitable extra premium.

Rating

The rating of excess of loss reassurances poses much the same sort of problems as apply to catastrophe covers for other classes of insurance.

Dr P. Strickler has pointed out that the liability of the reassurer depends mainly on two factors, namely:

(1) the frequency distribution of accidents causing the loss of M or more lives (where M is the minimum treaty limit); and

(2) the distribution of the retained sums at risk in the portfolio of the ceding company.[9]

Information on (1) is available from surveys into accidents causing multiple deaths carried out by the Metropolitan Life Insurance Company of New York from which the following function is derived:

$$A(x) = 8(100)^{1/x} x^{-\frac{1}{3}}$$

$A(x)$ is the annual number of deaths, for each million of the general population, from all accidents causing the death of x or more persons.

Thus the annual number of accidents, for each million of the population, claiming exactly x victims would be:

$$H(x) = \{A(x) - A(x+1)\}/x$$

and the probability, that if and when an accident occurred, it would involve exactly x victims, would be:

$$h(x) = H(x) / \sum_{x=1}^{\infty} H(x)$$

Given the above functions, and taking (1) the distribution of retained sums insured around the average sum at risk in the portfolio to be reinsured, and (2) the lower and upper excess of loss limits, Strickler was able to derive:

a net reinsurance premium (= expected cost of reinsured losses); and

a gross reinsurance premium (excluding the expense loading) based on the net premium plus a specified proportion of the standard deviation of the expected reinsured losses.

The premiums obtained by the Strickler formula, however, would need to be adjusted to allow for the following factors:

(1) Unless a company insured a large proportion of a population concentrated in a particular area, the probability of all x victims killed in a single accident being insured with that company would be small. Therefore the catastrophe reinsurance premium would need to be reduced accordingly.

(2) On the other hand a portfolio largely composed of group insurances would merit an increase in premium.

If the risk to be insured is very small so that the expense loading forms a large part of the total premium, or if the amount at risk is not expected to vary substantially, a flat non-adjustable premium may be quoted. Normally, however, premiums are adjustable but then, unlike non-life insurances, the ceding company's net retained premium income is an unsuitable base to which to apply the reassurance premium rate. A life reassurer's liability, as stated above, is based on the ceding company's ultimate net losses after deduction of reassurance recoveries and the relevant mathematical reserves. Therefore the measure of exposure normally used is the net sum at risk, which is defined in the specimen treaty in Appendix 13.2 as follows:

---

9 P. Strickler, 'Rückversicherung des Kumulrisikos in der Lebensversicherung', *The Transactions of the Sixteenth International Congress of Actuaries,* vol. 1 (1960), p.666.

Net sum at risk means the total sum assured in force payable on death under life assurance policies or reassurances covered by the Company, including additional benefits payable on accidental death, less any sums reassured payable on death placed with other offices, and less the total mathematical reserves held by the Company relating to such policies subject to any restrictions as stated in the first Schedule.

Besides allowing for the mathematical reserves held by the ceding company, the net sum at risk is not affected by the distribution of the reassured portfolio between high- and low-premium types of policy.

When the premium is adjustable, the ceding company pays at the commencement of each year a minimum premium, usually from two-thirds upwards of the expected annual premium, with the balance being payable four months later. The annual premium is then adjustable at the end of the year, the adjustment premium being calculated by multiplying the fixed reassurance premium rate by half the change in the net sum at risk at the end of the year. As noted in article 5, the reinsurer may require a non-adjustable treaty fee to cover his own management expenses.

Stop loss or excess of loss ratio reassurances

Reference was made on page 472 to the suitability of stop loss or excess of loss ratio reassurances as a means of protecting a company against the temporary fluctuations due to epidemics, natural disasters and so forth. Under a stop loss treaty the reassurer accepts liability for aggregate ultimate net losses (as defined above for excess of loss treaties) in excess of a fixed monetary amount per annum, subject to an upper limit, whereas under an excess of loss ratio treaty the reassurer's liability is expressed in terms of excess claims over a percentage of expected claims. The following specimen clause works principally on the excess of loss ratio principle but subject to lower and upper monetary limits. In accordance with usual stop loss reinsurance practice, the clause requires the reassured to participate in excess losses to the extent of 10%.

Insuring Clause. If the total of the Reassured's ultimate net loss, in respect of all losses occuring during the term of this agreement exceeds a deductible equal to 7.5% (seven point five per mille) the total sums assured in force (as finally determined) or £160,000 (One Hundred and Sixty Thousand Pounds Sterling) whichever amount is the greater, then the Reassurers agree to reimburse the Reassured for 90% (ninety per cent) of that part of its aggregate ultimate net loss which exceeds the said deductible up to but not exceeding £100,000 (One Hundred Thousand Pounds Sterling).
The balance of 10% (ten per cent) of the excess ultimate net loss together

with the first 7.5% (seven point five per mille) shall be retained net by the Reassured and not reassured in any way.

Although both types of cover have obvious attractions to a direct office, in practice their usage has been limited because of various inherent disadvantages. Like excess of loss treaties, contracts are normally subject to annual review; even guaranteed continuity of up to five years which one professional reinsurer is prepared to provide does not match the long-term liabilities assumed by a life office with equivalent reassurance protection. On the other hand it has been pointed out that as a company's portfolio of business expands its claims experience should become more stable so that the premium rate required for a stop loss reassurance should be reduced[10].

Normally war risks are excluded, though sometimes a reassurer, preferably operating outside the territory concerned and so not likely to be affected severely by any war involving its residents, may be prepared to provide war cover at an additional premium. If the ceding company's business is confined to 'safe' territories the exclusion of war risks may be waived free of extra charge.

The reassurer may also wish to exclude liabilities over which the ceding company has no direct control, such as liabilities assumed under automatic treaties and especially excess of loss reassurances. Moreover as the intention of a stop loss reassurance is only to protect a portfolio against unavoidable accumulations of claims during any one year, the reassurer may take the precaution of inserting in the treaty a clause along the following lines specifically excluding any increase in the ceding company's ultimate net losses due to errors or omissions in its underlying reassurance arrangments.

> *Net Retained Lines.* This agreement shall only protect that portion of any assurance or reassurance which the Reassured, acting in accordance with its established practices, retains net for its own account. Reassurer's liability hereunder shall not be increased due to an error or omission which results in an increase in the Reassured's normal net retention nor by the Reassured's failure to reassure in accordance with its normal practice, nor by the inability of the Reassured to collect from any other Reassurer any amounts which may have become due from them whether such inability arises from the insolvency of such other Reassurer or otherwise.

Two particular difficulties from a reassurer's standpoint associated with both stop loss and excess of loss ratio contracts are (1) possible changes in the ceding company's underwriting standards and (2) the

---

10 'Is individual excess reinsurance better than stop loss reinsurance?' *Quarterly Letter from the Nederlandse Reassurantie Groep,* July 1969, No. XV/59.

fixing of premiums. Changes in underwriting policy by a ceding company which obviously affect the reassurer's exposure (e.g. alterations in retentions or the issue of new types of policy) can be accommodated by an adjustment of the treaty terms; the problems arise when unknown to the reassurer the company relaxes its underwriting standards.

Premium rating problems arise from the volatility of loss experience and the reassurer's need for a substantial loading of the net premium because, as Hans Ammeter has pointed out, both the risk to be covered and the reassurer's expenses, though probably small in absolute value, are large relative to the net premium.[11] Therefore what is required is a system of rating that is capable of deriving gross premiums instead of leaving the loading factor to be fixed as some arbitrary percentage of the net premium.

Though loss experience on life portfolios may be more stable than for many non-life classes of insurance, the occurrence of fluctuations still makes ceding companies' own individual experiences unreliable bases for rating stop loss reassurances. Indeed it is the risk of fluctuations that creates the demand for such reassurances. Therefore, various attempts have been made to place rating on a sounder theoretical basis. Ammeter, for example, shows that the critical elements of a rating model are:

(1) The mean value of the number of claims in any year.

(2) The frequency function of the claims to be paid out.

(3) The degree of fluctuations in claims.

Ammeter then uses collective risk theory to obtain approximate evaluations of the distribution and frequency functions of the key variables to produce a rating model which should produce good results in many cases in practice. P.H. Kahn likewise uses collective risk theory to obtain a measure of the variance of claims in excess of a stop loss lower limit, and then advocates a loading factor for the reassurance premium (ignoring expenses) calculated as a percentage of the standard deviation of the excess claims.[12]

In practice no rating formula has gained universal acceptance as a method of calculating stop loss premiums.

---

11 Hans Ammeter, 'The calculation of premium rates for excess of loss and stop loss reinsurance treaties', in *Non-proportional Reinsurance,* ed. by S. Vajda (Arithbel SA, 1955).

12 Paul Markham Kahn, 'An introduction to collective risk theory and its application to stop-loss reinsurance', *Transactions of the Society of Actuaries,* vol. 14, part 1 (1962), p.400.

Methods of placing reassurance

Facultative reassurance

Traditionally British life companies reassured any business surplus to their own retentions by the facultative method. Nowadays because of the need of direct companies in Britain, America, Europe and many other parts of the world to minimize administration costs and to have automatic access to reassurance in order to accept business without delay in the face of competition from other offices, its use for life as opposed to annuity reassurances is largely confined to cases which fall outside the limits of a treaty or by companies without any treaty arrangements. Sometimes facultative cover may also be sought when an underwriter requires a second opinion about a case he has been offered.

Facultative cover may be arranged on either original terms (when the rate of commission paid by the reassurer is usually the same as that paid to the original agent) or the risk premium forms of reassurance. Whichever method is employed the reassurer's liability commences at the same time as the original policy comes into force.

The procedures laid down by the terms of the Reassurance Agreement 1900 for placing facultative reassurances on original terms are generally followed for risk premium reassurances too by both direct companies and professional reassurers. The rules require the company seeking to place the business (known as the principal office) to provide the reassurer (known as the guaranteeing office) with all material information, including copies of papers and previous proposals. In other words, the reassurer should have access to the same information for underwriting purposes as is available to the direct underwriter; that is, copies of the proposal form, medical reports, any specialists' reports, and the results of any investigations and financial evidence. The ceding company must also declare:

(1) The amount of assurance it already holds on the life to be assured.
(2) Its proposed retention on the new assurance.
(3) The terms upon which any existing assurance was written.
(4) Its proposed terms (including commission) for the new assurance.

If the ceding company becomes aware of any new material facts before the completion of the reassurance contract the reassurer must be told and will then have the right to withdraw his acceptance. Under the terms of the agreement, if the reassurance is not completed within one month of the reassurer's acceptance the ceding company must supply satisfactory evidence of the continued eligibility of the life to be assured: generally professional reassurers have to tolerate much longer delays on the business they write.

On completion the reassurance contract is evidenced either by a guarantee endorsed on to a copy of the ceding company's policy, or by a separate policy issued by the reassurer endorsed to the effect that it is a reassurance of a specified policy issued by the ceding company.

Normally a ceding company is not permitted to arrange any subreassurance without the consent of the facultative reassurer.

When there is a fairly regular flow of facultative business between two companies, the procedures for advising the reassurer of the completion of individual reassurances, renewals and accounting are largely identical to those used for treaty business.

Facultative obligatory agreements

These operate in the same manner as similar non-life reinsurance arrangements. They are employed by some of the smaller companies that do not have a sufficient flow of large policies to warrant effecting a normal treaty but wish to avoid having to place facultatively each reassurance they require. Although, within specified limits, a facultative obligatory contract enables a ceding company to obtain automatically any reassurance it needs from the time it accepts an assurance, it will be required to notify the reassurer of each risk it cedes.

Normally the ceding company is required to send copies of all relevant papers to the reassurer, though it may be agreed that, for example, copy papers are required only for amounts over a certain figure or for cessions involving substandard lives.

The agreement may provide for the reassurance to be either on original terms or on the risk premium basis. If desired, the reassurer may agree to different sections of the ceding company's business being reassured on different bases.

Before agreeing to become bound to accept whatever business the ceding company may want to cede, the reassurer must be satisfied about the reassured's underwriting standards, which he can continue to check throughout the course of the agreement from the details he receives of risks ceded. If the reassurer is dissatisfied with the quality of the business ceded and discussions fail to produce any improvement the agreement may be cancelled.

Normally facultative obligatory agreements are for an unlimited term but with provision for cancellation. In the event of cancellation by either party, reassurances already effected will remain in force for their natural term.

The terms offered by reassurers for facultative obligatory business are usually not so generous as for normal treaties. To counterbalance the likelihood of adverse selection in the risks ceded, the limits placed on the amounts that can be ceded and the rate of commission allowed are normally lower than those for equivalent treaties, though if a substantial volume of business has been built up over the years and experience has been satisfactory the reinsurer may be prepared to grant terms more in line with normal treaty business.

Preparation of renewal lists and accounts. Generally the procedures followed are as described below, though many exceptions are encountered in practice.

For United Kingdom business the preparation of renewal lists and accounts may be undertaken by either party, but usually it is done by the reassurer for individual risks and by the ceding company for group or block business. Whereas quarterly accounts used to be the norm, the introduction of computerized accounting systems has led to monthly accounts becoming more common for individual business. Accounts include details of new and renewal premiums, and claims payments. For reassurances on original terms they also include details of reassurance commission and surrender values paid.

For risk premium reassurances the reassurer usually calculates the premiums each year using a standard mortality basis. If the ceding company wishes to employ a different basis and is prepared to calculate the amounts at risk, or where a constant retention basis is employed, the ceding company will usually supply the reassurer with schedules of amounts at risk when sending details of new reassurances. Whichever method is used, the reassurer will incorporate the amounts at risk and premiums into the policy record, it then being relatively simple for a computer program to generate each year the amount at risk and premium for the preparation of the renewal list.

Usually provision is made for large claims (as defined) to be settled in cash upon payment of the original claim by the ceding company.

Treaties

With the pressure on direct companies to reduce their expenses, fully automatic treaties have become far more popular. A treaty may be arranged to provide any form of reassurance though most are on either original terms or the risk premium method. As noted above, when the reassurance is on original terms it is normally on a surplus basis. A specimen risk premium treaty is included in Appendix 13.2.

Scope. The scope of a treaty is a matter for negotiation. It may be agreed to include all business written by the ceding company or it may:
(1) be restricted to certain classes of business, such as temporary or

group life assurances; or

(2) exclude substandard lives, the ceding company making separate reinsurance arrangements for such business; or

(3) apply only to business written in a certain territory or territories.

Nowadays the general practice is to incorporate all of a company's business in one treaty. When business from more than one territory is included in the same treaty the cover may be expressed either in original currencies or in a common currency (e.g. the pound sterling).

Retentions. Different retentions may be specified in the treaty for different classes of business; for example, small companies often fix lower retentions for term assurances than for whole-life or endowment assurances. Also retentions may be varied according to the age of the proposer and according to the severity of substandard lives. If reduced retentions are not shown in the treaty for substandard lives or other special risks, the automatic cover provided by the reassurer is reduced in proportion to any reduction by the ceding company in its actual retention.

Reassurances. Reassurances in front of treaties are not permitted but ceding companies are allowed to effect catastrophe excess of loss reassurances to protect their net retentions. Indeed it may be desirable that such reassurances be arranged to protect small portfolios against adverse mortality fluctuations, particularly when business is obtained from confined geographical areas or from communities or groups of persons exposed to a distinct accumulation hazard.

Duration. The duration of life treaties is normally open-ended but subject to a cancellation clause. As in the case of facultative obligatory agreements, the cancellation clause normally stipulates that following the termination of the treaty by either party reassurances already ceded shall remain in force with the reassurer until their natural expiry, whether the reassurance be on original terms or the risk premium basis. Thus the reassurer will be able to recoup his expenses even in the event of an early termination of a treaty. In special circumstances, transfer of an existing portfolio may be negotiated, including the transfer to the new reassurer of reserves for original terms reassurances.

Procedures. Regardless of whether the reassurance is on original terms or the risk premium basis, it is nowadays unusual for ceding companies to supply bordereaux. Instead upon completion of an original assurance requiring reassurance a definite reassurance certificate will be prepared as part of the accounting procedure. The reassurer may prepare and supply to the ceding company forms like the specimen blank certificate designed for computerized accounts shown in Appendix 13.3, setting out the information he will require. The details of each risk ceded would then be filled in by the ceding company, and the form would be sent to the reassurer with a duplicate for signature and return as evidence of the reassurer's acceptance of the risk. When used for risk premium reassurances details of the amounts at risk and the reassurance premium for each year would be inserted in the schedule. Details of premium loadings and reductions (e.g. for females), changes in renewal commission terms, etc., would be shown under the heading 'observations'.

Though bordereaux may not be supplied, it is normal practice for copies of relevant papers (i.e. proposal form, medical reports, specialists' investigations and financial evidence) to be made available to the reassurer. Exactly what information is to be supplied is a matter for negotiation and will depend upon the relationship between the reassurer and the ceding company, particularly upon the degree of confidence the reassurer has in the ceding company's underwriting expertise and standards. So the requirements embodied in a treaty may range from the sending of copy papers for all cessions, or all cessions over a certain amount, through the stage of submitting papers only for substandard lives, to the sending of papers only when requested by the reassurer. Whatever form the requirement takes, copy papers are sent solely for the reassurer's information and do not affect the automatic cover provided by a treaty. On the other hand, if they should reveal any features which are unsatisfactory to the reassurer the matter may be discussed with the ceding company, and if no improvement can be achieved the reassurer's ultimate weapon is to exercise his right to terminate the treaty.

Accounting. The same accounting procedures are applied as for facultative obligatory treaties.

Reserves. Under reassurances arranged on the risk premium basis the reassurer only receives each year a premium sufficient to cover the mortality risk for the year so that there is no question of accumulating long-term reserves. However, under original terms reassurances the reassurer will accumulate part of the actuarial reserves applying to each policy reassured. Because of local insurance supervisory or other regulations, direct offices in many countries must account for the reserves relating to the gross business written, without deducting reassurances ceded. Therefore, it is necessary for the reassurer to deposit with the ceding company the reserves relating to the risks that have been ceded, either in cash or as securities. In the former case the treaty will normally stipulate that the reassurer shall be credited in the quarterly accounts with interest on those reserves allowing a margin in favour of the reassurer above the technical rate which the ceding company uses in the calculation of its own premiums and reserves. If securities are deposited, normally they would be in the currency of the contract so that their value remains unaffected by changes in foreign exchange rates. Interest or dividends on the securities in question would be paid direct to the depositing reassurer rather than be channelled through the treaty accounts.

Pools

In 1949 the first reassurance pool was formed in Britain to extend the range of life assurance available to diabetics. The pool is operated by the Mercantile and General Reinsurance Company but, apart from the Swiss Reinsurance Company, all of the other members are direct British life offices. Over the next few years similar pools were formed to provide cover for proposers suffering from high blood pressure and coronary disease. Reassurance business may be accepted by the managing reassurer for inclusion in the pools either on original terms or on the risk premium basis, the direct insurer writing the business on terms agreed with the reassurer after a study of the medical evidence. All or part of a risk may be reassured with the pools, any business accepted being divided between all of the members on an agreed quota share basis.

Today more capacity is available through normal market channels for handling the assurances of substandard lives, so further pools are unlikely to be formed. The pools were commenced on the basis that there was no associated impairment (e.g. rateable overweight or history of serious disease). This has in practice somewhat restricted their usefulness. Nevertheless the existing pools have played a valuable role in mobilizing capacity by spreading substandard business more widely and enabling each member of the pool to obtain a better diversified portfolio of such business than otherwise would have been possible. Moreover, over the years the pools have provided a wider experience on which to evaluate the various types of medical conditions and so decide on the terms to be applied to substandard risks.

Reassurance of substandard lives

The underwriting of assurances on substandard lives poses a number of problems, particularly for small companies that may not possess much experience of such business. Although life underwriters have the advantage of reliable mortality tables, care must be exercised in the selection of individual lives and in particular in identifying those suffering from any impairment which necessitates refusal or the quotation of special terms. The majority of cases handled by a company will be normal-health lives for whom standard terms can be quoted, but a minority will call for the advice of a medical officer with wide experience of life assurance underwriting.[13] When a small company does not have access to such advice within its own organization, arrangements may be made for a treaty reassurer to examine proposals and medical evidence for impaired lives and to decide on the terms to be quoted.

Nowadays instead of arranging a separate treaty for substandard business, it is the general practice to include all of a company's business within one treaty whether on original terms or the risk premium basis, although retentions and the automatic treaty cover provided may be reduced for substandard lives.

In cases where a separate treaty is arranged for substandard lives normal treaty terms are applied, though the treatment of reassurance commissions on extra premiums needs to be specified.

There are two basic ways of dealing with assurances for impaired lives—the charging of an additional premium or the imposition of a debt on the policy. In Britain the traditional way of charging a higher premium rate is to add a number of years to the proposer's attained age to obtain a rate from the standard rating table sufficient to cover the higher mortality risk. Alternatively the standard rate may be loaded either throughout the whole term or for the first x years. When the additional risk is handled by the imposition of a policy debt, so that only a proportion of the sum assured is payable on death, the amount of the debt will be reduced each year. The reader must be referred elsewhere for a discussion of the respective merits and demerits of each method[14]: here only their relevance to reassurance will be considered. It may be noted that when a debt is imposed, theoretically it would be appropriate for the ceding company to increase its retention since its net amount at risk is reduced by the amount of the debt, but in practice this is normally ignored. Independently of any permanent loading or debt, for certain impairments or temporary additional risks an office may charge for a limited period a temporary extra premium expressed as a level addition to the standard premium.

Original terms reassurances. Neither method presents any problems when the reassurance is effected on original terms—the reassurer will

---

13 For a discussion of this subject see R.D.C. Brackenridge, *Medical Selection of Life Risks* (The Undershaft Press, 1977), ch.4.

14 See, for example, Brackenridge, *Medical Selection of Life Risks.*

receive his due proportion of any extra premium or the deduction from the amount payable on death.

Risk premium basis. The basic assumption is that any extra premium, or the amount of a debt, in any year exactly matches the extra mortality risk in that year. It follows, therefore, that the extra premium, or debt should be apportioned between the ceding company and the reassurer in the proportion that the amount at risk retained bears to the amount at risk reinsured. Two situations can be distinguished:[15]

(1) When the sum reassured decreases each year by the increase in the value of the reserves relating to the initial sum reassured, i.e.

$$\frac{\text{Amount at risk reassured (A)}}{\text{Amount at risk (B)}} = \frac{(S-R)(1-V_t)}{S(1-V_t)}$$

where S = total original sum assured
R = total original retention
V_t = reserve per unit sum assured in year t

Clearly in this case the benefit of the extra premium or debt should be apportioned each year between the reassurer and the ceding company in the proportion that the initial sum reassured bears to the initial amount retained by the ceding company. So when a debt is imposed any claim payable by the reassurer would be reduced by his *pro rata* share of the policy debt. When an extra premium is imposed in effect the extra risk is being reassured on original terms so that the ceding company should receive normal reassurance commission thereon.[16] Since the changeover by British companies in October 1976 to a commission system for direct business based on premiums, normal reassurance commission is paid on extra premiums to reimburse the ceding company for the commission it will have paid to its agent.

(2) When the ceding company retains a constant amount at risk (see page 476) the reassurer is entitled to receive only a decreasing share of the extra premium or debt calculated as follows.[17]

$$\frac{A}{B} = \frac{S-SV_t-R}{S(1-V_t)}$$

With-profit policies

The reassurance of with-profit assurances creates special problems. If a reassurer accepts such business on original terms he will receive his share

15 Foster, 'Some observations on life reassurance', p.346.
16 Steeds, 'Life reassurance'.
17 Foster, 'Some observations on life reassurance'.

of the original premium including the bonus loading, and in return will be liable for the same share of the bonuses declared by the ceding company. The emergence of a surplus on a life fund from which bonuses are paid depends on a variety of factors, notably investment performance, mortality experience, the distribution of the portfolio between with-profit and non-profit policies and the expenses of administering the business, so making it unlikely that the overall experience of two companies will be identical. Therefore in return for a known additional premium the reassurer assumes an uncertain liability, so that it may be argued that the reassurance of with-profit policies on original terms is theoretically unsound.[18]

On the other hand, if a direct company reassures its with-profits business on original terms on a non-profit basis, although it retains all of the premium bonus loading it loses its share of any potential surplus arising from mortality experience and the investment of the non-profit actuarial reserves. It does, however, largely remain in control of the situation in that it controls the bonus declarations, though they must be sufficiently high to compete with other companies.

Despite the theoretical objections reassurances are frequently arranged on original terms with-profits, but the market capacity by way of reassurance is more limited than for reassurances arranged on a non-profit basis. Only rarely is such business reassured on original terms on a non-profit basis: in such cases the premium paid to the reassurer is based on the ceding company's equivalent non-profit premium rate.

Instead of reassuring on original terms, with-profit business can be handled by the risk premium method. Then the ceding company only loses the potential surplus due to favourable mortality experience, but such business would qualify for profit commission under automatic treaties.

Unit-linked contracts

The key feature of all of the unit-linked assurance contracts that have been developed in Britain since the end of the 1950s is the separation of the savings and protection elements. Instead of all of the premiums being paid into a general life fund, a small proportion is used to provide conventional assurance in the form of a minimum guaranteed sum assured payable on death and, sometimes, on maturity too. The balance of the premium is then invested on the policyholder's behalf in a unit trust, property or other designated securities so that he will obtain the

18 Ibid.

full benefits of good investment performance but at the same time carry the risks of capital losses and sometimes income fluctuations too.

Much of the business has been written by comparatively new companies which require substantial reassurance protection for the mortality risks they assume.

Since the introduction of such contracts there have been many changes in the benefits offered, and some contracts are now very complex. Consequently reassurance arrangements need to be tailor-made to meet individual requirements. For example, if the original contract undertakes (1) to invest a stated proportion of the premiums (so that a fixed proportion is available to cover expenses and to pay the risk premium for a decreasing term assurance), and (2) to pay a minimum sum assured *(a)* on early death and *(b)*, possibly a higher value, on maturity, the death strain for the ceding company on an individual contract will be the difference between the fixed sum payable on death and the current market value of units already allocated, plus or minus the reserve attributable to the payment of a level premium for a decreasing term assurance. Fluctuations in the market values of securities will therefore affect the death strain. Reassurance systems have been devised to deal with this situation. Basically the death strain and so the risk premium need to be recalculated at regular intervals. Such an enormous calculation task is possible with computers and it may be agreed that risk premiums be calculated, say, monthly to coincide with the revaluation of the underlying units.

The system just described would not, however, provide any protection for the maturity guarantee. The death strain as defined above is partly attributable to fluctuations in security values so that the reassurer would be assuming some investment risk. However, any shortfall in the unit values at maturity is entirely an investment risk which is outside the scope of the risk premium system.

Group life schemes

Even though group life and pensions business is conducted in Britain, Europe and North America mainly by the larger companies, its growth over the last 20 years has generated some demand for reassurance. Two problems are associated with such business. First, competition has forced up non-selection (free cover) limits to relatively high levels, so that most of the business is underwritten without medical evidence. Secondly, it is the oldest, and so generally least healthy, members of the scheme who tend to have the largest sums assured for which reassurance protection is required.

Consequently if reassurance were arranged on the conventional surplus basis, most of the business ceded to the reassurer would be for relatively high sums assured with no medical evidence. Moreover, unlike the ceding company, the reassurer would not have the benefit of the larger volume of business for the young, healthy members of group schemes. The only remedy is for the ceding company to reduce its retention sufficiently to enable the reassurer to obtain a wider spread, or for the reassurance to be arranged on a quota share basis.

Most British group life schemes are insured on a single premium (current cost) basis where each year's premium is just sufficient to cover the mortality risk for the year, plus a loading for expenses and commission. Only rarely is the alternative level premium method used because it is usually both more expensive, particularly if the insured group has a high staff turnover, and less flexible than the single premium basis under which any changes, such as increments in benefits or the termination of a scheme, can be dealt with far more easily. Consequently the reassurances of group life schemes in the United Kingdom are almost invariably on an original terms single premium basis.

For lives with benefits in excess of a scheme's non-selection limit it is normal market practice for full medical evidence to be made available to the reassurer (though he remains bound to accept his agreed share of the risk) and for the benefits in excess of the limit to be reassured on original terms using individual age-related premium rates. If the medical evidence reveals any impairment of the life to be assured, any premium loading will apply only to the amount of benefit in excess of the free-cover level.

Profit-sharing arrangements are another common feature of schemes covering large numbers of lives, whereby if the experience proves favourable, a proportion of the profit is returned to the assured. When the profit-sharing approach, or the retention-schedule method as it is called in North America, is used, the reassurer normally participates with the ceding office on a quota share basis. The reassurer works with the ceding office in devising the profit-sharing formula or retention schedule, and then participates in the experience of the scheme as a whole on a quota share basis.

Annuities

Whereas in life assurance the assurer is concerned with the risk of early death, under an annuity contract the prolongation of life beyond the expected age of the annuitant is a potential cause of loss. Thus a reduction in mortality rates at older ages will have an adverse effect on the performance of an annuity fund. However, the reassurance of annuities is on a relatively small scale. The demand for reassurance is in the main confined to the relatively few very large annuity contracts which are written.

Besides the relatively small number of contracts for which reassurance is required, a major problem with administering a treaty for immediate annuities is the need to obtain the reassurer's agreement to alterations in premium rates which, being linked to current interest rates, are constantly changing. Therefore immediate annuities are normally reassured facultatively. It may be added that because of the way in which the regulations for the taxation of annuity funds operate in the United Kingdom, professional reassurers are reluctant to enter into treaties which bind them to accept whatever business is ceded regardless of the tax position of their annuity funds.

Deferred annuities are very rarely reassured. This is partly because deferred annuities are generally for smaller sums than immediate annuities and partly because the decision whether to reassure can be deferred until the vesting date of the annuity. Deferral of the reassurance arrangements does, however, carry the risk that if interest rates have fallen since the purchase date of the annuity the ceding office will have to pay a commensurately higher price for reassurance than it charged its own annuitant.

Reassurance on original terms

Almost all reassurances of annuities are arranged on original terms whereby the reassurer accepts liability for the surplus over the ceding company's retention and in return receives a *pro rata* share of the purchase price less reassurance commission. The rate of commission allowed on facultative reassurances is the same as that paid by the ceding company to its agent, and reassurers are normally reluctant to allow an over-riding commission on treaties.

Reassurance on a risk premium basis

It is possible to reassure annuities on a modified risk premium basis designed to protect the ceding office against the financial effects of an annuitant living for a period longer than the life expectancy used to calculate the annuity consideration. The method, however, is complex and is rarely used in practice because the number of annuities a ceding company may need to reassure is usually too small to warrant the effort and expense involved.

Table 13.2. Immediate annuity reassured on modified risk premium basis.
Male aged 70, annuity £1,000 per annum, paid annually in arrear, Basis a (55) ultimate annuity table at 10%

(1) Age	(2) Reserve at start of year	(3) Interest at 10%	(4) Annuity payment	(5) Fund at end of year (2) + (3) − (4)	(6) Reserve at end of year	(7) Balance from reassurer (6) − (5)
	£	£	£	£	£	£
70	5,641	564.1	1,000	5,205.1	5,449	243.9
71	5,449	544.9	1,000	4,993.9	5,254	260.1
72	5,254	525.4	1,000	4,779.4	5,058	278.6
73	5,058	505.8	1,000	4,563.8	4,862	298.2
74	4,862	486.2	1,000	4,348.2	4,665	316.8
75	4,665	466.5	1,000	4,131.5	4,468	336.5
76	4,468	446.8	1,000	3,914.8	4,273	358.2
77	4,273	427.3	1,000	3,700.3	4,080	379.7
78	4,080	408.0	1,000	3,488.0	3,888	400.0
79	3,888	388.8	1,000	3,276.8	3,700	423.2
80	3,700	370.0	1,000	3,070.0	3,515	445.0

The example given in Table 13.2 illustrates how the method operates. It is assumed that the ceding company writes an annuity for a male aged 70 years for £1,000 per annum, paid annually in arrear. On the basis of the UK a (55) ultimate annuity table published by the Institute of Actuaries the net consideration, assuming an interest rate of 10%, is £5,641, though the purchase price payable would be loaded to cover expenses, etc.

If, for simplicity, it is assumed that the company reassured the longevity risk 100% it would pay the reassurer the purchase price less reassurance commission, and the reassurer would deposit with the company the required reserve of £5,641 shown in column 2 of the table to meet the expected annuity payments. The fund thus established would be credited with interest at the assumed rate of 10% (column 3) and debited with the annuity payment at the end of the year (column 4). In order to restore the value of the fund (column 5) to the amount of reserve required to purchase an annuity at the commencement of the next year (column 6) it would be necessary for the reassurer to contribute a sum equivalent to the mortality element of each annuity payment (column 7).

Besides receiving a share of the loading element of the original purchase price, the reassurer would be credited each year with interest on the remaining reserve shown in column 2 at a slightly (probably about ½%) higher rate than the assumed 10% to cover expenses and to provide a small profit margin. Furthermore if the annuitant should die early the reassurer would be entitled to the remaining reserve, but if the annuitant should live longer than his life expectancy at the inception, the accumulated payments from the reassurer would commence to exceed the return of reserve on death. With each year that passes, the reassurer's loss on the particular annuitant would further increase. If the reassurer's annuity fund is well balanced, the loss would be compensated by cases which do not reach the life expectancy. The value of reassurer's contributions to the ceding company is $1000e_{70}$, e_{70} being the expectancy, which is also the formula for an annuity at a nil rate of interest. Thus the ceding company absorbs the interest generated (including interest profit) leaving the reassurer to assume the longevity risk.

Fixing retentions

The key factors which a company should take into account in fixing retention limits have been discussed already in Chapter 9. Indeed the examples used in that chapter were based on life portfolios which present relatively simpler problems than most non-life business in that in the event of a claim occurring the insurer's liability is fixed — in other words, there is no element of uncertainty about the potential severity of loss. However, there are certain aspects of the nature of life business which merit further comment.

It may be assumed that the primary purpose of a life office in incurring the cost of purchasing reassurance is to obtain a relative stabilization of its mortality experience. Irving Rosenthal has listed five causes of deviation of actual mortality from the expected mortality assumed for underwriting purposes.[19] After examining the characteristics of each type of variation, he came to the following conclusions about their relationship to the fixing of retention limits for individual lives assured:

(1) *Relative chance fluctuations* are a function of portfolio size and the distribution of sums assured. The larger the portfolio, the smaller will be the relative fluctuations. On a portfolio of a given size and distribution of sums assured, an increase in retention limits will increase the relative chance fluctuations (see Chapter 9).

In fixing retentions there is no need to concentrate on the fluctuations within small sub-classes. What matters is the degree of fluctuation on the whole portfolio which 'is lower for an aggregation of small classes than the result secured by summing up the fluctuations for the individual classes'. Rosenthal also shows that the treatment of a portfolio as one big class subject to an overall average death rate will produce a conservative estimate of the chance fluctuations on the whole portfolio.

19 Irving Rosenthal, 'Limits of retention for ordinary life insurance', *The Record* (American Institute of Actuaries), vol. 36, part 1, no. 73 (1947).

(2) *Secular variations* can affect relative fluctuations in mortality experience only if over time there are substantially different alterations in the basic mortality rates for large risks compared with small risks. Therefore, in general, alterations in retention limits have no bearing on the problem of secular variations in mortality rates.

(3) *Catastrophic variations* can also be ignored when fixing individual retention limits.

(4) *Cyclical variations* in losses due to the influence on mortality of business cycles would appear to affect large risks unduly. Though the impact of such variations may be reduced by limiting retentions, a better remedy may be to improve underwriting controls.

(5) *Variations due to incorrect classification or inadequate knowledge of basic mortality* can be particularly heavy for extreme ages and impaired lives where a company may have neither sufficient experience of its own nor access to adequate market experience. Although substantial margins may be built into premiums for such risks, the deviation in the basic mortality rates from the underwriting standard may be such as to justify a downgrading of retention limits.

Fluctuations in losses due to catastrophes, although not amenable to reduction through limiting individual retentions, can be handled by catastrophe excess of loss and stop loss reinsurances. In both cases the distribution of policies by sums assured, and the probabilities of accidents causing multiple deaths, must enter into the determination of a company's retentions.

Actuarial techniques are more highly developed in life assurance than in other classes of insurance business, and various mathematical models have been devised to arrive at appropriate retention limits for a life fund. One example is Rosenthal's formula for calculating 'chance fluctuations funds', i.e. an amount sufficient within a certain limit of probability to cover any variation in the mortality experience in any year from expected losses due solely to chance fluctuations.[20] Nevertheless in practice retentions are generally still fixed in a more or less *ad hoc* fashion.

The weakness of all of the models developed to date is the assumption of an independence of risks, which is not true of most life portfolios. Even if in some cases the degree of interrelationship between the insured lives of a portfolio may be very small, it cannot be ignored. Consequently companies (after obtaining actuarial advice) still fix their retentions in the light of those factors which are common to other classes of business, that is:

(1) The capital and free reserves of the company.
(2) The size of the portfolio.

20 Ibid.

(3) The types and mix of business transacted.
(4) The margin that can be built in to premiums to provide for mortality risk.
(5) The price the company is prepared to pay for reinsurance.
(6) The other factors discussed in Chapter 9.

Arranging a reassurance programme

Each life company has its own peculiar reassurance requirements so that it is impossible to say that there is any one correct way to formulate a reassurance programme. Sometimes requirements will be so specific as to lead automatically to a given form of reassurance. In other cases the relative merits of the alternative forms of reassurance, and of placing those reassurances facultatively or by treaty, will not be so clear, so that the final choice will be more a matter of preference.

No further comment is required regarding the merits of the treaty method compared with facultative arrangements. As for the forms of reassurance, the following comments attempt to summarize the most important factors to be considered when choosing which form to adopt.

Original terms reassurances go some way to ease the new-business strain[21] particularly associated with some valuation bases. Therefore original terms reassurance can ease the financing problems of new and very young companies for whom new business will constitute a high proportion of their total business, and other companies with limited capital and free reserves that wish to secure a substantial volume of new business.

Generally it is cheaper to reassure temporary assurances on original terms than on a risk premium basis.

The risk premium method has the advantage of reducing premium outgo to the minimum, leaving the company with the savings element of premiums for investment. Therefore, it is an attractive method for companies with sufficient resources to finance new business production.

Hybrid arrangements may be a useful compromise for companies operating in countries with gross reserving regulations. The reassurance can be arranged essentially on original terms but leaving the ownership of the reserves on the reassured portion of the original portfolio with the

---

21 See page 474 for an explanation of this term.

ceding company. The resulting arrangement is then very similar to a risk premium reassurance but with a financing element through initial reassurance commission.

Excess of loss reinsurance is ancillary to original terms or risk premium cover in that it can provide the extra protection which a company may require if it is exposed to a significant accumulation risk. As the reinsurer is entitled to cancel an excess of loss cover it is not possible to rely on continuing cover being available at cheap rates.

Stop loss cover likewise offers reasonable ancillary protection to standard original terms or risk premium reassurances, but as an alternative it has severe drawbacks. Like excess of loss cover it presents the problems of a short-term cancellable cover for a long-term risk. Also a ceding company relying solely on stop loss cover would lose the underwriting and other assistance often provided by reinsurers.

Permanent health insurance

In Britain the supervisory authority groups permanent health insurance (PHI) with life assurance under the general heading of long-term business because, like life assurance, once such a sickness insurance has been accepted by an insurer, the terms cannot be amended and only the policyholder has the right to cancel. Elsewhere practice varies. In some European countries the business is classified as general (i.e. short-term) insurance business, and in North America both life and general companies may underwrite what is known as 'accident and health' or 'accident and sickness' insurance. Also in many countries although policies are non-cancellable, the premium charged for the class of business as a whole may be varied. Therefore reinsurance practice as described below for the UK sometimes differs in detail elsewhere.

The rapid growth of PHI business in Britain since the late 1960s has generated a demand for reinsurance at two levels. There is the usual demand for cover for large cases with sums insured in excess of the direct insurer's normal retention limit. Additionally some insurers newly embarking on writing such business seek the assistance of reinsurers with a specialist knowledge of underwriting and handling sickness claims. In the latter case reinsurers will often provide advice on suggested wordings for policies, forms, etc., and at the claims stage there is often much consultation on interpretation of policy wordings. Normally retentions are expressed in the form of a monetary amount of benefit per annum.

Like life assurance, permanent health insurances are written on both an individual basis and as group schemes. Although the two types of business share many common features there are differences which require separate consideration.

Individual policies

Market capacity is rarely a problem because of the limits placed on sums insured, but most new entrants to the market fix their retentions at relatively low levels so that there is a demand for reinsurance. Some companies are prepared to deal with the few large cases requiring reinsurance protection by arranging facultative reinsurances. Generally, however, most individual PHI reinsurances in Britain are effected by means of a surplus treaty on original terms, the reinsurer receiving for each risk ceded a *pro rata* share of the original premium less an overriding commission.

Claims settlement and administration costs. Under PHI contracts a major determinant of the number of claims that will be received is the deferred period; that is, the number of weeks of continuous disability before the income commences to be payable. Obviously the number of claims and thus the size of a reinsurer's administrative costs are inversely related to the length of the deferred period. With a short deferred period not only are more claims received but also the cost of handling short-term claims is disproportionately high compared to the benefit paid. Therefore when a company issues original policies with short deferred periods of less than, say, three months a modified form of original terms reinsurance may be arranged with a longer deferred period of perhaps six months. The reinsurer then only becomes liable on claims that reach the agreed period, and in return is paid a share of the premium based on the ceding company's premium rate applicable to the longer deferred period. As the reduction in the reinsurer's administration costs is reflected in the lower premium rate charged, there should be no change in the rate of reinsurance commission allowed.

At the other end of the claims scale are those cases where the policyholder remains incapacitated for several years. A company may seek to protect its account from the possibility that occasionally it may be committed to paying benefits for 30 or more years. Some companies seek 100% reinsurance for all claims that run for longer than, say, two or five years.[22] While reassurers are prepared to provide cover with a long deferred period, they usually require the ceding company to retain some interest in every reinsured risk throughout the duration of any claim.

22 R.J. Sansom, 'Practical PHI', *Journal of the Institute of Actuaries Students Society.*

Inflation provisions. Many PHI contracts now contain some form of inflation proofing in the form of escalation clauses, such as annual fixed percentage increases in policy benefits, annual increases in benefit during the duration of any claim, options to increase sums insured at fixed intervals, etc[2][3] Usually the insurer and reinsurer each accept liability for any escalation relating to their respective portions of the risk.

In order to exercise some control over potential liabilities, it is market practice for insurers to place lower initial acceptance limits on contracts containing escalation clauses, and some direct insurers slightly reduce their own initial retention limits too.

Modified risk premium method. Instead of proportional reinsurance on original terms, a small amount of PHI reinsurance is placed on a modified form of the risk premium method. It leaves reserves in the hands of the ceding company and thus is particularly useful where the company is subject to gross reserving regulations, or where under high inflationary conditions reserves can be invested locally in index-linked securities.

The morbidity risk for the PHI insurer is more complex than the mortality risk for the life assurer—a life assured can only die once but during the duration of a PHI policy he may suffer several periods of disability of varying lengths. However, like life assurance, PHI business leads to an accumulation of reserves from which claims can be paid, so than the risk run on a policy in any year is the expected cost of claims less the applicable reserves.

Thus when a PHI portfolio is reinsured on a risk premium basis the reinsurer will pay in respect of each claim that proportion of the benefit payable to the policyholder which the amount reinsured bears to the expected cost of claims in excess of the ceding company's retention less the applicable reserves. The reinsured thus pays the reinsurer the same share of the original premiums *less* (1) commission, (2) any increase in the reserves on the reinsured portfolio, (3) claims paid, and (4) any increase in claims reserves if the ceding company makes a specific reserve for claims in course of payment.

Group policies

Group schemes produce a larger demand for reinsurance than individual policies because amounts involved are likely to be larger, especially when the PHI benefit is associated with the waiver of pension premiums, and

23 For details see D.B. Biggs, 'Permanent health insurance', in *Handbook of Insurance,* ed. R.L. Carter. ch.2.4.

there is more pressure on direct insurers to provide cover for substandard lives.[24]

Besides the points already discussed for individual policies, group schemes present two particular problems for the reinsurer—free cover and profit sharing.[25]

Free cover. It is the universal custom to allow the major part of the benefits provided by any group scheme to be accepted without any evidence of health for employees actively at work.[26] Competition for group business pushes up non-selection limits so that often they are higher than the insurer's own retention. Consequently reinsurance is often required not only for those members of a scheme with sums insured above the free-cover limit for whom terms are fixed in the light of medical evidence, but also for others who are insured on a non-selected basis. As the latter group will include the more senior employees it will tend to comprise older, less healthy individuals.

Normal considerations apply to the reinsurance of peak risks over the free cover limit, e.g. the ceding company's underwriting experience and standards. Peak risks within the free-cover layer are a different matter. It is unreasonable to expect a reinsurer to accept such business on an unselected basis: some method must be found to enable the reinsurer to have a better spread of business.

If the scheme premium is calculated on a unit cost basis the only fair way of arranging the reinsurance for risks within the free-cover limit is on a quota share. Amounts above the free limit, for which individual details and medical evidence are available, could still be reinsured on a surplus basis, possibly as individual facultative reinsurances on a single premium basis.

In other cases a ceding company may resist quota share because of the loss of premium income it involves. Provided the company has a relatively low retention, e.g. £1,000 or £2,000 per annum, or is prepared to lower its normal retention to around that sort of figure for non-select business, it should be possible to obtain surplus reinsurance.

Profit sharing. Some group schemes are written subject to a profit-sharing agreement whereby, in return for an extra premium, the insurer at regular intervals will return a varying percentage of the amount by which net premiums exceed claims (including provisions for outstanding claims). Such agreements pose problems and are a likely source of conflict even on the original insurance—notably, provisions for

24 Sansom, 'Practical PHI'.
25 Ibid.
26 Biggs, 'Permanent health insurance'.

outstanding claims are very difficult to estimate.[27] They do, however, pose further problems for a reinsurer. Unless such a scheme is reinsured on a quota share basis it is difficult for the reinsurer to participate in the profit sharing arrangement for two reasons. First, if the scheme is reinsured on a surplus basis, the reinsurer is unlikely to obtain a sufficient number of members to provide the necessary balance for profit sharing to operate equitably. Secondly, as the surplus treaty results are unlikely to match the results of the original insurance it will be necessary to calculate separately the profitability of the reinsured portfolio.

Provided the peak risks do not comprise a significant proportion of the total scheme a possible solution is to arrange the reinsurance of the peak risks on a non-profit basis. The premium rate charged by the ceding company will then need to be adjusted to the equivalent non-profit rate for the purposes of calculating the reinsurance premium.

Duration of a treaty and other conditions

PHI treaties are normally arranged for an unlimited duration but with provision for termination by either party on giving three months' notice.

The main provisions applying to PHI treaties generally follow those applied to life treaties. One special feature is that upon cancellation the reinsurer remains liable for both existing cessions and any claims in course of payment until their natural expiry.

Generally treaties do not contain any special exclusions, reinsurers being content to rely on the limits and exclusions applied to original policies. Only if the reinsurer were unhappy about the geographical scope of a ceding company's operations would it normally be deemed necessary to insert any geographical limit in a treaty.

It is common practice to include both individual and group business in the same treaty.

27 Ibid.

Appendix 13.1 Main provisions of the Reassurance Agreement 1900

(1) The office placing the reassurance is known as the 'Principal Office'. The office to which the reassurance is offered is known as the 'Guaranteeing Office'.

(2) The Principal Office must disclose:
   (a) the amount of assurance it already holds on the life;
   (b) its proposed retention on the new assurance;
   (c) the terms applying to the new assurance;
   (d) the terms of any existing assurance;
   (e) all material facts at the time the reassurance offer is made, and also facts which emerge in the interval before completion. It must also:
      (i) furnish copies of all papers containing such information;
      (ii) give particulars of previous proposals and exhibit papers if required, and allow copies to be taken.

(3) The Guaranteeing Office may not retrocede any part of the risk without the consent of the Principal Office.

(4) The Guaranteeing Office is not on risk until it has intimated acceptance, nor until the Principal Office is on risk. After acceptance by the Guaranteeing Office it goes on the risk at the same time as the Principal Office receives the first premium. The Principal Office must not complete the risk after the expiry of one month from the date of the Guaranteeing Office's acceptance, unless the Guaranteeing Office is provided with satisfactory evidence that the life to be assured remains eligible for assurance.

(5) If before commencement of the risk the Guaranteeing Office receives information making it desirable to withdraw its acceptance, and accordingly informs the Principal Office in writing, the Guaranteeing Office's acceptance shall be void after the expiry of one week from the time of such intimation, or immediately the Principal Office withdraws its own acceptance or obtains an acceptance of the reassurance elsewhere, whichever happens first, unless in the meantime the risk of the Guaranteeing Office has commenced by reason of the Principal Office's risk having commenced.

(6) Upon becoming aware of the commencement of the risk, the Principal Office shall pay the first reassurance premium immediately or issue a notice to the Guaranteeing Office stating the amount and date of the risk.

(7) The reassurance contract shall be evidenced:
   (a) by a Guarantee endorsed on a copy of the Principal Office's policy; or
   (b) by a policy of the Guaranteeing Office endorsed to the effect that it is issued as a reassurance of the Principal Office's policy.

(8) The Guaranteeing Office shall pay the Principal Office a proportion of the stamp duty on the original policy.

(9) Where the Guaranteeing Office receives a premium for the reinsurance at the Principal Office's rate, the Guaranteeing Office shall follow the Principal Office in:
   (a) extra premiums charged and licences allowed, but the Guaranteeing Office shall be first consulted;
   (b) commutations or alterations of premium or adjustments of the sum assured or premium on account of misstatement of age, but the

Guaranteeing Office must first consent to any alteration involving the remission or reduction of any premium or modification of special terms imposed in lieu of extra premium;

(c) bonuses and their current cash values;

(d) surrender values, paid-up policy values.

(10) When the reassurance is at the Guaranteeing Office's own rate of premium, the Guaranteeing Office's conditions shall prevail for bonuses, surrender values, paid-up policy values, and alterations or commutations of premiums.

The Principal Office's conditions shall prevail for extra premiums charged, and licences allowed, and for adjustments on account of errors in statement of age.

(11) Where the rates are the same, the rates and conditions of the Principal Office shall be held to govern the reassurance.

(12) The premiums in respect of the reassurance shall be payable on the same dates as the premiums on the original assurance.

(13) The Principal Office may surrender the whole or any part of any reassurance.

(14) The rates of commission in default of special arrangements shall be:

(a) 10% of the first premium and 5% of the renewal premiums; or

(b) £1 per cent of the sum assured and 2½% of renewal premiums.

Appendix 13.2   Specimen treaties

A. Specimen risk premium treaty (with term assurances on original terms)

Article 1

Scope

This Agreement applies to the classes of life assurance business and supplementary benefits set out in the First Schedule which the Ceding Office accepts at the general conditions and, where applicable, rates of premium in force at the date of the Agreement as subsequently amended by the Ceding Office and accepted by the Reassurer.

Reassurances accepted by the Ceding Office will not be included hereunder unless mutually agreed otherwise.

Article 2

Retention and automatic cover

The Ceding Office agrees to cede and the Reassurer agrees to accept all business included in the Agreement up to the limits specified in the First Schedule.

In determining the retention of the Ceding Office the actual amount at risk under previous policies on the same life will be taken into account.

If the Ceding Office reduces its retention on any life below the amount stated in the First Schedule the automatic cover granted by the Reassurer will be reduced proportionately.

The Ceding Office will notify the Reassurer immediately of any increase in retention and such increase will apply to policies where risk is assumed on or after the date from which the increase takes effect. No cession previously made hereunder will be affected.

Should the Ceding Office receive a proposal for an amount in excess of its retention and the automatic cover granted by the Reassurer the excess may be offered facultatively to the Reassurer and if accepted the routine procedures set out in this Agreement will apply unless agreed otherwise.

Article 3

Currency

All cessions under this Agreement will be effected in the same currency as the original policy.

Liability

The liability of the Reassurer will commence simultaneously with that of the Ceding Office and, subject to any special provisions that may be made regarding the method of calculation of the amounts at risk for risk premium cessions, will cease at the same time as the liability of the Ceding Office ceases.

For all policies other than policies of a temporary assurance nature the amount at risk reassured in any policy year will be the difference between the original

510

amount of the cession and the reserve thereon at the beginning of the policy year calculated on the basis set out in the First Schedule.

For policies of a temporary assurance nature and for the forms of supplementary accident or disability benefits included within the terms of the Agreement the Reassurer agrees to follow to the extent of its liability the general conditions of the Ceding Office.

Article 4

Reassurance premiums

The basic rates of premium applicable to cessions reassured on the risk premium basis hereunder are set out in the Third Schedule. The premium for each policy year will be the product of the rate according to the age at the commencement of the policy year and the amount at risk for that year. If a policy is issued by the Ceding Office at a rate of premium for a higher age than the actual age at entry that higher age will be used to calculate the risk premiums. If a cession covers the mortality risk on more than one life and the sum assured is payable on the first death the rate of premium will be the total of the respective rates for the individual lives.

For all cessions of a temporary assurance nature the Ceding Office will pay to the Reassurer the annual rate of premium applicable to the original policy.

On all cessions the due proportion of any extra premiums payable under the original policy for any reason whatsoever will be payable to the Reassurer.

All premiums will be payable to the Reassurer annually in advance whatever the mode of payment of the premiums under the original policy.

The premium rates for the reassurance of any supplementary benefits falling under the provisions of this Agreement are stated in the First Schedule.

Commission and expenses

The Reassurer will pay to the Ceding Office commission at the rates shown in the First Schedule. Apart from this no commission, taxes or proportion of any expenses will be paid by the Reassurer except as provided in Article 7 and Article 12.

Article 5

Documentation

Subsequent to assuming risk, the Ceding Office will supply the Reassurer with sufficient information to enable the Reassurer to prepare a reassurance certificate or other agreed documentation as set out in the Second Schedule. Copies of all reassurance certificates or other agreed documentation will be sent as required to the Ceding Office.

For cessions specified in Article 5 of the First Schedule, immediately the Ceding Office assumes risk copies of the proposal and medical papers will be sent automatically to the Reassurer. For other cessions a copy of the proposal and medical papers will be sent to the Reassurer on request.

Article 6
Alterations

The Ceding Office will notify the Reassurer of any alteration to the original policy which affects the Reassurer's liability. In the event of a policy reassured under this Agreement being reduced in amount, the cession will be reduced proportionately from the same date, but a reduction of the sum assured under one of the Ceding Office's policies not reassured hereunder will not affect any cession on the same life. The Reassurer will refund to the Ceding Office any unearned reassurance premiums less commissions arising as a result of the alteration.

Cancellations

In the event of the cancellation of the original policy the Reassurer will refund to the Ceding Office any unearned reassurance premiums less commissions arising as a result of the cancellation.

Reinstatement

Should a policy which has lapsed be reinstated in accordance with the policy conditions, the cession hereunder will be automatically reinstated and the appropriate arrears of premium and interest will be payable to the Reassurer.

Article 7
Claims

In the event of a claim on a policy reassured hereunder the Ceding Office will notify the Reassurer immediately. All payments made by the Ceding Office within its policy conditions in respect of death, supplementary accident or disability benefit claims will be binding on the Reassurer to the extent of its liability. If a claim is settled for less than the full sum assured under the policy at the date of the claim the Reassurer will pay to the Ceding Office its proportion of the cost of the claim after deduction of the reserve applicable to the cession. In addition the Reassurer will be liable for its proportion of any legal costs and expenses incurred in the investigation of claims but excluding any expenses incurred by the Ceding Office's employees.

Where a debt or lien has been imposed on the original policy the Reassurer's liability will be determined by deducting from the current amount at risk a proportion of the debt or lien calculated in the ratio that the nominal amount of the cession bears to the sum assured under the original policy.

The Ceding Office will provide the Reassurer with details of the claim and the Reassurer will credit the Ceding Office with its share of the claim after production of proof of claim satisfactory to the Reassurer and notification of payment by the Ceding Office. Copies of the full claim documents need only be sent on request. All claims will be settled in the account unless the Ceding Office requests a separate remittance. Any settlement by separate remittance may be subject to the amount of the claim being set against any balances outstanding and due to the Reassurer.

Article 8

Accounts

Statements of account setting out all premiums, commissions, claims not paid by separate remittance and other items applicable to cessions effected, renewed, altered or cancelled during the period covered by the account will be prepared in accordance with the details set out in the First Schedule.

Settlement of the balance due as shown in the statements of account will be made in accordance with the details set out in the First Schedule. Alternatively the balance may be set against any other balances outstanding between the Ceding Office and the Reassurer.

Article 9

Errors and omissions

Any error or omission which occurs will not affect the validity of this Agreement and the mistake will be rectified upon discovery.

Inspection of records

The Reassurer may inspect at the offices of the Ceding Office all records and documents relevant to the business under this Agreement.

Article 10

Alterations to Agreement

Any alteration in the terms and conditions of this Agreement will be made by addendum or by correspondence attached to the Agreement embodying such alterations as may be agreed upon and the alteration will be regarded as part of this Agreement and equally binding.

Article 11

Duration of Agreement

This Agreement will take effect from the date stated in the First Schedule and is unlimited as to its duration but may be made inapplicable to future policies in whole or in part by either party giving three months' notice to that effect by letter, receipt of which will be immediately acknowledged by the other party. During the period of three months the Reassurer will continue to participate in all policies falling within the terms of this Agreement. The Reassurer will remain liable for all cessions existing at the date of expiry of the notice until their natural expiry unless the parties mutually decide otherwise.

Article 12

Arbitration

All disputes arising out of the above Agreement or concerning its interpretation or validity, whether arising before or after its termination, will be referred to two arbitrators, one to be chosen by each party.

If one party has appointed an arbitrator he may then serve notice upon the other party requiring that party to appoint another arbitrator. Unless within two calendar months after the date of serving such notice another arbitrator has been appointed, the arbitrator who has been appointed will at the request of the party appointing him proceed to hear and determine the matters in difference as sole arbitrator.

If both parties have duly appointed arbitrators, the arbitrators will before proceeding to hear the matters in difference appoint an umpire. If no umpire has been appointed within one calendar month after the date of appointment of the last arbitrator to be appointed, then the umpire will be appointed by the authority stipulated in the First Schedule upon the request of either party to this Agreement.

The Arbitration will be held at the place stated in the First Schedule and the award will be delivered in writing. The award will be final and binding on both parties.

The cost of the reference and award will be decided in the same manner as the matters in difference. The arbitrators and umpire may direct to and by whom and in what manner the cost or any part thereof will be paid with power to tax or settle the amount to be so paid.

The arbitrators and umpire will each be an official in a life assurance office or a partner in a firm of consulting actuaries.

This arbitration agreement will be construed as a separate and independent contract between the two parties and arbitration hereunder will be a condition precedent to the commencement of any action at law.

Article 13

Profit commission

At the end of the first year in which there are 200 risk premium cessions in force, the Reassurer will prepare a statement in the form of the following schedule, for the business ceded on the risk premium basis under this Agreement.

Schedule

Income under the Agreement	Outgo under the Agreement
1. Premium income for the current year.	1. Commission for the current year.
2. Reserve brought forward being 50% of the premium income for the preceding year.	2. Reserve carried forward being 50% of the premium income for the current year.
3. Loss carried forward (if any).	3. Loss brought forward (if any).
	4. Claims by death occurring during the current year.
	5. Expenses being 10% of the premium income for the current year.
	6. Profit (if any).

Provided the first 200 cessions are reached within three years of the commencement of this Agreement, the first statement will relate to the period since the date of effect of this Agreement. Subsequent statements will be prepared on an annual basis.

Only items applicable to risk premium reassurances will be included in the schedule. Items applicable to amounts retroceded by the Reassurer to other offices will be excluded from the schedule.

In the event of a profit being shown 35% of the profit will be payable to the Ceding Office.

In the event of a loss being shown the loss, together with any other losses, will be carried forward to subsequent years until extinguished and no profit commission will be payable during that period.

If, after the statement has been approved and the profit commission paid, further claims are notified relating to deaths occurring in the year to which the statement relates the statement will be recalculated and the necessary refund made to the Reassurer.

In the event of this Agreement being cancelled for new business the provisions of this Article will be cancelled from the same date.

First schedule

Article 1

Business covered by this Agreement

Article 2

Retention of Ceding Ofice

Automatic cover granted by Reassurer

Article 3

Basis of calculation of amounts at risk for risk premium cessions

Article 4

Premium rates for supplementary benefits

Commission

Article 5

Copy papers automatically required

Article 8

Preparation of accounts

Settlement of accounts

Article 10

Date of effect of Agreement

Article 11

Authority for appointment of umpire

Place of arbitration

Special Provisions

Made in duplicate and signed by both parties.
                    Signed for and on behalf of
this   day of   19   .

Signed for and on behalf of The XYZ Reinsurance Company Limited, London,
this   day of   19   .

Second Schedule
See Appendix 13.3.

Third Schedule
Premium rates.

B. Specimen life excess of loss reassurance treaty

Article 1
Definitions

The following definitions will apply in this Agreement:

Accidental death means any death caused solely through external, violent and accidental means, provided that such death occurs within 90 days of the accident.

Catastrophe means an event or series of related events which causes the accidental death of at least the number of lives, assured by the Company, specified in the First Schedule. Always provided that:
(1) Each catastrophe resulting from the perils of tornado, typhoon, windstorm, rainstorm, cyclone, hurricane or hail will include all losses occasioned by these perils arising out of one atmospheric disturbance during a continuous period of 48 hours.
(2) Each catastrophe resulting from the perils of earthquake, seaquake, tidal wave or volcanic eruption will include all losses occasioned by these perils arising during a continuous period of 72 hours.
(3) Each catastrophe resulting from any other perils whatsoever will include all losses occasioned by these perils arising during a continuous period of 168 hours.
The Company may choose the date and time from which any such period of hours commences and if any such event or series of related events is of greater duration than the above periods, the Company may divide that event or series of related events into two or more catastrophes, provided no two periods overlap and provided no period commences earlier than the date and time of the happening of the first recorded individual loss to the Company in that catastrophe.

Net sum at risk means the total sum assured in force payable on death under life assurance policies or reassurances covered by the Company, including additional benefits payable on accidental death, less any sums reassured payable on death placed with other offices, and less the total mathematical reserves held by the Company relating to such policies subject to any restrictions as stated in the First Schedule.

Ultimate net loss means the net sum at risk relating to those policies under which claims are paid by the Company resulting from any one catastrophe.

Article 2

Extent of cover

The Reassurer agrees subject to the terms, conditions and limitations hereinafter contained, to indemnify the Company to the extent of the agreed percentage as specified in the First Schedule for that part of the Company's ultimate net loss which exceeds the catastrophe retention of the Company as stated in the First Schedule. The sum recoverable under this Agreement in respect of any one catastrophe will not exceed the Reassurer's maximum liability per catastrophe as stated in the First Schedule.

In the event of more than one catastrophe leading to a claim under this Agreement arising within any consecutive 365 days, the Reassurer's liability during that period is limited to the amount stated in the First Schedule.

The maximum sum assured retained by the Company in respect of any one life will not exceed the individual retention of the Company as stated in the First Schedule. If the Company alters its individual retention the Reassurer will be notified immediately and the Agreement modified accordingly.

Article 3

Claims

In the event of a loss resulting in a claim under this Agreement the Company will notify the Reassurer as soon as possible. All claim settlements made by the Company will be binding on the Reassurer. Expenses incurred by the Company, excluding any expenses incurred by its full-time employees, in connection with the investigation and settlement or contesting the validity of claims or alleged claims which may be incurred will be included in the amount of the claim. However, the Reassurer will be entitled to participate in any recoveries in diminution of its share of any claim arising hereunder. All claims and expenses will be paid immediately by the Reassurer. Alternatively the claim may be set against amounts outstanding between the two parties and due to the Reassurer.

Article 4

Exclusions

The Reassurer will not be liable for claims arising under policies in respect of:
(1) War whether declared or not, invasion, acts of foreign enemies, hostilities, civil war, rebellion, revolution, insurrection, military or usurped power, riot and civil commotion.
(2) Aviation, except for passengers and crew of airlines or private flying purely

for transport purposes.

(3) Atomic energy and/or nuclear fission or reaction.

(4) Professional sports teams.

The following classes of business will not be covered under this treaty without the prior consent of the Reassurer:

(1) Any group scheme with membership greater than the number specified in the First Schedule.

(2) Any group scheme or group of persons under individual contracts subject to a special catastrophe hazard or an undue accumulation of risk.

(3) Non-proportional reassurances accepted by the Company.

Article 5

Reassurance premiums

At the commencement of this Agreement, and as soon as practicable after each subsequent treaty renewal date, the Company shall provide the Reassurer with full details of its net sum at risk. The annual premium payable by the Company to the Reassurer at the commencement of this Agreement and at each subsequent treaty renewal date will be the sum of the treaty fee and an amount equal to the product of the premium rate and the current net sum at risk. The treaty renewal date, the treaty fee and the premium rate are as specified in the First Schedule.

In addition if the net sum at risk has increased since the previous treaty renewal date a supplementary premium equal to one-half of the product of the premium rate and the increase in the net sum at risk during the previous treaty year will be payable to the Reassurer. Alternatively, if the net sum at risk has decreased since the previous treaty renewal date the Reassurer will refund to the Company an amount equal to one-half of the product of the premium rate and the decrease in the net sum at risk during the previous treaty year. The supplementary premium or refund in respect of the previous treaty year will fall due for payment with the annual premium for the current treaty year. In any year the annual premium plus any supplementary premium and less any refund of premium shall not be less than the minimum annual premium specified in the First Schedule.

Within one month of the commencement of this Agreement, and subsequently within one month of each treaty renewal date the Company shall make a provisional payment to the Reassurer equal to the minimum annual premium. Any balance of the annual premium will be payable to the Reassurer within four calendar months of the commencement of this Agreement for the first treaty year, and within four calendar months of the treaty renewal date for subsequent treaty years.

No commission, taxes or proportion of any expenses will be paid by the Reassurer except as provided in Article 3.

Article 6

Currency

For the purpose of this Agreement all premiums and claims will be expressed and payable in the currency specified in the First Schedule.

Net sums at risk in other currencies will be converted into the currency of this Agreement at the rates of exchange ruling on the relevant treaty renewal date. Losses in other currencies will be converted into the currency of this Agreement at the rates of exchange ruling on the date of the first recorded loss.

Article 7

Duration of Agreement

This Agreement will take effect from the date stated in the First Schedule and will remain in force for the period stated in the First Schedule. Thereafter, it may be renewed for further consecutive periods of one year, unless either party notifies the other party to the contrary in writing, receipt of which will be immediately acknowledged by the other party, at least 100 days before the Agreement is renewable. If this Agreement should be terminated while an event giving rise to a claim hereunder is in progress the Reassurer is liable for its share of the entire loss arising from such event, subject to the other conditions of this Agreement.

Articles 8-10

The remaining articles follow the wording of Articles 9, 10 and 12 in the preceding specimen agreement.

Appendix 13.3 Specimen life reassurance certificate

First Schedule

Article 1

Catastrophe: Number of lives

Net sum at risk: Modifications to cover

Article 2

Extent of cover
Percentage indemnification

Company's catastrophe retention

Reassurer's maximum liability per catastrophe

Reassurer's maximum liability within any consecutive 365 days

Individual retention of Company

Article 4

Exclusions
Reassurer's prior consent required for group schemes with membership greater than:

Article 5

Reinsurance premiums
Treaty renewal date

Treaty fee

Premium rate

Minimum annual premium

Article 6

Currency

Article 10

Date of commencement of Agreement

Duration of Agreement

14
Accounting and financial aspects of reinsurance

REINSURANCE

14
Accounting and financial aspects of reinsurance

Previous chapters have dealt with what may be called the underwriting side of reinsurance operations. Now the accounting arrangements and the financial aspects of reinsurance can be considered, albeit in rather broad terms. Although such a treatment of the subjects follows the organizational arrangements of most, if not all, ceding companies and reinsurers, it must be emphasized that there is a close interrelationship between the two sides of the business. The results of a treaty, for example, are dependent upon:

(1) The treaty provisions, such as whether the contract is on a run-off or clean-cut basis; the commission terms; the ceding company's rights to retain premium deposits (and the rate of interest, if any, payable thereon); the currencies in which accounts are to be settled; and so forth.
(2) Factors external to the treaty terms but nevertheless of financial importance, such as the level of investment yield both parties can obtain on funds, and the expenses of acquiring and managing the business.
(3) Control over the accounting arrangements, i.e. how quickly balances can be agreed and settled.

Therefore, the separate treatment here of the underwriting and financial aspects of reinsurance operations is merely for ease of exposition. In practice both must be considered together when planning a reinsurance programme and arranging treaties.

Accounting between ceding companies and reinsurers

The rendering of accounts

Reinsurance accounts are required for two purposes. First they provide a record of the financial transactions between the parties to a reinsurance contract, and so reveal the sums which at agreed intervals the reinsured is obligated to pay to, or is entitled to receive from, the reinsurer. Secondly they provide much of the data required for the preparation of underwriting statistics and the evaluation of individual treaties.

The precise details of the accounting arrangements are a matter for agreement between the parties, but practice broadly follows a standard pattern. The main differences lie in the treatment of facultative and treaty business, and the following comments are confined to non-life business, the accounting arrangements for life reassurance having been discussed in Chapter 13.

Facultative accounts

Almost invariably nowadays the ceding company is made responsible for the preparation of the quarterly accounts, though when a broker is employed he may do the work for the company. Set out in the account will be the amounts due to and from the reinsurer for all items falling within the period of account. Thus it will list:

Amounts due to reinsurer	*Amounts due from reinsurer*
Gross premiums for new reinsurances	Gross return premiums
Gross renewal premiums	Commission on premiums net of returns
Gross additional premiums	Claims (excluding claims paid in cash)

After confirmation by the reinsurer, the account will fall due for settlement within an agreed period.

Proportional reinsurance treaties

Traditionally the accounts for proportional treaties are prepared quarterly. Though very occasionally a longer period may be agreed, quarterly accounts remain more desirable from a reinsurer's point of view.

The reduction in the amount of information supplied by ceding companies to reinsurers regarding business ceded and losses means that responsibility for the preparation of the accounts must be placed on the ceding company. Basically the same aggregated information is required as for facultative reinsurances, as shown in the specimen account in Table 14.1.

Table 14.1. Specimen proportional treaty account

Period of Account	Treaty	Currency
. . . .	. . . . .	. . . .

Amounts due by reinsurer	Amounts due to reinsurer	
	Premiums less returns (Net of original charges)	
Reinsurance commission Premium taxes Fire brigade charges Any other specified deductions	Common account recoveries (losses)	
Reinsurance premiums for common account		
	Return premium reserve deposit	
Losses paid (less recoveries)	Interest on deposits	
Premium reserve deposit		
Tax on interest Balance due to reinsurer . . . . ———	Balance due from reinsurer . . . . ———	
Balance due from reinsurer Balance brought forward from previous account Settlements from ceding company	Balance due to reinsurer Balance brought forward from previous account Settlements by reinsurer	
	Cash loss settlements by reinsurer (Cash loss in paid losses)	
Liquid balance due to reinsurer . . . . ———	Liquid balance due from reinsurer . . . . ———	

The first part of the account records all items entering into the calculation of balances due between the parties, including losses paid by the ceding company, and the movements of premium and loss reserve deposits and interest payable thereon. Also any withholding tax on interest paid on deposits, or on reinsurance transactions paid by a ceding company as statutory agent for the reinsurer, will be included in the account, though sometimes it may not appear until an account subsequent to the date of payment by the ceding company.

The bottom part of the account itemises any balance brought forward from the previous account, any settlements already made by either party, and losses already settled in cash by the reinsurer, so leaving the final balance due for settlement. End of year accounts may also contain other items, such as movements in loss reserve deposits, profit commission, etc.

Some ceding companies prefer to break down the first part of the account into a *technical account* recording only premiums, commissions and losses, with the balance being transferred to a *current account* which will incorporate the movement of deposits, together with interest and tax payable thereon. Furthermore, portfolio movements may be included either in the technical accounts or in separate portfolio statements of account.

The withdrawal and taking over of portfolios raises some interesting issues in relation to the preparation of reinsurers' financial accounts.

If the reinsurer taking over a portfolio treats the portfolio consideration as premium income two points ought to be borne in mind. First the amount received will be net of reinsurance commission, and so for accounting consistency it should be grossed up for inclusion in the premium account, the difference being debited to commissions paid. Secondly, the reinsurer will have taken over a portfolio of risks which will have commenced in the previous year and which will usually run off during the current year. Therefore unless the portfolio includes any long-term insurances with periods of insurance running on into the next year, the consideration received should be excluded from the reinsurer's end of year calculation of the provision for unearned premiums to be carried forward to the next accounting year.

An outgoing reinsurer who returns to a ceding company a portfolio consideration likewise may treat it as a return of premium when the above arguments apply in reverse. In particular, because the reinsurer will have no continuing liability under the treaty, when he prepares his accounts it will be necessary to exclude from the premium income upon which the reserve for unearned premiums is calculated the whole of the premiums credited in respect of that treaty for the year in question. Calculation of the reserve on the basis of the premium income less only the portfolio consideration would result in over-reserving.

Perhaps a better way of dealing with the matter is to treat the transactions in accordance with what strictly they are—adjustments to unearned premium reserves. The reinsurer taking over the portfolio would then add the consideration received to his unearned premium reserve at the beginning of the current year, and the reinsurer from whom the portfolio is withdrawn would debit it against his reserves.

Time allowed for preparation and checking. Although some time must be allowed for the preparation and the checking of the accounts, it is in neither party's interest that settlement should be delayed unduly. Therefore the accounts clause will usually specify the times allowed for:

(1) The preparation and submission of accounts by the ceding company (usually two to three months after the close of each accounting period).

(2) Their confirmation by the reinsurer (usually 15 days to a month after receipt).

Provision may also be made for dealing with errors. It is difficult to eliminate errors entirely due to incorrect information having been supplied or figures being incorrectly transposed. Rather than delay settlement for the correction of minor errors it is better to settle immediately and adjust the next account as necessary.

Non-proportional treaties

The absence of individual cessions during the year and the practice of treating losses as cash losses payable individually by the reinsurer means that provisions regarding the preparation of accounts for non-proportional treaties can be relatively simple. Although sometimes provision must be made for adjustments to reserve deposits held by the ceding company and for profit commissions, generally only premiums have to be brought into account.

Treaties arranged on the basis of a flat non-adjustable premium obviously present the simplest accounting task. Far more often provision must be made for the payment of both a deposit premium at the beginning of the year and an adjustment premium at the end of the year based on the ceding company's eventually determined income for the year in question. The payment of a substantial deposit premium based on the amount of business the company expects to write during the year, but for which it has not yet received direct premiums, could place a severe cash strain on a ceding company. Therefore, when the amount involved is relatively large it is normal market practice for the parties to agree either to spread the payment of the deposit premium over four quarters or, if it is wholly payable at the beginning of the year, to fix the amount payable at some 10% to 20% below the anticipated final premium.

The following specimen accounts clause taken from an accident excess of loss treaty allows for the amount and method of payment of the deposit premium to be specified in the schedule.

> The Reinsured shall pay to the Reinsurer a deposit premium as provided for in the Schedule.
> As soon as possible after the end of each annual period of this agreement as stated in the Schedule but in any event within three months thereof, the Reinsured shall supply to the Reinsurer a declaration of its annual premium income as defined in article 3 fully subdivided by class of business and territory. The annual premium due to the Reinsurer under this agreement

shall be calculated in accordance with article 3 and after taking into consideration the deposit premium already paid in respect of the same period any premium adjustments due by the Reinsured shall be paid to the Reinsurer at the same time as the premium declaration is rendered. The premium adjustments shall be confirmed by the Reinsurer within one month of receipt and any premium adjustments due to the Reinsured shall be paid by the Reinsurer at the time of confirmation.

When a treaty covers overseas risks the same considerations regarding the treatment of premiums and losses in foreign currencies apply as for proportional treaties.

Standardized reinsurance accounts

Accounting between ceding companies and reinsurers is enormously complicated by the many accounting systems in use geared to the requirements of individual companies and their accounting facilities. Not only are systems designed to produce certain information in a particular way, but also many small companies still rely on manual accounting systems, whereas probably all large companies now employ computers to produce accounts and other financial data, though they use different accounting programs. The preparation of reinsurance accounts therefore has to be arranged to fit what are sometimes vastly different accounting systems. Obviously it would greatly simplify matters both for those involved in the design of accounting systems and for accountants responsible for the preparation and reconciliation of reinsurance accounts if a standardized account form could be produced. Reinsurers' and ceding companies' accounting systems could then be designed to produce all of the data in the form required, and a standard format would assist in the preparation and checking of accounts. Over the years several attempts have been made to introduce such account forms to the reinsurance market.

In 1964 the leading British reinsurance company took the initiative in preparing standardized reinsurance account forms which were designed primarily to act as the documentary accounting evidence to flow between ceding company and reinsurer, and also to act as the source document for the reinsurers' data processing department. This initiative met with a very good response from a large number of ceding companies. In 1967 the British Insurance Association formed a subcommittee to attempt to put the matter on a more formal basis. Three years later specimen forms were circulated to all British Insurance Association members but unfortunately this initiative met with little response.

The BIA subcommittee was disbanded in 1973 but quite recently some German ceding companies and reinsurers have taken the initiative yet again through the CEA (Comité Européen des Assurances). In May 1977 a formal subcommittee of the Productivity Working Group was set up and it is anticipated that this subject will now gain much more formal recognition not only in the United Kingdom but throughout Europe.

Settlement of accounts

Facultative accounts. Various sections of the London market have organized central accounting systems for the settlement of balances between insurers, and between insurers and brokers, including settlements for facultative reinsurances. Besides the systems operated by Lloyd's and the Institute of London Underwriters to deal with transactions between their members and brokers, a new Policy Signing and Accounting Centre was set up in 1976 to handle other non-marine business written in London (see Chapter 2). A feature of all these systems is that settlement is not delayed if any item is in dispute but any adjustment is carried forward to the next account.

Treaty accounts. The timing of settlements is a matter for agreement between the parties.

Non-proportional treaties present few problems. As shown in the specimen clause quoted on pages 527/528, normally the only items to be dealt with are the payment of an initial premium at the beginning of the treaty year and, if the premium is adjustable, the adjustment premiums due after the end of the treaty year. Settlement of the latter depends upon the preparation by the ceding company of its premium income and any other data on which the adjustments are to be made. Claims payments do not normally enter into the settlement of accounts in that they are payable on a cash basis.

The settlement of balances for *proportional reinsurance* treaties may be handled in two ways. Either settlement may be delayed until, say, 15 days after confirmation of the account by the reinsurer; or it may be agreed that if there is a balance due to the reinsurer it is to be remitted by the ceding company together with the account, whereas if the balance falls the other way it is to be paid by the reinsurer when confirming the account. The latter procedure is laid down in the following specimen accounts clause.

> The accounts between the Reinsured and the Reinsurer in respect of the business under this agreement shall be closed quarterly and rendered by the Reinsured as soon as possible thereafter but in any event not later than two months after the end of each quarter.

529

Accounts shall be confirmed by the Reinsurer within one month of receipt but inadvertent errors or omissions in the quarterly accounts shall not delay the payment of any balance due hereunder unless such errors or omissions have a major effect on the remittable balance. Any necessary correction shall be made in the next quarterly account rendered hereunder (except in those cases where the error or omission has a major effect on the remittable balance necessitating an immediate adjustment). Balances due to the Reinsured shall be paid at the time of confirmation and balances due to the Reinsurer shall be paid by the Reinsured at the same time as the accounts are rendered.

Amounts outstanding. In an era of high interest rates the opportunity cost to a creditor of outstanding balances can be substantial. For example, on an annual net cash inflow (i.e. premiums due less commissions and claims) of, say, £12 million spread evenly over the year, with interest rates at 10%, an extra one month's delay by ceding companies in settling their accounts would cost a reinsurer £100,000 in lost investment income; equally when a balance falls the other way a ceding company will lose from a late settlement. Therefore, there is a good case for including in all types of treaties a penalty clause such as the following, which makes either party liable to pay interest on any amount not settled within a specified time.

Any amounts due by either party under this agreement which are outstanding one month after the date on which settlement is due shall be subject to the payment of interest by the debtor as from the expiry of that one month's period of grace. Interest shall be calculated at the rate stated in the schedule and remain payable up to the day of the debtor effecting settlement unless the creditor shall amend or extend the one-month period of grace.

It is difficult in practice, however, to obtain agreement to such a provision, even if it is understood that it would be invoked only for serious delays in payment, and even then only if the delay was due to the offending party's own fault rather than the operation of exchange control regulations. Often any thought a reinsurer may have of including a penalty clause has to be abandoned in the face of competition for the ceding company's business.

Foreign currencies

Where a treaty covers overseas risks it should be made clear in the treaty (1) in which currencies accounts are to be rendered, including rates of exchange to be used, and (2) when the account itself is rendered in several currencies but settlement is to be in only one or two main currencies, the rate(s) of exchange at which the balances are to be converted.

Reference was made in Chapter 3 to the fact that the abandonment of fixed exchange rates in the late 1960s has considerably exacerbated the problems reinsurers experience in their international operations. Generally it is the reinsurer who tends to bear the foreign exchange risk in that now the normal practice is for accounts to be rendered in the currency of the ceding company, though settlement may be made in another currency at the rates of exchange applying at that date. Thus where the ceding company is operating in only one currency, any gains or losses arising from changes in its external value will fall entirely upon the reinsurer.

When a ceding company is writing business in several currencies, it is insufficient simply to specify that settlements under the treaty shall be made in the currency of the ceding company and leave the company free to choose the date at which to convert. To do so would leave the reinsurer's results even more at the mercy of the foreign exchange markets while offering the ceding company the possibility of windfall gains, as the following example illustrates.

Assume:

(1) A French company has effected a 50% quota share reinsurance on the London market for a block of direct insurance business it has written in the Ivory Coast.

(2) The rate of exchange at the inception of the treaty was 50 CFA francs = 1 French franc.

(3) The ceding company pays a claim for 1 million CFA francs at a cost of 20,000 French francs.

(4) The reinsurance accounts are to be rendered and settled in French francs.

The cost of the loss to the ceding company and the reinsurer respectively would be as shown in Table 14.2 if between the date of paying the original claim and the settlement with the reinsurer the exchange rate of the CFA franc varied as shown.

Table 14.2

| | Settlement with reinsurer | | |
	Total loss converted at date of treaty settlement F. Fr	50% of loss charged to reinsurer F. Fr	Balance of 20,000 Fr loss payment borne by ceding company F. Fr
The CFA franc:			
(1) Remains unchanged in value	20,000	10,000	10,000
(2) Appreciates 10% against the French franc	22,000	11,000	9,000
(3) Depreciates 10% against the French franc	18,182	9,091	10,909

In situation (3), the ceding company would avoid incurring an additional loss by converting at the rate of exchange prevailing when it paid the original claim.

There is no uniformity of practice regarding conversion rates. However, where the ceding company itself converts foreign premiums into its own currency, and so has to purchase foreign currency to meet claims, the treaty will usually stipulate that in its settlements with the reinsurer the ceding company shall convert premiums and claims at the same rates of exchange as applied to its own remittances. Alternatively the treaty may provide that reinsurance transactions relating to overseas business shall be settled at the rates of exchange prevailing on the last day of the month or quarter on which the ceding company prepares its accounts with its foreign branches or agencies, or the average rate of exchange for the month or the quarter.

Increasingly because of local supervisory regulations and in order to minimize foreign exchange risks, most insurance companies operating internationally keep assets in the currencies of origin so that only margins between assets and liabilities are exposed to the effects of currency fluctuations. It is then important for the treaty to lay down the rules for determining the rates of exchange to be employed. It may be added that when a treaty covering risks written in several currencies specifies that settlements shall be made in the currency of the ceding company, the latter has an element of choice which does not flow through to the reinsurer. The reinsured can decide on the currencies in which it will hold its assets, whereas the reinsurer receives payment in only one. Even if the reinsurer is permitted by exchange control regulations to convert premiums back into original currencies, he will incur the costs of doing so.

Few, if any, reinsurers are willing to accept unnecessary exchange risks in connection with North American business in view of the volume of American and Canadian risks reinsured through the international reinsurance markets and the leading role of the US dollar in the world economy. Therefore it is normal practice to require reinsurance accounts for such business to be prepared and settled in original currencies, even if the ceding company itself is not American.

An alternative to the system of settlements being made in the ceding company's own currency is for separate accounts to be kept for and settlements to be made in every currency involved. This system of multiple-currency accounts has been particularly popular with ceding companies on the Continent of Europe and, because of the slide in the external value of the pound sterling, over the last five years it has become more popular with UK reinsurers. It has advantages for both parties. The ceding company knows that its results will be independent of any fluctuations in foreign exchange rates, and the reinsurer can decide how to deal with that risk. He can either accept the risk involved in converting balances into his own currency, or he can minimize it by holding funds either in original or strong currencies, in so far as such practice is permitted by his own government's exchange control regulations. The major disadvantage of multiple-currency accounts is the administrative cost of keeping separate records of all of the items involved, preparing separate accounts and settling balances in the original currencies.

Premium and loss deposit reserves

Reference was made in Chapters 7 and 8 to the disadvantages a reinsurer incurs by agreeing to the ceding company retaining premium and loss reserve deposits. One effect is the adverse impact of such deposits on the reinsurer's cash flow if the deposit takes the form of cash withheld by the reinsured from premiums payable under a treaty. For the ceding company the retention of reserves provides additional financial benefits by easing the strain caused by any delays in the payment of premiums by policyholders and brokers—for the reinsurer there is a corresponding loss. However, the cash-flow effect should not be exaggerated. When during the first year a proportion of the premiums is being retained each quarter to build up a full year's reserves, obviously the reinsurer will suffer a substantial reduction in his cash inflow. Thereafter additional premiums will be retained only to cover (1) the premium reserve or loss reserve attributable to any increase in the volume of reinsurances ceded, or (2) an increase in the loss reserve due to a deterioration in experience. Thus after the first year the reinsurer should incur no further substantial loss of premium inflow, unless the total reinsurance premiums continue to expand from year to year.

The other major disadvantage for a reinsurer of cash deposits held by a ceding company is the loss of investment income which will be incurred in full each year the treaty remains in force. As noted in Chapter 7 two possible solutions are:

(1) for the ceding company to pay interest on deposits; or
(2) for the ceding company to accept the deposit of securities which will remain the property of the reinsurer who will thus be entitled to interest and dividends receivable thereon, and any capital profits (or losses) on the investments.

The second alternative has more to commend it to a reinsurer in that he retains a greater degree of control over his funds and can be sure of being able to obtain both the same yield and the same investment flexibility as is available to his ceding company and competitors. Moreover if the ceding company goes into liquidation, the reinsurer will be in a better position if he has deposited securities rather than cash.

On the other hand there are problems associated with the deposit of securities with ceding companies. Only certain types of investment—e.g. government securities—may be acceptable to the ceding company's supervisory authority. Also in some countries the deposited securities are treated as the property of the ceding company. If that concept (known as *pleine propriété*) is rigidly applied then it removes all of the advantages for the reinsurer of depositing securities. He is deprived of the commercial rate of interest earned on the securities, and for solvency purposes he can only show the face value of the deposit in his balance sheet, so that he loses the benefit of any capital appreciation but remains liable to augment the deposit if the market value of the securities should fall.

Regardless of any special problems, in every case the deposit of securities adds to administrative costs. Careful records have to be kept of where securities are deposited and of their market values relative to the changing size of the premium reserves to be covered.

Letters of credit offer a third alternative means of providing security for premium and loss reserves. They are in common use in North America and have gained limited acceptance in some other developed countries (e.g. the UK, the Netherlands and Italy), particularly for loss reserves. Instead of depositing cash or securities, the reinsurer arranges for a bank to issue to the ceding company a clean irrevocable sight letter of credit giving the ceding company the right to require payment up to a specified sum upon demand at any time prior to a stated expiry date. Normally the letter of credit is arranged with a bank established in the country of the ceding company, possibly to satisfy its supervisory authority. Thus provided the bank is of first-class standing the ceding company obtains the same guaranteed access to funds in the event of the failure of the reinsurer to honour his obligations as would be provided by a deposit.

The issuing of letters of credit possesses several advantages for the reinsurer. Once the terms and documentation for the first facility have been agreed with a bank, it is a relatively simple matter to extend it to the provision of similar drawing rights for other ceding companies. Moreover negotiations regarding terms are conducted with the banker instead of with the client ceding company. Provided the face value is set sufficiently high, normally the administration of a letter of credit need involve no more than an annual review of the amount of the reserve and, if necessary, an adjustment of the face value at the same time as the letter of credit is extended to a new date.

Letters of credit are also relatively cheap to operate, the banker normally charging an annual commitment fee expressed as a percentage of the face value. The reinsurer may provide the collateral security required by the banker either:

(1) by depositing an equivalent amount of cash (usually in the same currency) on a special deposit account on which the bank will pay a negotiated short-term rate of interest related to current market rates; or

(2) by depositing securities of equivalent value (or preferably a somewhat higher value to avoid the need for topping up if the market values of securities fall); or

(3) by a combination of (1) and (2).

Method (1) suffers the disadvantage that it involves the tying up of substantial sums in short-term deposits which offer no prospect of capital appreciation, and if any drawing is made on the letter of credit, interest will cease to be payable on the amount of the drawing. On the other hand, whereas interest receivable on deposits or securities may be subject to withholding taxes, generally such taxes are not levied on bank interest.

The taxation aspects of deposits also need to be considered in the case of overseas treaties. If funds are deposited overseas, whether as a cash deposit, or as a deposit of foreign securities, or as a collateral deposit made overseas as security for a letter of credit, the reinsurer's ability to offset overseas tax withheld on interest and dividends against his own domestic tax liability will depend upon the provisions in force relating to double taxation relief. Even if overseas tax is recoverable, the reinsurer will incur the expense of obtaining tax certificates.

Fortunately, the incidence of foreign withholding tax is nowadays generally mitigated by a world-wide network of double taxation agreements. Under the terms of the OECD (Organisation for Economic Co-operation and Development) Model Convention, withholding tax on interest is limited to 10%, and in the case of agreements made between developed countries, the tax rate is often reduced to zero.

The additional cost of deposits. Whatever form deposits take—cash, securities or letters of credit—they impose one further additional cost. By depriving the reinsurer of the freedom to locate his assets and distribute them between liquid and selected long-term securities solely in accordance with the needs of his business, deposits undermine in large measure the benefits to be obtained from the pooling of risks. The reinsurer will need to increase his free reserves in order to provide the same degree of security for ceding companies, and the cost of servicing that extra capital will increase the price of reinsurance.

Exchange control regulations

The results of an overseas treaty as revealed by the accounts may be of only academic interest if the reinsurer is unable to obtain possession of any balances due to him. All too often exchange control regulations place reinsurers in that position.

This subject is discussed in Chapter 15, so it is sufficient to note here that:
(1) Exchange control regulations may prohibit or impede the remittance of (*a*) premiums and loss payments, and (*b*) balances on accounts, the latter sometimes being treated as capital movements.
(2) Even if not officially prohibited, sometimes inordinately long delays may be suffered before remittances are authorized by a central bank.
(3) Exchange control regulations dealing with the investment of funds either in a country of origin, or in foreign currencies in a reinsurer's own country, may expose a reinsurer to a severe foreign exchange risk. Thus a foreign reinsurer may be placed at a considerable competitive disadvantage compared with domestic reinsurers.

Claims reporting and analysis

The accounts rendered between ceding companies and their reinsurers provide only a part of the information reinsurers require for the preparation of their financial accounts, and for checking the loss experience of treaties. Often two or more years may elapse between the occurrence of a loss and the appearance of any payment in the reinsurance accounts. Prior to the date of settlement the only information the reinsurer is likely to obtain about his potential liabilities is from the details of large claims and outstanding losses supplied by ceding companies in accordance with the claims-reporting provisions of treaties.

It is important that, for whatever purpose they are used, every effort should be made to ensure the accuracy of estimates of outstanding claims. There is no standard system of reporting loss data, and ceding companies vary considerably in the method and accuracy of the claims estimating procedures employed, so that any data supplied need careful analysis. Any underestimation of the provisions for outstanding claims included in a reinsurer's financial accounts will cause losses to be rolled forward into later years, whereas overestimating reduces profit in the year in question. Likewise, when calculating burning costs, underestimating of claims results in the deferral, and possibly the avoidance, of the full premium charge to the ceding company, as required by the terms of the treaty.

The importance of obtaining accurate estimates of outstanding claims can be gauged from Table 14.3 which is based on an analysis of a large UK direct insurance company's returns to the Department of Trade.

Table 14.3 An analysis of claims settlements (by amount) for claims occurring during 1970

	Percentage of total settlements during year	
Year of settlement	*Fire business* %	*Employers' liability business* %
1970	47.5	5.4
1971	43.2	22.6
1972	5.0	26.2
1973	2.0	14.8
1974	0.7	17.0
1975	0.6	6.9
1976	0.8	2.3
Outstanding at end 1976	0.2	4.8

Although at the end of 1970 less than half of the final cost of the fire claims incurred in that year had been settled, on the strength of loss adjusters' reports, etc., the company was able to produce a good estimate of the final settlement costs. Employers' liability business presents an entirely different picture; even by the end of the third year the company had paid little more than half of its final claims costs, and four years later still had claims outstanding, which it estimated would add an extra 5% to its total settlements cost.

Table 14.4 The flow of reinsurance premiums and claims for a typical underwriting year

Development year	Fire excess of loss Claims %	NPI* %	Accident excess of loss Claims %	NPI* %	Marine Claims %	NPI* %	Aviation Claims %	NPI* %
1	29	66	5	50	6	28	6	19
2	62	34	7	37	37	60	31	63
3	9		13	7	29	11	15	18
4			16	2	13	1	18	
5			16	2	6		6	
6			12	2	2		11	
7			10		3		6	
8			8		1		3	
9			5		2		2	
10			3		1		1	
11			2					
12			1					
13			2					
Total	100	100	100	100	100	100	100	100

*NPI = net premium income.

Source: F.E. Guaschi, 'Charting the financial course of a reinsurance company', in *Papers presented to the Third International Reinsurance Seminar* (Reinsurance Offices' Association, 1977).

Table 14.5 Incidence of notification and settlement of motor excess of loss reinsurance claims occurring in year N

Year	Percentage notified: In year	By end of year	Percentage (by numbers) settled: In year	By end of year
N	23.6	23.6	3.5	3.5
$N+1$	32.0	55.6	10.4	13.9
$N+2$	13.7	69.3	16.6	30.5
$N+3$	9.7	79.0	14.5	45.0
$N+4$	6.8	85.8	12.2	57.2
$N+5$	4.3	90.1	9.9	67.1
$N+6$	3.0	93.1	7.7	74.8
$N+7$	2.2	95.3	6.1	80.9
$N+8$	1.6	96.9	4.8	85.7
$N+9$	1.1	98.0	3.7	89.4
$N+10$ and later	2.0	100.0	10.6	100.0

The average settlement delays for reinsured claims are likely to be even longer than for the total claims on an original portfolio. Generally, and certainly in the case of excess of loss reinsurances, reinsurers are involved in only the larger claims which tend to take longer to settle than small claims. F. Guaschi has produced figures which confirm that is so in practice.[1] Table 14.4 is based on his company's experience which is likely to be much the same as that of any other professional reinsurer, and Table 14.5 records his analysis of motor excess of loss claims.

Two facts stand out from Tables 14.4 and 14.5:

(1) The importance of accurate estimating of outstanding claims varies between different classes of insurance, and a broad distinction may be drawn between short- (e.g. property) and long-tail (e.g. liability) classes. So, for example, according to Table 14.4 a 10% error in estimating outstanding claims at the end of year 2 would have resulted in the following degrees of error in the total figures for claims paid and outstanding:

Property account	0.9%	i.e. 10% of outstanding claims
Accident account	8.8%	
Marine account	5.7%	
Aviation account	6.1%	

(2) Although some delay inevitably occurs between the occurrence of events giving rise to claims and when they are reported to reinsurers, for some classes of business incurred but not reported (IBNR) claims are of major importance. Table 14.5 shows that some 3½ years after their occurrence, over 20% of the potential claims had not been reported to the motor excess of loss reinsurer.

Recognition of IBNR and claims settlement delays has led reinsurers—and accident reinsurers in particular—to turn to the use of so-called claims development statistics. Essentially ceding companies are required to supply statements of claims analysed according to year of origin, showing the amounts paid and outstanding at the end of each year for the last N years. The statements take the form shown in Table 14.6.

The London Institute Advanced Study Group suggested that such statistics should be obtained for the past five underwriting years,[2] but as Table 14.5 shows, five years' figures would be wholly inadequate for motor and other liability reinsurances.

The idea lying behind development statistics is that they can be used to estimate the value of IBNR and outstanding claims, whether required for the purpose of calculating premiums or for the preparation of accounts.

1 Table 13.3 *Accident Excess of Loss Reinsurance*, Mercantile and General Reinsurance Co. November 1972.
2 *Excess of Loss Methods of Reinsurance*, p.50.

Table 14.6

Underwriting year	N £	N+1 £	N+2 £	N+3 £	N+4 £	→	Final settlement year
t−4 Paid (to date)	—	2,000	6,000	12,000	14,000		
Outstanding	15,000	14,000	11,500	5,000	3,300		
Total	15,000	16,000	17,500	17,000	17,300		
t−3 Paid	—	2,500	6,600	11,500			
Outstanding	18,000	16,000	12,100	7,000			
Total	18,000	18,500	18,700	18,500			
t−2 Paid	1,000	5,000	9,000				
Outstanding	12,000	9,000	4,750				
Total	13,000	14,000	13,750				
t−1 Paid	—	6,000					
Outstanding	25,000	22,000					
Total	25,000	28,000					
t Paid	—						
Outstanding	21,500						
Total	21,500						

For example, if a ceding company's claims settlement statistics consistently showed the pattern of the accident claims in Table 14.4 then at the end of any year one could gross up the claims settled to date to obtain an estimate of the value of IBNR and outstanding claims. Thus, if at the end of a third year claims settlements were £8,000 the outstanding claims would be:

$$£ \left(8,000 \times \frac{100}{25}\right) - £8,000 = £24,000$$

In practice a reinsurer is far more likely to be presented with the sort of figures shown in Table 14.6 which provide no clear pattern on which to project claims costs. Possibly the upward trend in claims costs is due to an increase in exposures as measured by premiums, but there are dangers in expressing claims development statistics as ratios of claims to premiums paid. Such ratios are highly sensitive to variations in the force of market competition and premium rating levels, changes in retention levels, etc. Therefore in order to eliminate such influences, 'It is preferable to tabulate the relative progression of claims settled from one year of development to the next.'[3] The figures in Table 14.6 would then appear as in Table 14.7. Although the figures display less instability than

---

3 C.S.S. Lyon, 'The establishment of adequate reserves for outstanding and IBNR claims', in *Papers Presented to the Third International Reinsurance Seminar*.

Table 14.7 Amount of claims paid to end of Nth year of development as a percentage of claims paid to end of 2nd year of development

Underwriting year	N %	$N+1$ %	$N+2$ %	$N+3$ %	$N+4$ %
$t-4$	0	100	300	600	700
$t-3$	0	100	264	460	
$t-2$	20	100	180		
$t-1$	0	100			

the raw data of Table 14.6, they still hardly provide a firm base for any claims projection model. Possibly investigation may reveal that there has been some speeding up of claims settlements. It is noteworthy that at the end of the second and third years the percentage of claims paid to total claims paid and outstanding had risen as follows:

	$N+1$	$N+2$
$t-4$	12.5%	34.3%
$t-3$	13.5%	35.3%
$t-2$	35.7%	65.5%
$t-1$	21.4%	—

Such changes may be due to various factors, such as a change in the portfolio mix, or in legal or economic conditions which have induced the ceding company to attempt to settle claims faster. The reinsurer should be able to discover such facts and allow for them accordingly.

Other factors to be considered are the effects of inflation and exchange rate movements on claims development figures. If an account consists of business written in several countries, then the claims costs will be exposed to differential movements in exchange rates and inflation rates. Inflation presents an additional problem: if an excess of loss treaty does not contain a stability clause, over a period of years the cost of the excess claims falling within the treaty limits will have increased faster than the original claims. Consequently great care will be necessary in analysing claims in order to adjust the development statistics to a common monetary base.

If an individual ceding company's own claims development statistics are too unstable to provide a base for projecting estimates of its final settlement figures, a reinsurer may be able to draw on the experience of other ceding companies. Care would be necessary to select companies operating in the same territory and with a similar portfolio mix.

Whether development statistics or some other model is used for projecting the cost of IBNR and outstanding claims, it is important that the results be monitored by recalculating the final claims estimates at the end of each development year. If the estimated final figure increases from year to year, then the model can be regarded as too weak; conversely the estimates will fall if the model is too strong.

Reinsurance company's financial accounts

Normally a reinsurance company will be involved in the preparation of three sets of financial accounts:

(1) The end-of-year published accounts for shareholders prepared in accordance with the requirements of company legislation, supplemented by the requirements of other bodies. All UK registered companies must comply with the provisions of the Companies Acts 1948 to 1976, and the London Stock Exchange requires additional information to be published by quoted public companies. Similar requirements apply to companies registered in other countries.

(2) Accounts and returns in specially prescribed forms as required by insurance supervisory authorities in countries where it has established branch offices or subsidiary companies.

(3) Internal management accounts.

Additionally the revenue authorities may take (1) or (2) as the basis for the calculation of tax, subject to such adjustments as are required by the tax rules.

Before looking at the systems of accounting employed by reinsurers, some of the theoretical problems will be considered. Whether the object is to prepare accounts for shareholders, the supervisory authority, the revenue authority or a company's own management, a reinsurer encounters intractable problems in trying to reveal the transactions for the reporting year in the accounting statements for that year. Consequently there is no universally recognized method of accounting, and perfection remains an unattainable ideal.

At the crux of the problem lie the delays in the receipt of income and the payment of claims relating to any one underwriting year. Table 14.4 above gives some insight into the extent of the problems involved. The form of non-life insurance accounting employed in Britain evolved at a time when most of the business written by insurers consisted of fire insurance. Policies were issued for periods of 12 months renewable at quarter days, outstanding claims were amenable to reasonable estimation, and premium incomes grew only relatively slowly. The accounting forms which then evolved provided a reasonable, even if not 100% accurate, picture of each year's trading results. They are far less satisfactory for other classes of non-life insurance and reinsurance, as the following examples will demonstrate.

Example 1: proportional reinsurance. A reinsurer commences writing proportional property reinsurance treaty business. If it were possible to break down the accounting data rendered by ceding companies into separate underwriting years (and in practice it never is), the results of the business written over the first five years might appear as in Table 14.8.

Table 14.8 Underwriting year

| | Underwriting year | | | | | |
	1 £000's	2 £000's	3 £000's	4 £000's	5 £000's	Total £000's
Premiums	100.0	120.0	140.0	160.0	180.0	700.0
Losses	58.0	69.6	81.2	92.8	104.4	406.0
Commission and expenses	40.0	48.0	56.0	64.0	72.0	280.0
Profit	2.0	2.4	2.8	3.2	3.6	14.0
	100.0	120.0	140.0	160.0	180.0	700.0

Its ceding companies account for premiums and losses quarterly. Thus the percentage of the various items accounted for in each financial year in respect of treaties commencing or renewed in year t are as follows:

Year	Premiums %	Losses %	Commissions and expenses %
t	58	26	66
$t+1$	42	64	34
$t+2$	—	10	—

The reinsurer calculates his unearned premium reserve as 40% of premiums accounted for each year.

Early notification is required of large losses. It is assumed that, in respect of each underwriting year, at the end of the year provision is made for outstanding claims equal to one-third of the total claims for that year, and at the end of the second development year the provision is just equal to the claims paid in the third development year.

If it is assumed that no new business is written after the fifth year, the company's revenue account prepared in accordance with UK accounting practice would be as shown in Table 14.9.

Table 14.9 Property Proportional Revenue Account

	At end of year:							Total
	1 *£000's*	*2* *£000's*	*3* *£000's*	*4* *£000's*	*5* *£000's*	*6* *£000's*	*7* *£000's*	*£000's*
Premium income	58.0	111.6	131.6	151.6	171.6	75.6	—	700.0
plus unearned premium reserve at beginning of year	—	23.2	44.6	52.6	60.6	68.6	30.2	279.8
less unearned premium reserve at end of year	23.2	44.6	52.6	60.6	68.6	30.2	—	279.8
Earned premiums	34.8	90.2	123.6	143.6	163.6	114.0	30.2	700.0
Less:								
Claims paid and outstanding	34.4	64.9	76.5	88.0	99.7	42.5	—	406.0
Commission and expenses	26.4	45.3	53.3	61.2	69.3	24.5	—	280.0
Underwriting profit/loss (−)	− 26.0	− 20.0	− 6.2	− 5.6	− 5.4	47.0	30.2	14.0

Note: The item 'claims paid and outstanding' consists of claims paid *plus* the change in the provisions for claims outstanding. The underlying figures for each year are:

	Year						
	1	*2*	*3*	*4*	*5*	*6*	*7*
Claims outstanding	19.3	29.0	34.1	39.0	44.1	10.5	—
Change in claims outstanding	19.3	9.7	5.1	4.9	5.1	− 33.6	− 10.5
Claims paid	15.1	55.2	71.4	83.1	94.6	76.1	10.5
∴ 'claims paid and outstanding'	34.4	64.9	76.5	88.0	99.7	42.5	—

Example 2: non-proportional reinsurance. For a period of five years commencing in year 1 a reinsurer writes non-proportional accident reinsurance business with the results shown in Table 14.10.

The treaty years coincide with the reinsurer's financial year so that no provision need be made for unearned premiums. Deposit premiums are paid at inception and adjustment premiums are paid in subsequent years. All losses are settled within five years. The time distributions of the various items relating to treaties written or renewed at the beginning of year *t* are as shown in Table 14.11.

Table 14.10 Underwriting year

	Underwriting year					
	1 £000's	2 £000's	3 £000's	4 £000's	5 £000's	Total £000's
Premiums	100.0	120.0	140.0	170.0	200.0	730.0
Expected losses	92.0	110.4	128.8	156.4	184.0	671.6
Commission and expenses	6.0	7.2	8.4	10.2	12.0	43.8
Expected profit	2.0	2.4	2.8	3.4	4.0	14.6
Actual losses	101.2	121.4	128.8	153.3	178.5	683.2
Actual profit/loss ($-$)	-7.2	-8.6	8.4	6.5	9.5	3.0

Table 14.11

Year	Premiums %	Loss settlements %	Commissions and expenses %
t	75	10	83.3
$t+1$	14	23	8.4
$t+2$	5	30	8.3
$t+3$	4	28	—
$t+4$	2	9	—

In four of the five years actual losses differ from the expected losses, their development being as follows:

Underwriting year

1   Expected losses were underestimated by 10%, half of the error being recognized in year $t+1$ and half in year $t+3$.

2   Expected losses were underestimated by 5%, the error being recognized in year $t+2$.

3   Estimates proved correct.

4   At the end of year t outstanding claims were 8% overestimated. Actual losses were finally settled for 2% less than the expected total losses.

5   Actual losses were finally settled for 3% less than expected.

Preparation of the company's Revenue Account according to normal UK accounting practice would have produced the results shown in Table 14.12.

Table 14.12 Accident Non-Proportional Revenue Account

	1 £000's	2 £000's	3 £000's	4 £000's	At end of year: 5 £000's	6 £000's	7 £000's	8 £000's	9 £000's	Total
Premium income	75.0	104.0	126.8	157.1	187.6	44.5	19.6	11.4	4.0	730.0
Claims paid and outstanding	90.2	116.8	128.8	179.9	184.0	0	0	−11.0	−5.5	683.2
Commission and expenses	5.0	6.5	8.1	9.8	11.6	1.8	1.0	—	—	43.8
Underwriting profit/loss (−)	−20.2	−19.3	−10.1	−32.6	−8.0	42.7	18.6	22.4	9.5	3.0
Claims outstanding	80.1	161.5	219.1	289.4	338.4	204.4	96.3	21.5	—	
Change in claims outstanding	80.1	81.4	57.6	70.3	49.0	−134.0	−108.1	−74.8	−21.5	
Claims paid	10.1	35.4	71.2	109.6	135.0	134.0	108.1	63.8	16.0	
Claims paid and outstanding	90.2	116.8	128.8	179.9	184.0	0	0	−11.0	−5.5	

The two examples show how the underwriting results for each financial year as revealed by the accounts bear little relationship to the actual profitability or otherwise of the treaties written or renewed during those years. More specifically, on the proportional account:

(1) Delays by ceding companies in accounting for revenue result in the premium income figures shown each year being less than the premiums attributable to the corresponding underwriting year, so delaying the emergence of profit. (In practice the position is often even more confused. The reinsurer in many cases receives none of the data analysed into underwriting years.)

(2) The early notification of large losses, sometimes before the premiums for the relevant cessions have been accounted for, causes a further rolling forward of profits. Even after the third year the continuing growth of the business in years 4 and 5 results in losses being shown.

(3) The item 'claims paid and outstanding' is a prime example of the mixing of items relating to different underwriting years. Any under- or over-estimating of outstanding claims would have produced further distortions: for example, the additional loss due to a claim being settled for an amount in excess of the provision would fall in the year of settlement instead of in the year of occurrence.

And on the non-proportional account:

(1) All of the above points equally apply, but with even more force. In the example all claims are run off within five years, but under liability excess of loss treaties 20 years or more may elapse before the final cost of the losses occurring during a particular underwriting year are known. Differences between settlements and outstanding claims provisions, or revisions of such provisions, can substantially affect the results shown in the financial accounts throughout the whole run-off period.

(2) Delays in accounting for premiums are less of a problem than for proportional reinsurances, though adjustment premiums may still extend over several years.

Therefore, particularly in view of the lack of underwriting year data for proportional treaties, there is a strong case for employing different forms of accounting for proportional and non-proportional reinsurances.

Theoretically for proportional business there is much to commend the Lloyd's system of accounting whereby accounts are maintained on an underwriting year basis with each year's account being kept open for three years. Handled in that way the account for underwriting year 1 of Table 14.8 would appear as in Table 14.13.

Table 14.13 Revenue Account for year 1

Premiums:	£000's		Claims paid:		£000's
Year 1	58		Year 1	15.1	
2	42		2	37.1	
3	—	100	3	5.8	58
			Commissions and expenses:		
			Year 1	26.4	
			2	13.6	
			3	—	40
			Balance		2
		100			100

If the claims run-off period is longer than three years some system is needed to deal with claims still outstanding when the account is closed. The Lloyd's system is to reinsure outstanding liabilities at the end of the third year and charge the premium as part of the claims debited in the third year.

However, in practice any attempt to use the Lloyd's system would still be bedevilled by the lack of underwriting year data.

Practical financial accounting

Given the practical obstacles to compiling annual accounts along theoretically sound lines, compromise methods are employed for the preparation of reinsurance company financial accounts. In the case of companies operating internationally there are the additional complications arising from the varying legal and quasi-legal accounting requirements applying in different countries relating to the form of accounts, what information either must or need not be disclosed, and rules regarding such matters as the valuation of assets and liabilities, as applicable to their published accounts, tax accounts and supervisory returns. Also because the accounting practices which have evolved in one country are rarely applicable to others, reinsurers operating internationally need to record information in various ways in order to prepare different sets of accounts and returns conforming to the requirements of perhaps several supervisory authorities. For example, American companies find it difficult to fit overseas business into the annual statements laid down by the National Association of Insurance Commissioners (NAIC), and classifications of insurance business for accounting purposes differ considerably throughout the world.

Reinsurance companies operating in Britain are subject to the same accounting regulations as direct insurers in regard to the annual published accounts under the terms of the Companies Acts 1948 to 1976, and the supervisory returns to the Department of Trade under the Insurance Companies Act 1974 and the associated regulations. Since 1968 the supervisory requirements have developed in three directions:

(1) Companies have been required to provide far more information in the accounts and returns regarding their non-life business, though in many respects the details required still fall short of those required in North America.

(2) In granting authorization to either new companies or companies that wish to transact extra classes of insurance business, the Department can ask for more information at quarterly intervals in order to check progress.

(3) As progress is made within the EEC towards the establishment of a common market in insurance, so Britain's accounting regulations will be brought into line with agreed European standards, though substantial progress in that direction is unlikely for several years.

Here it is proposed to discuss only the accounting practices which are widely adopted in relation to published accounts.

Proportional reinsurances. Most specialist reinsurance companies now keep each year's account on a 'treaty year' basis, in the sense that the treaty year is the 12-month period covered by the contract with the ceding company that commenced in the accounting year under review. Each account is kept open for two years, or possibly longer. The figures for the first year are treated on a funded basis, and a balance is struck at the end of the second (or possibly the third) year after allowing for (1) outstanding claims and (2) the unearned premiums which may be calculated in accordance with the terms in the underlying treaties relating to unearned premium reserves. The accounts for the first two treaty years of Table 14.8 as prepared on that basis are shown in Table 14.14.

Table 14.14 Revenue Account for treaty year 1

	Year 1 (open) £000's	Year 2 (closed) £000's		Year 1 (open) £000's	Year 2 (closed) £000's
Unearned premium reserve brought forward	—	—	Losses paid	15.1	37.1
Reserve for outstanding claims brought forward	—	—	Commission and expenses	26.4	13.6
Funds brought forward	—	16.5	Unearned premium reserve	—	40.0
Premiums	58.0	42.0	Reserve for outstanding claims	—	5.8
			Funds carried forward	16.5	—
			Balance		−38.0
	58.0	58.5		58.0	58.5

Revenue Account for treaty year 2

	Year 1 (open) £000's	Year 2 (closed) £000's		Year 1 (open) £000's	Year 2 (closed) £000's
Unearned premium reserve brought forward	40.0	—	Losses paid	23.9	44.5
Reserve for outstanding claims brought forward	5.8	—	Commission and expenses	31.7	16.3
Funds brought forward	—	59.8	Unearned premium reserve	—	48.0
Premiums	69.6	50.4	Reserve for outstanding claims	—	7.0
			Funds carried forward	59.8	—
			Balance	—	−5.6
	115.4	110.2		115.4	110.2

Non-proportional reinsurances. Given the long claims reporting and settlement delays associated with some types of non-proportional reinsurances, the two forms of accounts in Tables 14.13 and 14.14 offer little improvement on the conventional one-year account when the final cost of the claims occurring in one year may not be known until 10, 15, 20 or even more years later. The solution some reinsurers have adopted is to treat the business for accounting purposes in the same way as life insurance; that is, to deal with it on a funded basis. The difference between the premiums received and the claims, commissions and expenses paid in any year is credited to (or debited against) a fund established to cover liabilities to ceding companies. Each year the fund must be valued in the light of the potential claims payable therefrom, any surplus then being transferred to the profit and loss account, while any deficit must be made good from reserves.

The funding method does mean that the surplus or deficit revealed on valuation each year will result from the development of claims arising over perhaps the past 20 years. External analysts will be unable to tie down performance to the results of individual underwriting years, and the company's own management will be able to do so only if development accounts are kept for individual underwriting years—which some reinsurers certainly do. [4]

Investment income

So far the treatment of investment income has been ignored, and no entries have been made in the specimen revenue accounts for that source of income. Although such treatment accords with the practice of most British insurance and reinsurance companies, the resulting revenue accounts present an incomplete picture of the performance of the business conducted by a reinsurance company.

The sources of a reinsurance company's investment income are (1) the funds held to cover liabilities to ceding companies (i.e. the reserves for unearned premiums and outstanding claims) which are generated by the business it accepts and so the premiums received; and (2) its capital and free reserves. Therefore there is a strong case for including the investment income attributable to (1) as part of the underwriting result, recognizing that in some instances it could be a negative figure. This point has long been a subject for argument, including the associated question of the treatment of realized and unrealized capital gains and losses, [5] so the general issue will not be pursued further here.

However, it must be emphasized that the way in which investment income is treated in a reinsurance company's financial accounts is a

---

4 F.E. Guaschi, 'Charting the financial course of a reinsurance company', *Papers Presented to the Third International Reinsurance Seminar*, (Reinsurance Offices' Association, 1977).

5 See, for example, *Prices, and Profits in the Property and Liability Insurance Industry* (Arthur D. Little Inc., ,967), and *Measurement of Profitability and Treatment of Investment Income in Property and Liability Insurance* (National Association of Insurance Commissioners, 1970).

question of considerable importance in relation to those classes of non-proportional reinsurance with very long claims settlement delays. Then investment income attributable to provisions for outstanding claims may be sufficient to convert a substantial underwriting loss into a respectable operating profit. And capital gains on technical reserves may add a further contribution to profit. The funding method of dealing with the financial accounts for non-proportional reinsurance business raises the issue in a specific way. Life companies value their liabilities taking account of future potential claim payments less the expected premiums attributable to the policies being valued and the expected investment income on the policy reserves. Arguably non-proportional reinsurance funds should be valued along similar lines, in which case it is essential that investment income should be brought into the revenue account. This question of discounting is now the subject of considerable discussion within reinsurance circles.

Taxation of reinsurance companies

Revenue authorities generally recognize that there are certain aspects of the business of insurers and reinsurers which require special treatment for the purpose of determining taxable profits.

Besides enacting special rules for determining profits, special arrangements may be made by the revenue authorities for handling insurers' and reinsurers' tax returns. In Britain the work is now centralized, being handled by six 'tax districts' in the City of London. Thus the six Inspectors in charge of the districts can acquire a specialist knowledge of the complexities of insurance business, and are known to meet occasionally to discuss points and problems of common interest. Matters of general policy are handled at the Head Office of the Inland Revenue by an insurance specialist who negotiates points of principle (e.g. the rules for the treatment of technical reserves and any changes in tax rules) on an industry-wide basis with the various trade associations, notably the British Insurance Association and the Life Offices' Association. Each Inspector is autonomous within his tax district and will strive to settle any problems that arise. However, he may consult the Revenue specialist at any time, and would feel obliged to refer matters of policy to the specialist.

Taxation and insurance supervision are quite separate matters in Britain and require the preparation of separate accounts drawn up in accordance with the respective regulations. Elsewhere the accounts prepared for the supervisory authority form the basis for determining tax liabilities (e.g. the United States), and in Canada the supervisory authority acts as agent for the revenue authority.

Generally revenue authorities distinguish between life (including annuity) business and other classes of insurance for the purpose of determining tax liabilities. Life business presents particular problems in two respects. Its long-term nature means that profits (or losses) emerge only over a very long period, and investment income and capital gains or losses on the realization of assets are both a large and a vital element in the performance and solvency of a life fund. Therefore, the Inland Revenue in Britain require life and annuity business to be kept separate from non-life business, and Parliament has enacted several special provisions in Finance and Taxes Acts and regulations dealing with the determination of tax liabilities for life business. Special rules apply in other countries too. A feature of those rules is the tax treatment of investment earnings including capital gains and losses. It is perhaps fortunate that relatively little life reassurance is conducted internationally, because if risks were reassured on original terms with foreign reassurers, differences in tax treatment could significantly alter the net-of-tax results of the reassurer compared with the ceding office.

Although most non-life contracts run only for one year, they still present certain special features, notably:

(1) Premiums received in one year may relate to periods of insurance overlapping previous or subsequent years.

(2) For some classes of insurance the final outcome of business written during a particular financial year may not be known with certainty until many years later. A notable example is liability excess of loss reinsurance where even after, say, five years a substantial proportion of the final settlements will still be outstanding, and where the fund for outstanding losses at the end of any year may exceed three times the net premiums written during the year. In Britain where corporation tax is normally payable within 9 months of the end of the accounting period, and assessed tax which is not paid at the due date attracts an additional interest charge, such long-tail business presents problems. It is impossible to get any clear idea of results by reference to the facts until two, three or even four years have elapsed, so that special concessions regarding the payment of interest have had to be negotiated with the Inland Revenue.

(3) Although investment earnings are not so large in relation to premium income as in life business, they still provide an important contribution to income.

The valuation of assets and liabilities is the key to the emergence of profits or losses on all classes of insurance business, and not infrequently the ideas of revenue authorities differ from those of supervisory authorities. Whereas the former are anxious to tax profits in the trading year to which they are attributable, the valuation rules of supervisory authorities concerned with maintaining margins of solvency not infrequently result in profits being rolled forward into later years.

It would be impossible to deal here with even the broad principles of insurance company taxation which differ from country to country and are subject to periodic change. A few general comments must suffice.

The first point to be made is that sometimes it may pay a company to split its business for accounting purposes and negotiate a tax treatment to follow the accounting treatment. An increasing number of British reinsurers are finding it advantageous to separate proportional from non-proportional reinsurance business for two reasons, as David Richards has explained: [6]

> First the proportional business is subject to considerable delay in receiving full information and great difficulty in estimating outstanding accounts at the end of one year. The Revenue account is therefore kept open for two years to enable a more accurate computation to be made.
>
> Secondly, excess of loss business is largely long-tail so that losses under reinsurance contracts do not develop for some years. As the contracts are usually on a losses occurring basis, there will be no need in most cases for any provision for unexpired risks, but the provision for outstanding claims including IBNR may easily amount to 300% of premium income.
>
> The non-proportional account is thus kept on a fund basis and a separate computation made for tax purposes.

Although over the long term the same taxable profit should emerge however accounts are presented, there is no benefit to be gained from paying tax before it is necessary to do so, unless possibly there is a firm expectation that tax rates may be increased substantially in future years.

A second point is the importance of maintaining adequate records to be able to substantiate claims for expenses and provisions. The basic proposition in UK tax law is that a liability is tax deductible in the year in which the liability arises, even though it may not be able to be quantified until a year later. In the same way a profit attaches to the year in which it was earned despite it being received some years later. The Taxes Acts then provide for releases of liabilities to be taxed in the year in which they are released and bad debts to be relieved in the year in which they are

6 D.E. Richards, 'General principles of insurance taxation', *Journal of the Insurance Institute of London*, vol. 65 (1977).

written off. Where a liability is not admitted (e.g. a compensation claim which goes to arbitration), the courts have decided that the deduction is due in the year in which the liability is established (i.e. when, in the above instance, the arbitrators decide that a liability exists) albeit that some years may pass before it is quantified.

It should be possible to determine *pro rata* provisions for unexpired risks with considerable accuracy now that computer programs are available, but the estimation of provisions for outstanding claims, and especially IBNR values, is far more open to dispute. Obviously a reinsurer is dependent upon adequate and reliable information being supplied by ceding companies regarding estimates of outstanding claims—hence the importance of claims-reporting clauses in treaties. However, experience should also permit the actuarial estimation of both outstanding claims and IBNR; evidence indicates that different claims-estimating formulae provide the best results for different classes of insurance business. Whatever method is used it must be capable of standing up to the critical appraisal of the revenue authorities, and in Britain IBNR provisions are only allowable if supported by statistical evidence to show that a liability does exist. When excess of loss treaties are written on a burning-cost basis, the burning-cost premium adjustment should be allowed for in the IBNR projection, and thus taxed in the original year of account though not received until later.

Management accounting

Although the financial state of a company is only one measure of corporate achievement, in many ways other aspects of performance are likely to be reflected in a company's financial results. For example, a discontented staff leading to high labour turnover will push up labour costs; and business growth will be revealed by revenue data. Therefore financial analysis can make an important contribution to effective management control. Far more detailed information is required, however, than is included in published financial accounts.

One technique that is frequently employed for management accounting purposes is to break down a company into smaller units, designating them as either 'cost' or 'profit' centres. The same organizational/accounting arrangements can be employed by a reinsurance company. Underwriting departments, divided by class of insurance and/or geographical areas, may be treated as separate profit centres.[7] Then various performance standards may be laid down for

---

7 G. Benktander, 'The underwriting of risks', in *Papers Presented to the Third International Reinsurance Seminar*.

each centre: for example, target rates of return may be set based on the free reserves required by each department to finance the business it writes.

Ideally the aim should be to break down the business into the individual treaties, though to do so is difficult. Generally the principles involved also apply to measuring the performance of larger profit centres. Therefore although the ensuing discussion relates specifically to evaluating individual treaties it is of wider application.

Obviously it is insufficient to view treaty results solely in terms of the balances on each year's accounts. There are other factors that need to be taken into account, notably:

(1) In view of the need to establish the true underwriting result for each year, the first point to be established is whether the balances on the treaty accounts accurately reflect the underwriting results attributable to each underwriting year. The distortions caused by mixing figures for different years have been pointed out in the preceding section on financial accounting.

(2) The level of investment earnings received by the reinsurer on the technical reserves attributable to the treaty. (Conversely, a ceding company when judging how much it is paying for reinsurance ought to take into account the difference between the interest it receives on any treaty reserves it holds and the rate of interest it pays to the reinsurer.)

(3) Which party obtains or carries any capital gains or losses on the treaty funds.

(4) Foreign exchange gains or losses incurred by either party on the business.

(5) The expenses incurred by the reinsurer in managing the business, including some part of his overheads.

(6) The tax treatment of investment earnings and profits, including whether double-taxation relief is available against tax levied overseas.

(7) The post-tax return needed by the reinsurer to service the funds (i.e. to pay dividends to shareholders and interest on long-term loans) held to finance the business. On a growing account earnings must be sufficient to provide for the required increase in free reserves. If an increase in premium income is solely the result of inflation it is unfair to expect shareholders to provide the extra finance required to write the same volume of business: tax rules regarding the calculation of taxable profits generally do not take this point into consideration.

In the case of overseas treaties there is the question too of whether the reinsurer is able to obtain control of and transfer back home balances on the accounts. Exchange control regulations may either block transfers or permit them only at penal rates of exchange.

Assigning costs to profit centres and treaties

Direct costs. The most important item under this heading is claims. As noted above, besides settled claims account must be taken of outstanding and IBNR claims too. Despite the long settlement time-lags associated with some classes of insurance, by using the sort of claims estimating models discussed earlier in this chapter, a reinsurer ought to be able to obtain a reasonably clear idea of the outcomes of the underwriting years of particular treaties long before the last claim is settled.

Other notable items that fall into the category of direct costs are the reinsurance and profit commissions, which on proportional treaties may absorb almost as much of the gross premiums as claims. The total reinsurance commission payable on a proportional treaty will usually be known at the same time as premiums are accounted for, unless it is payable on a sliding scale related to the treaty results. Profit commissions may not be known finally until several years after the end of the treaty year in question, though good estimation of outstanding claims will permit early estimation of what profit commission, if any, will be payable.

Management expenses present more difficulties. Mainly they consist of salaries and other labour costs of which some 50% – 60% may relate to staff engaged in the marketing, processing and administration of reinsurance contracts. It may be possible to allocate quite easily a small part of such direct costs to individual contracts, e.g. travelling costs incurred in visiting a ceding company, but generally any attempt to allocate staff time would necessitate the careful recording of time spent on dealing with individual contracts, which itself would be time-consuming and expensive. Moreover it may be argued that at the margin the cost of handling one more contract would be close to zero in that it would probably necessitate no increase in staff or other resources.

Indirect costs. The remainder of a reinsurer's expenses relate to such functions as central accounting, personnel, secretarial and general management expenses. There is no absolutely correct way of allocating such costs, even between the main classes of business. Certain principles can be established for the sake of consistency, but in the final analysis all involve arbitrary decisions. Should such costs, which in effect are fixed in relation to individual reinsurance contracts, be allocated on the basis of premiums, or claims costs, or according to variable costs, or by some other method?

Standard costing. An alternative approach to the problem may be through the use of standard costing techniques. Although the calculation of standard costs is not easy for any service industry, the technique can be used for insurance business.[8] Reinsurance, however, is probably far more difficult than many types of direct insurance. Generally the contracts handled by a reinsurer are very varied in their characteristics and there are the additional complications of the lack of standardization of the documentation required and volume of business covered by those contracts.

Before instituting elaborate costing techniques there are further factors to be considered. Often management expenses account for less than 10% of the premium under any contract, and in practice they play little or no part in the fixing of premiums for short-term business. Underwriters tend to be concerned far more with the state of competition, and the desire to acquire business which offers prospects of long-term premium growth and profits. Yet the potential current return on a treaty should not be ignored. Even if the price of acquiring new business in the face of keen competition is a likely short-term loss, the underwriter ought to have some idea of the price he is having to pay— and that means that he needs to have some clear ideas of the potential costs of the business compared with the income it will provide.

Fixing a performance standard

Besides claims and expenses there is one other factor to be considered in evaluating a treaty or a larger profit centre. Whether required by statute or simply dictated by commercial prudence, every reinsurer needs a certain level of free reserves relative to the volume of business written in order to provide a cushion against claims fluctuations. Every extra treaty will necessitate an increase, albeit not proportionate, in those reserves if the reinsurer is to maintain the same probability of ruin, and so the same degree of security for ceding companies. Therefore the cost of servicing that capital should be regarded as a charge against treaties.

That factor does pose a problem for a reinsurer operating internationally. The rate of return required on funds to meet dividends and interest charges will depend upon the levels of corporate tax payable on profits, and of local market interest rates and dividend yields. Both tax levels and interest rates vary significantly between countries. Therefore a company established in a country with high tax and interest rates could be in difficulties competing for business against reinsurers established in countries where interest rates and the dividends paid to shareholders may be several percentage points lower. On the other hand,

8 See S.S. Kapoor, 'Standard costing in insurance companies', *Policy Holder Insurance Journal*, vol. 91, no. 8 (23 February 1973).

if a treaty is charged with servicing its share of the reinsurer's capital and free reserves, it ought to be credited with a *pro rata* share of the investment yield on the funds representing those reserves, so that the difference would be much narrower.

The need of a reinsurer to earn sufficient to service its capital suggests an alternative approach to assessing treaties and profit centres. Instead of becoming involved in elaborate costing exercises which inevitably involve arbitrary allocation rules, it is easier to set a performance standard in the form of the minimum contribution which a treaty or centre must make to management expenses and capital service charges, after deducting from income claims, commissions and any other readily identifiable direct costs. During the 1970s many insurers and reinsurers have been constrained in the volume of business they can afford to write by the need to maintain solvency margins at a time when business has not been sufficiently profitable to generate additional free reserves. The use of contribution costing would at least focus attention on the comparative returns from different treaties, and enable a reinsurer to weed out those which clearly did not cover costs.

Whatever method of costing is employed, the other side of the equation is income. As indicated already, account must be taken of (1) all sources of income generated by a treaty, including investment income or interest on premium deposits; (2) taxation levied on that income; and (3) when income is received. Only by bringing non-premium sources of income into account can the results of different treaties be compared. The example in Table 14.15 illustrates this point.

Over three years it is assumed that two treaties produce the results shown in the table. Under treaty A the treaty reserves are deposited with the ceding company whereas under B they are held by the reinsurer.

Judged on Part 1 of the statement, treaty A would appear the more profitable, whereas after taking investment earnings into account treaty B produces a better result. If the timing of the cash flows were also allowed for by converting all of the items to present values, then the position may change even more one way or the other.

If a company is to be run efficiently all of the consequences of writing a treaty need to be considered. Underwriters cannot afford to look at only the technical aspects—the financial are equally important.

Table 14.15

	Treaty A		Treaty B	
	£	£	£	£
Part 1				
Premium income		500,000		500,000
less Commission	175,000		195,000	
less Losses paid and oustanding	280,000		280,000	
		455,000		475,000
		45,000		25,000
less tax at 50%		22,500		12,500
		22,500		12,500
Part 2				
Interest on premium and loss reserve deposits net of tax		15,000		—
Interest and dividends on funds held by the reinsurer net of tax		2,500		40,000
Contribution to management expenses and servicing capital reserves		40,000		52,500

REINSURANCE

15
International practice and problems

REINSURANCE

15
International practice and problems

A strong economic case can be made for spreading the insurance provided for certain risks amongst insurers drawn from more than one country. The benefits of doing so are self-evident for:

(1) Large risks where a single loss may account for a substantial proportion of (and in some cases more than) the total premium income of domestic insurers;[1]
(2) Catastrophe risks, notably where a country is so exposed to natural perils that a single event may destroy a significant part of its productive and other resources.

The international spreading of such risks relieves the local insurance industry of incurring losses beyond its financial capacity. Also it protects the country against random large foreign exchange losses in that claims payments received from abroad will help to finance the loss of exports and/or higher imports caused by the occurrence of the insured event, though premiums payable abroad will be a regular cost to the balance of payments.

It is impossible to consider here the respective merits of spreading risks internationally through direct insurance or reinsurance, but the benefits are not restricted only to the two cases cited above. An exceptional accumulation of smaller losses involving a large foreign exchange cost (such as the loss of imported or exported goods, or payments for liabilities incurred abroad) may place a strain on the balance of payments which it would be worth protecting by regular premium payments. There may be competitive advantages too from reinsuring abroad. International reinsurers may be able to offer lower premiums or a better service than can be obtained locally, or they may spur local companies into improving their performances. Finally, major reinsurance companies and brokers often provide considerable technical and training assistance for ceding companies. Frequently they take clients' employees

---

1 An UNCTAD study reported that 'One developing country has seven insurance policies covering its mining industry which account for 70% of its total premium income produced by all classes of insurance operated in that country.' *(Insurance of large risks in developing countries,* TD/B/C, July 1977).

into their own offices for training or second their own staff to work with their ceding companies.[2]

Yet despite those advantages, restrictions are increasingly being placed on international reinsurance transactions, particularly by the governments of developing countries. They take two main forms:

(1) Direct restrictions on the placing of reinsurances with foreign reinsurers.

(2) Indirect restrictions which put foreign reinsurers at a disadvantage in competing against local reinsurers.

Reasons for restrictions

Before considering the nature of the various types of restriction, it may help to try to understand the underlying reasons.

The barriers encountered by reinsurers are not generally erected by local companies anxious to protect themselves from foreign competition, but by governments and supervisory authorities. Their motives fall under four main headings:

(1) To protect local policyholders from the consequences of the insolvency of foreign reinsurers not under the control of the local supervisory authority.

(2) To build up a local insurance and reinsurance market, possibly as part of the planned growth and diversification of the economy.

(3) To protect the balance of payments and foreign exchange reserves from outflows of premiums and capital funds.

(4) To retain funds generated by insurance operations for local investment.

It would be difficult to quarrel with any of the objectives, and indeed the local retention of a larger volume of business may sometimes serve the best interests of all parties. In earlier chapters considerable emphasis has been placed on the desirability of ceding companies retaining a reasonable share of the risks they accept, in that if a company is substantially involved in the results of its business it will strive to maintain its underwriting standards. Also unnecessary fragmentation of business through coinsurance and reinsurance adds to total administrative costs.

It must be recognized too that developing countries have special needs which warrant special treatment. So it *might be* justifiable to accept the additional costs of short-term protective measures designed to facilitate

---

2 For an extensive discussion of the benefits see R.L. Carter and G.M. Dickinson, *Barriers to Trade in Insurance and Reinsurance* (The Geneva Association, 1976), and *Position Paper on International Insurance and Reinsurance* (Chamber of Commerce of the US, 1972).

the development of local companies, provided eventually they will be capable of withstanding competition unaided.

On the other hand, the interests of policyholders are not always best served by measures adopted in pursuit of wider economic objectives and, indeed, it may be that their interests are of minor consideration when the regulation of overseas reinsurance is under review.[3] Moreover there are sound reasons for believing that often the indirect economic costs of restrictions on international reinsurance transactions may outweigh the apparent benefits, as will be explained later. First, however, the various types of discriminatory measures employed against foreign reinsurers need to be explained.

Direct restrictions

An international reinsurer may either establish a branch office or a subsidiary company or appoint an underwriting agent in a country where it wishes to write reinsurance business, or it may transact such business on a so-called services basis from its head office. Direct restrictions therefore, take two forms:

(1) Those excluding foreign insurers and reinsurers from establishing in a country, or at best restricting their participation to a share in locally incorporated companies.

(2) Those prohibiting local insurers from placing reinsurances abroad.

Foreign or foreign-owned companies have been ejected from many countries as the result of policies of general nationalization and domestication. When foreign insurers have been permitted to retain a share in locally incorporated companies often they have been restricted to a minority interest, in some cases as low as 20%, with national interests holding the majority of the shares and exercising management control. Although local participation may provide access to more sources of business, it may also create problems, especially if the employment of expatriate staff is forbidden or severely curtailed.

South America led the way in placing restrictions on local companies reinsuring abroad. The state monopoly reinsurance institutions of Argentina, Brazil and Chile, for example, alone have the right to retrocede risks to foreign reinsurers. Elsewhere (e.g. Mexico) a certain proportion of all reinsurances must be placed locally before any business can be reinsured abroad. Now such restrictions are a common feature of the international reinsurance scene, particularly among developing countries.

3 J.A.S. Neave, 'The development of government involvement in reinsurance underwriting', in *Papers presented to the International Insurance Seminar, San Francisco, 1976.*

Indirect restrictions

There are many ways in which international reinsurance transactions, whether on an establishment or services basis, can be made more difficult or less profitable to either the reinsurer or ceding office. The following methods are the most common.

Localization of reserves. Extensive reference has been made in Chapters 7 and 13 to the deposit of premium and loss reserves. Generally requests for deposits arise from the regulations of supervisory authorities allegedly acting to protect the interests of local policyholders. Sometimes reinsurers, whether established in the country or otherwise, are compelled to maintain sufficient funds within the country to cover their liabilities to ceding companies. The regulations may also specify the types of securities (usually government securities) in which the funds shall be held.

Alternatively the pressure to deposit funds locally may be exercised indirectly through the solvency regulations applying to ceding companies. For example, whereas direct insurers may be permitted to deduct from premium and loss reserves an allowance for business ceded to local reinsurers, that concession may be withheld for reinsurances placed with 'non-admitted' reinsurers. Consequently foreign reinsurers are obliged to deposit premium, and perhaps loss, reserves with their ceding companies.

The results in both cases are that reinsurers' reserve funds are fragmented, and in order to provide the same global standard of security to all ceding companies they must maintain larger capital funds than otherwise would be needed. The servicing of that capital adds to the cost of reinsurance and thus the price of direct insurance.

Local incorporation. If establishment is permitted only through local incorporation, capital costs may be increased because a relatively larger capital may be required for a local company than for a larger group. Again that cost must be reflected in higher premiums or lower profit margins.

Taxation. Foreign reinsurers are exposed to discriminatory taxation in various, often complex, ways. In many instances the aim may be directed more towards reducing the loss of tax revenues than deliberately trying to reduce insurance imports.

Sometimes tax measures may deter ceding companies from placing business with foreign reinsurers. For example, premiums ceded abroad may not be deductible against income, so increasing the company's tax liability, as in Australia and New Zealand where the deduction of reinsurance premiums is disallowed unless they are included in a return by the reinsurer and taxed accordingly. Australia does, however, allow ceding companies to act as agents for non-resident insurers and pay tax on reinsurance premiums on the basis of an *assumed* profit of 10%. At least, under this latter arrangement the reinsurer can claim double-taxation relief, which is not available for any contribution he may be required to make towards a New Zealand ceding company's tax liability.

Elsewhere special taxes are levied on foreign suppliers of reinsurance. In some countries subsidiary companies, and particularly branch offices, of foreign insurers and reinsurers are subject to effectively higher rates of corporate tax than domestic companies. Some governments attempt to reach out and tax non-resident reinsurers on income which they claim originates in their countries: the Australian and New Zealand tax measures fall within that category.

The position regarding taxation of income arising on premium and loss reserve deposits has been covered already in Chapter 14.

Exchange control regulations. Most, if not all, countries impose exchange controls on the remittance of funds abroad for current trading transactions, and usually even more stringent controls are placed on capital movements. Such regulations can seriously impede the settlement of accounts for overseas reinsurances to the detriment of both ceding companies and reinsurers.

If ceding companies cannot remit balances to their reinsurers, then overseas reinsurers effectively face a one-way bet—if losses exceed premiums they will be expected to pay the balance, but without hope of receiving early payment if premiums happen to exceed losses. Restrictions on the investment of foreign balances may further exacerbate the position if reinsurers are thereby prevented from earning a reasonable return on their funds. However good may be the technical results of a treaty, it cannot be regarded as a financial success if the reinsurer is unable to obtain control of favourable balances. The problem can be particularly acute if for some reason the contract is retroceded so that the reinsurer is responsible for the payment to retrocessionaires of premiums he cannot himself obtain.

Even when no official exchange controls are imposed on the remittance of premiums, claims payments or reinsurance balances, inordinate administrative delays in obtaining authorization from a central bank can have much the same effect. In such circumstances, reinsurers may be unwilling to supply cover, and if ceding companies cannot obtain speedy settlement of claims they will be equally reluctant to purchase reinsurance from abroad. Some countries have imposed exchange control regulations which, by officially delaying the remittance abroad of reinsurance premiums, operate like deposit regulations.

Exchange control restrictions on capital movements may also adversely affect the profitability of overseas reinsurances. Restrictions have mainly been imposed by governments with weak currencies. However, during the 1970s countries with strong currencies (notably the German mark and the Swiss franc) have tried to protect themselves from capital inflows. Restrictions have been placed on the types of securities foreigners may purchase, and negative rates of interest have been charged on bank deposits. Though designed to deter 'hot money', reinsurance transactions have been caught by the same restrictions. Thus foreign reinsurers accepting business from those countries have been put at a disadvantage compared with domestic reinsurers. By holding reserves in other currencies the foreign reinsurer incurs a foreign exchange risk, and if he seeks to invest in the same currency as the liability he has accepted he will suffer a loss of investment income compared with domestic reinsurers.

Barriers to international trade are not erected solely by governments of importing countries, but by exporting countries too. This point is particularly important in relation to exchange control regulations. If reinsurers or brokers are required to surrender all premiums received in foreign currencies and hold balances in their domestic currency, then they lose the opportunity to match foreign liabilities with assets in the same currency. Such an interference with commercial judgment may not matter if the reinsurer's domestic currency is strong on the foreign-exchange markets, but the consequences can be near disastrous if the reinsurer is forced to hold a weak currency. The recent relaxation of UK exchange control regulations which now allow British reinsurers greater freedom to hold assets in original currencies was greatly welcomed throughout the London market.

Solvency regulations. Obstacles to overseas reinsurance transactions on a services basis may also be erected by the goverments of exporting countries through their own insurance solvency regulations. If foreign assets are deemed inadmissible for the purpose of establishing solvency then a reinsurer that accepts business from abroad must either maintain a higher level of free reserves or convert all foreign premiums into his own currency, in so far as that is possible.

Trends in restriction.

Generally over the last 30 years the political climate has become less favourable towards international insurance operations. Reinsurers have not fared as badly as direct insurers, but nevertheless the trend has been towards more restrictions at home and abroad. In particular, as ex-colonial territories have gained their political independence, so they have sought to establish their economic independence too. As part of that process most have attempted to create strong local insurance markets to reduce their dependence on foreign suppliers. Sometimes political ideology has played its part, but throughout the developing world attitudes towards insurance business have become increasingly inward looking, though UNCTAD has encouraged countries to cooperate at a regional level. [4]

There are signs, however, that perhaps attitudes are beginning to change. Although the discussions which have taken place over the years within the Organization for Economic Cooperation and Development (OECD) have not produced any real progress towards the liberalization of reinsurance trade, modest progress has been made elsewhere. As the first step towards the creation of a common market for insurance, in 1964 the European Economic Community issued its 'Directive for the abolition of restrictions on freedom of establishment and on the free supply of services of reinsurance and retrocession'. If developed countries lead the way in liberalization, developing countries may be encouraged to reconsider their positions, as two countries already have done. Egypt, after first 'Egyptianizing' and then in 1961 nationalizing its insurance industry, has now allowed foreign insurers to participate in two new direct insurance companies incorporated under its 1974 Free Zone legislation. South Korea is both denationalizing its state reinsurance corporation and relaxing its restrictions on foreign insurers. And in 1977 UNCTAD reported that: [5]

> Even the socialist countries of Eastern Europe, where purely national risks are not reinsured abroad, are thinking of resorting to foreign reinsurance in the near future to cover their large and technological risks.

The American government has come to accept the need for greater freedom in international trade in services, including insurance and reinsurance, and it appears quite likely that the matter will be taken up within the GATT (General Agreement on Tariffs and Trade). Arguably, while restrictions on trade in goods have been progressively reduced over the last 30 years, restrictions on trade in services have been allowed to grow because the effects have been imperfectly understood. Unlike visible trade, negotiators on invisibles have been unable to turn to any economic theory or reliable empirical evidence to support their

---

4 UNCTAD, *Reinsurance Problems in Developing Countries.*
5 UNCTAD, *Insurance of Large Risks in Developing Countries,* para. 32, p.10.

arguments. It is not possible here to attempt to remedy that position, but a few examples will serve to illustrate that often the case for restriction is far weaker than it may at first appear, and often costs may exceed the benefits.

The case for liberalization

Sometimes international reinsurance transactions are inadvertently caught by insufficiently selective legislation aimed at controlling other types of dealings. However, even when the intention is clear, the scanty evidence that exists suggests that not infrequently measures are introduced with a very imperfect understanding of their likely net effects.

Balance of payments

Measures aimed at reducing adverse balance-of-payments effects of reinsurance business are a case in point. Far too often the emphasis is placed on controlling premium outflows without appreciating either the offsetting inflows or that it may be only the balances on reinsurance accounts which cross the foreign exchanges. A recent study has shown that the balance-of-payments effects are far more complex than is frequently understood, and that the current account deficit in respect of insurance and reinsurance trade for all developing countries between 1972 and 1974 constituted only 2% of their overall deficit in respect of goods and services.[6] Similarly Professor Urbanski has estimated that the balance of payments effects of international reinsurance transactions for Austria (which though relatively small, is liberal in its approach to foreign reinsurers) is a net average outflow on current account equal to only 1 or 2% of domestic premium income, and in many years there is a new inflow of funds to cover losses.[7] Even an annual net outflow is not a sufficient reason *per se* for restricting foreign insurance - it may be a reasonable price to pay for security. Urbanski added that through international reinsurance very large losses can be paid 'without endangering any one company or even the economy of any one country'.

As previously noted, the latter point is of particular relevance to catastrophe risks. Following a disaster, claims payments from overseas reinsurers can help to provide the badly needed foreign currency a

---

6 G.M. Dickinson, 'International Insurance Transactions and the Balance of Payments, *The Geneva Papers,* no. 6 (October 1977).

7 H. von Urbanski, 'Reinsurance: Legend and Reality', *Die Industrie,* July 1977, reprinted in *The Review,* 26 August 1977.

country will need to repair the damage and restore its economy.

There are other points too that deserve consideration in assessing balance-of-payments effects. Given the degree of monetary instability experienced in recent years, many reinsurers have preferred to match assets and liabilities in the same currencies so that balances are often kept in countries of origin or in their currencies. Admittedly, developing countries may not have fared so well as developed countries which have both the volume of business and capital markets to facilitate investment locally. All countries, however, must consider the opportunity costs of attempting to develop local reinsurance facilities. If resources can be employed in alternative forms of production which may add more to exports or save more in imports than the net cost of purchasing reinsurance from abroad, then to attempt to build up local reinsurance institutions will result in a misallocation of scarce resources.

Security

At the beginning of this chapter the benefits of recourse to international reinsurance for the protection of very large and catastrophe-type risks were said to be self-evident. Yet governments still behave contrary to their own interests. For example, when insurers and reinsurers are obliged to hold funds locally, they are quite likely to be invested directly or indirectly in the physical assets which they are insuring. Generally that should not affect an insurer's solvency, provided the investment of its funds can be spread so widely that no one underlying physical asset accounts for more than a very small part of its total investments. However, funds held in respect of earthquake, windstorm, flood and other catastrophe insurances call for entirely different treatment. The only way in which an insurer or reinsurer can guarantee to be able to pay claims for widespread damage due to a natural disaster is to invest the funds in assets which will be unaffected by the occurrence of the event: that may necessitate investing funds abroad.

Costs of reinsurance

Besides the additional capital costs attributable to the fragmenting of reinsurers' reserves, there are other factors which tend to force up the price of reinsurance.

There are benefits to be gained from the formation of state reinsurance corporations, and local and regional reinsurance pools, but they can also increase total costs. Every additional link in the insurance production chain inevitably adds to total business acquisition and administration costs. In so far as state corporations and pools only act as a substitute source of reinsurance supply for business that otherwise would be handled by international reinsurers, they do not *per se* cause any unnecessary duplication of resources. The possibility of duplication arises when they take by way of compulsory cessions more reinsurance from their domestic insurers than they can handle themselves, and retrocede the balance. If those retrocessions are then used to bargain for the reciprocal exchange of business which reinsurers could well afford to retain for their own accounts, another unnecessary link is added to the production chain.

The formation of state corporations and pools can prove disadvantageous in other ways. If they reduce the volume and spread of proportional reinsurance available to international reinsurers, and if instead they require higher-level excess of loss covers for their own protection, then reinsurers' portfolios will become less balanced. Consequently the loadings required for excess of loss reinsurances must be increased accordingly. Frequently lower than market rates of commission are paid on compulsory cessions, though they are not reflected in the terms required by state corporations for their retrocessions. Then if direct insurers are allowed to cede any surplus abroad there is the temptation to overload their 'free' treaties in order to make up for the shortfall in reinsurance commission under the compulsory cessions. And international reinsurers may seek to recover their costs through higher premiums for the excess of loss treaties. The end result is that direct policyholders have to pay higher premiums for their insurances.

Indirect effects

It is, however, the indirect rather than the direct effects of restrictions which may be the most costly, but which are even more likely to be left out of the reckoning. The following examples will serve to illustrate this point.

If restricted access to international reinsurance markets results in a lack of adequate insurance cover, especially for new technologically advanced projects and processes, businessmen may be less willing to take risks, so reducing the efficient utilization of resources. Likewise, multinational corporations may be deterred from establishing, so perhaps depriving a developing country of badly needed external capital and technological know-how. In both cases the balance of payments is likely to suffer too.

Possibly subsidiaries of multinationals already operating in a country may seek through their parent companies insurance cover not readily available locally, if necessary by-passing regulations prohibiting overseas purchases of insurance by means of transfer-pricing arrangements.

Availability and innovation in the provision of insurance cover is one question, cost of cover is another. Competition remains the best spur to efficiency and it has been claimed that:[8]

> When all international contacts are denied to local companies by a national reinsurance monopoly, ... their competitive freedom is so stultified as to cause heavy overcharging to the public. A recent estimate of a typical case amounted to 50% in some branches but this overcharge probably exceeded 100% in other sectors.

The interests of insurance consumers

Although the interests of insurance consumers (and of persons otherwise affected by insurance, such as injured third parties) often may not be paramount when restrictions are being considered, they cannot be ignored. The extent to which the welfare of policyholders is likely to be impaired by restrictions on the supply or demand for foreign reinsurance depends on:[9]

(1) The degree and level of sophistication of local insurance needs.

(2) The extent to which the local market is capable of supplying those needs.

(3) The calibre of foreign insurers capable and, in the absence of such barriers, willing to supply those needs.

Apart from insurances against major catastrophe risks, notably natural disasters, the insurance needs of individuals and small traders can generally be met by local insurers. The needs of corporate buyers can be more complex. They require both wider and more flexible insurance cover, and a range of supporting services, such as advice on loss prevention and risk management, which small domestic companies are usually ill-equipped to provide. If large corporate buyers cannot obtain direct insurance from international insurers then the only way in which their needs are likely to be met is through the participation of international reinsurers. The possible consequences of the total exclusion of both foreign insurers and reinsurers have been considered above.

Besides contributing additional underwriting capacity and supporting services, major international reinsurers can play an important role too in the rating of large risks and specialist classes of insurance. Small domestic companies, particularly in developing countries, may possess neither an adequate spread of such business nor the experience to

---

8 Neave, 'The development of government involvement in reinsurance underwriting'.

9 R.L. Carter and G.M. Dickinson, 'Economic effects of restrictions on international trade in reinsurance' in *Papers Presented to the Third International Reinsurance Seminar,* (Reinsurance Offices' Association, 1977).

calculate premium rates.[10] In so far as accurate premium rating can influence loss-prevention decisions, the advice available to local insurers from major international reinsurers can improve resource allocation for the economy at large as well as helping to avoid cross-subsidization between different classes of policyholders.

Reference has been made already to the cost of reinsurance and thus the price original policyholders have to pay. Price, however, cannot be divorced from quality of service, so that free access to international reinsurance markets need not necessarily lead to lower original premiums. What corporate buyers of insurance may hope to gain is better value for the prices they pay.

A final aspect of policyholder welfare that merits further thought is security. As noted above, the fragmentation of reinsurers' reserve funds through compulsory deposits, etc., reduces the efficiency of capital utilization of foreign suppliers. In a period of economic instability it may also undermine the financial strength of foreign reinsurers, so creating the very problems governments seek to avoid. Sometimes it is ironic that governments are less willing to trust the financial probity and strength of major international reinsurers than their own, often comparatively very small, local insurers. What is badly needed is greater cooperation between supervisory authorities, and a climate of mutual trust in which they would be prepared to delegate responsibility for the supervision of international reinsurers to the supervisors of their countries of domicile. That would be a far more efficient solution than the present plethora of controls and regulations imposed by individual countries. It would even help if supervisory authorities would accept the returns prepared for the reinsurer's own supervisory authority instead of different returns, often in a very different form, having to be compiled for each country in which a company operates.[11]

The future

Reinsurance exists to spread risks, and in many instances the spreading of risks domestically is insufficient to provide the security policyholders and national economies require. Reinsurance conducted on an international scale has a vital role to play in fostering the economic welfare of all countries. It is to be hoped that the nationalistic trend that has swept around the world since the 1950s will be reversed in the remaining years of the 20th century.

10 UNCTAD, *Reinsurance problems in developing countries,* p.17.
11 Although supervision in the United States is exercised at the level of each state so that there are 51 supervisory authorities, the return submitted by a reinsurer to its home state is normally accepted in most other states.

If that is to happen then two things are necessary. First, politicians will need a better understanding of the costs and benefits of international reinsurance transactions. At a theoretical level the supporting economic analysis is now becoming available. What is badly needed is empirical evidence.

Secondly, many though not all of the barriers to trade that now exist were first devised by developed countries. They need to lead the way towards greater freedom for international reinsurance. Though developing countries may sometimes feel that they are in a special position, it is in their own interests not to pursue unthinkingly the restrictive examples set by some countries of the Western world.

REINSURANCE

Bibliography

Advanced Study Group of the Insurance Institute of London, *Excess of Loss Reinsurance*, Report by Advanced Study Group No 201, (Insurance Institute of London, March 1975).

H.Ammeter, 'The calculation of premium rates for excess of loss and stop loss reinsurance treaties', in *Non-proportional Reinsurance* edited by S.Vajda, (Arithbel, SA, 1955).

Sir J.Arnould, *A Treatise on the Law of Marine Insurance and Average*, 2nd edition, (Stevens and Sons, 1857).

M.H.Atkins, 'Simulation models in risk management', in *Handbook of Risk Management*, editors R.L.Carter and N.A.Doherty, (Kluwer-Harrap Handbooks, 1974).

P.H.Bartrum, 'Solvency and profitability', in *Policy*, (December 1977).

R.E.Beard, T.Pentikäinen and E.Pesonen, *Risk Theory, the stochastic basis of insurance*, 2nd edition, (Chapman and Hall, 1977).

R.E.Beard, 'A mathematical model for motor insurance', in *Mathematical Modelling*, editors J.G.Andrews and R.R.McClone, (Butterworths 1976).

R.E.Beard, 'Three R's of insurance—risk, retention and insurance', in *Journal of the Institute of Actuaries Students' Society*, Vol 15, Part 6, (1959).

J-M.Belloy and A.Gabus, 'A model for measuring the impact of inflation on motor insurance business', in *The Geneva Papers*, No 1 (The Geneva Association, January 1976).

B.Benjamin, *General Insurance* (Heinemann, 1977).

S.Benjamin, 'Simulating mortality fluctuations', in *Transactions of the XVII International Congress of Actuaries*, Vol 1 (1964).

G.Benktander, 'The calculation of a fluctuating loading for excess of loss reinsurance', in *The ASTIN Bulletin* (1975, Vol VIII, Part 2, p.272).

G.Benktander, 'The effect of inflation on excess layers', in *The Review* (12 January 1968).

G.Benktander, 'The principle of stability clauses in excess of loss reinsurance', in *Quarterly letter from the Nederlandse Reassurantie Groep*, No XIX/75, (August 1974).

G.Benktander, 'The underwriting of risks', in *Papers presented to the Third International Reinsurance Seminar*, (Reinsurance Offices' Association, 1977).

G.Benktander and C.O.Segerdahl, 'On the analytical representation of claims distributions with special reference to excess of loss reinsurance', in *Transactions of the XVI International Congress of Actuaries*, (1960).

D.L.Bickelhaupt, *General Insurance*, 9th edition, (Richard D.Irwin Inc., 1974).

D.B.Biggs, 'Permanent health insurance', in *Handbook of Insurance*, editor R.L.Carter (Kluwer-Harrap Handbooks, 1973 updated).

K.H.Borch, *The Mathematical Theory of Insurance*, (Lexington Books, D.C.Heath and Co. 1974).

K.H.Borch, 'An attempt to determine the optimal amount of stop loss reinsurance', in *Transactions of the XVI International Congress of Actuaries*, Vol 1, (1960).

K.H.Borch, 'The optimal portfolio of assets in an insurance company', in *Transactions of the XVIII International Congress of Actuaries,* Munich (1968).

W.H.Börner, 'An appraisal of the alternatives to the practice of reciprocity in reinsurance', a Bolesaw Monic Fund prize essay abridged in *Quarterly Letter of the Nederlandse Reassurantie Groep*, No XVI/61, March 1970.

R.D.C.Brackenridge, *Medical selection of life risks* (The Undershaft Press, 1977).

H.Bühlmann, *Mathematical Methods in Risk Theory* (Springer-Verlag, 1970).

J.Butcher, 'Insurance mergers—their effect on professional reinsurers', *Reinsurance* (September 1971).

J.S.Butler, *Punitive Damages and Reinsurance*, Reinsurance Offices' Association (1977). Also see *Reinsurance*, Legal Correspondent, in this section.

R.L.Carter, editor, *Handbook of Insurance*, (Kluwer-Harrap Handbooks, 1973 updated).

R.L.Carter, *Economics and Insurance* (P.H. Press, 1972).

R.L.Carter, 'Insuring for the future', in *Policy* (December 1976).

R.L.Carter and G.M.Dickinson, 'Economic effects of restrictions on international trade in reinsurance', in *Papers presented to the Third International Reinsurance Seminar at Cambridge*, April 1977, (Reinsurance Offices' Association).

R.L.Carter and G.M.Dickinson, *Barriers to Trade in Insurance and Reinsurance* (The Geneva Association, 1976).

R.L.Carter and N.A.Doherty, editors, *Handbook of Risk Management,* (Kluwer-Harrap Handbooks, 1975 updated).

F.de Carteret-Bisson, 'Contingency insurance', in *Handbook of Insurance,* editor R.L.Carter (Kluwer-Harrap Handbooks, 1973 updated).

Chamber of Commerce of the US, *Position Paper on International Insurance and Reinsurance* (Chamber of Commerce of the US, 1972).

G.Clayton, *British Insurance* (Elek Books, 1971).

R.Colinvaux, *The Law of Insurance,* 3rd edition, (Sweet and Maxwell Ltd, 1970).

W.C.Corbett, 'The insurance of aircraft and aviation risks', in *Handbook of Insurance,* editor R.L.Carter, (Kluwer-Harrap Handbooks, 1973 updated).

R.M.Cyert and J.G.March, *A Behavioural Theory of the Firm* (Prentice-Hall, 1963).

P.A.Dawson and M.Roberts, 'Credit Insurance', in *Handbook of Insurance,* editor R.L.Carter, (Kluwer-Harrap Handbooks, 1973 updated).

G.M.Dickinson, 'Concepts of probability and risk', in *Handbook of Risk Management,* editors R.L.Carter and N.A.Doherty, (Kluwer-Harrap Handbooks, 1975 updated).

G.M.Dickinson, 'International insurance transactions and the balance of payments' in *The Geneva Papers* No 6, (October 1977).

G.M.Dickinson, 'Risk and the law of large numbers', in *Handbook of Risk Management,* editors R.L.Carter and N.A.Doherty, (Kluwer-Harrap Handbooks, 1974 updated).

P.G.M.Dickson, *The Sun Insurance Office 1710-1960* (Oxford University Press, 1960).

W.A.Dinsdale, *Specimen Insurance Forms and Glossaries*, 2nd edition, (Stone & Cox, 1963).

J.A.Dixon, 'Captive insurance companies', in *Handbook of Risk Management* editors R.L.Carter and N.A.Doherty, (Kluwer-Harrap Handbooks, 1974 updated).

J.Dougharty, 'The History of Life Reinsurance in Great Britain'—an unpublished paper available from Mercantile and General Reinsurance Co. Ltd.

G.T.Foster, 'Some observations on life reinsurance' *Journal of Institute of Actuaries,* Vol LXXII, Part III (1946).

D.G.Friedman, 'Insurance and the Natural Hazards', in *The ASTIN Bulletin,* Vol. VII, Part 1 (December 1972).

D.E.W.Gibb, *Lloyd's of London* (Macmillan & Co., 1957).

C.E.Golding, *The Law and Practice of Reinsurance* (Stone & Cox, 1965 edition amended 1968).

C.E.Golding, *A History of Reinsurance* (published privately for Sterling Offices Ltd, 1927).

R.C.Goshay, 'Captive Insurance Companies' in *Risk Management,* editor H.W.Snider, (R.D.Irwin Inc. 1964).

T.R.Goulder, 'Self-insurance—the prospects' in *Insurance,* (February 1974).

M.Greenberg, 'International Problems and Possible Solutions', a paper read to the International Insurance Seminar, San Francisco (1976).

M.R.Greene, 'Trends in American liability insurance', *Sigma,* (Swiss Reinsurance Company, September 1977).

M.Grossmann, *Rückversicherung—eine Einführung* (Verlag Peter Lang, 1977).

F.E.Guaschi, *Accident Excess of Loss: an actuarial approach to the rating problem* (Mercantile and General Reinsurance Co. Ltd, 1969).

F.E.Guaschi, *Accident Excess of Loss* (Mercantile and General Reinsurance Co. Ltd, November 1972).

F.E.Guaschi, *Accident Excess of Loss* (Mercantile and General Reinsurance Co. Ltd, February 1975).

F.E.Guaschi, 'Charting the financial course of a reinsurance company', in *Papers presented to the Third International Reinsurance Seminar* (Reinsurance Offices' Association, 1977).

F.E.Guaschi, 'Non-proportional reinsurance', *Journal of the Institute of Actuaries Students' Society*, Vol 19, Part 1 (1970).

H.E.Gumbel, 'Arbitration under reinsurance contracts' in *Festschrift für Reimer Schmidt* editors F.Reichert-Facilades, *et al.*, (Verlag Versicherungswirtschaft E.V., 1976).

R.A.Handover, 'The London non-marine reinsurance market', *The Journal of the Chartered Insurance Institute*, Vol 64 (1967).

G.Hickmott, *Flixborough Disaster* (Mercantile and General Reinsurance Co. Ltd, 1977).

E.R.Hardy Ivamy, *General Principles of Insurance Law,* 3rd edition, (Butterworths, 1975).

G.T.Jones, *Simulation and Business Decisions,* (Penguin, 1972).

P.M.Kahn, 'An introduction to collective risk theory and its application to stop-loss reinsurance' in *Transactions of the Society of Actuaries,* XIV (1962) Part I.

S.S.Kapoor, 'Standard costing in insurance companies', *Policy Holder Insurance Journal,* Vol 91, No 8 (23 February 1973).

S.Kroll, 'The past, present and future of non-admitted insurance in the United States' in *Best's Review,* Property/Casualty Edition (November 1975).

L. La Bianca, 'Reinsurance, private insurance and the state', in *Post Magazine and Insurance Monitor* (27th May 1976).

A.M.Lanzone, 'Punitive damages—insurer and reinsurer, adversaries or partners?' in *Best's Review* Property/Casualty Edition, Vol 78, No 9, (January 1977).

J.Lavers, 'Underwriting information and the non-proportional account' in *Papers presented at the Third International Reinsurance Seminar,* (Reinsurance Offices' Association, 1977).

N.Legh-Jones, *MacGillivray and Parkington on Insurance Law*, 6th edition, (Sweet and Maxwell, 1975).

Arthur D.Little, Inc., *Prices and Profits in the Property and Liability Industry,* (Report to the American Insurance Association, 1967).

C.S.S.Lyon, 'The establishment of adequate reserves for outstanding and IBNR claims', in *Papers presented to the Third International Reinsurance Seminar,* Reinsurance Offices' Association, 1977.

P.Madge, 'Products liability insurance' in *Handbook of Insurance,* editor R.L.Carter (Kluwer-Harrap Handbooks, 1973 updated).

J.G.March and R.M.Cyert, *A Behavioural Theory of the Firm* (Prentice-Hall, 1963).

A.Mayes, 'Captive companies updated', *Policy Holder Insurance Journal,* Vol 90 (22 September 1972).

G.F.Michelbacher and N.R.Roos, *Multiple-line Insurers; their nature and operation,* 2nd edition, (McGraw-Hill, 1970).

S.Miller, 'The intermediary in international reinsurance' in *Papers presented at the International Reinsurance Seminar*, (Reinsurance Offices' Association, 1973).

J.H.C.Morris, *Dicey and Morris on Conflict of Laws*, 9th edition, (Stevens, 1973).

Munich Reinsurance Co., *The influence of inflation on insurance* (Munich Reinsurance Co. 1971).

National Association of Insurance Commissioners, *Measurement of Profitability and Treatment of Investment Income in Property and Liability Insurance*, (National Association of Insurance Commissioners, 1970).

J.A.S.Neave, 'International reinsurance: changing patterns in economic relationship' in *Policy* (May 1976).

J.A.S.Neave, 'Current problems of the reinsurance market' in *Policy Holder Insurance Journal*, Vol 89 (5 February 1971).

J.A.S.Neave, 'The development of government involvement in reinsurance underwriting', in *Papers presented to the International Insurance Seminar, San Francisco*, (1976).

J.A.S.Neave, 'Reinsurance today: a general survey' in *Journal of the Chartered Insurance Institute*, Vol 64 (1967).

Nederlandse Reassurantie Groep, 'Apportionment of liability excess of loss claims' *Quarterly letter from the Nederlandse Reassurantie Groep*, No XIX/73 (December 1973).

Nederlandse Reassurantie Groep, 'Indexed annuities—apportionment of claims between cedant and reinsurer' *Quarterly letter from the Nederlandse Reassurantie Groep*, No XIX/74 (May 1974).

Nederlandse Reassurantie Groep, 'Is individual excess reinsurance better than stop loss reinsurance?' *Quarterly letter from the Nederlandse Reassurantie Groep*, No XV/59 (July 1969).

Nederlandse Reassurantie Groep, 'The principle of stability clauses in excess of loss reinsurances—a brief outline' *Quarterly letter from the Nederlandse Reassurantie Groep*, No XIX/75 (August 1974).

P.M.North, *Cheshire on Private International Law*, 9th edition (Butterworths, 1974).

M.Parkington, *et al., MacGillivray and Parkington on Insurance Law*, 6th edition (Sweet and Maxwell, 1975).

'Problems of liability insurance' *Post Magazine and Insurance Monitor* (7 and 14 April 1977).

H.E.Raynes, *A History of British Insurance*, 2nd edition, (Pitman, 1964).

R.C.Reinarz, *Property and Liability Reinsurance Management* (Mission Publishing Co., 1969).

Reinsurance Legal Correspondent, 'Treaties: agreements to enter into future reinsurances?' in *Reinsurance* (March 1974). 'Looking at the reinsurance contract' in *Reinsurance* (April 1972). 'Compromise settlement' in *Reinsurance* (July 1970). 'Follow the fortune' in *Reinsurance* (October 1971). 'Contracts of Indemnity' in *Reinsurance* (August 1969). 'The intent of the parties' in *Reinsurance* (July 1972). 'Errors and Omissions clause' in *Reinsurance* (February 1970). 'Cut-through clauses are no short cut' in *Reinsurance* (November 1972). 'Winding-up and Set-off' in *Reinsurance* (May 1971). 'Are reinsurance agreements contracts of insurance?' in *Reinsurance* (February 1974). 'Agency-trade usages and customs' in *Reinsurance* (December 1970). 'Imputation of an agent's knowledge to his principal' in *Reinsurance* (July 1974).

Reinsurance: A Correspondent, 'Excess of loss rating science' in *Reinsurance* (January 1977).

Reinsurance Offices' Association, *Definition of Estimated Maximum Loss* (Reinsurance Offices' Association, 1974).

Reinsurance Offices' Association: Report by an International Sub-Committee of the Reinsurance Offices' Association, *Indexed Annuities and the Reinsurer* (Reinsurance Offices' Association, 1978).

Reinsurance Offices' Association, *1971 Monte Carlo Panel Discussion Papers* (Reinsurance Offices' Association, 1971).

F.M.B. Reynolds and B.J. Davenport, *Bowstead on Agency,* 14th edition, (Sweet and Maxwell, 1976)

The Review, 'Dangers inherent in reciprocity systems' in *The Review* Vol LXIX (25 November 1938).

D.E.Richards, 'General principles of insurance taxation' *Journal of the Insurance Institute of London*, Vol 65 (1977).

J.Ripoll, 'UNCTAD and Insurance' in *Journal of World Trade Law*, Vol 8, No 1 (January : February 1974).

N.R.Roos and G.F.Michelbacher, *Multiple-line insurers: their nature and operation*, 2nd edition, (McGraw-Hill, 1970).

I.Rosenthal, 'Limits of retention for ordinary life insurance' in *The Record*, American Institute of Actuaries, Vol XXVI, Part 1, No 73 (1947).

Royal Commission on Civil Liability and Compensation for Personal Injury, Report of the Royal Commission on Civil Liability and Compensation for Personal Injury, Vol 1 (HMSO 1978).

H.A.Simon, 'A behavioural model of rational choice' *Quarterly Journal of Economics* (February 1955).

H.A. Simon, 'Theories of decision-making in economics and behavioural science' in *American Economic Review* (June 1959).

A.J.Steeds, 'Life reassurance' in *Journal of the Institute of Actuaries Students' Society* Vol 12, Part 3, (March 1954).

P.Strickler, 'Rückversicherung des Kumulrisikos in der Lebensversicherung' in *Transactions of the XVI International Congress of Actuaries,* Vol 1 (1960).

L.Sudekum, 'The intermediary in international reinsurance' *Papers presented at the International Reinsurance Seminar* (Reinsurance Offices' Association, 1973).

B.Supple, *The Royal Exchange Assurance* (Cambridge University Press, 1970)

Swiss Reinsurance Co. (UK) Ltd, 'International survey of regulations governing motor insurance' in *Sigma,* Swiss Reinsurance Co. (11-12 November/December 1977).

A.Taylor, 'The property account—the truth, the whole truth and nothing but the truth' in *Papers presented at the Third International Reinsurance Seminar* (Reinsurance Offices' Association, 1977).

A.Taylor, J.Lavers and G.W.Croton, 'Underwriting information and the non-proportional account', in *Papers presented at the Third International Reinsurance Seminar.* (Reinsurance Offices' Association, 1977).

G.Taylor, *A survey of the principal results of risk theory.* A note deposited with the Institute of Actuaries Library.

K.R.Thompson, *Reinsurance*, 4th edition (The Spectator, 1966).

H.M.Tract, 'Accounting for reinsurance premiums by reinsurance brokers' in *Best's Review* Vol 78, No 8 (December 1977).

F.L.Tuma, 'The economics theory of reinsurance' in *Journal of the Insurance Institute of London* (1933).

UNCTAD, *Reinsurance problems in developing countries*, UNCTAD document TD/B/C.3/106/Rev. 1, (United Nations, 1975).

UNCTAD, *Insurance of large risks in developing countries* TD/B/C, (United Nations, July 1977).

H. von Urbanski, 'Reinsurance: Legend and Reality' in *Die Industrie* (July 1977) reprinted in *The Review* (26 August 1977).

M.Wolff, *Private International Law*, 2nd edition (Oxford Clarendon Press, 1950).

Index